State Oddities

State Oddities

AN ENCYCLOPEDIA OF WHAT MAKES OUR UNITED STATES UNIQUE

Nancy Hendricks

BLOOMSBURY ACADEMIC
NEW YORK • LONDON • OXFORD • NEW DELHI • SYDNEY

BLOOMSBURY ACADEMIC
Bloomsbury Publishing Inc
1385 Broadway, New York, NY 10018, USA
50 Bedford Square, London, WC1B 3DP, UK
29 Earlsfort Terrace, Dublin 2, Ireland

BLOOMSBURY, BLOOMSBURY ACADEMIC and the Diana logo are trademarks
of Bloomsbury Publishing Plc

First published in the United States of America by ABC-CLIO 2022
Paperback edition published by Bloomsbury Academic 2025

Copyright © Bloomsbury Publishing Inc, 2025

Cover photos: The world's largest Santa Claus statue at the Santa Claus House in North Pole, Alaska. (Richard Ellis/Alamy Stock Photo); Flintstones Bedrock City theme park and campground in Valle, Arizona. (Simon Leigh/Alamy Stock Photo); Dinosaur World in Cave City, Kentucky. (EUGENIO ROIG/Alamy Stock Photo)

All rights reserved. No part of this publication may be reproduced or transmitted in any form or by any means, electronic or mechanical, including photocopying, recording, or any information storage or retrieval system, without prior permission in writing from the publishers.

Bloomsbury Publishing Inc does not have any control over, or responsibility for, any third-party websites referred to or in this book. All internet addresses given in this book were correct at the time of going to press. The author and publisher regret any inconvenience caused if addresses have changed or sites have ceased to exist, but can accept no responsibility for any such changes.

Library of Congress Cataloging-in-Publication Data

Names: Hendricks, Nancy, author.
Title: State oddities : an encyclopedia of what makes our United States unique / Nancy Hendricks.
Description: Santa Barbara, California : ABC-CLIO, an imprint of ABC-CLIO, LLC, [2022] | Includes bibliographical references and index.
Identifiers: LCCN 2021061079 (print) | LCCN 2021061080 (ebook) | ISBN 9781440876691 (hardcover) | ISBN 9781440876707 (ebook)
Subjects: LCSH: U.S. states—Miscellanea. | United States—History, Local. | BISAC: HISTORY / United States / General | ARCHITECTURE / Buildings / Landmarks & Monuments
Classification: LCC E180 .H46 2022 (print) | LCC E180 (ebook) | DDC 973—dc23/eng/20220112
LC record available at https://lccn.loc.gov/2021061079
LC ebook record available at https://lccn.loc.gov/2021061080

ISBN: HB: 978-1-4408-7669-1
PB: 979-8-7651-3896-0
ePDF: 978-1-4408-7670-7
eBook: 979-8-2161-4882-1

To find out more about our authors and books visit www.bloomsbury.com
and sign up for our newsletters.

The publisher has done its best to make sure the instructions and/or recipes in this book are correct. However, users should apply judgment and experience when preparing recipes, especially parents and teachers working with young people. The publisher accepts no responsibility for the outcome of any recipe included in this volume and assumes no liability for, and is released by readers from, any injury or damage resulting from the strict adherence to, or deviation from, the directions and/or recipes herein. The publisher is not responsible for any reader's specific health or allergy needs that may require medical supervision or for any adverse reactions to the recipes contained in this book. All yields are approximations.

Contents

Preface ix
Introduction xi
Chronology xxi

Alabama	1
Alaska	9
Arizona	16
Arkansas	23
California	31
Colorado	39
Connecticut	47
Delaware	55
Florida	63
Georgia	71
Hawaii	79
Idaho	86
Illinois	94
Indiana	102
Iowa	110
Kansas	117
Kentucky	125
Louisiana	133
Maine	141

Maryland	148
Massachusetts	156
Michigan	163
Minnesota	170
Mississippi	177
Missouri	184
Montana	191
Nebraska	198
Nevada	206
New Hampshire	213
New Jersey	220
New Mexico	227
New York	235
North Carolina	243
North Dakota	250
Ohio	258
Oklahoma	266
Oregon	274
Pennsylvania	281
Rhode Island	289
South Carolina	296
South Dakota	303
Tennessee	310
Texas	318
Utah	325
Vermont	333
Virginia	340
Washington	347

West Virginia	**354**
Wisconsin	**361**
Wyoming	**369**
Appendix A: Timeline of the Thirteen Original English Colonies	*377*
Appendix B: Quick Reference Guide to Statehood Dates and State Capitals	*379*
Selected Bibliography	*381*
Index	*393*

Preface

State Oddities: An Encyclopedia of What Makes Our United States Unique takes a different kind of look at the American nation. Readers will find the uniqueness in each of the 50 states that are united under the banner of the Stars and Stripes, differences that residents of each state hold dear.

For example, depending on location, an elongated hard roll that is filled with a variety of meats, cheese, and vegetables might be called a grinder, a hero, a hoagie, an Italian, a po'boy, a submarine, or a torpedo. To wash it down, diners might request a carbonated soft drink they call cola, pop, or soda or even specify the trademarked brand name of a specific beverage ("Coke") when what they actually want is any one of a variety of fizzy drinks, contingent on the state in which they consume it.

In highlighting those differences, *State Oddities: An Encyclopedia of What Makes Our United States Unique* is arranged for the convenience of readers. The introduction sets the stage, painting a picture of the broad sweep of the American story. It offers a gateway to the country as it developed, a nation that today is filled with individual states than can be remarkably different from each other.

The chronology provides a clear reference for historical events as they happened. As readers will discover, the formation of the United States of America was not always an easy process, nor was it a quick one. The first state to be admitted to the Union was little Delaware in 1787, while exotic Hawaii did not attain statehood until 1959. A lot of quirky history happened in between.

The entries in *State Oddities: An Encyclopedia of What Makes Our United States Unique* are arranged alphabetically by state, focusing on customs and traditions that have developed in each. All material is vetted through official sources for the individual states rather than the hit-or-miss information often found on the internet.

In each entry, the basics for each state are covered in an introductory "Fact Box" that includes the date when it was granted statehood, its nickname, its capital city, its population, and what the natives call themselves. Population figures are round numbers according to the most recent information available from the U.S. Census Bureau.

Although this volume touches on the facts of how all 50 of the American states came to be united as one country, it is not a standard historical reference. In the "State History" section of each individual entry, readers will certainly find the basic story of each state. However, that story will also include firsts, foibles, peculiarities, and twists—in other words, oddities—that most locals know and love, even as they often tactfully gloss over any imperfections.

Readers will learn about the "Urban Legends" that each state holds dear. While there are a number of Bigfoot legends, the details can differ wildly across state lines.

"Iconic Foods" for each state are also included. Along with the aforementioned variation in naming an elongated sandwich, each state seems to have a special food that it claims as its own. "Arkansas Possum Pie" is a good example. By including a recipe for a state dish such as Possum Pie, visitors to Little Rock will be alerted as to whether their dinner will contain any actual roadkill.

"Odd Laws" will focus on bizarre points of jurisprudence in each state that may be rarely enforced but are still on the books. Although there are innumerable internet sites that claim to list these, the laws cited in this book have been vetted through official state and municipal legal codes for accuracy.

Anyone interested in "Unusual Destinations" will be able to make travel plans accordingly. Readers will discover the state where there is a historical marker where Elvis Presley, the "King of Rock and Roll," got a noticeably nonroyal haircut. They will determine whether there really is a museum where visitors often lick the walls as well as one that honors toilet seats. (Answer: Yes to both.)

There are "Words and Sayings" distinctive to each state that are known to natives, but less so to visitors. Readers will discover the state where "down" means "up" and also learn the proper response to both "O-H!" and "Rock Chalk!"

Sidebars will be sprinkled throughout, offering an array of quirky knowledge. For example, readers will discover the state where government officials formally acquitted a cow of arson a century later.

For those seeking more information, a brief "Further Reading" section at the end of each entry lists some of the source material utilized for each state, which readers may wish to explore in depth. A "Selected Bibliography" at the end of the volume provides a wide range of print and online materials.

State Oddities: An Encyclopedia of What Makes Our United States Unique will be useful to students studying different states, to teachers planning classroom activities, and to general readers who enjoy taking an eye-opening journey through the nation's fun side. In short, it offers a fascinating look at the character of America through the individuality of 50 very distinct states that are (mostly) united.

Introduction

America—a huge land with contrasts that can only be called staggering. Mountains and deserts, seacoasts and plains. Majestic cities and tiny towns. Some residents thriving amid the land's bounty; others barely surviving on raw, parched earth. Farmers of the land and fishers of the sea. Hunters in dense Northern forests and planters in the balmy South. East Coasters and West Coasters, as markedly unlike each other as from the masses in between. Wanderers prizing the freedom to roam versus close-knit communities with roots in one place for generations. A vast, dizzying whirlpool of different cultures, interests, religions, values, traits, and traditions.

And that was before Christopher Columbus set sail in 1492.

BEYOND THE OCEAN SEA

Any look at America's state oddities—the ways in which the 50 states are different from each other—must take into consideration how each was created. Even today, about 250 years after the nation's founding, a state that was created by English Puritans on the chilly coast of the Northeast is going be different from one established by Spanish grandees in the sizzling deserts of the Southwest. The question of how the states are different starts with knowing why, when, how, and by whom they were founded.

Many schoolchildren erroneously believe that American history began with Christopher Columbus in 1492, obscuring the fact that the story of the Americas goes back much further in time. Native American groups differed wildly from each other, developing their own cultures over thousands of years. Some were nomads, following wild game. Others built permanent settlements with homes laid out in a grid pattern.

To those Indigenous people, the Americas did not need to be discovered. The original inhabitants knew where they were and were content to be there. It was people from Europe who developed a thirst for sailing westward toward lands they had not known even existed.

Establishing themselves in what they called the New World, European colonizers laid the groundwork for what would ultimately become the United States of America, with all the variations that would emerge among its 50 states.

European explorers in the late 1400s and early 1500s ventured across what they called the "Ocean Sea," or today's Atlantic Ocean. What they found astonished the masses back home in Europe: a vast new land.

INTOXICATING

Recent discoveries have determined that an earlier group of Europeans beat them to it by about 500 years, if only briefly. Norsemen from Scandinavia had colonized Iceland and Greenland. Evidence has determined that in about the year 1000, these intrepid sailors, also called Vikings, pointed their longboats farther west until they reached the eastern coastline of today's North America.

Some sources claim they traveled as far south as today's Massachusetts, although most current scholarship places them as making landfall in Eastern Canada. There, a small number of men and women established a simple settlement.

Part of the attraction was what they found growing there. Native wheat could help ensure their survival by providing food. But they also found it was possible for a person to become intoxicated after consuming fermented berries that grew wild. Spotlighting this selling point, they envisioned a colony that nurtured wine making, calling their settlement Vinland in the hope of attracting other hardy (and hard-drinking) Norsemen.

However, relations with the Native people who already lived there varied from friendly trading partners to bloodthirsty foes. Ultimately, Viking settlements in North America vanished into the mists of time, leaving only tantalizing clues for present-day archaeologists.

SEEDS OF 1492

For several hundred years after exploration by the Vikings, Native people in North America continued living their lives as they had done for centuries. Both the Iroquois in the Northeast and Indigenous people in the Pacific Northwest built longhouses. Pueblo Indians of the arid Southwest inhabited adobes and cliff dwellings. Native Americans on the Great Plains lived as nomads, following the bison herds that were crucial to their survival. Cherokee villages of the Southeast often clustered near rivers, cultivating crops such as corn. Farther south in today's Central and South America, spectacular cities that rivaled London or Paris sparkled in the sun while mountaintop strongholds with terraced farms dominated what seemed to be the top of the world.

Native civilizations in the Americas had flourished for eons. With the arrival of Christopher Columbus, everything changed dramatically and tragically for the people who already lived there.

Thus, citing the year 1492 as the beginning of American history is inaccurate at best. In fact, the incentive for the European incursion into the Americas might well be said to have taken root decades earlier. The seeds were planted in the milestone year of 1453. If historical events had not coincided at that time, the year 1492 might be as uneventful to us today as any other random year in the centuries gone by.

In 1453, the Ottoman Turks conquered the city of Constantinople (today's Istanbul, Turkey), which was the main east-west conduit for trade between Europe and the Orient. When the Turks cut off the city, European merchants lost the ability to transport their goods to eastern markets. In addition, they no longer had access to coveted products from the Orient such as silk and spices.

Today, spices are often taken for granted. But for Europe in the Middle Ages, spices were what transformed food from being unappetizing at best to at least being palatable. With access by land cut off by the Turks, Europeans were desperate to find another way to the East.

3-G NETWORK

At the same time, Europe was becoming overpopulated. By 1453, it was running out of farmland to grow food as well as trees to use as building materials. Clean water for drinking was becoming scarce since waterways were often used by Europeans as a toilet and lakes as a toxic waste dump.

Moreover, with a strict class system, there were very few opportunities for average—or more likely, desperately poor—Europeans to better themselves.

An Italian known today as Christopher Columbus was an excellent sailor who was willing to risk everything on his belief that the world was not flat but was a round sphere. Therefore, he believed that by sailing west, he could reach the Orient.

The idea was not new, having been theorized for decades. However, Columbus was the one who was willing to not only take the bet but also persuade royal sponsors to finance the trip. After decades of rejections by the various royal courts of Europe, Columbus finally convinced King Ferdinand and Queen Isabella of Spain to be his backers.

In 1492, Columbus set out on his epic voyage. After two months, jittery crew members were trying to convince him to turn back. Suddenly, they spotted land. What they found were the islands of the Caribbean, but Columbus thought it had to be China, Japan, or India (thus calling the Natives "Indians").

Returning to Spain with the news of a landmass that could be reached by sailing west, Europe was aflame with excitement over his discovery. Many planned accordingly. They felt it was a way to earn a fortune based on tales of gold that needed only to be scooped up from the ground. It was a way for the pious to spread the Christian religion among Natives who were presumed to be pagans. And it was a way for men without prospects in Europe to have the chance of advancing themselves toward a glorious future.

Europeans who came after Columbus risked their lives sailing westward in tiny boats. They knew that even the voyage itself could end in death, not to mention what they might encounter when they landed. Why? Because they had compelling reasons to do so.

In the smartphone age of the early 21st century, "3-G" referred to the third generation of devices. Amid the New World fever of the early 1500s, there was another 3-G network that drove European explorers toward America: God, gold, and glory.

VESPUCCILAND THE BEAUTIFUL

Christopher Columbus went to his grave in 1506 believing he had found Asia, not a completely new hemisphere. It is primarily for that reason that the landmasses today known as North, South, and Central America are not called by some variation of his name, such as "Columbia." Since he successfully made many other demands of his royal sponsors, such as receiving money and titles, it is plausible that he would have also wished the lands he discovered to be named for him. No doubt he did not seek that recognition because he thought the lands already had names, such as Cathay (China) and Zipangu (Japan).

In 1497, Italian mapmaker Amerigo Vespucci sailed on an expedition to what he determined were lands that were unknown to Europeans, and not actually Asia. Vespucci charted the Atlantic coastline of today's South America before returning to Europe, where he published colorful accounts of his explorations that became very popular in the early 1500s. Some historians cite a publication written in Latin around 1507 in which another mapmaker who had read Vespucci's account applied a name to the lands that were described. That mapmaker suggested naming the newly discovered landmass as Amerige or America, roughly translated as "Amerigo's land." By 1532, the name "America" was being applied by mapmakers to the continents of the Western Hemisphere.

Amerigo Vespucci himself died in 1512, rendering it unknown if he was aware of being recognized in such a way. In any case, his first name was the one that was used for the continents of the Western Hemisphere, not the harder-to-spell "Vespucciland," something for which many Americans owe a debt of thanks.

SPAIN TAKES THE LEAD

In Europe's land rush for territory in the New World, Spain took an early lead. Juan Ponce de León came to the Americas with the second voyage of Christopher Columbus in 1493. By 1513, Ponce de León was leading the first-known European expedition to today's Florida, which he claimed for Spain. No mention of Ponce can omit his alleged search for the Fountain of Youth in the flower-covered land he called "La Florida." However, modern historians claim that no documented evidence of such a quest by Ponce actually exists (nor, presumably, does such a fountain).

Ships carrying Spanish conquistadors arrived regularly in the New World, bringing two secret weapons that terrified unsuspecting Indigenous people who had never seen anything like them: guns and horses. In 1521, with the fall of the Aztec city of Tenochtitlan (today's Mexico City), Spaniards looked to expand the reach of what they were calling "New Spain."

Francisco Vázquez de Coronado heard reports that there were Seven Cities of Gold somewhere to the north of Mexico City. In 1540, Coronado led a Spanish expedition into the region that is now the Southwestern United States. They discovered the Grand Canyon, clashed with local Indians, and laid claim to new lands for the king of Spain. However, they found no cities made of gold, just dusty pueblos. Without procuring the precious metal, Coronado's expedition was labeled a failure by Spanish authorities. However, gold or no gold, through ventures such as his, New Spain would ultimately grow to encompass current American states such as Arizona, California, Colorado, Nevada, New Mexico, Utah, and Texas, as well as parts of Idaho, Kansas, Louisiana, Mississippi, Montana, Oklahoma, and Wyoming.

MISSIONS TO METROPLEX

Spanning such a vast territory across North America, there was little feeling of a cohesive identity among Spanish colonists. The sense of individuality later manifested itself as part of the differences among the 50 states. Rather than thinking of themselves as citizens of New Spain, the Spanish colonists generally saw themselves as residents of individual places such as California or Florida, isolated and apart from each other.

In some areas, the Spanish presence became more enduring than in others. Beginning in 1519, Spain began building missions and forts (called "presidios") in New Spain. Not counting the Alamo in Texas, which has become part of the nation's mythic history, for modern-day Americans, the most significant of these were established in California, which was claimed as Spanish territory in 1542.

To thwart the incursion of Russians moving south into California from Alaska, the Spanish established 21 missions and military outposts between 1769 and 1833. They were set approximately 30 miles apart, about a day's journey on horseback. Ultimately spanning 600 miles north to south near the coastline, the California Mission Trail formed the foundation for cities that retained their Spanish saints' names, many of which are familiar to most people today. They include Santa Barbara, Santa Cruz, San Diego, San Francisco, San Juan Capistrano, and San Luis Obispo. El Pueblo de Nuestra Señora la Reina de los Ángeles ("The Town of Our Lady the Queen of the Angels") evolved into the glitzy metroplex today known as Los Angeles.

On America's Eastern Seaboard, in 1565, Spanish admiral Pedro Menéndez de Avilés founded St. Augustine, Florida. That city went on to become known as the oldest continuously inhabited settlement established by Europeans in the contiguous United States.

By 1610, when the Palace of the Governors was built by the Spaniards in Santa Fe as the seat of government in today's New Mexico, others were clamoring to get in on the act.

HOLLAND AND SWEDEN AND FRANCE—OH MY!

Not to be outdone by Spain, other European countries wanted their own foothold in the New World. In 1609, Holland established a Dutch colonial presence in what they called New Netherland, which ran along the Hudson River Valley up to today's Albany, New York.

That endeavor ended abruptly in 1664, when English warships landed in the harbor of the village of New Amsterdam (present-day New York City), demanding that the Dutch in New Netherland surrender. With Dutch governor Peter Stuyvesant being unpopular among the colonists, his subjects refused to fight under his leadership, surrendering without firing a shot. England quickly rechristened today's Big Apple in honor of the Duke of York. The speed with which the renaming took place was possibly the first instance of a "New York Minute."

Even with their relatively brief presence, Dutch colonists provided the future United States of America with a memorable historical snippet. In 1626, the Dutchman Peter Minuit is said to have purchased Manhattan Island from a group of Native Americans for goods that were calculated to be worth around $24 (about $1,000 today). But the important questions are *who* the Native Americans were and *what* they thought the transaction meant—almost certainly, not the same thing as the Dutch. Some historians speculate that they might have been a group of Natives from elsewhere who were just passing through, chuckling all the way back home that they had gotten the best of the strangely dressed rubes. In any case, it made a good story that went on to become a beloved highlight of America's cultural mythology.

In 1638, Sweden established the colony of New Sweden along the Delaware River in what are now parts of Delaware, Maryland, New Jersey, and Pennsylvania. The Swedish South Company was a business consortium that had been formed the year before with a very clear profit motive.

The Swedes allied themselves with the Susquehannock people, joining the Native Americans against the English colony in Maryland that was led by Lord Baltimore. The English had the last laugh when the Swedish Navy, involved in a European war, could no longer protect Sweden's colonies in America.

In 1655, New Sweden formally incorporated itself into New Netherland, an arrangement that lasted only until the English conquered the Dutch there in 1664. Some Swedes still kept arriving in their nation's former colony to live among their countrymen, but any remnants of New Sweden came to an end when it was assimilated into William Penn's charter for Pennsylvania in 1682.

France was a major player in the North American land rush. After several attempts at permanent French colonies that did not survive, René-Robert Cavelier, Sieur de La Salle explored the Ohio River Valley and the Mississippi River Valley in 1682. Reaching the Gulf of Mexico at the approximate site of today's New Orleans, he claimed the entire territory for France in the name of King Louis XIV, calling it La Louisiane in honor of the monarch.

The French were primarily trappers and traders. They generally maintained good relations with the Natives who became their business partners. France established trading posts, forts, and settlements that would go on to become major American landmarks like the city of New Orleans.

However, after the French and Indian War in which France was defeated by Britain, the French influence in the Americas declined. This became more pronounced after the Louisiana Purchase of 1803 when France sold her holdings to the United

States, doubling the size of the new American nation. The French presence can still be found in place names around the country including cities such as Baton Rouge, Boise, Des Moines, and Detroit. Even "Chicago" has a French pronunciation.

THE RUSSIANS WERE COMING . . .

In 1732, Russian merchants and fur trappers arrived in North America, establishing outposts in Alaska. By 1799, the Russian Orthodox Church was sending missionaries to convert the Natives, building churches as the Russians expanded their territory in the Pacific Northwest to a region more than twice as large as Texas.

The Russians were primarily interested in hunting fur-bearing animals, having depleted such creatures in Siberia by overhunting. Proceeding to do the same thing to the furry animals of North America, the Russians kept moving southward in search of more hapless targets. They eventually established an outpost in 1812 at today's Bodega Bay in Northern California, near San Francisco. As the Spanish overseers in California saw it, the Russians were coming.

It was this southward movement by the Russians toward the Spanish colonies in California that stimulated a significant response by Spain. By 1769, there was growing apprehension among the Spaniards about Russian traders and settlers encroaching farther into California. As noted previously, Spain authorized the construction of Roman Catholic missions and military outposts in California. The Spanish outposts that evolved in response to the Russians ultimately developed into major California cities.

The question of Russian expansion into North America became moot in 1867. At that time, Russia sold Alaska to the United States at a cost of a little over $7 million, or about 2¢ an acre. Some critics called the land sale "Seward's Folly," named for Secretary of State William Seward, who authorized the deal. If Seward's critics were still around in 1896 when gold was discovered in the region, they may have reconsidered their position.

. . . BUT THE ENGLISH WON

Joining the land rush in the New World, England planned to establish settlements in the safe middle ground on America's East Coast that lay north of the Spanish in Florida and south of the French in Canada.

The English would ultimately emerge victorious. Most schoolchildren are familiar with two dates marking the English colonization of America. The first was 1607, denoting the establishment of Virginia, the first permanently settled English colony on the North American continent. The other is 1620, when Plymouth Colony in Massachusetts was founded by the Pilgrims who sailed on the *Mayflower*.

Some colonists from England came to America for religious freedom, at least the freedom to practice their own religion if not to tolerate anyone else's. Some new arrivals came strictly for profit. Still others emerged from English prisons, destitute villages, or the mean streets of London with nothing to their name except the dream of a better life. In other words, the English colonists continued the 3-G tradition: God, gold, and if not glory, at least a chance for survival.

The Dutch, French, and Swedish colonies were eventually absorbed under English rule. Even so, most of the thirteen colonies that became states as we know them today still bear many vestiges of their previous landlords (see Appendix A).

CRAZY QUILT

Tens of thousands of new residents arrived in America during every decade of the 1700s alone. They came from all over Europe, including English Catholics, French Protestants (called Huguenots), Germans, Irish, Scots, and Welsh. Many despised the other groups. A great number of new arrivals settled in with people of their own kind who were already here, such as the Pennsylvania Dutch (from the German word Deutsch, meaning "German") who clustered in that state's Lancaster County. These later arrivals came for a variety of reasons, generally continuing the 3-G tradition: God, gold, and/or the glory of making something better of themselves beyond what they ever would have had in Europe.

After the American Revolution, new states were added regularly. Like the original Northern colonies, new states in the North were often mountainous with a thin rocky layer of soil that was best suited for small family farms. Northern states therefore leaned toward an economy that was based on manufacturing and trade, jobs that could be performed when the weather turned too cold for subsistence farming. Many of the Northern states had been settled primarily for religious and/or political freedom, often sharing a common heritage based on the English model.

Meanwhile, the South enjoyed a warmer climate with rich fertile soil that could support huge plantations based on a single cash crop like cotton or tobacco. Southern colonies were often settled by companies eager for profits, which soon found that the free labor of untold thousands of enslaved people improved their bottom line. Each plantation tended toward being self-sufficient, without much need to develop manufacturing industries in their agriculturally based economy.

As more states were added west of the original thirteen colonies, there grew to be noticeable friction between the westerners who were carving a primitive subsistence out of the wilderness and their sophisticated East Coast counterparts who were several generations removed from such hard manual labor. New states in the Southwest reflected their Spanish heritage, while those in the Northeast and the Pacific Northwest could almost have been French Canadian.

When the framers of the Constitution came together after the American Revolution in 1789 to shape a document that would be used to govern the new nation, what they found was a crazy quilt of fellow delegates. Each state had its own agenda, primarily based on its economy and the characteristics of its people. Modern historians often express astonishment that such a landmark document as the U.S. Constitution could be constructed from such a wide gulf of contrasts.

In the centuries to follow, differences were often blurred by time, growth, technology, and successive waves of immigration. Still, with such diverse origin stories, a variety of unique personalities evolved for each of the 50 states. It is therefore no wonder that America's individual states are in some ways as different as they are alike.

Further Reading

Gear, Kathleen O'Neal, and W. Michael Gear. *Vikings in North America: Pursuing the Myth of Paradise*. New York: Tor Books, 2015.

Kreitner, Richard. *Break It Up: Secession, Division, and the Secret History of America's Imperfect Union*. New York: Little, Brown, 2020.

Marshall, Bill (editor). *France and the Americas: Culture, Politics, and History*. Santa Barbara, CA: ABC-CLIO, 2005.

Shorto, Russell. *The Island at the Center of the World: The Epic Story of Dutch Manhattan and the Forgotten Colony That Shaped America*. New York: Doubleday, 2004.

Vinkovetsky, Ilya. *Russian America: An Overseas Colony of a Continental Empire, 1804–1867*. New York: Oxford University Press, 2014.

Weber, David. *The Spanish Frontier in North America: The Brief Edition*. New Haven, CT: Yale University Press, 2009.

Chronology

Circa 15,000 BCE	Ancient people migrate to North America, presumably into today's Alaska from Siberia.
Circa 1000	Norsemen are the first-known Europeans to set foot on the continent of North America.
1453	Ottoman Turks cut off east-west trade route between Europe and the Orient.
1492	Christopher Columbus, sailing for the king and queen of Spain, makes landfall in the Bahamas, sparking European exploration and colonization of the American continents.
1513	Spaniard Ponce de León leads first-known European expedition to today's Florida.
1521	Fall of Tenochtitlan in present-day Mexico spurs Spaniards to look toward exploring territories to the north, in what would become today's American Southwest.
1532	Amerigo Vespucci of Italy is recognized on early maps for his popular descriptions of the New World, which starts being called "America" in his honor.
1540	Francisco de Coronado leads Spanish expedition into today's American Southwest.
1542	California is claimed as a Spanish territory.
1565	Spaniard Menéndez de Avilés establishes St. Augustine in present-day Florida, the oldest continuously occupied European settlement in North America.
1587	England establishes Roanoke settlement led by John White in today's North Carolina; it becomes known as the "Lost Colony" due to unexplained disappearance of its people.
1607	Jamestown, Virginia, is founded by John Smith; it becomes first permanent English settlement in the Americas. In present-day New Mexico, Pedro de Peralta of Spain founds La Villa Real de la Santa Fe de San Francisco de Asís (Royal Town of the Holy Faith of Saint Francis of Assisi), today's Santa Fe.
1609	The Dutch establish New Netherland in the Hudson River Valley as far north as today's Albany, New York.

1610	Palace of the Governors in Santa Fe becomes seat of government for Spanish province of New Mexico, making Santa Fe the oldest continuous state capital in the United States.
1619	First recorded enslaved people from Africa are transported to North America, landing near Jamestown colony.
1620	Plymouth Colony is founded in Massachusetts by English "Pilgrims."
1626	Dutchman Peter Minuit allegedly buys Manhattan Island from Natives for $24 in goods.
1629	Massachusetts Bay Colony is founded by English Puritans. New Hampshire is founded as an English colony.
1632	Maryland is founded as an English colony.
1638	New Sweden, along the Delaware River, is founded as a Swedish colony.
1651	Province of Carolina is founded as an English colony, but due to its size, it will later be divided into North Carolina and South Carolina.
1655	New Sweden formally incorporates itself into the Dutch colony of New Netherland.
1663	Rhode Island is founded as an English colony.
1664	English ships land at New Amsterdam (today's New York City), forcing the Dutch to surrender New Netherland to England. Delaware is founded as an English colony. New Jersey is founded as an English colony. New Amsterdam is renamed New York. Three English settlements are merged to become the Connecticut Colony.
1675	Native Americans in today's New England fight colonists in what is called King Philip's War, running through 1678.
1681	Pennsylvania is founded as an English colony.
1682	Final remnants of New Sweden are incorporated into William Penn's charter for Pennsylvania. René-Robert Cavelier, Sieur de La Salle, explores Ohio River Valley and Mississippi River Valley, claiming the entire region that he calls "La Louisiane" for France.
1691	Massachusetts Bay Colony merges with Plymouth Colony.
1729	North Carolina is chartered as an English colony. South Carolina is chartered as an English colony.
1732	Georgia is founded as an English colony. Russian merchants and fur trappers arrive in North America, establishing outposts in Alaska.
1739	Large slave uprising called Stono Rebellion (sometimes called Cato's Rebellion) takes place in Stono, South Carolina.

CHRONOLOGY

1763	Following victory over France in the French and Indian War, Britain wins territory west to the Mississippi River. Pontiac's Rebellion, an uprising of Native American tribes against British rule after French and Indian War, takes place in the Great Lakes region. Proclamation of 1763, issued by England's King George III, claims land west of America's Appalachian Mountains for the Crown, spurring discontent by prohibiting settlement by colonists.
1769	Spanish authorities begin building 21 missions and military outposts in California.
1770	British troops kill five American colonists in "Boston Massacre," including Crispus Attucks, an African American whom some consider to be the first casualty of America's war for independence.
1773	Phillis Wheatley, an enslaved woman from Boston, becomes renowned as the first female African American to publish a book of poetry.
1774	After Britain closes Boston Harbor and sends troops to Massachusetts, the First Continental Congress is formed by American colonists.
1775	George Washington leads army of colonists to fight for independence from British rule in the American Revolution.
1776	On July 4, the Declaration of Independence is endorsed by the Second Continental Congress, proclaiming that the thirteen American colonies are separating from British rule.
1781	The thirteen American colonies form a loose alliance under the Articles of Confederation.
1783	British army surrenders, ending the American Revolution.
1784	Treaty of Paris is ratified, formally granting independence to the American colonies by freeing them from British rule.
1786–1787	Led by Daniel Shays of Massachusetts, Shays' Rebellion raises doubt about decentralized government in dealing with civil unrest.
1787	Constitution of the United States of America is ratified, replacing Articles of Confederation. Statehood for Delaware, New Jersey, and Pennsylvania.
1788	Statehood for Connecticut, Georgia, Maryland, Massachusetts, New Hampshire, New York, South Carolina, and Virginia.
1789	Statehood for North Carolina. George Washington is unanimously chosen as first president of the United States.

1790	Statehood for Rhode Island.
1791	Statehood for Vermont.
	First 10 amendments, called Bill of Rights, are added to the Constitution to guarantee individual freedoms.
1792	Statehood for Kentucky.
	Tax protest in Pennsylvania called Whiskey Rebellion begins; runs through 1794.
	Eli Whitney's patent on cotton gin increases market for more enslaved people to be brought to America.
1796	Statehood for Tennessee.
1797	John Adams becomes president.
1800	White House becomes official residence of the president of the United States.
1801	Thomas Jefferson becomes president.
1803	Statehood for Ohio.
	France sells "La Louisiane" (Louisiana Territory) to the United States, almost doubling America's size with land including current states of Arkansas, Iowa, Kansas, Missouri, Nebraska, and Oklahoma plus portions of Colorado, Louisiana, Minnesota, Montana, New Mexico, North Dakota, South Dakota, Texas, and Wyoming.
1808	U.S. Congress bans further importation of slaves, although last known slave ship bringing captives from Africa to the United States is the *Clotilda*, arriving in 1860.
1809	James Madison becomes president.
1811	Native American army led by Shawnee chief Tecumseh fights the United States, allying themselves with the British in War of 1812.
1812	Statehood for Louisiana.
	War of 1812 between the United States and Britain is won by the former in 1815.
	Russians establish settlement at today's Bodega Bay near San Francisco, with Fort Ross becoming headquarters of Russian California.
1816	Statehood for Indiana.
1817	Statehood for Mississippi.
	James Monroe becomes president.
1818	Statehood for Illinois.
1819	Statehood for Alabama.
1820	Statehood for Maine and Missouri.
1825	John Quincy Adams becomes president.
1829	Andrew Jackson becomes president.
1831	Nat Turner leads rebellion of enslaved people in Virginia.
1836	Statehood for Arkansas.

1837	Statehood for Michigan. Martin Van Buren becomes president. Battle of the Alamo in Texas.
1838	Trail of Tears begins, forcing about 60,000 Native Americans to relocate from their homes in Southeastern United States to territories in the West.
1841	William Henry Harrison becomes president. John Tyler becomes president upon death of William Henry Harrison.
1845	Statehood for Florida and Texas. James Polk becomes president. New York newspaper editor John O'Sullivan coins the phrase "Manifest Destiny" for alleged divinely ordained expansion of the United States to the Pacific.
1846	Statehood for Iowa. Mexican American War begins, running through 1848. Former slave Frederick Douglass begins publishing antislavery newspaper, *North Star*.
1848	Statehood for Wisconsin. In Mexican Cession, the United States receives present-day California, Nevada, and Utah, plus parts of Arizona, Colorado, New Mexico, and Wyoming. Seneca Falls Convention in New York is first women's rights conference in the United States. Gold discovered in California.
1849	Zachary Taylor becomes president. Harriet Tubman escapes from slavery, becomes leader of Underground Railroad.
1850	Statehood for California. Millard Fillmore becomes president upon death of Zachary Taylor.
1851	Sojourner Truth, former African American slave, delivers "Ain't I a Woman" speech at Ohio Women's Rights Convention.
1853	Franklin Pierce becomes president.
1854	In Gadsden Purchase, the United States pays Mexico for portions of present-day Arizona and New Mexico.
1857	James Buchanan becomes president. U.S. Supreme Court's *Dred Scott* decision denies citizenship to enslaved people or free Blacks who are descendants of slaves.
1858	Statehood for Minnesota.
1859	Statehood for Oregon.
1861	Statehood for Kansas.

	Abraham Lincoln becomes president.
	Confederate States of America formed upon secession from the Union by Alabama, Arkansas, Florida, Georgia, Louisiana, Mississippi, North Carolina, South Carolina, Tennessee, Texas, and Virginia.
	America's Civil War begins at Fort Sumter in Charleston, South Carolina.
1863	Statehood for West Virginia.
1864	Statehood for Nevada.
1865	Confederacy is defeated, ending the Civil War.
	Andrew Johnson becomes president after assassination of Abraham Lincoln.
	Under Thirteenth Amendment, slavery is abolished in the United States.
1867	Statehood for Nebraska.
	United States purchases Alaska from Russia.
1868	Fourteenth Amendment overturns *Dred Scott* decision, granting citizenship to all persons born or naturalized in the United States, including freed former slaves.
1869	Ulysses Grant becomes president.
	Transcontinental railroad is completed, spurring new growth of the United States.
	Susan B. Anthony and Elizabeth Cady Stanton establish National Woman Suffrage Association.
	Territory of Wyoming gives women the right to vote.
1870	Fifteenth Amendment gives African American men the right to vote.
1872	Victoria Woodhull, candidate from the Equal Rights Party (with running mate Frederick Douglass), is the first woman to run for president.
1876	Statehood for Colorado.
1877	Rutherford B. Hayes becomes president.
1881	James Garfield becomes president.
	Chester A. Arthur becomes president after assassination of James Garfield.
1885	Grover Cleveland becomes president.
1889	Statehood for Montana, North Dakota, South Dakota, and Washington State.
	Benjamin Harrison becomes president.
1890	Statehood for Idaho and Wyoming.
1893	Grover Cleveland becomes president for second, nonconsecutive term.
1896	Statehood for Utah.
	Gold discovered in Yukon.

	U.S. Supreme Court's *Plessy v. Ferguson* decision rules that racial segregation is constitutional, ushering in "Separate but Equal" policies of Jim Crow era.
1897	William McKinley becomes president.
1898	Spanish American War.
	Guam, Puerto Rico, and the Philippines become U.S. territories following victory by the United States in Spanish American War.
	Hawaii is annexed by the United States.
1901	Theodore Roosevelt becomes president after assassination of William McKinley.
1904	Panama Canal Zone acquired by the United States.
1907	Statehood for Oklahoma.
1909	William Howard Taft becomes president.
1912	Statehood for Arizona and New Mexico.
1913	Woodrow Wilson becomes president.
1916	Jeannette Rankin of Montana is first woman elected to the U.S. House of Representatives; is not reelected until 1940.
1917	The United States enters World War I.
	U.S. Virgin Islands acquired by the United States.
1920	Under Nineteenth Amendment, American women earn the right to vote.
	Prohibition bans manufacture and sale of alcoholic beverages under Eighteenth Amendment; repealed by Twenty-First Amendment in 1933.
1921	Warren Harding becomes president.
1923	Calvin Coolidge becomes president upon death of Warren Harding.
1924	Indian Citizenship Act gives Native Americans the right to U.S. citizenship, although some states bar Native Americans from voting until 1957.
1929	Herbert Hoover becomes president.
	Stock market crashes, sparking Great Depression of the 1930s.
1932	Hattie Caraway of Arkansas is first woman elected to the U.S. Senate; is reelected in 1938.
1933	Franklin Delano Roosevelt becomes president.
1934	"Dust Bowl" environmental and economic disaster in mid-America begins.
1939	World War II begins in Europe.
1941	The United States enters World War II after Japanese attack on Hawaii's Pearl Harbor.
1945	Harry Truman becomes president upon death of Franklin Roosevelt.

	Germany and Japan surrender, ending World War II.
1946	Cold War begins between the United States and Soviet Union.
1949	Margaret Chase Smith of Maine becomes first woman to serve in both houses of U.S. Congress, having been elected to House of Representatives in 1940 and the Senate in 1949.
1950	The United States enters Korean War, which runs through 1953.
1953	Dwight Eisenhower becomes president.
1954	U.S. Supreme Court's *Brown v. Board of Education* decision rules that racial segregation in American public schools is unconstitutional.
1955	Rosa Parks, an African American, ignites protest movement by refusing to give up seat on city bus to white male. Official beginning of U.S. involvement in Vietnam War.
1959	Statehood for Alaska. Statehood for Hawaii.
1961	John F. Kennedy becomes president.
1963	Civil rights leader Martin Luther King delivers "I Have a Dream" speech. Lyndon Johnson becomes president after assassination of John F. Kennedy.
1965	Voting Rights Act outlaws disenfranchisement of African American voters.
1967	Thurgood Marshall is first African American appointed to U.S. Supreme Court. Edward Brooke of Massachusetts becomes first African American elected to U.S. Senate since Reconstruction.
1968	Civil rights leader Martin Luther King is assassinated. Presidential candidate Robert Kennedy is assassinated.
1969	Richard Nixon becomes president. American astronaut Neil Armstrong becomes first person to walk on the moon.
1973	Vietnam cease-fire agreement signed.
1974	Richard Nixon resigns as president in wake of Watergate scandal. Gerald Ford becomes president upon resignation of Richard Nixon.
1977	Jimmy Carter becomes president.
1981	Ronald Reagan becomes president. Sandra Day O'Connor is first woman appointed to U.S. Supreme Court.
1983	Sally Ride becomes first American woman in space.

1989	George H. W. Bush becomes president.
1993	Bill Clinton becomes president.
2001	George W. Bush becomes president.
2009	Barack Obama becomes first African American president.
2016	Hillary Clinton is first female presidential candidate for major political party.
2017	Donald Trump becomes president.
2021	Joseph Biden becomes president.

State Oddities

Alabama

FACT BOX

Nicknames: Yellowhammer State and Heart of Dixie
Statehood Granted: 1819
Capital: Montgomery
Population: 4,900,000
State Motto: *Audemus jura nostra defendere* (Latin: "We Dare to Defend Our Rights")
What Natives Call Themselves: Alabamans or Alabamians

STATE HISTORY

Alabama, the state that begins the alphabetical array of the list of America's 50 states, got its name the way many did: from the Indigenous people who had lived there for centuries.

Among the Native Americans living in Alabama at the time European explorers arrived were such people as the Chickasaw, Choctaw, and Creek, along with a tribe whose name was transcribed by Europeans as the Alabamu, Alibama, and Alibamo, among other variations, as well as Albaamaha in the Natives' own language. The state's name was therefore derived from the people who lived there before eventually being forced to leave.

The first documented visit by Europeans to present-day Alabama was an expedition led by Spanish explorer Hernando de Soto in 1539. De Soto claimed the region for the king of Spain as part of "La Florida," the peninsula to its southeast that had been discovered in 1513 by another Spaniard, Ponce de León. De Soto encountered long-established villages inhabited by the Native people who were already living in what became today's Alabama. They included those who built platform mounds, similar to earthwork pyramids and often used for religious purposes, which remain in evidence today as part of the Alabama Indigenous Mound Trail.

In the 1600s and 1700s, the territory of today's Alabama was contested by two other European powers, apart from Spain. Through charters issued in both 1663 and 1665, the English king, Charles II, awarded land grants in the region as part of England's Province of Carolina.

France, which was England's longtime enemy, also established a foothold in the region. In 1702, the French founded Fort Louis de la Mobile led by Jean-Baptiste Le Moyne de Bienville. Building near the mouth of the Mobile River, this settlement was abandoned by 1712 due to repeated flooding. However, for most of its existence, it was the seat of government for New France, the French colonial presence in North America.

Despite the flooding at Fort Louis de la Mobile, France was determined to retain its presence in the area. The French settlers moved to higher ground nearby, rebuilding their colony. Naming the new site Fort Condé in 1723, it developed into present-day Mobile, Alabama, which claims the title of being the first permanent European settlement in the state.

Perhaps of even greater cultural significance is the fact that in 1703, Fort Louis de la Mobile held the first organized celebration of Mardi Gras (Fat Tuesday) in the New World. Today's Mobile, where the Fort Louis settlement was reestablished, claims the distinction of holding America's first Mardi Gras, earlier than the arguably more famous event in New Orleans, Louisiana, where the first recorded Mardi Gras parade was in 1837.

Along with competing with each other to be the primary allies and trading partners with Alabama's Native Americans, the English and French brought their traditional European squabbles to the New World. What became known as the

Mobile, Alabama, claims to have held the first Mardi Gras parade in the New World, which it celebrated in 1703. Historians place it earlier than the first recorded Mardi Gras parade in New Orleans, Louisiana, that took place in 1837. (The George F. Landegger Collection of Alabama Photographs in Carol M. Highsmith's America, Library of Congress)

French and Indian War (1754–1763) was the North American arm of the Seven Years' War in Europe between the two nations. The English victory in that conflict brought control of many French possessions in the New World to England, including today's Alabama.

With the coming of the American Revolution (1775–1783), Native Americans in Alabama fought on both sides. After victory by the patriots, large-scale colonization by Americans began in Alabama as Natives were forced off their land.

Becoming America's 22nd state in 1819, Alabama based its economy on the mass cultivation of cotton by enslaved people from Africa.

In the run-up to the Civil War (1861–1865), Alabama was central to the South's growing sentiment for secession, or withdrawing from the Union. In March 1861, the South's secession convention was held at Montgomery, Alabama, the city known to many today as the birthplace of the Confederacy. Alabama was the first to ratify the constitution of the Confederacy, thus becoming the first official member of the Confederate States of America on March 13, 1861. Before moving to Richmond, Virginia, the Confederate government made Montgomery its first capital.

There was some dissent early in the secession process among small farmers in Alabama's northern hill country. Popular sentiment there leaned toward establishing their own neutral state called Nickajack. After the Civil War broke out, however, the idea did not materialize.

When the war ended, the rise of the Industrial Revolution transformed the nation in the late 1800s. Birmingham, Alabama, became a booming center of the iron industry in the twentieth century.

Alabama can claim a unique event in 1954 when there was a bit too much heavy metal in the state. An Alabama woman was napping on her couch when she was struck by an 8.5-pound meteorite that crashed through her roof. She survived with only bruises, and today Alabama is known as the only state to have one of its residents confirmed as being hit by a meteorite.

Alabama's meteorite victim might have benefited from another Alabama "first" if it had come sooner. In 1968, the first emergency call in the nation using the new 911 system was placed in Haleyville, Alabama.

Alabama is also home to the nation's one-of-a-kind center for selling unclaimed luggage from America's airlines. For more than 50 years, contents of lost or abandoned suitcases have been shipped to Scottsboro where around a million items are for sale to the public in the huge building. The facility adds about 7,000 new items *every day* and attracts more than a million customers each year.

If those customers are doing their Christmas shopping, it is entirely fitting to do so in Alabama. It was the first state to declare Christmas a legal holiday, doing so in 1836. The federal government eventually followed Alabama's lead, declaring December 25 to be a national holiday in 1870.

Another unique feature of Alabama pertains to Mobile's Mardi Gras parade. Instead of colored beads, people on floats in Mobile throw Moon Pies into the crowd. Moon Pies are sweet treats consisting of two large round graham cracker cookies with marshmallow filling in the center, dipped in a flavored coating, usually

> ### "Sweet Home Jacksonville"?
>
> Not many Alabamans can sing the official state anthem "Alabama," which was adopted by the state's legislature in 1931. If pressed, many people today would consider the state's anthem to be the iconic song "Sweet Home Alabama" by the rock group Lynyrd Skynyrd. Sample lyrics include *"Sweet home Alabama / Lord, I'm coming home to you."* Few people realize that the songwriters, several members of the Lynyrd Skynyrd band, were not from Alabama at all—the band members were all from Jacksonville, Florida. Not even the group's namesake, their high school gym teacher Leonard Skinner, was from Alabama. However, through the years, the song's popularity became so closely associated with Alabama that its renown and connection to the state continues to be sweet indeed.

chocolate. Although the snack is made in Tennessee, it has become associated with Alabama mythology as the state's preferred lunch. This adds a new dimension to the phrase "Sweet Home Alabama," which has been seen on its license plates since 2009.

With a 2002 film titled *Sweet Home Alabama*, it seems as though the movie would have been produced in Alabama. Its title was derived from the hit song of the same name by Southern rock band Lynyrd Skynyrd. However, in a development that was unsettling to many Alabamans, even though the story was set in a fictional Alabama town, the movie was primarily filmed in neighboring Georgia.

URBAN LEGENDS

The **Boyington Oak** can be found in Mobile's Church Street Graveyard. The Southern live oak tree is growing from the burial site of a man named Charles Boyington who was laid to rest in a pauper's grave in 1835. According to legend, Boyington was executed for the murder of another man during an alleged robbery. Boyington repeatedly swore he was innocent, but he was condemned to a sentence of death. Before his execution by hanging, Boyington is said to vow that a mighty oak tree would grow from his grave, emerging from his pure heart, as proof that he was not guilty. A tree eventually did so. It can still be seen today, commanding a spot where visitors claim to hear the ghostly cries of the dead Mr. Boyington, still proclaiming his innocence.

A month before her 16th birthday in 1837, the teenage Sally Carter visited her sister's plantation home, Cedarhurst Mansion, in Huntsville. At what should have been a festive time, Sally suddenly passed away after a brief illness and was buried on the grounds. Although her life was short, Sally Carter is said to have lived on in the afterlife, apparently stretching out her visit to Cedarhurst indefinitely. The legend is alleged to have been born in 1919 when a young man who was a guest in the house claimed that he had a strange dream while sleeping in Sally's former bedroom during a thunderstorm. A ghost identifying itself as Sally Carter reportedly asked him to go prop up her headstone, which she said had fallen during the storm. The next morning, he walked to the gravesite where Sally's tombstone had indeed tumbled over during the heavy storm. Before her grave was moved to an unknown location in 1982 to make way for a town house community at Cedarhurst, many Alabamans say that visiting **Sally Carter's Grave** at night became a rite of passage. Some say that despite the relocation of her body, Sally Carter's uneasy spirit remains at Cedarhurst.

The **Witch in the Woods** is said to inhabit the thicket near Gadsden, Alabama. According to local legend, a disheveled woman will appear to daring souls who are walking in the densely forested Hinds Road area at night, claiming she has sold her soul to the devil. In the early 1900s, a woman is alleged to have lived alone in a nearby shack. Whenever a child in town went missing, the reclusive woman was said to have been responsible. Finally, a vigilante mob went to her shack by the dead of night and burned it with her inside. Local citizens swore they heard a terrifying cackle echoing over the town as they watched the glow from the flames engulf the woman and her shabby home. Soon after, the spirit of the Witch in the Woods was said to appear to those who venture into her territory at night.

ICONIC ALABAMA FOOD

The originator of **Lane Cake** was Emma Rylander Lane, of Clayton, Alabama. The rich confection became associated with the state after being mentioned in Harper Lee's classic book *To Kill a Mockingbird*, set in Alabama. In 2016, Lane Cake became Alabama's official state cake. Some cooks prefer the convenience of prepared frosting, as seen below, while others make their own. The cake's filling traditionally includes cherries, coconut, pecans, and raisins that are soaked in bourbon, brandy, or wine. However, brandy flavoring is used in this recipe:

Lane Cake (Serves 10)
1 cup butter, softened
2 cups white sugar
1 tsp vanilla extract
3¼ cups all-purpose flour
1 Tbsp baking powder
¾ tsp salt
1 cup milk
8 egg whites
Prepared frosting

Filling
½ cup butter

1¼ cups white sugar
8 egg yolks
½ cup water
1 tsp brandy flavoring
1 cup chopped pecans
1 cup raisins
1½ tsp light corn syrup
½ cup chopped candied cherries
½ cup flaked coconut

1. While preheating oven to 350°F, grease and flour four 8-inch round cake pans, then mix butter, sugar, and vanilla together in a bowl until fluffy.
2. Combine baking powder, flour, and salt before adding to butter mixture in three parts alternately with the milk, beginning and ending with flour.
3. Beat egg whites until stiff, then gently fold egg whites into batter. Spread batter evenly into four pans. Bake at 350° for 25 minutes or until toothpick inserted in the center comes out clean. Let layers cool before spreading Lane Cake filling between layers.

Filling
4. Put the butter and sugar in the top of a double boiler and beat together, away from heat. Add egg yolks and beat well, then stir in water and brandy flavoring.
5. Place over boiling water, stirring until thickened. Add cherries, coconut, pecans, corn syrup, and raisins. Combine all ingredients and remove from heat, letting the filling cool before spreading between cake layers.
6. Frost the cake according to directions.

Source: Adapted from https://www.allrecipes.com/recipe/7613/lane-cake/.

ODD LAWS

According to legal sources, it is unlawful in Alabama to wear a fake mustache in church. The rationale is said to be that it could cause laughter in a house of worship. Alabama police are not reported to be overly zealous about enforcing this law, nor is it known how often the law is broken.

Possibly along similar lines, according to Alabama Code, a person in a public place who fraudulently pretends "by garb or outward array to be a minister of any religion, or nun, priest, rabbi or other member of the clergy" is guilty of a misdemeanor. Infractions could earn the offender a $500 fine and up to a year in jail, regardless of the intent.

As the first capital of New France, the city of Mobile has a proud history that includes hosting the oldest annual Mardi Gras celebration in the United States. Situated on the Gulf Coast and mindful of the Gulf's ecosystems that are important to the economy, Mobile may also have been ahead of the environmental curve when the city enacted an ordinance stating that the use of nonbiodegradable plastic-based confetti is prohibited. That also includes risking prosecution by spraying the substance known as Silly String, which some offenders seem to find indispensable for a Mardi Gras parade.

UNUSUAL DESTINATIONS

Although it is in an isolated location, the **Coon Dog Cemetery** near Cherokee, Alabama, attracts visitors from all over to mingle among the occupants of what is said to be the only cemetery in the world designated specifically for these registered hunting dogs. There are more than 300 canines buried there, all of whom appear to have been much loved by the humans for whom they were "man's best friend." Observers often especially note the names of the deceased, such as Hardtime Wrangler, Preacher, and Strait Talk'n' Tex. Some are members of the same family, such as Blueflash and Blueflash Jr. A few have simple names like Sam, while others, like "Bragg the Best East of the Mississippi River," are self-explanatory. Some graves are marked with humble wooden crosses, while others have elegantly etched granite markers. All are strangely touching.

The **Largest Office Chair** does not belong to an internet magnate or wealthy investment banker. Since 1981, it has loomed above the parking lot of Miller's Office Furniture in Anniston, Alabama. Store owner Leonard "Sonny" Miller had it built to attract attention and stimulate business. Standing taller than a three-story building, the massive chair is said to be constructed from 10 tons of steel that are held in place by a similar tonnage of concrete. The structure is an exact model of a standard office chair manufactured by the Hon Company, a brand sold in Miller's store. In 1982, Miller's supersized seat earned a coveted spot in the official *Guinness Book of Records* where it rested on its laurels as the World's Largest Office Chair. Alabama was sitting pretty until 2003 when it lost its throne to a company from Italy that built a larger one. However, Alabama can still take pride in holding the American record for this seat of power.

For a different kind of seat, the award-winning **Restrooms at Perry Lakes Park** in Marion, Alabama, comprise a destination that has been known to leave many Alabamans flushed with pride. Called "Toilet Experiences" by the designers, they are three separate restroom facilities that were designed and built by architecture students at Auburn's Rural Studio, a program offered through Alabama's Auburn University. Created to blend into the natural environment, the Perry Lakes Park facilities were finalists in the 2015 competition to be named "America's Best Restroom" sponsored by the Cintas Corporation. Reflecting the style of the rustic pavilion at Perry Lakes Park, the first option in answering nature's call ascends to 50 feet and is understandably called the Tall Toilet. The second, with two lengthy cantilevered walls that include a tree within their placement, is named the Long Toilet. The third is called the Mound Toilet, which is said by Rural Studio to be "captured in the earthen septic system of the bathroom complex." Officials stress that while all three are essentially open air, they are designed for privacy as well as aesthetics. Concerned guests are informed that they will be able to see out from their vantage point but people outside allegedly do not have the same kind of view looking in.

DISTINCTIVE ALABAMA WORDS AND SAYINGS

Bama: Abbreviation of the word "Alabama," especially as it pertains to University of Alabama athletics.

Dolphin Island: What some children mishear for "Dauphin Island," a popular Alabama vacation spot. The resort embraces the error by featuring a dolphin on promotional materials, which is probably more family friendly than its original name of Massacre Island.

Tide: Not a laundry detergent or the rise and fall of sea levels on the coast, but the nickname for the University of Alabama's "Crimson Tide" athletics program, whose exhortation is "Roll, Tide!"

"We Are the Tigers Who Say 'War Eagle!'": Auburn University battle cry that often has to be explained to confused outsiders, since the school's mascot is a tiger. Along similar lines, the University of Alabama, known as the Crimson Tide, has an elephant for a mascot. State residents proudly say it's an Alabama thing.

Further Reading

Bridges, Edwin. *Alabama: The Making of an American State*. Tuscaloosa: University of Alabama Press, 2016.

"Lane Cake." *Encyclopedia of Alabama*. Accessed October 29, 2021. http://www.encyclopediaofalabama.org/article/h-1340.

Windham, Kathryn Tucker. *Jeffrey's Latest 13: More Alabama Ghosts*. Huntsville, AL: Strode Publishers, 1982.

Alaska

FACT BOX

Nickname: The Last Frontier
Statehood Granted: 1959
Capital: Juneau
Population: 730,000
State Motto: "North to the Future"
What Natives Call Themselves: Alaskans

STATE HISTORY

Most experts believe that about 15,000 years ago, the first humans came to Alaska from present-day Siberia following animal herds. They were able to travel on what has been called the "Bering Land Bridge" between Russia and Alaska, which was utilized until Ice Age glaciers melted and sea levels rose to cover it. Today, their probable descendants include Alaska's Indigenous people such as Aleuts, Eskimos, and Inuits.

In 1741, Alaska was discovered during a Russian expedition led by Vitus Bering. The name "Alaska" was derived from the Russian interpretation of the Aleut word *Alyeska*, essentially meaning "great land." By 1784, Russian settlements were established in Alaska to exploit fur-bearing animals.

However, the Russian government lost interest in maintaining an outpost in Alaska when overhunting depleted the supply of pelts. In 1867, Russia agreed to a purchase offer by America's secretary of state William Seward of about $7 million—less than 2¢ an acre. Many Americans of that era called the sale "Seward's Folly," imagining a worthless frozen wasteland.

However, the glitter of gold in the Alaska Territory motivated some to reconsider their opinion. In 1872, the year of Seward's death, gold was discovered near Sitka. Thousands of prospectors flooded into Alaska seeking gold deposits that regularly kept being discovered in the region through the late 1800s. The Klondike Gold Rush of 1897–1900 alone brought more than 100,000 prospectors to Alaska.

In 1942, Alaska's Aleutian Islands were invaded by Japan, taking more than a year for American troops to recapture them for the United States. It is known as the only World War II battle to be fought on American soil.

> ### Sightseeing Seward
>
> William Henry Seward (1801–1872) was far better known in his own time than today and may reign as one of America's unsung heroes. He was regarded as a leading candidate for the presidency in 1860, losing the nomination to Abraham Lincoln. Seward then graciously campaigned for Lincoln. After winning the election, President Lincoln appointed Seward as secretary of state. In that post, Seward helped prevent Britain and France from intervening on the Confederate side in the Civil War. Suffering serious injuries in the assassination plot that killed Lincoln, Seward never fully regained his health. After leaving office in 1869, Seward wanted to spend his last days traveling. He visited Alaska that same year, and after returning home, he spoke publicly about the wonders he had seen there. In an unusual move for that era, he had gone to Alaska simply to seek out the region's natural beauty, not for business purposes. Therefore, many Alaskans today regard Seward as Alaska's first tourist.

In 1959, the Alaska Territory became America's 49th state. This was good timing, since less than 10 years later, "black gold"—oil—was discovered at Alaska's North Slope at Prudhoe Bay. Today, Alaska accounts for about a quarter of all oil produced in the United States, giving Alaskans a unique distinction among the 50 states: free money. Based on oil production, each year, every qualifying Alaska resident receives a check called the Permanent Fund Dividend (PFD). Over the years, individual annual payments have ranged from about $300 to more than $2,000.

Alaska is the only American state to call its 19 local governmental units "boroughs," not counties. Alaska reigns as the largest state in the Union, often a source of chagrin for Texas, which is half the size of Alaska.

The state is unique in having coastlines on three major seas: the Arctic Ocean, Pacific Ocean, and Bering Sea. Many Alaskans have plenty of time to contemplate not only the waters but the nature all around them. Due to its far-North location, it is the only state in the Union with areas that get up to 24 hours of daylight in summer. Therefore, parts of Alaska comprise America's own "Land of the Midnight Sun."

Conversely, in winter, some places in Alaska have 24 hours of night. Northern Alaska towns such as Barrow can go more than two months without seeing the sun rise in winter and about three months in summer without seeing a sunset.

It is not quite as extreme in other parts of the state, where there are generally a few hours of sunshine during winter and vice versa. But even in the centrally located city of Fairbanks, there are only a few hours of sun per day in winter and about three hours of darkness in summer.

All that sunshine from June through August has an uncanny effect on Alaska's crops. Even though winter temperatures in Alaska can range from 0°F to −30°F from November to March, temperatures in summer can reach well above 80°F.

With the combination of summertime sunshine for 20 hours a day plus Alaska's fertile soil, massive crops emerge.

Cabbages with a weight of more than 100 pounds and pumpkins that tilt the scales at 1,000 pounds have sprung forth in Alaska, along with 30-pound stalks of broccoli and carrots that weigh 10 pounds each.

Alaska has a few more things that other states cannot match. As the home of Denali, rising over 20,000 feet, Alaska can boast the highest mountain peak in North America. It is also home to America's most remote point in all the 50 states, the Ipnavik River National Petroleum Reserve, which is situated a lonely 120 miles from the nearest habitation.

In one of the oddest manifestations of Alaska's geography, it is said to be the northernmost, westernmost, *and* easternmost point of the United States. Generally, there is no argument about Alaska being the farthest north and west. However, the Aleutian island of Semisopochnoi lies west of the 180° longitude meridian that separates the Western Hemisphere from the Eastern Hemisphere and is therefore so far west that it can technically be considered *east*. It is a point of trivia that often annoys people from Maine who prefer to think of their state as the easternmost point of the United States. However, Alaska wins on a technicality.

URBAN LEGENDS

Consisting of some of the most barren wilderness in the world, the **Alaska Triangle** is the state's version of the Bermuda Triangle. Located in Northwest Alaska, more than 20,000 people are said to have vanished there over the past 50 years. Some claim that the victims are being consumed by mythological evil spirits such as the Keelut or Qalupalik who lure them to their death. Some blame an electromagnetically influenced "vile vortex." When the small plane carrying U.S. congressmen Mark Begich and Hale Boggs disappeared without a trace in 1972, conspiracy theories abounded. Such theories and urban legends are more dramatic than the likely cause: man versus nature. In a barren artic wilderness, nature often wins. With Alaska being home to hundreds of communities that are accessible only by air or water, many Alaskans own small aircraft that they use for basic transportation, much like cars. The state's weather can be extremely variable all year, especially in winter, and light airplanes with little instrumentation can crash in inaccessible places. Some say that if the massive blanket of snow, primeval forests, and apparently bottomless lakes were to disappear, a well-preserved mass grave of accident victims would emerge. Others prefer to blame it on demons.

As with many areas around the world, Alaska has its own version of Bigfoot. The **Alaskan Hairy Man** is said to stand over 10 feet tall; be covered with coarse, shaggy hair; have elongated arms; and emit a foul smell, although there is little documented evidence of anyone getting close enough to catch his scent. According to legend, the Hairy Man is a descendant of mythological creatures known as the Tornits. The trouble is alleged to have started back in the mists of time when the peaceful relationship between the Tornits and Inuits came to a halt in an incident that apparently involved a damaged kayak. Since that time, the fate of hunters in the wilderness who go missing is often attributed to vengeful Tornit spirits personified by the Hairy Man.

During the Alaska gold-rush era, the long arctic nights often gave rise to sharing ghost stories. A popular tale centered on the abandoned **Baranof Castle** in Sitka. As home of the territory's Russian governors, it was the site where the Russians lowered their flag in 1867, officially transferring Alaska to the United States. After its abandonment, Baranof Castle allegedly became haunted by the apparition of what was said to be a beautiful Russian princess wearing a dark old-fashioned dress. Spooky tales arose, with newspaper articles eventually repeating the story. It seems that that the ghostly "Lady in Black" was the daughter of an aristocratic Russian governor who forced her to marry a man she did not love. On her wedding night, she reportedly killed herself, leaving her spirit to wander the deserted castle after midnight. In rebuttal, historians could find no evidence of any such family, but they were often dismissed as killjoys.

Whether the urban legends involve the **Kushtaka, Keelut, Ircenrraat,** or **Qalupalik**, these mythological creatures are alleged to prey on unsuspecting humans. The Kushtaka are shape-shifters who are said to look like a cross between an otter and a human male. Perhaps with a nod to the lovable otters, some stories describe the Kushtaka as helpful to humans. However, most portray them as deceptive creatures that mimic the screams of women and children drowning in the sea, luring fishermen to their deaths. The Keelut, said to prey on those traveling at night, is described as a black dog that is hairless except for profuse hair on its feet, making tracks that disappear in the snow. Native to the Alaskan tundra, Ircenrraat are said to be small humanoid creatures who are mischief-makers, disorienting travelers in the wilderness before trapping them in underground lairs. Finally, the Qalupalik live in the frigid waters of the Alaska coastline, having scaly, green skin; long, dark, wet hair; and unnaturally long fingernails. They are said to entice children to the water's edge by humming cheerfully to attract attention before dragging the child under the waves, never to be seen again.

ICONIC ALASKAN FOOD

Many Alaskans consider the quintessential Alaskan food to be **King Crab**, a world-class delicacy. King crabs are large deep-water creatures that are harvested from the Bering Sea off the Alaskan coast and the waters of the Aleutian Islands. There is often significant risk involved from drowning or hypothermia for those on the fishing boats. The commercial harvest season is short, lasting only a few weeks. King crabs are fierce crustaceans who claim the sea floor as their hunting grounds, wielding a set of large claws and three pairs of powerful legs. Their succulent meat is found within the shells of the legs. King crabs are usually flash frozen on the fishing boats, ultimately arriving to consumers in that state. Many aficionados favor preparing them as follows:

> **Steamed Alaskan King Crab** (Yields as many crab legs as desired)
> King crab legs (as many as desired)

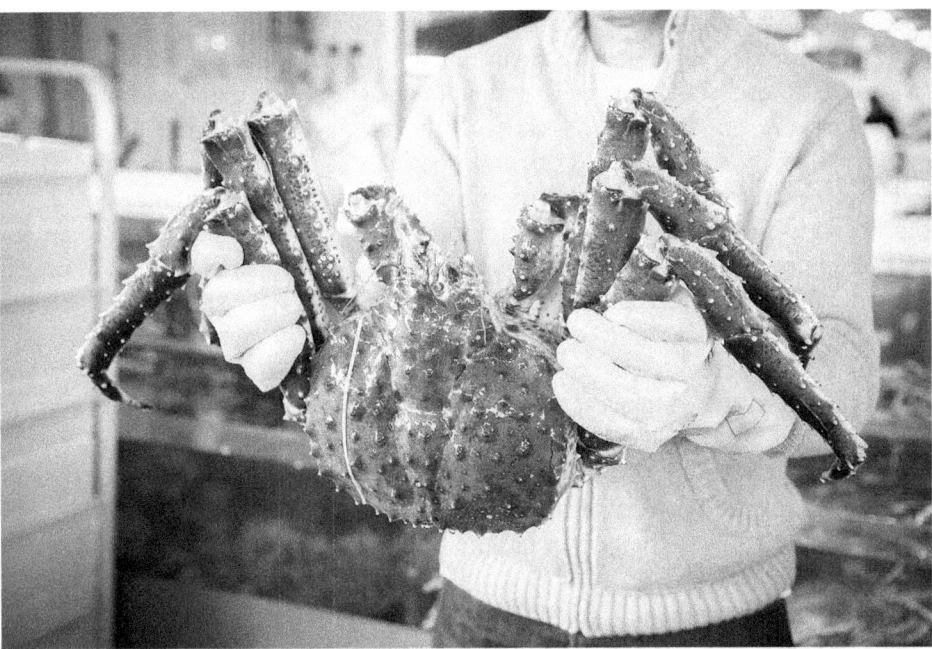

Alaska is famous for its King Crab, a large deep-water creature that wields a huge set of claws and three pairs of powerful legs. Harvesting them off the Aleutian Islands is often dangerous for those on the fishing boats. (Nuvisage/Dreamstime.com)

  2 cups water
  1 Tbsp salt
  Garlic butter
  Lemon wedges

1. Add water and salt to a large pot until the pot is about a third of the way full, then bring to a boil.
2. Place King Crab legs in a colander or on a rack over the rapidly boiling water.
3. Cover with a lid.
4. Cook for 6–10 minutes so the crab legs are completely heated, which can often be determined if they "smell cooked."
5. Serve with garlic butter and lemon wedges.

Source: Adapted from https://www.alaskankingcrab.com/blogs/resources/how-to-cook-alaskan-king-crab.

ODD LAWS

According to Alaska statutes, the moose (known by its formal name from the Latin as *Alces alces*) is the official state land mammal. Having such an elite status, the moose can be found at the center of a number of the state's laws, which Americans in other locales might consider to be somewhat odd. Unlike most other deer species, a moose is a solitary animal that does not gather in a herd. Sometimes a loner can wander into domestic environments where it is not welcome. Alaska's "Nuisance Moose" statute states that an animal shall not be destroyed "if a practicable alternative exists for the relocation of the moose to suitable habitat where the moose will not be a nuisance." It does not specify how that might be accomplished.

However, any moose relocation cannot involve an airplane. One Alaska law prohibits pushing a live moose out of a moving airplane. Nor is it legal to search for moose from an airplane on the same day that a person plans to hunt, although hunters can "scout" the night before and hunt the next day (although, often, the moose might well have moved). Incidentally, while a hunter is taking aim at a moose, it is illegal to whisper in that hunter's ear.

In other Alaskan ordinances, it is unlawful to wake a bear just to shoot a picture of it. However, if a bear is wide awake, it is legal to shoot it with a gun.

Speaking of weaponry, the sale of stun guns to children is banned in the state of Alaska. In addition, whether or not a child is involved, carrying a concealed slingshot is unlawful unless the person has the proper license to do so.

UNUSUAL DESTINATIONS

The **Hammer Museum** in Haines, Alaska, claims to have 2,000 hammers on display. Calling itself the world's first museum dedicated to preserving the history of the hammer, it is strangely fascinating as it ties the history of this useful tool into the history of humans. Even the sign atop the building is made of hammers, and a giant hammer stands in front, so the building is hard to miss. Hammers from around the world, in every shape and size, can be seen. Curious visitors will also discover some of the different uses hammers have had through time, ranging from ancient to modern, and sizes from 2 inches to 20 feet. Museum officials note that they have many more hammers in storage, so this family-friendly spot is not just a one-time-only destination. Visitors should be attentive to planning the time of their visit, since the Hammer Museum is only open from May to September.

Interested parties will also have to time their visit carefully to coincide with the date of the annual **Outhouse Races** in Anchorage. Usually held in late February as part of the annual Fur Rendezvous, the Outhouse Race is a highlight of the festival and is precisely what the name implies. Squads of five people, often with unprintable team names, push or pull outhouses that are mounted on skis over the city's frozen roadways. Each entry must include a rider inside as well as an obligatory roll of toilet paper. It is considered the world's largest such event, attracting contestants who build their outhouse specifically with aerodynamics in mind and must pass a prerace inspection to make sure it is structurally sound. Various skills are involved, including solid construction, strength of team members, and coordination in rounding curves on the icy streets on the way to the finish line. The coveted Toilet Paper Holder trophy is awarded to those who wipe out the competition to become Number One.

Despite its name, the town of North Pole, Alaska, is near Fairbanks, more than 1,500 miles south of Earth's actual geographic North Pole. However, it *can* boast the **Santa Claus House**, a Christmas-themed gift shop that is known for having the world's largest statue of Santa plus a small herd of domesticated reindeer under the watchful gaze of the 42-foot-tall Saint Nick. It is open year-round for those who can't get enough of Christmas. Each year, Santa Claus House is ground zero for hundreds of thousands of children's letters to Santa as well as thousands more from grown-ups who want the town's postmark on their Christmas cards. Santa Claus House provides customers with a variety of styles for "Santa" to send letters to children at various stages of their lives and displays some letters to Santa that have been received over the years since the shop's inception in 1952. The town of North Pole itself, with its Christmas-themed street names, was created in hopes of attracting a toy manufacturer to jump-start its economy. Although that did not materialize, Santa Claus House serves as a stand-in, providing children around the world with the knowledge that the zip code of North Pole, Alaska—99705—is the one to use for Santa.

Travelers who enjoy being photographed at unusual city limits signs might consider a visit to **Eek, Alaska**. Thoroughfares from that town run to Quinhagak to the south and Tuntutuliak to the west. With the village of Eek originally known as Apokagamiut, "Eek" is considered by most to at least be simpler to pronounce. Incidentally, the town's name is derived from an Eskimo word meaning "two eyes" and is not a reaction to seeing its average winter temperature, which hovers around zero.

DISTINCTIVE ALASKA WORDS AND SAYINGS

Bush: Areas of Alaska unreachable by roadway and therefore must be reached by either airplanes or boats in summer and snow machines (see below) in winter.

Cheechako: Essentially a "tenderfoot," or a person who is new to Alaska and ignorant of how things work there.

Nanook: Variant on the native word for "polar bear," sometimes applied to local sports teams such as those at the University of Alaska in Fairbanks.

Snow machine: Alaskan term for what is usually called a "snowmobile" elsewhere in the United States.

Sourdough: An Alaskan who has lived in the state for a very long time, even if not actually born there.

Further Reading

Devereaux, James P. *Spirits of Southeast Alaska: The History and Hauntings of Alaska's Panhandle*. Kenmore, WA: Epicenter Press, 2018.

Farrow, Lee A. *Seward's Folly: A New Look at the Alaska Purchase*. Fairbanks: University of Alaska Press, 2016.

Naske, Claus, and Herman Slotnick. *Alaska: A History*. Norman: University of Oklahoma Press, 2014.

Arizona

FACT BOX

Nickname: The Grand Canyon State
Statehood Granted: 1912
Capital: Phoenix
Population: 7,300,000
State Motto: *Ditat Deus* (Latin: "God Enriches")
What Natives Call Themselves: Arizonans

STATE HISTORY

For thousands of years, the land in today's Arizona was home to Native American people, including tribes such as the Hopi and Navajo. Spaniards began arriving in 1539, with the first documented exploration of the region made by a Franciscan friar, Marcos de Niza. Attracted by tales of gold, Francisco Vázquez de Coronado's expedition arrived the following year. Searching in the heat while wearing about 30 pounds of gilded armor, the only gold they found was Arizona's scorching desert sun.

Today's Arizona was claimed by Spain as part of its empire, but the number of settlers remained relatively small. Then the area became known to Americans when tens of thousands passed through today's Arizona, lured by the 1849 California Gold Rush. Many returned when their luck in the gold fields did not pan out.

During the remainder of the 1800s, Arizona was absorbed by the United States. In 1863, the Arizona Territory was created by the U.S. government. It was none other than President Abraham Lincoln who approved the final name of "Arizona" for the territory, although Gadsonia, Montezuma, and Pimeria had all been considered. Ultimately, Arizona joined the Union in 1912, making it the 48th and last of the contiguous states to be admitted.

Today, Arizona is revered by many as a unique state full of staggering natural wonders, plus a rich Native American– and Hispanic-based culture. It has the kind of natural treasures that are found nowhere else: the Grand Canyon, the Painted Desert, Petrified Forest, parts of Monument Valley, the red rocks of Sedona, and the vertigo-inducing undulations of Antelope Canyon. The mythical Old West still lives in restored Arizona towns such as Tombstone.

One Arizona landmark goes back even further than the Old West: England's London Bridge. In 1963, with the British planning to replace the structure that dated back to 1825, the London City Council agreed to its purchase by an American industrialist who had London Bridge dismantled, shipped, and reassembled as a tourist attraction in Lake Havasu City, Arizona.

Along with the apparent mirage of spotting London Bridge amid Arizona's desert landscape, the state is one of the few that can truthfully claim that a visitor may go snow skiing in its mountains in the morning and water skiing on one of its lakes that same afternoon. Alongside its flat, desolate landscape that would look at home on the planet Mars, Arizona has more than 30 snowy mountain peaks that tower higher than 10,000 feet in elevation.

Arizona is the only state that contains parts of all four North American deserts—the Chihuahua, Great Basin, Mohave, and Sonoran—having the most diverse plant and animal life of all the deserts in the world. In spite of—or perhaps because of—such barren desert regions, within Arizona's borders are Lake Mead and Lake Powell, America's two largest man-made lakes. Arizona can also boast the only one of the seven natural wonders of the world that is in the United States: the Grand Canyon.

This unique, mystical state is also a land of contradictions. Iconic Arizona figures are not always what they appear to be. For example, the first "white man" to arrive in Arizona was actually a Black man. An enslaved person from Africa was sent by the viceroy of New Spain to scout lands north of Mexico after several Spaniards declined to tackle the daunting, barren waste. Usually said to be called Esteban, he left Mexico City in 1539, traveling ahead of a party led by Friar Marcos de Niza in search of the golden Seven Cities of Cibola. Esteban was reported to have been killed by Native Americans, although some accounts favor the theory that reports of his death were greatly exaggerated so he could gain freedom from slavery and live among the Indians.

With much of the Old West's iconography being based on cowboys, Arizona's first great cattleman was actually a woman: Eulalia Elias, a Mexican American who established the first major cattle ranch in Arizona, the Babacomari, in 1832.

Another myth-shattering Arizona oddity is that America's most famous gunfight, which took place in the town of Tombstone in 1881, did not actually take place at the O.K. Corral. This legendary altercation between Wyatt Earp and his brothers with their friend Doc Holliday against the McLaury brothers and Billy Clanton occurred at a vacant lot *behind* the O.K. Corral on Tombstone's Fremont Street between Fly's Photography Gallery and the William Harwood house. However, most people would agree that the "Gunfight at the Vacant Lot next to Fly's" might not sound as colorful.

Further, Arizona is unique in having not only a nation within its borders but also a nation within a nation. Covering more than 27,000 square miles, the major portion of the Navajo Nation is in Northeastern Arizona. With a population of about 175,000 people, it is the largest area of land held by an Indigenous Native American tribe in the United States, almost equivalent to the combined area of Connecticut, Delaware, New Hampshire, New Jersey, and Rhode Island.

> **Time Will Tell**
>
> In the United States, setting the clock ahead one hour during the warmer months of the year ("Spring Forward") is called Daylight Saving Time. The Uniform Time Act of 1966 was decreed by Congress to theoretically save energy by adding an extra hour of daylight to summertime evenings and subtracting one from summer mornings. Most areas of the United States observe the practice, but Arizona claimed an exemption in 1968. With summer temperatures in much of Arizona soaring over 100°F, it is said that no energy is conserved by running air conditioners an extra hour in the hottest part of the day. Depending on destination, to make matters more confusing for travelers on a time-critical schedule, Arizona's Navajo Reservation observes Daylight Saving Time, but the Hopi Reservation, completely surrounded by the Navajo Nation, does *not*, thus necessitating changing clocks back and forth several times en route.

The Hopi Reservation, at about 2,500 square miles, is located entirely within the Navajo Nation. Arizona is also home to other large Native American enclaves, including the Gila River and Salt River Indian Communities of the Pima and Maricopa, the San Carlos Chiricahua Apache Reservation, and the White Mountain Apache Reservation.

One more oddity involves a widely copied internet item stating that it is illegal to hunt camels in Arizona. Legal experts note that while such a law may have existed in the past, it is no longer on the books. If it was, there was indeed a historical basis for this law. In 1855, American secretary of war (later Confederate president) Jefferson Davis ordered herds of camels to be imported from the Middle East to haul supplies for military bases in America's desertlike western territories such as Arizona. However, after the Civil War broke out in 1861, Davis was out of office and out of favor. Then, the completion of the transcontinental railroad in 1869 made the camels unnecessary. Left to forage the Arizona deserts on their own, they may have at least been safe from being hunted.

URBAN LEGENDS

With its unnerving name, the legendary town of Tombstone, Arizona, allegedly has its share of specters from the past stalking its dusty streets. One site is especially known for hosting visitors from the afterlife: the **Bird Cage Theater**, which is called Tombstone's most haunted spot. The Bird Cage opened in 1881, soon after the legendary gunfight at the O.K. Corral. It later served as a saloon, gambling hall, and brothel, operating 24 hours a day, 365 days a year. In 16 different deadly gunfights and grisly knife fights, almost 30 people lost their lives at the Bird Cage. Today, its walls are riddled with about 150 bullet holes. Some "fallen women" are said to have succumbed to drink, drugs, or disease or killed themselves out of despair. Today, their ghosts are said to be joined at the Bird Cage by other uneasy spirits who, when alive, suddenly and violently exchanged the town of Tombstone for another kind of tombstone.

Shape-shifting **Skinwalkers** are said to be powerful medicine men who departed from benign spiritual ways to become evil reflections of the Navajo Nation's values. Skinwalkers have a reputation for being malevolent creatures that can kill humans using mental powers. Some travelers driving at high speeds through lonely, barren regions on deserted Arizona highways claim to hear tapping on their window and then turn to see a zombielike creature looking in, apparently wanting to ride shotgun. The legend of the Skinwalkers is deeply ingrained in Arizona culture, particularly among the Navajo. Skinwalker lore has been known to be used in court as an alternative theory of the crime by defendants accused of especially gruesome murders. Skinwalkers even have their own alleged stomping grounds, a place known as Skinwalker Ranch where inexplicable paranormal-type events are said to have taken place. With a number of books, films, and television shows spotlighting Skinwalkers, the creatures may be ready for their close-up, but few humans would probably care to see them.

In the 1800s, a family allegedly lived south of Kingman, Arizona, near the bottom of what is today called **Slaughterhouse Canyon**. The father would leave home for days or weeks at a time to try prospecting or simply in search of food. One day, it is said that the father did not return. His family, left alone in the canyon, descended into starvation. The mother was driven to madness seeing her children wither away for lack of food and hearing their pitiful cries that echoed across the canyon walls. Unable to bear their suffering, she is said to have killed the children. She then took her own life, which some say was done after she changed into her wedding dress. According to the legend, those who visit Slaughterhouse Canyon at night will not only feel the mother's anguish but hear the pathetic cries of the family who perished there, echoing through the canyon.

ICONIC ARIZONA FOOD

Being home to the Navajo Nation, Arizona has enjoyed the influence of Native American cultures in its foods. A unique item that is well known in Arizona is a puffy flatbread called **Navajo Fry Bread**. It can be eaten as an appetizer with a light spread or as an accompaniment to a meal like any bread. But it can also shift into a starring role as a main dish by being used as the base for tacos, wraps, or other sandwiches. Fry bread can even become a dessert by sprinkling it with sugar or cinnamon. Whatever role it plays, the basic preparation, as seen below, is the same.

Navajo Fry Bread (Yields 10 pieces)
2 cups bread flour
2 tsp baking powder
¼ tsp salt

¼ cup powdered milk
1 cup hot water
Oil for frying

1. Mix dry ingredients in a bowl, then slowly add hot water. Mix with fingers until it forms a ball that pulls away from sides of the bowl.
2. Add flour or water as needed to create dough that is not too sticky, then cover and let the dough rest for 10 minutes.
3. Pour about an inch of oil in a large skillet. After setting a thermometer on the edge of the skillet, heat until it reaches 375°F.
4. Pinch off pieces of dough about the size of golf balls. Flatten each ball, then gently roll or stretch out the edges to form disks that are 5–6 inches across and ¼ inch thick.
5. Make a small hole in the middle of each disk to prevent the dough from "ballooning."
6. Lay disks of dough in the hot oil so they do not stick together. Press each one down with tongs so hot oil flows over the top of the dough.
7. Fry until golden brown around edges, then turn over and cook for a few seconds until the other side looks the same.
8. After placing each on paper towels to blot excess oil, repeat the cooking process until all the disks of dough are fried.

Source: Adapted from https://www.aspicyperspective.com/easy-navajo-fry-bread.

ODD LAWS

Anyone who has seen a Western is familiar with the saguaro cactus. Some think of the plants with "arms" as majestic, others as slightly goofy. But whatever impression they make on observers, saguaros are protected by Arizona law. According to the state's legal code, a person who moves a saguaro that is more than four feet tall from its original growing location must have a permit, tag, and seal before doing so, or the person will face the consequences. Destroying one through construction work or roadbuilding is also prohibited, along with shooting one for target practice. Violation is punishable by a fine and/or jail time. However, in one documented case, a 500-pound saguaro took the law into its own hands by falling on a man who was trying to push it over, killing him.

Saguaros are native to Arizona, so their protection might be understandable. However, "crane games" can be found everywhere across the nation, such as at arcades, fairs, and supermarkets. These are the boxlike cubes in which the player pays to maneuver a crane over a pile of toys to try grabbing one as a prize. According to Arizona statute, it is unlawful for a person to be caught altering or maintaining a crane game so that the claw is unable to grasp the exposed prizes as well as displaying prizes in a crane game so that the claw is physically incapable of grasping the prizes, misrepresenting the value of prizes in crane games, using cash or currency as prizes in crane games, or awarding prizes in crane games that are redeemable for cash or currency. It is not known how severe the crane game problem was in Arizona before this law was enacted to protect its citizens.

An even more difficult conundrum is what sort of criminal behavior spurred the enactment of the following succinct statute in the Arizona legal code: "State Neckwear: 'The Bola tie shall be the official state neckwear.'" Sometimes called a bolo or shoestring necktie, this item of clothing consists of cord or braided leather with decorative metal tips and secured with an ornamental clasp or slide. For trivia buffs, the metal tips are called aiguillettes, although there is nothing in the statute that regulates them. It is not known what caused the statute to be enacted by the Arizona Legislature in 1971. The law does not specify what the penalty for infractions might be. Hopefully, it does not involve a saguaro cactus.

Anyone who has seen a Western is familiar with the saguaro cactus, with its distinctive "arms." The saguaro (pronounced suh-WARR-oh) is protected by Arizona law. (Muriel Kerr/Dreamstime.com)

UNUSUAL DESTINATIONS

To some, the **Boneyard** at Davis-Monthan Air Force Base near Tucson is virtually sacred ground. It is the place where airplanes go to die or at least to go into retirement. With more than 4,000 aircrafts, it is the largest facility of its kind in the world. This aviation graveyard is managed by the Air Force through its Aerospace Maintenance and Regeneration Group. Old military aircraft and other types of planes are stored indefinitely. Some are demilitarized for display purposes, others are stripped for parts, and a few are restored somewhat to be ready for service if needed. It is the only such facility open to the public, but it can only be seen on a bus tour. Photography is permitted through the bus window, since visitors are not allowed off the vehicle. It may be just as well, because at the Boneyard, grown men have been known to become teary eyed at the sight.

Arizona boasts a number of places that re-create its storied Western past, but travelers can go even farther back, all the way to prehistoric times (at least the fictional version) at **Flintstones Bedrock City**. Located near the town of Williams, Arizona, Flintstones Bedrock City features life-size replicas of characters and structures based on the popular television program that ran from 1960 to 1966. Some visitors consider this destination to be home of American TV's original "rock" stars.

Most people would probably not seek Santa's workshop in the Arizona desert. But near Kingman, on the highway leading to Las Vegas, is the abandoned **Santa Claus, Arizona**. All that is left of a proposed Christmas-themed town are a few rickety vandalized buildings and the remains of "Old 1225," a derailed children's train that once featured festive hand-painted pictures of Santa and his elves but today is defaced by graffiti. The ghost town had been planned in the 1930s by a real estate developer as a tourist destination, resort, and land sales office for those who wanted to enjoy Christmas cheer year-round. The town of Santa Claus even appeared in a 1950 short story called "Cliff and the Calories" by prominent science fiction writer Robert A. Heinlein. Even that could not save the deteriorating townsite. Today, the sad remains on the roadside are a curiosity, but probably not a place for impressionable children, even those on their way to Vegas.

DISTINCTIVE ARIZONA WORDS AND SAYINGS

Chubasco: Torrential rainfall in late summer that might be called a "monsoon" elsewhere.

Haboob: Large, intense dust storm.

"It's a dry heat": Classic Arizonan's response to unrelenting summer temperatures of well over 100°F, which some say is less debilitating than humidity-ridden hot weather in sultry Louisiana or even the Chicago Loop in the steamy season.

Saguaro: Name of the iconic long-limbed cactus, which, if mispronounced, is a tip-off that the speaker is not a native Arizonan. The letter g is silent; thus, the word is pronounced "suh-WARR-oh."

Stravenue: Combination of the words "street" and "avenue" that is familiar to Tucson residents as a diagonal roadway running between the two.

Further Reading

Crutchfield, James. *It Happened in Arizona: Remarkable Events That Shaped History*. Lanham, MD: Rowman & Littlefield, 2017.

Hirsch, Rebecca. *What's Great about Arizona?* Minneapolis, MN: Lerner Publications, 2015.

Trimble, Marshall. *Arizona: A Cavalcade of History*. 2nd edition. Tucson, AZ: Rio Nuevo Publishers, 2003.

"Why Arizona Opts Out of Daylight Saving Time." *ASU Now*. Arizona State University, March 8, 2018. https://asunow.asu.edu/20180305-discoveries-why-arizona-has-opted-out-daylight-saving-time.

Arkansas

FACT BOX

Nickname: The Natural State
Statehood Granted: 1836
Capital: Little Rock
Population: 3,000,000
State Motto: *Regnat populus* (Latin: "The People Rule")
What Natives Call Themselves: Most use "Arkansans," although some prefer "Arkansawyers."

STATE HISTORY

With its rocky hill country in the northwest and fertile Mississippi delta in the southeast, Arkansas has been called a state with a split personality. That notion even extends to what the natives call themselves, whether "Arkansans" or "Arkansawyers."

Indigenous people first arrived in today's Arkansas more than 12,000 years ago. Later, Native American tribes included the Chickasaw, Osage, and Quapaw. Living among them was a group of Native Americans that is today called the Plum Bayou tribe. They built mysterious mounds as tall as five-story buildings, as seen today at Arkansas's Toltec Mounds State Park.

In the late 1600s, French explorers arrived in the lower Mississippi Valley. The first successful European settlement in today's Arkansas was called "Poste de Arkansea," or Arkansas Post. It was founded on the Arkansas River by Henri de Tonti, an explorer who had traveled in North America with René-Robert Cavelier, Sieur de La Salle, from 1678 to 1686.

On their expeditions, they canoed down the Mississippi River to its mouth, claiming the lands it touched for King Louis XIV of France, dubbing it "La Louisiane." For establishing the first settlement in the state that endured, many historians consider Henri de Tonti to be the "Father of Arkansas."

The Frenchmen interpreted the Native name for the region to sound something like "Akansa" or "Arkansea," evolving into "Arkansas." Even though the word basically contains the word "KAN-sas," like the nearby state, it is pronounced "AR-kan-saw."

Few of the early inhabitants of today's Arkansas cared much about proper pronunciation. They were rough hunters and trappers who barely noticed when the region bounced between ownership by France, then Spain, then France again, and finally the United States as part of the Louisiana Purchase in 1803.

The American government in Washington thought that today's Arkansas would be a good place for new settlements west of the Mississippi River. Veterans of the U.S. Army who fought against the British in the War of 1812 were offered land grants as a bonus for their service. Reports filtered back east that the land in Arkansas was rich in great forests teeming with game, which sounded promising to potential settlers.

One can only imagine the reaction of newcomers arriving at the site of their land grants in Northeastern Arkansas. What they found after their arduous journey was not land but water—as far as the eye could see. The forests they had expected were bare treetop branches poking above vast brackish swamps.

What the settlers had *not* heard back east was that the New Madrid Earthquake of 1811–1812 was so severe that it made the Mississippi River run backward for a time, submerging thousands of acres of collapsed land, some of which simply disappeared into the river. Their land grants were at the bottom of a huge dismal swamp. Even today, a great swath of Northeast Arkansas called the "Sunken Land" remains under water.

This unexpected situation disrupted settlement in the Arkansas Territory among the small farmers who had expected to carve homesteads out of the now-submerged forests of the state's northeast section. Some moved westward to the mountainous region of Northwest Arkansas where they could try their luck farming the rocky ground. Others looked to the fertile soil of the Mississippi River delta in Southeast Arkansas, establishing plantations that ultimately relied on slave labor.

By the time Arkansas was granted statehood in 1836, it was already experiencing a cultural and economic divide. Arkansas entered the Union as a slave state, which was supported by wealthy landowners in the southeastern part of the state but was unpopular among small farmers in the hill country of the northwest.

There were money problems in Arkansas almost from the beginning. Cash-strapped small farmers in the hilly northwest felt they were asked to shoulder more than their fair share of the economic burden than the big planters of the southeast who grew ever wealthier through the free labor of enslaved people.

In early 1861, many Arkansas residents wanted to avoid the coming Civil War. Even after some other Southern states seceded, Arkansas voted to stay in the Union. But when President Lincoln ordered the state to send troops, Arkansas officially joined the Confederacy. Once again, popular sentiment was split between pro-Unionists in the northwest and wealthy slaveholders in the southeast who supported the Confederates.

When the Civil War ended in 1865, the state's economy was in tatters, leaving Arkansas in long-term poverty. Toward the latter 1800s, a certain image of Arkansas emerged that was based on a popular song and painting called *The Arkansas Traveler*. This image focused on isolated "hillbillies" subsisting in the Ozark

> **Take the Money and Run**
>
> A year after gaining statehood in 1836, there was a banking scandal in Arkansas that was made worse by the Panic of 1837, a nationwide depression. Then came what seemed like a windfall for Arkansas—about $15 million in today's dollars. The downside was that the United States almost lost of one of its national treasures, the Smithsonian Institution. In 1838, Congress decided to earn interest on the funds left by James Smithson to establish a museum. The U.S. Treasury invested the money in bonds issued by the new state of Arkansas. However, the cash vanished after arriving in the state, never to be seen again. Thanks to an impassioned plea by Massachusetts statesman John Quincy Adams, Congress grudgingly restored the Smithsonian's endowment from the federal budget. There is no documented evidence that Arkansas ever repaid the bonds or who in Arkansas made off with the original Smithsonian funding.

Mountains of North Arkansas. The result was the stereotype of shiftless (and often toothless) Arkansans. This was not appreciated in areas of Arkansas such as Little Rock, the state's capital and cultural center.

Many Arkansans claim their state is the home of America's first national park. In 1832, the U.S. Congress established Hot Springs Reservation, known for its warm waters that were said to have beneficial effects on health; today it is called Hot Springs National Park. It was the first piece of land to be protected by the federal government for recreational use by the public.

Dating back to its earliest days, Arkansas has traditionally been the home of some colorful characters. In the early 1900s, the nationally known temperance advocate, ax-wielding Carrie Nation, moved to the Arkansas town of Eureka Springs. Renowned for smashing up establishments that sold alcohol, after Nation's death, her home in Eureka Springs, aptly called Hatchet Hall, was turned into a museum.

With the coming of the 20th century, headlines about Arkansas could be found in the nation's mass media. One episode was the alleged discovery of a lost civilization in the state. Throughout the 1930s, an Arkansas man sold artifacts that he claimed to have miraculously unearthed. Among the alleged 5,000-year-old relics, the most famous and photogenic was a small statue called King Crowley, named for Crowley's Ridge, where it was said to be found. However, sales dropped when the "discovery" was debunked by national experts, including archaeologists from the Smithsonian Institution.

In an arguably more substantial development, in 1932, an Arkansan named Hattie Caraway became the first woman elected to the U.S. Senate as well as the first woman reelected to the Senate, which she did in 1938. Caraway served until 1945 and was esteemed by Arkansans for her efforts, especially assistance to education.

The outlook for Arkansas looked bright after World War II when wealthy Winthrop Rockefeller, of the Standard Oil fortune, bought land on Petit Jean Mountain near Little Rock, moving there from New York. Rockefeller established his niche in

Arkansas business, culture, and politics, serving as governor from 1967 to 1971. His efforts toward progress helped promote the state's motto at the time, "Land of Opportunity," as well as countered lowbrow Arkansas humor on national radio shows such as *Lum and Abner*.

During the Cold War era, the federal government constructed 18 nuclear launch sites in Arkansas. In 1965, and again in 1980, there were accidents at two of the Arkansas underground missile silos, which some said could have destroyed Middle America. Others felt the devastation would probably just have been confined to vaporizing Arkansas. Neither scenario came to pass, but once again, Arkansas was the subject of national headlines.

The name of one particular colorful character from Arkansas sprang into the nation's consciousness in the 1970s. Businessman Sam Walton created a retail store called Walmart. The company expanded worldwide from its headquarters in the small Northwest Arkansas town of Bentonville, where it remains to this day. Walmart's annual shareholder meeting attracts about 20,000 people from around the globe and is held not in the concrete canyons of New York City but amid the mountains of Northwest Arkansas.

As if that distinction were not enough, several towns in Arkansas claim the title of "World Capital" of something or other, such as Alma (spinach), Hope (watermelons), Malvern (bricks), Mount Ida (quartz), and Mountain Home (folk music). For almost a century, the town of Stuttgart, Arkansas ("Rice and Duck Capital of

Sam Walton of Arkansas created Walmart, which expanded into a multi-million-dollar global phenomenon. The huge corporation is still based in the small Arkansas town of Bentonville. (Andreistanescu/Dreamstime.com)

the World"), has hosted the World Championship Duck Calling Contest. It is said to be the largest and longest-running competition for humans adept in the art of mimicking feathered fowl.

URBAN LEGENDS

The superstar of Arkansas's urban legends is the **Fouke Monster**, otherwise known by its stage name the **Beast of Boggy Creek**. The small town of Fouke, Arkansas, is alleged to be the home of this large hairy Bigfoot-type creature with glowing red eyes. It was said to have attacked members of a local family and their hunting buddy, receiving its name from a reporter whose story went nationwide. Despite the creature's bulk, he apparently moves surprisingly fast, at least too quickly to be captured on film. Using a stand-in, the movie *The Legend of Boggy Creek* catapulted this Arkansas monster to fame. Billing itself as a "docudrama," this low-budget horror film barely missed being in the top 10 highest-grossing films of 1972, going on to become a cult classic. It also spawned the films *Return to Boggy Creek* (1977), *Boggy Creek II: And the Legend Continues* (1985), *Boggy Creek: The Legend Is True* (2010), and *The Legacy of Boggy Creek* (2011). It is also the focal point of Arkansas's annual Fouke Monster Festival, dedicated to this homegrown creature and other celebrity cryptids.

Arkansas is home to three separate urban legends involving ghostly lights. Best known is the story of the **Gurdon Light** near Little Rock, which is a mysterious glow floating above isolated railroad tracks outside town. Its blue-white light is said by some to look like a lantern. Believers claim it belongs to a railroad worker who was decapitated by an oncoming train and now swings his railway lantern along the tracks looking for his missing head. Holding second place in the pantheon of Arkansas's ghostly lights is the tale of the **Dover Lights**. This emanation occurs in an isolated valley of the Ozark Mountains and is allegedly only visible from a nearby overlook. The legend ascribes the lights to the restless spirits of Spanish soldiers who died looking for treasure. Finally, like Gurdon's, the **Crossett Lights** are also attributed to a ghostly railroad worker who haunts the area but which some skeptics attribute to swamp gas.

According to the legend of the **Old Malco Theater** in Hot Springs, a 19th-century traveling magician who was performing at the theater asked for a volunteer from the audience, selecting a young woman named Clara. Placing a silk sheet over her as part of the trick, he commanded her to "disappear," which she did. However, no matter how hard the magician tried, it is said that he could not make her reappear. According to the legend, no one ever saw or heard from her again except for the disembodied sound of a woman crying in the theater's unoccupied basement. It is said that the cellar's supernatural occupant is Clara, ready to return from her lengthy disappearing act.

Honorable mention goes to the **Texarkana Moonlight Murderer** who attained celebrity status with a 1976 horror film about his alleged exploits, *The Town That Dreaded Sundown*. Even though the unsolved murders took place on the Texas side of the town, which straddles the state line, the movie was made by an Arkansan who brought glory to his home state by representing the gore as taking place on the Arkansas side. Claimed by both Arkansas and Texas, this enduring legend has spawned dozens of books and movies.

ICONIC ARKANSAS FOOD

Nothing quite says "Arkansas" like **Arkansas Possum Pie**. As seen in the recipe below, no marsupials are injured in its preparation. The name comes from the phrase "playing possum," or pretending to be something you're not. In this case, it looks fairly plain on the outside but is stuffed with a rich filling that is hiding, or "playing possum" inside.

Arkansas Possum Pie (Serves 8)
Pecan Shortbread Crust:
1 cup flour
½ cup melted butter
¼ cup brown sugar
¾ cup chopped pecans

Cream Cheese Layer:
6 oz softened cream cheese
½ cup powdered sugar
2 tbsp heavy cream

Pudding Layer:
1 cup sugar
⅓ cup cocoa powder
3 Tbsp cornstarch
2 Tbsp flour
Pinch of salt
3 egg yolks
2 cups whole milk
2 Tbsp butter
1 tsp vanilla

Whipped Cream Topping:
½ cup heavy whipping cream
2 Tbsp powdered sugar
½ tsp vanilla
1–2 Tbsp chopped pecans
Grated chocolate

1. After preheating oven to 350°F, combine melted butter with flour, brown sugar, and pecans. Press into 9-inch pie pan. Bake 15–20 minutes until crust begins to brown around edges, then remove from oven and allow to cool completely.

2. Mix cream cheese, heavy cream, and powdered sugar until smooth. Spread over bottom of cooled pie crust.
3. Combine cocoa powder, cornstarch, flour, salt, and sugar.
4. In separate bowl, whisk egg yolks and milk, then add to cocoa powder mixture.
5. Cook 7–10 minutes over medium heat, whisking constantly until mixture begins to bubble and thicken. Remove from heat, add butter and vanilla, and stir until butter is melted. Refrigerate 30 minutes before spreading over cream cheese layer. Cover with plastic wrap before refrigerating for four hours.
6. Beat heavy cream with powdered sugar and vanilla. Spread over chilled pudding layer. Before serving, sprinkle with chopped pecans and chocolate shavings.

Source: Adapted from https://houseofnasheats.com/arkansas-possum-pie/.

ODD LAWS

In a 2018 addition to the Arkansas Code, the state's General Assembly determined that the proper pronunciation of the state's name should be three syllables, "with the final 's' silent, the 'a' in each syllable with the Italian sound, and the accent on the first and last syllables." This is risky for those unsure of their Italian sounds as well as grammarians who question two accented syllables in a three-syllable word. The penalty for unlawful pronunciation is not specified.

In 2016, the Little Rock Code of Ordinances amended an earlier law that outlawed sounding the horn on a vehicle at any place where cold drinks or sandwiches are served after 9:00 p.m. It currently prohibits "yelling, hooting, shouting out at any time or place in a manner to annoy or disturb the peace." It is unclear whether an unwritten exception for hooting is allowed for spirited responses to Arkansas Razorback football games.

UNUSUAL DESTINATIONS

With no pun intended, the crown jewel is **Crater of Diamonds State Park** in Murfreesboro, Arkansas, the only active diamond mine in the nation. Visitors can dig for their own gems, often with remarkable results. Three diamonds that are among the largest ever found on Earth came from Arkansas.

The **Elvis Haircut Historic Site** at Chaffee Crossing can be found at the reception center for the now-closed Fort Chaffee. It's where Elvis Presley, the "King of Rock and Roll," got his nonroyal army buzz cut in 1958. There is an annual anniversary celebration, when hardcore fans of the King can often be found scuttling around, searching for a previously unseen scrap of hair from the monarch of modern music.

In 1900, a colorful character named William "Coin" Harvey aimed to make his fortune by building a resort in Rogers, Arkansas, called **Monte Ne**. The resort was intended to combine a health retreat with a relaxation spa, but both failed. Ultimately, Monte Ne was submerged by a lake that was formed by a federal dam project. Today, in dry seasons, visitors can see the tops of Monte Ne's stone structures as if they have arisen from the dark waters as a ghostly testament to Coin Harvey's dream gone wrong.

For those who prefer dreams that went very, very right, there is the **Walmart Museum** in Bentonville, located in the original "Walton's 5–10" building. The exhibits tell the story of Walmart's rise into a worldwide dynamo with this unpretentious little Northwest Arkansas town remaining as its base. Visitors to the museum are encouraged to touch the door handle of Sam Walton's beloved 1979 pickup truck parked outside. According to legend, it will impart the gift of Sam's frugality, if perhaps not his multimillion-dollar success.

DISTINCTIVE ARKANSAS WORDS AND SAYINGS

Arkansas Toothpick: A really, really big knife.

Cattywompus: Tilted, not straight (apparently unrelated to "Wampus Cat," below).

Chimley: What in other states is a fireplace fixture called a "chimney."

Might near: Almost, with proper Arkansas pronunciation being "maht nur," as in "it's maht nur suppahtime."

Rackensack: An Arkansan, often not in the best sense.

Wampus Cat: Said to have six legs, able to utilize four for running and two for fighting.

Further Reading

Bolton, Charles. *Arkansas, 1800–1860: Remote and Restless.* Fayetteville: University of Arkansas Press, 1998.

Lorne, Lorraine. "Virtually Legal." *Arkansas Law Notes.* Fayetteville: University of Arkansas Law School, 2007.

Sutterfield, Ragan. "How Arkansas Almost Killed the Smithsonian." *Arkansas Life*, March 6, 2014. https://arkansaslife.com/how-arkansas-almost-killed-the-smithsonian.

Whayne, Jeannie, Thomas A. DeBlack, George Sabo III, and Morris S. Arnold. *Arkansas: A Narrative History.* Fayetteville: University of Arkansas Press, 2014.

California

FACT BOX

Nickname: The Golden State
Statehood Granted: 1850
Capital: Sacramento
Population: 40,000,000
State Motto: *Eureka* (Greek: roughly meaning "I Found It!")
What Natives Call Themselves: Californians

STATE HISTORY

California exudes a mythology all its own, standing unique among the 50 states as a land of dreams. After all, it is from California that for more than a century, the Hollywood "Dream Factory" has projected the concept of the American Dream to even the most remote spots around the globe. It is the place sought by desperate Americans of the Depression era in the 1930s who traveled the same westward route of the wagon trains in the 1800s that preceded them. They were all following the sun toward what they imagined was the Promised Land of California. There was no place farther west for them to go.

Today, California is not only the home of that same Hollywood Dream Factory but also the land of Silicon Valley, which jump-started the information age and continues to flex its technological muscle around the world. Like Hollywood, it projects an image of the American Dream, often with the refinement of being the California Dream.

No single descriptor can contain California. It ranges from the sunbaked cauldron of Death Valley to the sparkling pools of Beverly Hills. It is rimmed on the west by the rugged Pacific coastline in its northern reaches to the surfboard-laden swells of the south. California is farms and films, palm trees and pastures. It is majestic scenery, mineral wealth, mountains, deserts, serenity among giant redwood trees, and smog-choked commutes amid massive highway cloverleafs.

Apart from being the most powerful cultural influence in the world by virtue of Hollywood and Silicon Valley, its economy is one of the world's largest. According to 2018 statistics, if California had been an independent country, its gross domestic product would have ranked behind only China, Germany, Japan, and the United States.

STATE ODDITIES

California's Hollywood movie industry projects an image of the American Dream around the world. It is an ideal that is often also the California Dream. (Corel)

California has become familiar to the rest of the world through innumerable movies that have been set there, everything from *American Graffiti* to *Zorro*.

Fiction runs in its blood. California has been compared to the fictional utopia called "Shangri-La" that was portrayed in the 1933 novel *Lost Horizon*. Shangri-La was imagined as a place of perfect weather, ageless people, and continuous harmony among its residents—a paradise on earth.

Although the real-life California cannot boast all the attributes of the fictional Shangri-La, it is ironic that California began its life as we know it today after being named for a work of fiction. In 1510, a popular Spanish novel titled *The Adventures of Esplandián* told of a make-believe island called "California" that was described as an earthly paradise. When Spanish explorers arrived at today's Baja California in the 1500s, they thought it was an island, naming their discovery after the glorious mythical land in the book.

California was claimed as a Spanish territory in 1542. Before long, Russia sought to expand its empire. By 1639, Russian explorers were sailing the northern Pacific Ocean on voyages of discovery. Russia's emperor ordered Vitus Bering to find lands bordering the northern Pacific for the exploitation of natural resources. After Bering spotted today's Alaska in 1741, Russia claimed that North American territory. The Russians kept moving southward from Alaska along the Pacific coastline in search of more fur-bearing animals to kill for their pelts.

There are some who say that at that particular point in history, the Russians became indirectly responsible for California's growth, specifically the rise of such world-class cities as Los Angeles and San Francisco.

> **Starry-Eyed**
>
> Probably every American movie star and television personality has called California home at one time or another. Even its public schools churn out celebrities. The roster of notable alumni from Hollywood High School alone is too lengthy to list. Even the less famous Van Nuys High School can claim former students such as Marilyn Monroe and Robert Redford. Many Americans learned the geography of greater Los Angeles from classic TV shows including *The Beverly Hillbillies, CHiPs, Fresh Prince of Bel-Air, L.A. Law*, and *77 Sunset Strip* as well as more current programs such as *All Rise, Black-ish, Curb Your Enthusiasm, NCIS: Los Angeles*, and *Modern Family*. Remarkably, even California zip codes are stars, as demonstrated by *Beverly Hills 90210*, or the more recent version that only needed to be called *90210*. Many Americans who cannot remember their own zip code recognize that one at a glance.

The unsung catalyst was today's small California community of Bodega Bay. In the early 1800s, the Russians kept moving southward into California. After the Russians established an outpost in 1812 at Bodega Bay near today's San Francisco, it caught the attention of Spanish authorities. The Spaniards who controlled California had been building Catholic missions there as early as 1769, but when the Russians arrived at Bodega Bay, Spain quickly authorized building a chain of 21 California missions and military outposts heading north. They were set about 30 miles apart, or a day's journey on horseback, eventually running for 600 miles near the coast.

Those mission sites gave rise to major California cities like Los Angeles, San Diego, and San Francisco as well as upscale communities such as today's Carmel, Monterey, Santa Barbara, San Juan Capistrano, and San Luis Obispo. Ground zero for California's Silicon Valley is San Jose, located within Santa Clara County, both derived from the missions that were located there.

Meanwhile, little Bodega Bay, the town that could be said to have started it all with the incursion of the Russians, did not rise to become a massive urban center. However, it eventually attained its own pinnacle of fame by becoming a movie star through films being set there, such as *The Birds, The Goonies, I Know What You Did Last Summer*, and, ironically, *The Russians Are Coming, The Russians Are Coming*.

In 1848, a treaty was signed that ended the Mexican War, awarding today's state of California to the United States. In the days before rapid communication, the timing would prove momentous. Apparently unbeknown to Mexico, 10 days before the treaty was finalized, gold was discovered at Sutter's Mill in Coloma, California. It went on to become one of the richest veins in the world. The California Gold Rush brought hundreds of thousands of people flooding into California between 1848 and 1855, accelerating the process of statehood, which was granted in 1850. It also proved disastrous for California's Native population, including the Chumash and Shasta people, who were decimated.

The unstoppable state of California grew by leaps and bounds. Its northern and southern portions developed very distinct personalities that today they do not always coexist harmoniously. Few other states have such a marked contrast between two geographical regions. Northern California, often called "NorCal," is personified by San Francisco. Southern California, or "SoCal," generally runs from Santa Barbara southward through Los Angeles to San Diego.

Southern California is sun-kissed, sparkling with a celebrity culture of glamour and trendiness. Tech-driven Northern California, especially the Bay Area around San Francisco, is more "chilled out," and not just due to its frequently nippy weather. Often, the only things that the two regions seem to agree on is that San Francisco should never be called "Frisco," nor should their mutual home state of California be called "Cali."

Sometimes said to be ungovernable and unmanageable, the Golden State still continues to glow like its dazzling Pacific sunset. With all its oddities, California remains a beloved icon, totally unique among the other American states.

URBAN LEGENDS

The **Dark Watchers** are said to be huge shadowy humanlike phantoms lurking among the Santa Lucia Mountains. They can allegedly only be seen around twilight, standing on the mountaintops like ghostly figures staring expressionlessly over people below. The Dark Watchers instantly vanish if they are approached. But on the plus side, they apparently do not harm travelers who stay on the pathways and mind their own business.

The **Elizabeth Lake Monster** is said to be found just outside the town of Lancaster in Los Angeles County. The lake has been called the spot where Satan kenneled a favorite pet. This particular pet is allegedly about 50 feet long with bat wings, a bulldog's head, and the neck of a giraffe. Reports from locals dating back to 1880 claimed it smelled rancid, like decaying flesh. At the bottom of the lake, which lies directly over the San Andreas Fault, is allegedly a passageway to hell.

At the iconic **Hollywood Sign**, there is an urban legend about a ghostly Lady in White with skeletal features who haunts the structure with its 45-foot-tall white block letters. It is thought to be the apparition of long-dead actress Peg Entwistle who fatally threw herself off the sign's letter *H* in 1932. Hollywood itself is not only the world's Dream Capital but also claims a few visions found in nightmares. Silent film superstar Rudolph Valentino died tragically in 1926 at the age of 31, but he was apparently not ready to leave show business. His ghost has allegedly appeared at Falcon's Lair, his former home, as well as the costume department at his old workplace, Paramount Studios. The long-dead Rudy is also known to drop by the Hollywood Knickerbocker Hotel, occasionally in the company of Marilyn Monroe.

The powerful **Santa Ana Winds** are so painfully hot and dry that some Southern California residents feel they are being hit by a massive incessant hair dryer that is set on "high." As the winds race from the desert to the coast, they inspire the urban legend that people act unpredictably, become violent, and commit the kinds of acts found in classic LA noir crime novels. On top of what is alleged to be an increased homicide rate, the urban legend credits these "Devil Winds" with causing earthquakes.

ICONIC CALIFORNIA FOOD

Cioppino (pronounced "chuh-PEA-no") is a seafood dish that was said to be created in San Francisco by Italian fishermen who would combine the day's leftover fish into a rich stew for dinner. The usual version contains a mixture of seafood such as clams, crabmeat, shrimp, scallops, squid, mussels, and white fish as available that can be added to this basic recipe:

> **Cioppino** (Serves 4)
> 2 Tbsp extra-virgin olive oil
> 1 medium shallot sliced thin
> Kosher salt and freshly ground black pepper to taste
> Pinch of dried red chili flakes
> 1 tsp dried oregano
> 2 medium garlic cloves, minced
> 1 (28 oz) can whole peeled tomatoes
> 1 cup red wine
> ¾ lb cod or flounder
> ½ lb each scallops and/or shrimp, peeled and deveined
> ½ cup fresh parsley

1. Heat oil in a 12-inch skillet before adding shallot and pinch of salt, stirring until softened. Add garlic, chili flakes, and oregano, and cook together about 30 seconds.
2. Add tomatoes, crushing with wooden spoon until they soften, then add red wine and bring to a simmer, cooking until sauce begins to thicken, about 8–10 minutes.
3. Add seafood, cover, and stir occasionally to break up the fish.
4. Season with salt and pepper to taste. In serving bowls, top with parsley and serve with lemon wedge and bread if desired.

Source: Adapted from https://www.seriouseats.com/recipes/2013/08/easy-cioppino-recipe.html.

ODD LAWS

In California, where cars are king, drivers are prohibited from watching television or videos while driving, no matter how bored they might be with their daily commute. The law specifies a ban on both entertainment and business applications, so claiming to get a head start on the workday probably won't carry much weight in court.

Incidentally, California drivers planning to send their car to work while they stay home still have to mind the speed limit. Driverless cars cannot exceed speeds over 65 miles per hour at any time of day and/or during inclement weather.

Pedestrians in San Francisco have to be mindful of the law in terms of what they are carrying. In the City by the Bay, a municipal statute makes it unlawful to transport manure through the public streets. In addition, it is illegal to carry bread in an open basket through the streets of San Francisco, a law that also extends to cakes and pastries.

Two towns have odd laws concerning height. In the community of Walnut, California, flying a kite higher than 10 feet off the ground is prohibited. Then there is the municipal code of Carmel, which bans wearing shoes "having heels more than two inches in height or with a base of less than one square inch unless the wearer has obtained a permit for them." Theoretically, the ordinance is aimed at preventing lawsuits from stiletto-shod strollers tripping on irregular pavement. Shoe permits are available without charge at Carmel's City Hall.

UNUSUAL DESTINATIONS

In 1859, gold was discovered at a small mining settlement by prospectors, including W. S. Bodey. On his way to get supplies, Bodey perished in a blizzard. After a richer vein of gold was uncovered in 1876, Bodey's mining camp exploded into a boomtown. Although the town was named for him, it was misspelled. Today, **Bodie, California**, near Lake Tahoe, is a ghost town like so many boom-and-bust communities of the Gold Rush era. At one point, about 7,000 people lived in Bodie, but once the gold began to dwindle, so did the population. Today, the ghost town is in a state of what is called "arrested decay." Stores remain exactly as they were when abandoned, their shelves still stocked with goods. The eerie townsite even comes with its own curse: if any items are taken, bad luck will follow. It is said that some visitors later return what they took, along with written apologies intended to remove the curse. It is not known if the curse was placed by Mr. Bodey himself, insulted at the misspelling of the town named for him.

Some people feel that the heavily saline Salton Sea has an eerie, apocalyptic aura. They might therefore wonder if it is an appropriate location for the **International Banana Museum**. This unusual destination is located in the desertlike surroundings of a town called Mecca, California, on the shoreline of the largely dry Salton Sea. Within its bright yellow walls are innumerable figurines, pictures, sculptures, and toys along with banana-centric furniture, stuffed animals such as monkeys eating bananas, and all manner of banana figures. More than 25,000 banana-related items are displayed. Guests are encouraged to pose for a photo opportunity next to a giant banana statue, and are even invited to borrow something from the museum's stock of banana-themed clothing, hats, and wigs. Visitors can order a chocolate banana milkshake or a scoop of homemade banana ice cream in order to be fully immersed in the banana-rama experience. There are an overwhelming number of banana-related objects for visitors to enjoy before they split from the Banana Museum and peel out.

Cynics might claim that the show business culture of Los Angeles is figuratively populated by saber-toothed tigers and giant sloths. However, at the **La Brea Tar Pits** in LA's Hancock Park, there literally are such creatures, and more. There are a few other tar pits in the world, in places such as Azerbaijan and Venezuela, but the La Brea Tar Pits in California can claim to be the superstar of these gooey time capsules where Ice Age fossils are sealed in natural asphalt. This unusual destination feels even more unnerving by virtue of being within the massive urban metropolis of Los Angeles. More than three million fossils as large as mammoths have been discovered there. They met their doom by wandering into the unforgiving muck that bubbles up from deep underground. Visitors can explore the on-site museum, where they might learn that even the name of the La Brea Tar Pits is odd. "La brea" means "the tar" in Spanish; therefore, saying "The La Brea Tar Pits" literally—and redundantly—means "The The Tar Tar Pits."

Over the years, the **Winchester Mystery House** in San Jose has earned a special place in the pantheon of unusual destinations. Sarah Winchester, widow of arms manufacturer William Winchester, commissioned construction on the house in 1886. Believing she would be haunted by the ghosts of those killed by Winchester rifles, she had contractors continue building nonstop to confuse evil spirits, which the builders did until her death in 1922. At that point, the 200-room house contained doors that open into thin air, mismatched levels, secret passageways galore, and staircases that lead to a dead-end at the ceiling. It is unknown whether the Winchester house confused any dark spirits, but today it certainly has that effect on tourists.

DISTINCTIVE CALIFORNIA WORDS AND SAYINGS

City, the: San Francisco, at least to residents of the Bay Area. For them, San Francisco is *never* called "Frisco," and there is only a grudging recognition that New Yorkers refer to Manhattan as "the City."

Dude: This all-purpose word has been co-opted by the rest of the nation, but it retains its California roots.

Industry, the: For Southern Californians, it is unnecessary to say someone works in movies, television, show business, the entertainment field, or any variation therein. It is always simply "the Industry." Everybody knows which one.

Surfer speak: An entire vocabulary in itself. For example, words meaning "great" or "cool" have many surfer-derived variations, including "awesome," "epic," "rad," "stellar," and so on, about which the speaker can be *stoked* (excited) unless things get *gnarly* (crazy, intense, horrible, risky, or shocking).

The (plus a number): Southern Californians do not refer to highways such as the Santa Monica Freeway by their names. Instead, they use the Interstate Highway System's numerical designation, so a driver might be told to take "the 10" (Santa Monica Freeway), "the 405" (San Diego Freeway), and so on.

Further Reading

Krist, Gary. *The Mirage Factory: Illusion, Imagination, and the Invention of Los Angeles.* New York: Crown, 2018.

Rolle, Andrew, and Arthur Verge. *California: A History.* 8th edition. Malden, MA: Wiley-Blackwell, 2015.

Rubin, Saul. *Northern California Curiosities: Quirky Characters, Roadside Oddities and Other Offbeat Stuff.* Guilford, CT: Globe Pequot, 2005.

Rubin, Saul. *Southern California Curiosities: Quirky Characters, Roadside Oddities, and Other Offbeat Stuff.* Guilford, CT: Globe Pequot, 2004.

Colorado

> **FACT BOX**
>
> **Nickname:** The Centennial State
> **Statehood Granted:** 1876
> **Capital:** Denver
> **Population:** 5,800,000
> **State Motto:** *Nil sine numine* (Latin: "Nothing without Providence")
> **What Natives Call Themselves:** Coloradans

STATE HISTORY

By the mid-1500s, when Spanish explorers arrived in the region that became today's state of Colorado, they were relative newcomers. The Spaniards followed thousands of years of previous occupants.

Artifacts denoting permanent residency by Native American people in today's Colorado have been found, some dating from more than 11,000 years before the birth of Christ. Many people consider the superstars of Colorado's ancient people to be the Anasazi who built massive cliffside communities that fascinate present-day visitors.

The Anasazi, whose name is usually translated as "Ancient Ones," anchored a major civilization. Their reign lasted for a thousand years, usually said to be around the years 200–1300, long before Columbus was born. Archaeologists ponder how Anasazi people of all ages, from children to the elderly, managed the routines of daily life back and forth from their cliff dwellings carved high into the mountainside. Apparently, they did so successfully, obtaining sources of food and water that allowed them to thrive.

However, suddenly and without warning, the Anasazi disappeared, which scientists claim happened within a single generation. Somewhere around 1300, the Anasazi vanished, abandoning their majestic cliffside dwellings. The key seems to have been the availability of water. When a prolonged drought struck, famine followed. The timing of the drought was especially bad, with the Anasazi reaching their highest population level at that point.

Another Colorado treasure left by ancestral people who inhabited the region until about the same time is the UNESCO World Heritage Site at Mesa Verde

National Park. Located in Colorado's Montezuma County, the four-story Mesa Verde cliff city is the largest and one of the best-preserved archaeological sites in the United States. With more than 5,000 individual points of interest, including 600 cliffside dwellings, guests at Mesa Verde are permitted to climb ladders into the lodgings that were carved by hand into the solid rock face.

Even those ancient people were relative newcomers compared to the former lords of Colorado: dinosaurs. At Dinosaur National Monument in Northwest Colorado, the remains of the giant prehistoric creatures are embedded in exposed rock. Visitors can spot fossils in various conditions, from those that are still encased in stone to skeletons that are fully assembled.

All these forebears had come and gone before the Spanish arrived in 1540. The Spaniards named Colorado for the Rio Colorado ("Red-Colored River") that ran through it, claiming the future state as part of the Spanish Empire.

Colorado's Ancestral Puebloan people such as the Anasazi and those at Mesa Verde inhabited cliffside dwellings carved into the mountainside. Then, suddenly, the people disappeared. (Sherwood Imagery/iStockphoto.com)

Ownership of the region proceeded to swing among various claimants, from Spain to France to the United States, which ultimately acquired the area containing today's Colorado in 1803 as part of the Louisiana Purchase.

Spain was still contesting claims in the region in 1806 when Zebulon Pike led a U.S. Army reconnaissance expedition into Southern Colorado. He was arrested by the Spaniards but eventually released, earning the last laugh by having the landmark mountain Pikes Peak near Colorado Springs named for him. Incidentally, grammarians may wish to note that since 1890, Pikes Peak has officially been spelled without the possessive apostrophe (as in "Pike's") by both the state of Colorado and the U.S. Board of Geographic Names.

However it was spelled, Pikes Peak attained national recognition in the days of the Old West. The slogan "Pikes Peak or Bust" was painted across many of the covered wagons in westward-bound wagon trains.

After the United States settled squabbles with Spain, the Territory of Colorado eventually came together from various geographical bits and pieces through the 1800s. Some would-be prospectors passed through Colorado when they crossed the Rocky Mountains on their way to the gold fields of the West during the California Gold Rush between 1848 and 1855. Some, however, decided to cut the trip short after discovering that Colorado itself held a wealth of gold and silver beneath its picturesque landscape. As mines were dug beneath Colorado soil, mining towns sprang up on top of it.

Even the American Civil War (1861–1865) could not slow Colorado down, with a major silver strike emerging in 1864. Following the coming of the transcontinental railroad in 1869, Colorado and its riches were linked to the rest of the nation. More silver strikes followed in the late 1800s.

In 1876, Colorado was admitted to the Union as the 38th state. There were no other states admitted to the Union that year. As it happened, that year was when the 100th anniversary, or centennial, of American independence in 1776 was being celebrated. Therefore, Colorado adopted "the Centennial State" as its nickname. In fact, it was the only state admitted to the Union in the entire decade of the 1870s.

More gold and silver strikes followed, along with significant fortunes being made in copper. One of the Colorado "copper kings" was J. J. Brown. His wife, Margaret, later gained worldwide fame as "the Unsinkable Molly Brown" for her heroism following the sinking of the doomed ocean liner *Titanic*.

After Colorado's mining industry declined in the 1890s, the state's economy was in jeopardy. However, Colorado was rich in other things, especially its natural wonders. Hotels sprang up as tourism boomed amid the state's clean mountain air.

For some people, visiting Colorado was a matter of life and death. During the Industrial Revolution in the late 1800s and early 1900s, Northern cities became crowded and polluted. Those conditions made an ideal setting for the spread of tuberculosis, called "TB." The lung disease was highly infectious, incurable, and

Shining Through

The night before Halloween in 1974, a tourist who needed lodging stumbled upon the Stanley Hotel in Estes Park, Colorado. The hotel was about to close for the winter, and he later wrote about the eerie sensation of there being no other guests, especially noting the hotel's winding, empty corridors. That guest was master of the macabre, Stephen King. After a disturbing dream that night about his young son, he got up and outlined the plot for what ultimately became his best-selling book and subsequent hit movie, *The Shining*. King's novel featured a fictional hotel inspired by the Stanley, which was haunted by evil spirits and their victims. Today, at Colorado's real-life Stanley Hotel, which opened in 1909, *The Shining* is continuously available on television in the guest rooms all day—and for the fearless, all night.

often deadly. Doctors advised TB patients to go to a sanitarium in dry, sunny climates for their health. Those who could afford to do so often chose Colorado with its majestic scenery and pure mountain air. In the 1880s, Colorado started to be nicknamed "the World's Sanitarium."

Today, Coloradans often consider their home to be a unique place with a distinctive mindset among its residents. It is the only state known to have turned down the Olympic Games after being named host city. In 1976, the Winter Olympics were planned for Denver, but almost two-thirds of Colorado voters chose not to welcome the prestigious worldwide athletic event due to the costs, pollution, and influx of people into the city and state.

Denver can at least claim truthful advertising in its city slogan. At 5,280 feet above sea level—exactly 1 mile—Denver accurately calls itself the Mile High City.

In the 1960s, an aspiring folk singer chose the city's name as his own and is today one of its "favorite sons": the late John Denver. Along with "Where the Columbines Grow" (from 1915), the Colorado legislature named John Denver's valentine to Colorado, the hit song "Rocky Mountain High," recorded in 1972, to be one of two official state songs.

URBAN LEGENDS

Denver's **Cheesman Park** lies atop an old cemetery, making for an urban legend that is spooky enough. The historical facts are worse. In 1893, the city hired a man to remove thousands of bodies to make way for the park, with his contract specifying him to put the bodies into fresh coffins. The man decided he could make a bigger profit if he bought inexpensive child-sized coffins, hacking up the adult bodies before stuffing them into the tiny caskets. Some didn't entirely fit. Residents were appalled at the sight of scattered bones and body parts on the ground. After city officials canceled his contract, they simply bulldozed over open graves and desecrated bodies. Today, it is said that the park is haunted by the spirits of the dismembered, who cannot rest in peace.

Red Rocks, near Morrison, Colorado, is a magnificent natural stone formation, where concerts are often held. Along with popular musicians, there is a resident celebrity at Red Rocks: the **Hatchet Lady**. Some say she appears as a headless spirit who does not like finding young people in the throes of romance at Red Rocks, scaring them with a hatchet in her hand. Others claim she was a homeless woman living in a nearby cave who killed children venturing too close to her makeshift abode, hiding their severed bodies among the rocks. Still others say the legend grew after a real-life local woman would pull her coat over her head and carry a hatchet to scare away unworthy suitors enamored of her daughter.

The **Hotel Colorado** in Glenwood Springs is known for its alleged hauntings by a former maid who was killed by a jealous lover. Another urban legend centers on the paranormal activities of a supernatural being with an apparent goal of being an interior decorator. During the renovation of an empty room at the hotel, newly pasted wallpaper was found the next morning, pulled down from the wall and rolled up on the floor. After reapplying it, the same thing happened the next day. Finally, different wallpaper samples were placed on the bed when workers left for the evening. The next morning, all the samples were on the floor—except one. That wallpaper pattern was the one they used in the room, and it remained in place without further incident.

St. Elmo Ghost Town near Buena Vista can be explored by visitors interested in the boom-and-bust culture of Colorado mining communities. Along with abandoned buildings dating from the 1880s, they might also catch a glimpse of past resident Annabelle Stark, who may still be a town booster for St. Elmo. It is said that Annabelle was sheltered by her parents from the rowdy males of the mining town. She eventually married a man from a nearby community, but apparently, the match was not successful. Two years later, in 1924, Annabelle returned to St. Elmo, where her declining years matched those of the town. As an old woman, rifle in hand, she was said to roam the empty streets of St. Elmo to deter vandals. After her death in 1960, more than half a century ago, there are still reports of seeing Annabelle's apparition peering out the window of her now-abandoned home, a silent sentinel.

ICONIC COLORADO FOOD

Coloradans are said to love **Green Chili**—on just about everything. Also known as Chili Verde, the dish gains its rich green color from tomatillos. Some like to serve it over burritos, or with beans and rice. However, burgers, omelets, pizza, and even chocolate cake are fair game by diners, who might also eat green chili by itself, spooning it up like soup. Whether consumed alone or as a condiment, this is the basic recipe:

> **Colorado Green Chili** (Serves 6)
> 1 Tbsp olive oil
> 1½ lb cubed pork
> Salt and pepper to taste
> 1 large yellow onion, diced
> 4 cloves garlic, minced
> 2 cups chopped roasted green chiles
> 1 can (14.5 oz) diced tomatoes with juice
> 1½ cups tomatillo salsa
> 5 cups chicken broth
> ½ tsp dried oregano
> Pinch ground cloves
>
> 1. Heat olive oil in a large pot over medium-high heat, placing pork in the hot oil after seasoning with salt and pepper to taste. Cook until golden brown on all sides, about seven minutes.

2. Remove pork; set aside. Stir in onion and garlic, reducing heat to medium and cooking until onion softens and turns translucent, about five minutes.
3. After returning pork to the pot, stir in the green chiles, chicken broth, diced tomatoes with juice, tomatillo salsa, oregano, and cloves, then bring to a low boil over medium heat.
4. Reduce heat to low, cover, and simmer 20 minutes.
5. Remove two cups of liquid with no pork cubes in it, pour into a blender, and puree until smooth. Pour back into cooking pot and let simmer until pork is tender, at least 30 minutes.

Source: Adapted from https://www.allrecipes.com/recipe/214191/colorado-green-chili-chile-verde/.

ODD LAWS

In Colorado, it is entirely permissible to buy alcohol on Sunday, but anyone who gets tipsy and decides it would be the perfect day to buy a car is in for disappointment. The state of Colorado does not permit the sale of automobiles on Sundays. The law applies to dealerships as well as selling cars at what are called "premises or residences." Violating the law can result in a fine, six months of jail time, and/or having a motor vehicle dealer's license revoked. On the other hand, if a Coloradan is in the mood to buy tires or other automotive accessories on Sunday, it is perfectly legal to do so.

Those who own a piece of medieval weaponry called a catapult would be well advised to refrain from using it in the city of Aspen. The town's municipal code prohibits hurling things at buildings or people through the use of bows, blowguns, catapults, or slingshots, as well as throwing rocks and even snowballs. Shooting firearms at a building is also frowned upon. It is not known if a massive catapult-launched snowball fight at some point in Aspen's history may have gotten out of hand, spurring this piece of legislation.

Speaking of altercations, the municipal code in the city of Boulder contains a section governing "Use of Fighting Words." Under this provision, the code states that no person "shall, with intent to harass, annoy, or alarm another, repeatedly insult, taunt, or challenge another in a manner likely to provoke a disorderly response." The law then becomes even more specific: "If the person to whom such insult, taunt, or challenge is directed is a police officer, there is no violation of this section until the police officer requests the person to cease and discontinue the conduct, but the person repeats or continues the conduct." In other words, it seems to be OK to verbally abuse police officers in Boulder, but only until they ask you to stop.

UNUSUAL DESTINATIONS

In one way, the **Lee Maxwell Washing Machine Museum** in Eaton, Colorado, is an interesting collection of more than 1,400 antique washing machines. But on a more profound level, the Maxwell collection is a visual image of the history of women's rights and freedom from the constant back-breaking labor of washing the family's clothing by hand. Washing machines played a part in the struggle. Maxwell, a retired electrical engineering professor, earned the Guinness World Record for having the world's largest washing machine collection, a pursuit he began in 1985. The earliest vintage washing machine in Maxwell's collection dates to 1840. They come from not only the United States but also other countries around the globe. Maxwell feels the historical contributions of washing machines have been overlooked, convincingly offering his collection as a testimonial.

Most visitors expect to see the purple mountains' majesty that Colorado is known for, but few are prepared for a sight that looks more like North Africa than North America. Consisting of almost 150,000 square miles in area, **Sand Dunes National Park** is located southwest of Pueblo, Colorado. The park is home to the tallest sand dunes in North America, including the Star Dune that is higher than a seven-story building. Visitors can immerse themselves in the sandy experience by climbing the dunes, hiking across them, or sliding around on them using a sandboard, similar to a snowboard. Although Colorado's snow-covered Sangre de Christo Mountains can be seen as a backdrop, summer temperatures on the sand can reach 150°F, so guests are welcome to splash in the park's Medano Creek amid the sand, forming what seems like America's biggest beach.

Near the town of Hooper, the state of Colorado is home to the **UFO Watchtower**. Having virtually no light pollution in the area, the 10-foot-tall watchtower is built to make use of the high elevation. Among many UFO watchers, it is said to be the best place in the world to search for unidentified flying objects in the clear night skies. In addition to the watchtower's observation platform with its 360° view, there is a campground where visitors can relax as they scan the stars. There is also a Healing Garden that attracts psychics who claim that two large vortexes were formed after the watchtower was built. Additionally, there is a dome-shaped visitor center where guests can read accounts from local residents who attest to seeing strange happenings in the sky.

DISTINCTIVE COLORADO WORDS AND SAYINGS

Flatlanders: Out-of-staters from lower elevations, especially derisive of those who have trouble driving Colorado's winding, snow-covered mountain roads.

Fourteener: This refers to more than 50 of Colorado's mountain peaks that are taller than 14,000 feet.

Front Range: The relatively less mountainous region of Eastern Colorado, home to such cities as Boulder, Colorado Springs, and Denver.

Jerry: Used by native Coloradans to describe someone who is new to the ski slopes and does not practice accepted mountain etiquette.

Transplants: Newcomers who relocate from elsewhere to Colorado.

Western Slope: Anything west of the Continental Divide in the Rocky Mountain range, which bisects Colorado.

Further Reading

Abbott, Carl, and Stephen J. Leonard. *Colorado: A History of the Centennial State.* 5th edition. Boulder: University Press of Colorado, 2013.

Getz, Charmaine Ortega. *Weird Colorado: Your Travel Guide to Colorado's Local Legends and Best Kept Secrets.* New York: Sterling, 2010.

Maxwell, Lee. *Save Women's Lives: History of Washing Machines.* Eaton, CO: Oldewash, 2003.

Pittman, Rebecca. *The History and Haunting of the Stanley Hotel.* Loveland, CO: Wonderland Productions, 2015.

Connecticut

FACT BOX

Nickname: The Constitution State
Statehood Granted: 1788
Capital: Hartford
Population: 3,600,000
State Motto: *Qui transtulit sustinet* (Latin: "He Who Is Transplanted Still Sustains")
What Natives Call Themselves: Connecticuters

STATE HISTORY

The word "Connecticut" is a European interpretation of the Native American word "quinetucket," used to designate today's Connecticut River. That does not explain the bane of schoolchildren for generations: why Connecticut is spelled with the second *c*.

For a state that is small in size, Connecticut packs a powerful punch. It has traditionally enjoyed a high standard of living in addition to the kind of culture that inspired books and movies such as *The Stepford Wives*, which was said to be inspired by the author's Connecticut community.

Today's state of Connecticut was inhabited for generations by Native people, including the Mohegans and the Pequots. In 1633, the Dutch West India Company established a small settlement called Fort Hoop where today's Hartford stands, claiming the region to be part of the Dutch colony of New Netherland.

The official Dutch presence in Connecticut was short lived. The first English colonists arrived in 1636, creating three settlements: Hartford, Wethersfield, and Windsor. Those three Puritan colonies were combined into one under a royal charter in 1662.

The "Fundamental Orders of Connecticut," which was adopted at that time to govern the colony, is said by some historians to be the first written constitution in the New World, establishing a democratic representative government in 1662. Advocates of neighboring Massachusetts have been known to dispute the claim, citing the Mayflower Compact, signed in 1620, as the first such governing document. However, the Fundamental Orders of Connecticut gave its (male) colonists more voting rights and increased eligibility to run for elected positions than the Mayflower Compact did.

Thus, Connecticut claimed its nickname of "the Constitution State." That name may be preferable to another possibility, one in which Connecticut definitely had the early edge on Massachusetts: "the Witch Hunt State."

The Connecticut Witch Trials took place from 1647 to 1663. As the first large-scale witch prosecutions in the American colonies, Connecticut's version predated the 1692–1693 witch trials in Salem, Massachusetts, by decades—and lasted longer. As in Salem, female colonists, who had been ignored in the Fundamental Orders of Connecticut, were overwhelmingly the victims of execution. To secure convictions, evidence in the Connecticut trials was said by officials to be easily obtained through what were called "battering interrogations," a process that is no doubt self-explanatory.

Along with holding the dubious distinction of being the first of the American settlements to foster witch trials, Connecticut held a unique status as a colony that basically had a colony of its own. The Connecticut Western Reserve was a large swath of land in today's Northeastern Ohio that was claimed by the Connecticut Colony. The reserve had been granted to Connecticut through its charter from England's King Charles II in 1662. From its East Coast location, Connecticut was granted land in America "from sea to sea." Since no one at the time knew the location of what is today known as the Pacific Ocean, the Connecticut Reserve extended only as far as Lake Erie. The grant came with the stipulation that the king would receive one-fifth of all gold and silver that was mined in the colony.

That arrangement became moot following the American Revolution. After ratifying the U.S. Constitution in 1788, Connecticut became the fifth state admitted to the Union. It traded the Western Reserve to the new U.S. government in return for paying the state's war debts. Today, the Connecticut Western Reserve is recalled in institutional names such as Case Western Reserve University in Ohio.

"Listen, My Children, and You Shall Hear / of the Midnight Ride of . . . *Sybil Ludington?*"

Connecticut is able to boast its own Paul Revere, a 16-year-old girl named Sybil Ludington (1761–1839). All night on April 26, 1777, she galloped on horseback through cold, heavy rain to alert colonial militiamen that British forces were coming. The Americans had a supply depot at Danbury, Connecticut, so it was especially important to rally the sleeping patriots to defend it from capture. Some historians claim that Revere got the credit because his ride was in 1775, two years earlier, but proud Connecticuters claim that Sybil was completely erased from history due to her shortcoming of being a girl. Memorial statues have been erected to the brave teen who rode through the pitch-black night for 40 miles (twice the distance of Revere's ride), ultimately saving the day for America.

Connecticut prospered in the years following the Revolution and into the industrial age, with wealth derived from its factories, fisheries, seaports, and textile mills. After the outbreak of World War I in 1914, Connecticut became a major supplier of armaments for the American military. Three Connecticut companies—Colt in Hartford, Remington in Bridgeport, and Winchester in New Haven—produced half the weaponry used by the U.S. Army. From that time, Connecticut's arms manufacturers held a dominant market share for private gun owners as well as the military.

Connecticut later became known for its production of helicopters, jet engines, and nuclear submarines. To some, an even more significant claim to fame is being the state where the beloved PEZ candy is manufactured.

With a statewide population today that is less than the city of Los Angeles, Connecticut may be unique for the number of "firsts" that can be claimed by such a relatively small state. For example, Connecticut is home to the oldest U.S. newspaper still being published. Today's *Hartford Courant* began life as the *Connecticut Courant* in 1764.

The Scoville Memorial Library in Salisbury, Connecticut, is the oldest public library in the United States. Established in 1803, it was the first library in the United States open to the public free of charge and is still in operation today.

Mary Kies of South Killingly, Connecticut, was the first woman to receive a U.S. patent, which she did in 1809. Her patent was awarded for an innovative way to weave straw with silk and other threads in making women's bonnets.

In 1878, the New Haven District Telephone Company published the first telephone book. Containing just 50 names, it was a service offered to citizens of that city who subscribed to the world's first telephone exchange service.

Although the title is said to be hotly contested, Connecticut is believed by many to be the home of the first hamburger, dating back to 1895. Louis' Lunch (punctuated that way) in New Haven is still doing a sizzling business today, claiming to be the first restaurant to serve hamburgers. Its founder, Louis Lassen, was selling food items from a wooden cart in 1895. His descendants say a customer rushed up, exclaiming that he was in a hurry and for Louis to "slap a meatpuck between two planks and step on it!" Ground steak was indeed slapped between two pieces of toast, the hurried customer was happy, and a slice of history was made. Five generations later, Louis' Lunch is operated by family members in a tiny (and usually jam-packed) square brick building where a No Ketchup sign is prominently on display. Those who request the condiment may be invited to "have it their way" elsewhere.

In 1937, Connecticut became the first state to issue permanent license plates for cars. Two years later, people could look to the skies when, in 1939, Igor Sikorsky designed the world's first practical helicopter, taking flight at Stratford, Connecticut. Sikorsky Aircraft went on to become a major supplier of helicopters for both military and civilian use. The company continues to employ thousands of people at its Connecticut plants.

It took just 15 years for the novelty of the helicopter to give way to the marvels of the nuclear age. In 1954, the *USS Nautilus* became the world's first

STATE ODDITIES

In 1954, the *USS Nautilus* became the world's first nuclear powered submarine. It was built in Groton, Connecticut, where America's nuclear navy is based. The United States Coast Guard Academy is nearby at New London, Connecticut. (U.S. Navy)

nuclear-powered submarine. It was built in Groton, Connecticut, where America's nuclear navy is based. The United States Coast Guard Academy is nearby at New London.

In a spirited response, Connecticut was one of two states (along with Rhode Island) that never ratified the 18th Amendment, or Prohibition, in 1919. That legislation mandated America's ban on alcohol. Like the Connecticut Colony's percentage of gold and silver owed to the king of England, that omission also became moot with the passage of time.

URBAN LEGENDS

The abandoned **Bara-Hack** near Pomfret, Connecticut, is reportedly haunted by residents who lived there in the late 1700s. Around that time, residents encountered economic hardships and moved away. Today, only a few stone foundations and cellars remain, but the urban legend has it that any visitors who stumble upon the site are greeted by floating orbs, ghostly sounds, and strange lights. Reportedly, the sound of children's laughter is followed by the appearance of a ghost baby in a tree.

At another abandoned Connecticut community, **Dudleytown**, the remnants are also limited to cellar holes and stone foundations. Founded in the mid-1700s, the town only boasted about 25 people at its peak in the 1850s. The legend is that the site was cursed after its founders, the Dudley family, tried to dethrone England's King Henry VIII, a major offense since rulers were allegedly anointed by God. Their town was therefore said to be cursed with famine, cold, and constant darkness. Geographically, the town is surrounded by large hills that tended to block the sun and keep it chilly. In addition, it was built atop rocky soil that was not suited to farming. Even with those facts, the urban legend tilts toward the story of the curse.

The town of Winsted has spawned its own version of a resident Bigfoot-type hairy creature. First mentioned in 1895, there have been alleged sightings of the **Winsted Wildman** well into the 21st century, perhaps accidentally coinciding with the rise of the internet. Local residents have claimed to spot a six-foot-tall creature covered with thick black hair that jumps from the bushes along deserted roads. All the reports denied that it could have been a bear, with the urban legend maintaining that it was the specter of a long-ago escaped mental patient or an extraterrestrial who is able to jump between galaxies, vanishing without leaving any tracks.

Honorable mention among urban legends goes to Connecticut's mythic animal called the **Nauga**. During the 1960s, there was an advertising campaign for an artificial leather upholstery material called Naugahyde that was produced in the town of Naugatuck, Connecticut. The ads, meant to be humorous, claimed that Naugahyde was made from the skin of an animal called a Nauga that was unlike other animals in having the ability to shed its skin without causing any harm to itself or being slain for its hide. Some folks apparently took it literally, turning marketing fantasy into urban myth.

ICONIC CONNECTICUT FOOD

For some people, the idea of **New Haven–Style Clam Pie** provokes visions of marine mollusks baked in a sugary crust and topped with whipped cream. It is actually a rich pizza that has plenty of clams but no tomato sauce. Many Connecticut residents call it the best pizza in America. Some cooks prefer to make their own crust from scratch, but this version uses prepared refrigerated pizza dough that can be found at the grocery store. For cooks lucky enough to have them, fresh clams can be substituted.

New Haven–Style Clam Pie (Serves 4)
1 can prepared pizza dough
¼ cup grated Pecorino Romano cheese
1 can (6.5 oz) chopped clams, drained and rinsed
1 can (10 oz) whole baby clams, drained and rinsed
2 cloves garlic, chopped
½ tsp dried oregano
½ tsp crushed red pepper flakes

2 Tbsp chopped parsley
1 Tbsp extra-virgin olive oil

1. Preheat oven according to directions for prepared pizza dough.
2. Spread uncooked dough on pizza stone to create about a 12-inch circle.
3. Leaving ¾-inch border on uncooked dough to form the crust, sprinkle cheese followed by clams, garlic, and oregano.
4. Bake according to directions for prepared dough, usually 12–14 minutes, until cheese is melted and crust is golden brown.
5. Sprinkle crushed red pepper flakes and chopped parsley on the pizza, then brush the crust with the olive oil. Let cool for two minutes before cutting.

Source: Adapted from https://iamahoneybee.com/2020/01/21/new-haven-style-white-clam-pizza/.

ODD LAWS

A search of current Connecticut state codes casts doubt over innumerable internet sites that claim it is illegal there to store town records near alcohol. Such a law had indeed been passed in 1949 as Section 30-97, which stated that town and probate records shall not be kept where liquor is sold. However, Section 30-97 was repealed in 2002. On the other hand, the Connecticut statute that follows it, Section 30-98, is still on the books. It states that liquor is not to be furnished to prisoners. Therefore, potential lawbreakers need to be are aware that there is no Happy Hour in jail.

A law passed in Southington, Connecticut, prohibits the aerosol polymer resin product known as Silly String at public events. As in the case of many laws that seem odd, this one has a basis in past events. It started at Southington's annual Apple Harvest Festival in 1996. Onlookers armed with Silly String squirted it at marchers in the parade before moving on to spray town monuments. Along with the substance damaging musical instruments and being difficult to clean up afterward, the dyes in the product discolored cars, clothing, and memorials. The slippery plastic strands also caused a problem for police officers riding in the parade trying not to lose control of their motorcycles. It should be noted that Silly String is only banned at public events, not in private homes.

Some people love clowns, while others definitely do not. According to the Connecticut State Police, it is not actually illegal to dress as a clown, but it is very much against the law to do so "with the intent of causing alarm." In 2016, there was a bizarre series of occurrences in Connecticut during which individuals dressed as what were said to be evil clowns struck fear into communities by their malicious acts and then posted videos on social media sites. Some involved accosting people who were paying their respects at cemeteries, while other reports claimed the creepy clowns tried to lure children into the woods. Along with being illegal in Connecticut, the World Clown Association has condemned such acts.

UNUSUAL DESTINATIONS

Gillette's Castle in East Haddam has been called a fairy tale vision, medieval gothic mash-up, Victorian folly, or simply "weird." Its walls, insulated with paper and seaweed, were built like a stage set, lacking mortar or studs, and were said to be an architectural wonder for not simply collapsing. The structure, with its fieldstone exterior, is one of Connecticut's top tourist attractions. It was built by actor William Hooker Gillette (1853–1937), whose signature onstage role was Sherlock Holmes, and there is no shortage of ego or stagecraft in the building's construction. Gillette designed trick locks for each of the 47 doors, mirrors that let him view guests downstairs from his bedroom upstairs, and secret passageways allowing him to suddenly vanish or make an unexpected dramatic entrance, startling guests. A footnote for trivia buffs is that Gillette's leading lady on his most successful Sherlock Holmes theatrical tour, running from 1929 to 1932, was actress Peg Entwistle. She jumped to her death from the Hollywood sign in 1932, soon after the tour ended.

The **Glass House** in New Canaan has been the subject of innumerable jokes about "throwing stones." In 1948, architect Philip Johnson began construction on the glass rectangle, which some said looked like a giant upside-down fish tank. He lived in it until his death in 2005. It could not be seen from the road, but even so, trespassers made it necessary to post a guard at Johnson's see-through house. All living areas and bedroom spaces are entirely surrounded by walls of clear glass, with Johnson stating that the wooded landscape all around the house served as its "wallpaper." Today, guided tours are available for the public. Visitors of all ages have one overriding question: *"What about the bathroom?"* A tall brick cylinder runs from floor to ceiling, enclosing the home's restroom facilities, the only part of the house that is not open for the world to see.

Holy Land USA in Waterbury began as a faith-inspired vision in 1955. It was intended to be an 18-acre theme park with 200 miniature structures inspired by Bible passages, including the Garden of Eden, the Stations of the Cross, and scenes in the life of Jesus. The plan also included mini-replications of Bethlehem and Jerusalem as well as an Israelite village from around the time of Christ. Overlooking it all was a five-story cross and an illuminated sign (similar to the Hollywood sign in Los Angeles) that read "Holy Land USA." After attracting tens of thousands of visitors annually in the 1960s and 1970s, the park closed to the public in 1984. It fell victim to vandalism as well as bad press when an especially gruesome murder was committed under the cross. Guests are sometimes able to attend services for Mass, which is offered there occasionally, but it is always best to check first.

DISTINCTIVE CONNECTICUT WORDS AND SAYINGS

Apizza: What the rest of the world calls "pizza"; said to be derived from Italian immigrants arriving in New Haven who spoke a Neapolitan dialect and pronounced the word "a-BEETS."

Grinder: A long sandwich that is elsewhere called a hero, hoagie, or submarine and that seems to have no relation to the Neapolitan dialect.

Tag sale: The event that in other parts of the country is called a garage sale or yard sale.

UConn: Pronounced "Yukon" like the Arctic territory, but in Connecticut refers to the University of Connecticut, located in the town of Storrs.

Further Reading

Abbott, E. F. *Sybil Ludington: Revolutionary War Rider*. New York: Square Fish, 2017.

Farnsworth, Cheri. *Haunted Connecticut: Ghosts and Strange Phenomena of the Constitution State*. Mechanicsburg, PA: Stackpole Books, 2006.

Roth, David Morris. *Connecticut: A History*. New York: W. W. Norton, 1979.

Delaware

FACT BOX

Nickname: The First State
Statehood Granted: 1787 (the first to gain statehood, as reflected in its nickname)
Capital: Dover
Population: 980,000
State Motto: "Liberty and Independence"
What Natives Call Themselves: Delawareans

STATE HISTORY

For such a small state (only Rhode Island is smaller), Delaware is unique in having been America's very *first* state, as well as being fought over by so many for so long.

Today's Delaware was originally home to Native American people, including the Lenni Lenape and Susquehanna. After various groups of Europeans arrived, conflicts began. Without regard for the Native people who were already living there, today's Delaware was first claimed by the English based on the North American voyages of John Cabot back in 1497.

The Dutch also staked a claim in Delaware subsequent to explorations in 1609 by Henry Hudson, who sailed on behalf of the Dutch East India Company. Establishing trading posts in what is today's Delaware starting in the 1620s, the Dutch were the first Europeans to create actual settlements there. One, Zwaanendael, or "Swan Valley," was founded in 1631 and later evolved into the town of Lewes, Delaware.

In 1638, Sweden established an outpost at a place they called Fort Christina, which became today's city of Wilmington, Delaware. Known as the first Swedish settlement in North America, Fort Christina was named after Sweden's Queen Christina (portrayed fictionally in the classic Greta Garbo movie).

The Dutch waged war on Delaware's Swedish colonies, overthrowing the Swedes in 1655. Then the English in turn ousted the Dutch in 1664, establishing their own presence.

Delaware's current incarnation is often said to be part of the "Delmarva" region, an amalgam of the state names of Delaware, Maryland, and Virginia. There were recurring squabbles with other colonies over ownership of various portions of

Delaware, including an ongoing feud with Pennsylvania that was not resolved for several hundred years.

Tiny Delaware persisted, launching its own identity. This perseverance may have come from its namesake, English colonial governor Baron De La Warr (1577–1618), who ruled the vast territory of Virginia at the time. In a bit of historical trivia, Baron De La Warr was the great-grandson of Mary Boleyn, sister of Anne Boleyn, one of history's most notable names. De La Warr served as an adviser for Anne Boleyn's daughter, Queen Elizabeth I of England.

In 1610, De La Warr outfitted three ships and 150 men at his own expense to sail for the New World, being appointed "governor-for-life" of the region that included today's Delaware. In that role, De La Warr replaced the prior colonial government, which had been instituted by another notable, Captain John Smith.

Baron De La Warr died at sea on his way back to America from a trip to England, but his legacy lives on in the name "Delaware." It was applied to not only the state but also the bay, the river, and an entire group of people, the Native tribe also known as the Lenni Lenape.

With Delaware ultimately being named for Baron De La Warr, it may be a relief to schoolchildren through the years for whom spelling a state named for the original Dutch colony of "Zwaanendael" might be a challenge.

It was due to a colonial-era boundary dispute involving Delaware that one of America's most significant political and cultural demarcations occurred. Surveyors Charles Mason and Jeremiah Dixon were instructed to determine the location of Delaware's boundaries beyond dispute. Their report, issued in 1768, designated a line below which Delaware was officially situated. Placed below the "Mason-Dixon line," Delaware was therefore considered part of the nation's South. However, Delaware remained in the Union during the Civil War. Ironically, a small boundary dispute remained between Delaware and its neighbor to the north, Pennsylvania, until 1921, well after the Civil War and even after America fought in World War I.

Tiny Delaware went on to establish itself as the "first" in a number of areas. Even though the Battle of Cooch's Bridge was the only skirmish of the American Revolution to be fought in Delaware, it was deeply symbolic. For the first time, the new American flag that is known today as the Stars and Stripes was flown in battle.

While many of its citizens supported the American cause, Delaware was also the site of an insurrection by loyalists, who were colonists remaining loyal to England. "Cheney Clow's Rebellion" in 1778 was spurred by a battalion of American soldiers who were said to have "foraged" for supplies from local farms. Some farmers objected to their provisions being taken, including one named Cheney Clow who constructed a fort on his property near today's city of Dover, Delaware. There was a skirmish between Clow's loyalists and a patriot militia, leaving one man dead on each side. More soldiers of the Continental Army arrived, burned Clow's fort, and captured many of the loyalists. After the Revolution, Clow was indicted for treason by the state of Delaware and hanged.

Many Americans erroneously think of Delaware in connection with the classic painting *Washington Crossing the Delaware*. During the American Revolution in

> **What Della Wore**
>
> The first exposure to the state of Delaware for many schoolchildren has traditionally been a novelty song popularly known as "What Did Della Wear?" written in 1959. Under its official title of "Delaware," the tune became a hit record for Perry Como in 1960 with its references to 15 of the United States. Of the puns on state names, Delaware is the most prominent. The song begins by asking the question "What did Della wear, boy, what did Della wear?" and responding with her apparel said to be "a brand-new jersey." There are other questions, including one asking what did Missus sip (answer: a mini-soda), but Delaware is the one that is often indelibly burned into people's minds.

1776, General George Washington and his troops did indeed cross the Delaware River, but it was from Pennsylvania to New Jersey, not actually in the state of Delaware.

In 1787, Delaware became the first of the original thirteen colonies to ratify the U.S. Constitution and was the first to be granted statehood. Its nickname, "the First State," became official in 2002 by an act of the Delaware legislature following an appeal by first graders at a Wilmington, Delaware, elementary school.

Even though the state of Delaware has the fewest number of counties in the United States (three in all: Kent, New Castle, and Sussex), it did not let its diminutive size hamper its prosperity in the years following the American Revolution. A major factor came when Éleuthère Irénée Du Pont stepped off the boat in America from France and established a factory on the Brandywine River near Wilmington, Delaware, in 1804. The company that still bears his name is one of the largest chemical companies in the world.

No mention of Delaware would be complete without noting the significance of the Du Pont family to the state. Its extended family tree also includes a smattering of Astors, Rockefellers, and Vanderbilts through marriage, bringing an upscale panache to Delaware.

In 1813, the oldest African American church in the United States was chartered in Wilmington, Delaware, as the Union Church of Africans. The following year, the Big August Quarterly, named for the church's annual summer conference, was first held. Enslaved people and free Blacks from around the region were able to come together to pray, sing, and rejoice in their faith. Held annually in downtown Wilmington, the Big August Quarterly is still celebrated, making it the oldest such religious and cultural festival in the nation.

Connecting the Delaware River with Chesapeake Bay, the Chesapeake and Delaware Canal was opened in 1829, bringing Delaware to the world. Starting in 1899, the business world came to Delaware with the passage of the state's General Corporation Law. Under this business-friendly statute, more than half of America's publicly traded businesses are incorporated in Delaware. Today, the state is home to more corporations than people.

URBAN LEGENDS

While New York may claim the story of the Headless Horseman of Sleepy Hollow, Delaware can boast not one but two such decapitated demons, even though their haunting ground is the less lyrically named **Cooch's Bridge** at Newark, Delaware. According to the urban legend, the head of a British soldier was detached by an American cannonball during the Revolutionary War battle at the bridge. Some people have claimed to see his spirit on foggy nights, trudging around the battlefield looking for his lost head. Wandering somewhere nearby is said to be the ghost of an American soldier whose head was blown off by a British cannonball in the same battle. He too allegedly haunts Cooch's Bridge in search of a severed skull.

During the Civil War, today's inactive **Fort Delaware** at Delaware City was used as a prison to confine Confederate soldiers. The island fort had a reputation of being impossible for prisoners to escape. It had been built for about 500 troops, but by the end of the Civil War, about 33,000 Confederate prisoners were packed in with little food or water nor any beds, sleeping on the floor of rat-infested dungeons. Thousands died. One of the desperate prisoners was said to be a young drummer boy who tried to escape by hiding in a coffin. The unsuccessful plan led to the boy being buried alive. Today, it is said that visitors can hear the sound of the boy's desperate spirit, still dutifully playing his drum.

The neighboring Delaware towns of Felton and Frederica both lay claim to the area's resident **Ghost Dog**, sometimes called the Fence-Rail Dog because it is said to be as long as a fence rail. Reports dating back to the early 1900s claim to have encountered a spectral canine with glowing red eyes appearing at the roadside. With the rise of the automobile later in the century, reports from nighttime drivers increased, possibly because local pedestrians and travelers on horseback had traditionally tended to avoid the area after dark. The legend states that an angry tenant murdered his landlord. The killer then ground up the body and fed it to his dog. Later events may have confirmed the adage "You are what you eat." The Ghost Dog allegedly started to appear and said to have glowing red eyes and a giant bushy tail, perhaps a spectral variation of the phrase "bright eyed and bushy tailed." Adding spice to the urban legend, the body of water flowing through the Ghost Dog's turf is the Murderkill River.

ICONIC DELAWARE FOOD

Unlike their puffy cousins from the South, **Delaware Slippery Dumplings** are large rectangles of dough that are rolled very thin, resembling large noodles. They are then cooked in chicken broth, to which chicken can be added to make Delaware Chicken and Dumpling Soup. The meatless version below is chock-full of slippery dumplings plus a few tasty vegetables for a hearty soup that is known by

Delawareans to be the perfect thing on a cold winter day. Some cooks may wish to make their own chicken stock, but the version below uses prepared chicken broth.

Delaware Slippery Dumpling Soup (Serves 8)
2 containers (48 oz) chicken broth
½ tsp each salt and pepper
1 Tbsp garlic powder
2 carrots, peeled and sliced
2 celery stalks, sliced
1 onion, sliced into eighths
Shredded parsley for garnish, or sliced green onion if preferred

Dumplings
2 cups all-purpose flour (along with a little more on hand for dusting)
½ tsp salt
¼ cup vegetable shortening
½ cup warm water

1. While broth, spices, and vegetables simmer to a low boil, make dumplings by combining flour and salt, then add shortening. Mix by hand until mixture feels coarse, adding warm water sparingly until a soft dough is formed.
2. Dust flour on cutting board, then knead the dough about four minutes before wrapping kneaded dough in plastic wrap.
3. Allow dough to rest for 15 minutes, then dust more flour on cutting board before rolling out the dough as thinly as possible.
4. Cut dumplings into rectangles of about 2 by 3 inches, then lightly dust them with flour.
5. Drop dumplings individually into boiling broth, ensuring they do not stick together.
6. Cover and boil the dumplings at medium heat for about 15–20 minutes.
7. Add garnish of choice before serving in warm bowls.

Source: Adapted from https://explorecookeat.com/delaware-chicken-and-slippery-dumplings/.

ODD LAWS

A law that remains on the books in Delaware is a said to be unenforced and possibly unconstitutional, but nonetheless, it states that "R-rated" movies shall not be shown at drive-in theaters. When drive-ins declined after their peak of popularity as family entertainment during the postwar years, some owners began showing more adult-oriented fare at their drive-ins, capitalizing on the seclusion afforded by viewing in the privacy of a personal car. People living nearby began to complain that X- and R-rated movies on the drive-in screens were visible to children.

Delaware's law, passed in 1974, was typical of others passed around the country around that time by prohibiting films at drive-ins that were not suitable for minors, although Delaware's is the only one cited by legal scholars that specifically banned R-rated movies. Such laws have been known to be overturned in other states, but Delaware's law remains. The legality of the statute may be moot, as Delaware's last known drive-in closed in 2008. However, the onslaught of COVID-19 starting in March 2020 brought about suggestions that drive-in movies might be reinstated, so the Delaware law could still be put to the test.

In the town of Rehoboth Beach, Delaware, it is unlawful for people to change clothes in their personal vehicle. This law specifies vehicles in a public place, so theoretically, changing outfits in a car parked in a private garage would not be a violation if anyone should choose to do so. Municipal codes also prohibit disrobing on the beach or under the boardwalk, which might be considered understandable, although changing into or out of a bathing suit in a public restroom is also prohibited, raising the possibility of wending one's way home in a soggy swimsuit.

Delaware law also maintains that getting married on a dare is grounds for an annulment. This statute is sometimes incorrectly interpreted as being illegal in Delaware to get married on a dare, which is not true. What the actual law does is provide weight to a section on Delaware's Petition for Divorce/Annulment Form that asks when the petitioner learned his or her marriage was based on a practical joke or dare.

UNUSUAL DESTINATIONS

The **Futuro House**, situated at the Eagle Crest Aerodrome in Milford, Delaware, can be best described as "*E.T.* Meets *Mad Men*." These round, prefabricated homes were marketed during the late 1960s as being totally cool. Today, only a handful of Futuro houses still survive around the world. Created in 1968, the flying-saucer-shaped residences were promoted as modernistic vacation getaways in which people climbed inside through an airplane-style hatch entrance. The Futuro was constructed of fiberglass-reinforced polyester plastic, measuring 13 feet high by 26 feet in diameter. While the structure is certainly eye-catching in a retro sort of way, a significant limitation to a Futuro home was that they came with neither electricity nor plumbing. The surviving structure in Delaware attracts a number of Futuro fans each year, presumably having been fitted with those conveniences, as it appears to be inhabited as a private residence at least part of the time.

Each year in late June, Delawareans and visitors to the state do not have to travel to Pamplona, Spain, for the excitement of the Running of the Bulls. To be accurate, the annual event at Delaware's Dewey Beach is singular: **the Running of the Bull**. It is also less dangerous than the Spanish version, since the Delaware sprint is two humans in a bull costume. Even so, participants strive to preserve the spirit of the event in Spain by dressing themselves in the traditional Pamplona white clothing with red bandanas. There are also less traditionally garbed entrants in bikini tops. Running with the bull ensues, accompanied by the cheers of the crowd on the

With only a small handful still surviving around the world, the flying-saucer-shaped Futuro House, such as the one in Milford, Delaware, was marketed in the 1960s as a modernistic vacation getaway. (Jef Wodniack/Dreamstime.com)

sidelines. After about 10 minutes, everyone adjourns to various seaside establishments for refreshments. Organizers stress that no humans in animal costumes are harmed during this event.

Last alphabetically but certainly not least in the level of oddity is the **Zwaanendael Museum** in Lewes. Along with housing such displays as what is said to be a petrified mermaid, the Zwaanendael Museum was created to honor Delaware's first European settlement, Zwaanendael (Dutch for "Swan Valley"), founded 1631. There is no documentation of mermaids, petrified or otherwise, being among the Dutch settlers, but the museum is still known for its quirkiness. One point of interest is the museum's odd description of how the colony met its demise in 1632, which may be a classic of understatement. Citing Delaware Historical and Cultural Affairs, the settlement was burned to the ground and the 28 colonists killed by Native Americans as the "result of a cultural misunderstanding between the Dutch and Native people in the area."

DISTINCTIVE DELAWARE WORDS AND SAYINGS

Baggin' up: Responding with tremendous laughter, as in a hilarious joke that had listeners "baggin' up" (termed "cracking up" elsewhere).

Beach, the: The entire Delaware coast, not one specific sandy location.

Cousint: Including but not limited to the child of an aunt or uncle, this is someone distantly related who would usually be called a "cousin," without the *t*.

Slower Lower: The region of the state south of the Chesapeake and Delaware Canal, an area that is more agriculturally oriented and Southern in nature. Sometimes the word order is reversed into "Lower Slower" and sometimes abbreviated as "LSD" (Lower Slower Delaware).

Further Reading

Duffy, Jim. *Eastern Shore Road Trips: 27 One-Day Adventures on Delmarva (Volume 1)*. Cambridge, MD: Secrets of the Eastern Shore, 2016.

Martinelli, Patricia. *Haunted Delaware: Ghosts and Strange Phenomena of the First State*. Mechanicsburg, PA: Stackpole Books, 2006.

Words, Russell C. *So, You're Moving to Delaware!: A Handbook to Being a Delawarean*. Flat Rock, NC: Cruden Bay Books, 2014.

Florida

FACT BOX

Nickname: The Sunshine State
Statehood Granted: 1845
Capital: Tallahassee
Population: 22,000,000
State Motto: "In God We Trust"
What Natives Call Themselves: Floridians

STATE HISTORY

Readers of such authors as Dave Barry, Edna Buchanan, and Carl Hiaasen understand that compared to the other 49 states of the Union, Florida can be called . . . different.

Florida was the first area of what became mainland United States to be explored and settled by Europeans. This incursion by Spain took place more than a century before the English aboard the *Mayflower* landed at Plymouth Rock in 1620.

Although most textbooks have traditionally tended to begin the narrative of Florida's history with the arrival of the Spaniards in 1513, there were already thousands of Native people living there. These included the Apalachee, Calusa, and Mayaimi tribes, with the Seminole arriving later.

The Native people who lived in Florida when the Europeans arrived were relative latecomers. In 1998, during an excavation in downtown Miami to build a luxury condominium, hundreds of mysterious holes were discovered in a layer of limestone bedrock. Twenty-four of the largest holes comprised a perfect circle almost 40 feet in diameter. The human teeth and ancient tools that were discovered on the site were radiocarbon dated back to around the time of Christ. The unknown origin of the prehistoric site has led to its nickname "America's Stonehenge." Some people ascribed its origins to space aliens. In any case, the state of Florida purchased the land as a historical museum and protected archaeological site.

When the Spaniard Juan Ponce de León spotted the peninsula in 1513, he named it Florida, a Spanish term referring to flowers, many of which grew abundantly in the lush landscape.

> ### "Youth"-ful Appearance
>
> In 1513, Spanish explorer Juan Ponce de León (1474–1521) won a place in the history books as the discoverer of Florida, along with becoming the center of a 500-year-old legend. The story goes that Ponce staked a claim in Florida for Spain while allegedly searching for the mythical Fountain of Youth, which was said to grant immortality to those who drank from it. The reality is much less romantic, having to do with political squabbles. To discredit Ponce and his supporters by making him look foolish, a Spanish politician spread the fake Fountain of Youth story after Ponce de León's death, making it difficult for the deceased explorer to deny it.

The Spaniards founded the settlement of St. Augustine, Florida, in 1565, making it the oldest continuously occupied European-based city in the United States. (Santa Fe, New Mexico, a rival for the longevity title among American cities, was founded in 1607.)

England, which was Spain's European rival, began gaining a foothold on the East Coast of America in the early 1600s. The Spanish presence in America's southernmost peninsula became something of an annoyance to the English. As the 1600s and 1700s wore on, Florida gained a reputation as a haven for enslaved people escaping from England's North American colonies as well as a base of operations for Native Americans launching attacks on English settlements.

In 1819, U.S. secretary of state (and future president) John Quincy Adams succeeded in purchasing Florida from Spain at a cost of about $5 million. Worth almost $85 million in today's dollars, it would currently work out to about two dollars an acre.

With an increased number of settlers moving into Florida during the 1800s, removing Native Americans became a priority for the United States. Tribes that were not already destroyed by disease or violence were forcibly moved west of the Mississippi River.

After gold was discovered in neighboring Georgia in 1828, prospectors came to Florida assuming that the precious metal would be there too, but found none. Experts today claim there are no known gold deposits whatsoever in Florida, making it unique among the 50 states. However, the Florida coast turned out to be a rich source of gold-laden Spanish shipwrecks as well as enticing tales of buried treasure.

In 1845, Florida was admitted to the Union as the 27th state. Being south of the Mason-Dixon line, it was declared a slave state and was no longer a sanctuary for people escaping enslavement.

Until the early years of the 20th century, permanent settlements in Florida were relatively few. But Florida is the only state that borders both the Atlantic Ocean and the Gulf of Mexico, so with its abundant sunshine even in winter, it attracted wealthy vacationers from cold Northern states to loll temporarily on its shores.

However, due to Florida's summer heat, much of the state was considered uninhabitable until the mid-20th-century advent of air conditioning. In the early 1900s, most Floridians lived within 50 miles of the Georgia border, and Florida's economy was based largely on agriculture.

Starting in 1920, that all began to change with a phenomenon that made Florida unique among the other states: the Florida Land Boom. In the 1920s, Florida was promoted as the American Riviera. Better railroad connections, easy credit, general prosperity in America, and a nationwide advertising campaign created a hot market in Florida real estate speculation. By 1925, land prices rose until new buyers could not afford to make the investment and existing owners could not sell. Then, in 1926, a deadly hurricane destroyed much of South Florida, killing hundreds of people. It was followed by another killer hurricane in 1928. Due to the storms, at least tens of thousands were injured and/or left homeless in Florida. With bank failures and the stock market crash in 1929, the Florida land craze of the 1920s ended as the Great Depression of the 1930s began. Many historians consider Florida in the 1920s and 1930s to be the nation's most significant real estate boom-and-bust.

America's World War II years (1941–1945) saw Florida, with its year-round temperate weather, become home to a number of military bases. After the war ended, Florida was chosen as the site of an exciting new program for America. A sleepy East Florida spot called Cape Canaveral became the nation's rocket test site due to its location on the ocean, proximity to the equator, temperate weather, and

Cape Canaveral, Florida, became known world-wide as the center of America's NASA space program. Television brought Florida's space shots to people around the globe. (Chris Kelleher/Dreamstime.com)

distance from heavily populated cities. In the 1950s and 1960s, Cape Canaveral, Florida, became known worldwide as the center of America's space program. The rise of the television industry brought Florida's space shots into homes around the globe.

In addition, the postwar years saw the rise of commercial jet airliners. Fast, affordable air travel put Florida within the reach of average American vacationers from across the nation.

Amid the country's general prosperity, convenient transportation to Florida became even more attractive, beginning in 1971 with the opening of Walt Disney World in the central Florida town of Orlando. Benefited by inexpensive land and the ability to expand its theme parks, the Disney complex changed the nature of Florida tourism, which had previously centered on coastal regions, making Florida a worldwide tourist destination.

Due to the pervasiveness of stories in the news media, Florida today has the distinction of being considered by many to be unique in its status as a rather unusual state. Innumerable books and websites center on strange doings in the Sunshine State. Among other contributing factors, some theorize it is partly due to the weather, with Florida's constant heat and humidity interrupted only by the panic-inducing devastation of regular hurricanes.

Many people across the nation are familiar with the "Florida Man" phenomenon. It is based on actual headlines that many people claim are indicative of odd behavioral patterns among Floridians, such as "Florida Man Attacks Father with Pizza."

A number of Florida towns proclaim themselves to be the "capital of the world" for some type of distinction. For example, Wausau, Florida, claims to be the "Possum Capital of the World," complete with a commemorative stone marker. However, the nearby town of Chipley, about 10 miles away, also lays claim to the possum-related honorific.

In the small East Florida community of Cassadaga, there are so many self-styled clairvoyants, mediums, mystics, psychics, seers, and other spiritualists who have gathered there that it has been nicknamed "the Psychic Capital of the World."

Florida is known worldwide as a haven for retirees, but also for its serial killers. It has hosted iconic figures like Henry Ford and Thomas Edison, who were next-door neighbors at their Florida vacation homes. Gangster Al Capone died at his estate in Miami, and designer Gianni Versace was murdered in front of his Miami mansion.

The Salvador Dali Museum in St. Petersburg, Florida, is dedicated to the surrealist painter whose most famous works include melting clock faces. Some say such surrealism is perfectly at home in the unique state of Florida.

URBAN LEGENDS

The **Devil's Chair** can be found in the town of Cassadaga, which is called Florida's spiritualism center. Most of Cassadaga's psychic activity is said to have its basis in positive energy, but one local landmark has attracted another type of element.

Many people believe that sitting in the brick "Devil's Chair" at Cassadaga's Lake Helen Cemetery at midnight will bring about a visit from Satan himself. However, Beelzebub is said to apparently get thirsty from working around fire and brimstone. Placing a full can of beer on the Devil's Chair will result in the can being empty the next morning, which might be attributed to Satan building up a thirst from his evil activities or possibly just a parched passerby.

The **St. Augustine Lighthouse** was home to a private citizen who served as lighthouse keeper until the government wanted control of the facility. Angry at being offered a paltry sum of money for his property, followed by the threat of being forcibly evicted by the government, he swore never to leave. Apparently, the old lighthouse keeper was true to his word. According to the urban legend, some visitors to the lighthouse today claim to spot the ghost of a grizzled elderly man in old-fashioned clothing. This spectral senior citizen is sometimes accompanied by the smell of cigars, which the lighthouse keeper was known to favor and the sound of invisible footsteps on the empty lighthouse stairs.

Florida's **Skunk Ape** is also known by other equally descriptive labels, such as the Abominable Florida Apeman, Stink Ape, Swamp Ape, Swamp Cabbage Man, and Swampsquatch. As the name might suggest, this giant Bigfoot-type creature emits a foul skunk-like odor. In the creature's defense, after living in the swamps for decades, that might not be unexpected. Since the 1960s, there have allegedly been thousands of reported sightings of this hairy humanoid in South Florida. The legend has led to the founding of the Skunk Ape Research Headquarters in Ochopee. The resident researcher collects Skunk Ape reports, investigates sightings, and displays relevant exhibits. In 1977, a "Skunk Ape Bill" was introduced into the Florida legislature to make it a crime to "take, possess, harm or molest anthropoid or humanoid animals." The law did not pass. Therefore, at this writing, the Skunk Ape remains an unprotected species and, as such, fair game.

ICONIC FLORIDA FOOD

Starting in the 1950s, **Key Lime Pie** was widely promoted as Florida's "most famous treat." In 2006, the Florida legislature formally named key lime pie as the official pie of the state of Florida. Some people think the delectable confection is a pie made with limes and simply named for the exotic Florida Keys. However, the key lime is a specific type of fruit (*Citrus aurantifolia*) that, with its thin yellow rind, is more tart and aromatic than the typical grocery-store lime. Key lime juice is a pale yellow, making the filling in a true key lime pie light yellow, not green. This adaptation calls for the real thing, but it also allows for a substitute:

> **Key Lime Pie** (Serves 8)
> 1 package (8 oz) cream cheese, softened
> 1 can (14 oz) sweetened condensed milk
> ½ cup key lime juice or regular lime juice
> 9-inch prepared graham cracker crust

2 cups whipped topping
Sliced key lime as garnish (optional)

1. In a large bowl, beat cream cheese until smooth.
2. Blend in milk and lime juice, then transfer to crust.
3. Cover and refrigerate for at least four hours.
4. Top with whipped topping and lime slices just before serving.

Source: Adapted from https://www.tasteofhome.com/recipes/easy-key-lime-pie/.

ODD LAWS

According to Florida statutes, doors to all public buildings must open outward. While this might appear to hinder the creative vision of some architects, the law is not meant to stifle imagination. With the number of tourists in Florida along with residents of all ages and backgrounds, this legal requirement is meant to minimize congestion in case of a fire or other emergency. Anxious people simply have to push outward to escape rather than pulling inward, which would create congestion and a greater degree of danger in getting everybody out safely. Florida's "Door Law" is sometimes cited on the internet as a strange legal requirement, but anyone trying to make it out of a burning building quickly might find a great deal of merit in it.

On the other hand, people riding an elephant through the streets might find one Florida law annoying, forcing them to carry change if they choose to conduct their daily business from atop a pachyderm. It states that if a person ties an elephant to a parking meter, the meter must be fed and the standard parking fee paid exactly as if the four-legged ride in question were a motor vehicle.

Agriculture in Florida is big business, and the state takes a special interest in its oranges. It is therefore unlawful to ship oranges under the auspices of allegedly being Florida grown when they are not. This would seemingly include pretending that a fruit basket sent to envious folks back home contains citrus from the Sunshine State but instead consists of the kind of foreign-grown oranges that might be found being hawked somewhere along I-95.

In other food-related legalities, Florida motorists are free to take roadkill home. It would seem to be open season on squashed possums, raccoons, and squirrels. However, before acquiring a dead deer from the roadside, the Florida Wildlife Commission must be notified if said deer is out of season. Incidentally, Florida law maintains that if a motorist dies after colliding with a pet deer that is also killed, the animal's owner cannot sue the driver's estate.

UNUSUAL DESTINATIONS

In the waters near Marco Island in Southwestern Florida lies the abandoned **Cape Romano Dome Home**, giving the seascape a distinctive otherworldly aura. The island on which it was originally built is now underwater, as rising ocean levels cut off the home from Cape Romano. The Dome Home is a complex of six concrete igloos on stilts that today are accessible only by sea. Despite the stilts that have managed to keep its rounded pods above water, the Dome Home is slowly being submerged by the Gulf of Mexico. Some observers claim it was constructed by aliens or a secret cult, but the truth is more mundane, having been built in 1981 as a retreat for a wealthy family. Its rounded domes withstood hurricanes, but it was ultimately rendered unlivable by the effects of rising sea levels that some environmentalists claim is a preview of the future.

At the historic **Haile Homestead** in Gainesville, more than 12,500 words written on every surface of the house seem to illustrate the adage that "the handwriting is on the wall." In this case, the scrawls are the work of the family who lived in the plantation house that was built by slave labor in 1856 and remains one of Florida's last surviving antebellum homes. After the final descendants of the 15 Haile children departed, the house and land were left dormant in the 1930s. It languished until it was discovered again in the 1970s when it was noted that all the family members had taken to writing on the walls, not just the scribbling of toddlers. Dating back to the 1850s, there are doodles, growth charts, inventories, journals, lists, names of party guests, notes, and random thoughts. Today it is a destination that is open to the public, many of whom ask a simple question: *Why?*

For those who cannot decide whether to go diving or attend a concert over the weekend, the annual **Underwater Music Festival** at Big Pine Key provides both at once. It was created to raise awareness of the Looe Key Reef, which is part of the only living coral barrier reef in North America. Listening to the ethereal sound of music as it travels through water, hundreds of divers and snorkelers can enjoy a unique experience. For landlubbers and boaters above sea level, the music is broadcast simultaneously by a local radio station. The Beatles have proven particularly popular, with their recordings of such songs as "Octopus Garden" and "Yellow Submarine" being special crowd-pleasers along with one year's guest appearance by "Ringo Starfish."

DISTINCTIVE FLORIDA WORDS AND SAYINGS

Bugs: Elsewhere, small insect life-forms. In Florida they are creatures so big that they are said to often be mistaken for alligators.

Chad: In Florida, not a boy's name or an African nation, but a small bit of paper that can affect an election ballot and change the course of history, particularly the "hanging" variety.

Keys: Island chain off the southernmost Florida coast, not the items used to start a car or unlock a door.

Lovebugs: Not really loved by anyone, this is a name given to the insects that wreak havoc on car windshields with their messy splatters.

Further Reading

Becnel, Tom, and David Grimes. *Florida Curiosities: Quirky Characters, Roadside Oddities and Other Offbeat Stuff.* 2nd edition. Guilford, CT: Globe Pequot, 2006.

Gannon, Michael. *The History of Florida.* Gainesville: University Press of Florida, 2018.

Shaer, Matthew. "Ponce De Leon Never Searched for the Fountain of Youth." *Smithsonian Magazine*, June 2013. https://www.smithsonianmag.com/history/ponce-de-leon-never-searched-for-the-fountain-of-youth-72629888/.

Wright, James D. *A Florida State of Mind: An Unnatural History of Our Weirdest State.* New York: Thomas Dunne, 2019.

Wynne, Nick, and Richard Moorhead. *Paradise for Sale: Florida's Booms and Busts.* Charleston, SC: History Press, 2010.

Georgia

FACT BOX

Nickname: The Peach State
Statehood Granted: 1788
Capital: Atlanta
Population: 10,600,000
State Motto: "Wisdom, Justice, Moderation"
What Natives Call Themselves: Georgians

STATE HISTORY

Trivia buffs may wish to note that the answer to (a) the youngest of the thirteen original colonies, (b) the southernmost of the original English colonies, and (c) the largest state east of the Mississippi River all have the same name: Georgia.

By the time the colony was founded in 1733 after being named for Britain's King George II, today's state of Georgia already had a long history of Indigenous people going back more than 12,000 years. Native American groups that eventually gathered in permanent agriculturally based villages included the Apalachee, Creek, and Cherokee.

After European colonization, many Cherokee adopted the English language, the colonial American way of life, and the Christian religion, sometimes sending their children to Northern missionary schools to be educated. Despite their efforts to adapt, the presence of the Cherokee in Georgia would end tragically when they faced the choice between forced removal west of the Mississippi River or annihilation.

The earliest Europeans in today's Georgia were the Spanish in 1526. However, their only attempt to form a permanent settlement, San Miguel de Gualdape, lasted only six weeks. African people brought there by the Spaniards constituted the first documented instance of Black slavery in North America. In 1526, the enslaved people at San Miguel de Gualdape led the first slave rebellion in the continental United States.

By the mid-1600s, English settlers from the Carolina Colony were crossing into today's Georgia, sometimes engaging in the slave trade of Blacks and Native Americans.

Today's Georgia was founded as an English colony in 1733, with its first settlement in Savannah. A member of England's Parliament, James Oglethorpe, saw a way to offer a fresh start for Britain's "worthy poor," especially debtors who could hardly repay their debts while languishing in prison. There was also a military aspect: creating Georgia was seen as a buffer zone against the Spanish in Florida.

At the time of its founding, Georgia was the only one of England's North American colonies in which slavery was expressly forbidden. Also banned were rum and lawyers. However, in 1742, rum was made legal in Georgia. Slavery was legalized next, in 1751, when it was found that there were huge profits to be made on cotton plantations with slave labor. By 1789, Georgia required an oral examination and evidence of good moral character to become an attorney; therefore, lawyers were also presumably legal at that point.

In 1788, Georgia became the fourth state to ratify the U.S. Constitution. In 1829, when gold was discovered in Georgia, white settlers demanded the right to seize Native lands. Subsequent to America's Indian Removal Act in 1830, thousands of Native American people died on the forced march westward in 1838 that came to be called the Trail of Tears.

Seceding from the Union in 1861, Georgia was one of the original Confederate states. In 1864, it suffered from the devastating scorched earth policy of Union general William Tecumseh Sherman's "March to the Sea" from Atlanta to Savannah. In 1870, Georgia became the last of the Confederate states to be restored to the Union.

Like the rest of the Deep South, Georgia struggled with the effects of the Civil War and Reconstruction. However, by the mid-20th century, with the advent of air conditioning that made Georgia's summer heat bearable, Atlanta became a leader in the nation's booming Sunbelt economy.

One of Georgia's most prominent businesses was established in 1886 by Atlanta resident John Pemberton: Coca-Cola. Popularly called "Coke," it was a local product that made good through the next century to the point that today its red-and-white logo is said to be the most recognizable image around the world.

Georgia also became a leader in modern communications. It was there that Ted Turner's empire was born. Along with cable television channels based in Atlanta such as Superstation TBS, TNT, and Turner Classic Movies, Turner created the groundbreaking 24-hour news channel called the Cable News Network (CNN).

Even though Atlanta is generally considered a world-class city and home of the busiest airport in the United States, Georgia is never far from its agricultural roots. It is nicknamed "the Peach State" for its bounteous harvest of the fuzzy fruit, and on New Year's Eve, traditionally a giant peach is dropped from a tower in Atlanta as Georgians count down to the New Year, although the event went on hiatus around the time of COVID-19.

Many people around the globe were introduced to Georgia as the setting of the iconic book and movie *Gone with the Wind*. Although considered controversial today for its portrayal of antebellum society, the film's burning of Atlanta scene is often etched in people's minds. Today, Marietta, Georgia is home to a *Gone with the Wind* museum containing original costumes and memorabilia.

Children at the Coca Cola Museum in Atlanta, Georgia. Coca-Cola, one of Georgia's most prominent businesses, was established in 1886 in Atlanta. Today its red and white logo is said to be the most recognizable image around the world. (Corel)

History was made when today's Wesleyan College in Macon, Georgia, was founded in 1836. It was the first college in the world chartered specifically to grant degrees to women.

Georgia is also known by many as the birthplace of America's Civil Rights Movement. The Martin Luther King Jr. National Historical Park in Atlanta consists of several sites, including the King Center, Dr. King's boyhood home, and the original Ebenezer Baptist Church where he was pastor.

Lumpkin County in North Georgia was the site of one of the very first gold rushes in the United States. In 1828, gold was discovered in Auraria, Georgia, near today's town of Dahlongea. Being in Cherokee territory, this discovery led to the passage of the Indian Removal Act of 1830.

Like many boom-and-bust mining communities, Auraria is currently a ghost town. However, a footnote to the story is that in 1848, when gold was discovered at Sutter's Mill in California, former Auraria resident Jennie Wimmer, a cook, was the first person to verify that the California gold was authentic. From her time in Georgia, she was the only person at Sutter's Mill who knew how to perform the proper tests.

Savannah, Georgia, became widely known through the book and movie *Midnight in the Garden of Good and Evil*, spotlighting local oddities that only added to Georgia's mystique.

> ### Just an Old Sweet Song
>
> "Georgia on My Mind" is a classic song written in 1930 by musician Hoagy Carmichael and his friend Stuart Gorrell, both of whom were from Indiana and had met at Indiana University. Although neither hailed from Georgia, in 1979, the Georgia legislature designated the tune to be the official state song. After penning the words to one of the most haunting ballads of all time, Gorrell became a banker and was not known to write another lyric in his life. The song received a fair amount of notice over the years, but the most popular version came in 1960 when it became a hit record by Ray Charles who was indeed born in Georgia—ironically in 1930, the same year the song was created.

URBAN LEGENDS

Legend has it that millions of dollars in buried treasure are hidden somewhere on Georgia's **Blackbeard Island**. It is named for pirate Edward Teach (circa 1680–1718), who was nicknamed "Blackbeard." Over the centuries, rumors have abounded about treasure that he looted from seagoing raids in the early 1700s. The island where he allegedly stashed the goods was designated with Blackbeard's name on a survey map as early as 1760, since he and his men were known to frequent the area. During his prime, Blackbeard was notorious for being a highly skilled pirate. If the centuries-old rumors of buried treasure are true, he was apparently also a master of concealment. As of this writing, no riches have been found on the island that bears his name, so if Blackbeard stashed his treasure there, he hid it extremely well. Held by the federal government since 1800, Georgia's Blackbeard Island is currently a national wildlife refuge. The last documented search for Blackbeard's fortune to be approved was in the 1880s, but it did not reveal any buried treasure. No other hunts have been authorized since then. If the island's resident alligators and sea turtles have come across any of Blackbeard's millions, they are keeping the news to themselves.

The urban legend of Augusta's **Haunted Pillar** is so persuasive that few people want to believe it was actually a fiction created in 1931 by a press agent who was hired to stimulate the town's economy by attracting tourists. The story went that a stone pillar at a marketplace in downtown Augusta was cursed in the 1800s by a preacher who was angry at being banned from "exhorting" at its foot. He allegedly laid a curse about being struck by lightning on anyone who tried to move the pillar as well as those who even touched the pillar briefly. When a tornado tore through the town in 1878, the storm demolished everything in its path except the pillar, which the preacher was said to have predicted—at least according to a newspaper story later planted by the press agent. The urban legend continues even after 2016, when the pillar was destroyed after being hit by a car. A handsome historical marker stands in its place, citing the local tradition of any person's contact with the town's "haunted pillar" to be doomed.

Dublin, Georgia, is often said to be a town with great charm, being named for the city in Ireland and carrying on the Irish theme in much of its imagery. However, it is at the center of an urban legend that has nothing to do with the Emerald Isle unless the isle in question is located on the far side of the galaxy. Dublin, Georgia is said to contain the portal to another universe called "**Kcymaerxthaere**" (apparently pronounced "Kcymaerxthaere"). According to the legend, Kcymaerxthaere is a parallel universe that has much in common with our familiar planet Earth, although it has different laws of physics and unique types of living things. Believers in search of this portal to another universe were traditionally guided to a marker on the side of what was called, at seven stories high, the tallest building in Dublin. However, in 2018, the portal between Dublin and Kcymaerxthaere became harder to find for true believers after the marker was removed when the building was renovated. Even so, the urban legend lives on.

ICONIC GEORGIA FOOD

Although Georgia is renowned for the bounty of peanuts and Vidalia onions that are among its best-known crops, Georgia officially calls itself "the Peach State." There is not only a Peach County but also dozens of thoroughfares having the word "Peachtree" as part of their name in the city of Atlanta alone. Not surprisingly, a special Georgia food is **Peach Cobbler**, as seen in this recipe:

Georgia Peach Cobbler (Serves 8)
½ cup unsalted butter
1 cup all-purpose flour
2 cups sugar, divided in half
1 Tbsp baking powder
Pinch of salt
1 cup milk
4 cups fresh peaches, sliced
1 Tbsp lemon juice

1. Preheat oven to 375°F.
2. Melt the butter in a 9 by 13 inch baking dish.
3. Combine flour, baking powder, salt, and one cup of the sugar before adding milk, stirring until the dry ingredients are moistened.
4. Pour over buttered baking dish but do not stir.
5. Bring remaining cup of sugar plus peach slices and lemon juice to a boil over high heat, stirring constantly, then pour over batter but do not stir.
6. Bake at 375° for 40–45 minutes or until golden brown. Serve warm or cool, with or without whipped topping or vanilla ice cream, according to taste.

Source: Adapted from https://sweetstateofmine.blogspot.com/2011/07/georgia-peach-cobbler.html.

ODD LAWS

According to the 2010 Georgia Code, it is unlawful to use language in the presence of another person that would tend to provoke violent resentment, or in the official terminology of the Georgia law, to be "fighting words." Along similar lines, Georgia Code also prohibits using obscene, profane, or vulgar language in the presence of a person under the age of 14, including via telephone. This statute does not specify whether such inflammatory language is also prohibited on the internet.

Georgia Code prohibits removing any human body part from the scene of a death or dismemberment. This law applies only to civilians who are not there acting in a professional capacity. Law enforcement officials and emergency medical personnel are exempted from this rule in the course of performing their official duties. It is not known what prompted this provision—that is, a rash of body parts disappearing from their last known location in the possession of interested, yet ghoulish, onlookers.

The city of Kennesaw, Georgia, made national news in 1982 when it passed an ordinance that was widely interpreted as all Kennesaw residents being ordered to have a gun. Technically, the Kennesaw ordinance requires every head of household residing in the city limits to maintain a firearm and ammunition. The stated purpose of the law was to provide for the emergency management of the city as well as the safety, security, and general welfare of the town's inhabitants. However, the Kennesaw statute was publicly said to have been passed in response to an ordinance in Morton Grove, Illinois, that prohibited handgun ownership in the city limits. The Morton Grove law was repealed after being ruled unconstitutional, although the Kennesaw law remains in effect, though usually unenforced. It was noted in a subsection of the Kennesaw ordinance that conscientious objectors whose personal beliefs or religious doctrines oppose maintaining firearms are exempted. The law also does not apply to those citizens who are suffering from a mental disability, who are convicted of a felony, or who are "paupers."

UNUSUAL DESTINATIONS

Expedition Bigfoot is located in Cherry Log, Georgia, which can be found in the mountains north of Ellijay. There, it is said, visitors can be exposed to the mythical creature, although probably not up close and personal. Despite the word "Expedition" in its name, suggesting the great outdoors, the 4,000-square-foot museum consists of indoor exhibits. It claims to display Bigfoot artifacts along with information on sightings, the origins of Bigfoot legends, and a reference library for the academically minded. This venue also encourages people to share confidential testimonies of encounters with Bigfoot, Sasquatch, Yeti, or other such oversized hairy beasts. The Expedition Bigfoot website states that all are welcome at the museum, leaving the question of Bigfoot's existence up to the individual, regardless of whether one is a "skeptic, believer, or 'knower.'"

When it comes to truth in advertising, **Goats on the Roof** is on solid ground. Abbreviated simply as "Goats" by the owners, the facility is located in the community of Tiger, which can be found in the mountains of Northeast Georgia. "Goats" is said by many sources to be the quintessential North Georgia road-trip stop. It bills itself as a country store that sells items including homemade fudge, ice cream, souvenirs, T-shirts, and what is said to be Amish furniture. However, the namesake attraction is about a half-dozen live goats who roam freely on top of the building. There are interconnected walkways, playhouse-type towers, and suspension bridges on which the goats can travel from roof to roof, eat real grass, and look down on visitors. Guests can become official Goat Rangers, sending food up to the roof via pulleys, including one that is powered by pedaling an attached stationary bicycle, possibly for those who already consumed an overabundance of the homemade fudge.

The **Georgia Guidestones** can be found in Elberton, Georgia, near the South Carolina state line. Sometimes called the "Stonehenge of the South," the Guidestones are a series of tall granite monuments that are said to have been commissioned in 1980 by what was called a "mysterious stranger." Inscribed on five slabs are 10 suggested guidelines for civilization that are written in eight modern languages: Arabic, Chinese, English, Hebrew, Hindi, Russian, Spanish, and Swahili. Short messages can also be found in four ancient languages: Babylonian, classical Greek, Egyptian hieroglyphics, and Sanskrit. On the granite slabs, which are almost 20 feet tall, are such pieces of advice as "Avoid petty laws and useless officials," "Balance personal rights with social duties," and "Unite humanity with a living new language." Because of the mysterious origins of the slabs and their suggestions that include matters such as population control, the Guidestones have been the subject of controversy and conspiracy theories.

Honorable mention must go to **Barbie Beach**, which can be found in the town of Turin. In 2005, a local couple cleared an area of their front yard to create a sandy beach where numerous Barbie dolls and G.I. Joe action figures are posed in various configurations, such as playing volleyball. Although it is in the front yard of a private residence, visitors are welcome to see what is happening on the Barbie Beach scene, where the action changes regularly. The attraction has even been the subject of a documentary that was screened at the Cannes Film Festival.

DISTINCTIVE GEORGIA WORDS AND SAYINGS

404: Elsewhere, the annoying "Page Not Found" error on the internet, but in Georgia, it refers to a section of metro Atlanta via its telephone area code.

Alanna: Georgia's largest city, Atlanta. Sometimes the first syllable is dropped, so it is further refined into "Lanna."

Hotlanta: A reference to Atlanta often used by tourists that is roughly held in the same disdain as outsiders saying "Frisco" for San Francisco.

Overhauls: The bibbed garment, usually made of denim, that is worn by farmers and other workers; called "overalls" elsewhere.

Underground: Not the subway system in London, England, but a mixed-use shopping and entertainment district in Atlanta that is mostly above the ground.

Further Reading

"Barbie Beach." *Chattahoochee Heritage*. Accessed November 25, 2021. https://www.youtube.com/watch?v=YVzC5bEI09M.

Greer, Chris. *Georgia Discovered: Exploring the Best of the Peach State*. Guilford, CT: Globe Pequot, 2020.

McDonald, Janice. *Georgia Off the Beaten Path*. 11th edition. Guilford, CT: Globe Pequot, 2016.

Meyers, Christopher, and David Williams. *Georgia: A Brief History*. Macon, GA: Mercer University Press, 2012.

Sullivan, Buddy. *Georgia: A State History*. Charleston, SC: Arcadia Publishing, 2010.

Hawaii

FACT BOX

Nickname: The Aloha State
Statehood Granted: 1959
Capital: Honolulu
Population: 1,400,000
State Motto: *Ua Mau ke Ea o ka 'Āina i ka Pono* (Hawaiian: "The Life of the Land Is Perpetuated in Righteousness")
What Natives Call Themselves: Hawaiians

STATE HISTORY

In Key West, Florida, there is a buoy-shaped marker with big letters proclaiming "Southernmost Point" followed by smaller letters specifying "Continental USA." For trivia buffs, it is the state of Hawaii that can actually boast the southernmost town in the 50 states, Nā'ālehu, which is farther south geographically than Key West.

Lying in the Pacific Ocean, one of the ways Hawaii is unique is by virtue of being the only state made up entirely of islands: Kauai, Lanai, Maui, Molokai, Oahu, and Hawaii, which is often called the "Big Island" to avoid confusion. As the only U.S. state located outside North America, it is home to the most isolated people in the world, being more than 2,500 miles from Los Angeles.

Formerly a U.S. territory, it was the most recent state to join the Union when it became the 50th state in 1959. With its year-round warm tropical climate and majestic natural beauty, Hawaii is an exotic spot that is unique among the states.

The 50th state is said to derive its name from Hawai'iloa, a figure from its native mythology. About 1,500 years ago, Polynesian explorers are believed to have sailed to Hawaii from Pacific islands such as Bora Bora and Tahiti. The islands of Hawaii were under the control of various tribal groups until 1795, when the Battle of Nuuanu solidified the quest to unite the islands by Kamehameha, who was the founder of the Kingdom of Hawaii.

In 1810, Kamehameha I became king of the Hawaiian Islands, with the Kamehameha dynasty ruling Hawaii until 1874.

The first documented contact by Europeans came with the arrival of British explorer James Cook in 1778. He honored his sponsor, the Earl of Sandwich, by naming today's Hawaii as the "Sandwich Islands." Incidentally, that same Earl was also the namesake of the popular food item that, allegedly at his request, is meat tucked between two slices of bread.

Captain Cook's reports about the tropical paradise attracted Europeans. As in the case of North America, South America, and the Caribbean, they brought European diseases such as influenza and smallpox. After centuries of isolation, native Hawaiians had no immunity to these illnesses. By 1820, more than half the native Hawaiian population had perished.

Influence by the United States grew exponentially through the 1800s when businessmen and Christian missionaries planted roots in Hawaii. After Americans assumed active roles there in commerce and politics, Hawaii officially became a territory of the United States in 1898.

Some established large agricultural operations, including James Drummond Dole, whose pineapple plantation was created in 1903. By the early 1960s, the majority of canned pineapple sold around the world came from Hawaii.

Coffee emerged as a cash crop for Hawaii at the same time when special blends were becoming a worldwide obsession. The altitude, climate, sheltered slopes, and volcanic soil on Hawaii's Kona Coast were found to be ideal for cultivating coffee beans. Hawaii is the only American state to grow coffee on a commercial scale.

The Aloha State is also the only one in which there are two official languages: English and Hawaiian. Before the arrival of missionaries in the early 1800s, Hawaii had no written language. Cultural milestones such as births, deaths, genealogy, history, and a who's who of Hawaiian heroes were passed through the generations via chants, poetry, and songs. Even one of Hawaii's most popular features, the hula dance, told a story.

In the 20th century, one particular export from the islands caught on in a major way: the ancient Hawaiian sport of surfing. Between 1912 and 1924, native Hawaiian Duke Kahanamoku was a five-time Olympic medalist in swimming. Kahanamoku gave swimming exhibitions around the world, at which he also demonstrated surfing. By the time Kahanamoku died in 1968, surfing was known even to the most landlocked Americans.

With the Hawaiian Islands having been ruled for years by a monarchy, its kings and queens occupied a residence fit for royalty. Today, the state of Hawaii is the home of America's only true royal palace. Under the Kamehameha dynasty, Honolulu's Iolani Palace was built in 1882, serving as the official home of the Kingdom of Hawaii's ruling family.

The dynasty ended with Queen Liliuokalani. She ruled from 1891 until the overthrow of the Hawaiian monarchy in 1893, which according to historians, was prompted by powerful American plantation owners. Queen Liliuokalani was imprisoned in her bedroom at Iolani Palace for almost a year following the overthrow. She passed away in 1917, and the palace is currently a museum. In the upstairs bedroom where Queen Liliuokalani was imprisoned, guests and staffers have reported hearing the unexplained sound of Hawaiian music or chanting.

There is an old saying that buying land is the best investment because "they're not making any more of it." Hawaii is unique in that new land actually *is* being created every day. The state itself was formed by the awesome power of volcanoes that rose from the floor of the Pacific Ocean millions of years ago to create the islands.

Today, Hawaii is one of the few places in the world where visitors can come face to face with an active volcano while it is in the process of forging new land areas through the cooling of its lava flow. Scientists say that one of them, Maunaloa, is not only the most massive mountain on earth, but it is also deceptive by covering half of Hawaii Island. Other volcanoes in Hawaii include Hualalai, Kohala, and Maunakea along with the landmark Leahim, better known as Diamond Head. Another, Kilauea, is said to be the most active volcano known anywhere in the world. Kilauea, the volcano that helped create much of the Hawaiian Islands, continues to erupt as of this writing. In 2019, it was announced that lava from Kilauea added 875 acres of volcanic land to Hawaii in one year alone.

Queen Liliuokalani ruled from 1891 until the overthrow of the Hawaiian monarchy in 1893, when the dynasty ended. Liliuokalani was imprisoned in her bedroom at Iolani Palace for almost a year following the overthrow. (Hawaiian Historical Society)

Many Americans got to know the 50th state through hit television shows such as *Hawaii Five-0* and *Magnum, P.I.* Hawaii regularly appears on lists of places Americans most want to visit before they die.

URBAN LEGENDS

Even amid its sunny tropical beauty, Hawaii has a dark side. One urban legend concerns the **Night Marchers**, said to be the spirits of ancient Hawaiian warriors who have been cursed to stalk the islands for eternity. Some say these ghostly soldiers haunt former battlefields and religious sites as well as relentlessly seek to avenge their deaths. Others state that the Night Marchers are searching for an

> ### Aloha, Shirt!
>
> Also called a Hawaiian shirt, aloha shirts began appearing in Hawaii in the 1920s. It is said that local Japanese women adapted surplus kimono fabric to make lightweight men's shirts with festive tropical images like palm trees. When Hawaiian shirts hit the mainland, they became all the rage. Part of the attraction was "snob appeal." It made the wearer look as if he had been able to vacation in the Islands, or at least that he had something in common with celebrities who did. After World War II, military personnel who had been in Hawaii enjoyed the cool comfort of the shirts along with their general cheeriness. After Elvis Presley wore one in the 1961 movie *Blue Hawaii* and Tom Selleck sported them on the television series *Magnum, P.I.*, it seemed everyone was saying "Aloha" to Hawaiian shirts.

entrance into the spirit world. People who claim to have encountered the Night Marchers report that they move in a single line, carrying torches and weapons while blowing conch shells, chanting, and playing war drums. Onlookers must lie down in submission and never look the Night Marchers in the eye, or else they will face being condemned to join the undead warriors of the night for all eternity.

The **Nu'uanu Pali Highway** on Oahu is host to a "hot dog" of an urban legend. The story goes that Kamapua'a, a half-man/half-hog fertility god, romanced the fire goddess Pele. Following their breakup, they agreed to split the island in half as a kind of mythological version of community property. One result of their split is that taking pork from one side of the island to the other would symbolically break the agreement with the half-hog deity. Some people driving across the island on the Nu'uanu Pali Highway who are carrying hot dogs for lunch have claimed their cars mysteriously stalled. After they threw the pork product out the window, their vehicles started up again. Some believers say that after the car stalls, an old woman with a dog will appear. Feeding the pork product to the canine will allow drivers to continue on their way.

The aforementioned fire goddess **Pele** is at the center of several Hawaii urban legends. As a shape-shifter, Pele is said to be capable of appearing in various guises, sometimes as a young woman and, at other times, as an old woman with long white hair. According to the legend, she is said to test the kindness and welcoming spirit of the Hawaiian people and therefore must be greeted with a friendly "Aloha." If she is walking by the side of the road in her old woman manifestation, drivers must offer to give her a ride. After getting her settled in the car, she will sometimes inexplicably vanish. But if she is not offered a ride, the driver is cursed with bad luck. Many Hawaiians feel that giving a ride to an old woman is always a nice thing to do, even if she is not Pele.

Honorable mention must go to the **Curse of the Lava Rocks**. As fire goddess, Pele oversees the islands' volcanoes. If any visitors abscond with lava rocks from Hawaii Volcanoes National Park, it is said that they will be cursed by Pele to suffer bad luck. Graciously, she offers a reprieve to overzealous tourists by lifting the curse if the purloined pebbles are returned. Some claim that the legend actually originated with a park ranger who got tired of seeing parts of his park disappear. In any case, hundreds of lava rocks are mailed back each year in an attempt by pilfering persons to free themselves from the curse.

ICONIC HAWAIIAN FOOD

Like grits in America's Southern states, **Poi** is a traditional starchy side dish that might best be described as an acquired taste. Poi is made by mashing boiled taro root and mixing with water until it reaches a desired consistency. Although some say taro, a tuber plant, is slightly sweet and nutty in its natural state with a potato-like texture, poi is bland when served plain. Diners tend to season it according to personal tastes, whether with salt and pepper, garlic, soy sauce, or even sugar. When faced with plain poi, many diners encountering the pale purple dish tend to prefer it with a bite of pork or salmon. Here is how poi is made:

> **Hawaiian Poi** (Yields 3 cups)
> 1½ lb unpeeled taro root
> 2 qt water, with additional 1¼ cups water held aside
>
> 1. In a medium saucepan, boil 2 qt water.
> 2. Peel taro, discard skin, then roughly chop the remaining taro.
> 3. Add chopped taro to the boiling water and cook about 40 minutes until tender.
> 4. Drain, then cool for 15 minutes.
> 5. Adding one cup water, mash cooled taro with a stone pestle or potato masher, or place taro and water in a blender, processing until smooth.
> 6. Add remaining ¼ cup water, a tablespoon at a time, until poi reaches desired consistency.

Source: Adapted from https://www.myrecipes.com/recipe/poi.

ODD LAWS

Perhaps in an effort not to block any of Hawaii's majestic natural scenery, billboards are outlawed on the islands. Lest any creative advertisers attempt to skirt the law, the legislation is quite specific in terms of what is prohibited, defining a billboard as any board or similar structure, "whether free-standing or supported by or placed against any wall or structure, which is designed or used for the principal purpose of having outdoor advertising devices placed, posted, or fastened upon it." Such advertising is unlawful if it is meant to draw the attention of the public through "writing, picture, painting, light, model, display, emblem, sign, or similar device situated outdoors."

Plastic bags are also banned in Hawaii in order to keep them off the beaches and out of the waters that surround the islands. In 2015, Hawaii became the first of the 50 states to prohibit the distribution of single-use plastic bags at places such as convenience stores, groceries, and even major retailers. Some businesses provide paper bags at checkout, although a few stores do not offer any bag at all. Therefore, islanders know it is always a good idea to carry a light, reusable tote in their pocket or purse. "Bring Your Own Bag" stickers are usually posted in stores as a reminder for unsuspecting tourists.

Discovering whether a store will provide a bag to carry goods is often a bit of a gamble. That is one of the few forms of gambling permitted in Hawaii. The state does not permit casinos, horse races, lotteries, sports betting, or even bingo games that can be considered "exploitive conduct." Casual bets between friends are exempted from being considered criminal offenses, but other than that, residents and tourists do not have to worry about inadvertently wandering into a casino and losing their (Hawaiian) shirt. Ironically, the state's prohibition on gambling has created an interesting footnote as cited by travel professionals who note the top destination for Hawaiian residents who leave the islands on holiday. Where do people who live in paradise tend to go on vacation? Answer: Las Vegas.

UNUSUAL DESTINATIONS

When visiting stunningly beautiful Hawaii, some people want to see . . . algae. The **Algae Growing Ponds** at Kailua-Kona, Hawaii, are algae production tanks the size of football fields that are spectacular when seen from above, such as on an airplane or helicopter ride. Conditions surrounding the facility on the Kona coast are ideal for cultivating the mineral-rich organism that can be sold as ingredients for nutritional products. In a spot where there had been only barren black lava rock, today dozens of the huge multicolored tanks of algae occupy about 90 acres. The red, green, orange, and blue ponds each contain an average of more than 100,000 gallons of algae culture, which is a lot of algae. The facility has a visitor center where scientific programs are offered. Tours are also available. However, the best views of the algae ponds are from above, and it is said that satellite images of their stunning colors are best of all.

When many people think of pineapples, they think of Dole. However, in addition to the prickly fruit, the name is now also synonymous with giant mazes for fans of complex garden labyrinths. The **Dole Plantation's Pineapple Garden Maze**, located off the Kamehameha Highway in Wahiawa, Hawaii, is the current record holder as the largest such maze in the United States. Made from more than 14,000 colorful and often fragrant Hawaiian plants, the three-acre maze runs for over two miles of pathways. Stations along the way provide clues to successfully completing the maze, which is one of only a few such permanent installations in America. To add the thrill of competition, the names of those with the fastest times through the maze are posted at the entrance. Most visitors complete it in about an hour, although the record time is seven minutes. The elaborately artistic layout of the maze is best seen from above, especially the garden at its center which is, not surprisingly, in the shape of a pineapple.

Most people have heard that if life hands you a lemon, make lemonade. At **Post-a-Nut** in Hoolehua, Molokai, postal employees facing downsizing used not lemons but coconuts. Requirements of the U.S. Postal Service demand that in order to be mailed, items must have strong packaging. It is difficult to think of anything stronger than coconut shells—even the most voracious sorting machines have trouble damaging them. When told by postal authorities in 1991 that their small post office was going to be downgraded, the woman who was postmaster had the idea of mailing local coconuts for visitors as a unique postcard/souvenir. They currently mail about 3,000 a year, with the small post office having been expanded to accommodate heavy tourist traffic. Art supplies to decorate and address the coconuts are free. The only cost is about $20 for postage, depending on weight. After being inspected to make sure they are free of leaks and insects, the coconuts are delivered globally to spots as remote as Antarctica. For many visitors, the best part of going to this post office is the chance to interact with local residents picking up their mail. For them, "going postal" is a plus.

DISTINCTIVE HAWAII WORDS AND SAYINGS

Aloha: One of the most often used of all Hawaiian words, it can mean "Hello" or "Goodbye" but can also express kindness, welcome, and affection.

Chee hoo! What a Hawaiian might shout when excited, similar to "Yee-haw!" on the mainland.

Howzit? Often accompanied by the word "braddah" (colloquial for "brother"), this is a Hawaiian slang term similar to "What's up?"

Mahalo: Thank you.

Mele Kalikimaka: For lucky December tourists, this is Hawaiian for "Merry Christmas."

Pau Hana: The part of the day after working hours, dedicated to relaxation and socializing.

Pupu: Appetizers. A selection of appetizers is called a Pupu Platter, which is sometimes included at bars and restaurants in Pau Hana specials, much like Happy Hour.

Further Reading

Brokaw, Teddy. "The History of the Hawaiian Shirt: From Kitsch to Cool, Ride the Waves of Undulating Popularity of a Tropical Fashion Statement." *Smithsonian Magazine*, May 2020. https://www.smithsonianmag.com/innovation/history-hawaiian-shirt-180974598/.

Haley, James L. *Captive Paradise: A History of Hawaii*. New York: St. Martin's Griffin, 2015.

Moore, Susanna. *Paradise of the Pacific: Approaching Hawaii*. New York: Farrar, Straus and Giroux, 2015.

Thompson, Judi. *Supernatural Hawaii*. Atglen, PA: Schiffer Publishing, 2009.

Idaho

> **FACT BOX**
>
> **Nickname:** The Gem State
> **Statehood Granted:** 1890
> **Capital:** Boise
> **Population:** 1,800,000
> **State Motto:** *Esto perpetua* (Latin: "Let It Be Perpetual")
> **What Natives Call Themselves:** Idahoans

STATE HISTORY

Idaho is one of the few states with a "panhandle," a narrow strip of territory that projects outward from the main part of the state. Bordering on Canada at its northernmost point, the relatively isolated Idaho Panhandle asserts itself by observing the Pacific Time Zone even though the rest of the state is on Mountain Time.

Idaho was originally inhabited by ancient Native American people. Excavations around the state have revealed evidence of human habitation there from at least as long as 14,000 years ago. Arrowheads found in today's Idaho rank among the oldest verified artifacts in America.

The state boasts a wealth of ancient relics and remnants of the prehistoric past, including the Morley Nelson Petroglyphs. As opposed to pictographs, which are ancient images painted on cave walls, petroglyphs are carved directly onto the surface of the rock. Archaeologists date Idaho's petrographs to about 12,000 years ago. Natural oxidation created color variations that have rendered them both historic and artistic.

Today, some of their descendants may still remain. Idaho's federally recognized Native American tribes include the Coeur d'Alene, Nez Percé, Shoshone-Bannock, and Shoshone-Paiute.

The arrival of European settlers was presaged by the early presence of Spanish explorers, who ventured into Idaho beginning in 1592. When the Lewis and Clark Expedition crossed Idaho in 1805 and came back again in 1806, they encountered Spanish-speaking Native Americans.

Lewis and Clark were followed by French Canadian fur trappers who traded with the Native Americans in the region. This incursion by French-speaking traders resulted in numerous Idaho place-names derived from the French language, such as

Boisé (meaning "wooded") and Coeur d'Alène ("heart of an awl," a colloquialism for a tough skinflint of a trader). The French speakers also dubbed local Native Americans as Nez Percé, meaning "pierced nose," a look favored by the tribe.

Landlocked Idaho may be unique on the mainland for the number of Hawaiian islanders who came to the state. They arrived to look for work in the Pacific Northwest, and local historians claim that in the mid-1800s, almost the entire staff of Fort Boise was from the Hawaiian Islands. The name of Idaho's Owyhee County resulted from an Americanized rendering of the word "Hawaii."

After several short-lived settlements sprang up, Lewiston is said to be Idaho's first permanent community. It was established in 1861, just two years before Idaho Territory was officially acknowledged by the United States. In 1890, Idaho was the 43rd state to be admitted to the Union.

Idaho is unique for having a range in elevation than runs from Borah Peak at almost 13,000 feet high to the state's lowest point just over 700 feet in Lewiston. It can also boast a more diverse topography than most states, with a landscape that includes deep clear lakes, fast-moving rivers, steep canyons, and snow-capped mountains. Hells Canyon (which claims no apostrophe in its name) is the deepest gorge on the North American continent. Shoshone Falls plunges down from a height that is taller than the Niagara Falls.

Even with Idaho's remarkable prehistoric habitation, stunning topography, and awe-inspiring natural beauty, there is one thing that immediately comes to mind for most people when they think of Idaho: potatoes.

Idaho is known for its potatoes, which are trademarked to ensure their reputation for quality. Idaho's combination of clean air, clear water, mineral-rich soil, warm days, and cool nights contribute to its superior spuds. (Hannator92/Dreamstime.com)

Officially, the correct form should be written as Idaho® potatoes. According to the Idaho Potato Commission (IPC), true Idaho potatoes are trademarked. With the state producing about a third of America's entire crop of potatoes, the unassuming spud is responsible for bringing in a huge part of the Idaho economy. Marketed with a "Grown in Idaho®" seal, the strict trademarking is meant to assure consumers that they are purchasing what the IPC calls genuine, top-quality Idaho® potatoes, not impostors.

The history of potatoes in Idaho is recounted in detail by the Idaho Potato Museum at Blackfoot, Idaho (with the enticing slogan "Free Taters for Out of Staters!"). Although there were earlier attempts, museum experts cite a particular potato crop documented in 1860 as being the most significant for the state's future.

Idaho's potato crop grew by leaps and bounds each decade. A unique combination of elements made Idaho the tops in taters: clean air, warm days and cool nights, mineral-rich volcanic soil, and ready availability of clear water.

A murkier topic is why Idaho is called "Idaho." A self-proclaimed businessman named George Willing is said to have lobbied the federal government in 1860 for the territory to be named "Idaho," claiming that it was derived from the Shoshone term "Ee-da-how," meaning "sunrise" or "gem of the mountains." Later, however, Willing confessed that he had simply made up the name, being inspired by a girl named Ida. Therefore, some people claim that the state's name might justifiably be called an "Idahoax."

URBAN LEGENDS

The **Bear Lake Monster** is a legend that concerns an underwater creature associated with Idaho's Bear Lake, on the Utah border. As in the tradition of the Loch Ness Monster, the massive Bear Lake creature is said to have a neck so long that it can extend its head onto land and devour unsuspecting humans on the shore. In a unique variation, some versions of the tale maintain that it has evolved into being amphibious, with its forays out of water and onto land making it doubly dangerous. Many believers may not be familiar with the backstory about the Bear Lake Monster. In 1868, an article appeared in the *Deseret News* stating that local Native Americans told of a huge serpentlike creature called the "Water Devil" inhabiting the waters of Bear Lake, adding that white settlers declared they saw it with their own eyes. Even after the author of the article soon admitted it was a hoax, reports of sightings continued. Today, a tourist boat in the shape of a green monster plies the waters of Bear Lake with passengers no doubt hoping to get up close and personal with the "Water Devil."

The **Massacre Rocks Water Babies** are said to be the spirits of small vengeful children who sometimes manifest themselves as miniature murderers. Massacre Rocks is a state park near Pocatello, with a beauty that belies the gruesome legend. It is said that ancient Native Americans who were suffering a severe famine decided that since there was not enough food to sustain more people, newborn babies would be drowned in the river. After being submerged, the irritated infants

> ### Area 52?
>
> When U.S. Navy officers refer to a place as the American submarine force's most important body of water, few would envision Idaho, which at its closest point is 350 miles from the ocean. However, due to its size and incredible depth, Idaho's Lake Pend Oreille is home to a naval test site that is similar to the open ocean but with far less background noise, not to mention nosy foreign ships. At more than 40 miles long and over 1,000 feet deep, Lake Pend Oreille is where new configurations and stealth technology for America's nuclear submarines are tested. One new submarine design was so unusual that after a long-range photo of it was taken, rumors abounded that there was a prehistoric sea monster prowling Lake Pend Oreille. The faux fiend was quickly dubbed "the Paddler." Today, there are those who believe Idaho's Lake Pend Oreille is just as mysterious as Nevada's Area 51.

transformed themselves by growing fins and gills, eating small fish to survive. There have been alleged reports of seeing what looked like water spirits playing in the river of the Massacre Rocks area. Occasionally, the terrifying toddlers play rough by trying to lure humans to their death. Today it is said that on a dark night, nearby visitors can sometimes hear the eerie sound of a baby crying.

The **Owyhee Mountain Dwarves** are alleged to be other miniature-sized monsters. Again attributed to Native American legends, they are reported to be about two feet tall but not remotely cute. Living in caves, they are said to be cannibalistic, vicious, and strong, with a special fondness for kidnapping children. The malevolent midgets have tails that they try to hide by wrapping them around their bodies to assure a person, especially a child, that it is safe to come closer. At that point, the unsuspecting prey becomes dinner for the dwarves. Hikers in the Owyhee Mountain Range are cautioned to be observant—and be sure to look down.

ICONIC IDAHO FOOD

Although Idaho's official nickname is the Gem State, many people refer to it as Spud Central. Potatoes are virtually synonymous with Idaho, comprising a major part of the state's economy. For that reason, true potatoes from Idaho are trademarked, as seen in the recipe below. The IPC recommends eating potatoes in all forms, including the classic baked version. The IPC strongly advises against wrapping them in foil, but instead piercing the skin with a fork before baking. For a potato-y treat that is twice as good, here is a recipe for **Idaho Twice Baked Potatoes**:

Idaho Twice Baked Potatoes (Serves 4)
4 Idaho® russet potatoes
1 tsp olive oil

½ cup sour cream
Bacon, cheese, chives, garlic, nutmeg, onions, and/or jalapeños to taste
Salt and freshly ground pepper to taste
Milk as desired for consistency

1. While preheating oven to 400°F, wash and dry potatoes, then pierce skin of each potato 2–3 times with a fork.
2. Rub each potato lightly with a small amount of olive oil, then salt generously.
3. Using a baking pan or cookie sheet, bake potatoes for 50–60 minutes or until tender when pierced with a fork.
4. Wearing an oven mitt to hold hot potatoes, scoop out the interior of each, and place potato flesh in a medium bowl, leaving potato skin as shell.
5. Mash the potato flesh with potato masher.
6. Add sour cream and seasonings, then combine all until smooth, adding a small amount of milk for smooth consistency if needed.
7. After turning oven to 325°F, use a spoon to fill potato shells with the potato flesh mixture.
8. Place filled potatoes on baking sheet and bake for 18–20 minutes until heated through.

Source: Adapted from https://idahopotato.com/recipes/basic-twice-baked-idaho-potatoes.

ODD LAWS

As noted, Idaho takes its potatoes very seriously. A state law codifies what may and may *not* be called Idaho Deluxe, Idaho Standard, and Idaho Utility potatoes. Not only is misrepresentation unlawful, but there are very detailed specifics that must be followed. The statute asserts that Idaho Deluxe potatoes shall be "well shaped, free from freezing injury, blackheart, and soft rot or wet breakdown and from damage caused by dirt or other foreign matter, sunburn, second growth, growth cracks, air cracks, internal disorders, cuts, shriveling, sprouting, scab, blight, dry rot, rhizoctonia, other disease, insects or mechanical or other means." Legal experts believe the law, which has been on the books since 1941, was proposed by lobbyists to protect the industry's brand image rather than being sought by concerned state legislators fearing Idaho getting a bad reputation for shoddy spuds.

Insofar as other edibles, cannibalism is not only frowned upon in Idaho, but it is illegal under state law—with one important exception. According to the Idaho Code, willfully ingesting the flesh or blood of a human being is unlawful. However, if the accused can prove that the action was the only apparent means of survival in extreme life-threatening conditions, it could be a viable defense to avoid being charged with a felony. The defendant must be able to substantiate that the other person died of natural causes, such as freezing to death, *before* the alleged cannibalism took place.

If such a grisly act takes place in Pocatello, Idaho, it apparently must be perpetrated in a cheerful manner. In a 1948 law that remains on the books, the city of Pocatello passed what was presumably a tongue-in-cheek regulation making it illegal not to smile within the city limits. After an especially harsh winter that apparently put Pocatellans in a bad mood, the City Council passed an ordinance forbidding "pedestrians and motorists to display frowns, grimaces, scowls, threatening and glowering looks, gloomy and depressed facial appearances, generally all of which reflect unfavorably upon the city's reputation." Since that time, Pocatello has been called the U.S. Smile Capital, sponsoring a yearly celebration that includes a poster contest for elementary schoolchildren, a smile competition, and mock arrest of those who flaunt the smile mandate. Perhaps as a result of these happy faces, the American Association of Retired Persons (AARP) named Pocatello one of the best places in the nation to retire. Incidentally, the Pocatello City Council meetings are live-streamed, so citizens can make sure their elected officials practice what they preach.

UNUSUAL DESTINATIONS

The **Bates Motel** in Coeur d'Alene, Idaho, is not actually known to be the site of bloody stabbings in the shower, but it has nonetheless gained residual fame from its Hollywood namesake. It was originally used as officers' barracks for the nearby Farragut Naval Training Station beginning in 1942. After World War II ended, the barracks facility was no longer needed, and it was sold in 1946 and converted into a motel known as the Roadway Inn. Its connection to the shorthand for horror might have been nonexistent if it had not been resold soon afterward to a local accountant named Randy Bates. The proud Mr. Bates promptly renamed his new business venture as the Bates Motel. Robert Bloch, author of a 1959 thriller novel *Psycho*, allegedly stayed at the motel, making note of the name. When the 1960 Alfred Hitchcock movie *Psycho* was released, the motel's name achieved immortality. At this writing, Idaho's 13-room Bates Motel is still in business, attracting guests who often request Room 1 or Room 3, where strange noises and spooky unexplained occurrences are said to take place. However, the showers have—so far—been free of fatalities.

Tidying up after a bloody assault in the shower would be just the thing for the **Museum of Clean** in Pocatello. It is the only known museum of its kind in the country, with visitors claiming it to be unexpectedly fascinating. Some enter the massive 74,000-square-foot building expecting to see a collection of brooms and wash buckets. However, with a wide range of artwork, displays, exhibits, printed materials, and interactive demonstrations, guests are immersed in the entire notion of cleanliness, which in some ways is a relatively modern concept. Cleaning products are certainly included in the facility, which takes up an entire city block, but according to its website, the Museum of Clean is meant to spotlight the idea of cleanliness itself, such as clean air, clean eating, clean water, clean homes, clean minds, clean thinking, clean language, clean jokes, clean communities, and a clean world. They even include "clean politics" in their mission, which is something that might have to be seen to be believed.

Idaho's 1,000-foot-long lava tube called the **Shoshone Ice Caves** is the largest such cave system in the world that is open to the public. One of the most unique natural cave formations on Earth, the frozen stuff in the Shoshone Ice Caves is 30 feet thick, encased in a sea of jagged lava rock between 8 and 30 feet high. The ice was caused by cold air flowing through the lava tubes, freezing subterranean water. Hovering at a constant temperature between 24°F and 32°F year-round, the cave remains permanently frozen, which visitors find refreshing on a hot summer day but a bit chilly during an Idaho winter. Some legends claim that the Shoshone Ice Caves are passageways between the land of the living above ground and the spirit world below.

Honorable mention must go to any place that makes visitors feel as if they have left the planet Earth and been transported to the surface of the Moon. In addition, the site—along with its visitors—might be vulcanized at any time. According to the National Park Service (NPS), the 600-mile ocean of ancient solid lava that forms the **Craters of the Moon National Monument**, midway between Boise and Yellowstone National Park, not only looks otherworldly, but in addition, according to NPS, "yesterday's volcanic events are likely to continue tomorrow." For over about 2,000 years, oozing lava flows have created a lunar landscape of cinder cones, spatter cones, and lava tubes and rivers as well as petrified trees that left their charred, dying impressions in the lava rock. Some were encased in the lava before expiring, leaving vertical molds that, like the ruins of ancient Pompeii, are somehow poignant reminders of mortality.

DISTINCTIVE IDAHO WORDS AND SAYINGS

Fry sauce: Newcomers to Idaho are often baffled when this is requested, most often for fried potatoes. Basically, it is a mixture of ketchup and mayonnaise, with further refinements that might include ground mustard, onion powder, paprika, salt, sugar, vinegar, and Worcestershire sauce to taste.

Jockey box: What Idahoans call the glove compartment in a car; said to be derived from chests attached to the side of Old West chuck wagons for holding feed or water.

Potato drop: A variation of New York's Times Square Ball Drop at midnight on New Year's Eve, this event at the Idaho State Capitol involves a giant potato and always seems to please the spec-taters.

Tots: Anywhere else, these are small children. In Idaho, they are a beloved deep-fried cylindrically shaped potato product called Tater Tots® made by the Ore-Ida company.

Treefort: Not a citadel among the branches, but the five-day Treefort Music Festival in Boise that is usually held around Spring Break.

Whistle pigs: Idahoan for prairie dogs and/or ground squirrels. The Idaho Fish and Game Department requires a hunting license to shoot whistle pigs, if anyone would want to.

Further Reading

Derig, Betty. *Roadside History of Idaho*. Missoula, MT: Mountain Press, 1996.
Schwantes, Carlos Arnaldo. *In Mountain Shadows: A History of Idaho*. Lincoln: University of Nebraska Press, 1991.
Stapilus, Randy. *Idaho Myths and Legends: The True Stories Behind History's Mysteries*. Lanham, MD: Globe Pequot, 2020.

Illinois

> **FACT BOX**
>
> **Nickname:** The Prairie State (however, the Illinois legislature also adopted "Land of Lincoln" as the official state *slogan*)
> **Statehood Granted:** 1818
> **Capital:** Springfield
> **Population:** 12,700,000
> **State Motto:** "State Sovereignty, National Union"
> **What Natives Call Themselves:** Illinoisans

STATE HISTORY

There are indications that today's state of Illinois has been inhabited by humans for thousands of years. Although documented evidence of most habitation has been lost to the mists of time, Illinois can boast two notable exceptions.

The first, a three-acre excavation at the Koster Site, south of Eldred, Illinois, has revealed 7,000 years of continuous habitation. At the second, located near present-day Collinsville, the Cahokia site has proven itself to have been one of the nation's largest and most significant Native American centers. Cahokia, designated a National Historic Landmark, is especially noted for its urban complex with a 50-acre plaza plus more than 100 hand-built ceremonial mounds, among the largest in North America. Most intriguing to many people today is what is called Cahokia's "Woodhenge," a planned design consisting of timber posts that functioned much like England's Stonehenge in cultural and cosmological significance. Most sources date the Cahokia civilization between the 1200s and 1400s, but suddenly the people mysteriously vanished.

The Illini tribes followed, allegedly giving the state its name when early French explorers and missionaries adapted it from the Native American language. Present-day Illinoisans often favor the interpretation of the word that means "tribe of superior men." However, according to the Illinois State Museum, the name may have originated as the Native word *ilinwe*, meaning "he speaks in the ordinary way."

However it evolved, the current spelling of "Illinois" began appearing after French explorers Jacques Marquette and Louis Jolliet explored the Illinois River in 1673. Marquette, a Jesuit missionary, founded a mission called Grand Village of the Illinois near the present town of Utica, Illinois.

Soon, more French explorers arrived, including René-Robert Cavelier, Sieur de La Salle. They began setting up trading posts and forts such as the one at the site of present-day Peoria in 1680. Illinois was claimed by France as part of its North American holdings until 1763, when it passed to the British after they defeated France in the French and Indian War.

At that point, today's Illinois was part of a plan by Britain to reserve territory in what was then the West for Native Americans. George Rogers Clark, who fought for American independence on the then Northwest Frontier during the Revolutionary War, claimed Illinois for America in 1778. After the United States won the revolution, settlers began arriving in Illinois, swelling the population to the point that by 1818, there were enough inhabitants for Illinois to become America's 21st state.

Having attained statehood, Illinois needed a state capital. Originally, it was the village of Kaskaskia. Some Kaskaskia residents might have suspected it was only temporary when they noticed the state's business being conducted at a small rental property. Starting in 1819, the town of Vandalia served as the state capital. However, in 1837, a group of state legislators from Sangamon County successfully lobbied for the Illinois capital to move permanently to Springfield, coincidentally located in Sangamon County. The Springfield boosters were led by a state representative named Abraham Lincoln, who would later be heard from again.

In a footnote to history, Kaskaskia may have lost its chance to be the Illinois state capital, but it gained another distinction. In 1838, John Willis Menard was born there. In 1868, Menard became the first Black American ever elected to the U.S. House of Representatives.

Meanwhile, the 1830s were seeing another significant birth. On the banks of the Chicago River and Lake Michigan, the town of Chicago was organized in 1833. Chicago's population grew from about 200 at its founding to more than 6,000 by

Moo-t Point

On October 8, 1871, what started as a small fire in Chicago was fueled by high winds until it became an inferno that raged for three days, destroying much of the city and claiming at least 300 lives. Known as the Great Chicago Fire, it was traditionally said to have been started by Mrs. Catherine O'Leary's cow kicking over an oil lantern. Although the reporter who wrote the newspaper article pointing the finger at the pair later admitted he made up the cow-and-lantern story, the unfortunate lady and her bovine carried the stigma of guilt. However, 126 years later, the Chicago City Council voted in 1997 to clear the falsely accused Mrs. O'Leary and her cow. By that time, however, both were deceased and were therefore unable to celebrate their exoneration. Incidentally, on that hot, dry, windy October day in 1871, three other major fires also occurred along Lake Michigan at the same time as the Great Chicago Fire. No cattle were known to have been involved.

the end of the decade. For a number of years, it was acknowledged as the world's fastest-growing city. After the Erie Canal was completed in 1825, Chicago—and therefore Illinois—would become connected to the world.

Although Illinois has traditionally been about 80 percent farmland, it became renowned for its booming urban metropolis of Chicago. When the Great Chicago Fire of 1871 left only a handful of buildings standing, help for the beleaguered city poured into Illinois from around the globe.

In the 1920s, Illinois was home to a benchmark of popular culture. It was during the Prohibition era of the "Roaring Twenties" that Chicago became synonymous with gun-toting gangsters and the winking acceptance of bootlegging, violence, corruption, and crime. Mob boss Al Capone self-promoted himself into notoriety as the state's most famous citizen.

Illinois can boast a number of superlatives. In 1881, Aurora, Illinois, became the first U.S. city to use an all-electric street lighting system to illuminate the entire community. The first modern skyscraper, the Home Insurance Building, was built in 1885, not in New York but in Chicago.

In 1942, the Atomic Age was ushered in when the University of Chicago was the site of the first sustained nuclear chain reaction. Many of those scientists went on to work at the top-secret Los Alamos atomic bomb project.

But for many, the most significant achievement took place in 1960 when the world's first McDonald's hamburger franchise was opened in Des Plaines, Illinois.

Illinois seems to have an ability to foster new beginnings, whether from the devastation of a cataclysmic fire or fueling the grand ambitions of an average citizen such as Abraham Lincoln, whose first public office was as postmaster in New Salem, Illinois.

In addition, Illinois is the only state that is home to a show business superlative by virtue of the crucial question "Will it play in Peoria?"

URBAN LEGENDS

The **Ghost Lady of Kennedy Hill Road** solidified a spot in the urban legends of Illinois in the early 1980s. Sometimes called the Phantom Woman, she is famed for her nocturnal wanderings along the rural Kennedy Hill Road, near Byron, Illinois. This spectral female gained a following in large part due to reports of her various stages of dress, or rather *undress*. In the midst of a cold Illinois winter, it struck some alleged observers as odd that a woman would be strolling back and forth on the roadway either (a) in nothing but a short skirt, (b) in black underwear, or (c) in the altogether, sporting no clothing whatsoever. The local newspaper reported speculations that it may have been the ghost of a woman who was buried nearby. Others guessed it might be a mentally ill person who had run away. Another proposed explanation was that it was really a man wearing the clothing of his dead girlfriend. In any case, the scantily clad wanderer vanished with the coming of spring, but the urban legend lives on.

The legend of the **Murphysboro Big Muddy Monster** resonates in its Illinois hometown. Reports in the early 1970s attest to the experience of a Murphysboro couple who were parked near a boat ramp, suddenly encountering a large, nonhuman figure approaching them and making a terrifying noise. After the couple reported the incident, law enforcement officials were skeptical. However, when police went to the scene, they saw large footprints and heard horrifying sounds. Newspaper reports were followed by other accounts of a frightening nonhuman creature with matted hair. After a time, the reports died down. However, the story of the Big Muddy Monster is recounted on the official website of the town of Murphysboro, complete with scans of police reports and photos taken by the Murphysboro Police Department. The tale is recounted periodically in local news media with the chilling footnote that the case file on Murphysboro's Big Muddy Monster remains open.

The story of the **Piasa Bird**, pronounced "PIE-a-saw," is a local legend in Alton, Illinois, that can be traced back to 1673 when Father Jacques Marquette was recording his journey down the Mississippi River with Louis Jolliet. He described tales of a birdlike monster with horns, red eyes, and a tail so long it wrapped around its body. The beast, dominating the River Bend area, was allegedly named "the Piasa" by Illini Indians, meaning a bird that devours men. It appears that Marquette did not have an actual firsthand sighting of the creature, but instead he described the Piasa Bird monster from a painting of it high on the Mississippi River bluffs where Alton now stands. His written account depicts a beast as large as a calf, having horns like a deer, a face like a man, and a body covered with green, red, and black scales. Over time, the original rock painting faded, but due to a local effort, it was restored so that once again, the Piasa Bird dominates all it surveys from its perch on the bluffs.

Honorable mention among urban legends is a man who self-promoted his notoriety into becoming a legend in his own time: Chicago mobster **Alphonse "Al" Capone**. The cigar-smoking gangster of the Roaring Twenties died in 1947 and was buried in the family plot at Mount Carmel Cemetery in Hillside, Illinois. Although there is a large stone monument at the Capone family burial site, Al's grave marker itself is simple, inscribed only with "Alphonse Capone | 1899–1947 | My Jesus Mercy." Some say the mob kingpin's penchant for publicity endured after death. The legend is that the ghost of Capone will chase away visitors to his gravesite if they do not show proper respect. Often, that deference is shown by placing gifts on his grave, including flowers, bottles of alcohol, and, of course, a cigar.

ICONIC ILLINOIS FOOD

If a frankfurter looks as if it had been dragged through a vegetable garden, it is probably a **Chicago-Style Hot Dog**. According to sources celebrating the culinary canine, two young immigrants from Austria-Hungary brought their recipe for wieners to Chicago for the World's Columbian Exposition in 1893. Today, Chicago's signature frank, also called a "red hot," is served up by at least 2,000 vendors in the Windy City alone as well as elsewhere in the state. There are said to be more wiener stands in Chicago than the city's top three name-brand hamburger franchise

STATE ODDITIES

If a frankfurter looks as if it's been dragged through a vegetable garden, it is probably a Chicago-Style Hot Dog. With seven toppings combining elements that are crispy, crunchy, spicy, and sweet, there are definite rules about its construction. (Bhofack2/Dreamstime.com)

outlets combined. With seven toppings designed to combine elements that are crispy, crunchy, spicy, and sweet, there are definite rules about constructing a Chicago-style hot dog, starting with the most notorious: absolutely no ketchup. In addition, the all-beef frank itself must be made with a natural casing that provides the distinctive "snap" when bitten. Some sources also specify a poppy seed bun for the open-face creation.

Chicago-Style Hot Dog (Serves 1)
One 2 oz all-beef frankfurter
One high-gluten bun
Ample supply of yellow mustard, sweet green pickle relish, chopped white onion, tomato slices, kosher dill pickle spear, sport peppers (mild bite-size chile peppers), and celery salt.

1. Steam or boil frankfurter.
2. Steam bun until warm.
3. Place cooked frankfurter on steamed bun in an open-face arrangement.
4. Add the toppings in this order: mustard, relish, onion, tomato, pickle, sport pepper, and celery salt.

5. The pickle spear should rest between the frankfurter and the bottom half of the bun.
6. Optional: handful of fresh, warm French fries on top.

Source: Adapted from https://chicago.seriouseats.com/2012/03/the-serious-eats-chicago-dog-style-guide.html.

ODD LAWS

According to a 1923 state law, the official language of Illinois is "American." After the bill was passed by the Illinois General Assembly, the state's law-abiding citizens may have wished to comply but were not quite sure what the "American" language was. Teachers in Illinois continued to instruct their classes in English, yet none were known to be prosecuted. In 1969, a subsequent act of the General Assembly quietly replaced the word "American" with "English." According to legal experts, the term "American language" remains in some Illinois legislation from the past. However, it is generally said that the statute is purely symbolic.

From 1858 to 2002, the city of Joliet, Illinois, was known as the home of one of the nation's most feared prisons, Joliet Correctional Center. Even tough Prohibition-era gangsters tried to avoid being incarcerated there. Therefore, in the minds of many people, Joliet is not a town to be trifled with when it comes to law and order. The Joliet Code of Ordinances states unequivocally that "the only official, correct and proper pronunciation and spelling of the name of this city shall be JO-li-et; the accent on the first syllable, with the 'o' in the first syllable pronounced in its long sound, as in the words 'so,' 'no' and 'foe,' and any other pronunciations to be discouraged as interfering with the desired uniformity in respect to the proper pronunciation of the name of this city." The fine for the misdemeanor is five dollars. Apparently, some municipal officials were peeved at hearing the town's name pronounced as "Jolly-ETTE" (as in the words "get," "set," and "threat").

According to Illinois law, it is illegal to hang "obstructions" from the rearview mirror of an automobile. One case went all the way to the Court of Appeals for an infraction that traffic officials claimed "might have been obstructing the driver's view." It was a Catholic rosary.

In other transportation-related legalities, when riding a bicycle in Mendota, Illinois, it is unlawful to remove both hands from the handlebars, or feet from the pedals, or to practice "acrobatic or fancy riding on any street."

UNUSUAL DESTINATIONS

Whether spelled "catsup" or "ketchup," the tangy tomato-based condiment is strictly banned from the state's iconic Chicago-style hot dog. However, in the town of Collinsville, Illinois, catsup is proudly celebrated. Since 1949, a popular tourist attraction is what Collinsville claims to be the **World's Largest Catsup**

Bottle. Rising to a height of 170 feet and listed on the National Register of Historic Places, it is painted to resemble a bottle of Brooks Catsup and had served as the water tower for the nearby Brooks Catsup manufacturing plant. Each summer, the World's Largest Catsup Bottle Festival takes place with a volunteer Catsup Bottle Crew welcoming guests with enough tomato-based merchandise and photo opportunities as if to taunt, "In your face, Chicago dogs!"

For enthusiasts of scuba diving, the first destination that comes to mind for a unique diving experience is not usually Illinois. However, **Mermet Springs** at Belknap, Illinois, has been called the "Key West of the Midwest." Covering more than eight acres with its watery depths, this spring-fed stone quarry is a full-service dive site that also provides scuba training for the uninitiated. It offers submerged visitors an underwater petting zoo where they can approach friendly freshwater fish. Divers can explore sunken objects such as planes, trains, and automobiles that have all been submerged as items of interest, including sunken boats, a school bus, and a tractor. One of the most popular is a 22-ton Boeing 727 that was used in filming the 1998 movie *U.S. Marshals*. The nose of the aircraft lies beneath 50 feet of water, about the depth of a five-story building. The plane's hollowed-out fuselage allows divers a unique swim-through experience that some claim cannot be matched even in the Florida Keys.

In addition to human law enforcement officials, the city of Rockford, Illinois, can claim to be protected by the **Rockmen Guardians**, a towering group of four 12-foot-tall statues made entirely from boulders. Each one looks fierce, striking an intimidating pose showing villains they are ready for battle should the need arise. Created in 1987, they are stationed at Rockford's Sinnissippi Park. Weighing hundreds of pounds, each Guardian is made completely from boulders that are secured with cement. Even though made of rock, they seem to have unique heroic personalities of their own, belying their stone construction. One of the Rockmen appears to be the leader, holding a battle-ready sword also made of rock. Observers say the Rockmen appear to be wearing suits of armor over battle skirts, which, along with the upper-body tone, has led to the speculation that two of the figures are female. In any case, the Rockmen Guardians of Illinois may be considered gender neutral and ready for action.

DISTINCTIVE ILLINOIS WORDS AND SAYINGS

Cheese toasties: Known elsewhere as grilled cheese sandwiches.

Horseshoe: Not footwear for an equine, but an Illinois delicacy that is an open-faced sandwich consisting of thick-sliced toasted bread, a hamburger patty or other meat, cheese sauce, and French fries on top. A smaller portion, should the diner be so inclined, is called a pony shoe.

Gym shoes: Known elsewhere as sneakers or tennis shoes.

Jimmies: The little sprinkles often found atop an ice cream cone.

Pop: Not one's father, but a carbonated soft drink of any variety.

Salty: Embarrassed, upset, or generally perturbed, often over something trivial.

Washroom: Otherwise known as the bathroom or restroom. True Illinoisans are said to pronounce the first syllable "warsh."

Further Reading

Banash, Stan. *Roadside History of Illinois*. Missoula, MT: Mountain Press, 2013.
Bowen, Rich, and Dick Fay. *Hot Dog Chicago: A Native's Dining Guide*. Chicago: Chicago Review Press, 1983.
Danzer, Gerald. *Illinois: A History in Pictures*. Urbana: University of Illinois Press, 2011.
Taylor, Troy. *Haunted Illinois: Ghosts and Strange Phenomena of the Prairie State*. Mechanicsburg, PA: Stackpole, 2008.

Indiana

FACT BOX

Nickname: The Hoosier State
Statehood Granted: 1816
Capital: Indianapolis
Population: 6,800,000
State Motto: "The Crossroads of America"
What Natives Call Themselves: Hoosiers

STATE HISTORY

When television shows want to portray an average depiction of mid-America, they often look to Indiana for typical small-town life. A few recent series involving Indiana include *The Middle*, *Parks and Recreation*, *Stranger Things*, and *The Unbreakable Kimmy Schmidt*. Although small-town life is often symbolized by Indiana, for one weekend a year, the state goes global when it becomes the center of the universe for auto racing fans.

The Indianapolis 500 auto race, usually abbreviated as the Indy 500, has origins going back to 1909. The annual event is traditionally held at the Indianapolis Motor Speedway over Memorial Day weekend in May. Many consider the Indy 500 to be in the top tier of championship car racing. Incidentally, the original organizers settled on 500 miles because it was the estimated distance a race car could be driven all day before darkness fell.

Along with that distinction, Indiana can claim its uniqueness among the 50 states in another important way. Indiana is the only one whose inhabitants are not known by having part of the state's name in their designation, such as Texans or New Yorkers. Anyone born in Indiana or who is a current resident is considered a "Hoosier." And it's official. After lobbying by Indiana congressmen, in 2017, the U.S. Government Publishing Office changed the official designation for Indiana residents from "Indianans" to "Hoosiers." The only question is, "What's a Hoosier?"

A number of theories have been suggested over the years, with varying degrees of plausibility. One is that it is a corruption of "Who's there?" a question no doubt asked by isolated log cabin dwellers on the Indiana frontier. It is also attributed to various languages from Old English to Hindustani as well as an alleged Native

Each year, Indiana is the center of the universe for auto racing fans with the Indianapolis 500, usually called the Indy 500. Many consider the event to be the top tier of championship auto racing. (Christopher Smith/Dreamstime.com)

American word for "corn," although it does not seem to exist in any known Native American dialect.

The most credible story comes from the Indiana Historical Society, which cites "Hoosier" as originating in states like Virginia, where it meant a backwoodsman or a country bumpkin. The society notes a popular 1833 poem by Indiana resident John Finley, originally from Virginia. Finley's poem was titled "The Hoosier's Nest" and immortalizes a *"Hoosier's Nest / In other words, a buckeye cabin."*

The state of Indiana itself was named for its original Native American inhabitants, with a meaning essentially being "Indian land," which it was for thousands of years. Native inhabitants created a vibrant civilization there, with large agriculturally based settlements, ceremonial spaces, and public plazas. Today, archaeological evidence can be seen at the 600-acre Angel Mounds State Historic Site near Evansville. More than 2 million artifacts were collected during excavations. The site is not named for its original inhabitants, but rather the surname of a family of settlers who purchased farmland in 1852 where the present archaeological site is located.

When Europeans arrived in today's Indiana, Native inhabitants included the Illini, Miami, and Shawnee. The first European who was said to arrive was French explorer René-Robert Cavelier, Sieur de La Salle. In 1679, he traveled through the area near today's South Bend, Indiana. French Canadian traders soon followed, exchanging goods with the Native Americans in return for furs. Vincennes, established in 1702, was the site of Indiana's first trading post.

In the latter part of the 1700s, Indiana's Native American tribes allied themselves with the French Canadians during the French and Indian War (1754–1763). With the British victory in 1763, France lost lands in North America including what would become today's Indiana, placing the Native Americans there under the jurisdiction of Great Britain.

In 1783, when the British were in turn defeated in the American Revolution, they ceded Native American lands in the Great Lakes region to the newly formed United States. In 1800, the U.S. Congress divided what was then termed the Northwest Territory into several areas, including what they called the Indiana Territory.

In 1810, with white settlers pouring in, Shawnee chief Tecumseh began urging Native tribes to band together in resisting white settlement on Indian lands. Future president William Henry Harrison quelled the unrest, resulting in a footnote to history with the American victory at 1811's Battle of Tippecanoe.

Indiana became the 19th state of the Union in 1816. Although it can today boast more interstate highways per square mile than any other state, much of Indiana remains farmland. Each year, usually about half of Indiana's cropland is planted with corn, resulting in its distinction as the producer of a fifth of the popcorn supply in the entire nation.

The Hoosier state proudly notes that aircraft pioneer Wilbur Wright was born near Millville, Indiana (brother Orville was born in Ohio). Another point of pride is that legendary aviator Amelia Earhart spent the final two years of her known life on the staff of Indiana's Purdue University. She mysteriously disappeared during her historic around-the-world flight in 1937. Today, Purdue houses the world's largest collection of Earhart artifacts.

One unique tidbit of Indiana history combines its heritage of both farming and aviation. In 1972, a year after the infamous skyjacking in Oregon by a man the news media called "D. B. Cooper," an Indiana farmer tending his soybean field found a moneybag containing $500,000 in cash. It was the ill-gotten gains of a copycat skyjacker whose moneybag got away from him as he was parachuting over Peru, Indiana. The loot landed in the Indiana field, and the skyjacker was later arrested.

In a footnote that some call an example of Hoosier integrity, the farmer returned the money to authorities. For his honesty, the airline offered the farmer and his wife a free trip to the destination of their choice. Stating they would not even set foot in a crop duster to go to the next county, the farmer declined. On the other hand, his selfless act won a spot in the *Guinness Book of World Records* as the most cash ever returned to its owner.

URBAN LEGENDS

Gary, Indiana, is the epicenter of one of the state's most enduring urban legends, the **Carolina Street Demon House**. Due to its alleged spirit population, it has been called the "House of 200 Demons." In 2011, the site made national news after

> **Pup-ular Culture**
>
> For all the state's fine attributes, when many people think of Indiana, the first thing that comes to mind is the name of a beloved icon of popular culture, the fictional character "Indiana Jones." As part of the story line, the hero's formal name is Henry Walton Jones Jr. The character was the brainchild of real-life writer/producer George Walton Lucas Jr. In the movie *Indiana Jones and the Last Crusade*, the character reveals that he has always preferred being called "Indiana," which was the name of a family dog he loved as a child. Incidentally, "Indiana" was also the name of an Alaskan malamute owned by Lucas. When Lucas drove his car around town, the large, long-haired canine would ride in the passenger seat, reminding Lucas of a copilot and thus giving rise to another icon: the *Star Wars* character Chewbacca.

there were reports by the inhabitants that a boy living there was walking backward up a wall in the house, a girl was levitating from her bed, and a shadowy apparition skulked around the living room. Possession by the devil was said to be the problem, although three exorcisms failed to evict the archfiend. After an appearance on the television program *Ghost Adventures* in 2014, the home was demolished, leaving only a lively urban legend behind.

In the region called the Indiana Dunes, fronting Lake Michigan near Chesterton, the legend about **Diana of the Dunes** reigns supreme. She was alleged to be a beautiful woman who lived alone near the shore. Unfortunately, she opened her heart and her home to a man who eventually poisoned her. Through the years, a ghostly looking female is said to run naked along the shore before vanishing into the lake where fishermen have reported a nude woman in the water. Locals embraced the legend of the woman they dubbed Diana of the Dunes. Today the scantily clad Diana lives on as an urban legend that inspires visitors to keep an eye out for bathers in the buff.

The abandoned **Stepp Cemetery** near Bloomington may be small, with only about two dozen old grave markers, but it is the site of an enduring urban legend. The story goes that a young mother lost both her husband and daughter to death in a short period of time. The woman, in full mourning attire, took to visiting their gravesite at the lonely Stepp Cemetery, sitting on a tree stump and sobbing. After her own death, which some say was by suicide, she was buried with her loved ones. But according to the legend, visitors to Stepp Cemetery after dark can still hear the mournful sounds of her sobbing.

Honorable mention goes to two Hoosier theaters that come with their own urban legends. At the beautifully restored **Fowler Theater** in Fowler, Indiana, there are reports of disembodied voices in the theater when it is empty, eerie noises, lights inexplicably turning on and off by themselves, mysterious shadows, and unattended doors opening and slamming that are attributed to the ghost of its original owner when it was built in 1940. The **Elkhart Civic Theatre** in Bristol, Indiana, is said to be haunted by a long-dead family. The former handyman, his wife, and two daughters lived in the basement of the theater during the hard times of the Great Depression in the 1930s. The urban legend features the somewhat off-putting allegation that nowadays, the ghost of the handyman likes to hang around the women's dressing rooms.

ICONIC INDIANA FOOD

In 2009, the Indiana Senate made **Hoosier Pie** the unofficial state pie. It is, therefore, hard to argue about the status of the delectably sweet dessert in the hearts of Indiana residents. Also known as sugar cream pie, this is no low-calorie health food. On the other hand, it added a touch of sweetness for many Hoosiers during the otherwise bleak Great Depression in the 1930s. It became known as a "desperation dessert" because it did not require fresh fruit, eggs, or other ingredients beyond those that most cooks already had in their pantry, even in hard times. Today, there is a Hoosier Pie Trail spotlighting Indiana eateries that feature their version of the creamy treat. While traditional cooks may wish to make the pie crust from scratch, this recipe uses ready-made crust that should be prepared according to the instructions on the package.

> **Hoosier Pie** (Serves 8)
> 9-inch prepared pie crust (either flour based or graham cracker crumb)
> 1 cup sugar
> ¼ cup cornstarch
> 2 cups whole milk
> ½ cup butter, cubed
> 1 tsp vanilla extract
> ¼ tsp ground cinnamon
>
> 1. Prepare pie crust as directed on package.
> 2. Preheat oven to 375°F.
> 3. Combine sugar and cornstarch in a large saucepan, then stir in milk until smooth.
> 4. Bring to a boil, then reduce heat, stirring constantly for about two minutes until thickened and bubbly.
> 5. Remove from heat, stir in butter and vanilla, transfer to crust, and sprinkle with cinnamon.
> 6. Bake 15–20 minutes until golden brown, then cool on a wire rack at least 15–20 minutes more before refrigerating several hours until thoroughly chilled.

Source: Adapted from https://www.tasteofhome.com/recipes/sugar-cream-pie/.

ODD LAWS

Indiana is serious about its wildlife as well as what is considered sporting. Under state code, it is unlawful to catch a fish by using one's bare hands. Other prohibited methods not only make bare hands appear sporting but also give the fish a fighting chance. Unlawful means of catching fish in Indiana include shooting them with a gun, spearing them with a crossbow, blasting them with dynamite or other explosives, zapping them with an electric current, or utilizing any substance that has a tendency to "stupefy or poison fish." The law also prohibits using a weir or a seine, for those who know what they are. In addition, a person may not ice fish or, as the law states, "attempt to ice fish," through a hole greater than 12 inches in diameter. Under the law, any structure used for ice fishing must be temporary and "shall be removed from the ice before the ice leaves."

Under Indiana law, a person wishing to see a hypnotist must get a referral from a licensed physician, psychologist, or dentist unless the desired procedure is to quit smoking or lose weight. Overseeing such activities is Indiana's state-authorized Hypnotist Committee, which consists of three hypnotists, one licensed physician, one licensed psychologist, and an Indiana resident not associated with hypnotism in any way other than as a consumer. Presumably, the consumer on the committee either got an approved referral or was only interested in weight loss or smoking cessation to avoid being censured by the other members of the group.

Citizens who innocently enter a liquor store hoping for a nice cold soft drink or a chilled bottle of water are in for a disappointment. Under Indiana law, liquor stores can only sell warm sodas or, as the state code specifies, "uncooled and uniced" carbonated soda, ginger ale, mineral water, grenadine, and flavoring extracts. Such establishments can sell alcohol and tobacco products with impunity, but a cool, thirst-quenching can of ginger ale is forbidden.

Indianapolis, home of the world-famous motor speedway, apparently likes its cars fast and its horses slow. Municipal code states that no horse shall be driven or ridden on any street in the city "at a speed in excess of 10 miles per hour." The rationale is that horses are considered to be vehicles in the eyes of the law and must therefore be regulated. Horses may not be left unattended, unhitched, or "insecurely fastened upon any street or public place." Moreover, the animal cannot be left in an area that is a No Parking zone for cars. The penalty for doing so renders the four-legged scofflaw "subject to all applicable provisions regulating motor vehicles at any such time and place." In other words, the horse could be towed.

UNUSUAL DESTINATIONS

The **RV/MH Museum and Hall of Fame** in Elkhart is especially popular with those who have an interest in honoring the past and present of the RV (recreational vehicle) or MH (manufactured housing or motorhomes). There are historical exhibits, photos, and memorabilia of past behemoths of the highway as well an

RV/MH showroom that features gleaming new models. In addition, there is a Hall of Fame gallery, films about RV/MH history, and an event center where the annual RV/MH Hall of Fame Induction Banquet is held. The museum houses early RV/MH models as well as a particularly popular exhibit: the 1931 "housecar" presented by Paramount Studios to Hollywood actress Mae West.

Along with giant recreational vehicles, Indiana seems to enjoy items on a massive scale. The **World's Largest Ball of Paint** in Alexandria is home to—there is no other way to put it—the world's largest ball of paint. In its own display barn next to a private home, the project started in 1977 when the homeowner encouraged his young son to paint a baseball with the same blue paint as the house. From that humble beginning, the family began adding coats of paint each day until it is currently almost 15 feet around and weighs well over two tons. After calling for an appointment, visitors can choose their preferred color, add a layer of paint to the ball, have their photo taken, and sign the guest book, which is presently in its seventh volume. There are about 25,000 coats of paint on the ball, including those added by celebrities like the Oak Ridge Boys. T-shirts are available with the obvious slogan, "I Painted the World's Largest Ball of Paint."

Along the same oversized lines, Columbus, Indiana, is home to the **World's Largest Toilet**. It's an interactive exhibit in which visitors can slide through the plumbing all the way to the bottom. As part of the Kids Commons museum, the colossal commode is said to be fun for all ages. In a friendly Indiana gesture, there is no admission charge just to take a picture with the gigantic john.

Indiana is also home to what must surely be the world's largest group of **Trees That Spell "Studebaker."** In South Bend, the former test track for Studebaker automobiles is now a public park. Saplings that were planted in 1937 to spell out the word "Studebaker" are now fully grown. Admittedly, the effect is not quite as impressive from ground level, adding a new twist to not seeing the forest for the trees. However, visitors with access to aircraft claim that from above, the Studebaker-spelling trees are a sight to behold.

DISTINCTIVE INDIANA WORDS AND SAYINGS

B-Rip: Abbreviation for Broad Ripple Village, a popular entertainment and shopping district in Indianapolis, known for late-night hot spots boasting the slogan "We're open if you are."

Indy: What Indiana residents may call the city of Indianapolis, but not the state of Indiana itself. Those Indiana residents are called "Hoosiers," not "Indianans."

Naptown: Once meant as an insult, now a term of endearment for Indianapolis.

"Ope": An all-purpose word along the lines of "Oops," often used when accidentally bumping into someone.

Puppy chow: Not dog food but a popular dish for humans to consume at Indiana parties. The sweet treat consists of butter, Chex cereal, peanut butter, powdered sugar, semisweet chocolate, and a dash of vanilla extract.

Region, the: Indiana's northwestern area near Chicago. Residents of Indiana's Lake County in the Region are often considered part of the Chicago metropolitan area.

Further Reading

Madison, James H. *Hoosiers: A New History of Indiana.* Bloomington: Indiana University Press, 2016.

Thomas, Phyllis. *Indiana Off the Beaten Path: A Guide to Unique Places.* Guilford, CT: Globe Pequot Press, 2012.

Willis, James A. *Haunted Indiana: Ghosts and Strange Phenomena of the Hoosier State.* Mechanicsburg, PA: Stackpole Books, 2012.

Iowa

> **FACT BOX**
>
> **Nickname:** The Hawkeye State
> **Statehood Granted:** 1846
> **Capital:** Des Moines
> **Population:** 3,200,000
> **State Motto:** "Our Liberties We Prize and Our Rights We Will Maintain"
> **What Natives Call Themselves:** Iowans

STATE HISTORY

The Native American people in Iowa when Europeans arrived included the Ioway, for whom the state is named. Eventually, the Ioway people were removed from the state that bears their name.

Frenchmen Jacques Marquette and Louis Jolliet arrived in 1673, becoming the first-known European explorers in today's Iowa. At the time of their expedition, Iowa was unclaimed by any European power, although there were English, French, and Spanish settlements nearby. Subsequently, France planted its flag, and Iowa became part of its North American holdings called the Louisiana Territory.

One of the repercussions surrounding the French and Indian War (1754–1763) took place in 1762. At that time, France secretly transferred the land in its Louisiana Territory to Spain so the region would not fall to the British.

The French influence still remains in Iowa through such place-names as Dubuque, a city named for explorer Julien Dubuque, and Des Moines, Iowa's capital city, referring to *moines*, the French word for monks, a group of whom lived nearby.

After the transfer to Spain, not much changed in Iowa. French traders were permitted to deal in furs and establish trading posts, but there were not many permanent settlers. Europeans again manipulated the map of North America in 1800, when French leader Napoleon Bonaparte made a treaty with Spain to regain France's claim on the Louisiana Territory.

Following America's independence, the Louisiana Purchase took place in 1803, bringing Iowa along with 14 other of today's states under American control. Soon settlers began arriving, with Iowa being granted territorial status in 1838. In 1846, Iowa became the 29th state in the Union.

Plans for new towns were laid out across the state to accommodate incoming settlers. When the railroad arrived in Iowa starting in the mid-1840s, Iowa's population grew by leaps and bounds. Place-names were no longer based in the French language as many "town fathers" gave a nod to the original inhabitants of the region. Its nickname, the Hawkeye State, is said to be a reference to Native American chief Black Hawk.

Some white settlers adapted what they understood to be Indian terms. Town founders thought the word "Villisca" was a derivation of "pretty place" or "pleasant view" in the Native tongue. They gave the name to their new town in 1858, but apparently, they had misheard rather badly. According to local sources, the Native word actually means "evil spirit." Ironically, Villisca gained national notoriety for a horrific ax murder that took place there in 1912, a crime that remains unsolved.

Although Iowa is today often considered to be one of the safest places to live, the state was often a crossroad for violent criminals hoping to "rob and run" from tiny banks in small Iowa towns. In 1871, members of the Jesse James gang were said to have been the culprits in a bank robbery at Corydon, Iowa. After that incident, the famed Pinkerton Detective Agency of Chicago was hired, beginning its relentless pursuit of the James gang.

Notorious outlaws John Dillinger, "Pretty Boy" Floyd, and the Clyde Barrow-Bonnie Parker gang all crossed into Iowa to rob banks during the 1930s. Perhaps underestimating Iowa law enforcement, they had bloody shoot-outs with local police. In Dexter, Iowa, the Barrow gang barely survived a hail of bullets from Iowa police in 1933. That famous encounter severely wounded Bonnie and Clyde; was fatal to Clyde's brother, Buck; and resulted in the capture of Buck's wife, Blanche, who was blinded in the gun battle.

Iowa became known for achievements other than crime, however. The state is often cited for its efforts in civil rights. The Mars Hill Church near Ottumwa, Iowa, a log cabin constructed in 1857, was an active stop on the Underground Railroad in which enslaved people attempted to make their way to freedom. Noted abolitionist John Brown is said to have brought two wagonloads of enslaved people there before his ill-fated attack on Harper's Ferry in 1859.

Iowa was also ahead on school desegregation. In 1868, soon after the Civil War, the state ruled that "separate but equal" schools were unlawful. This was more than 80 years before the U.S. Supreme Court's *Brown v. Board of Education* decision in 1954 did the same thing for the rest of the nation.

As opposed to other states, married women in Iowa received property rights in 1851. In addition, the Iowa Supreme Court ruled in 1869 that women should be allowed to practice law, making an Iowan, Arabella Mansfield, the first female attorney in the United States.

The Iowa Department of Economic Development proudly points out that the world's first electronic digital computer was created at Iowa State University in 1937. If that achievement is considered by some to be the "greatest thing since sliced bread," it was also an Iowan, Otto Rohwedder, who invented the bread slicer in 1912.

Iowa is often cited for its efforts in civil rights. The Mars Hill Church near Ottumwa, a log cabin constructed in 1857, was a stop on the Underground Railroad in which enslaved people made their way to freedom. (Gloria Moeller/Dreamstime.com)

URBAN LEGENDS

Iowa is home to not one but *two* urban legends involving **Black Angels**. At the Fairview Cemetery in Council Bluffs, the story is that anyone who touches the hand of the Black Angel statue at the Ruth Anne Dodge memorial will be the next to die. Some claim that it is not even necessary to touch the statue, maintaining that anyone who so much as looks into the Black Angel's eyes at midnight will soon be dead. Erected in 1918, locals say that there have been strange occurrences such as the statue leaving its pedestal to hover over the cemetery grounds. The other Black Angel resides at the Oakland Cemetery in Iowa City. Sculpted to honor a local family, the eerie tales surrounding this memorial statue have led to its being dubbed "the Angel of Death." Once again, looking into its eyes at midnight is said to bring a fatal curse to the viewer. The statue, originally gold, gradually turned black over time, starting with the eyes. This sparked dark tales including one about a skeptical man who touched the Black Angel statue and immediately died of a heart attack. Some add to the tale by claiming that the statue's strange powers emanate from one of the family members who was alleged to be a witch, cursing the statue in order to protect her gravesite.

People walking their dog across the **Roseman Covered Bridge** in Winterset often report the animal going on alert with hackles rising on its back, as if in the presence of something it sensed to be very wrong. According to the legend, in 1892 an escapee from the Madison County Jail was cornered inside the covered bridge with police at both ends. After hearing a bloodcurdling scream from inside

> ### Aquaman and Superman are from . . . Iowa?
>
> Most people think of Superman as being born on the planet Krypton and raised as "Clark Kent" in Kansas. However, Iowa can lay its own claim to the Man of Steel. In addition, the Hawkeye State can also claim Aquaman as one of its own. Jason Momoa, title character of the 2018 movie *Aquaman*, and Brandon Routh, star of *Superman Returns* in 2006, both attended high school in Norwalk, Iowa. Before joining forces in the Justice League, the superheroes were teammates in the 1990s on the Norwalk Warriors varsity soccer team. The town of Norwalk is not far from Woolstock, Iowa, birthplace of actor George Reeves, who was the first to star as Superman on television in the 1950s. Incidentally, a 1947 episode of the *Superman* radio serial and a 1949 *Superboy* comic places the town where Clark Kent was raised in Iowa. Suspiciously, his home state was later changed to Kansas.

the bridge, the officers rushed in from both ends to find that the convict had apparently vanished into thin air. Today, there have been reports of eerie laughter and unexplained cold spots inside the bridge. Some have also claimed to see an apparition there that might have been the escaped convict, whose spirit may still be on the run.

Near the Iowa town of Burlington is **Stony Hollow Road**, a thoroughfare that comes with an urban legend containing all the best elements of such tales. According to locals, who are said to avoid this stretch of road at night, back in the 1800s, a young woman named Lucinda planned to meet her beloved at the cliffs along Stony Hollow Road so they could elope. The object of her affections never showed up, breaking her heart and causing her to throw herself off the cliff to her death. Adding a touch of irony, some say the reason Lucinda's young lover was unable to meet her was because his horse-drawn wagon had gotten stuck in the mud along the way. Today, according to the legend, some intrepid people venturing down the road at night have reported seeing the specter of a woman covered in blood. In addition, some claim that saying the name "Lucinda" three times will cause her ghost to appear atop the cliff. If she lays a rose at the feet of the one who summoned her, that unlucky person will die the next day.

ICONIC IOWA FOOD

A beloved food in the Hawkeye State originally began as a menu item called a Loose Meat Sandwich at Iowa's longtime popular eatery Maid-Rite. An Iowa tradition since 1926, the Maid-Rite restaurant inspired a generic version that today is simply called a **Maidrite** (one word). Even the friendliest Hawkeye might become annoyed by an outsider calling the sandwich a sloppy joe—Iowans are quick to point out that there is a difference. According to connoisseurs, the Maidrite is an unformed burger, featuring tender slow-cooked beef simmered in seasoning and served on a warm, slightly sweet bun. Different cooks tend to have their own special version, often involving various combinations of chicken broth, onion, and vinegar along with "secret herbs and spices," capping it off with optional toppings such as cheese and pickles, but rarely ketchup. This recipe is a good example:

> **Maidrite Sandwich** (Serves 4)
> 1 lb ground beef, preferably 85/15% lean
> 1 onion, chopped
> 1 beef bouillon cube
> ½ cup water
> Ground pepper to taste
> 1½ Tbsp soy sauce
> 1½ Tbsp Worcestershire sauce
> Optional: Dash of apple cider vinegar, light brown sugar, and/or mustard to taste

1. Sauté beef and onions on medium heat until cooked through, then skim fat before returning to pan.
2. Add other ingredients, and simmer about 10 minutes, stirring frequently with wooden spoon.
3. Scoop onto warmed buns.
4. Add optional toppings to taste, such as cheese, mustard, pickles, and/or fresh chopped onions.

Source: Adapted from https://iowagirleats.com/you-know-youre-from-the-midwest/.

ODD LAWS

When people think of the rickshaw-type conveyance called a pedicab, which transports passengers not by being motorized but by means of human power, they often think of such vehicles amid the massive urban sprawl of places like Shanghai and Singapore. Their first thought is not usually Cedar Rapids, Iowa. However, a municipal ordinance known as the Cedar Rapids Pedicab Code regulates those simple vehicles within the city limits. The ordinance defines a pedicab as a wheeled vehicle, powered by pedals, that carries passengers for hire. It mandates that a license is required from the Cedar Rapids City Clerk to operate the vehicles, which resemble big tricycles. Not only must a rate sheet be posted so that is it clearly visible to potential passengers before they climb aboard, but an estimate of the fare is required to be given in advance of the trip. The law forbids the pedicab operator to collect a rate more than the specified amount, not that any friendly Iowans would do that.

It is widely reported on the internet that the Iowa legislature once passed a resolution ordering the cafeteria at the state capitol building to serve corn bread. With the state often cited as the nation's top producer of corn, that regulation may have seemed reasonable to supporters of such legislation as a nod to the state's top crop. However, if such a mandate was enacted, it does not appear in current Iowa legislative statutes. Moreover, research reveals that at this writing, the eatery known as the Iowa State Capitol Cafeteria does not serve hot meals, only a variety of sandwiches. The bread choices are white, wheat, and marble rye. The latter might please fans of the old *Seinfeld* television series, but others may feel it does not say "Iowa" as corn bread would.

UNUSUAL DESTINATIONS

According to its website, the **National Hobo Museum** in Britt, Iowa, began as the dream of three lifelong hobos who wanted to preserve the history of their breed by forming the Hobo Foundation in the 1970s. The museum became a reality in the 1980s with a donated box of artifacts and a monetary gift from an unknown benefactor, thought to be a former hobo. Today, the museum houses memorabilia, photographs, and other objects pertaining to the hobo lifestyle plus a theater that shows a hobo documentary. The gift shop features souvenirs including what are said to be authentic hobo-made crafts. The museum also seeks to educate visitors on facts such as the difference between hobos and individuals who are termed "bums" or "tramps" in addition to stressing that the hobo lifestyle is not confined to the Great Depression. The museum is also the centerpiece of the annual National Hobo Convention held each summer since 1974, where one of the highlights is crowning the Hobo King and Hobo Queen. The convention is embraced by the townspeople of Britt. It is currently organized by the local Chamber of Commerce, which some might feel is a bit too structured for free-spirited hobos. But for those involved, the partnership seems to work out fine.

Even in peaceful Iowa, crime is not unknown. In 1885, the town of Council Bluffs experimented with a new type of jail that was said to be safer for both jailers and prisoners. It also appealed to thrifty Iowans by being less costly to operate than standard jailhouses. Officially called the Pottawattamie County Jail but better known as the **Squirrel Cage**, it consists of a three-story rotating cell drum inside a cage that has only one opening per floor. Some preferred to couch it in friendly sounding terms like "a lazy Susan design," with prisoners in pie-shaped cells. In theory, only a single jailer was needed to operate the hand crank that moved the massive mechanism. However, arms and legs of both guards and prisoners were lost when the building's bedrock would periodically shift, throwing gears out of balance. The Squirrel Cage was in continuous use until 1969, when it became a popular museum and tourist attraction.

For those who thrive on gory true crime, the **Villisca Ax Murder House**, often called "The Scariest Place in Iowa," is hard to beat. It had once been a happy home until all the members of the well-liked family of Mr. and Mrs. Josiah Moore were horribly murdered in a bloodbath during the summer of 1912. Villisca, Iowa, was—and is—a peaceful small town, but it was also the site of this inexplicable slaughter that remains unsolved to this day. On that fateful morning over a hundred years ago, eight bloody corpses were found in their beds with their skulls bashed in by an ax. Among the six dead children were two young friends who had stayed overnight after a program at church. When news of the massacre spread, the National Guard had to secure the site from curiosity seekers who took souvenirs (including possible clues) from the crime scene. Today, visitors can tour the restored home with its backyard cemetery and even make reservations to spend the night.

A bit more whimsical is what is billed as the **World's Largest Popcorn Ball** in Sac City, Iowa. It is currently constructed from about 2,000 pounds of popcorn, more than 4,900 pounds of sugar, 2,500 pounds of corn syrup, and a dash of lecithin. It has to be rebuilt periodically by dedicated volunteers since it is stored in a shed that is not hermetically sealed. The popcorn ball crew also has to work on keeping Sac City's spot in the record books. By periodically increasing the size of the popcorn ball, they can continue claiming the title of World's Largest against those who might try to usurp the crown. The present version measures about 24 feet around and stands over eight feet tall, weighing around 10,000 pounds. The nearby Sac City Museum and outdoor Museum Village feature an array of historical items that are said to allow guests to feel they have stepped back in time, possibly before colossal popcorn balls were in vogue.

DISTINCTIVE IOWA WORDS AND SAYINGS

Going gravel: Taking a dusty back road to avoid highway traffic as much as possible.

Got the holler tail: Said to be the condition of a person who is in a bad mood.

Parking ramp: What most other places call a parking deck or parking garage. Even though Iowa has a well-deserved reputation for being rural, major towns like Des Moines have a number of cars needing a place to park.

RAGBRAI: To outsiders, this may sound like something reminiscent of filmdom's *Thor: Ragnarok*. However, Iowans recognize this popular annual event sponsored by the *Des Moines Register* newspaper. The weeklong competition, formally known as the "**R**egister's **A**nnual **G**reat **B**icycle **R**ide **A**cross **I**owa," has been a summertime tradition in Iowa since 1973. Running from the Missouri River on the state's western side to the Mississippi River on the east, RAGBRAI is the largest, longest, and oldest multiday recreational bicycle touring event in the world.

Further Reading

Jones, Eric, and Dan Coffey. *Iowa Curiosities: Quirky Characters, Roadside Oddities and Other Offbeat Stuff*. Guilford, CT: Globe Pequot, 2009.

Lewis, Chad, and Terry Fisk. *The Iowa Road Guide to Haunted Locations*. Eau Clair, WI: Unexplained Research Publishing, 2007.

Schwieder, Dorothy. *Iowa: The Middle Land*. Iowa City: University of Iowa Press, 1996.

Kansas

> **FACT BOX**
>
> **Nickname:** The Sunflower State
> **Statehood Granted:** 1861
> **Capital:** Topeka
> **Population:** 3,000,000
> **State Motto:** *Ad astra per aspera* (Latin: "Through Hardship, to the Stars")
> **What Natives Call Themselves:** Kansans

STATE HISTORY

Kansas is often said to be the very embodiment of Middle America. It has found its way into the pantheon of popular culture, from the tune in *South Pacific*, "I'm as corny as Kansas in August," to the line from *The Wizard of Oz*, "We're not in Kansas anymore," synonymous with strange new surroundings apart from someplace familiar and down to earth.

Kansas is frequently cited as being the geographic midpoint of mainland United States. Some states dispute this, but experts say that Kansas lies in the geodetic center of the country, a measurement that takes the actual curvature of the earth into consideration rather than a flat map. Signage near Lebanon, Kansas, marks the spot.

To Native inhabitants of today's Kansas such as the Arapaho, Cheyenne, and Comanche, none of that was relevant. They simply enjoyed the bountiful life that the region provided. The state's early residents were the descendants of Indigenous people who arrived in today's Kansas about 7,000 years before the birth of Christ.

Many Indigenous people eventually formed agriculturally based societies centered on the cultivation of maize, or corn, although the land also provided resources for hunting and foraging.

In 1541, the first-known European to visit today's Kansas was the Spanish explorer Francisco Vázquez de Coronado. His venture into Kansas was noteworthy for two reasons. First, in his futile search through the American Southwest for the mythical seven cities of gold, it was in Kansas that Coronado ultimately lost the conviction that he would find them. He is said to have turned around and headed back to Mexico from a place currently called "Coronado Heights," near present-day

Lindsborg, Kansas. Pieces of Spanish chain mail have been found in Kansas, relics of the despondent explorers.

The other significant result of Coronado's trek into Kansas was introducing the Native American tribes of the Great Plains to horses. The Natives immediately recognized the advantages of possessing this four-legged marvel, acquiring horses from the Spaniards and radically changing both the lifestyle and mode of warfare for Plains Indians.

At first, that warfare primarily took the form of skirmishes between rival Native tribes. As the massive region containing Kansas, known today as the Louisiana Territory, seesawed between claims of ownership by France and Spain, there was little settlement there. The first documented white settlers did not arrive until 1812, after most of Kansas was acquired by the United States in the Louisiana Purchase of 1803.

The region was named for the Kansas River, which itself was named after the Kansa tribe of Native Americans who had made their home along its banks. Kansas was a prime crossroad for the opening of the Old West. Between around 1820 and 1880, the migration westward brought people and goods across Kansas via the Santa Fe Trail. Today, historians point out that wagon ruts are still visible in the Kansas prairie.

When the Kansas-Nebraska Act was passed by the U.S. Congress in 1854, the region was opened to increased settlement. Kansas was deeply entangled in the conflict over slavery as the nation hurtled toward war. Both antislavery and proslavery groups arrived, each hoping Kansas would swing their way as either a free state or a slave state. In the deadly violence that followed, the territory became known as Bleeding Kansas, which some historians cite as a microcosm of the Civil War that followed.

In 1861, as a free state, Kansas joined the Union to become the nation's 34th state. After the end of the Civil War in 1865, waves of settlers poured into Kansas. The state was a central point in the mythology of the Old West. Legendary figures like Wyatt Earp, Wild Bill Hickok, and Bat Masterson served as lawmen in Kansas towns, such as Dodge City.

In the aftermath of the Civil War, many African Americans

In the late 1800s, Kansas became central to the mythology of the Old West. Legendary figures like Wyatt Earp (pictured here second from left, bottom row) served as lawmen in Kansas towns such as Dodge City. (National Archives)

> **Planes on the Plains**
>
> When Dorothy left the Land of Oz to return home to Kansas, she traveled in a balloon. Considering the fact that according to the state's Department of Commerce, Kansas is known as the "Air Capital of the World," she might simply have taken a plane. Many of the greatest figures in aviation have called Kansas home, including Walter Beech, Clyde Cessna, and Amelia Earhart. Charles Lindbergh lived there as a barnstormer. During World War II, aircraft factories in Kansas produced one out of every nine U.S. warplanes. Today, Wichita, Kansas, is known worldwide as the home of such top-tier aircraft manufacturers as Beechcraft, Cessna, and Learjet. With Kansas also being the fictional home of Superman, an observer could well exclaim, *"Look, up in the sky! It's a bird! It's a plane! It's . . . wait, it IS a plane!"*

made Kansas their home. Their legacy produced notable native Kansans, including Gwendolyn Brooks, the first African American to receive a Pulitzer Prize; prominent Black author Langston Hughes; and Hattie McDaniel, the first African American to win an Academy Award. The famed Buffalo Soldiers, composed entirely of African Americans, were based at Fort Leavenworth, Kansas.

In addition, *Brown v. Board of Education*, the landmark 1954 Supreme Court decision that dismantled the racial doctrine of "separate but equal" in the United States, got its start with plaintiffs in Topeka, Kansas.

URBAN LEGENDS

Fort Leavenworth, Kansas, was established in 1827 and remains the oldest active U.S. Army base west of the Mississippi River. Through the years, a number of urban legends have sprung up there, including alleged hauntings by various ghosts. One of the most famous is the apparition of Catherine Sutler. During the 1880s, she and her family were on their way West in autumn, stopping for the night at Fort Leavenworth. Catherine sent her son, Ethan, and daughter, Mary, to collect firewood. The children never returned. After a search, Catherine's husband was determined to continue traveling to their new home in the West. Refusing to join him, Catherine stayed at Fort Leavenworth so she could continue looking for the children. According to the legend, she searched through the winter, calling their names as she made her way through deep snow. Eventually, she died of pneumonia. The legend maintains that in the depths of winter, an apparition in old-fashioned clothing will appear at Leavenworth National Cemetery, calling the names "Ethan" and "Mary."

In the town of Hutchinson, Kansas, a dedicated local librarian is said to have remained on the job at the **Hutchinson Public Library** even after her death. Ida Day Holzapfel was head librarian between 1915 and 1954. Neither patrons nor staffers were spared from her reprimand if they disturbed the silence of the library.

Ida died a year after she retired, but according to the legend, soon there were said to be strange incidents involving ghostly apparitions. One of the most widely reported came from a young librarian who had been quietly humming as she filed documents in the basement. Suddenly, the apparition of a stern-faced old woman emerged from the shadows, hissing "What are you doing?" at the startled employee who had forgotten Ida's edict of silence.

Any spot that becomes known as one of the "Seven Gateways to Hell" no doubt exemplifies the definition of an urban legend. In 1974, the quiet little **Stull Cemetery** in Stull, Kansas, was the subject of a Halloween story in the student newspaper at the nearby University of Kansas. With the headline "Legend of Devil Haunts Tiny Town," the article was an attention-getter, particularly being written the same year that *The Exorcist* was a popular movie. The story cited what were said to be "well-known" legends about the devil appearing at Stull Cemetery at various times of the year, including the equinox, conveniently near Spring Break. With the story later being copied repeatedly on the internet, the Stull Cemetery took on the notoriety of being one of the "Seven Gateways to Hell." Those who believe the legend claim that the cemetery has been the meeting place for witches and satanic cults, leaving it cursed for all time. The urban legend has left a trail of vandalism and stolen tombstones at sad little Stull Cemetery as the story continues to live.

ICONIC KANSAS FOOD

Although some people might think the most iconic Kansas food would be the famed Kansas City steak, others point out that the beefy fare in question is indigenous to Kansas City, Missouri. Many Kansans lean toward their home state's preference for the **Bierock**, a handheld combination of beef and cabbage stuffed in a fluffy roll that makes a hearty all-in-one meal. It originated among Kansas farmers with Eastern European origins who usually had most of the ingredients already on hand.

> **Bierock** (Yields 24 servings)
> *Dough:*
> 10½ cups all-purpose flour, divided
> 1 package (¼ oz) active dry yeast
> ½ cup sugar
> 2 tsp salt
> 2½ cups water
> 1 cup whole milk
> ½ cup butter, cubed
> 2 large eggs
>
> *Filling:*
> 2 lb ground beef

1 large onion, chopped
2 tsp salt
1 tsp white pepper
2 lb shredded cabbage, cooked and drained

1. In a large bowl, prepare dough by combining sugar, salt, and yeast with four cups flour; mix well and set aside.
2. In a saucepan, heat water, milk, and butter just until butter melts. Remove from heat and cool before combining with flour mixture, then add eggs. Blend until moistened, gradually stirring in enough remaining flour to make the dough firm.
3. Knead on a floured surface about 10 minutes before placing in a greased bowl and turning once to grease top. Cover and let rise in a warm place about 1 hour until doubled, then punch dough down and let rise again until almost doubled.
4. Mix filling by browning beef with onion, salt, and pepper; drain before adding cabbage, then set aside.
5. Divide the dough into quarters, then roll each piece into a rectangle about 10 by 15 inches, then cut into 5-inch squares. Spoon about ⅓ cup filling onto each square.
6. Bring the four corners up over the filling; pinch together tightly to seal. Repeat with remaining dough and filling, then place on greased baking sheets.
7. Bake at 375°F for 30 minutes or until brown.

Source: Adapted from https://www.tasteofhome.com/recipes/bierocks/.

ODD LAWS

In suburban Derby, Kansas, riding a horse or other animal down any road is against the law. Animal-drawn vehicles are also prohibited unless they are part of a parade or other public event. On the other hand, a potential rider requesting special permission from the chief of police might obtain a waiver permitting that person "to ride or allow a horse or other animal upon a designated boulevard, road, street, or drive, or upon public ground during certain designated hours and under supervision of the police department." Lest the rider become overconfident with this elite status, "all respects of the Standard Traffic Ordinance" must be obeyed.

If would-be animal riders in Derby are disappointed at being turned down by the chief of police, those persons cannot take out their frustration on a vending machine, even if it steals their money. In Derby, hitting or damaging a vending machine is illegal. That also goes for assaulting larcenous parking meters.

In Topeka, it is illegal to drive a car through a parade. Not in a parade, but *through* a parade. Police cars or other authorized emergency vehicles can do so if needed, but other drivers must wait patiently on the sidelines until the parade passes by. It is not known if this was a problem in the past, but anything "conspicuously designated as a parade" in Topeka is off-limits to through traffic.

Another moving violation in Topeka is driving a herd of cattle through town. Despite the proud Kansas heritage of the Old West, Topeka's municipal code bans "any herd of cattle, horses, mules or swine, or any flock of sheep, upon any street within the city."

Topeka also forbids screaming at a haunted house. The city code states that visitors to any haunted house "must be orderly at all times, and it shall be unlawful for any person attending such haunted house to create a disturbance." Some say that treating a haunted house like a library would tend to defeat its scream-inducing purpose, but that's the law in Topeka.

Down the highway in Wichita, people must get a permit from the city if they wish to take dirt from the airport. In the interest of full disclosure, this anti-dirt-snatching ordinance also applies to public streets, alleys, or parks, although it does make special mention of the airport. City employees or contractors are permitted to indulge in a land grab if they are performing their job, such as constructing a sewer. Therefore, this exemption may also include the proverbial Wichita lineman.

UNUSUAL DESTINATIONS

The **Kansas Barbed Wire Museum** in La Crosse may sound a bit dull to some, but the sharp twisted metal is recognized by historians as having changed the American West forever. At last count, the museum has more than 2,400 varieties of barbed wire along with hundreds of antique tools for fences. Many visitors to the museum have to be reminded that the advent of barbed wire in the West often spurred bloody vendettas, vigilante raids, and murder. For example, the "Fence Cutting Wars" in the 1880s led to state and federal legislation addressing fence building as well as fence cutting. This unusual Kansas museum highlights the fact that barbed wire was a small invention that tamed the West in a big way, bringing about the end of the cowboy era.

The **Kansas Underground Salt Museum**, also called "Strataca," truly lives up to its name. The museum is built 650 feet under Hutchinson, Kansas, in one of the world's largest deposits of rock salt. Visitors descend beneath the earth's surface in a 90-second elevator ride to explore underground salt deposits that are said to have been formed 275 million years ago. Museum officials have collected artifacts from the 67 miles of caverns, such as relics that were left in place from past salt mining. Whatever the temperature or weather conditions are topside on the Kansas prairie, the mine remains a constant 68°F, with a relative humidity of around 45 percent. To add to the experience, visitors are required to wear a hard hat and a rescue breather on their trip underground. Although salt is mined at other places in the United States, none of them are open to tourists. The Kansas Underground Salt Museum therefore adds a new meaning to the term, "Just another day in the salt mines."

The **World's Largest Ball of Twine** in Cawker City has to fight to hold its title. So far, it has done the job admirably. By the time of his death in 1974, a Cawker City resident had created a ball made of more than 1 million feet of twine, measuring over 10 feet in diameter. Fellow citizens of Cawker City not only honored his efforts by constructing an open-air gazebo to house his creation but also initiated an annual "Twine-a-thon," during which community members add more twine to the massive ball, which is currently more than 40 feet around. By a recent measurement, its height is estimated at over 10 feet, tipping the scales at more than 20,000 pounds and growing. Competitors in other states claim specifics such as the heaviest twine ball, largest nylon twine ball, and largest ball of sisal twine built by a single person. As of this writing, Cawker City, Kansas, holds two titles: "Ball of Twine with the Largest Circumference" and "Largest Ball of Sisal Twine Built by a Community." In addition, the Cawker City creation earned celebrity status by being a subject of the comic strip *Doonesbury* during 2012 and being cited in the 1983 movie *National Lampoon's Vacation*.

In Lucas, Kansas, a unique attraction may be in the running not only for its distinctive area of interest but also for having the strangest museum name. The **World's Largest Collection of the World's Smallest Versions of the World's Largest Things** (helpfully abbreviated as **WLCoWSVoWLT**) is housed in a museum located on the town's Main Street. The artifacts also go on the road with a display bus tour that bills itself as The World's Largest Collection of the World's Smallest Versions of the World's Largest Things Traveling Roadside Attraction. It's the brainchild of an artist who calls herself "one of America's foremost experts on the World's Largest Things." In addition to miniatures, she created the full-size World's Largest Souvenir Travel Plate from an old satellite dish. Celebrating all things massive (though downsized), the attraction features a rare collection that includes miniature replicas of exhibits running from baseball bats to bulls that are billed as the world's largest. Honoring fellow Kansans, it also includes a mini-model of the World's Largest Ball of Twine, no doubt the Sunflower State's version in Cawker City.

DISTINCTIVE KANSAS WORDS AND SAYINGS

EMAW! Stands for "Every Man a Wildcat," the official slogan and battle cry of Kansas State University athletics.

Kansas City: In many other places, this refers to a major city in Missouri. To Kansans, it means the one in Kansas.

Kellogg: When Kansans "take the Kellogg," it does not refer to cereal. This six-lane stretch of U.S. Highway 54 runs through Wichita, being named for Milo B. Kellogg, the city's first civilian postmaster.

Manhattan: In Kansas, this is the "real one," being the state's eighth largest city. Many Kansans understand that there is also another one in New York.

Rock Chalk! This chant-and-response is used by supporters of University of Kansas Jayhawks athletics, with the appropriate reply being "Jayhawk!"

Further Reading

Grant, R. G. *Flight: The Complete History of Aviation*. New York: Penguin Random House, 2017.

Heitz, Lisa Hefner. *Haunted Kansas*. Lawrence: University Press of Kansas, 1997.

Miner, Craig. *Kansas: The History of the Sunflower State*. Lawrence: University Press of Kansas, 2002.

Ringer, Roger L. *Eccentric Kansas: Tales from Atchison to Winfield*. Charleston, SC: History Press, 2019.

Kentucky

FACT BOX

Nickname: The Bluegrass State
Statehood Granted: 1792
Capital: Frankfort
Population: 4,500,000
State Motto: "United We Stand, Divided We Fall"
What Natives Call Themselves: Kentuckians

STATE HISTORY

England's Queen Elizabeth II, who presumably could have any wish fulfilled, once stated publicly that one of her dreams was to visit Kentucky. Her Majesty's wish list specified attending the Kentucky Derby, which she was eventually able to do in 2007.

Any state named as a dream destination by the Queen of England must be a special place. Indeed, each year Kentucky is in the global spotlight with the running of thoroughbred racing's Kentucky Derby.

Some historians claim that the state's name evolved from a Native American term for meadows. The famed Kentucky bluegrass that may have covered those meadows can sometimes be a source of disappointment to visitors who expect to see azure-colored landscaping. Although bluegrass is actually green, it is named for the buds that can appear blue in the springtime.

Below ground, Kentucky can boast Mammoth Cave, the longest-known cave system in the world.

Kentucky was part of the vast Mississippi River Valley region claimed for France in 1682 by explorer René-Robert Cavelier, Sieur de La Salle. In the 1700s, increased white settlement led to skirmishes with Native Americans such as the Shawnee who already lived there.

Kentucky can claim America's oldest university west of the Allegheny Mountains, with Lexington's Transylvania University, chartered in 1780. At that time, today's Kentucky was part of Virginia, having been established as Kentucky County in 1776. However, the desire for independence and statehood culminated in 1792, with Kentucky becoming the nation's 15th state.

With its distinctive spires, Churchill Downs in Louisville is home of the world-famous Kentucky Derby. Each year on Derby Day, Kentucky is in the global spotlight for this premier event in thoroughbred racing. (Courtesy: Kentucky Department of Travel)

When the Civil War broke out in 1861, Kentucky became known as a border state, as opposed to the Deep South. Although the state officially remained neutral throughout the war, the South nevertheless admitted Kentucky into the Confederacy, being represented by a star on the Confederate battle flag.

Mary Lincoln, wife of Union president Abraham Lincoln, endured harsh criticism during the Civil War. As a native of Lexington, Kentucky, she was accused by Northerners of being a spy for the Confederacy and condemned by the South for being a traitor to her southern homeland. Mary publicly supported her husband's efforts to hold the Union together.

In 1863, during the Civil War, an infamous feud broke out between the Hatfield family of West Virginia and McCoys of Kentucky. The Civil War ended before the feud, which ran through 1891.

Kentucky did not secede, so after Reconstruction, it never had to regain its statehood as part of the Union. However, like the myth of bluegrass, Kentucky is technically not a state. Along with Massachusetts, Pennsylvania, and Virginia, Kentucky calls itself a "commonwealth." Evolving from English common law, the term traditionally refers to government based on the common consent of the people. In America, a commonwealth is the equivalent of a state.

From its beginnings, Kentucky became known for something that took its place alongside the state's blue grass: "liquid gold." Bourbon, made primarily from corn,

> ### Kentucky vs. Kentucky
>
> One of the great ironies of the American Civil War was that the leaders of the opposing sides, Abraham Lincoln for the Union and Jefferson Davis for the Confederacy, were both born in Kentucky. In fact, they were born only about 100 miles apart. Lincoln was born in 1809, near Hodgenville. Davis had been born the previous year in Fairview. Lincoln was called "Abraham" in honor of the grandfather who had moved the family to Kentucky. Jefferson Davis was named for President Thomas Jefferson of Virginia, which had previously claimed Kentucky as one of its counties. In 1842, Lincoln married Mary Todd of Lexington, Kentucky. Davis's first wife was the daughter of Kentuckian Zachary Taylor. Though Abraham Lincoln and Jefferson Davis were adversaries in what many consider the nation's most tragic war, today their statues both stand in the rotunda of Kentucky's capitol building.

was born in Kentucky and is America's only native spirit. The distillation method was probably brought to Kentucky in the 1700s by British settlers. Ironically, its name seems to refer to the ruling Bourbon dynasty of France, which was Britain's traditional enemy. Today, Kentucky is the source of 95 percent of the world's bourbon. According to the Kentucky Distillers Association, in 2020, the quantity of bourbon aging at Kentucky distilleries (about 9 million barrels) is approximately twice the state's population of 4.5 million people.

A major source of pride for the state began in 1875 when the first Kentucky Derby was run. However, for many people, a different kind of "horse power" also earns bragging rights for the state. In 1981, the General Motors assembly plant for the Chevrolet Corvette sports car moved to Bowling Green, Kentucky, becoming the only facility to produce the beloved Corvette.

The nearby National Corvette Museum in Bowling Green is a unique institution dedicated to the much-loved sports car. Corvette enthusiasts, along with the Bowling Green community, were aghast in 2014 when the Kentucky limestone on which the museum was built gave way, opening a 30-foot-deep sinkhole beneath the facility. In what some said was Kentucky "can-do" spirit, a viewing window was built into the museum's floor, offering a look at the cave-in below and the spot where eight 'Vettes took a tumble.

Kentucky is home to the unique tradition of "Burgoo." This thick, highly seasoned stew usually starts with meat, corn, onions, and tomatoes, but there is a wide variation of recipes among individual cooks. Burgoo is often prepared in Kentucky at social gatherings or fundraisers where attendees bring one or more ingredients. Both Lawrenceburg and Owensboro, Kentucky, claim to be the Burgoo Capital of the World.

Burgoo usually contains the kind of "secret herbs and spices" that would gladden the heart of Kentucky's Colonel Harland Sanders, founder of Kentucky Fried Chicken, another distinction that gained the state worldwide fame. Based in

Louisville, the first KFC franchise opened in the United States in 1952. Today there are KFC franchises worldwide, from Albania to Zimbabwe.

URBAN LEGENDS

Joining its Bigfoot-style counterparts elsewhere, Kentucky's **Hillbilly Beast** is a classic urban legend that allegedly goes back to the days of pioneer Daniel Boone, who is said to have had a personal encounter. The apelike Hillbilly Beast supposedly makes its home in the foothills of Eastern Kentucky. Like Bigfoot, it is extremely large and covered with dark matted hair. According to the legend, it has glowing yellow eyes, smells repulsive, and is said to "glide" when it runs as opposed to taking big galumphing strides as might be expected from a huge hairy Sasquatch. A distinctive feature of the Hillbilly Beast is its ferocious howl that has been described as sounding something like a tornado siren. According to the legend, the Hillbilly Beast has been known to attack humans, although few have claimed to have spotted the Beast in person.

At the **Pope Lick Trestle Bridge**, people have been drawn to their death by a devilish legend that keeps attracting thrill seekers who are determined to check it out. The story is that a half-goat, half-man creature lives beneath the railroad trestle over Pope Lick Creek in Fisherville. The horned Goatman allegedly lures people onto the bridge into the path of a passing train. Some curiosity seekers are under the impression that the trestle is no longer used by the Norfolk Southern Railway. Actually, it is heavily traveled, carrying locomotives that are notoriously hard to stop. Depending on the specific version of the legend, the Goatman uses hypnosis or calls for help in a childlike voice or jumps up and down to attract his victims. Then he allegedly attacks them with a bloody ax or simply terrifies them so badly that they end up in front of a train or over the side of the bridge. Regardless of the folklore, there have been some very real deaths among monster hunters who trespass onto the railway trestle to go looking for the Goatman. Therefore, in that respect, this particular myth has claimed more real lives than most urban legends.

On **Sleepy Hollow Road** near Louisville, no headless horsemen are known to be involved, but according to the urban legend, other goings-on are so spooky, there might as well be. In fact, there are several legends about this curving two-mile stretch of roadway. The best known is that after dark, a hearse will suddenly materialize out of thin air on the two-lane country road. The hearse is said to speed up and drive directly at approaching cars, which are then run off the road, dropping 30 feet into the ravine below. The second version involves a certain point along the road at which alleged satanic rituals have taken place. The third tale involves an old woman, called by locals "the Sleepy Hollow Witch," who appears to be standing in the middle of the road when a driver comes around a blind curve. Some drivers who swerved to miss her said they ended up hitting a guardrail; others, who had no time to swerve, claim to have driven right through her. The last tale, and most intriguing to many, is that traveling along Sleepy Hollow Road will produce a time warp. Drivers have claimed to enter the road at a certain time, drive for about five minutes, and then come out on the other end not minutes, but hours later.

Honorable mention goes to the **Phantom Police Officer** of Narrows Road in Erlanger, Kentucky, who was said to be killed by a car during a routine traffic stop in the 1950s but is allegedly still on the job, at least on the midnight shift. At that hour, it is said that a ghostly specter in a 1950s-era police cruiser will appear and pull over drivers who are behind the wheel of the same make of car as the one that had hit him. Most of the time, he disappears as he walks to the person's car, although some drivers say he spoke to them before disappearing as he walked away. The good news is that in all the tellings, no driver was actually given a ticket by the phantom patrolman.

ICONIC KENTUCKY FOOD

Hands down, it's the **Hot Brown**. The story goes that in the 1920s, Louisville's legendary Brown Hotel attracted more than a thousand people to each of its regular dinner dances. When the event ended in the wee hours of the morning, guests went to the hotel restaurant for something to eat. There, the chef decided to create something unique, a more alluring signature dish than a traditional ham-and-eggs breakfast. The Hot Brown, an open-faced turkey sandwich with bacon and special sauce, was the result. Today, it is a Kentucky tradition that has found global acclaim. The recipe below is adapted from the source, Louisville's historic Brown Hotel:

Hot Brown (Serves 2)
2 oz butter
2 oz all-purpose flour
8 oz heavy cream
8 oz whole milk
½ cup plus 2 Tbsp grated Pecorino Romano cheese (reserved)
Pinch ground nutmeg
Salt and pepper to taste
14 oz thick-sliced roast turkey breast
4 slices thick Texas Toast–type bread with crust trimmed
4 slices bacon, fried crisp
Dash paprika
Dash parsley

1. Preheat oven to 350°F.
2. In 2 qt saucepan, melt butter and slowly whisk in flour until it forms a thick paste, which should be cooked for about 2 minutes over medium to low heat, stirring frequently.

3. Whisk in cream and milk, and cook over medium heat about 2–3 minutes, until cream begins to simmer.
4. Remove sauce from heat, and slowly whisk in cheese until mixture is smooth. Add nutmeg, salt, and pepper to taste.
5. Place two slices of toast in an oven-safe dish, covering each with half the turkey before pouring on the sauce and sprinkling with remaining cheese.
6. Bake in the oven for 20 minutes until cheese begins to bubble and brown.
7. Remove from oven, cross two bacon slices on top, sprinkle with paprika and parsley, and serve immediately.

Source: Adapted from https://www.brownhotel.com/dining/hot-brown.

ODD LAWS

According to Kentucky law, no reptiles are permitted to be handled during religious services. If worshippers are apprehended while doing so, there might have to be a second collection. The law clearly states that any person who "displays, handles or uses any kind of reptile in connection with any religious service or gathering shall be fined not less than fifty dollars ($50) nor more than one hundred dollars ($100)." This statute applies equally to crocodiles, lizards, snakes, and turtles.

Fines are also levied for those who show their displeasure at public speakers, nor is jail out of the question. Penalties range from a fine of $50 to $500 and/or imprisonment for six months to a year. The statute covers verbal heckling as well as more physical expressions of disagreement. According to state law, interfering or interrupting a speaker addressing a public audience is unlawful. This includes "insulting or offensive language or opprobrious epithets applied to the speaker." In addition, the law states that a listener with an opposing viewpoint may not show displeasure with the speaker by "throwing missiles of any kind at him." It is unclear what the penalty might be if the speaker is a "her" as well as whether the missile in question is a bouquet of roses.

Also according to state law, it is not permissible to "sell or exchange, display, or possess living baby chicks, ducklings, or other fowl or rabbits which have been dyed or colored . . . in any quantity less than six (6)." Wrongdoers who think small by dyeing less than a half dozen are subject to a fine.

Mention must be made of an allegation on the internet that Kentucky law forbids hunting from a moving vehicle unless the game animal is a whale. A search of Kentucky statutes makes provisions for vehicles in some circumstances, but there is no mention of whales apart from one in the state's game and fish regulations. Referencing hunters going after elk, it is stated that "a cow's 'mew' call is surprisingly high-pitched and nasally, sounding somewhat like a whale's vocalization." The guideline goes on to suggest learning to imitate whale sounds. This could be difficult to do locally since Kentucky has not been underwater for more than 400 million years.

UNUSUAL DESTINATIONS

As the name suggests, **Dinosaur World** in Cave City is a prehistoric theme park. In a natural outdoor setting, visitors can stroll among life-size dinosaur statues. Each figure has a nearby description offering helpful details about its species. There is also an indoor museum exhibiting prehistoric fossils along with informational displays with facts about dinosaurs, plus common questions and answers. There are interactive features as well as a dinosaur-themed playground for children. The park reassures young visitors and their parents that they will not become a dinosaur's dinner. Dinosaur World also encourages guests to bring a cooler, drinks, and snacks with them along with what they call "friendly" dogs on a leash.

In Munfordville, **Kentucky Stonehenge** may be less of a mystery than its ancient counterpart in England, but is still a strangely compelling destination. Around the year 2000, Munfordville's former town mayor trekked around the nearby Hatcher Valley, covering more than 1,000 acres in his travels. There, he located large rocks that looked like suitable candidates for immortality, bringing them back home. He created this landmark in his yard, which is located in a quiet residential neighborhood. Like the original in England, the rising sun casts appropriate shadows at dawn of the summer solstice. Visitors can park on the street and then wander around the impressive mini-monoliths amid decorative shrubbery. The construction project had enough stones left over to also create rock displays, including "Earth Mysteries," "Garden of Gethsemane," and "Twisted Rock." At this free attraction, all the owner asks is to refrain from touching or climbing the rocks and not to visit after dark.

The level of enjoyment by visitors to **Vent Haven Museum** in Fort Mitchell, Kentucky, may be based on their fondness for ventriloquism and ventriloquists' dummies, the latter also being called "ventriloquial figures." As what the website calls the world's only museum dedicated to ventriloquism, this attraction celebrates the history of the art by displaying a wide variety of memorabilia. It also sponsors ventriloquist events. Along with almost a thousand dummies from around the world, there are artifacts, mementos, posters, and photographs. The attraction, which opened in 1973, began as the personal collection of one man who was dedicated to ventriloquism. Amateur ventriloquist William Shakespeare Berger spent more than 40 years amassing an assortment of items dating back to the 19th century. Upon his passing, the collection was opened to the public. The museum is also the centerpiece for those attending the annual Vent Haven ConVENTion where hundreds of professional and amateur ventriloquists come together with their inanimate (but talkative) sidekicks.

DISTINCTIVE KENTUCKY WORDS AND SAYINGS

Betty: In Kentucky, it's not necessarily a girl's name but a fruit-based dessert, similar to a cobbler, called a Brown Betty.

Churchill: Not the former British prime minister, but Churchill Downs, home of the world-famous Kentucky Derby, or simply "The Derby" to Kentuckians.

Thunder: Kentuckians know it to be "Thunder over Louisville," an airshow and fireworks display that kicks off each year's Kentucky Derby Festival and is said to be the largest annual fireworks display in North America. At other times of the year, "thunder" may also be the sound made during a storm—but not near Derby time.

"Unbridled Spirit": Although Kentucky's official nickname is the Bluegrass State, its registered trademark combines two of the state's main attributes: bourbon and thoroughbred horses.

Ville, the: Shorthand for "Louisville," neatly solving the problem of whether the city's name should be pronounced "LOO-a-ville" or "LOO-ee-ville."

Further Reading

Brown, Alan. *Haunted Kentucky: Ghosts and Strange Phenomena of the Bluegrass State*. Mechanicsburg, PA: Stackpole Books, 2009.

Craig, Berry. *Hidden History of Kentucky in the Civil War*. Charleston, SC: History Press, 2010.

Harrison, Lowell, and James Klotter. *A New History of Kentucky*. Lexington: University Press of Kentucky, 1997.

Louisiana

FACT BOX

Nickname: The Pelican State
Statehood Granted: 1812
Capital: Baton Rouge
Population: 4,700,000
State Motto: "Union, Justice, Confidence"
What Natives Call Themselves: Louisianans or Louisianians

STATE HISTORY

As noted in the Fact Box, the official state motto of Louisiana is "Union, Justice, Confidence." However, there are some who might say that a better choice would be the often-heard phrase "Laissez les Bons Temps Rouler," French for "Let the Good Times Roll."

Louisiana is often seen not only as a place where good times roll but also as the most "foreign" state of the Union. It is the land of bayous and beignets, of Cajuns and Creoles, of gumbo, jambalaya, po'boys, Tabasco, voodoo, zydeco, and streetcars named Desire.

For trivia buffs who are asked how many counties there are in Louisiana, the answer is "None." In Louisiana, the 64 corresponding units of local government are called "parishes" rather than counties. It is the only state with such designations, stemming from subdivisions of the Catholic Church, the predominant religion of Louisiana's previous owners, France and Spain.

Before the French and Spanish arrived, Native Americans were the inhabitants of Louisiana. Indigenous groups lived there for thousands of years, creating the earliest mound complex in North America, earthworks that were generally used for ceremonial purposes. Today's mound site at Watson Brake, Louisiana, has been dated to more than 3,000 years before the birth of Christ. Indigenous nations in today's Louisiana at the time of European arrival include the Caddo, Choctaw, and Natchez.

The first-known Europeans came to Louisiana in 1543 when Hernando de Soto of Spain followed the Mississippi River to the Gulf of Mexico. Native Americans pursued the Spaniards down the river, firing arrows at them day after day. This resulted in numerous deaths and injuries among the Spaniards, whose interest in Louisiana rapidly faded.

In 1682, French explorer René-Robert Cavelier, Sieur de La Salle claimed the entire territory drained by the Mississippi River for France. La Salle named the vast region La Louisiane, later known as the Louisiana Territory, to honor France's King Louis XIV.

In 1714, the French founded the town of Natchitoches, making it the oldest permanent European settlement in today's Louisiana. Five years later, in 1719, French ships carried the first enslaved African people to Louisiana. Mass cultivation of cotton and cane sugar proved profitable for landowners with a huge unpaid labor force. Untold thousands of captive Africans were transported to Louisiana.

France quietly transferred La Louisiane over to its ally, Spain, when things looked grim during its conflict with England in the French and Indian War (1754–1763). It was in 1765, during Spanish rule, when a chapter of history took place that would prove fundamental to Louisiana's culture. Thousands of French-speaking people were expelled from Canada by the victorious British. Coming from an Eastern Canadian region called Acadia, they were transported to a brutally different world in Louisiana. The Acadians who survived found their name abbreviated into an Americanized pronunciation that evolved into "Cajuns."

Louisiana got a new proprietor in 1800 when Spain secretly transferred ownership back to the French. Soon, however, when France wanted money to fight a war under Napoleon Bonaparte, La Louisiane was offered to the newly created United States of America. In 1803, the sale was finalized into what became known as the Louisiana Purchase. All or parts of what would become 15 states, including the state of Louisiana, were acquired for less than three cents an acre.

In 1812, Louisiana joined the Union as the nation's 18th state. Due to its prior history, Louisiana became home to a rich mix of cultures, including African, Cajun, Creole, French, Haitian, Native American, and Spanish in addition to newly arrived American settlers. It produced a cultural diversity for Louisiana that many find to be unequaled among the 50 states.

From Louisiana's early days, importing enslaved African people was an accepted practice in order to provide free labor for large landowners. A shortage of white European women led to marriages that produced a growing population group known as mulattos, or people with a mixture of ethnic ancestries. Another group, Creoles, denoted people who were born in Louisiana. At first, the label was applied to native-born Europeans such as the French and Spanish. It was eventually also applied to mixed-race descendants of African slaves and Native Americans who were born in Louisiana.

Part of that mélange was ultimately reflected in religious practices through the kind of cultural exchanges that became voodoo. Many enslaved people came from West Africa and Haiti where they had developed a belief system originally called "vodun." In Louisiana, voodoo mingled with Catholicism to form a kind of hybrid faith.

> ### Long Time, No See
>
> Historians have written that Huey Long, governor of Louisiana from 1928 to 1932, had a unique way of financing his political campaigns. It is said that state employees had to deduct up to 10 percent of their salary to Long's campaign fund in return for job security. This deducted cash, which was generally called a "DEE-duct," was placed in a locked chest called the Deduct Box, which was said to eventually contain about a million dollars. Only Long knew where it was hidden. Some sources believe it was in a safe at the Roosevelt Hotel in New Orleans. Others claim Long buried it somewhere in the countryside or submerged it in a Louisiana bayou. One day Long was asked by a trusted adviser where the Deduct Box was hidden, but Long said they would discuss it later. Before that happened, Long was dead. As of this writing, the Deduct Box has not been found, although there is a replica in the Roosevelt Hotel lobby.

Louisiana seceded from the Union in 1861 but was soon defeated by the North as part of its strategy to control the Mississippi River. The federals who controlled Louisiana designated it to be a Union state.

Today, Louisiana is an extraordinarily popular tourist destination. Colorful locales offer signature festivals, such as that at Breaux Bridge, which calls itself "Crawfish Capital of the World," and at Mamou, calling itself the "Cajun Music Capital of the World." During Mardi Gras time, the population of New Orleans generally swells from about 390,000 to more than a million. Amid the boisterous crowds, the proverbial good times are definitely said to roll.

URBAN LEGENDS

A story that began in the 1930s and still manages to hold its mythological status is the **Devil Man** that was said to roam the New Orleans area at night, terrorizing young couples. The creature, which was said to suddenly appear and quickly vanish into thin air, had bright pink ears, long black horns, and horrible huge eyes. It is said that when accosting the victims, it could induce what were called "temporary deaths" in which people's lives would flash in front of them. One version of the tale involves a policeman who was said to have apprehended the creature and put it in jail, but when the officer walked outside the jailhouse, the monster was standing in front of him. The policeman fired his gun at point-blank range, but the bullets bounced off the creature, who threw the ammunition back at the officer. Later, when a local resident was arrested for unlawfully discharging a firearm, he claimed that he did so in self-defense to ward off the Devil Man.

Grunch Road, a dead-end dirt roadway that leads into the woods east of New Orleans, is said to be the home of creatures that are half human and half monster. The **Grunch** are said to have resulted from inbreeding among deformed human dwarves deep in the bayous. The tale cautions drivers not to get out of their car if they see what looks like an injured goat by the roadside. The Grunch are alleged to use goats to lure unsuspecting victims out of their vehicle before capturing the humans, draining their blood, and turning them into Grunch gourmet dinners.

A mythical Louisiana monster with a more melodic name is the **Rougarou**. This half man, half wolf is said to wander the swamps in search of human blood. It is alleged that after an encounter, unfortunate victims will themselves become Rougarous. Folklorists maintain that the legend followed early French settlers and French Canadians to Louisiana centuries ago based on the werewolf mythology of Europe. One early version of the tale involved the Rougarou attacking Catholics who did not uphold Lent. In whatever incarnation, the Rougarou took on some degree of celebrity status in popular culture when it was featured as part of the story line on an episode of the television series *NCIS: New Orleans*.

Honorable—or dishonorable—mention goes to a modern-day urban legend that circulated following the devastation of Hurricane Katrina in 2005: the **Drowned Looter**. It seems that a number of people had a friend, or a friend of a friend, who allegedly saw it firsthand. A looter was said to have broken into an empty home in New Orleans that was knee-deep in water after the hurricane. The owners had evacuated, so the looter easily gathered up their valuables in a pillowcase, escaping into the backyard. However, the looter did not know there was an in-ground swimming pool in the yard where he thought there were only a few feet of water. Stepping into the deep end of the pool by mistake, and unable to swim, the looter drowned. The owners allegedly returned home after the storm to find his dead body floating in the pool, still clutching the pillowcase full of their valuables.

ICONIC LOUISIANA FOOD

Some call it a thick soup, some call it a stew, but what is certain is its place at the heart of Louisiana culture. The dish, which was formally designated by the Louisiana legislature as the official state cuisine in 2004, incorporates the state's name right in the title: **Louisiana Gumbo**. There are many variations on this mouthwatering muddle of ingredients, but it almost always begins by cooking butter and flour to form a thick paste called a roux (pronounced "roo"). Next comes meat or seafood, spices, tomatoes, and a mix of vegetables, primarily okra. The recipe below features fresh Gulf shrimp and blue crabs for those lucky enough to get them.

Louisiana Gumbo (Serves 10)
1 cup melted butter
1 cup flour
2 onions, diced
1 cup lump crab meat
1 stalk celery, diced

1 seeded green bell pepper, diced
2 cloves garlic, minced
1 cup fresh okra, sliced
1 sprig fresh thyme leaves
2 qt shellfish stock
2 bay leaves
1 lb medium shrimp
1 cup shucked oysters
6 blue crabs
1 cup minced green onions
Salt, pepper, Tabasco, Worcestershire, and Creole spices to taste
6 cups cooked rice

1. Heat butter in a large heavy pot over high heat, then whisk in the flour until it sizzles. Reduce heat to medium, and continue whisking about 20 minutes until roux is browned.
2. Add onions, stirring with wooden spoon. Lower heat, and continue stirring about five minutes until roux turns dark brown.
3. Add lump crab meat and stir briefly, then add celery, bell peppers, garlic, and okra. Increase heat to medium and stir about three minutes before adding bay leaves, stock, and thyme.
4. Stir and bring to a boil, then reduce heat to low and simmer for 45 minutes, stirring occasionally.
5. Add blue crab meat, oysters, shrimp, and green onions, then cook for 15 minutes. Remove bay leaves before seasoning with salt, pepper, Creole spices, Tabasco, and Worcestershire to taste. Serve in bowls over cooked rice.

Source: Adapted from https://www.louisianatravel.com/culinary/recipes/louisiana-seafood-gumbo-recipe.

ODD LAWS

Under Louisiana statutes, stealing an alligator is considered theft, resulting in a possible jail sentence for the perpetrator. The infraction also includes taking an alligator's skin, or any part of an alligator, whether dead or alive.

Slightly less intimidating than a live gator is the tiny crawfish. However, no matter how small the miniature lobsterlike creature looks, stealing crawfish could generate a jail term of up to 10 years. Louisiana law prohibits taking crawfish that belong to another person by any means. Selling the purloined decapod for a profit is especially frowned upon. Although the statute refers to the freshwater crustaceans as "crawfish," the law covers any of their other aliases, such as crayfish, craydids, crawdaddies, crawdads, freshwater lobsters, mountain lobsters, mudbugs, or yabbies.

Although Louisiana is often considered America's epicenter of voodoo, the state provides mandates for practitioners that could result in up to 25 years in jail or a fine up to $25,000 if violated. A section of the state code called "Ritualistic Acts" was enacted for the preservation of "public peace, health, morals, safety, and welfare," covering what it specifies as ceremonies, initiations, observances, performances, practices, or rites. The act specifically forbids "the ingestion of human or animal blood or human or animal waste."

In New Orleans, the law bans fortune-telling, or in the language of the municipal code, "pretending to tell fortunes." It covers the use of cards, hands, or other methodology. While absolving religious worship, the law prohibits claiming the power to predict the future as well as solving romantic problems or finding hidden treasures. It also frowns on pledges to locate missing people and bans claiming to "bring together the bitterest enemies, converting them into staunchest friends."

Sometimes bitter enemies do not turn into staunch friends, resulting in a physical altercation. Such an assault could end in a jail term if false teeth are involved. Louisiana law considers biting someone while wearing dentures to be aggravated battery since the perpetrator is using something that is legally considered a weapon.

UNUSUAL DESTINATIONS

On May 23, 1934, a young couple stopped at a café in the small rural town of Gibsland, Louisiana. They bought a fried bologna sandwich and a BLT to go, but before they could finish their sandwiches, they had a date with destiny. A few minutes later, the couple—Depression-era bandits Clyde Barrow and Bonnie Parker—met their demise in a bullet-riddled car at the hands of law enforcement. Today, the **Bonnie and Clyde Ambush Museum** in Gibsland, about eight miles from the actual site of the roadside bloodbath, is housed in the building that was formerly the café where they bought their last meal. There are displays, photos, and artifacts, including Bonnie's hat as well as some of the gang's firearms. Visitors can also get directions to a monument down the road marking the alleged spot of the outlaws' last stand. In addition, the museum is the centerpiece of the annual Bonnie and Clyde Festival each May near the date of their death. It comes complete with reenactments, minus live ammunition and dead bodies.

Death is a constant at **Saint Louis Cemetery No. 1** in New Orleans. Because of the city's low elevation, the dead are often laid to rest in aboveground mausoleums instead of being buried. Visitors to the cemetery must be accompanied by a licensed tour guide, but even with an escort, some people tend to become spooked in such an unsettling atmosphere. Created in 1789, the cemetery occupies a small piece of land in the city's old section. It is therefore crowded with tombstones for what are said to be tens of thousands of the dead. The most sought-after tomb is that of voodoo queen Marie Laveau. After dying in 1881, she attracts not only tourists but also believers in voodoo who come to offer gifts and ask for favors.

In Morgan City, the International Petroleum Museum and Exposition is more commonly called the **Rig Museum**. There, visitors are invited to explore a real

At Saint Louis Cemetery No. 1 in New Orleans, the dead are often laid to rest in above-ground mausoleums instead of being buried because of the city's low elevation. Among thousands of tombs is the gravesite of voodoo queen Marie Laveau where people come to ask for favors. (Karen Foley/Dreamstime.com)

offshore drilling rig called "Mr. Charlie," which operated in the Gulf of Mexico from 1954 to 1986. Guests can explore the rig and learn about the lives of crew members involved in the offshore petroleum industry. According to museum staff, the "Mr. Charlie" exhibit is the only place in the world where the public can step aboard an authentic offshore drilling rig. The museum also displays artifacts and offers information about the history and global impact of offshore petroleum drilling, which staffers claim to be a Cajun-born industry.

At Avery Island, Louisiana, there is no question about the Cajun influence. The island, located on the Gulf Coast, is home to a wide variety of wildlife in its marshlands. However, to many people, it is better known as the center of the universe by virtue of being the site of the McIlhenny Company, better known as the **Tabasco Sauce Factory**. Visitors can tour the facility where the world-famous hot sauce is made and even get a firsthand view of the fields where the spicy peppers are grown. At this red-hot destination, guests receive what is called a "seed to sauce" experience. There is information on the history of both Tabasco sauce and the McIlhenny family who have made it on Avery Island for more than five generations since 1868. At the on-site restaurant, visitors can also sample classic Cajun and Southern dishes that are, needless to say, seasoned with what the company calls the Tabasco family of flavors.

DISTINCTIVE LOUISIANA WORDS AND SAYINGS

Cher: Not the legendary singer but a Cajun term of endearment that is similar to "my dear." If preferred, it can sometimes take the form of "cherie."

Fais-do-do: A rollicking Cajun dance party, often lasting through the wee hours.

Gris gris: Voodoo amulet that is believed to bring good luck and/or protect the wearer from evil.

Lagniappe: Pronounced "lan-YAP," it means a little something extra that is given as a gift or bonus, like an extra donut when buying a dozen.

N'Orleeyuns, N'Orlins, Noo Orleens, Noo Orlins, Noo Orleyuns: Acceptable pronunciations of New Orleans.

Further Reading

Allured, Janet, and Michael S. Martin. *Louisiana Legacies: Readings in the History of the Pelican State*. Malden, MA: Wiley-Blackwell, 2013.

Stuart, Bonnye. *It Happened in Louisiana: Remarkable Events That Shaped History*. Guilford, CT: Globe Pequot, 2015.

Wall, Bennett, and John Rodrigue (editors) and Light Townsend Cummins, Judith Kelleher Schafer, Edward F. Haas, and Michael L. Kurtz. *Louisiana: A History*. 6th edition. Malden, MA: Wiley-Blackwell, 2014.

Maine

> **FACT BOX**
>
> **Nickname:** The Pine Tree State
> **Statehood Granted:** 1820
> **Capital:** Augusta
> **Population:** 1,400,000
> **State Motto:** *Dirigo* (Latin: "I Direct" or "I Lead")
> **What Natives Call Themselves:** Mainers

STATE HISTORY

It might be said that America's day begins in Maine. Each morning, Eastern Maine is the first place in the contiguous United States to see the sunrise.

Located in the far northeast corner of the nation with a craggy shoreline that faces the Atlantic Ocean on the east, Maine is surrounded on two sides by Canada. It is attached to the rest of the continental United States by a border with New Hampshire.

Away from the shore, the state's massive timberlands lie to the west. According to the U.S. Department of Agriculture, Maine is the most forested state in the nation, with almost 90 percent of its land covered by trees.

There are also daunting mountains, with Maine's mile-high Mount Katahdin being the northern terminus of the Appalachian Trail. There are some who say that even after successfully hiking all the way from its southernmost point in Georgia, the Maine leg of the trail is the hardest.

That may be because there is a lot of Maine to cover. The state is larger than all five other New England States combined. One single Maine county, Aroostook, is bigger than Connecticut and Rhode Island put together.

Much of today's Maine was the result of Ice Age glaciers, including its soil structure and rock formations. After the ice retreated, Indigenous tribes such as the Kennebec and Penobscot occupied the land for thousands of years.

There are those who believe that Norsemen may have visited Maine around the year 1000, but the first European settlement in the region is generally felt to have been established by the French in 1604. At St. Croix Island, on Maine's border with Canada, France attempted to create a permanent colony. During the first winter, half of the French colonists perished. The survivors moved elsewhere, with the remains of their settlement later burned by the British.

In England, two expeditions set sail for America in 1607. One group went down in history by establishing Jamestown, Virginia. The other was led by George Popham, who planned to create an English settlement on the coast of Maine. However, in about a year, the dejected inhabitants of the Popham Colony returned to England. The combination of cold climate, rocky soil, and unfriendly relations with Native Americans caused its demise. Various other English settlements that were established along the Maine coastline during the early 1600s also faltered.

During this time, the territory's name became known as Maine. The first documented usage came in 1622 when an English royal charter declared that a group of colonists intended "the Province of Maine" to be the name of their future home in America. By 1665, "Maine" was being entered into official records. In 2001, the Maine legislature approved a resolution declaring that the state was originally named after the French province of Maine. For trivia buffs, Maine is the only American state with a name of only one syllable.

Although they were unconnected physically, Maine was originally part of the Massachusetts colony. Possibly because of its relative isolation and difficult conditions, by the early 1700s, only a handful of European settlements survived in today's Maine. There were mixed loyalties during the American Revolution (1775–1783), with some Maine residents supporting the English homeland.

Maine played a significant part in the War of 1812, with much of its land being occupied by British forces who hoped to annex it into Canada. After America's victory in that conflict when it ended in 1815, Britain ceded Maine to the United States.

Maine was still part of Massachusetts until 1820. At that time, the residents of Maine voted to become a separate state. Under the Missouri Compromise of 1820, one of the most controversial pre–Civil War acts of Congress, Maine was admitted as the 23rd state. It joined the Union as a free state at the same time that Missouri was admitted as a slave state in order to maintain the balance of power between North and South in the U.S. Senate.

During the Civil War (1861–1865), the 20th Maine Volunteer Infantry Regiment attained immortality under the command of the state's future governor, Joshua Lawrence Chamberlain. At the Battle of Gettysburg in 1863, Maine's troops famously kept the Union Army from being flanked by the Confederates.

During the Industrial Revolution of the late 1800s, Maine stayed largely agricultural. Today, residents of Maine's heavily wooded rural interior still find themselves relatively isolated, both from the state's coastal cities and from each other. Away from the water where large cities such as Augusta and Portland are located, many inland roads are impassable in winter with annual snowfall that averages between 60 and 110 inches, taller than the average human. Maine is famous for violent storms called "Nor'easters" that have been known to drop at least 10 inches of snow in a single day.

No doubt related to its weather, the state became the birthplace of earmuffs in 1873 when a teenager from Farmington, Maine, invented them. In 1912, Leon

Leonwood ("L. L.") Bean carried it a step forward by founding his namesake outdoor apparel company in Freeport, Maine, that is still based there.

URBAN LEGENDS

The legend of the **Cursed Tomb of Colonel Buck** began in the late 1700s when Colonel Jonathan Buck, founder of Bucksport and a justice of the peace, allegedly fell in love with a woman who became pregnant with his child. Buck supposedly forced her to leave town and raise the baby alone. After several years in destitution, the woman returned to Bucksport, asking the colonel for help. Instead, he is said to have condemned her as a witch, sentencing her to be burned at the stake. During the ensuing fire, the story goes that her leg fell off and rolled beyond the flames. The woman is said to have cursed Buck, crying out, "Your tomb shall bear the mark of a witch's foot for all eternity!" After Colonel Buck's death in 1795, his tomb indeed shows a mysterious stain in the form of what some say is a woman's leg. Despite repeated attempts to remove it, the stain keeps coming back. Today there is a small parking area nearby so that visitors can get a kick out of being photographed with the leggy legend.

With its lengthy coastline, Maine is home to maritime urban legends, including two notable **Lighthouse Hauntings**. At the Wood Island Lighthouse, it is said that the structure is haunted by the ghost of fisherman who killed his landlord in 1896 during an alcohol-fueled altercation over unpaid rent. The remorseful murderer later committed suicide inside the Wood Island Lighthouse. Soon, Wood Island Lighthouse keepers began reporting the sound of moaning and seeing unexplained shadows even though they were alone at the time. It is said that the manifestations belong to the repentant fisherman. The second urban legend takes place at the Seguin Island Lighthouse—a lonely, isolated structure that was the home of a lighthouse keeper and his wife. Noting that the woman became severely depressed from the loneliness, the husband arranged for a piano to be shipped to the island, hoping it would not only cheer his wife but provide entertainment on long, dreary nights. It is said that only one piece of music was included with the piano, which the wife was determined to master, playing it over and over again. Even when the husband had new music brought from the mainland, the wife stuck with the one piece she knew. Eventually, the lighthouse keeper is said to have gone mad from the incessant melody, destroying the piano with an ax. When the wife tried to stop him, he killed her with the same ax. Sorrowfully realizing what he had done, he then killed himself. Locals, wondering why the lighthouse was not lit, rowed to the island and discovered the gruesome scene. Today, it is said that visitors to the isolated spot can still hear the sound of an eerie song on a ghostly piano, no doubt over and over.

Honorable mention goes to the **Mount Hope Cemetery** in Bangor, which was established in 1836 and is the final resting place for about 30,000 of the departed. Today, some visitors report seeing unexplained shadows and ghostly figures roaming the grounds. That itself makes for a fine urban legend, but Mount

Maine-ly Murder

There's just something about the brooding backwoods of Maine, which comprise most of the state away from the coastline. Two of television's most memorable mystery programs were based in Maine. The spooky, vampire-laden *Dark Shadows* took place in the fictional town of Collinsport, Maine. The long-running *Murder She Wrote* was based in Cabot Cove, Maine, a fictitious town where the carnage was so extreme that it earned a spot among real-life law enforcement officials as shorthand for an unusual spike in local murder rates. However, the king of Maine-style mayhem is the aptly named Stephen King. Most of the books by King, a lifelong Mainer, are set in his home state. Some include fictional towns that tourists eagerly seek but never find, such as Chamberlain, Chester's Mills, Derry, Haven, and Ludlow. King wrote *Carrie*, his first novel, while teaching school in Bangor, Maine, the town where he still resides. On the home's heavy wrought-iron fence, drop-in guests are discouraged by foreboding black metal bats.

The aptly-named king of Maine-style mayhem is master of the macabre Stephen King, pictured here. Most of his best-selling books are set in his home state of Maine, where he still resides. (Nufather/Dreamstime.com)

Hope attained true immortality when it served as the location for filming the 1989 movie *Pet Sematary*, based on the book by Maine's native son Stephen King.

ICONIC MAINE FOOD

When it comes to food, the word that often springs to mind with "Maine" is "lobster," with the word that often follows "lobster" being "rolls." The classic cooking technique for **Maine Lobster Rolls** involves either boiling or steaming the lobster. Many cooks prefer steaming for lobster rolls, as in the recipe below, since steaming is said to yield meat that is more tender and flavorful as well as preventing the danger of overcooking. Although lobster rolls contain very few ingredients, the sweet lobster meat itself must reign supreme and not be overwhelmed by the accompaniments.

Maine Lobster Rolls (Yields 4)
2 lobsters (about 1½ lb each), steamed
3–4 Tbsp high-quality mayonnaise
Dash of freshly squeezed lemon juice (optional)
Sea salt and freshly ground black pepper to taste
4 leaves of Boston lettuce
4 New England–style hotdog buns, flat sided and split on top
2 Tbsp unsalted butter, softened

1. After steaming lobsters, remove tail and claw meat, then cut meat into ½-inch chunks. Refrigerate until chilled.
2. After chilling, discard any liquid that has drained from the meat, then gently toss lobster with mayonnaise so the lobster is coated, but not weighed down by the mayonnaise.
3. Season to taste with salt and pepper if needed. If more "tang" is desired, add a dash of fresh lemon juice.
4. Cover the lobster mixture, and refrigerate at least 30 minutes, up to 6–8 hours.
5. When ready to serve, butter the sides of the hotdog buns, and grill on preheated griddle at medium heat about 1–2 minutes per side, until toasted.
6. Place a lettuce leaf in each griddled bun, then mound each with ¼ of the lobster mixture. Serve immediately.

Source: Adapted from https://stripedspatula.com/maine-lobster-rolls.

ODD LAWS

Numerous internet sites circulate the tale that the Maine legislature passed an official state law making it illegal to add tomatoes to clam chowder. Some accept it as fact, while others dismiss it as an urban legend. The truth actually lies somewhere in between. In 1939, a Maine assemblyman did indeed attempt to pass legislation outlawing tomatoes in clam chowder. The bill never became law, but the sentiment remains—as unwary visitors might discover if they attempt to order tomato-y Manhattan Clam Chowder in Maine.

In the town of Wells, Maine, it is unlawful to place an advertisement in a cemetery. Under the municipal code, such commercialism is included under "Prohibited Acts." The code bans willful defacement, disfigurement, marking, or tampering with anything on cemetery grounds that is designed as a memorial. Advertising signs are also prohibited on fences, railings, or other prime locations near the dead, who are notoriously unenthusiastic consumers.

In Freeport, Maine, it would definitely be unlawful to display cemetery advertisements promoting the sale of mercury fever thermometers. Under the town's municipal code, the sale of mercury thermometers to patients and the general public is prohibited, except by prescription, including online retail. If such a thermometer does manage to be obtained, the ordinance states that the manufacturer must supply clear instructions on handling the thermometer to avoid breakage as well as how to clean up afterward if all else fails.

Maine, having the largest moose population in the contiguous United States, has some fairly stringent laws about its wildlife. According to Maine statutes, possession of either monk parakeets or mute swans is prohibited. Moreover, under the statute, a permit is required to have certain animals as pets, specifically including elephants, giraffes, hippos, hyenas, and long-nosed armadillos.

Most laws take care not to promote or otherwise single out private businesses, but the municipal code in the town of South Berwick, Maine, makes an exception. As directly quoted from the local statute, "No person shall park a vehicle at any time upon any of the streets or parts of streets described: Main St. (West) in front of Dunkin Donuts to a point 25 feet south." It makes a succinct exception as follows, again quoting directly: "Police only."

UNUSUAL DESTINATIONS

Among the deserts of the world, several generally come to mind, such as the Sahara or Gobi. But Maine . . . ? The Pine Tree State is not what most people envision when they think of parched, arid, sandy places. But the **Desert of Maine** in Freeport has been a destination for the curious since 1925. It is one of those cases of making lemonade when life hands out lemons. Owned by a family of farmers since 1797, the soil gradually wore away due to erosion, exposing 40 acres of underlying glacial silt that resembles a desert. A special point of interest is a springhouse that was built in 1938; by 1962, it was completely covered by drifting sand dunes. Today, the Desert of Maine offers a campsite, tours, and a photo opportunity with a giant statue of a camel, an animal that is not native to Maine.

The **International Cryptozoology Museum** (ICM) in Portland claims to be the world's only museum exploring the study of what the owner calls "hidden animals." At the ICM, Bigfoot, Sasquatch, Yeti, and the Loch Ness Monster are joined by their lesser-known cousins such as the Kraken, Mothman, Myakka, and Jersey Devil. On display are artifacts, photographs, replicas, and specimens such as alleged footprint casts, hair samples, and fecal material. For many visitors, the prime photo opportunity is having their picture taken while standing next to the Crookston Bigfoot, which weighs 300 pounds, stands over eight feet tall, and is said to be life-size for that particular species.

For those who enjoy all sorts of large creatures, especially when they are made of milk chocolate, **Lenny the Chocolate Moose** at Len Libby Candies in Scarborough makes the ideal photo opportunity. Pun aside (think of chocolate "mousse"), Lenny is said to be the world's largest moose made entirely of chocolate. Visitors can watch a video about the creation of Lenny, who is the life-size 1,700-pound milk chocolate star of what is called an edible animal habitat. Nearby are some dark chocolate bears coexisting with Lenny around a blue-tinted white chocolate pond. It must be noted that Maine has the largest moose population in the contiguous United States. Technically, Alaska has more, but it is unknown if any are made of chocolate.

Wild Blueberry Land in Columbia Falls spotlights another incredible edible. Inside what is called the World's Largest Blueberry, fans of the tasty blue fruit will find a bakery, café, and gift shop. Visitors tend to be delighted (and therefore are not blue) when they discover a tempting array of all things blueberry: homemade baked goods such as blueberry muffins and scones along with ice cream, jams, and sauces. Maine's wild blueberries comprise a major part of the state's economy and are certainly integral to Wild Blueberry Land.

Honorable mention goes to the **Umbrella Cover Museum** at Peaks Island, Maine. Visitors must take a ferry to reach the museum, which fans say is part of its charm. The facility was born when the owner noticed that the sheathlike covers on new umbrellas are discarded almost immediately and never seen again. This museum, which houses about 2,000 umbrella covers, is "dedicated to the appreciation of the mundane in everyday life" as well as finding wonder and beauty in the simplest things. Curating what is called the world's first and only umbrella cover museum, its director states, "There is always a story behind the cover."

DISTINCTIVE MAINE WORDS AND SAYINGS

Ayuh: This variation of "yes" or "yeah" is so representative of Maine that some think it should be on the state flag. It can actually mean more than just an affirmative answer, serving as a general acknowledgment.

County, the: Of Maine's 16 counties, only one is known by virtually everyone in the state without needing to say the actual name: Aroostook, the largest county east of the Mississippi River.

Down: Up. As in "Down East." With the term said to have evolved from sailing terminology, a person from Northern Maine is often called a "Down-easter."

From away: Anyone not born and raised in Maine, preferably going back three generations.

Italian: Not necessarily someone from sunny Italy, but a sandwich called a "sub" or "hero" elsewhere and often sold at bait shops in Maine.

Further Reading

Gratwick, Harry. *Hidden History of Maine*. Charleston, SC: History Press, 2010.
Griffin, Nancy. *How Maine Changed the World*. Guilford, CT: Globe Pequot, 2017.
Woodard, Colin. *The Lobster Coast: Rebels, Rusticators, and the Struggle for a Forgotten Frontier*. New York: Penguin Books, 2005.

Maryland

FACT BOX

Nickname: The Old Line State
Statehood Granted: 1788
Capital: Annapolis
Population: 6,000,000
State Motto: *Fatti maschii, parole femine* (Italian: "Manly Deeds, Womanly Words," which some Maryland officials translate as "Strong Deeds, Gentle Words")
What Natives Call Themselves: Marylanders

STATE HISTORY

One of the first things visitors to Maryland tend to notice is the state flag, which is unique among the 50 states and felt by many to be extremely cool. Maryland's flag, dating from the 1600s, is based on the heraldic banner of England's Lord Baltimore. Therefore, in keeping with the time frame, it may be altogether fitting that a Maryland law signed in 1962 declared the official state sport to be *jousting*.

In 1632, Lord Baltimore was granted a royal charter for present-day Maryland by England's King Charles I. The site was an appealing one, lying on the American seacoast halfway between the northern and southern colonies. For the settlement's name, Lord Baltimore originally proposed "Crescentia" from the Latin, symbolizing growth. However, the king preferred "Terra Mariae," or Mary Land, to honor his wife, Henrietta Maria, known in England as Queen Mary.

The king won, but at least it seemed to be an appropriate name since Queen Henrietta Maria was Roman Catholic, and the colony was created as a refuge for English Catholics who were being persecuted.

When the first colonists arrived at today's Maryland in 1634, they found Native Americans who had been there for thousands of years, such as the Lenape, Piscataway, and Shawnee.

Maryland's early economy was based on tobacco plantations. At first, laborers could be recruited among indentured servants from England who exchanged work for their passage to the New World. However, as plantations grew larger to generate increased profits and as the number of indentured laborers arriving from England decreased, enslaved people from Africa were brought to Maryland, which grew to depend on slave labor for prosperity.

By the mid-1700s, there was ongoing border strife between Maryland and its neighbor, Pennsylvania. Between 1763 and 1767, two surveyors, Charles Mason and Jeremiah Dixon, were tasked with setting official boundaries. The borders they set, later known as the Mason-Dixon Line, not only formalized Maryland's boundary but also became the figurative line of demarcation between America's Northern and Southern states.

During the American Revolution (1775–1783), Maryland's troops distinguished themselves so highly that according to tradition, George Washington was particularly impressed with the state's soldiers, who were called the "Maryland Line." It is said that Washington himself dubbed Maryland "the Old Line State."

Maryland's unique state flag, dating from the 1600s, is based on the heraldic banner of England's Lord Baltimore who founded the Maryland colony in 1632. (StockNinja Studio/Dreamstime.com)

In 1788, Maryland became the seventh state admitted to the Union. Maryland then donated some of its land for the creation of America's capital city, Washington, DC.

Even though Maryland was south of the Mason-Dixon Line, the state remained in the Union during the Civil War (1861–1865). In April 1861, secessionists attacked federal troops who were marching through Baltimore, Maryland, on their way to Washington, DC, marking the first bloodshed of the war.

Maryland enjoyed prosperity after the Civil War. With its close proximity to the nation's capital, it has traditionally attracted a number of influential residents.

Along with Annapolis, Maryland, being the home of the U.S. Naval Academy, the Maryland State House in Annapolis can boast its own place in history. Construction on the building was begun in 1772, prior to the American Revolution. Not only does the building feature an imposing dome, but a lightning rod on top is said to have been made by Benjamin Franklin himself. The Maryland State House served as the U.S. Capitol in 1783 and 1784 and remains America's oldest state capitol building still in continuous legislative use.

As many schoolchildren know, America's national anthem was written by Francis Scott Key, who was a Maryland lawyer. The story is that he wrote *The Star-Spangled*

> **De-lighted**
>
> During the War of 1812, the coastal town of St. Michaels, Maryland, was a major target for the British fleet moving up Chesapeake Bay. With St. Michaels being the site of strategic shipyards and having an American militia unit stationed there, townspeople knew they would be under heavy attack by enemy bombardment. Under cover of darkness, the people of St. Michaels blacked out their house lights, hanging bright lanterns on treetops outside town. Seeing those decoy lights, the British overshot the town so badly that only one house was struck by a cannonball. St. Michaels became known as "the Town That Fooled the British." Another Maryland town, Havre de Grace, is known for the high quality of duck decoys made there, even being home to a Decoy Museum. Although Havre de Grace calls itself the Decoy Capital of the World, there are some who might say the honor should go to St. Michaels.

Banner during the War of 1812 while watching the bombardment of Fort McHenry in Baltimore Harbor. Key, who is buried in Maryland, was a distant cousin of the Jazz Age writer F. Scott Fitzgerald. Alongside, his equally headline-making wife, Zelda, the author of *The Great Gatsby*, is also buried in Maryland.

The unmarked gravesite of Lincoln assassin John Wilkes Booth is said to be located in his family's cemetery plot in Baltimore, where Booth grew up. The grave of another player in the assassination story, Samuel Mudd, the doctor who treated Booth's broken leg, can also be found in Maryland.

However, many sources would claim that the most famous gravesite among the celebrity dead of Maryland is legendary author Edgar Allan Poe, who is said to have created the horror genre in fiction. Poe died in 1849, but starting in the 1930s, a Baltimore tradition was the annual appearance of an unidentified black-clad person dubbed "the Poe Toaster." Until 2010, when the yearly nocturnal visits ceased, a shrouded figure arrived during the wee hours of each January 19, Poe's birthday. After toasting the writer with a glass of cognac, roses were left at Poe's grave along with the unfinished bottle of cognac.

One of the roses was said to be for Poe's beloved young wife Virginia, whose remains were almost lost when the cemetery where she had been laid to rest in 1847 was destroyed. In a Poe-like development during 1883, an admirer of the author reportedly rescued Virginia's bones just at the moment when they were about to be discarded as "Unclaimed," storing them under his bed. In 1885, her remains were reburied along with her husband's.

In the tapestry of African American history, Maryland plays a significant role through the legacy of such towering figures as Frederick Douglass and Harriet Tubman. Both were able to escape a life of slavery in Maryland, devoting their lives to helping other enslaved people. Douglass was a national leader in the abolitionist movement, speaking and writing eloquently about the plight of people condemned to slavery. Tubman repeatedly returned to the South after her own escape, courageously rescuing dozens of slaves via the network of safe houses known as the Underground Railroad. According to the Maryland Office of Tourism, "Maryland is the most powerful Underground Railroad storytelling destination in the world," with the state being the location of numerous historic sites as well as tours honoring Douglass and Tubman.

Maryland was also the home of surveyor Benjamin Banneker, an African American who helped establish the boundaries of Washington, DC, in 1791. Continuing Maryland's legacy in Black history, in 1967, Thurgood Marshall of Baltimore became the first African American Justice on the U.S. Supreme Court.

URBAN LEGENDS

Scotland may have its Loch Ness monster, nicknamed Nessie, but Maryland's Chesapeake Bay has its own alleged sea monster: **Chessie**. The aquatic urban legend of Maryland is said to have begun in 1936 when a helicopter crew said they spotted "something reptilian and unknown in the water." From that nondescript beginning, various future sightings have been claimed. A video made in 1982 purports to capture something brownish moving from side to side. Some sources note that misguided manatees from Florida have been spotted in Chesapeake Bay. In any case, Maryland has adopted the legend of Chessie to promote the bay's environmental health. Maryland's Department of Natural Resources uses a friendly-looking cartoon image of Chessie in their educational materials to promote protecting the resources of Chesapeake Bay and cutting down on pollution.

For believers in the **Curse of Moll Dyer**, a young woman in Leonardtown, Maryland, was cut down in her prime, not by pollution but by her neighbors. During the late 1600s, some Marylanders may have taken the Salem Witch Trials in Massachusetts (1692–1693) too much to heart. Villagers accused Moll Dyer of witchcraft, chasing the young woman out of her home on a frigid winter night. Her dead body was later found frozen to a large stone where she had stopped to rest from her pursuers. The legend has it that her spirit haunts the town in search of the men who caused her death and that no crops will grow near the spot where she died. Far from spurning the legend, Leonardtown has embraced it. In 1972, the boulder where Moll allegedly died was moved from the woods to the Leonardtown Courthouse lawn. According to the legend, those who approach it may become dizzy and faint. Through the names of Moll Dyer Road and a local creek, Moll Dyer's Run, the persecuted woman has also been honored, albeit posthumously.

Maryland's Beltsville Agricultural Research Center was opened in 1910 by the U.S. Department of Agriculture (USDA). According to a longtime urban legend, the **Goatman** was a research center scientist whose experiment involving goats went horribly wrong, resulting in a bizarre mutation. The Goatman legend lives on as half human and half animal who manages to wield an ax as he stalks the back roads of Beltsville, attacking everything from dogs to automobiles and frightening amorous teenagers in parked cars. The Goatman story has been repeated not only in local newspapers but also in the *Washington Post* to the point where the USDA publicly denied any accidental goat mutations at the Beltsville facility by one of its scientists, whose name may or may not have been Billy.

ICONIC MARYLAND FOOD

Maryland is famed for its bounty of Chesapeake blue crabs. After all, it was named the official crustacean of Maryland and is at the center of the state's largest commercial fishery. Native Americans and the European settlers who colonized the Chesapeake Bay area in the 1600s found the blue crab to be an important food item. Many Marylanders even know how to tell the genders of blue crabs apart by utilizing nearby landmarks: the abdomen of the male is shaped like the Washington Monument, while that of a mature female looks like the dome of the U. S. Capitol building. The state is known for its classic **Maryland Crab Cakes** as seen in this recipe:

> **Maryland Crab Cakes** (Yields 6 cakes)
> 1 lb lump Maryland crabmeat
> ½ cup bread crumbs
> 1 egg, beaten
> 5 Tbsp mayonnaise
> 1 Tbsp finely chopped parsley
> 1 Tbsp Worcestershire sauce
> 1 tsp prepared mustard
> 1 Tbsp Old Bay seasoning
> Corn oil for frying

1. Mix together bread crumbs, egg, mayonnaise, parsley, Worcestershire sauce, mustard, and seasoning.
2. Pour mixture over crabmeat, folding in carefully by hand so as not to break up the lumps of crabmeat.
3. Form by hand into six cakes and pat until just firm.
4. Deep-fry in corn oil at about 350°F for 2–3 minutes until cakes are golden brown.

Source: Adapted from https://www.visitmaryland.org/article/Maryland-Crab-Cakes-Recipe.

ODD LAWS

Even though Scotland proudly claims the purple thistle as its national emblem, the prickly plant can get Maryland residents in trouble with authorities. Under state law, thistles have been declared "prohibited noxious weeds" and are banned from being grown on any property in Maryland, including backyard gardens. The rationale, according to the Maryland Department of Agriculture, is to protect farmland and lawns from the invasive plant. Offenders can be prosecuted by the State's Attorney and sentenced to fine and/or imprisonment. Incidentally, Scotland remains partial to the thistle even if it is shunned in Maryland, and for good reason. According to legend, Norse invaders were sneaking up on a Scottish army encampment one night when a barefoot Norseman stepped on a prickly thistle. He yelled out in pain, the Scotsmen were alerted to the danger, and Scotland was saved.

If the sore Norseman had been in the city of Rockville, Maryland, and yelled out a bad word when his foot met the thistle, he would have been breaking the law. In Rockville, it is unlawful to "profanely curse and swear or use obscene language upon or near any street, sidewalk or highway" within the hearing of other people. The Rockville Municipal Code considers it disorderly conduct.

The city of Rockville also frowns upon people stepping in its public fountains, presumably even to ease the pain of a foot stabbed by a prickly plant. Apart from specifically designated swimming pools, no person may "wade or otherwise immerse any part of his body in any City-owned fountain." Rockville residents should not even think about tossing "trash, debris or any other matter whatsoever" into a city-owned fountain because that would be unlawful too.

Once again in Rockville, some might say the Christmas spirit is on shaky legal ground if homeowners celebrate by festooning their property with a massive display of Christmas lights. Under the Rockville Municipal Code, doing so may be considered "unreasonable operation of outdoor illumination devices." The law aims to prohibit interfering with "the use or enjoyment of abutting or nearby property." Therefore, it is gracious to offer a friendly holiday greeting to neighbors in Rockville as long as it is not accompanied by a mammoth light show.

So as not to single out Rockville, in 1982 the people of Garrett Park, Maryland, voted overwhelmingly to ban the processing, production, storage, transportation, disposal, or use of nuclear weapons in their town. Under its Municipal Code, Garrett Park is officially a "Nuclear Free Zone," with violators subject to a $100 fine. The law must be obeyed to avoid any fallout.

UNUSUAL DESTINATIONS

There are those who believe that Dr. Samuel Mudd was a coconspirator in the murder of Abraham Lincoln, just as there are supporters who maintain that the doctor was simply a Good Samaritan in the wrong place at the wrong time. The **Dr. Samuel Mudd House Museum** in Waldorf, Maryland, may offer clues for both groups. Dr. Mudd treated assassin John Wilkes Booth's broken leg after Booth killed Lincoln at Ford's Theater in 1865. Subsequently, Mudd was incriminated in the assassination plot and narrowly avoided execution, being sentenced to life in prison. After ultimately being pardoned, Mudd returned to the home that is today the museum bearing his name. It houses many Civil War–era artifacts that were there the night Booth dropped in. Visitors may also learn the truth of whether the phrase, "His name is mud," signifying an unpopular person, was derived from Dr. Sam.

Not to be confused with "cryptozoology" (the study of alleged creatures such as Bigfoot), "cryptography" is the art of writing and breaking codes. Affiliated with America's top-secret National Security Agency (NSA), the **National Cryptologic Museum** is said to be the first public museum of the nation's intelligence service. Located near NSA headquarters in Annapolis Junction, Maryland, the museum's collection includes displays illuminating the machines and code-breakers assigned to solving their puzzles. Some artifacts predate the American Revolution. The important role of women, African Americans, and Native Americans are highlighted as well as codes used by hobos. One of the most popular attractions is the exhibit of working models of the German Enigma machines from World War II, which are available for visitors to try out.

The **Nutshell Studies of Unexplained Death** are not named for an individual named Nutshell, but as its founder stated, they were created to "convict the guilty, clear the innocent, and find the truth in a nutshell." Throughout the first half of the 20th century, Mrs. Frances Glessner Lee dedicated herself to advancing forensics to help solve crimes. While death and dollhouses are not often a natural pairing, she created miniature dioramas of crime scenes for police and coroners whose investigative resources were limited. Today the perfectly proportioned Nutshell Studies are located in the Maryland Medical Examiner's Office at Baltimore. They are based on actual crime scenes, with tiny details such as bullet holes and overturned cups as well as miniature corpses in a wide range of gruesome positions. The Nutshell Studies are still used as training tools and are available for viewing by appointment through the Medical Examiner's Office. Mrs. Lee and her crime scene creations have been integral to plotlines in such hit television programs as *CSI* and *NCIS* and were the subject of a documentary titled *Of Dolls and Murder*. In addition, Mrs. Lee is said to be partly the inspiration for supersleuth Jessica Fletcher on TV's *Murder, She Wrote*.

DISTINCTIVE MARYLAND WORDS AND SAYINGS

Bawlmer: An acceptable two-syllable pronunciation of "Baltimore." Some go even further, using "Nap" as a one-syllable abbreviation for "Annapolis."

Chicken Necker: An individual who is not from Maryland's eastern shore, a phrase said to be derived from visitors to the oceanfront who often use chicken necks to catch crabs from the pier.

Merlin/Marilyn: Neither a mythical magician nor a filmland icon, both are accepted ways of pronouncing "Maryland."

Snowball: Not necessarily a projectile to be thrown in wintertime, but a summertime treat made from shaved ice and sold from stands that pop up across Maryland.

Terps: Shorthand for Terrapins, mascot for University of Maryland athletics. It honors the diamondback terrapin turtles that inhabit the Chesapeake Bay region, with an aggressive turtle in the Terps logo appearing to be a distinctly Ninja-looking warrior.

Them O's: Referring to the Baltimore Orioles baseball team, as in "How 'bout them O's?"

Further Reading

Brugger, Robert. *Maryland, a Middle Temperament: 1634–1980*. Baltimore, MD: Johns Hopkins University Press, 1988.

Chappelle, Susan. *Maryland: A History*. Baltimore, MD: Johns Hopkins University Press, 1986.

Hedberg, Jacqueline Simmons. *Plantations, Slavery and Freedom on Maryland's Eastern Shore*. Charleston, SC: History Press, 2019.

Massachusetts

FACT BOX

Nickname: The Bay State
Statehood Granted: 1788
Capital: Boston
Population: 7,000,000
State Motto: *Ense petit placidam sub libertate quietem* (Latin: "By the Sword We Seek Peace under Liberty")
What Natives Call Themselves: Bay Staters (official), Massachusites (traditional)

STATE HISTORY

For centuries, present-day Massachusetts was occupied by Native Americans who constructed longhouses for their homes. The Native people cultivated beans, corn, and squash to accompany a diet that relied on hunting and fishing. Fishing would remain vital to Massachusetts, with Cape Cod not only named for a fish but also shaped like a fishhook.

When Europeans arrived in the 1600s, the Native American groups inhabiting today's Massachusetts included the Narragansett, Wampanoag, and Massachusett. The state's name was derived from the latter tribe.

In 1620, a ship called the *Mayflower* arrived near present-day Plymouth, Massachusetts, carrying people who would form the first permanent English colony in New England. Today called the Pilgrims, they founded their settlement for religious reasons as opposed to the first successful English colony in North America, the for-profit Jamestown in Virginia, which had been established in 1607.

One of the most popular narratives in the American tradition is the story of the first Thanksgiving. According to legend, Wampanoag people under their leader Massasoit helped the Pilgrims survive, celebrating with them in 1621 as they shared a meal to give thanks.

Numerous place-names in Massachusetts commemorate the Native culture that had thrived there for centuries. However, their names were often all that remained after being decimated by European-borne diseases such as influenza and smallpox, to which they had no resistance. In the winter of 1623, Massasoit himself became ill.

The Pilgrims were followed by English Puritans who established the Massachusetts Bay Colony near today's city of Boston in 1630. They had been harassed in England for their religious beliefs and were seeking tolerance in their New World colony. That tolerance did not often extend to those whose beliefs were different from their own.

As the 1600s progressed, more English colonists arrived in Massachusetts. A conflict known as King Philip's War took place from 1675 to 1676 as Native American tribes in Massachusetts fought against the influx of Europeans. The war was named for a Wampanoag chief whose father was the deceased Massasoit. Not all the newly arrived colonists coexisted as peacefully with the Natives as the Pilgrims had. Some historians report a tremendously high casualty rate among Native Americans as a result of King Philip's War, with some Native survivors being sold into slavery.

According to legend, Native American people under their leader Massasoit (portrayed here in a statue) helped the Pilgrims survive. They shared a meal to give thanks that evolved into today's Thanksgiving holiday. (Marcos Souza/Dreamstime.com)

Early Massachusetts settlers dealt no less harshly with each other. In 1692 and 1693, the town of Salem saw many of its citizens accusing fellow colonists of witchcraft. Sometimes the victims' alleged crimes were the result of religious differences; others were based simply on a squabble with a neighbor. At Salem, several hundred people were accused of witchcraft, with the majority being women. Of the 19 who were executed, 14 were women. Many others died in jail.

In the late 1700s, Massachusetts became virtually synonymous with the movement toward American independence. Crispus Attucks was an African American who was killed at what was called the Boston Massacre in 1770, becoming known to many as the first casualty of the American Revolution. Events such as the Boston Tea Party in 1773 escalated into the opening salvos of the Revolution at the Massachusetts towns of Lexington and Concord in 1775. Such notables as John Adams, Samuel Adams, and John Hancock all hailed from Massachusetts, which, in 1788, after the American victory, became the new nation's sixth state.

Technically, Massachusetts calls itself a commonwealth. As a holdover from English Common Law, a "commonwealth" was generally defined as government by the people, although in reality, it is equivalent to other American states.

In the years leading to the Civil War, Massachusetts was a center of intellectualism, literary achievement, and abolitionist spirit. Notable residents from that era include Frederick Douglass, Ralph Waldo Emerson, Henry David Thoreau, and Sojourner Truth. After the war began, Massachusetts was the first state to recruit an African American regiment, the 54th Massachusetts Infantry, spotlighted in the 1989 film *Glory*.

After the Civil War, Massachusetts adapted quickly to the Industrial Revolution.

As one of the first American colonies to be established, Massachusetts has a long history, which has led to its being able to boast a number of "firsts." In the first part of the 1600s alone, Massachusetts can claim to have been the site of the first public park in America, Boston Common, created in 1634. The Boston Latin Grammar School, founded in 1635, was the first American public secondary school. America's first university, Harvard, was established in 1636. In 1639, Boston was the site of the first free public school in America and also became home to the first American public library in 1653.

Those achievements in such a short time are all the more extraordinary considering that the Pilgrims arrived in 1620 and the Massachusetts Bay Puritans in 1630. Both groups had to spend a lot of time building homes, carving farms out of the wilderness, growing food, and trying to survive Massachusetts winters.

Massachusetts continued its tradition of landmark achievements for the nation and the world. In 1876, the first telephone was demonstrated by Alexander Graham Bell in Boston. The first American subway system was built in 1898 in Boston, much to the chagrin of some New Yorkers whose own official subway system did not open until 1904. In Auburn, Massachusetts, Dr. Robert Goddard built and launched the world's first liquid-fueled rocket in 1926, ushering in the Space Age. Pioneering work in computers took place at the Massachusetts Institute of Technology (MIT) starting in 1927. Harvard is first in the world for its number of Nobel laureates, with MIT close behind.

However, some sports fans cite another notable "first." In 1891, the first basketball game took place in Springfield, Massachusetts. Physical education instructor James Naismith wanted something that could be played indoors during the cold Massachusetts winter. The first game consisted of using two peach baskets and a soccer ball, from which the name of the game was derived. Play had to be stopped each time a point was scored so the janitor could bring a ladder and retrieve the ball from the peach basket. Through later refinements, no janitors were needed.

URBAN LEGENDS

The **Bridgewater Triangle** in Southeast Massachusetts consists of about 200 acres near the Freetown-Fall River State Forest that is said to be one of the most haunted forests in the world. According to the legend, supernatural occurrences in the

> ### Of Bee Gees and Buckaroos
>
> Many people find that one of the most haunting classic rock songs is *Massachusetts*, by the Bee Gees. The musicians, who grew up in Australia, had never been to Massachusetts when they wrote the song. They composed it on a sightseeing boat ride around New York City during their first U.S. tour, choosing the name because they liked the sound of the word "Massachusetts." It topped the charts in America as well as abroad where it became the first number-one hit single by a non-Japanese artist on Japan's official hit chart. Some feel it was even more of a cross-cultural phenomenon when it was recorded by American country singer Buck Owens, born in Sherman, Texas. Many Massachusetts residents find the song to be a fitting tribute to their state and, once heard, is almost impossible to get out of one's head.

Bridgewater Triangle abound. There have been reports of unidentified flying objects (UFOs) as well as balls of fire, giant snakes, poltergeists, floating orbs of light, and Bigfoot sightings. One of the claims is that the Triangle is home to "Thunderbirds," which are said to be giant flying creatures resembling pterodactyls, with wingspans of around 10 feet. The urban legend maintains that the Bridgewater Triangle was cursed by Native Americans due to their treatment by the colonial settlers who encroached on their ancestral land.

Pukwudgies, said to be small humanlike creatures, may sound like something out of the *Harry Potter* series (which indeed they are), but were known to the Wampanoag people centuries before. According to the urban legend, they are tricksters with smooth gray skin who inhabit swampy areas of Eastern Massachusetts. Standing about 2–3 feet tall, they can appear and disappear at will; in fact, the word "Pukwudgie" is said to be translated from the Wampanoag as "little wild man of the woods that vanishes." The legend maintains that they were once friendly to humans, until something unknown happened to turn the Pukwudgies bad. They are said to attack human victims with spears, blind people with sand, launch poison arrows, start fires, and use magic to lure people to their deaths by pushing them off cliffs. There are references to Pukwudgies in Massachusetts resident Henry Wadsworth Longfellow's epic poem *The Song of Hiawatha*. However, for many, the ultimate accolade may be as the name of one of four houses of witchcraft and wizardry in J. K. Rowling's *Harry Potter* universe.

At **Scargo Lake** near Dennis, Massachusetts, an urban legend evolved from Native American lore. It is said that the spirit of a Native American princess mourns her lost love by haunting the lake, where visitors report hearing the sounds of crying or moaning. A variation is that the mythical princess dug a hole in the ground, with the dirt she removed forming Scargo Hill. The hole was said to fill with water during autumn rains, drowning the princess but canonizing her as a sacrifice that keeps the present-day lake stocked with a bountiful supply of fish. For those who prefer their urban legends to come stocked with aliens, there have been reports that a UFO crashed into the lake in 1971. Ever since that allegedly otherworldly incident, locals are said to have noted eerie sounds and strange lights emanating from the depths of the lake's waters.

ICONIC MASSACHUSETTS FOOD

When a lowly bean becomes designated by the Commonwealth of Massachusetts as an official food, and a major American city such as Boston gains the nickname "Beantown," it is not surprising that **Boston Baked Beans** are so closely related to Massachusetts. The connection goes back to colonial times. Historians note that religious beliefs in the Massachusetts Bay Colony discouraged cooking on the Sabbath, which ran from sundown Saturday to sundown Sunday. Baked beans made a warm, filling supper on Saturday night with leftovers that could be eaten, while still warm from the fire, as a hearty Sunday morning breakfast. Salt pork and bacon were eventually substituted for the bear fat that was originally used in colonial days.

> **Boston Baked Beans** (Serves 6)
> 2 cups dried navy beans
> ½ lb salt pork or bacon, chopped and divided
> ⅓ cup granulated sugar
> ⅔ cup dark molasses
> 1 tsp dry mustard
> 1 tsp ground white pepper
> 1 tsp salt

1. Soak beans overnight in cold water.
2. Preheat oven to 400°F.
3. Place beans in a heavy saucepan and fill with water to cover by about half an inch.
4. Boil 25–30 minutes, until just tender. To test, place a bean between thumb and forefinger and pinch; if done, the outer shell should slip off. Drain, rinse, and reserve the liquid.
5. Place half the pork at the bottom of a large ovenproof pot, then add beans, sugar, molasses, dry mustard, white pepper, salt, and reserved liquid. Top with remaining pork.
6. Cover and bake about 4½ hours, stirring occasionally and adding more water as needed. Let beans rest 30 minutes before serving.

Source: Adapted from https://newengland.com/today/food/boston-style-baked-beans/.

ODD LAWS

With so many graveyards that go back to colonial days, Massachusetts takes its cemeteries seriously. Filmmakers wanting to capture the spooky ambiance of places like the Salem burial ground for their movie or television show would do well to note that it is illegal to make a film or even take photos for commercial purposes without the previous consent of cemetery trustees. Under the law of the commonwealth, violators could be subject to a $1,000 fine or even a jail term of up to six months.

According to Massachusetts General Law, assuming the role of would-be music arranger is unlawful if the song being adapted or cut is the national anthem. Nor should people even think about dancing to it. The pertinent section of the Massachusetts statute is worth quoting: "Whoever plays, sings or renders the 'Star Spangled Banner' in any public place . . . other than as a whole and separate composition or number . . . or renders the 'Star Spangled Banner,' or any part thereof, as dance music, as an exit march or as a part of a medley of any kind, shall be punished by a fine of not more than one hundred dollars." Sticklers may note that according to the website https://starspangledmusic.org/the-facts/ ("Celebrating the History of the U.S. National Anthem"), there should be a hyphen between the words "Star" and "Spangled," and that the word "The" is part of the title, neither of which is seen in the Massachusetts statute.

Under Massachusetts law, there is a fine for cursing at athletic events. This was perhaps enacted due to the extreme passions exhibited by fans of such teams as the Boston Red Sox. The language of the law is curious: "Whoever, having arrived at the age of sixteen years, directs any profane, obscene or impure language or slanderous statement at a participant or an official in a sporting event, shall be punished by a fine of not more than fifty dollars." It is not known if cussing is perfectly legal for fans who are 15 years old or younger.

UNUSUAL DESTINATIONS

"Art too bad to be ignored" is the slogan of the **Museum of Bad Art** in Somerville. It may be just the thing for those who have ever wandered through an art gallery and felt they could do better. The museum, known by its acronym MOBA, proudly claims it is the world's only museum dedicated to collecting, exhibiting, preserving, and celebrating bad art "in all its forms." After acquiring its first piece in 1994, not at an art auction but from a trash can, the Museum of Bad Art now fills two galleries. According to its website, MOBA's prestige as a repository of bad art has gone beyond Massachusetts to become a worldwide presence. The website claims that a newspaper in New Delhi, India, included the Museum of Bad Art in their list of the six best museums in the world.

The **O'Reilly Spite House** in Cambridge, Massachusetts, lives up to its name. In 1908, a Cambridge resident named Francis O'Reilly offered to sell his small parcel of land to his neighbor. The neighbor presumed that the plot was too small for anyone to build something on and therefore did not feel the need to spend any money buying it. Mr. O'Reilly, not taking kindly to this cavalier treatment, *did* in fact build on it—a long house just eight feet wide—to spite the miserly neighbor. However, it was not the first such spite house in the Bay State. At 10 feet wide and four stories tall, the **Skinny House** in Boston was built soon after the Civil War as a result of an uncivil war, the kind that can literally turn brother against brother. In this case, while one man went off to serve the Union, his brother served himself by building a sprawling house that took up most of the land they were to have jointly inherited. The returning soldier then built his tiny but tall residence on one of the few spots still available on the property, one which conveniently blocked the brother's sunlight and views of the harbor. Like the O'Reilly House, this diminutive domicile is currently occupied, is frequently photographed, and tends to bring a chuckle to passersby who believe in the power of spite when it comes to one-upmanship.

True to its name, the **Paper House** in Rockport is constructed entirely of newspaper. Elis Stenman started constructing it in 1922 as a summer home. He had a close relationship to paper at that point since he was the mechanical engineer who designed the machines that make paper clips. Stenman began building the house himself as a hobby, and the paper was originally meant to serve as insulation. Eventually, not only was the entire house made from more than 100,000 sheets of paper, but also furniture such as chairs, a desk, and a piano. One of the few exceptions is the fireplace, for obvious reasons. The newspapers are varnished to hold up to the elements, as anyone whose morning paper ever disintegrated on the lawn after being soaked by a sudden rain might appreciate. Visitors to the house not only enjoy the feat of structural engineering but also read headlines in newspapers that are almost a century old.

DISTINCTIVE MASSACHUSETTS WORDS AND SAYINGS

Barrel: A trash can.

Bubbler: The kind of fountain that provides drinking water. Proper pronunciation is "bubblah."

Cape, the: In Massachusetts, it's not a garment worn by Batman, but a place: Cape Cod. The usage is similar to "the Vineyard," which is not a field for growing grapes but the island of Martha's Vineyard.

Frappe: In no-nonsense Massachusetts, the final *e* is silent. This is the ice cream-and-milk dairy treat known elsewhere as a milkshake.

Green Monster: Standing almost four stories tall, this is the high left-field wall at Boston's Fenway Park, home of baseball's Red Sox. Its great view makes it a preferred seating area for many die-hard fans who do not mind ducking when an errant ball sails their way.

"Pahk the Cah in Hahvahd Yahd": No collection of sayings unique to Massachusetts would be complete without this legendary phrase in its true Boston pronunciation.

Further Reading

Brown, Richard D., and Jack Tager. *Massachusetts: A Concise History*. Amherst: University of Massachusetts Press, 2000.

Johnson, Claudia Durst. *Daily Life in Colonial New England*. Santa Barbara, CA: ABC-CLIO, 2017.

Muckenhoupt, Meg. *The Truth about Baked Beans: An Edible History of New England*. New York: New York University Press, 2020.

Michigan

> **FACT BOX**
>
> **Nickname:** Great Lakes State
> **Statehood Granted:** 1837
> **Capital:** Lansing
> **Population:** 10,000,000
> **State Motto:** *Si quaeris peninsulam amoenam circumspice* (Latin: "If You Seek a Pleasant Peninsula, Look around You")
> **What Natives Call Themselves:** Michiganders

STATE HISTORY

Michigan is the only state in the nation that borders four out of the five Great Lakes. Its shape is bounded by Lake Erie, Huron, Michigan, and Superior. Only Lake Ontario finds itself untouched by the Michigan shore. It is no surprise that the state's nickname is the Great Lakes State, although some people insist on calling it the "Wolverine State." Adding a bit of confusion, "Pure Michigan" is the phrase on the state's current standard license plate.

Michigan's name is said to be based on *michi gami*, a Native American term for "large lake." At the time when French explorers claimed the region for France in the early 1600s, they encountered tribes like the Ojibwa who had lived there for thousands of years.

When France was defeated in the French and Indian War in 1763, the area came under British rule. Then, after Britain in turn lost the American Revolution in 1783, the region containing present-day Michigan was ceded to the United States. Britain still had territorial grievances, and it was not until the end of the War of 1812 that British claims to portions of the territory were resolved.

Not long after that came a conflict that resulted in Michigan's unique configuration, making it the only American state to consist of two peninsulas. The Toledo War (1835–1836) was an altercation between the Michigan Territory and the adjoining state of Ohio. Michiganders and Ohioans fought over what was called the Toledo Strip, which each believed belonged to them. The U.S. Congress offered a solution: if the Michigan Territory ceded rights to Ohio for the small Toledo Strip, Michigan would be granted statehood and receive the virtually uninhabited Upper Peninsula, although it was felt to be relatively worthless.

Sunshine on a Cloudy Day

Established in 1959, Detroit's Motown Record Corporation was the dream of Detroiter Berry Gordy (1929–), going on to become the world's most successful independent record label. Its name blended the words "motor" and "town," a nickname for Detroit as the center of America's automotive industry. Originally headquartered in Gordy's home and today a major tourist destination, the studio attracted a lineup of artists hailing from Detroit that had some people wondering if there was something special in the city's rarefied air. A small sample includes Detroit natives Smokey Robinson and the Miracles, the Four Tops, the Temptations, Martha Reeves and the Vandellas, Diana Ross, and the Supremes. Fellow Motown artist Aretha Franklin came to Detroit at age two and Stevie Wonder at age four. As an African American–owned label, the Motown Sound played a major role in the integration of popular music amid the racial unrest of the 1960s, serving as ray of sunshine amid the storm clouds of the era.

Originally headquartered in Berry Gordy's home and today a major tourist destination called "Hitsville USA," Detroit's Motown Sound played a major role in the integration of popular music amid the racial unrest of the 1960s. (Winstonyarde/Dreamstime.com)

Michigan was admitted to the Union in 1837 as America's 26th state and may have felt it got the last laugh when rich copper and iron deposits were found along with the huge timber resources of the Upper Peninsula. Periodically, there are proposals in the Upper Peninsula to make it America's 51st state, to be called "Superior," but so far, it remains part of Michigan, connected by a bridge.

In the 20th century, Michigan's economy boomed when Detroit became the center of the automotive industry, both in the United States and around the world. With more miles of freshwater shoreline than any other state in the nation, it is also a prime vacation destination, attracting thousands of tourists each year to its pristine lakes, wooded campgrounds, and picturesque Mackinac Island where visitors often feel they have gone back in time.

With a nod to its Native American and French heritage, a popular poster in the Great Lakes State comes with the tagline "*You know you're from Michigan when you can pronounce Mackinac, Charlevoix, Ypsilanti, and Sault Ste. Marie without batting an eye.*" Helpful hint: MACK-in-awe, SHAR-la-voy, Ip-sill-ANN-tee, and SOO-saint-ma-REE, respectively.

URBAN LEGENDS

A popular urban legend in Michigan involves a tall, menacing creature with piercing eyes and a screaming howl who roams the North Woods. Neither a Bigfoot nor a werewolf, the creature is described as being eerily doglike, earning it the name **Dogman**. The origin story is based on an admitted hoax by a Traverse City radio station in 1987. However, listeners began calling the station with stories that they had actually had experiences with the Dogman or knew someone who did. One caller claimed that he had a personal encounter with the beast in 1938. Some reported that rumors of the Dogman went back as far as the early 1800s when French fur traders in the North Woods reported seeing a creature with a dog's head and the body of a man. Similar reports in 1878 came from lumberjacks who claimed to have seen the same type of beast. The Dogman tale grew in 1987 when police reported that an isolated cabin in the North Woods had been attacked by what seemed to be a large dog. After a film called *The Michigan Dogman* was produced in 2012, the legend took on a new life.

The **Old Presque Isle Lighthouse** between Lake Huron and the Straits of Mackinac was built in 1840 to help ships safely navigate the channel. However, it deteriorated within 30 years, so a new Presque Isle Light was built nearby. The Old Presque Isle Lighthouse was stripped of its wiring and converted into a museum in 1977, employing a couple named George and Lorraine Parris as caretakers. Apparently, George took the job seriously and steadfastly refused to leave his post, even after his death in 1991. Despite the lens in the light having been removed decades earlier, Lorraine said she saw the Old Presque Isle Lighthouse brightly lit in 1992, which defied all natural—and electrical—laws. Since that time, others, including sailors across the harbor, have reported seeing a golden glow from the lighthouse, a phenomenon for which the coast guard does not have an official explanation. Some have claimed to see a figure in the lantern room. Perhaps it is George, still on duty, helping others navigate the dangers of life even after he has left it.

A village named Paulding lies near a town suspiciously called Sleepy Hollow in the Upper Peninsula. Amid heavy woods, a stretch of road suddenly stops, leaving baffled motorists facing a sign from the U.S. Forestry Service that states, "This is the location from which the famous **Paulding Light** can be observed. Legend explains its presence as a railroad brakeman's ghost, destined to remain forever at the sight of his untimely death." Strict grammarians note the federal government's misuse of the word "sight" (the power of seeing or something that can be seen), maintaining that it should be "site" (a particular place or area of ground). In any case, would-be observers of the mysterious light are directed to focus their eyes on a spot beyond a clearing through the trees. It is said that the Paulding Light has been seen almost nightly since 1966. Some give credence to ghostly tales of the supernatural causing the phenomenon; others believe it is something as unexciting as swamp gas. Still others, including scientific investigators, chalk it up to car headlights on a nearby highway.

There is probably no swamp gas or automotive illumination prompting underwater sightings of Michigan's **Torch Lake Monster** beneath the waters of Torch Lake in the township of Antrim County. Stretching almost 20 miles, Torch Lake is the longest inland lake in Michigan, providing plenty of room for underwater monsters to skulk around. The sparkling lake is among the most popular vacation spots in the state, having deep, clear waters that can seem to change from iridescent green to deep turquoise, spurring comparison to a Middle American version of the Caribbean. It may not be a coincidence that the urban legend of the Torch Lake Monster is often said to have been helped along by staffers at a summer camp on the lakeshore. The story that was told around the campfire seems to have originated with a counselor there in the 1960s. A song emerged to accompany the tale, with such lyrics as "One eye is brown, one eye is blue / His body covered in icky green goo." Some descriptions of the Torch Lake Monster say it has the body of a lizard combined with the head of a cat. Monsters aside, Torch Lake itself is a breeding ground for eerie tales. It is the deepest inland lake in Michigan, which some maintain is "bottomless." Torch Lake's topography is said to connect it to nearby Grand Traverse Bay via underwater tunnels that run through the rock. Stories recount the unnerving discovery of people who had drowned in Torch Lake but their bodies washed up in Grand Traverse Bay, which some call supernatural and others call geology.

ICONIC MICHIGAN FOOD

Michigan Style Pasties, pronounced "PASS-tees," are essentially a savory filling of seasoned meat and vegetables wrapped in a folded pastry pocket. It is said that the dish was brought to Michigan in the 1800s by miners from Wales and Cornwall, England, where pasties were a traditional meal for the men deep in the mines. At lunchtime, the miners could take a pasty from their lunch box, place it on a shovel, heat the bottom on a flame, and warm up their tasty, filling meal. Depending on the cook, it is traditionally made with some combination of beef, diced potatoes, onion, and turnips or rutabaga. Pasties have become so associated with the state that there is an annual pasty festival in the town of Calumet, Michigan, where festival-goers enjoy the traditional dish as seen in this recipe:

Michigan Style Pasties (Yields 6 pasties)
4 cups flour
2 tsp plus 1 Tbsp salt
1¼ cups chilled lard, cut into ¼-inch bits
10–12 Tbsp ice water
2 lb round steak, trimmed and cut into ¼-inch cubes
5 medium potatoes, peeled and coarsely chopped
3 medium turnips, scraped and cut into ¼-inch cubes
1½ cups finely chopped onion
1 tsp freshly ground pepper

1. While preheating oven to 400°F, combine flour, lard, and 2 tsp salt in a large, chilled bowl. Mix quickly with fingers until it looks like coarse meal.
2. Add 10 Tbsp ice water, mix, and shape dough into a ball. Add 2 Tbsp more water if dough crumbles.
3. Divide dough into six equal balls, dust them with flour, wrap in waxed paper, and chill one hour.
4. Combine beef, potatoes, onions, turnips, pepper, and 1 Tbsp salt, mixing well.
5. On lightly floured surface, roll out balls of dough, one at a time, into a circle about ¼-inch thick. Use a plate or pot lid about nine inches in diameter as a guide to cut the dough into rounds with a sharp knife.
6. Spread about 1½ cups meat mixture on one side of round; then fold other side of the round over that, pressing edges together snugly.
7. Place formed pasties on baking sheet, then cut small slashes on the tops before baking about 45 minutes, or until pasties are golden brown.

Source: Adapted from http://www.hu.mtu.edu/vup/pasty/recipes.htm.

ODD LAWS

Michigan prides itself on the passion of its football fans. Fans who choose to ride a train to or from a big game should be aware of a law enacted in 1913. According to the Michigan Legislative Code, intoxicated persons may not climb aboard or be allowed to stay on the train in an inebriated state. According to the law, offenders may find their adult beverages impounded by the conductor and the alcohol taken to the nearest station agent, who will provide a receipt for the confiscated contraband. Within 10 days of the inebriated incident, offenders can return to the station agent to retrieve their liquid spirits. However, if the offense is deemed by the train conductor to be especially serious, the matter can be taken to court where the penalty could be a $100 fine and/or up to 90 days in jail. Hundreds of thousands of people are said to ride trains in Michigan each year. Amtrak has more than 20 train stations in the state, including those at Ann Arbor, East Lansing, and Detroit, homes of the University of Michigan, Michigan State

University, and the NFL's Detroit Lions, respectively. It is not known how often this law is enforced.

If a Sunday afternoon pastime involves looking for a car rather than riding the train, there is a Michigan law that might squelch the buying trip, even in the state that is home to America's automotive industry. Michigan's Legislative Code forbids a person or company "to engage in the business of buying, selling, trading or exchanging new, used or second-hand motor vehicles," or offering to do so, "on the first day of the week, commonly called Sunday." The law dates back to 1953, when the automotive assembly lines of Detroit led the world. Present-day proponents of keeping the law cite such concerns as dealership staff spending time with their families, employee morale, impact on customer relationships, and inability to finance the deal on Sunday with banks and auto insurance companies being closed. Some dealers, especially in smaller counties, are said to open on the Sabbath, while others observe the never-on-Sunday rule.

Along with buying a car on Sunday, Detroiters might do well to stifle the desire for all-night bowling. The Detroit Municipal Code outlaws bowling alleys from operating in the city, via "any place or room where bowling lanes are located" after 3:00 a.m. or before 7:00 a.m.

UNUSUAL DESTINATIONS

At **Dinosaur Gardens Prehistoric Zoo** in Ossineke, visitors can walk among dinosaurs, or at least their replicas. The 25 life-size reproductions of prehistoric birds and dinosaurs include a brontosaurus that is more than 80 feet long and weighs over 60,000 pounds. Guests can explore 40 acres of "No-Boundaries" exhibits to see what life was like when dinosaurs ruled. The park invites visitors to imagine the Michigan landscape when it was covered by a prehistoric sea as glaciers retreated, as well as the time when mastodons roamed the land. Guests can do additional roaming of their own amid non-prehistoric amenities such as putt-putt golf and a frozen yogurt bar. Dinosaur Gardens Prehistoric Zoo in Ossineke should not be confused with the Prehistoric Forest Amusement Park in Onsted, Michigan, which is the site of what remains from an abandoned dinosaur theme park that fell victim to highway rerouting and vandalism, ultimately going extinct just like the dinosaurs.

Marvin's Marvelous Mechanical Museum in Farmington is true to its namesake Marvin Yagoda, who spent 50 years collecting all manner of coin-operated games and automata from the oldest gypsy fortune-telling machines of the early 1900s to laser hologram video games from the 1990s. Many visitors find the museum to be delightfully overwhelming to the senses, with its clanging cacophony of sound and the flashing neon of machines. Exhibits include model airplanes, old arcade games, robots, and slot machines along with advertisements, animation, and other mechanical marvels that make Marvin's so memorable.

In Michigan, the fictional lumberjack Paul Bunyan is big—literally and figuratively. Huge statues of the hulking Bunyan can be found all around the Great

Lakes State. In alphabetical order by locale, they include what is called the **Paul Bunyan Made of Car Parts** in Alpena, the **Paul Bunyan Statue** in Manistique, **Barrel Chested Bunyan** in Oscoda, and **Big Sitting Bunyan** in West Branch. In Ossineke, **Paul Bunyan and Babe the Blue Ox** is over 25 feet tall, with his mythical sidekick Babe weighing in at almost five tons and standing more than 10 feet tall, larger than most standard oxen. At St. Ignace, a seated **Paul Bunyan and Babe the Blue Ox** statue is situated behind a fence to discourage visitors trying to sit on Paul's spacious lap.

Anyone who has ever felt off balance should feel right at home at the **St. Ignace Mystery Spot**. At this roadside attraction in St. Ignace, Michigan, visitors experience a place where gravity seems to behave irrationally, tall people appear shorter, and the slant of a cabin does strange things to one's equilibrium. According to an on-site sign, the story is that surveyors exploring Michigan's Upper Peninsula claimed that their surveying equipment was not working according to the laws of nature. They reported that the malfunctions only occurred in a circle about 300 feet in diameter. Visitors today find what seem to be odd physical sensations and optical contradictions. Some people believe it is the result of a prehistoric meteor's electromagnetic field or a mysterious magic circle. However, experts maintain that a site such as St. Ignace is the result of an oddly tilted environment as well as people standing on a slanted floor, causing the senses to react in an unusual fashion. In any case, the St. Ignace Mystery Spot is one of Michigan's top—if slightly off-kilter—tourist attractions.

DISTINCTIVE MICHIGAN WORDS AND SAYINGS

Fudgies: Tourists, especially those who spend lots of time in gourmet fudge shops such as those on Mackinac Island.

Michigan Left: A right turn immediately followed by a left to complete a U-turn. It is said to keep traffic from backing up at intersections.

Mitten: Michigan's Lower Peninsula because, on a map, it appears to be shaped like a mitten.

Thumb: Continuing the mitten theme, this is the thumb-shaped area of Michigan's eastern shore on the Lower Peninsula, which Michiganders often use to describe the location of their hometown.

U.P., the: Michigan's Upper Peninsula.

Yooper: Someone who resides in the U.P.

Further Reading

Barber, Sally. *Myths and Mysteries of Michigan*. Guilford, CT: Globe Pequot Press, 2011.

Burcar, Colleen. *It Happened in Michigan: Stories of Events and People That Shaped Great Lakes State History*. Lanham, MD: Globe Pequot, 2019.

Rubenstein, Bruce, and Lawrence Ziewacz. *Michigan: A History of the Great Lakes State*. Malden, MA: Wiley-Blackwell, 2014.

Minnesota

FACT BOX

Nickname: "Star of the North" is the official nickname, although "Land of 10,000 Lakes" is the unofficial yet popular alternative
Statehood Granted: 1858
Capital: St. Paul
Population: 5,700,000
State Motto: *L'Étoile du Nord* (French: "Star of the North")
What Natives Call Themselves: Minnesotans

STATE HISTORY

Many Americans came to know what they perceived to be the state of Minnesota through a program that was broadcast from 1974 to 2016 by National Public Radio (NPR) stations. Titled *A Prairie Home Companion*, it was aired live from the Fitzgerald Theater in St. Paul. A beloved feature was the segment called "News from Lake Wobegon," with the latest update from the fictional town of Lake Wobegon, Minnesota. There, it was claimed, the women were strong, the men good looking, and all of the children above average.

Those above-average children would know that although the state's official nickname is "Star of the North," Minnesota is often called the "Land of 10,000 Lakes." That claim may sound like an exaggeration, but it is actually an understatement. According to the Minnesota Department of Natural Resources, there are more than 11,000 major lakes measuring 10 acres or more, plus a multitude of smaller ones. The department notes that Minnesota has an impressive 90,000 miles of shoreline, more than California, Florida, and Hawaii combined.

Minnesota's lake-filled landscape is due to prehistoric ice sheets scraping enormous quantities of rocks and soil as the Ice Age glaciers retreated northward. Over time, the depressions were filled by rainwater to become Minnesota's legendary lakes.

Subsequently, Native people moved into in the area of today's Minnesota where they lived amid its bounty for thousands of years. European fur traders and missionaries began arriving following explorations in the region by Frenchmen including Pierre-Esprit Radisson during the 1650s.

Native tribes encountered by the Europeans included the Dakota and Ojibwe tribes. Most sources credit the Dakota language for the words that became the name of the state: "Mní sóta," loosely translated as "blue water." The aquatic prefix can also be found in other names around the state, such as Minnetonka ("big water") and Minnehaha ("curling water" or waterfall).

French explorer René-Robert Cavelier, Sieur de La Salle gave the state its nickname when he charted the Mississippi River, with the source of the Mississippi generally accepted as being at Lake Itasca in Clearwater County, Minnesota. La Salle dubbed the region "L'etoile du Nord," French for "Star of the North." The phrase became Minnesota's official motto, being emblazoned on its Great Seal in 1858 when it became America's 32nd state.

Within a few years of statehood, railroad lines began crisscrossing Minnesota, carrying goods and settlers. Waves of European immigrants arrived in Minnesota during the late 1800s and early 1900s after hearing of its plentiful farmland. Many came from places like Germany and Scandinavia, finding Minnesota not only to be amenable to their existing agricultural skills but also to have a winter climate that was not much different from what they were used to back home.

In fact, these hardy settlers not only endured the cold but embraced frigid conditions to the point that present-day Minnesotans have made ice fishing one of the state's top pastimes. After the lakes freeze solid in January and February, entire villages of ice fishing houses emerge atop the frozen lakes, complete with makeshift streets and lighting along with the kind of sociability that is warm even if conditions are not.

No one can deny that Minnesota gets cold in winter. Temperatures have dropped as low as −60°F. Yet, Minnesota summers have been known to exceed the usual standards of balminess, once reaching 114°F.

The standard of living in Minnesota is among the highest in the United States, with its people considered some of the best educated in the nation. The first children's department in an American library was created at the Minneapolis Public Library in 1889. With neighboring St. Paul, the "Twin Cities" are known for culture with amenities such as the Guthrie Theater in Minneapolis, the largest regional playhouse in the country. Notable St. Paul residents have included writer F. Scott Fitzgerald and playwright August Wilson, who premiered many of his plays there.

Apart from cultural pursuits, Minnesotans also gravitate toward getting outdoors. In a state known as the "Land of 10,000 Lakes," it may not be a surprise that Minnesota has more recreational boats than any other state, boasting one vessel for every six people.

What actually *may* be surprising is that Minneapolis is said to have more golfers per capita than any other city in the nation, even though they can only play outdoors for a relatively short time each year.

The world-famous Mayo Clinic in Rochester, Minnesota, was founded in 1864. Since that time, Minnesota has been a global center of medical innovation. The oxygen mask was invented in 1935 by three Mayo Clinic physicians. The first open heart surgery and first bone marrow transplant were performed at the University

> ## Mother of Invention
>
> Some Minnesota boosters claim that the innovative spirit of its people is something in the water, which is understandable in a state with thousands of lakes. Others point to Minnesota offering the nation's first free legal assistance program for inventors seeking a patent. In any case, Minnesota has been the birthplace of a staggering array of inventions including armored cars, automatic pop-up toasters, Bundt pans, masking tape, microwave popcorn, oxygen masks, Post-it notes, rollerblades, Scotch tape, snowblowers, snowmobiles, and water skis. Of greater importance to some is that Minnesota's Frank Mars introduced the Milky Way candy bar, Snickers, and Three Musketeers. It must also be remembered that in 1937, the Hormel Company of Austin, Minnesota, introduced the meat product called Spam. Since that time, more than eight billion cans of Spam have been sold. Still made in Minnesota, Spam is currently available in 43 countries around the world, including South Korea, where it is considered a delicacy and is often given to friends as a gift. Minnesotans can be proud.

of Minnesota in 1952 and 1958, respectively. The external artificial cardiac pacemaker was invented in 1957 by Minnesotan Earl Bakken in his garage.

According to naturalists, Minnesota is home to more than 50 different species of mosquitoes. Most people would think that one species is enough, but between mosquitoes in summer and arctic temperatures in winter, Minnesotans rose to the challenge. Southdale, built in 1956 in the Twin Cities suburb of Edina, was America's first enclosed climate-controlled shopping center. With a concept that was new at the time, some have included its developer among the most influential architects of the 20th century.

Not a state to rest on its laurels, Minnesota went a step further in 1992 with the opening of the Mall of America in Bloomington. It is the biggest shopping mall in the United States, having more than four miles of storefront footage. To put it in perspective, Minnesota's Mall of America is the size of 78 football fields and is large enough to hold 32 jumbo jet airplanes.

Ironically, in a state known for frigid winters, in 1914, the first home in America to have air conditioning was in Minneapolis.

URBAN LEGENDS

The small town of Vergas, Minnesota, is renowned in a big way for its very own urban legend. The **Hairyman of Vergas Trails** is said to be eight feet tall, has long scraggly hair, emits a musty smell, and walks barefoot as he stalks the woods around the Vergas Trails. Some believe that the tale evolves from an old hermit who lived in the woods, adopting a frightening appearance to keep people away from his shack. The most often-repeated encounter story involves a local resident who was driving in the woods when suddenly the Hairyman allegedly jumped in front of the car and punched dents in its hood, which were visible when the driver got back to town. Another report came from two teens who were snowmobiling near an old cabin when what they described as a beast-like creature sprang out at them, holding a large stick and standing barefoot in the snow. The town has cheerfully embraced the legend with what is called the annual Vergas Hairyman 5K event, at which T-shirts are available proclaiming, "I outran the Hairyman."

Many locales have their own alleged resident underwater monster, notably the one that is said to skulk beneath Scotland's Loch Ness. However, in keeping with the state's general reputation for friendliness, **Pepie the Lake Pepin Serpent** at Lake City, Minnesota, is known for its good nature. For decades there have been rumors of an aquatic monster being spotted in the lake, but swimmers are reassured that they can splash in the water unmolested. A family-friendly Pepie Fest brings visitors to the lakeshore where none have been known to succumb to any sea serpents. Still, the stories persist, including those by a contemporary boat captain who claimed to have seen the beast lurking in the depths. In 1871, there were reports of a monster swimming on Lake Pepin, but the urban legend goes back to the time before Minnesota existed as a state. The story goes that when traveling on Lake Pepin, Native Americans would beach their birchbark canoes on the shore in order to exchange them for thicker dugout boats. The conventional wisdom was that even a friendly sea monster could easily puncture less sturdy crafts as they plied the waters of its home.

The **Wendigo**, a supernatural creature that allegedly makes its home in the thick forests of Northern Minnesota, is far less friendly than Pepie. The Wendigo is said to display a rude tendency to dine on human flesh. Said to be about 15 feet tall, the monster has a curious shape in which it is allegedly too thin to be seen from the side. But with a head-on view, the monster is every bit as big and scary as monsters tend to be. The legend evolved from a Native American tale of a creature or evil spirit living in the deep woods. It not only has a taste for eating humans but also has been said to turn them into fellow Wendigos. Although there are no known family-friendly festivals honoring the Wendigo, it attained a bit of cultural currency when it appeared in Marvel Comics' *Incredible Hulk* #162 in April 1973 and again in issue #180 in October 1974. As if costarring with the Hulk was not enough of an accolade, the creature of this particular urban legend lends its name to the medical term "Wendigo psychosis." This obsession is described as displaying an intense craving for human flesh and the fear of becoming a cannibal.

ICONIC MINNESOTA FOOD

In some places, people might call it a casserole. But in Minnesota, it is recognized immediately as the state's quintessential cuisine item: the **Hot Dish**. It's a combination of meat, vegetables, and canned cream soup, ideally topped off with a generous portion of cheese and heaping helping of Tater Tots. Not only does the Hot Dish almost always make an appearance at church suppers, family gatherings, and potlucks in the state, but it is also the centerpiece of cook-offs to see whose version is the undisputed champ. While there may be as many variations as there are Minnesota cooks, the recipe below is a fine example of the Hot Dish in all its glory:

Minnesota Hot Dish (Serves 8)
1 lb ground beef
1 medium onion, chopped
1 can (10½ oz) cream of mushroom soup
1 can (10½ oz) cream of chicken soup
½ cup milk
1 package (16 oz) frozen mixed vegetables
1 package (16 oz) frozen Tater Tots
1½ cups cheddar jack cheese

1. Brown ground beef with the onion and drain fat before stirring in the soups, milk, and vegetables.
2. Transfer the mixture to a 9 by 13 inch baking dish and arrange Tater Tots on top.
3. Bake in preheated 350°F oven for about 30 minutes, until the mixture is bubbly and the Tater Tots are brown and crisp.
4. Sprinkle the cheese over the Tater Tots, return the dish to the oven, and bake an additional 10–15 minutes until the cheese is melted.

Source: Adapted from https://www.minnesota-visitor.com/minnesota-hot-dish-recipes.html.

ODD LAWS

Hopeful ride seekers are sometimes confused by the Minnesota law that states, "No person shall stand in a roadway for the purpose of soliciting a ride from the driver of any private vehicle." They are puzzled as to whether hitchhiking itself is outlawed, or merely standing in the road to do so, which most would agree is the classic methodology for hitchhiking. Soliciting contributions from occupants of vehicles that are stopped at an intersection is also unlawful. In a subsection, the law goes on to state that it is forbidden for people to stand on a roadway in order to solicit employment or business, which puts employees waving signs at a disadvantage. A gray area would be the tall inflatable "wind puppets" that presumably do not contain humans inside.

Many people erroneously interpret Minnesota law to be a groundbreaking step forward in pest control by declaring mosquitoes to be a "public nuisance." Even if the state's law enforcement officials could apprehend the annoying insects and lock them up, the law actually declares the public nuisance to be the *areas* where mosquitoes incubate or hatch, not the mosquitoes themselves. However, many people would gladly step forward to make a "citizen's arrest" if the law was ever amended to make the irritating pests themselves illegal.

UNUSUAL DESTINATIONS

People who have always had a desire to drive a tank will enjoy the appropriately named **Drive A Tank** at Kasota, Minnesota. Along with calling itself one of the few "recreational tank driving experiences" in the world, this facility offers a variety of packages with opportunities that go well beyond simply driving a tank. The upgrade packages are labeled in military-type terminology such as 3 Star, 4 Star, 5 Star, and Sherman. The various options include driving a tank over a car, driving a tank over two cars, and driving a tank through a house, which in this case is a mobile home rather than an owner-occupied dwelling in a nearby neighborhood. The website claims that they are the only known company offering this kind of activity to the public in the United States. In addition, it proclaims itself to be the only place in the world that is not owned by a government entity where guests can also shoot a fully automatic historic machine gun under one roof. Drive A Tank is available for birthday parties, holiday celebrations, and weddings as well as bachelor and bachelorette parties. With some workplaces compared to a war zone, corporate events are also welcome.

The tiny town of Wykoff, Minnesota, is home to fewer than 450 people, but it has a big attraction: **Ed's Museum**. Edwin Julius Krueger owned the Jack Sprat Food Store and was also what might be euphemistically be called a "collector." He apparently kept everything and threw away nothing. When Ed died in 1989, he left the store and all of its contents to the town of Wykoff on the condition that it would be turned into a museum. As volunteers noted to their dismay as they were hauling out six big truckloads of trash, Ed also kept the remains of his deceased cat Sammy in a cardboard box. Sammy is still there, along with other items in the museum, which is chock-full of 20th-century advertisements, antiques, artifacts, and posters, including one that states, "Meat Builds Them Up for the BATTLE OF LIFE" [sic]. Visitors to Wykoff who find they will need several days to pore through the displays at Ed's Museum are in luck. Nearby is the original 1913 City Jail, which today serves as a Bed-and-Breakfast. Although there are still bars on the windows, guests are able to check out whenever they want.

Austin, Minnesota, is home to the **Spam Museum**, which has dubbed itself "the world's most comprehensive collection of spiced pork artifacts." Hormel Foods Corporation, based in Austin, has produced the popular canned precooked meat product since 1937. The Spam Museum traces the story of Spam's origin and its place in world culinary culture. The museum houses an interactive exhibit where visitors learn about all the different varieties of Spam. Family members touring the facility are also invited to compete in a mock assembly of cans of Spam. In the gift shop, there are hundreds of Spam-branded items. However, for many, the highlight of their visit is being offered bites of Spam, commonly known as "Spamples."

At the Spam Museum in Austin, Minnesota, the highlight for many is being offered free "Spamples" by volunteer guides, known as "Spambassadors." The globally-known spiced meat product is still produced in Minnesota. (Adrianadh/Dreamstime.com)

These edible tidbits are offered by the museum's volunteer guides, known—obviously—as "Spambassadors."

Honorable mention goes to the bronze figure honoring the plucky heroine of TV's classic *Mary Tyler Moore Show*. Located in downtown Minneapolis, the **MTM Statue** captures an iconic moment in the opening credits of the sitcom that ran from 1970 to 1977. The show broke new ground by having an unmarried working woman as the lead character. It was also not set in the usual TV locations of New York or California, opting instead for Minnesota. Some local residents claim it put Minneapolis on the map. Today, fans of all generations can photograph themselves imitating Mary as she throws her hat in the air, celebrating the sheer joy of life and "turning the world on with her smile."

DISTINCTIVE MINNESOTA WORDS AND SAYINGS

Cities, the: Minneapolis and St. Paul.

Don'tcha know: Quintessential Minnesotan slang for "Don't you know," often used at the end of a declarative sentence.

Not that cold: Very cold.

Uff da: Also spelled "uffda," "oofda," or "oofdah," among other variants, this exclamation can be used in a number of situations, such as feeling dismayed, overwhelmed, relieved, surprised, or tired.

You betcha: Indicates a general sense of acceptance, agreement, or understanding.

Further Reading

Lass, William E. *Minnesota: A History*. New York: W. W. Norton, 2000.

Ortler, Brett. *Minnesota Trivia Don'tcha Know!* Cambridge, MN: Adventure Publications, 2014.

Stansfield, Charles, Jr. *Haunted Minnesota: Ghosts and Strange Phenomena of the North Star State*. Mechanicsburg, PA: Stackpole Books, 2012.

Mississippi

FACT BOX

Nickname: The Magnolia State
Statehood Granted: 1817
Capital: Jackson
Population: 3,000,000
State Motto: *Virtute et armis* (Latin: "By Valor and Arms")
What Natives Call Themselves: Mississippians

STATE HISTORY

Mississippi is largely defined by the iconic river that forms the state's western border. Like the Mighty Mississippi itself, the name of the state is generally said to have evolved from the Native American terminology for "big river," usually transliterated as *misi-ziibi*.

Much of its iconography pertains to the region of the state popularly known as the Mississippi Delta. This is actually a bit of a misnomer, since the actual delta at the mouth of the Mississippi River lies on the Gulf Coast, about 300 miles to the south. The Mississippi Delta flatlands are part of an alluvial plain that has been formed over the centuries by regular flooding by the Mississippi and Yazoo rivers. Running about 200 miles long and 70 miles wide, it contains some of the most fertile soil in the world. A popular saying is that the Mississippi Delta runs between the lobby of the Peabody Hotel in Memphis and south to Catfish Row in Vicksburg, Mississippi.

The Native Americans who lived in the area for thousands of years understood the importance of the "big river." Using it as a watery highway, trade took place among the various regional tribes, including the Biloxi, Natchez, and Yazoo, whose names live on in the state's locales.

One tribe, called the Plaquemine culture, lived in today's Mississippi around the years 1200–1730. They constructed the Emerald Mound as a place of worship, making it the largest sacred mound in the region and one of the largest in North America. Located near the town of Stanton, Mississippi, this archaeological site spans more than eight acres and has been named a National Historic Landmark.

There are those who say that the mound site was still under construction when the first documented European expedition into the territory arrived in 1541.

Spanish explorers under Hernando de Soto passed through the state near today's Natchez, Mississippi, and are said to be the first Europeans to see the Mississippi River.

However, it was not until 1699 that the first permanent European settlement in today's Mississippi was established. Formed by French settlers under Pierre d'Iberville, it was located on the Gulf Coast and called Fort Maurepas, today known as Old Biloxi.

Natchez, which was founded in 1716 by the French, went on to become a major Mississippi River town. The Natchez Trace, running more than 400 miles between Natchez, Mississippi, and Nashville, Tennessee, was a vital link between the Eastern United States and the Mississippi River. Prehistoric animals had "traced" a path that was later followed by Native Americans and European explorers before it became an important trade and emigration route by Americans. In addition to being the oldest permanent settlement on the Mississippi River, Natchez is said to have once boasted more millionaires among its residents than any place in America except New York City.

In the years surrounding the French and Indian War (1754–1763), France, Spain, and Britain all claimed today's Mississippi at one point or another. When America won the War of Independence in 1783, the region was ceded by Britain to the United States. In 1817, Mississippi became the 20th state admitted to the Union.

A colony called "Mississippi in Africa" was founded during the 1830s in today's Liberia on land purchased by a group called the Mississippi State Colonization Society. In his will, the owner of Prospect Hill Plantation in Jefferson County, Mississippi, freed the people who were enslaved on his properties, arranging for supplies and passage to the current African country of Liberia. Through the 1840s, several hundred free Americans of color emigrated from Mississippi to the settlement. There are descendants of the "Mississippi in Africa" settlers who live in Liberia to this day.

In 1861, Mississippi became the second state to secede from the Union as one of the founding members of the Confederacy. Following the Northern victory in the Civil War and the Reconstruction era, Mississippi rejoined the Union in 1870.

Well into the 20th century, Mississippi's economy remained agriculturally based, particularly in the fertile land of the Mississippi Delta. Along with crops, that region also nurtured one of America's most significant musical forms, called the Delta blues. Much of it sprang from the poverty of farm workers living there, especially sharecroppers. Relatively inexpensive musical instruments such as harmonicas and guitars (often secondhand or homemade) joined with soulful vocals to create an emotionally compelling sound.

At a spot called the Crossroads in Clarksdale, Mississippi, three giant blue guitars mark the highway intersection where an unsuccessful singer named Robert Johnson allegedly sold his soul to the devil in exchange for making him one of the greatest blues musicians of all time. Some say that whether or not diabolical forces were at work, he succeeded.

In addition to Johnson, a small sample of Mississippians reflect American music in all its forms, from opera to the Grand Ole Opry: Jimmy Buffet, Mickey Gilley, Faith Hill, B. B. King, Leontyne Price, Charley Pride, Britney Spears, Conway Twitty, and Tammy Wynette. In addition, Tupelo, Mississippi was the birthplace of the "King of Rock and Roll," Elvis Presley.

Mississippi also produced actors Morgan Freeman and James Earl Jones as well as media superstar Oprah Winfrey. It was the home of iconic American writers including William Faulkner, John Grisham, Eudora Welty, Tennessee Williams, and Richard Wright.

In a footnote to history, the concept of selling shoes in boxes by the pair—left foot and right foot, which was something new—originated at a shoe store in Vicksburg, Mississippi, in 1884. At the time, it was definitely a step forward.

Mississippi can claim Mamie Thomas, who became America's first female rural mail carrier in 1914. She drove her buggy to deliver mail in an area near Vicksburg.

Another "favorite daughter" is Burnita Shelton Mathews of Hazelhurst, Mississippi, who was the first female federal judge in the United States, serving from 1949 until her death in 1988.

Mississippi's Vicksburg National Cemetery is the second largest such burial ground in the country, second only to Arlington National Cemetery.

Historians note that Mississippi did not ratify the U.S. Constitution's 19th Amendment, granting women voting rights, until 1984, which was 64 years after other female American citizens were allowed to vote. When Mississippi's all-male state Senate approved it in 1984, they called it a "housekeeping measure."

URBAN LEGENDS

King's Tavern in Natchez is one of the town's oldest buildings, being constructed in the late 1700s. It remains a popular restaurant and is said to be haunted by the spirit of a beautiful young serving girl named Madeline. According to the legend, Madeline was being romanced by the tavern's owner, Richard King, but disappeared shortly after Mrs. King discovered the affair. Local lore holds that Mrs. King killed Madeline and hid the girl's body behind the tavern's walls. That tale was gruesome enough, but when restoration work was being done in the 1930s, *three* mummified bodies were found hidden in the wall behind the tavern's fireplace. Along with the remains of two men and one woman, a jeweled dagger that was assumed to be the murder weapon was also discovered. The men were not identified, but the woman was said to be Madeline. Believers in the legend of the doomed serving girl have reported seeing an eerie reflection suddenly appearing in a mirror at the tavern. This specter is said to be the long-dead Madeline who never left her place of employment.

According to the legend of Mississippi's **Pascagoula River**, it played a role in the fate of the small Pascagoula tribe, Native Americans who mysteriously went extinct. One evening, it is said that the Pascagoula learned that their enemies, the Biloxi tribe, were planning to attack at first light. The Pascagoula knew they were outnumbered and are said to have pondered their inevitable fate of being slaughtered or enslaved. Local lore has it that they chose another alternative: mass suicide. According to the legend, under cover of darkness, the entire tribe held hands while chanting a song of death as they walked into the Pascagoula River, women and children first. By the time the last voice could be heard no more, the entire tribe had drowned. Today, the legend of the "Singing River" remains. It is said that during late evening, the sound of eerie music seems to be emanating from under the water.

In Yazoo City's Glenwood Cemetery, there is a gravesite containing a tombstone that is broken in large pieces. According to the legend of the **Witch's Grave**, an old woman who lived on the Yazoo River in the 1880s would use witchcraft to lure fishermen to her shack, where she killed them. Investigating reports, the local sheriff entered her cabin where he found a cache of bones. When he confronted her with the grisly evidence, she ran away. The sheriff is said to have pursued her into the swampland where she became trapped in quicksand. As she sank to her death, she is alleged to exclaim that in 20 years, she would return and burn the town to the ground. In 1904—said to be 20 years later—a massive unexplained fire did indeed consume the town. When locals visited Glenwood Cemetery soon after the fire, they noticed that the large chain surrounding her gravesite had been broken, with her tombstone in pieces. A new chain and gravestone were installed, only to break like the originals. According to the legend, every time they are repaired, the same thing happens. A somewhat peevish marker was erected by the town: *"On May 25, 1904, the Witch of Yazoo City broke out of these curious chain links surrounding her grave and burned down Yazoo City. Writer Willie Morris' classic 'Good Ole Boy' brought national renown to this vengeful woman and her shameful deed."*

ICONIC MISSISSIPPI FOOD

Outside Mississippi, the definition of "mud" refers to the result of mixing dirt with water. However, in the Magnolia State, it means the iconic dish, **Mississippi Mud Pie**. There are a number of origin stories, but most are centered on the rich dessert's resemblance to the dark soil along the banks of the Mississippi River, which runs through the state. Many cooks pride themselves on their own variations, but the basic formula can be seen in this recipe:

> **Mississippi Mud Pie** (Serves 12)
> 1 cup all-purpose flour
> 1 cup chopped pecans
> ½ cup butter, softened
> 1 package (5.9 oz) instant chocolate pudding mix
> 1 package (8 oz) cream cheese, softened
> 1 cup confectioners' sugar
> 1 container (16 oz) frozen whipped topping, thawed and divided
> Chocolate curls and toasted chopped pecans to taste

1. While preheating oven to 350°F, beat flour, pecans, and butter in a large bowl until blended to form the crust.
2. Press crust mixture into the bottom of a 9 by 13 inch baking dish and bake until golden brown, about 15 minutes. Remove to a wire rack, and cool completely.
3. Prepare chocolate pudding according to package directions, and let stand for five minutes.
4. Beat cream cheese and sugar together in a bowl until smooth, then fold in one cup whipped topping.
5. Spread cream cheese mixture over cooled crust, then spread pudding over cream cheese layer.
6. Top with remaining whipped topping, then add chocolate curls and pecans on top.

Source: Adapted from https://www.eater.com/2016/4/30/11490356/what-is-mississippi-mud-pie.

ODD LAWS

Although cattle rustling is traditionally identified with the Old West, it features into the criminal code of Mississippi, which is often considered part of the New South. The rationale is the same in both places: money. Under Mississippi's legal code, it is a felony to steal cattle or other livestock, including horses, sheep, and swine. Whether the theft takes place by masked outlaws under cover of darkness or through misrepresentation or other fraud, the temptation to make easy money via someone else's four-legged property can come with a high price tag. Under Mississippi law, there is a fine of between $1,500 and $10,000 along with a prison term of one to five years "regardless of the value of the livestock." In addition, restitution must be made to the owner, not only for actual financial loss but also for loss of income, court costs, attorney's fees involved in recovering the stolen livestock, and/or current replacement value if the cows do not come home.

It is also against the law in Mississippi to willfully disturb "any congregation of persons lawfully assembled for religious worship." For such an outburst, the culprit could incur a $500 fine and/or a six-month jail term. Incidentally, the offender is subject to apprehension not only by an officer of the law but also by a private individual in a "citizen's arrest" without a warrant.

Under Mississippi law, the penalty for such a sacrilegious disturbance would increase if the perpetrator protested being arrested by proceeding to "profanely swear or curse, or use vulgar and indecent language." Furthermore, it would do no good at all for the malefactor to attempt a defense of being under the influence. According to Mississippi state law, if a person is drunk in any public place, in the presence of two or more persons, "he shall, on conviction thereof," be subject to a possible fine of up to $100 along with a 30-day jail term. The law does not specify the consequences if "he" is a "she."

UNUSUAL DESTINATIONS

True to its name, the **Apron Museum** in Iuka, Mississippi, is the only museum in the United States that is dedicated to aprons and, possibly more important, to the stories they tell. Thousands of aprons, some dating back to the Civil War, are on display alongside more contemporary exhibits such as aprons with a Star Wars theme. The museum, which has been featured in *Ripley's Believe It or Not*, also interprets aprons embellished with ruffles and bows as an art form. Since aprons have also been worn by blacksmiths, butchers, carpenters, chefs, printers, shopkeepers, and backyard barbecuers, the museum does not focus solely on the role such garments played for women through the ages. While some of the aprons are made from old flour sacks, the displays also demonstrate how the wealthy could afford more elaborate aprons as status symbols. Some of the most poignant displays include a handwritten letter from the donor, giving the history of the apron and the person who wore it.

At **Frog Art Farm** in Fayette, the whimsical sculpture garden is filled with lovable one-of-a-kind figures of frogs. Each folk art frog is painted in bright, lively colors and is completely unique, appearing to have its own distinctive personality. Their creator, artist Louise Cadney Coleman, places the wooden statues in fun settings. Thus, the visitor will find frogs fishing from a dock, playing musical instruments such as drums or banjos, or simply enjoying little houses with a view of the pond. The words "charming" and "whimsical" are often heard from smiling visitors.

Another whimsical Mississippi site is **PlayGarden Park** behind the Itawamba County Courthouse in the town of Fulton. Here, smiling bronze sculptures of large coins and small houses await. The simple sculptures, which can only be described as "sweet faced," are scattered around a downtown park that welcomes the young and young at heart. Rather than being clustered in plain view, part of the attraction is turning a corner and coming across one of the statues peeping out of bushes, standing on a rock, or sitting on the railing of the park's gazebo. Visitors

Many people honor Mississippi as the birthplace of Kermit the Frog. The town of Leland, Mississippi, recognizes Kermit and his creator Jim Henson through the annual Leland FrogFest. (Carrienelson1/Dreamstime.com)

> ### Hop on over to Leland
>
> The Chamber of Commerce in Leland, Mississippi, is justly proud of its proximity to one of the world's largest agricultural research stations. However, many people honor the town as the birthplace of a small green creature that went on to achieve worldwide fame. Jim Henson (1936–1990), creator of the Muppets, grew up in Leland, where he spent a lot of his childhood playing in the neighboring swamplands. Locals claim it was there that he got the inspiration for his most famous creation, the original Muppet, Kermit the Frog. A historical marker in town reads, "Birthplace of Kermit the Frog," noting on the plaque that Henson was sometimes joined on his swampy sojourns "by his friend, Kermit Scott." The town of Leland embraces both Henson and Kermit (the amphibian) through the annual Leland FrogFest, which features art displays, live music, a 5K race (with contestants running, not hopping), and food venues spotlighting Delta cuisine. Frogs' Legs may or may not be included on the menu.

are greeted by a larger version of the coin sculptures with their arms linked. Older guests might discern a subtle message regarding capitalism, while children are satisfied to frolic in the park's playground. Many guests describe the statues as being "weird," "wonderful," or some variation thereof, but most visitors at least end up grinning, which is a priceless gift in itself.

DISTINCTIVE MISSISSIPPI WORDS AND SAYINGS

Delta: Neither the Greek letter nor the airline, but the richly fertile section of the state between the Mississippi River and the Yazoo River.

Finer'n frog's hair: A response to an inquiry about one's health. If frogs had hair (which they don't), the conventional wisdom is that it would be invisible and therefore extremely fine.

Gimme some sugar: No need to pass the sweetener, just "give me a kiss."

Go on up the road a ways: A method of giving directions, with the exact length of "a ways" being undetermined but felt to be understood by the listener.

Ole Miss: Not an elderly single woman, but the University of Mississippi.

Further Reading

Brown, Alan. *Haunted Natchez*. Charleston, SC: History Press, 2010.
Gioia, Ted. *Delta Blues: The Life and Times of the Mississippi Masters Who Revolutionized American Music*. New York: W. W. Norton, 2009.
Kirkpatrick, Marlo Carter. *Mississippi Off the Beaten Path: A Guide to Unique Places*. Guilford, CT: Globe Pequot, 2015.
Mitchell, Dennis J. *A New History of Mississippi*. Jackson: University Press of Mississippi, 2014.

Missouri

> **FACT BOX**
>
> **Nickname:** The Show Me State
> **Statehood Granted:** 1821
> **Capital:** Jefferson City
> **Population:** 6,200,000
> **State Motto:** *Salus populi suprema lex esto* (Latin: "Let the Good of the People Be the Supreme Law")
> **What Natives Call Themselves:** Missourians

STATE HISTORY

Missouri received its name by way of the Native American people who lived there before Europeans arrived. The Missouri secretary of state claims that the name was derived from a tribe called the Missouris. Experts translate it along the lines of "village of the large canoes" or "big canoe people," although the word is popularly said to mean "muddy water."

Being drained by two of the nation's major waterways, the Missouri River and the Mississippi, the state would be no stranger to muddy water. River travel has long been associated with Missouri, becoming a huge part of its lifeblood. The Mississippi River presents a rich panorama of history for the state that is personified by the works of Missouri author Samuel Langhorne Clemens, better known as Mark Twain. He describes his boyhood in the book *Life on the Mississippi*, having grown up in the port town of Hannibal, Missouri. Hannibal is said to have inspired its fictional counterpart in Twain's novels *The Adventures of Tom Sawyer* and *The Adventures of Huckleberry Finn*.

The river was important to the state's people long before that. At Sugarloaf Mound in St. Louis is a ceremonial mound built between the years 600 and 1300 by ancient people who also constructed the earthworks at the famed Cahokia Mounds across the river in Illinois.

After French Canadian settlers arrived in today's Missouri, they founded the town of Ste. Genevieve in 1735. Located at what they thought would be an ideal spot on the Mississippi River, it is often cited as the first organized European settlement in present-day Missouri. However, the riverfront location that seemed ideal also spelled the demise of Ste. Genevieve. Following devastating floods, such as one in 1785, the town moved to its current location about a half mile inland.

Founded in 1764, St. Louis went on to become a major port on the Mississippi River and a gateway to the West at exactly the time when the nation was expanding. In 1850, St. Louis became one of the 10 largest cities in the country. It was the first top 10 appearance of any American city west of the Mississippi River, holding its rank until 1960.

After the region containing today's Missouri was briefly ruled by Spain, the United States acquired it from France in 1803 as part of the Louisiana Purchase. Would-be settlers from both America and abroad came to the Missouri Territory in droves.

In the years before the Civil War, the issue of slavery became a flash point for Missouri. Under the Missouri Compromise of 1820, Maine was admitted to the United States as a free state at the same time as Missouri, where slavery was permitted.

Missouri author Samuel Clemens, better known as Mark Twain, grew up in Hannibal, Missouri. The town inspired the locale for Twain's classic novels, *The Adventures of Tom Sawyer* and *The Adventures of Huckleberry Finn*. (Library of Congress)

In 1821, Missouri became the nation's 24th state. It was the first state admitted to the Union that was entirely west of the Mississippi River. For decades, Missouri played a central role in America's expansion. It was the starting point of such vital links to the Old West as the Butterfield Overland Mail Route, California Trail, Pony Express, Oregon Trail, and Santa Fe Trail.

Missouri's designation as a slave state led to one of the most famous and hotly debated Supreme Court cases in U.S. history. Commonly known as the *Dred Scott* Decision, it centered on Scott, an enslaved man from Missouri. In 1857, the Supreme Court ruled that the Constitution of the United States did not grant citizenship for Black people, whether enslaved or free. Black Americans were therefore legally denied the constitutional rights enjoyed by U.S. citizens. Taney County, Missouri, home of the popular tourist spot Branson, was named for Chief Justice Roger Taney, who handed down the decision.

Nonetheless, Missouri went on to become prominent as the home of many notable African Americans. In 1871, Joe Penny, a freed Black man, used his life savings to buy land from his former master in Saline County, Missouri. There, he founded the first incorporated Black town in the nation. During a time when African Americans were not permitted to own land in some parts of the country, Pennytown was a beacon of hope for people who had formerly been enslaved. After reaching a peak population of about 1,000 residents by the early 1900s, it went into decline until all that remained was a historic church which was later added to the National Register of Historic Places.

The world of music is well represented by Missourians including Josephine Baker, Chuck Berry, Scott Joplin, Charlie "Bird" Parker, and Tina Turner. In addition, playwright Langston Hughes hailed from Joplin, Missouri.

No discussion of Missouri is complete without a reference to its nickname, "the Show Me State," which appears on its license plates. Most sources cite a speech made in 1899 by a Missouri congressman who stated, *"Frothy eloquence neither convinces nor satisfies me. I'm from Missouri, and you have got to show me."* However, some naysayers contend that the phrase "Show Me" in relation to Missouri was already in use before that time. Other descriptors have also been used for Missouri, including "the Cave State," for its thousands of underground caverns, and "the Mother of the West," for its importance as a base for the nation's westward expansion.

Another question that often arises is whether the state's name is pronounced Miz-OO-*ree* or Miz-OO-*ruh*. Some say the distinction is demographical, with the "uh" sound more prevalent in rural areas. Others say it is generational, with younger folks favoring "ee." Without definitive guidelines, it is said that in order to appeal to as many voters as possible, politicians sometimes pronounce "Missouri" both ways at various times in the same speech.

However, there is no debate over the official state dinosaur, which contains "Missouri" right in its name. The *Hypsibema missouriense* was a prehistoric duck-billed dinosaur having about 1,000 teeth. It was discovered near Glen Allen, Missouri.

Another discovery may have more widespread fame. Missouri's official state dessert, the ice cream cone, was introduced during the 1904 World's Fair in St. Louis. It is said that an ice cream vendor ran out of cups, so he asked a nearby waffle maker to roll up some "cones" made of waffles to hold the ice cream. That same World's Fair in Missouri is also said to have introduced the world to cotton candy and iced tea.

URBAN LEGENDS

In the 1970s, a popular book and movie called *The Exorcist* captured America's imagination, at least the spooky side of it. What many people do not know is that the **Exorcist House** was not in Washington, DC, as it was in its fictionalized setting, but on a quiet suburban street in St. Louis, Missouri. According to the legend, in 1949, Roman Catholic priests were called upon to perform a series of exorcisms on a 13-year-old boy who became known under the pseudonym "Roland Doe" to protect his identity. It is said that the boy was playing with a Ouija board when he was apparently patched through to the dark side. It was feared that the boy became possessed by Satan, who caused terrifying things of the satanic variety to happen in the house. The priests eventually seemed successful in removing the spirit of

> ## Walt's World
>
> Missouri can boast a long list of notable residents, but arguably, more people have experienced a look at the Missouri childhood of one "favorite son" than any other. Walt Disney (1901–1966) moved with his family to the small town of Marceline, Missouri, when he was about four. There, young Walt found what he called his "Dreaming Tree," spending time under the cottonwood sketching woodland animals that came his way. Walt sold his very first drawing to a neighbor in Marceline. After he became a worldwide juggernaut, his Missouri childhood came to be represented at all Disney theme parks by Main Street USA, which is inspired by downtown Marceline. At Disneyland in California, Walt kept a private apartment atop the firehouse on Main Street USA. Today, a lamp is kept glowing there to symbolize that Walt's spirit is still alive and, by extension, that of Marceline, Missouri.

the devil from the boy, since the family was said not to be bothered by Beelzebub again. Today the house is a private residence apparently without incident, but the urban legend lives on.

Hitchhike Annie is the name of an apparently harmless ghost in an urban legend that is well known to many Missourians. She is described as being a young woman with long brown hair, pale skin, and wearing a white dress. The ghoulish girl allegedly roams the area of St. Louis that lies between the city's Calvary Cemetery and Bellefontaine Cemetery. When the sun is setting, she is said to flag down unsuspecting motorists and ask for a ride up the street. She is then said to disappear when the car reaches Bellefontaine Cemetery, never quite completing the journey.

Many states seem to have a Bigfoot legend, and Missouri is no exception. **Momo**, which is a nickname for "Missouri Monster," is said to be about seven feet tall with glowing orange eyes and an allegedly pumpkin-shaped head, all covered with black fur. It is said to have been sighted as it skulked along the Mississippi River, with those getting close enough to catch a scent reporting that the creature emits a foul odor. According to the legend, it gets its thrills by killing animals and scaring humans. However, it may have gotten an even bigger thrill when the 2019 film *Momo: The Missouri Monster* was released.

ICONIC MISSOURI FOOD

Ravioli is a popular food in itself, but Missouri expanded on the theme by creating a delicacy that is said to be served in most of the state's restaurants, especially in the St. Louis area. Aficionados of **Toasted Ravioli** scrupulously compare the best places to indulge in the crisp, warm, pillowy pockets. When visiting dignitaries arrive, this is the dish that is generally served as an appetizer, although many people find they can make a full meal of the pasta puffs. As a convenience, it is sold at the deli counter of many grocery stores, but the dish can easily be replicated at home. For dipping, homemade marinara sauce can be made from scratch, but any favorite prepared spaghetti or pizza sauce can be used, as seen in this recipe:

Toasted Ravioli (Yields 12 appetizer servings)
2 eggs, lightly beaten
¼ cup milk
16–20 oz frozen meat- or cheese-filled ravioli, freshly thawed
1 cup seasoned fine dry bread crumbs
Oregano to taste
Vegetable oil for frying
1 jar (24 oz) prepared tomato sauce
Grated Parmesan cheese to taste

1. Preheat oven to 300°F.
2. In a small bowl, combine eggs and milk.
3. Dip each thawed ravioli patty into egg mixture and then into bread crumbs mixed with oregano to coat on both sides.
4. In a heavy 3 qt saucepan, heat two inches of vegetable oil to about 350°F.
5. Fry coated ravioli, a few at a time, in hot oil about two minutes or until golden brown, turning once. Using a slotted spoon, remove ravioli from hot oil, and drain on paper towels.
6. Keep the already-cooked ravioli warm in 300° oven while frying remaining patties.
7. Meanwhile, gently warm the tomato sauce.
8. Remove all ravioli from oven and sprinkle each with Parmesan cheese.
9. Serve immediately with warm tomato sauce for dipping.

Source: Adapted from https://www.midwestliving.com/recipe/appetizers-snacks/missouri-toasted-ravioli/.

ODD LAWS

Internet wisdom can be found in items along the lines of Missouri residents allegedly not being legally able "to worry about squirrels" in the Show Me State. The actual amended ordinance in Excelsior Springs, Missouri, is that residents may not "*worry* squirrels," as in "bothering" the furry little creatures, not worrying *about* them. The current town law places squirrels, along with starlings and pigeons, in the category targeted by the Elimination of Pests ordinance, which presumably would bother squirrels a great deal. However, procedures are in place to give the animals a fighting chance. In areas of town where the city director believes such pests are sufficient to create a public nuisance, a licensed exterminating company must apply for a permit good for 30 days in which "disposal" may take place through "humane and sanitary methods."

Another internet rumor is that it is illegal to leave an unattended car running in Missouri due to the fact that it may scare the horses. Actually, the city of Springfield has outlawed the act of leaving a car running while unattended, though for different reasons. Specifically, no driver or individual in charge of a car may let it stand unattended without first stopping the engine, locking the ignition, and removing the key. The penalty for flouting this ordinance could involve up to a $1,000 fine. The rationale has nothing to do with equine anxiety, but with a rash of car thefts in Springfield causing problems for law enforcement. Almost half were being swiped when car keys were left in the vehicle and/or it was left running and unattended. The ordinance does not apply to delivery vehicles in the process of making a drop-off, which may be good news for hurried drivers of big parcel service trucks, which, if stolen, would at least be easier to spot and apprehend.

In Kansas City, bright outdoor lighting might be a deterrent to car theft if it does not shine too brightly. A municipal ordinance specifically titled "Glare" states that all outdoor lighting must be reflected away from residences and streets. Helpful exemptions include airport runway and aviation safety lights required by the Federal Aviation Administration (FAA) as well as warning lights on radio, communication, and navigation towers. Local residents in the holiday spirit will be glad to know that "temporary holiday light displays" are also acceptable in Kansas City amid the festivity of the season, as long as they are only short term.

UNUSUAL DESTINATIONS

The **Glass Labyrinth** in Kansas City, Missouri, is a maze with seven-foot-high walls that are made of clear glass one inch thick. Those in the know suggest that rookies avoid trying to hurry through the maze because it is harder than it looks—there is only one way in and one way out. Newcomers to the maze are also advised keep a hand in front of themselves to avoid unexpectedly running into the clear walls with their head, creating a "Bonk!" sound that is said to amuse onlookers.

Independence, Missouri, was once known across the nation as the home of U.S. president Harry Truman, the only Missourian to become the chief executive. Today, the town can also boast **Leila's Hair Museum**, which displays hundreds of examples of what is called a lost art form: weaving human hair into decorative objects. During the Victorian era, women would entwine hair into such items as bookmarks, buttons, jewelry, wall hangings, and wreaths. Some of the most poignant items are those that were made as a remembrance from the hair of loved ones who passed on, especially children who died young. Many of the century-old items at Leila's are accompanied by descriptions that tell their stories.

Speaking of stories, as its name may suggest, there is an interesting one about the **Nuclear Waste Adventure Trail** at Weldon Spring, Missouri, officially titled the Weldon Spring Site Remedial Action Project Disposal Cell. At one time, it was the setting of the largest explosives factory in America, later becoming the home of a facility that refined uranium for nuclear bombs in the Cold War era. After that came to a halt, what remained was more than a million cubic yards of contaminated rubble including asbestos, mercury, polychlorinated biphenyls (PCBs), radioactive uranium, radium, and good old-fashioned TNT. Today it is a tourist attraction. Visitors are invited to climb the man-made mountain via a pathway leading to the top. Underneath, the nuclear waste is said to be safely entombed, as illustrated in the Visitors Center through a cross-section display of the layers that make up the hill. Some guests are reluctant to climb the "adventure trail," even though admission is free.

Honorable mention among unusual destinations in Missouri goes to a handful of the state's "World's Largest" designations. **Maxie, the World's Largest Goose**, resides in Sumner, Missouri, but is not the feathered variety. Instead, it is a 4,000-pound fiberglass fowl standing 40 feet tall, heralding Sumner as the self-styled "Wild Goose Capital of the World." Visitors can feast their eyes on the **World's Largest Fork**, a pillar of the community in Springfield. The **World's Largest 20th Century Pecan**, the size of a bus, is a concrete kernel found in Brunswick, Missouri. After some contention for the title of "world's largest," the four-story-tall **World's Largest Rocking Chair on Route 66** is seated in the town of Cuba, Missouri. Finally, the **World's Largest Small Electric Appliance Museum** in Diamond, Missouri, proudly displays more than 7,000 diminutive items including blenders, hair dryers, hot plates, irons, mixers, popcorn poppers, and razors. Fans of unusual small appliances should not miss the "hot dog electrocuter."

DISTINCTIVE MISSOURI WORDS AND SAYINGS

Arch: Neither a curved geometrical shape nor the iconography of a famous fast-food franchise, but the Gateway Arch in St. Louis, which was completed in 1965 and is the world's tallest arch.

Mizzou: Affectionate reference to the University of Missouri.

Provel: Little-known outside Missouri, this processed cheese product is a blend of cheddar, swiss, and provolone, having a low melting point and gooey texture that Missourians love.

Put out: Angry.

Sundah: The Missouri pronunciation of hot-fudge-topped ice cream in a dish.

Further Reading

Brown, John W. *Missouri: An Illustrated Timeline—200 Years of Heroes and Rogues, Heartbreak and Triumph*. St. Louis, MO: Reedy Press, 2020.

Christensen, Lawrence, Brad Lookingbill, and William E. Parrish. *Missouri: The Heart of the Nation*. 4th edition. Hoboken, NJ: Wiley-Blackwell, 2019.

Taylor, Troy. *Haunted Missouri: Ghosts and Strange Phenomena of the Show Me State*. Mechanicsburg, PA: Stackpole Books, 2012.

Montana

FACT BOX

Nickname: Big Sky Country
Statehood Granted: 1889
Capital: Helena
Population: 1,070,000
State Motto: *Oro y plata* (Spanish: "Gold and Silver")
What Natives Call Themselves: Montanans

STATE HISTORY

As the state's name implies, there are a lot of mountains in Montana, which was named by Spanish explorers who called the region Montaña del Norte, or northern mountains. Similarly, as Montana's "Big Sky" nickname suggests, there are a lot of wide open spaces under seemingly endless skies. Although Montana is the nation's fourth largest state, it is one of the smallest in terms of population, having about the same number of people as the city of Phoenix, Arizona.

However, Montana has plenty of nonhuman residents. It is said to be home for a wider variety of animal species than any other state in the country, with at least 100 species of mammals alone, such as bighorn sheep, bobcats, caribou, and elk.

The state is unique geologically by having a "Triple Divide." At the Continental Divide in the Rocky Mountains, water flows westward from one side and eastward from the other. However, Montana's Triple Divide makes it the only state in the nation to have water not only flowing toward the Atlantic Ocean in the east and the Pacific Ocean in the west, but also flowing northward from Montana's Triple Divide to the Arctic Ocean by way of Hudson Bay.

Montana's Yellowstone River is the longest free-flowing undammed river in the contiguous United States. The Missouri River, the nation's longest, begins at the intersection of the Gallatin, Jefferson, and, Madison Rivers in Montana.

Montana shares a northern border with Canada at the 49th parallel. For trivia buffs, the 49th parallel also runs through Paris, France, although some say that latitude can seem a bit colder in Montana. In 1916, the temperature in Montana dropped 100° on a single January day—from 44°F to 56°F *below zero*—setting a world record for the greatest temperature change ever recorded in a single day.

Even the snow is larger in Montana. The largest measurable snowflake fell during a Montana storm in January 1887. At more than 15 inches in diameter and tipping the scales at eight inches thick, it holds the top spot in *Guinness World Records*.

With its vast wide open spaces, Montana contains a variation in terrain from peaks to prairies. Having a state motto meaning "Gold and Silver," Montana has traditionally been rich in natural resources. As far back as 10,000 years ago, Indigenous people migrated across the region to follow the great herds of bison, on which their existence depended.

The Louisiana Purchase in 1803 secured Eastern Montana for the United States. During the Lewis and Clark Expedition in 1805, the explorers covered more miles within today's Montana than in any other state. Western Montana was the subject of a dispute with the British until the Oregon Treaty was signed in 1846.

With the United States claiming what it felt was clear title to the land, white settlers and traders soon arrived in today's Montana. Their activities put them into direct conflict with the Native Americans who were already there. Fur-bearing animals, on which the Indians depended, were decimated, especially the bison. Contact with whites also brought deadly diseases for which the Natives had no immunity.

The first permanent white settlement in today's Montana was founded at St. Mary's in 1841, although trading posts had been established earlier in the 1800s. When gold was discovered in 1852, prospectors flooded in. Around the same time, settlers traveling westward on the Oregon Trail often remained amid Montana's beauty.

In 1864, Congress officially created the Montana Territory. By 1889, the region's increased population qualified Montana for statehood, joining the Union as the 41st state.

Montana's Native Americans were often moved to reservations far away from their traditional homes. The extermination of the bison herds on which they depended often also spelled the demise of Native people.

The removal of Montana's Native Americans frequently came after conflicts with the state's white population. Clashes between the U.S. Army and Native Americans in Montana include Red Cloud's War (1866–1868), the Blackfoot Massacre (1870), Great Sioux War (1876–1877), Nez Percé War (1877), and Battle of Crow Agency (1887).

However, one particular battleground in Montana has assumed an iconic spot in America's mythic history: Custer's Last Stand, more formally known as the Battle of the Little Bighorn. Taking place on June 25–26, 1876, along the Little Bighorn River in Southeastern Montana, the battle between Native Americans and the Seventh Cavalry Regiment of the U.S. Army under George Armstrong Custer resulted in a stunning defeat for the white American soldiers. Discounting a warning from scouts, Custer ordered an attack on an Indian village that ultimately led to the death of more than 200 men in his command. Through popular books, lectures, and paintings, Montana's Battle of the Little Bighorn and the flamboyant Custer have lived on through the years.

Another larger-than-life individual associated with Montana is media mogul Ted Turner, who is best known for founding television stations such as CNN and Turner Classic Movies. Originally making his fortune in Atlanta, Georgia, Turner began buying property in Montana. His estate eventually covered about two million acres, making him one of the nation's largest private landowners.

One significant feature of Ted Turner's holdings in Montana is his cultivation of bison in an attempt to bring them back from the brink of extinction. Turner has said he wanted to help restore the great herds of bison that roamed the plains by the millions before they were decimated by white men until only about 200 were left. By some estimates, Turner's efforts have nurtured about 50,000 of the animals.

In addition to encouraging other landowners to raise the animals, Turner has also spread Montana's iconography across America in an innovative way: Bison Burgers. With restaurants called Ted's Montana Grill across the country, he has helped to popularize the meat, providing an incentive for ranchers to actively grow their herds.

Montana was apparently home to other animals. A giant Tyrannosaurus skeleton that was recently unearthed in Montana is one of only a few virtually intact T. Rex skeletons and one of the largest ever found in the world.

A sapphire from Montana called a "Yogo" is the only gemstone from North America that is found in Britain's Crown Jewels. Found only in Montana, Yogo sapphires are ranked among the very finest in the world, with a unique natural cornflower blue color.

Often incorrectly termed "buffalo," millions of bison once roamed Montana. The extermination of the bison herds on which they depended also spelled the demise of Native people. Some Montana ranchers are trying to bring the animals back from the brink of extinction. (Isselee/Dreamstime.com)

> ### Timing Is Everything
>
> In 1916, Montana's Jeannette Rankin (1880–1973) became the first woman elected to the U.S. Congress. That achievement was notable enough, but 1916 was *four years before* American women even had the right to vote. Rankin was an outspoken advocate for civil rights, child welfare, and women's rights, as well as being strongly anti-war. Soon after her Congressional term began, she joined 50 members of the U.S. House of Representatives in voting against America entering World War I in 1917. She was the one who was singled out for harsh criticism and was voted out of office. She was finally able to return to Congress 24 years later, but the bad news was that it occurred in 1941, just in time to vote on America's entry into World War II. Again, she opposed going to war, this time the only member of Congress to do so. She was denounced mercilessly and did not run for reelection. To date, Rankin remains the only woman ever elected to Congress from Montana.

However, there are some Montanans who would suggest that the state's real treasure is the perseverance of its people, including its women who labored side by side with men to build the Big Sky State.

URBAN LEGENDS

Since the late 1880s, there have been numerous reports each year of something fishy in Montana's Flathead Lake, specifically the **Flathead Lake Monster**. It is said that there have been hundreds of alleged sightings of the mysterious creature that apparently has a home in the huge lake. Measuring 200 square miles in area, Flathead Lake is the largest freshwater lake west of the Mississippi River, thus providing plenty of room for an underwater behemoth to stretch out. The Flathead Lake Monster is described as having an eel-like body with multiple humps on its back. According to reports, it is up to 40 feet long with piercing black eyes and brown or blue-black skin. With a nod to "Nessie," the Loch Ness Monster in Scotland, local Montanans have come to think of their state's Flathead Lake Monster as "Flessie."

Arguably the most poignant Montana legend involves the **Ghosts of Little Bighorn**. Commonly called Custer's Last Stand, Montana's Battle of the Little Bighorn took place in 1876, securing a spot in America's national psyche for decades to come. The clash between Native Americans and the U.S. Army's Seventh Cavalry ended in the violent death of around 300 soldiers and Natives combined. Today at the Little Bighorn Battlefield National Monument, both sides are honored. It is said that the ghostly spirits of Natives and soldiers have been spotted by observers, along with hearing the sound of bugles, rifle fire, screams, and war cries.

Drivers traveling at night between Great Falls and Benton on Montana's Highway 87 are urged to keep alert. The **Hitchhiker of Black Horse Lake** is said to haunt that stretch of road, startling unsuspecting motorists. The phantom hitchhiker has been described as wearing denim and having long black hair. According to the legend, his body suddenly thuds up onto the hood of the driver's car, hitting the windshield as if a pedestrian had been struck by the car. When the driver pulls over, there is no one to be found, nor is there damage to the vehicle. It is said that the vanishing victim is the ghost of a man who was indeed hit by a car one night on that highway many years ago, and the violent reenactment is his spirit wandering the roadway from the great beyond.

ICONIC MONTANA FOOD

In the mountains of Montana, it is not unusual to see people hiking with empty containers. They are meant to carry wild huckleberries, Montana's signature fruit. Similar to blueberries but with a distinctive depth of flavor, the round purple berries can be found across Montana in dishes such as ice cream, jam, muffins, pancakes, huckleberry vinaigrette dressing, pork with huckleberry glaze, and "huckleberry burgers." The annual Huckleberry Days Arts Festival in Whitefish, Montana, leaves no doubt as to the loyalty of Montanans to their beloved berry, which can be found in such dishes as this recipe for **Montana Wild Huckleberry Pie**:

> **Montana Wild Huckleberry Pie** (Serves 5)
> 2 prepared crusts to form top and bottom of a 9-inch pie
> 3 Tbsp flour
> ¾ cup sugar, with some in reserve to add if berries are very tart
> 4 cups fresh huckleberries
>
> 1. Preheat oven to 450°F.
> 2. Mix flour and sugar with the huckleberries, then set aside.
> 3. Fit the pastry dough into a 9-inch pie pan to form bottom crust, then brush the edge of the crust with cold water.
> 4. Pour the berry mixture into the bottom piecrust.
> 5. Place the upper crust on pie, pricking with a fork. Press the crusts together, trimming and fluting the excess dough at the rim of pie pan.
> 6. After baking the pie at 450° for 10 minutes, reduce heat to 350° and bake about 40 minutes more.

Source: Adapted from http://www.dvo.com/recipe_pages/best-from-the-plains/Montana_Huckleberry_Pie.php.

ODD LAWS

In keeping with the policy of many businesses and municipalities, the town of Billings, Montana, prohibits bringing firearms to city council meetings or other public assemblies. But Billings goes a step further, perhaps as a nod to the state's mining industry. In addition to prohibiting weapons in government buildings, concealed or unconcealed/with or without a permit, Billings also prohibits toting explosives. In a state where the mining industry used mass quantities of explosives for decades, the town leaders of Billings might have concerns that a few leftovers might be lying around. The Billings municipal code clarifies its position by affirming its concern over the security of city council proceedings and the safety of its participants, specifically outlawing explosives "where such possession intimidates, terrifies or endangers another human being," which explosives have a tendency to do.

There are also concerns over concealment in the town of Kalispell, but not weaponry: pool tables. That town's municipal code renders it unlawful for any place of business where there is a pool table or billiard table to place "any screen, blind, curtain, shutter, painted, colored or ground glass or any article of furniture or any obstruction that would prohibit the view of such pool table or billiard table from the street in front of such room or place of business wherein is kept any of the tables above described." In other words, apparently passersby must have an unobstructed view of pool tables lest they possibly mistake a billiard hall for an ice cream parlor. Or perhaps it is to persuade strollers that they might enjoy a rousing game of pool. It is not known what manner of issue prompted this city statute.

In the city of Helena, another type of recreation is available for those who know what it is and confine themselves to playing during daylight hours. According to the Helena municipal code, "No person shall play or engage in the game of folf . . . at nighttime in any area within the business improvement district that has not been sanctioned as a designated folf course by the city." In other places, the sport is commonly known as disc golf or Frisbee golf. Played with round discs, usually plastic and about the size of a pie pan, it basically simulates the game of golf. Players compete by aiming at a target or "hole," throwing a disc toward the target, then throwing again from where the previous throw landed, and so forth until the target is reached. Many municipal recreation areas in America have such courses set up, but at least in Helena, adding to the challenge by playing after dark is a definite bogey.

Speaking of recreation, honorable mention is awarded to the city of Helena. According to the municipal code, it is unlawful to use a lawn sprinkler for recreational purposes if the recreational activity involves using it for "the annoyance of passersby" i.e., getting them wet. In other words, it is against the rules to use a lawn sprinkler as a Super Soaker.

UNUSUAL DESTINATIONS

For those who enjoy getting up close and personal with toxic waste, the **Berkeley Pit** in Butte, Montana, is the place to go. The site is a former open-pit copper mine that is more than a mile long, a mile wide, and almost 2,000 feet deep. It holds the result of hundreds of million tons of waste from the mine and continues to be filled by water from nearby aquifers. The noxious brew contains high concentrations of toxic chemicals such as arsenic, cadmium, copper, iron, and sulfuric acid. It is said that if a person were to drink some of the toxic water, death would result from the effect of corroding the digestive system from inside. Boasting an adjacent gift shop, the Berkeley Pit is a tourist attraction. For a small admission fee, visitors can go out on the viewing platform to check it out, although it is not known if there are any nearby water fountains.

Grasshopper Glacier in Park County, Montana, lives up to its name. This rapidly disappearing glacier is filled with extinct grasshoppers who are perfectly preserved in the ice. It sits about 11,000 feet above sea level and is strangely colored, not the pure white or icy blue of most glaciers, but variegated swirls. Tens of millions of grasshoppers—actually, locusts—are entombed in the ice. The current theory is that centuries ago, billions of locusts were migrating over the Rockies when they were trapped by a winter storm that kept them frozen in time. Their species, called Rocky Mountain Locusts, went extinct over a century ago and today's frozen forebears may vanish as well. Due to climate change, Grasshopper Glacier has melted from a length of more than five miles about a hundred years ago to less than a mile today. Visitors are therefore encouraged to see it soon.

For those who wish to see a classic example of the frontier "can-do" spirit, **Havre Beneath the Streets** in the town of Havre, Montana, is just the thing. In 1904, a massive fire burned much of the town to the ground, including most of its business district. Shop owners therefore moved their businesses down to the basement, constructed a web of underground tunnels, created what was essentially an "underground mall," and thrived. Most of it was carved out by Chinese workers. Today, tour-goers will see what remained from those businesses, including a butcher shop, dentist's office, pharmacy, saloon, and soda fountain. Visitors can also get a glimpse of other slices of history, such as the opium dens and speakeasies that were served by the underground tunnels.

DISTINCTIVE MONTANA WORDS AND SAYINGS

Back east: Anything east of the Plains States.

"Cowboy up!" Advice for someone, usually a male, to deal with a difficult situation rather than complaining. In a similar vein, "cowgirl up!" can be used for Montana females.

Gumbo: Not the succulent soup, but Montana slang for the state's slick, slippery mud that can become virtually impassible when wet, and as hard as concrete when dry.

Nice speakin' atcha: Goodbye.

Outfit: Pickup truck. New female residents of Montana are often stunned to hear an auto mechanic say there's a problem with their outfit.

Further Reading

Enright, Kelly. *America's Natural Places: Rocky Mountains and Great Plains.* Santa Barbara, CA: ABC-CLIO, 2010.

Howard, Joseph Kinsey. *Montana: High, Wide, and Handsome.* Revised edition. Lincoln, NE: Bison Books, 2003.

Stevens, Karen. *Haunted Montana: A Ghost Hunter's Guide to Haunted Places You Can Visit—If You Dare!* Helena, MT: Riverbend Publishing, 2007.

Nebraska

FACT BOX

Nickname: Cornhusker State
Statehood Granted: 1867
Capital: Lincoln
Population: 2,000,000
State Motto: "Equality before the Law"
What Natives Call Themselves: Nebraskans

STATE HISTORY

To many schoolchildren, Nebraska is best known as half of the Kansas-Nebraska Act, which created the Kansas and the Nebraska territories in 1854. The historical significance of that law lies in its provision for "popular sovereignty," in which the local citizens, rather than the U.S. Congress, would determine whether or not slavery would be permitted in their territory. There were deadly conflicts in "Bleeding Kansas" as pro- and antislavery factions clashed. However, that kind of bloodshed did not take place in Nebraska, which was far enough north to be a free territory under the terms of the Missouri Compromise of 1820.

Nebraska became America's 37th state in 1867. As with most of the nation, its history went back thousands of years. Today's Nebraska was traversed for centuries by Indigenous people who followed the great herds of bison on which they depended for survival. Native people migrated regularly along the flat swath of mid-America currently called the Great Plains, which encompasses all of today's Nebraska.

Following the arrival of Europeans in North America, control of the region containing Nebraska was disputed among Britain, France, and Spain, although France and Spain did not have a viable presence there. After winning its independence in the American Revolution and again defeating the British in the War of 1812, the United States claimed the region. When Fort Atkinson in today's Nebraska was established in 1819, it was the first U.S. Army post west of the Missouri River.

Although some people think of the region as calm and uneventful, those people have never lived through a Nebraska storm. Nature provides much of the drama in

Nebraska. With most of the state situated on the vast treeless prairie of the Great Plains, there is nothing to stand in the way of fierce thunderstorms, tornadoes, and blizzards as they roar across the land. The ceaseless Chinook winds are so unrelenting that they are said to have driven people mad.

In the 1860s and 1870s, tens of thousands of settlers moved into Nebraska. They were in search of the free land that was granted by the American government under the Homestead Act of 1862. Historians estimate that around 75,000 permanent settlers came to Nebraska during the year 1872 alone, with even more arriving in 1873.

Those new arrivals were often stunned to discover that there were few trees on the prairie. Therefore, many adopted the Native American practice of constructing their homes from sod, which at the time was plentiful. Some were unfazed by the lack of trees, finding it easier to clear the land for farming and ranching. New technology brought the advent of barbed wire, steel plows, and windmills to the prairie, which encouraged the development of more acreage. The coming of the railroads brought greater numbers of people to Nebraska as well as providing a system for shipping to distant markets, which led to an increase in still more farming and ranching.

However, beginning in 1874, Nebraska suffered a series of catastrophic invasions by hungry grasshoppers. To some, it seemed to be a plague of biblical proportions. Innumerable millions of the flying insects ate crops, contaminated water, killed livestock, and even endangered trains by making the tracks slick with their oily bodies. The landscape was utterly decimated each time the skies turned black with the returning swarms. Years of back-breaking work were often destroyed in hours.

However, things seemed to be turning around in the early years of the 20th century. With agricultural mechanization, farmers could easily plow up the land and add to their holdings. However, like the hungry grasshoppers, this too would prove to devastate Nebraska's farmers. In the drought year of 1931, without any sod to hold it down, the dry, loose soil started blowing away. As the Dust Bowl annihilated the Great Plains from Nebraska to Texas, hundreds of thousands of acres of Nebraska farmland was said to simply blow into the Gulf of Mexico. In Nebraska, the Dust Bowl did not end until drenching rains came in 1939.

Nebraska rebounded from the agricultural devastation, going on to become a leader in other industries such as meatpacking. Many residents left the rural countryside for more urban areas such as Nebraska's largest city, Omaha, and the state capital of Lincoln.

It was Omaha that formed the basis for much of the state's development in other fields, often being ranked near the top of American cities in terms of Fortune 500 companies and high-tech hubs.

One Fortune 500 company that has become closely identified with Omaha and the state of Nebraska is Berkshire Hathaway. Its chairman and CEO, Warren

Buffett, is considered one of the most successful investors in the world as well as one of its richest people. Financiers around the globe closely follow Buffett's investment picks and his interpretation of market trends. Throughout his stellar career, he has continued to live modestly in Nebraska, earning him the nickname "the Oracle of Omaha."

It is often surprising to people that a well-known symbol of sophistication did not hail from London or New York. Movie star Fred Astaire (born Frederick Austerlitz) first took dance lessons in his hometown of Omaha, going on from Nebraska to become Hollywood's personification of grace and elegance.

Nebraskans often claim their state as home of Kool-Aid, the TV dinner, and the Rueben sandwich (although New Yorkers dispute the latter).

However, there is one indisputable oddity about Nebraska that sets it apart from all the other American states: its legislative system. Nebraska is the only state in the nation to have just a single legislative body instead of two. Other places have two independent lawmaking bodies that meet in separate chambers, usually called a state Senate and state House of Representatives. But since 1937, Nebraska's state legislature, called the "Unicameral" (from the Latin, meaning "one chamber"), has been felt to be more streamlined and cost-efficient than having two separate bodies. Nebraskans may not always agree with the Unicameral's decisions, but it's hard to argue with its efficiency.

Nebraska is unique in having only one state legislative body instead of two (i.e. a state Senate and House of Representatives). Nebraska's statehouse, pictured here, is called the "Unicameral," which is Latin for "one chamber." (Paul Brady/Dreamstime.com)

> ### Law and Order
>
> Richard "Two-Gun" Hart (1892–1952) was a noted Nebraska lawman who gained his nickname "Two-Gun" after a series of daring raids against bootleggers during Prohibition. In addition to destroying illegal stills, during the course of his outstanding career in law enforcement, Hart was credited with arresting at least 20 wanted killers and apprehending many other dangerous criminals. Hart became a justice of the peace after his career as a Prohibition agent, living a quiet life in Homer, Nebraska, where he later died peacefully. He had come to Nebraska at age 16 after an incident in New York City during a street gang fight when Hart defended his younger brother by pushing an attacker through a plate glass window. Fearing retribution, he fled New York and changed his name to Hart in honor of his idol, movie star William S. Hart. Incidentally, the younger brother whom Hart was protecting was named Al, and his family name before he changed it was "Capone." Richard Hart went on to be a Nebraska lawman, while brother Al became the criminal world's Public Enemy Number One.

URBAN LEGENDS

The 300-foot-tall **Blackbird Hill** overlooking the Missouri River near the town of Macy, Nebraska, was not named for feathered friends but was christened in honor of Chief Blackbird, a leader of the Omaha tribe. The hill served as distinctive landmark for river travelers through the years. However, its claim to fame is an urban legend about love that went bad. It is said that every year on October 17, a woman's chilling screams echo from Blackbird Hill. That was the date when the legend was born, involving a romantic triangle with a particularly unhappy ending. It seems that years before, a young woman had fallen in love with a young man who went to seek his fortune before they could marry. However, he never returned. After waiting several years, the heartbroken young woman married an older man. One day, by coincidence, her young suitor appeared at their farm, recognized her as his lost love, and explained he had been shipwrecked. The young couple planned to leave together, and she asked her husband to release her from their marriage. The husband's negative response was characterized by attacking her with his hunting knife. Aghast, the younger man watched him carry her bleeding body to the cliff atop Blackbird Hill, clutching it as he jumped into the river. Today Blackbird Hill is said to be possessed by the spirit of the murdered woman, crying out in anguish on the date when she met her untimely death.

In the early 1900s, the teacher at Portal School, a one-room schoolhouse in the small Nebraska town of Portal, may have had her own unique ideas about classroom management. According to the urban legend, she snapped one day. Barring the door, she took up a hatchet and murdered each of her young charges by chopping off their heads and placing the decapitated craniums on their desks. Then she methodically cut out their hearts, went to a nearby bridge, and threw the hearts into the water. Today, locals call it Heartbeat Bridge because it is said that while crossing it, the shuddering boards sound like the still-beating hearts that were tossed into the creek below. The schoolhouse was relocated to the nearby town of Papillion, where its name is whispered to be the **Hatchet House**. Despite the continuing urban legend, there is no record of a mass murder taking place at this school. The building was moved due to frequent flooding, and Portal eventually became a ghost town. Today, the old schoolhouse is used for field trips to presumably illustrate Nebraska history, although some teachers report improved behavior by students after they visit.

The post office in the small town of Valentine, Nebraska, undergoes an annual upsurge in mail when thousands of cards arrive in order to be re-mailed with a special postmark for Valentine's Day. However, another claim to fame by the town that is home to fewer than 2,800 people is much less romantic. Its oldest standing building, Centennial Hall, was built in 1897 and used to house the **Valentine Public School**. It is currently serving as a museum, which today is said to be haunted. According to the urban legend, the building is occupied by the ghost of a former student who was the victim of a bizarre, fatal crime. In 1944, a girl who attended the school played clarinet in the band. The story goes that she died after someone poisoned its reed, so when she began playing the instrument, the deadly poison took effect. Neither a motive nor a suspect has ever been documented. This "cold case" has led to reports of seeing the murdered girl's disgruntled ghost wandering the halls, apparently seeking justice. There is also said to be the sound of music coming from the school's old band room, a place where there have not been any musical instruments for years.

ICONIC NEBRASKA FOOD

There are some who believe that the only thing better than a grilled cheese sandwich would be a grilled cheese sandwich that is *deep-fried*. Many of those people reside in Nebraska, where the iconic state dish is known as a **Cheese Frenchee**. Thought by some to have received its name because of a passing resemblance to the French-derived croque monsieur, the Cheese Frenchee became a Nebraska staple in the 1950s due to its popularity at a restaurant called King's Food Host. The restaurant vanished, but Cheese Frenchees remain in the hearts and taste buds of Nebraskans. It even manages to incorporate a food item that pays tribute to the Cornhusker State by being dipped in cornflakes before frying, making it gooey on the inside and crunchy on the outside.

> **Cheese Frenchees** (Serves 3)
> 6 slices American cheese
> 6 slices white bread
> Miracle Whip or mayonnaise to taste
> 1 egg

½ cup milk
¾ cup flour
1 tsp salt
1 cup finely crushed corn flakes, replenishing supply as needed
Oil for deep frying

1. Prepare three standard grilled cheese sandwiches, using two slices of cheese for each and mayonnaise or Miracle Whip to taste.
2. Cut crusts off the sandwiches, and slice them diagonally into four triangles each.
3. Combine egg, milk, flour, and salt.
4. Dip each triangle into egg mixture before coating on all sides in a small bowl of corn flake crumbs.
5. Deep-fry in oil at about 375°F until golden brown; serve immediately.

Source: Adapted from https://www.justapinch.com/recipes/main-course/other-main-course/cheese-frenchee.html.

ODD LAWS

With a population of almost 50,000 people, the city of Grand Island, Nebraska, is not exactly a "one-horse town." But like the rest of the state, its roots lie firmly in the Old West. Anyone planning a trip to town might be well advised to "hold your horses" if the mode of transportation is four-legged and the proposed route involves downtown city streets. According to the town's municipal code, horses, mules, oxen, or other draft animals are prohibited on thoroughfares that comprise the town's central business district. That includes not only riding the animal but also walking or tethering. Permission may be granted if the city's chief of police is notified at least 12 hours prior to the trip and if it will not "interfere with, or endanger, the normal traffic or use of the streets," not to mention endangering the animal itself.

The town of Kearney, Nebraska, also cannot be accused of "horsing around." Its city code does not actually ban horses from its downtown district or require special permission to park, but it says somewhat obscurely that if a "vehicle is horse-drawn, the horses shall be turned at right angles to the vehicles and in the direction in which traffic on that side of the street is moving." In the interest of fairness, even cars and trucks have to follow the rules—no backing to the curb is permitted except when actually loading or unloading, "and in no case longer than the actual time required."

In the town of Hastings, the municipal code hygienically forbids spitting on the sidewalk. According to city officials, there is no recent history of complaints, citations, or any other penalties for public expectoration. However, the law is on the books and goes beyond spitting on the sidewalks of Hastings, also including crosswalks as well as "steps, approaches or stairways leading to any public building or place of public gathering in the City." Visitors to Hastings would be well advised to plan ahead during allergy season; tobacco chewers should make their own arrangements.

UNUSUAL DESTINATIONS

The pride of York, Nebraska, is an institution known as **Lee's Legendary Marbles**, carefully organized by owner Lee Batterton. Its collection, said to be the largest in the world, revolves around about a million marbles, those diminutive balls of colored glass generally used for playing games. Besides the marbles themselves, there are exhibits of marble information and memorabilia. Along with the general public, individuals who self-identify as serious collectors will find a lot to love, and possibly purchase, since the museum also sells rare and antique marbles dating back to the early 1800s. A few unique marbles in the collection that were made before World War I contain uranium. In the unlikely event that visitors tire of being surrounded by marbles, even uranium-filled ones, there are also board games from olden days, vintage lunch boxes, coins from the past, and antique watches.

As might be deduced by its name, the **National Museum of Roller Skating** in Lincoln, Nebraska, is home to what is said to be the world's largest collection of historical roller skates. Established in 1980, it is the only museum of its kind, not just in the nation but also around the globe. Spotlighting roller skating as recreation, sport, and business, the exhibits include skates through the years as well as artwork, books, costumes, films, photos, trophies, and other skating memorabilia from 1819 to present. The display groupings include artistic skating, inline skating, roller derby, and speed skating plus a difficult-to-categorize pair of jetpack skates developed in 1956 but which never quite found a niche with the public. On the other hand, the museum's friendly slogan, "Come Roll with Us!" makes it a destination that has found a place in the hearts of skating fans—that's just the way they roll.

Seekers of the **World's Largest Porch Swing** will find it in Hebron, Nebraska. It was built by local citizens in 1985 to compete for the title of "Nebraska's Fourth of July City." The award never quite materialized, but the massive porch swing did. Tourists often stop by this attraction, seating 16 adults or 24 children, to have a swinging time.

Honorable mention among offbeat Nebraska destinations is the **Hay Bale Rest Area** in Alliance. To call it rustic is an understatement. While the state of Nebraska has more conventional highway rest stops, this open-air facility is constructed of a small pile of hay bales. On top are a lounge chair and a toilet. There are no other amenities.

DISTINCTIVE NEBRASKA WORDS AND SAYINGS

Aksarben: "Nebraska" spelled backward. Dating back to a group of boosters in 1895, the word is still seen today, including a development called Aksarben Village in Omaha.

Der Viener Schlinger: Sausage-shaped shoulder-mounted gun that shoots wrapped hot dogs into the crowd at Cornhusker football games.

Dorothy Lynch: The name of a salad dressing, sometimes affectionately called "sweet tangy orange goo," used in Nebraska as dipping sauce or even a substitute for mayonnaise in pasta salads.

Market rats: Teens who hang out at the Old Market entertainment district in Omaha.

Runza: Nebraska's meat-and-cabbage-filled baked pocket sandwich (similar to Bierocks in Kansas) with the word based on a German dialect for a round belly.

Further Reading

Luebke, Frederick. *Nebraska: An Illustrated History.* 2nd edition. Lincoln, NE: Bison Books, 2005.

Nebraska History. Accessed December 10, 2021. https://visitnebraska.com/things-to-do/history.

Olson, James C., and Ronald Naugle. *History of Nebraska.* Lincoln: University of Nebraska Press, 2015.

Nevada

FACT BOX

Nickname: The Silver State
Statehood Granted: 1864
Capital: Carson City
Population: 3,000,000
State Motto: "All for Our Country"
What Natives Call Themselves: Nevadans

STATE HISTORY

The state's name comes from the Spanish word "nevada," meaning "snowy," a reference to the icy peaks of the region's Sierra Nevada ("snowy mountains").

Although known for its deserts, it often comes as a surprise for people to learn that Nevada is one of the top five most mountainous states in America, along with Colorado, New Mexico, Utah, and Wyoming.

Even with such a diverse topography, much of Nevada is inhospitable for human habitation. Nearly three-quarters of Nevadans live in the area around Las Vegas, far exceeding the next largest urban environment, Reno, or, as it calls itself, the "Biggest Little City in the World."

Native Americans, including the Paiute and Shoshone tribes, inhabited the region before Spanish explorers like Francisco Garcés arrived in the late 1700s. Today's Nevada was annexed by Spain in 1804 and then by Mexico in 1821.

In 1847, pioneers from the Church of Jesus Christ of Latter-day Saints (LDS), or Mormons, founded a settlement in today's Nevada, calling it the State of Deseret. The word "deseret" is said to appear in the Book of Mormon, usually referring to "honeybee," a symbol of industriousness.

After the United States acquired the region following the Mexican War in 1848, the discovery of gold in neighboring California brought both permanent settlers and get-rich-quick prospectors. Some of the latter were disappointed not to find gold, but those who persevered found one of the country's richest veins of silver, called the Comstock Lode, near Virginia City, Nevada, in 1859. Today, Nevada is officially known as the Silver State in homage to the wealth it brought.

Nevada became America's 36th state in 1864. It was one of two states admitted to the Union during the Civil War, the other being West Virginia.

> ### You Say Ne-VAHH-duh, I Say Ne-VADD-uh
>
> Amid the many subjects that are debated by Americans, one is at the forefront in the state of Nevada. It has been known to bring heated criticism upon visiting politicians and has merited urgent communications from Nevada governors to campaigners from their own political party, advising them on the matter before they come to the state and doing so in order to prevent losing votes based on one important issue. The issue is this: how to pronounce the word "Nevada." It is true that by adhering to the Spanish word for the state, meaning "snowy," it would be pronounced Ne-*VAHH*-duh. However, the Spaniards departed a few centuries ago. When Americans arrived, they preferred Ne-*VADD*-uh. In the latter Americanized pronunciation, the second syllable rhymes with "mad"—which is what sensitive locals might become if the name of their state is mispronounced.

In the anything-goes atmosphere of Nevada's mining communities, unregulated gambling was commonplace. In 1931, Nevada's state legislature officially legalized open gambling. The law was passed one week after the federal government approved a huge construction contract to build today's Hoover Dam. The project was to be built near a small, dusty Nevada town called Las Vegas, Spanish for "the meadows."

After land was auctioned in what became today's downtown Las Vegas, it was founded as a city in 1905. The small town prospered amid the combination of legalized gambling and the massive influx of construction workers between 1931 and 1936, when the dam was completed.

Opportunities for profits in Nevada did not go unnoticed. In the 1930s, mobster Benjamin Siegel saw the potential in Las Vegas, a vision that expanded after World War II ended in 1945. The rise of air travel in the prosperous postwar era meant that visitors from around the country could enjoy the Las Vegas experience if, as Siegel thought, it was done right. Along with legalized gambling, this meant good food, luxurious hotels, and top entertainers.

After Siegel's flagship hotel, the Flamingo, opened in 1946, others followed. Soon, the civic tolerance for various forms of "adult entertainment" in Las Vegas earned it the title of "Sin City." Visitors from around the world came to Nevada with the hope of having a blast.

Many were able to experience a blast of a different kind. In the 1950s and early 1960s, Nevadans and visitors to Las Vegas were able—even encouraged—to view mushroom clouds from nuclear weapons that were being tested at the nearby Nevada Test Site. The billowing radioactive clouds were touted as a spectacular attraction available nowhere else in the United States. Special tour packages and novelty drinks at hotels during bomb-watching parties were part of the fun in Las Vegas, which boasted a new nickname, "Atomic City." It was later determined that radioactive nuclear fallout posed a health risk to observers, even those who were a long distance away.

Nuclear testing as a tourist attraction has been merely one unique factor in Nevada. Having less than 10 inches of rain per year, Nevada is known as America's driest state. In an additional bit of trivia, Reno, Nevada, is farther west than Los Angeles, California, as maps will attest.

Nevada even has its own legal holiday when state, county, and city government offices are closed, along with most schools, libraries, and businesses like banks. It is called Nevada Day, commemorating the state's admission to the Union on October 31, 1864. Being observed on the last Friday in October, Nevada Day bumps Halloween to another date if a conflict arises.

In whatever way Nevadans choose to celebrate their day off on Nevada Day, it is not recommended that they plan a visit to the zone popularly known as Area 51, located near Groom Lake, Nevada. The famed Area 51 is a top-secret facility that is part of the Nellis Air Force Base complex. This restricted military installation has served as a test facility since the 1950s, but is better known for being at the center of conspiracy theories involving unidentified flying objects (UFOs) and extraterrestrials.

For decades, the U.S. government did not admit Area 51 even existed. It currently insists there are no little green men or any other types of aliens residing there. The military says Area 51 is classified for reasons of national security, which only adds fuel to the fire. Believers in the conspiracy theory remain convinced that all the secrecy must mean it is a hotbed for interplanetary activity.

Some sources claim that the actual use of Area 51 is at least as exciting as visitors from outer space. It is said that the facility is a top-secret test site for experimental aircraft, albeit the kind that stays relatively close to our planet. Those wishing to find out for themselves by visiting or photographing Area 51 will be met by explicit signs stating that such incursions will be met with fines and/or jail time. Armed patrols reinforce the point. However, there are many other out-of-this-world spots to visit in Nevada.

URBAN LEGENDS

Elvis is still in the building at the Westgate Hotel in Las Vegas, or so the urban legend goes. It was formerly called the Las Vegas Hilton, and prior to that, it was the International. In 1956, Elvis Presley made his Las Vegas debut at the New Frontier Hotel, which billed him as "the Atomic Powered Singer." He was on the lineup with comedian Shecky Greene and the Freddy Martin Orchestra, both of whom were better received by the Vegas crowd than the King of Rock and Roll. However, by 1969, when Elvis started playing the International/Hilton each year, millions of adoring fans flocked from around the world. Today, the ghost of Elvis, who died in 1977, is said to repay the compliment by manifesting itself at the hotel in spectral form, wafting near the showroom and leaving observers all shook up.

One night in 1870, five masked men held up the Central Pacific Overland Express train on its way to Reno with $40,000 worth of gold intended for a mine payroll. Only about 150 gold coins were recovered, but even after the robbers were caught and imprisoned, not one was willing to reveal the whereabouts of the gold. The men were believed to have buried their loot in Six Mile Canyon or along the bank of the Truckee River near Reno. After serving their sentences, four of the robbers vanished, never to be heard from again. Jack Davis, thought to be the ringleader, was released later, but was killed during an attempted Wells Fargo stagecoach robbery. Today, according to the legend of the **Lost Gold of the Overland Express**, the loot is still allegedly buried somewhere in Six Mile Canyon or near the Truckee River. Treasure hunters have sought it for years without success. Some say the ghost of Jack Davis protects his ill-gotten gains by appearing as a screaming white phantom to frighten away anyone seeking the hidden treasure he will never be able to spend.

At **Robb Canyon** near Reno, it is said that the mutilated bodies of three men and a woman were discovered in the 1970s at the remote location. Their brutal murders have never been solved. According to legend, intrepid hikers descending into the canyon will encounter all manner of supernatural phenomena, including cold spots, full body apparitions, screams, and shadowy figures stalking them. The visitors are usually rendered disoriented, at which point they are eager to either film the paranormal activity or get out of the canyon as quickly as possible.

Also near Reno, an urban legend concerns the **Water Babies of Pyramid Lake** who are said to lure unlucky fishermen to their deaths. Each year, anglers tend to vanish into the depths of the lake without their bodies ever being recovered. The urban legend maintains that centuries ago, the Water Babies were ill-formed premature fetuses that were interred by Native Americans in the lake, which is one of the largest in Nevada. The angry spirits of these terrifying tots are said to produce the cries of invisible babies from beneath the surface of the water. When a fisherman leans over the side of the boat to investigate, the ghostly wails are replaced by the sound of a *splash*.

ICONIC NEVADA FOOD

In many listings of each state's iconic food, there may be a photo of gumbo (Louisiana) or lobster rolls (Maine), for example. But for Nevada, some sources, often with tongue in cheek, show a photo of an empty plate. That's because casino towns like Las Vegas or Reno rely heavily on the kind of all-you-can-eat buffet where diners start with an empty plate, adding piles of food precariously as they go down the line. In some places, there may be more than 500 items on a single buffet, everything from delicate crepes to smoked pork belly. But there is one special item that Nevada seems to have made its own: **Shrimp Cocktail**, as seen in the recipe below. Thanks to flash freezing and air transport, it is said that more than 50,000 pounds of shrimp are consumed in landlocked Nevada per day, more than the rest of the country combined.

Nevada Shrimp Cocktail (Serves 4)
Packaged shrimp boil mix
2 lb jumbo shrimp

1 cup ketchup
⅓ cup horseradish
1 Tbsp lemon juice
⅛ tsp black pepper
Lemon wedges to garnish

1. Boil water and packaged shrimp boil in a large pot.
2. Add raw frozen peeled and deveined shrimp.
3. Turn off heat, allowing the shrimp to sit in the hot water for about 10–15 minutes until they turn a light pink, then drain and chill.
4. When shrimp is completely cooled, mix remaining ingredients together in a bowl.
5. Toss the shrimp into the sauce and serve in individual glass dishes with a lemon wedge. If preferred, place the sauce mixture in individual dishes, then array the shrimp around its edges for dipping.

Source: Adapted from https://lazygastronome.com/nevada-shrimp-cocktail/.

ODD LAWS

An advertising campaign once proclaimed that what happens in Vegas stays in Vegas. However, under Nevada law, what happens in Vegas may actually end up on driving records across the country. Many states treat traffic offenses as civil infractions, in which offenders pay a fine and are essentially done with it. However, even for out-of-state tourists, driving offenses in Nevada are classified as misdemeanors under the criminal code. A conviction could conceivably have consequences back home for matters of employment or in seeking a professional license. In addition, Nevada courts may order repeat offenders to pay for and attend driver training school, which some perpetrators consider dire punishment.

There are those who might try to avoid possible traffic infractions by avoiding cars altogether and finding alternate means of transportation. However, they would do well to consider the Las Vegas municipal code before planning their route. On Fremont Street, unicycles are forbidden, along with other modes of transportation such as skateboards, roller skates, and even shopping carts. Nor is it permitted to revel in a unicycle-free environment by twirling in a hula hoop. They are forbidden too.

Nevada is not all nightlife and neon. Under state law, respect must be paid to both archaeology (the study of human history by excavating ancient sites and artifacts) and paleontology (the study of fossilized animals and plants). Under Nevada statutes, each April is designated as Paleontological Awareness Month, followed by Archeological Awareness and Historic Preservation Month in May. Activities include an annual proclamation by the governor calling upon schools, nonprofit groups, and state and local entities to work toward preserving Nevada's archaeological and paleontological resources. Some sites are singled out for special recognition, including Tule Springs in Southern Nevada, where remains have been found of extinct animals such as mammoths and American camels. Ichthyosaurs, not to be outdone, have been designated by legislative statute as the official state fossil.

UNUSUAL DESTINATIONS

With a smile from Lady Luck, sometimes even a mistake can turn into a winner. Such is the case of the **Fly Geyser** near the town of Gerlach, Nevada. A combination of human error mixing with natural geothermal pressure has created a water spout that not only shoots an impressive surge of water into the air but, thanks to a mineral buildup, also manages to turn the geyser into rainbow-colored hues. About a hundred years ago, an effort was made to drill for water there in hopes of irrigating potential farmland in the desert. The drillers did hit water, but at a temperature of about 200°; they determined it was too hot to use for irrigation. Later, a geothermic energy company sank a test well at the same site, but like Goldilocks, they found that it was not hot enough for their purposes. Their sealing cap did not hold, and another geyser spurted forth. Today, drop-in visitors are not permitted on the private land, although Friends of Black Rock/High Rock host regular nature walks on the property with its too hot/too cool geysers.

Some eye-catching phenomena are cool, but unlike the geysers, are not *too* cool; in fact, they are "just right." In Las Vegas, the **Neon Museum** is a cool yet eye-popping extravaganza of all things neon. Its mission is to collect and preserve iconic Las Vegas signs for artistic, cultural, and historic purposes. There is a light projection exhibit inside the gallery along with an outdoor display called the Neon Boneyard, which features hundreds of old neon signs. There are also exhibits of blueprints, photographs, and oral histories by original neon art creators, because according to staffers, every sign at the Neon Museum tells a unique story. They have a big canvas to work from: the Las Vegas Strip is only about four miles long, but is said to have more than 75,000 miles of neon.

For more flashing lights, the **Pinball Hall of Fame** has them, along with dinging bells and the chance to indulge in some serious button-pushing. Located in Las Vegas, the Pinball Hall of Fame is home to hundreds of machine games. They are predominantly pinball, but also include others such as sports-themed games and even one with a safe-cracking theme. Visitors can pay the going rate on the machines and play the games, with any proceeds being donated to charity.

There are no flashing lights in the ghost town of **Rhyolite**, Nevada. In fact, there are no lights at all. The boomtown was born in 1904 but was dead by 1916, when, like the fate of many bustling mining communities, the mines played out. Abandoned and left to the desert, today the town is home to a crumbling bank, general store, jail, and train depot, with their tattered shells being all that remain of Rhyolite's past glory. When the lights of Rhyolite went out in 1916, ghosts of the past were all that stayed behind. Today, tourists can walk the empty streets, although a few movie companies have come to town. They are usually filming a Western or an apocalyptic glimpse of America's future, which looks as bleak as Rhyolite itself.

After it was abandoned, the boom town of Rhyolite, Nevada, became a ghost town. Today, only tourists walk the empty streets, unless a movie company is filming a bleak vision of America's future. (Larry Gevert/Dreamstime.com)

DISTINCTIVE NEVADA WORDS AND SAYINGS

Burners: Not the parts of a stove that heat up to cook food, but the tens of thousands of participants at the annual Burning Man alternative arts festival in the Northwest Nevada desert.

Chapel: In most places, a small place of worship, but due to lax nuptial requirements in Nevada, it's a spot for a quick wedding that might involve an Elvis impersonator for an added touch of class.

Nickel: Gambling parlance for $500, not the 5¢ coin in a change purse.

Spaghetti Bowl: Hardly a tasty Italian pasta treat; in Nevada, it's the highway maze of on- and off-ramps at the interchange of I-15 and US-95.

Strip: Elsewhere, it may be a sliver of paper or wood, but in Las Vegas, it's the gaudy four-mile stretch of neon and casinos that locals tend to avoid at all costs.

Further Reading

Green, Michael S. *Nevada: A History of the Silver State*. Reno: University of Nevada Press, 2015.

Moreno, Richard. *Nevada Myths and Legends: The True Stories behind History's Mysteries*. 2nd edition. Lanham, MD: Globe Pequot, 2019.

Online Nevada Encyclopedia. Accessed November 13, 2021. https://www.onlinenevada.org.

New Hampshire

FACT BOX

Nickname: The Granite State
Statehood Granted: 1788
Capital: Concord
Population: 1,400,000
State Motto: "Live Free or Die"
What Natives Call Themselves: New Hampshirites

STATE HISTORY

Every four years, tiny New Hampshire is buried by an avalanche. It's not the kind with fluffy white snow but a landslide of presidential candidates, campaign managers, hangers-on, and news media of all varieties. There are even some curious visitors who want a firsthand glimpse of the election's early field of candidates and potential president.

The New Hampshire presidential primary is the first of the nationwide party primaries. Although the Iowa caucuses come first, it is said that Iowa is more informal, while the Granite State holds an actual primary election. Winners in New Hampshire can capitalize on their success by eliciting campaign contributions, while some candidates who do poorly in New Hampshire often drop out. Still others may try a different strategy as they go forward.

In any case, every four years, New Hampshire is spotlighted by national politicians and the news media. This is where many campaigns live or die based on the outcome, appropriately enough, since New Hampshire is the Live Free or Die state.

Although New Hampshire's official nickname is "the Granite State," referring to its exceptionally hard rock formations, many people are more familiar with the iconic New Hampshire state motto that appears on its license plates: "Live Free or Die."

The phrase is said to have been adapted from a toast written in 1809 by General John Stark, a New Hampshire hero in the American Revolution. Unable to attend a military reunion in person, he sent his toast by letter, stating *"Live free or die: Death is not the worst of evils."* As a popular motto of the French Revolution, "live free or die" was already in use at the time. Not only does the New Hampshire motto serve

Quote Shakespeare or Die?

There are some who say that the Granite State's motto, "Live Free or Die," is the one every other state wishes it had. The phrase was adopted as the official New Hampshire motto in 1945 and is one of the few state mottos that many other Americans know. In great part, this is due to what some consider a sentiment akin to the free-spiritedness of bikers on the open road. However, the backstory of the phrase includes something more likely to be found in a book of sonnets. A poem first published in 1803 called *It Is Not to Be Thought Of* by English romantic poet William Wordsworth (1770–1850) contains the line "We must be free or die, who speak the tongue that Shakespeare spoke," a phrase not likely to be found on the bumper sticker of a Harley.

Some say that New Hampshire's motto, "Live Free or Die," is the one every other state wishes it had. The phrase is one of the few state mottos that many Americans know, even if they do not know their own. (Thomaspajot/Dreamstime.com)

as a catchy title for action movie sequels, it describes what the locals feel to be their general character.

The region, known for its daunting winters, had been home for centuries to Native American people such as the Androscoggin and Pennacook. English explorers are said to have visited the area as early as 1600, although the first permanent settlements like present-day Dover were not established until the 1630s.

Historians note that arguably the most important feature of the early New Hampshire colony was its 18-mile strip of Atlantic coastline. It is shorter than that of any other state that touches the sea. Through that small but significant piece of New Hampshire seashore, settlers could arrive, and trade could be maintained.

Some New Hampshirites are quick to point out that as one of the original thirteen colonies, New Hampshire supported the American Revolution even before the war officially started. Although there was only one Revolutionary War battle fought in New Hampshire, it was an important one. A 1774 raid by the Americans on the British fort at Portsmouth, New Hampshire, secured cannons and gunpowder, which was said to be used by the patriots at the Battle of Bunker Hill the following year. Incidentally, it was Paul Revere himself who alerted the New Hampshire colonists that British reinforcements were soon to arrive at the fort, allowing the Americans to stage their successful raid. Revere's ride from Boston to Portsmouth was even longer than his more famous dash through Lexington and Concord and took place several months prior.

New Hampshire was the first of the original thirteen colonies to establish a government independent of Great Britain, which it did in 1776. It was also the first to establish its own state constitution, which it did that same year. When it came time for the former colonies to decide on their support of the U.S. Constitution, New Hampshire was the ninth state to do so, becoming the last necessary state needed to bring the document into effect.

If New Hampshirites hold their heads high based on those events, they can also do so by virtue of being home to the tallest peak in the Northeastern United States, Mount Washington. At almost 6,300 feet tall, it is well over a mile high. Mount Washington is so prominent that early explorer Giovanni da Verrazano cited it in his ship's log after spotting its peak from the Atlantic Ocean in 1524.

Although New Hampshire can boast a dozen other mountain peaks over a mile high, Mount Washington is the one that can claim the title of "world's worst weather," something many hikers have found to their dismay. Since records began in 1849, there have been about 150 deaths on Mount Washington. Some are due to avalanches, but almost all the rest are weather related. Hypothermia is the usual culprit, and not only in winter. The record low on Mount Washington in the balmy month of May was two degrees below zero. Along with winds that can reach well over 200 miles per hour, temperatures on Mount Washington can drop below freezing at any time.

During the growing season, however, things improve, allowing crops to flourish. New Hampshire claims the distinction of being the place where Scottish settlers planted the first potato crops in America, which they did in 1719. Accordingly, New Hampshire's state vegetable is the white potato.

It is generally felt that while potatoes are greatly loved everywhere, taxes are not. Along with New Hampshirites not having to pay state income tax, there is also no sales tax.

True to the state's motto of "Live Free or Die," New Hampshire is the only state without enforceable laws that require wearing seat belts in a vehicle and is therefore the only state where seat belts are not mandatory.

Another type of transportation may have chosen to visit New Hampshire, with or without seat belts. On September 3, 1965, it is said that an unidentified flying object, otherwise known as a UFO, made its presence known at Exeter, New Hampshire. Several upstanding townspeople, including two local police officers, reported the sighting of a large, brightly lit unknown object hovering above the fields near town.

After authorities were notified, U.S. Air Force officials claimed that the alleged UFO was merely the usual nighttime illumination from nearby Pease Air Force Base. After sundown, one Air Force officer came to Exeter to prove his point. With a crowd of New Hampshirites looking on, the officer radioed the base for the lights to be turned on. Everyone waited and . . . nothing happened. Irate, he yelled into his walkie-talkie to turn the lights on *now*! The base immediately responded that all the lights *were* on. Amid the jeers of the crowd, the officer roared off in his staff car. It is not known if he was wearing a seat belt. An annual event in New Hampshire commemorates what is called "the Incident at Exeter."

URBAN LEGENDS

As might be inferred from the name, the **Devil Monkey** is said to be a demonic-looking primate with fierce teeth, powerful claws, and a tendency to emit terrifying howls. According to legend, the creature is known for making its home in the area around the small New Hampshire town of Danville. There have allegedly been sightings in the woods near Danville that go back to the 1950s. In 2001, about a dozen local citizens are said to have reported personal sightings of the Devil Monkey, giving the appalling ape a higher profile. Suddenly, the sightings stopped, with rumors flying that the Devil Monkey departed the glare of the spotlight in Danville. It was said that the demon's destination might be a less populated area of the White Mountains, terrain that would offer more privacy, which was apparently more appealing to the publicity-shy creature.

Cemeteries are always hot spots for urban legends, and the **South Street Cemetery** in Portsmouth is no exception, especially when combined with a wrongful execution and vindictive victim. It is said that Ruth Blay, a young schoolteacher, was sentenced to death in 1768. She had become pregnant out of wedlock, not a pleasant fate in colonial days, and gave birth to a stillborn baby. Neither knowing what to do nor having anyone to turn to, she buried the remains under the schoolhouse floor. A student apparently saw what she had done and reported her. According to legend, the governor was going to pardon Ruth to save her from execution. However, the sheriff executed her earlier in the day, which some said was to avoid interfering with his lunch. The expected pardon arrived just after she was killed. Today, Ruth's ghost is said to haunt South Street Cemetery so that no one else buried there can rest in the kind of peace that she was denied.

In the backwoods of New Hampshire's Coos County, hard against the Canadian border, a strange creature known as the **Wood Devil** reigns supreme, at least according to legend. Similar to the ubiquitous Bigfoot or Sasquatch in other states, the seven-foot-tall Wood Devil is more streamlined, having a slender silhouette and cloaked in light gray fur. Because the Wood Devil is said to be slim and trim, verifiable sightings have traditionally been notoriously difficult. The streamlined creature is said to simply outrun his pursuers, who have to content themselves with a glimpse of huge footprints.

ICONIC NEW HAMPSHIRE FOOD

With a nod to New Hampshire's neighbor Canada, where the origins of the dish lie, **Poutine** is not only consumed in mass quantities by New Hampshirites but also celebrated with the state's annual Poutine Festival. Some feel the dish tastes better than it sounds: thick fries and cheese curds slathered in hot brown gravy. For those unfamiliar with cheese curds, they are a natural by-product that occurs in the process of making cheese when the milk clots and can be cut into cubes. The flavor of cheese curds is about the same as mild cheddar, but curds have a springy, more rubbery texture. True to its place in the hearts of New Hampshirites, according to the website for the state's Poutine Festival, the event's slogan is "Live Free and Eat Poutine."

> **Poutine** (Serves 4)
> 1 qt vegetable oil for frying
> 1 container (10.25 oz) prepared beef gravy
> 5 medium potatoes
> 2 cups cheese curds

1. While oil is heating in a deep fryer or heavy skillet, cut potatoes into thick slices for fries.
2. Warm the gravy in saucepan on medium heat to almost boiling.
3. When oil is hot enough for frying, gradually add the potato slices and fry until light brown, about five minutes.
4. Remove fries from the hot oil and place them on a plate that is thickly lined with paper towels to drain.
5. Transfer the fries to a warm serving platter, then sprinkle the cheese over them.
6. Ladle hot gravy over the fries and cheese, then serve immediately.

Source: Adapted from https://www.allrecipes.com/recipe/79300/real-poutine/.

ODD LAWS

State legal codes in New Hampshire are called Revised Statutes Annotated (RSAs). By using the RSA coding system, interested parties can ferret out relevant legislative statutes. If they are hunters, one thing they can *not* do is ferret out animals from the safety of their dens. Ferrets are small mammals who are cousins to weasels and, with their sharp teeth and killer instincts, can be fierce predators. New Hampshire RSAs ban the use of hunting with ferrets because it is felt to violate the basic rules of "fair chase."

Certain entertainers also have to abide by what the state considers the rules of fair play. New Hampshire statutes prohibit any "showman, tumbler, ropedancer, ventriloquist or other person" from charging money to exhibit "feats of agility, horsemanship, sleight of hand, ropedancing or feats with cards, or any animals, wax figures, puppets or other show, or promote any public competition." Potential performers must first utilize their feats of agility to go to the office of the town council in the locale where they plan to demonstrate their skills. There, they must obtain a license before dazzling the locals with ropedancing or anything else.

Some disappointed New Hampshirites might seek other forms of amusement if they find they are unable to be entertained by a nonlicensed puppet show or wax figures. In that case, they should be aware that some nighttime activities are banned under the legal codes of the state. Anyone apprehended between dusk and dawn for collecting seaweed from the shore "below high-water mark" will be deemed guilty of a violation of the law.

UNUSUAL DESTINATIONS

For those craving a return to the golden days of their youth when they spent hour upon hour in video game arcades, a magic carpet of sorts can be found at the **American Classic Arcade Museum** (ACAM) in Laconia, New Hampshire. Billing itself with the tagline "The Games You Grew Up With," ACAM is both a final resting place for many of the beloved machines and a time warp in which visitors can continue playing more than 250 classic video games from Asteroids to Zaxxon. Guests learn about the history of original arcade games and can try their luck on more modern incarnations. With hundreds of coin-operated machines at ACAM, visitors should be able to find their favorites from the Golden Age of arcade games, including Pac-Man, Q*Bert, and Space Invaders, to name a few. While the museum acknowledges that video games can arguably be played at home, its mission is to provide the true classic arcade experience, which means being surrounded by all the glory of clanging bells, flashing lights, and the triumphant shouts of fellow players who attain the highest scores.

An outcropping of land called **Mystery Hill** can be found in the woods near Salem, New Hampshire. This 30-acre complex of monolithic granite blocks contains a maze of sunken chambers and passageways as well as stone structures with obscure writings on them, lending the site its nom-de-plume, "America's Stonehenge." Theories of its origin range from Native Americans to ancient European explorers, as well as simply being the product of a hoax. Even the hoax theory has its variations, such as colonial farmers with too much time on their hands or 20th-century entrepreneurs. The attraction is part of a recreation zone that is open to the public. For those seeking even more diversion, the recreational area also includes snowshoe trails and an alpaca farm.

It would be hard to find a destination with a less appealing name than **Smuttynose Island**. Located about six miles off the New Hampshire coast, it has a history of unpleasant events, including deadly shipwrecks. The island is best known for a horrific murder that took place there in 1873, culminating in what newspapers of the time called "The Crime of the Century." After two young women were brutally butchered, a local fisherman named Louis Wagner was executed, although he vehemently swore his innocence. It is said that Wagner's angry ghost still haunts the site. The island can be reached only by small boat, but for those who prefer their macabre destinations to be more landlocked, the graves of the women slaughtered at Smuttynose Island can be found onshore in the town of Portsmouth.

Honorable mention goes to the **Elm Street Cemetery** in Milford, New Hampshire, where there is what at first appears to be a simple white gravestone. It is a worthy destination due to its painstakingly etched 150-word inscription from the early 1800s. As seen here—completely verbatim—the carved-in-stone accusation by the deceased's husband does not hesitate to name names: *"Caroline H., Wife of Calvin Cutter, M.D., Murdered by the Baptist Ministry and Baptist Churches As follows: Sep't. 28, 1838; aged 33. She was accused of lying in church meeting by the Rev. D. D. Pratt and Deacon Albert Adams. Was condemned by the church unheard. She was reduced to poverty by Deacon William Wallace. When an ex-parte council was asked of the Milford Baptist Church, by the advice of their committee, George Raymond, Calvin Averill, and Andrew Hutchinson, They voted not to receive any communication on the subject. The Rev. Mark Carpenter said he thought as the good old Deacon said, 'We've got Cutter down and it's best to keep him down.' The intentional and malicious destruction of her character And happiness as above described destroyed her life. Her last words upon the subject were 'Tell the Truth and The Iniquity will come out.'"*

DISTINCTIVE NEW HAMPSHIRE WORDS AND SAYINGS

Hornpout: What New Hampshire residents call a catfish.

Kanc, the: Much easier to spell and pronounce than "Kancamagus," one of New Hampshire's most scenic highways.

Old Man, the: What granite cliffs on Cannon Mountain were said to resemble and therefore called the Old Man of the Mountain, even after the rock face collapsed in 2003.

Quill pig: New Hampshire-ism for what is elsewhere called a porcupine.

Slower than cold molasses moving uphill in January: Really slow.

Further Reading

Jones, Eric. *New Hampshire Curiosities: Quirky Characters, Roadside Oddities and Other Offbeat Stuff*. 2nd edition. Guilford, CT: Globe Pequot, 2011.

Morison, Elting, and Elizabeth Forbes Morison. *New Hampshire: A History*. Nashville, TN: American Association for State and Local History, 1976.

Whitney, D. Quincy. *Hidden History of New Hampshire*. Charleston, SC: History Press, 2008.

New Jersey

> **FACT BOX**
>
> **Nickname:** The Garden State
> **Statehood Granted:** 1787
> **Capital:** Trenton
> **Population:** 8,900,000
> **State Motto:** "Liberty and Prosperity"
> **What Natives Call Themselves:** New Jerseyan is official, but New Jerseyite is more commonly used

STATE HISTORY

Anyone who has ever played the classic board game Monopoly is already familiar with some significant New Jersey real estate. When the game was first marketed in 1935, the format was based on the real-life streets of Atlantic City, New Jersey.

Today's New Jersey is the most densely populated of the 50 states. However, for many centuries, New Jersey was home to Native American people such as the Lenni Lenape. In relatively small tribal groups, they made use of the rich resources of the land. Adapting to the natural environment, they based their culture on its abundant opportunities for fishing, hunting, and gathering.

Europeans began arriving in the early 1600s. The Dutch became the first Europeans to claim lands in today's New Jersey, part of the colonial empire they called "New Netherland." One of their primary purposes was to pursue trapping and fur trading with the Natives. The first Dutch colony in the current New Jersey, Pavonia, was established in 1630. As more settlers arrived, European-borne diseases such as influenza, malaria, and smallpox decimated the local Native American population.

Soon the Dutch would lose their grip on today's Garden State. In 1664, an English fleet sailed into New York Harbor, easily annexing New Netherland for Britain.

England's King Charles II divided the lands among his supporters. They included his brother, the Duke of York, for whom New York was named. Other friends of the king had come from the island of Jersey in the English Channel. They had been loyal to the monarch through the English Civil War (1642–1651), with the grateful monarch rewarding them with their own land grant in America, today's New Jersey.

European settlers steadily arrived, drawn by fertile lands and bountiful fishing. In colonial days, New Jersey began its ascent into the national consciousness with a number of "firsts." Even though the state is often eclipsed by neighboring New York and has been the subject of barbs by late-night comedians, some people consider New Jersey to have the superior distinction of being home to America's first brewery, established in 1642 at Hoboken.

New Jersey was one of the thirteen original colonies rebelling against Great Britain during the American Revolution (1775–1783). In fact, more Revolutionary War battles took place in New Jersey than any in other state. Clashes in today's New Jersey include the Battle of Trenton in 1777, which gained a noteworthy place in history by being commemorated in the iconic painting *Washington Crossing the Delaware*.

During the Revolution, in 1783, the New Jersey town of Princeton briefly served as the nation's capital. It was there that America's delegates to the Continental Congress learned the war was officially over when the Treaty of Paris was signed. Following quickly behind Delaware and Pennsylvania, New Jersey was the third state to ratify the U.S. Constitution in 1787. In 1789, the Garden State was the very first to ratify the first 10 amendments to the Constitution, known as the Bill of Rights.

Along with being the site of America's first brewery, Hoboken is distinguished by being home to America's first official supper club, founded in 1796, with what is arguably the ultimate membership roster of any social group: Aaron Burr,

Important Revolutionary War battles in New Jersey include the Battle of Trenton in 1777. It gained a place in history after being commemorated in the iconic painting, *Washington Crossing the Delaware*. (Joe Sohm/Dreamstime.com)

Alexander Hamilton, and George Washington. However, in 1804, Burr quite unsociably killed Hamilton in a duel at nearby Weehawken, New Jersey.

In the summer, many early Americans adjourned to what is known as the oldest seaside resort in the United States. Cape May, New Jersey, became a fashionable holiday destination starting in the mid-1700s.

The town of Hoboken again stepped to the forefront in 1846 when the first-ever recorded baseball game was played there, complete with recognizably modern rules.

Many movie buffs consider New Jersey to be the film industry's original version of Hollywood. In 1903, much of the footage for *The Great Train Robbery*, the world's first narrative film, was shot in New Jersey. The movie is considered a major milestone in film history, one that revolutionized the movie industry for all time. Incidentally, a brand-new way to watch films also made its debut in New Jersey. The first drive-in movie was born in 1933 at Camden.

Another revolutionary event began in New Jersey with the very first Miss America Pageant in 1921. It was held at New Jersey's Atlantic City, where the contestants had plenty of room to strut in their swimsuits since Atlantic City is home to the world's longest boardwalk.

Miss America is sometimes considered part of the nation's pop culture royalty, but New Jersey has also been home to the real thing. Joseph Bonaparte, former king of Naples and king of Spain, as well as brother of Emperor Napoleon of France, moved to Bordentown, New Jersey, in the early 1800s. His former highness lived what appeared to be a pleasant suburban life. In a show of goodwill and the New Jersey spirit, his neighbors referred to him simply as "Mr. Bonaparte."

URBAN LEGENDS

The legend of **Captain Kidd's Treasure** extends back to about the year 1700 and has not loosened its grip on the popular imagination in all that time. Captain William Kidd, who was accused of being a notorious pirate in his lifetime, was no stranger to New Jersey, especially the Jersey Shore where his ships could regularly be spotted. In fact, he married a wealthy New Jersey woman whose presence in his life is sometimes invoked in the mindset of *cherchez la femme* (basically, "look for the woman behind the trouble"). Through her connections, Kidd believed he had permission from the king of England to capture French vessels and seize their loot, as long as he split it with the Crown. Whether justified or not, the authorities soon accused Kidd of piracy due to his alleged hoarding of some of the profits, so he set off for Boston to clear his name. Along the way, he is said to have buried about $20,000,000 in today's money at various New Jersey locales such as Cape May, Cliffwood Beach, Del Haven, Sandy Hook, and Toms River. Treasure hunters who believe the legend still look for it. Incidentally, Kidd was unable to prove his innocence and was publicly hanged in 1701. In fact, he was actually hanged *twice*. On the first attempt, the rope broke, and Kidd survived. However, minutes later (no doubt with a stronger rope), the second try at his execution was successful.

According to local legend, the **Ghost Train** passes through Newark's Broad Street Station on the 10th day of each month at midnight. The spectral railway

> ### New Jersey Is for Brainiacs
>
> Despite late-night comedians taking potshots at New Jersey, Thomas Edison and Albert Einstein, who are generally considered the two greatest brains of the 20th century, chose New Jersey to be their homes. In 1876, Edison (1847–1931) established his first laboratory in Menlo Park, New Jersey, where many of his world-changing inventions, such as the light bulb, were developed. Einstein (1879–1955), who settled at Princeton, New Jersey, in 1933, is usually regarded as the most important scientist of the 20th century by revolutionizing physics with his famous equation, $E = MC^2$ (energy equals mass times the speed of light squared). Both of these New Jerseyites were unafraid to try new ideas, as seen in Einstein's quote *"A person who never made a mistake never tried anything new"* and Edison's *"I have not failed 10,000 times; I've successfully found 10,000 ways that will not work."*

is said to be operated by an engineer who was killed on those tracks in the late 1800s, a date that was the 10th day of the month. Periodically, local newspapers and ghost-hunting websites revive the story. They tend to repeat a tale that at one point, lost in the mists of time, hundreds of witnesses allegedly reported hearing the ghostly sound of the train whistle along with the frenzied clank of iron wheels against the rails, but saw no locomotive nor any sign of life as the ethereal engine roared by.

Far and away, the most famous New Jersey urban legend is the **Jersey Devil**. The Bigfoot of the Garden State is said to be a horned creature with clawed hands, cloven hooves, a goat's head, the wings of a bat, and, for the finishing touch, a forked tail. Known to emit bloodcurling screams, it is said to reside in New Jersey's Pine Barrens region. The legend ascribes the demon to a Native American woman from a local tribe. In the early 1700s, she was said to have given birth to her 13th child, a hideously deformed offspring who managed to flee into the woods soon after its birth. Alleged sightings reached a peak in the early 1900s, coincidentally around the time when cheap tabloid newspapers were on the rise. Some published not only the sensational story but also artists' renderings of the entity. Fast-forwarding to 1982, New Jersey's NHL hockey team named themselves the New Jersey Devils in an homage to the beast, complete with a dauntingly stylized logo. Fans, perhaps honoring the creature as much as the game, seem to have a penchant for face-painting in order to support the team, as popularized in an episode of the classic TV series *Seinfeld*.

ICONIC NEW JERSEY FOOD

It must first be stated that **Salt Water Taffy** does not actually contain salt water. This beloved candy was originally produced at the seaside resort of Atlantic City on the Jersey Shore starting in the 1880s and perhaps simply seemed to taste better in the salty air. Glycerin is added to give it the familiar creamy texture. Although Atlantic City has had its ups and downs over the decades, one constant has remained: Salt Water Taffy is still sold along the city's boardwalk.

> **Salt Water Taffy** (Yields about 50 one-inch pieces)
> 2 cups sugar
> 2 Tbsp cornstarch
> 1 cup light corn syrup
> 2 tsp glycerin
> ¾ cup water
> 2 Tbsp butter
> 1 tsp salt
> 1 tsp vanilla, lemon, maple, or mint flavoring as preferred
> 3 drops food coloring as preferred

1. In a large saucepan, mix sugar and cornstarch together.
2. Use a wooden spoon to stir in the corn syrup, glycerin, water, butter, and salt, then place the saucepan over medium heat, stirring until the sugar dissolves and mixture begins to boil.
3. Let it simmer undisturbed until it reaches about 270°F, then brush the sides of the pan with a pastry brush dipped in warm water while the syrup cooks.
4. Remove saucepan from the heat, then add flavoring and food coloring. Stir gently and pour onto a greased cookie sheet to cool.
5. When the taffy is cool enough to handle, grease hands with oil or butter for what many call the fun part by pulling the taffy until it is light colored and has a satiny gloss, which should take about 10 minutes.
6. Roll the pulled taffy into a long rope, until it is about ½ inch in diameter, then cut it with a butter knife into pieces that are about 1 inch long.
7. Let the pieces sit for about 30 minutes, then wrap them in wax paper or plastic wrap and twist the ends of the wrapper to secure.

Source: Adapted from https://www.exploratorium.edu/cooking/bread/recipe-taffy.html.

ODD LAWS

In the postwar prosperity of 1949, the New Jersey legislature passed the Retail Gasoline Dispensing Safety Act. It seemed a logical companion to the inexpensive gasoline that was common at the time, to provide jobs for attendants at what were called "service stations," and to protect the safety of the state's consumers. Therefore, the New Jersey law banned drivers from pumping their own gas. Other states did the same around that time but later overturned those laws, allowing self-service. Today, self-service is the norm across the country, with the exception of New Jersey, where it is still against the law for drivers to pump their own gas.

Some New Jerseyites consider it a badge of honor not to have any idea how to work a gas pump. Supporters of the law claim that repealing it would mean thousands of gas station employees losing their jobs. Opponents counter those assertions by claiming that allowing people to fill their own fuel tanks would lower gas prices for everyone. Still other Garden State residents are no fans of higher gas prices but point to the sublime feeling of staying warm and dry in their car on a cold rainy day, uttering the magic words "Fill 'er up."

For those who wish to avoid the gas pumping conundrum altogether by relying on four-legged horsepower, there are other laws to obey. New Jersey statutes assert that no person may drive a horse attached to a sleigh on a highway unless there are a sufficient number of bells attached to the horse's harness to give warning of its approach. To the surprise of many, this law is not a carryover from olden days before the horseless carriage; it was enacted in 2016. Perhaps by virtue of being such a new area of jurisprudence, no test cases are known that have codified what the "sufficient number" of bells might be.

Finally, for residents of Blairstown, New Jersey, who wish to avoid transportation-related issues completely by staying home to sit beneath a pleasant shade tree, the township's Municipal Code has a few words to say about that. In Blairstown, shade trees may indeed be planted, but "no street-side trees may be planted that obscure light and air," which has some law-abiding citizens scratching their heads. Trees must be properly trimmed by the owners, but if not, citizens are prohibited from taking the law into their own hands regarding light-and-air issues by clipping the trees of adjoining premises without the consent of the property owner.

UNUSUAL DESTINATIONS

Targeting those who feel nostalgic for the days of the Cold War's nuclear bomb–threat era in the 1950s, the **Atomic Fallout Shelter Theater** in Wall Township, New Jersey, takes visitors back to those days of yesteryear. With its barrels of water, cement floor, cinder block walls, emergency communication equipment, Geiger counter to measure radioactivity in the air, and shelves stacked with what were called survival crackers, the Fallout Shelter recreates the feel of what was thought to be a responsible American family's refuge in case of atomic attack. Other points of interest include the presentation of government public service films such as *Duck and Cover* and *Radiological Defense*.

There are those who notice an unoccupied piece of big highway construction equipment by the side of the road and immediately wonder if the keys are in it. However, unauthorized persons taking one for a spin could face unpleasant consequences. Happily, **Diggerland USA** in West Berlin, New Jersey, bills itself as a "construction amusement park," where heavy machinery such as backhoes, bulldozers, excavators, and front-end loaders are there for the fun of it. Grown-ups and children who are under adult supervision can take the wheel, along with working the handles, levers, lifts, pedals, and all manner of controls to operate heavy equipment. During the warm-weather months, there is also a water park if anyone happens not to be in the mood to drive the specially engineered big rigs. Thus, Diggerland calls itself the only combined construction theme park and water park in America.

True to its name, the **Spoon Museum** at Lambert Castle in Paterson, New Jersey, is home to the world's largest collection of decorative spoons. Lambert Castle was built in 1892 as the home of a prosperous New Jersey silk merchant. Today, all four floors of the impressive structure are open to the public with displays including period furnishings in the various rooms, art galleries, and historical exhibits. However, for many visitors, the high point is the spoon collection itself, said to be the largest in the world. The museum holds more than 5,000 spoons gathered between 1882 and 1966 that commemorate persons, places, areas of interest, and special events, which rotate regularly for display. To many people, perhaps the highest accolade for New Jersey's Spoon Museum is the fact that it was once a clue on the beloved television game show *Jeopardy*.

Another *Jeopardy* clue might be as follows: "This 1938 radio program scared the nation into thinking that Martians had landed in Grover's Mill, New Jersey." The correct response would be "What is Orson Welles's broadcast of *War of the Worlds*?" Under Welles's direction, the Mercury Theatre's broadcast of October 30, 1938, was meant to be a fictional Halloween treat-or-treat novelty. But Welles and his talented gang of actors were so believable that many Americans were driven into a panic. The national frenzy over supposed alien landings is commemorated at the **War of the Worlds Monument** in West Windsor Township, New Jersey.

DISTINCTIVE NEW JERSEY WORDS AND SAYINGS

AC: Not a reference to air conditioning or alternating current, but an abbreviation for New Jersey's fabled seaside resort town of Atlantic City.

Boards, the: Neither smoothly cut wood nor examinations like the College Boards, but a shortened version of "Boardwalk," something for which Atlantic City is world famous.

Down the shore: The beach, specifically the Jersey Shore, as in "This weekend we're going down the shore."

Jughandle: New Jersey-ism for highway exits that curve tightly to the right, forming a shape like the handle of a jug and allowing drivers to eventually turn left.

Ripper: This beloved New Jersey treat is a deep-fried hot dog in which the frying process causes its casing to rip open.

Further Reading

Genovese, Peter. *New Jersey State of Mind*. New Brunswick, NJ: Rutgers University Press, 2020.

Lurie, Maxine, and Richard Veit (editors). *New Jersey: A History of the Garden State*. New Brunswick, NJ: Rutgers University Press, 2018.

Martinelli, Patricia, and Charles Stansfield Jr. *Haunted New Jersey: Ghosts and Strange Phenomena of the Garden State*. Mechanicsburg, PA: Stackpole Books, 2004.

New Mexico

FACT BOX

Nickname: Land of Enchantment
Statehood Granted: 1912
Capital: Santa Fe
Population: 2,100,000
State Motto: *Crescit eundo* (Latin: "It Grows as It Goes," i.e., ever-increasing progress)
What Natives Call Themselves: New Mexicans

STATE HISTORY

Many visitors to New Mexico agree wholeheartedly with the state's nickname, Land of Enchantment. New Mexico tends to attract all types of people, from tourists to celebrities. There are artists who claim that even the light is different there.

Today's New Mexico was originally inhabited by Native Americans for thousands of years. The first-known residents were discovered to be members of the ancient Clovis culture, dating from about 12,000 years ago. Native American groups including the Hopi, Navajo, and Ute were living in the region when Europeans arrived in the 1500s.

As opposed to Plains Indians, who were nomadic, the Spaniards noticed that tribes in the region they called Nuevo Mexico lived in permanent villages. "Pueblo," the Spanish word for a town, came to describe the villages in which they lived, the Native American people who lived in them, and their style of architecture, which was adobe structures built from dried mud bricks that stood up well in the dry climate.

By the time Spanish conquistador Coronado arrived in the region during the 1540s, he had heard tales of the mythical Seven Cities of Cibola, where he believed he would win gold and glory. He found neither.

Nonetheless, Spain added the current American Southwest to its empire. Santa Fe, the state capital of today's New Mexico, was founded in 1610, 10 years before the Pilgrims landed at Plymouth Rock. Santa Fe remains the oldest continuous state capital in the United States.

Reflecting its original inhabitants, New Mexico today is one of the three states with the highest population of Indigenous people, along with Alaska and Oklahoma.

New Mexico was integral to the 19th-century concept of Manifest Destiny, the doctrine that America should spread across the continent from the Atlantic to the Pacific. When Mexico won its independence from Spain in 1821, New Mexico became a Mexican territory, but only for a relatively short time. After America's victory in the Mexican War of 1848, New Mexico was annexed by the United States.

In 1853, the Gadsden Purchase allowed the United States to acquire more land in the Territory of New Mexico. In 1861, during the Civil War, the Confederate Army claimed some of the New Mexico Territory. Its New Mexico Campaign was an attempt to control the Southwest and open access to California for the Confederacy. However, after the Union victory at New Mexico's Battle of Glorieta Pass in 1862, the Confederates were turned back.

It took another half century for New Mexico to be admitted as America's 47th state, which it did in 1912. Its state flag was officially introduced in 1925, which some people feel was worth the wait. Its red sun symbol on a field of gold is often cited as one of the most distinctive banners in the nation.

Having almost no natural water sources, New Mexico remained relatively unpopulated and isolated. This was still the case when one of the most world-changing events of the 20th century took place there. During World War II, strangers began arriving at the nondescript address of 109 East Palace Avenue in Santa Fe. From there, the newcomers were surreptitiously transported to the nearby secret facility at Los Alamos. They were the nation's leading scientists, working on the ultra-secret Manhattan Project that developed America's atomic bomb.

New Mexico can claim the distinction of being the site of the world's first nuclear bomb explosion, which occurred on July 16, 1945. The test blast's epicenter was at Alamogordo, New Mexico, on barren land known locally as Jornada del Muerto, roughly translated from the Spanish as "Path of the Dead Man."

A few years later, the town of Roswell, New Mexico, became an epicenter of its own as the nation's hot spot for unidentified flying objects (UFOs). What is usually called the "Roswell Incident" refers to an event in 1947 when rumors flew that debris at a crash site near Roswell had come from outer space. The U.S. military claimed that the object was a weather balloon, although originally there was conflicting information in the local press, such as headlines boldly stating that the air force had captured a flying saucer. As the years went by, conspiracy theories abounded in the popular media, asserting not only that an alien spacecraft had crash-landed but also that its extraterrestrial occupants had allegedly been seized by the military who engaged in a massive cover-up. Later, declassified military reports pointed to the object being a nuclear test surveillance balloon. Still, New Mexico's "Roswell Incident" remains one of the most popular UFO-related legends.

If the object really did contain extraterrestrial travelers, perhaps they were attracted by New Mexico's incredibly diverse landscape. Its terrain includes not only arid regions such as the Chihuahuan Desert but also the soaring peaks of the Sangre de Cristo Mountains. In between, population studies reveal only about 12 people per square mile, indicating that there are many more sheep and cattle living in the state than people.

404 Error, Not Found

Many trivia buffs have lost elite status over the question of where software giant Microsoft got its start. Most immediately answer "Seattle," while some sense a trick and say "Redmond, Washington." The correct answer is Albuquerque, New Mexico. The exact address was 115 California Street NE, in a small nondescript storefront. There, in 1975, when most Americans were using typewriters, Paul Allen (1953–2018) and Bill Gates (1955–) founded Microsoft, originally called Micro-Soft, to produce computer software. Albuquerque was the home of their first major customer, but they soon had others. In 1979, they moved the company to the Seattle area because Allen and Gates had grown up there and were tired of making the long trip home to visit friends and family. In addition, they felt they could recruit more programmers in the Pacific Northwest. Like the innocuous storefront at 109 East Palace Avenue in Santa Fe, the drop-off address for scientists creating the first atomic bomb, a big bang was coming. Today, a plaque marks the first Microsoft office in Albuquerque, although the plaque has repeatedly been stolen and, like many computer errors, is not always found.

Santa Fe is the highest capital city in the United States, situated about 7,000 feet above sea level. Its Palace of the Governors is the oldest occupied building in the nation. Santa Fe remains one of the few state capital cities not to have a major airport. There are a few flights on small planes from Santa Fe Regional Airport, but local residents seem to prefer their hometown without a bustling airport and jumbo jets flying in and out.

While Santa Fe keeps a lid on airborne traffic, the state's largest city, Albuquerque, is renowned for being a place where the sky's the limit. Each year, the city hosts the International Balloon Fiesta, the world's largest hot air balloon event. Visitors are often awestruck by the sight of hundreds of colorful hot air balloons wafting majestically over the New Mexico landscape as far as the eye can see.

Even the official state creatures of New Mexico have an air of the exotic about them. The state insect is the Tarantula Wasp, with neither word sounding pleasant. On the other hand, the state bird is none other than the Great Roadrunner, a cartoon classic. This juxtaposition of scary insect and lovable bird is pure New Mexico.

URBAN LEGENDS

Dating back to the late 1970s, the urban legend involving alleged **Aliens Under Dulce** maintains that there is a secret military base concealed under the small New Mexico town of Dulce (population: about 2,750 and almost entirely Native American). Dulce lies on the Jicarilla Apache Reservation, near the Colorado border. What adds to the exotic atmosphere is not only that the base is hidden under Dulce's Archuleta Mesa, but that the operation is allegedly a joint venture between humans and extraterrestrials. Sounding suspiciously like the plot of the 2011 movie *Cowboys and Aliens*, there had allegedly been a gun battle at some point in the past between humans and extraterrestrials. That skirmish led to a truce with the combatants deciding to work together in a secret underground lair. Tales of human abductions began to circulate, with Dulce residents claiming to see moving lights and unidentified flying objects in the sky, culminating in the Dulce Base UFO Conference in 2016 at the local casino hotel. The convention managed to stimulate tourism but did not include tours of any underground facilities.

The **Chupacabra** (pronounced choo-pa-COBB-ruh) is a said to be a monster that feeds off the blood of livestock, essentially a Dracula of domesticated animals. The monster's culinary taste seems partial to goats, leading to its name in Spanish meaning something along the lines of "goat-sucker." While physical descriptions of the hideous creature vary, none of them are very appealing. Not reaching the heights of a true Bigfoot, it is said to be about the size of a small bear, with a spiky row of exterior spines that reach to the base of its tail. There are those who state that artists' renderings make the head of the Chupacabra look similar to the monster in the 1954 movie *Creature from the Black Lagoon*. Some biologists and wildlife management officers claim that Chupacabras are actually wild dogs afflicted with the mange. Still, the legend persists.

As in the neighboring state of Arizona, arguably the superstars of New Mexico mythology are the **Skinwalkers**. These evil humanoid witches are able to transform after dark into animals. After having died and passing into the realm of the dead, shape-shifting Skinwalkers are said to adopt the guise of a coyote, fox, or wolf, attacking people who had been close relatives of the deceased. Some feel this is cause for being nice to family members at all times. In any case, the Skinwalker tradition is a longtime feature of Navajo folklore and has spawned a number of books, movies, and television shows in mainstream popular culture.

ICONIC NEW MEXICO FOOD

New Mexico's most iconic foods are often said to be a blend of Native American, Mexican, and Spanish cuisines simmered with French, Italian, and down-home Southern influences. By adding classic New Mexico touches such as red and green chiles as well as blue corn, the unique flavor medley is as enchanting as the state's nickname would imply. One of the classic New Mexico dishes is **Posole**, a stew that is generally a combination of pork cooked with red and/or green chiles along with hominy, or coarse-ground corn that is boiled and soaked in an alkali solution. Hominy lovers are quick to state that it tastes better than it sounds, especially in Posole, which is often considered such a special treat that it is served on New Year's Eve, holidays, weddings, and other festive occasions.

>**Posole** (Serves 5)
>1½ lb pork stew meat, cut into ¾-inch cubes
>1 large onion, chopped

2 Tbsp canola oil
2 garlic cloves, minced
3 cups beef broth
2 cans hominy (15½ oz each), rinsed and drained
2 cans (4 oz each) chopped green chiles
1 or 2 red jalapeno peppers, seeded and chopped
½ tsp salt
½ tsp ground cumin
½ tsp dried oregano
¼ tsp black pepper
¼ tsp cayenne pepper
½ cup fresh cilantro, minced
Blue corn tortilla strips

1. In a large heavy pot, cook pork and onion in oil over medium heat until meat is no longer pink, then add garlic and cook another minute before draining.
2. Stir in broth, hominy, chiles, jalapeno, salt, cumin, oregano, pepper, and cayenne, then bring to a boil.
3. Reduce heat; cover and simmer for 45–60 minutes or until meat is tender.
4. Stir in the cilantro.
5. Serve with blue corn tortilla strips.

Source: Adapted from https://www.tasteofhome.com/recipes/land-of-enchantment-posole/.

ODD LAWS

New Mexico has a long history of colorful residents, from Spanish grandees to Hollywood superstars. The New Mexico legislature decided to stamp down any hot blood that might arise among its more excitable citizens by making dueling with deadly weapons illegal. In fact, to avoid even the possibility of bloodshed in the streets, the law goes a step further. In New Mexico, it is unlawful to even challenge someone to duel with a deadly weapon or to accept such a challenge. It's also against the law if the presumptive duel never takes place, no matter the circumstances in the heat of the moment of the challenge. That goes for the individuals who serve as seconds as well. When enforcing this law in the town of Roswell, it is not known if the definition of "deadly weapons" might include laser swords, light sabers, or ray guns from a galaxy far, far away.

In the town of Deming, lest anyone be overcome with extreme curiosity about their neighbors, municipal statutes render it unlawful to "look, peer or peep into or be found around or within the view of any window or other means of viewing into any occupied building, other than *his* own residence." Some people may speculate whether the gender-specific language gives females a free pass to peep.

Also in Deming, specifically in the town's Mountain View Cemetery, the municipal code makes it clear that lots at Mountain View Cemetery "shall be used for no other purpose than the burial of the human dead." It is not known what prompted this statute.

UNUSUAL DESTINATIONS

At the **American International Rattlesnake Museum** in Albuquerque, there is no question that rattlesnakes are the main attraction. For those who avoid that particular living creature in favor of the fine arts, snake-related artwork is also on display. According to the museum, it houses the most diverse collection of rattlesnakes in the world. Live displays of 34 different species abound, alongside rarities such as albino snakes and snake skeletons, a look at the rattlesnake's place in popular culture, and snake fangs that are available for purchase in the gift shop. As if to show the positive side of rattlesnakes, there are also displays of creatures that make rattlers look sweet-natured, such as the Gila Monster, which chews on its prey to inject as much poison as possible into the victim's bloodstream. Anyone struggling with ophidiophobia, or fear of snakes, may wish to bear all this in mind before visiting.

Similarly, the **Chile Pepper Institute** at New Mexico State University in Las Cruces specializes in one subject and does it well. Founded in 1992, the institute

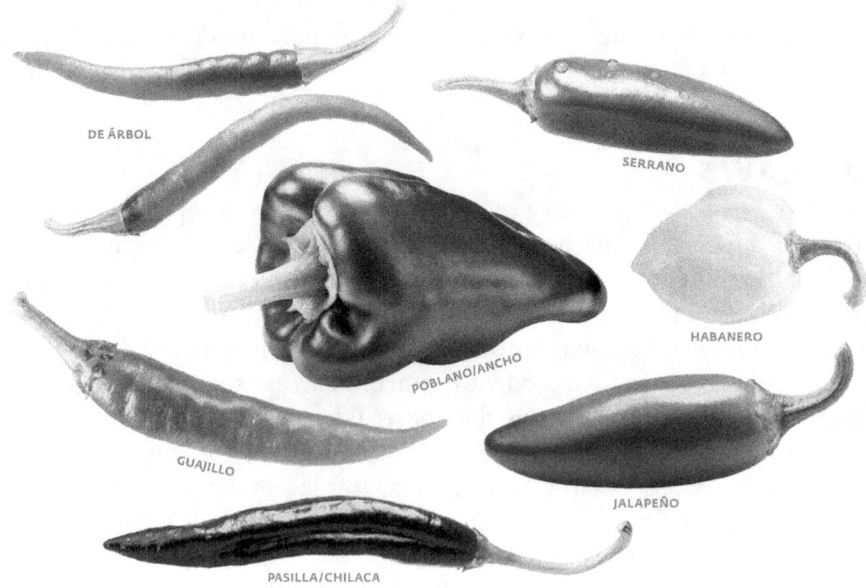

The Chile Pepper Institute at New Mexico State University claims to be the only international nonprofit organization devoted to chile peppers. For many, the garden where hundreds of the plants grow in a rainbow of colors is the most stunning attraction. (Maxim Tatarinov/Dreamstime.com)

claims to be the only international nonprofit organization devoted to education and research related to capsicum, or chile peppers. Among the indoor displays are chile pepper art, books, chile research posters, and what the museum states are hundreds of high-demand, hard-to-find chile pepper seed varieties. The visitor center store sells an array of chile products, running from expected items such as hot sauces, to the surprising, such as brownie mix made with one of the hottest peppers in the world. For many, the most stunning attraction at the Chile Pepper Institute is its garden, where more than 150 different pepper varieties grow in a rainbow of colors that dazzle the eye as well, presumably, as the taste buds.

No mention of attractions in New Mexico can omit the **International UFO Museum and Research Center** in Roswell. The town itself, with a population of about 48,000 earthlings, has embraced the UFO mythos with alien-themed mailboxes, murals, and street lamps, along with statues of little green men hanging around town—at least most people presume they are statues. Even the golden arches of a top fast food franchise in Roswell stand amid a unique UFO-shaped facility. According to its website, the UFO Museum was organized to inform the public about what has come to be known as "the Roswell Incident," when aliens are said to have landed nearby. Furthermore, the museum claims to be dedicated to collecting materials and up-to-date information on all unexplained phenomena related to UFO research. Not surprisingly, many of its visitors describe the museum's attractions as being "out of this world."

For those who prefer more down-to-earth novelties, honorable mention goes to the **World's Largest Pistachio** at Alamogordo, New Mexico, or, as some prefer to call it, "the really big nut." Constructed of concrete, at 30 feet tall, it is about the height of a three-story building. The light-green paint job is strangely realistic, but inedible. Pistachio lovers can quell their cravings at the adjacent Pistachio Tree Ranch and Winery Gift Shop. Among items for purchase are homemade pistachio milkshakes along with an homage to its home state, chile-chocolate-pistachio brittle for those who are nutty about chiles, chocolate, and pistachios.

DISTINCTIVE NEW MEXICO WORDS AND SAYINGS

Burque: Nickname for Albuquerque, where residents are called Burqueños. The acronym ABQ is also a quick reference for this hard-to-spell city.

"Eeeeeee . . .": An all-purpose interjection that, depending on context, might express everything from agreement to disappointment, and from fear to happiness as in "Eeeeeee, this posole is good!"

Red, green, or Christmas? Santa Claus is not coming to town. Diners are being asked whether they want their meal with red chile, green chile, or both (red and green being Christmas colors). In New Mexico, "None of the above" is not usually an option.

Viga: Rough-hewn wooden beams running across interior ceilings and often protruding from the exterior of many homes in the Land of Enchantment. Not to be confused with **Kiva**, a style of ceremonial room or a fireplace common to New Mexico.

Further Reading

Chávez, Thomas E. *An Illustrated History of New Mexico*. 2nd edition. Albuquerque: University of New Mexico Press, 2002.

De Aragón, Ray John. *Enchanted Legends and Lore of New Mexico: Witches, Ghosts and Spirits*. Charleston, SC: History Press, 2012.

Mulhouse, John M. *Abandoned New Mexico: Ghost Towns, Endangered Architecture, and Hidden History*. Charleston, SC: Arcadia Publishing, 2020.

Sanchez, Joseph, and Robert L. Spude. *New Mexico: A History*. Norman: University of Oklahoma Press, 2013.

New York

FACT BOX

Nickname: The Empire State
Statehood Granted: 1788
Capital: Albany
Population: 20,000,000
State Motto: *Excelsior* (Latin: "Ever Upward")
What Natives Call Themselves: New Yorkers

STATE HISTORY

Upon hearing the words "New York," many people immediately think of the teeming urban metropolis on Manhattan Island. For some, it is ingrained through such tag lines as "Live from New York—It's *Saturday Night!*" Similarly, seeing a title such as *West Side Story*, no one has to ask, "Which west side?"

While other American cities may be known as the capital of a particular industry, such as Hollywood for movies or Detroit for cars, New York City has it scaled down to individual streets, such as Broadway for theater and Wall Street for finance.

Yet the state also comprises a huge triangle-shaped monolith called "Upstate" that rises north of Manhattan Island, teeming with farms and foliage, woods and wilderness, rivers and rural life. That too is New York.

Upstate or downtown, today's New York has always been prime real estate. Before Europeans arrived, the region was home to Native American people such as those who formed what was called the Five Nations or Iroquois Confederacy: the Cayuga, Mohawk, Onondaga, Oneida, and Seneca.

The Lenape people controlled the region around today's New York Harbor, and by doing so, found themselves at the center of a beloved centuries-old America saga.

It began in 1624 when the Dutch West India Company established the colony of New Netherland, which comprised present-day New York as well as parts of Connecticut and New Jersey. A small Dutch settlement called New Amsterdam flourished on the southern tip of today's Manhattan Island. As evidenced in a document written in 1626, the Dutchmen believed they had made a good purchase by buying Manhattan Island from the Native Americans for the equivalent of $24.

PETER MINUIT AND WALTER VAN TWILLER
1626–1637

THE PURCHASE OF MANHATTAN ISLAND.

In 1626, as depicted in this scene, Dutch colonists thought they were buying New York's Manhattan Island from Native Americans for the equivalent of $24. Historians believe otherwise. (Library of Congress)

However, many historians believe the Dutch, who were usually sharp traders, got conned. There is evidence that the Natives with whom they bartered were just passing through, with no claim whatsoever on the land they "sold." In any case, experts presume that the Natives, whoever they were, simply believed they were permitting the Dutch to have hunting and fishing rights, not approving a bill of sale.

In 1664, when English ships sailed into New York Harbor, none of that would matter, since the Dutch were forced to yield their colony to the British. The days of Dutch New Netherland were at an end.

The region was renamed New York, in honor of England's Duke of York, the future King James II. It was one of the original thirteen colonies, with the populace being about evenly split in its loyalties during the American Revolution. The British occupied New York City throughout the war, making it their base of operations.

Part of the reluctance of many colonial New Yorkers to join the American cause was due to strong business ties with England. New York was the only colony not

> **Supreme Wisdom**
>
> In 1998, a case came before the U.S. Supreme Court that reflected the origin stories not only of several sitting justices but also of untold millions of Americans. The question was whether Ellis Island, port of entry for masses of immigrants in the 20th century, is in New York or New Jersey. Ellis Island is located near the Statue of Liberty in New York Harbor. However, most maps show it to be within the official boundary line of New Jersey. Both New York and New Jersey claimed portions of the island that were expanded due to landfill. New Yorkers on the Supreme Court, including Justices Ruth Bader Ginsburg, Elena Kagan, and Sonia Sotomayor, joined the majority in the 6–3 decision holding that Ellis Island belongs to *both* New York *and* New Jersey, depending on location. For example, the Main Building, housing the Ellis Island National Museum of Immigration, is in New York, but New Jersey has sovereign rights over filled-in lands on its side of the Hudson River. Unusually for a Supreme Court decision, apparently everyone was happy with the Solomon-like arrangement.

to vote for the Declaration of Independence, with its delegates claiming they were not authorized.

After the war ended, New York did ratify the U.S. Constitution in 1788, although it was among the final three to do so. New York City became the site of America's first presidential inauguration when George Washington took the oath of office in 1789, and the city served as the nation's capital until 1790.

From that time, New York City hurtled forward to the top tier of world-class cities. Despite periodic proposals to escape Albany's rule by seceding, New York City remains firmly attached to the Empire State.

URBAN LEGENDS

Like the 2006 movie title *Snakes on a Plane*, the urban legend known as **Alligators in the Sewers** tells the whole story. According to the tale, New York City kids who went on vacation with their families to Florida brought back baby 'gators as pets. But when the reptiles started to outgrow Manhattan apartments, they were said to be unceremoniously thrown into the toilet and flushed away—right into the city's vast sewer system. There, the alligators are said to have adapted, eventually spawning more of their kind. Today, there are periodic retellings of a 1935 *New York Times* article claiming an alleged eight-foot-long alligator was found in a city sewer manhole. The urban legend has been celebrated permanently in the form of a sculpture at Manhattan's 14th Street subway station in which the reptile appears to be devouring a small child—perhaps recognizing the same tot who tossed him into the toilet.

The Empire State often seems to do a lot of things on a larger scale than other places. That includes urban legends concerning Loch Ness Monster–type creatures skulking in the waters of its lakes—not just one, but three. The first, nicknamed **Champ**, is said to dwell beneath Lake Champlain in Upstate New York. Local towns celebrate Champ at annual festivals and have included the creature in tourism campaigns. Despite attempts to locate Champ by using scientific equipment to verify the sea monster's existence, Champ currently lives only in the realm of urban legend. The second such creature, **Georgie**, is the alleged beast of Lake George, also in Upstate New York. At one point, a local resident swore publicly that he had caught the 10-foot-long serpent but later put a dent in the saga by admitting his story about catching Georgie was a hoax, or in other words, a rather large fish tale. Finally, there is **Old Greeny** who is believed to undulate in the deep waters of Cayuga Lake where it is said that the lake bottom descends to a depth below sea level. Along with reported sightings over the years, the Greeny legend's "proof" has been linked to mysterious waves that are seen on the lake even on calm days. Spoilsports tend to dismiss the existence of Old Greeny as hardly a lake monster but simply a large sturgeon.

One longtime urban myth concerns coins that turn into murder weapons when tossed from the observation deck of the 102-story Empire State Building in Manhattan. The story goes that **Dropping a Penny** from the top of the venerable tower is enough to kill a passing pedestrian below due to the speed of its downward acceleration from such a height. Believers have likened its impact to that of a bullet. The problem is that the myth has been debunked on numerous occasions. Still, it seems to hold its place as a cautionary lesson about dropping things off high places when people are strolling below, as well as innumerable puns along the lines of "Heads or Tales."

What is arguably the granddaddy of New York's urban myths is the legend of **Sleepy Hollow**. According to the tale, during the late 1700s in a quiet upstate village near Tarrytown, a Hessian soldier was allegedly struck by a cannonball during the American Revolution, blowing his head off. One dark night, schoolmaster Ichabod Crane was said to have been accosted by the ghost of the Headless Horseman, prompting Ichabod to leave town rather hurriedly and never be seen again. The tale of the Headless Horseman, however, stayed on. He lives today through a local "Legend Weekend" festival, is commemorated in a large sculpture on the road to Tarrytown, and perhaps most significant to many, is the mascot of the town's football team, sometimes called America's scariest high school mascot.

ICONIC NEW YORK FOOD

While delicious dishes from around the world can be found in New York, there are those who claim that the state's most iconic food is the classic donut-shaped hard roll called the **Bagel**. The unique step in their preparation is boiling them before baking. They can be made with a multitude of toppings, or can be enjoyed plain, with butter or cream cheese, or whatever feels right.

New York Bagels (Yields 8 medium-sized bagels)

2 tsp active dry yeast
4½ tsp granulated sugar
1¼ cups warm water
3½ cups bread flour
1½ tsp salt
Cooking oil as needed

1. Pour sugar and yeast into ½ cup warm water, then let sit for five minutes before stirring to dissolve the mixture.
2. After mixing flour and salt in large bowl, make a well in the middle and pour in sugar/water/yeast mixture.
3. Add ⅓ cup warm water into the well, then stir and mix, adding extra water if needed.
4. Knead the dough on floured surface for about 10 minutes until dough is firm, elastic, and smooth.
5. Lightly brush bottom and sides of large bowl with oil, add the dough, and turn it to coat before covering the bowl with a damp dish towel. Let rise in warm place for an hour until the dough has doubled in size, then punch the dough down and let it rest for another 10 minutes.
6. Divide the dough into eight equal pieces, shaping each into a round. Press each dough ball against work surface, pulling the dough into itself to shape a round ball.
7. After coating a finger in flour, gently press it into center of each dough ball to form a ring, then place each dough ball on lightly oiled cookie sheet and cover with damp dish towel. Allow to rest for 10 minutes while preheating oven to 425°F.
8. Bring large pot of water to a boil before reducing heat to simmer. Then, use slotted spoon to lower bagels into water until they float to the top.
9. After a minute, flip them over to boil for another 1–2 minutes.
10. When all bagels have boiled, transfer them to an oiled baking sheet and bake for 20–25 minutes until golden brown, then cool on a wire rack.

Source: Adapted from https://www.sophisticatedgourmet.com/2009/10/new-york-style-bagel-recipe/.

ODD LAWS

Each year, New York City attracts legions of would-be entertainers who flock to its concrete canyons hoping to fulfill their dream of a career in acting, comedy, dance, or music. Often, their road to success is paved with unpaid performances to hone their craft. However, potential puppeteers must make sure that the honing does not take place in their house or apartment. Under a 2006 New York City statute, it is unlawful to use "any window or open space" in a residence "to exhibit to the public upon the street, or the sidewalk thereof, any performance of puppet or other figures." The puppeteering perpetrator is subject to a $25 fine and/or 30 days in jail. If the latter, the municipal code does not specify if puppet shows could be performed for fellow inmates.

Tourists and passersby in Manhattan's Times Square have been known to feel overwhelmed by the sheer number of costume-clad figures promoting photo opportunities for cash. Elmo, Minnie Mouse, and other characters are portrayed by individuals who sometimes combine panhandling with manhandling. In an attempt to limit their impact, a New York law makes it illegal for two or more mask-wearing persons to gather in public, specifically in "a mask or any face covering which blocks or hides their identity." Some exposure of the face must be in evidence, possibly for later identification in a police lineup. Along with exceptions for private parties, allowances were made for mask mandates in the age of COVID-19. But the law remains on the books.

New Yorkers are often accused of talking too fast, walking too fast, and doing many other things too fast, giving rise to the concept of the "New York Minute." But even New Yorkers in a big hurry must slow down to a crawl in situations where many would wish to put pedal to the metal. People who are late for work or otherwise impatiently stuck behind a sanitation vehicle, no matter how slow moving or foul smelling, cannot speed past it without being in violation of New York law. Under the Slow Down to Get Around law, drivers must proceed very, very slowly around garbage trucks when the vehicle's safety lights are flashing. Ignoring the law could result in a fine up to $100 and/or 15 days in jail, a place where that famed "New York Minute" could feel a lot slower.

UNUSUAL DESTINATIONS

For cutting-edge entertainment, the **American Museum of Cutlery** in Cattaraugus, New York is, of course, a cut above. The local region had once been home to almost 200 companies that produced cutlery, which is basically anything that has a sharp edge. There are currently only a few such factories left in town. However, today Cattaraugus is home to a corporation that bills itself as "the original paper lollipop stick manufacturer" and may someday have its own museum. At the Museum of Cutlery, there are displays of knives not only from Cattaraugus's past but from a variety of eras and locations around the globe, some offering a slice of life from the 1600s and even the pre-Columbian world. The museum points out that sharp-edged tools cleared America's forests, fed and clothed the nation's pioneers, and helped to win our freedoms, and are therefore hardly a dull subject. Many of the knives on display tell personal stories, including a pocket knife carried by a local Civil War soldier at the battle of Gettysburg and one that went through World War II strapped to the leg of a torpedo bomber pilot in the Pacific. Other knives tell additional stories that will "whet" the appetite to learn more.

The iconic U.S. highway known popularly as Route 66 ran from Chicago to California, and therefore did not cross through New York. However, for those who want the experience of what was called the "Mother Road" but don't want to leave the Empire State, the mini Route 66 in the upstate town of Speculator, New York, should suffice to "get their kicks." **Route 66 Village** was constructed to re-create the days before the age of interstate highways. All the structures in Route 66 Village are no more than 96 square feet, since anything over 100 would have required a building permit. The miniature town consists of a barbershop, church, gas station, general store, ice cream parlor, post office, and schoolhouse, complete with miniscule inkwell desks. Each was built with wood scraps and tends to delight visitors by serving as a tiny time machine.

The **New York Earth Room** in Manhattan takes visitors on another time-traveling journey, this one going back to eons before the bustle of dirty urban streets took the place of actual dirt. The 3,600-square-foot gallery space in the middle of New York City's trendy SoHo contains 250 cubic yards of rich dirt spread almost two feet thick. The 280,000 pounds of well-watered soil have been called an "interior sculpture." However, many people enjoy simply being in touch with a serene element of nature that has the rich smell of the unspoiled outdoors rather than the sights, sounds, and other kinds of smells that are present in the rest of the city. Guests need only to press a buzzer at the front door to arrange a visit to the Earth Room and be transported to this sanctuary of peace and quiet.

Honorable mention goes to another unlikely oasis in the grimy, bustling Big Apple, one that has been nestled in Bryant Park near the New York Public Library for 25 years. It is a most unlikely place of its kind in any setting, much less an urban maelstrom like Manhattan. The lavish **Public Restroom in Bryant Park** is light years away from what one might expect in such places, some of which are often too unspeakable for words. Guests using the Bryant Park facilities enjoy the utmost in civility: classical music, colorful paintings, fresh flowers, and even restroom attendants. Some preplanning is required, since there are usually long lines to get in. It is funded by private donations, so New Yorkers do not have to worry that their tax dollars are being flushed away.

DISTINCTIVE NEW YORK WORDS AND SAYINGS

City, the: With due respect to San Francisco, New Yorkers believe there is only one: the Big Apple, Gotham, Manhattan, the City That Never Sleeps, NYC.

Fuhgedaboudit: This New York adaptation of "Forget about it" (pronounced fuh-GED-uh-boww-dit) can mean anything from "Definitely" to "No way!"

Not fuh nuttin': Another New York mutation, this time of "not for nothing." It is generally utilized when giving an opinion, in the sense of, "Just sayin'."

Schlep: Can be used as a verb meaning to carry, or as a noun to describe someone felt to be a loser, as in "He's such a schlep!"

Upstate: The huge portion of New York that lies above the City.

Further Reading
Editors of New York Magazine (authors). *The Encyclopedia of New York*. New York: Simon & Schuster, 2020.

Eisenstadt, Peter, and Laura-Eve Moss. *Encyclopedia of New York State*. Syracuse, NY: Syracuse University Press, 2005.

Klein, Milton (editor). *The Empire State: A History of New York*. Ithaca, NY: Cornell University Press, 2005.

Revai, Cheri. *Haunted New York: Ghosts and Strange Phenomena of the Empire State*. Mechanicsburg, PA: Stackpole Books, 2005.

North Carolina

FACT BOX

Nickname: Old North State, although some argue for Tar Heel State
Statehood Granted: 1789
Capital: Raleigh
Population: 10,500,000
State Motto: *Esse quam videri* (Latin: "To Be, rather than to Seem")
What Natives Call Themselves: North Carolinians

STATE HISTORY

As later inhabitants would discover, the region that is today's North Carolina has traditionally been able to boast an appealingly long coastline, complete with the shelter of the Outer Banks with their miles of beaches.

Archaeologists estimate that Native American people lived in the region for about 10,000 years. When Europeans arrived, beginning in the 1500s, Native people in today's North Carolina included the Cherokee, Pamlico, and Tuscarora tribes.

After the discovery of the New World, Spanish explorers such as Juan Pardo attempted to claim the land in today's North Carolina for Spain. Taking his expedition several hundred miles into the interior around 1567, Pardo founded Fort San Juan at Joara, in what is currently Burke County, North Carolina, nestled in the foothills of the Blue Ridge Mountains. It was the first European settlement in the interior of North Carolina and was soon joined by additional forts to the west. However, when those fortifications did not survive, Spain opted to concentrate its colonization efforts farther south, in Florida.

North Carolina was attractive to other European nations aiming for a North American empire. In 1584, Queen Elizabeth I of England granted a charter sanctioning settlement in present-day North Carolina.

The most famous attempt went down in history not because of its success but because it disappeared, becoming America's original "cold case" mystery. The fate of what has become known as the Lost Colony of Roanoke, North Carolina, remains unsolved. Founded in 1587, all 115 members of the settlement, led by John White, vanished without a trace. Theories range from drought, disease, and Native American raids to alien abductions—or the colonists simply moving someplace else.

North Carolina's Ocracoke Inlet was the haunt of notorious pirate Edward Teach, better known as Blackbeard, pictured here. After being killed, Blackbeard's head was publicly displayed. (Photos.com)

One small member of the Lost Colony who became a big name in history books is Virginia Dare, born in 1587. She is known as the first English child to be born in today's United States, but she disappeared along with the rest.

Eventually, other settlements were more successful, allowing North Carolina to become one of the original thirteen colonies. King Charles II of England granted a colonial charter in 1663 for a huge province to be called "Carolina," from the Latin word "Carolus," honoring his late father, King Charles I. In 1712, the province of Carolina was split between two portions, North Carolina and South Carolina.

The economy of the North Carolina colony was based on agriculture as well as the export of lumber to England for shipbuilding. The volume of seagoing traffic back and forth across the Atlantic attracted nautical bandits to the Carolina shores.

Some of the region's most notorious pirates of the early 1700s included Jean Lafitte, Calico Jack Rackham, and, the most infamous of all, Edward Teach, better known as Blackbeard. North Carolina's Ocracoke Inlet was said to be Blackbeard's favorite hunting ground. He could lie in wait for inbound or outbound oceangoing vessels that had to pass through the inlet. His strategy became so well known that it was at Ocracoke where Blackbeard met his death in 1718 in an attack ordered by the colonial governor. Afterward, Blackbeard's head was severed from his body and publicly displayed, both for his killer to collect the reward and as a warning to other would-be pirates.

In the later 1700s, many residents of North Carolina supported the English side as the American Revolution approached. However, in 1776, North Carolina's three delegates signed the Declaration of Independence.

After the Revolution, in 1789, North Carolina became the 12th state to ratify the Constitution.

With the approach of the Civil War, some Southern states began seceding from the Union. North Carolina was the last of the Confederate states to do so, while its neighbor, South Carolina, had been the first.

> ### A Matter of Perspective
>
> The Massachusetts towns of Lexington and Concord usually claim to have lit the first spark of the American Revolution. However, residents of the Tar Heel State are often quick to point out that the Battle of Moores Creek Bridge, near Currie, North Carolina, was the site of the war's first Patriot victory. In 1776, local citizens who were mostly Scottish Highlanders loyal to the British charged across Moores Creek Bridge wielding broadswords. Patriots on the other side opened fire with cannons. The decisive American victory prevented the British from gaining early control of the Southern colonies. In addition, it demonstrated the effectiveness of cannons against broadswords. The Battle of Moores Creek (spelled without an apostrophe by National Park Service staffers who maintain the site) is sometimes called the "Lexington and Concord of the South." Proud North Carolinians, however, may refer to Lexington and Concord as the "Moores Creek of the North."

North Carolina suffered the greatest number of casualties in battle during the war, with more than 20,000 of its men being killed. An additional 21,000 succumbed to disease.

After the Civil War, North Carolina struggled to emerge from the devastation. A large segment of its population moved away from the coast, pursuing agriculture inland to form a vital part of the state's postwar economy. The Industrial Revolution that took place in the late 19th and early 20th centuries brought forth the development of factories in North Carolina, based in large part on cotton mills.

In the late 1800s, railroads connected the state to the rest of the nation, but it was a revolutionary new mode of transportation that gave North Carolina the slogan that can still be seen on its license plates: *First in Flight*. Amid the coastal dunes of Kitty Hawk, North Carolina, two brothers named Orville and Wilbur Wright succeeded in their attempt at what is called the first successful controlled and sustained heavier-than-air flight in 1903.

In the later part of the 20th century, an area of North Carolina popularly called the Research Triangle took shape. With a number of universities in the region, the cities of Durham, Chapel Hill, and Raleigh became national leaders in scientific and technical research. Meanwhile, the city of Charlotte, North Carolina, emerged as a major national financial center.

North Carolina is blessed with two major hubs of tourism, which is an important economic element for the state. Not only are the Appalachian and Blue Ridge Mountains a draw for visitors, but the beaches of the Outer Banks off the Carolina coast exert a pull on tourists where pirates once ruled the waves.

Through its long history, North Carolina has been proud of the number of "firsts" attributed to the state. Established in 1776, the town of Washington in Beaufort County, North Carolina, is said to be the first in the United States to be named for America's first president, George Washington. In 1793, the University of North Carolina became the first public university in the United States. America's first outdoor drama, *The Lost Colony*, has been staged every year in Manteo, North Carolina, since 1937.

However, for many, North Carolina holds a place in their hearts as being the site of Babe Ruth's first professional home run. He did so on March 7, 1914, in the town of Fayetteville. It was there that the young rookie George Herman Ruth, playing for the Baltimore Orioles, earned the nickname "Babe."

The 255-room Biltmore Estate in Asheville, North Carolina, is known as the nation's largest privately owned home, popularly called "America's Castle."

Far removed from wealthy castle-dwellers is the average North Carolinian who is known by a simpler term: "Tar Heel." Its origins can be traced to early North Carolina's distinction as a producer of tar, made from the state's abundant pine trees, a substance that was vital to shipbuilding. During the Civil War, North Carolina soldiers were teased about having tar on their footwear, but they—and the rest of the state's residents—embraced the term as an affectionate nickname as unique as the state itself.

URBAN LEGENDS

North Carolina has its own version of the rumored "chupacabra," a monstrous creature that allegedly attacks livestock. The legend of the **Beast of Bladenboro** began in 1954 when there were numerous animal mutilations near this small North Carolina town. Some livestock as large as cattle and horses were allegedly found with their jaw broken or removed and the blood drained from their dead bodies. Reports from supposed witnesses claimed that the beast was about the size of a large wildcat, but more monstrous in appearance. Suddenly, the attacks stopped as abruptly as they had begun. For a half century, the Beast of Bladenboro legend remained just that—a legend. Then, in 2006, the attacks allegedly began again, with livestock mutilated in the same way as the 1954 version, adding a retro touch to this urban legend.

As opposed to the Beast of Bladenboro, the **Brown Mountain Lights** in Burke County, North Carolina, can be easily spotted, which does not make them any less of an urban legend. Aliens, unidentified flying object (UFO) abductions, and Native American ghosts are all part of the mythos surrounding the Brown Mountain Lights. Visitors to the Brown Mountain Overlook late at night report strange orbs in different colors and sizes that appear to rise from the trees of the Pisgah National Forest, "dancing" above the mountaintops. Some claim that the lights have a sort of intelligence about them by seeming to follow onlookers. Reports of one observer who came too close to the lights maintain that he collapsed, regained consciousness several days later, and displayed what some felt were signs of having been abducted by a UFO. Although skeptics attribute the phenomenon to marsh gas, the Brown Mountain Lights were featured in a 1999 episode of *The X-Files* on television as well as playing a starring role in the 2014 movie *Alien Abduction*. It is unknown if marsh gas has any movie or TV credits.

In Chatham County near Bear Creek, a 40-foot scorched circle in the middle of the woods is called **Devil's Tramping Ground**. It is said that Satan ascends to Earth there, pacing around the circle and even dancing while plotting his evil deeds. According to the tale, nothing will grow in the circle, dogs will bark and refuse to get close, and defiant campers pitching a tent there have claimed to see strange figures lurking in the woods at night, after which the campers are said to never feel quite sane again. Items left in the circle are reportedly found the next day, inexplicably tossed outside its boundary. So far, neither scientists nor ghost hunters have been able to crack the mystery of the Devil's Tramping Ground.

ICONIC NORTH CAROLINA FOOD

According to the North Carolina SweetPotato Commission, the Tar Heel State is the nation's top producer of sweet potatoes. Most North Carolinians save room for dessert if it's **Sweet Potato Pie**. Here is the recipe, endorsed by the commission itself:

North Carolina Sweet Potato Pie (Serves 8)
Prepared piecrust for 9-inch single-crust pie
2 medium sweet potatoes, peeled and cubed
⅓ cup butter, softened
½ cup sugar
2 large eggs at room temperature, lightly beaten
¾ cup evaporated milk
1 tsp vanilla extract
½ tsp ground cinnamon
½ tsp ground nutmeg
¼ tsp salt

1. While preheating oven to 425°F, flute edges of prepared piecrust and refrigerate.
2. Place sweet potatoes in a medium saucepan, adding water to cover, then bring to a boil.
3. Reduce heat, and cook, uncovered, about 15 minutes or until tender.
4. Drain sweet potatoes, return to pan, and mash them until they are smooth, before cooling to room temperature.
5. Cream butter and sugar together in a bowl, then add eggs and mix well.
6. Add 2 cups mashed sweet potatoes, milk, vanilla, cinnamon, nutmeg, and salt. Mix well and pour into the prepared crust.
7. Bake for 15 minutes, then reduce heat to 350° and bake until a knife inserted in the center comes out clean, about 35–40 minutes. Cool on a wire rack.

Source: Adapted from https://www.tasteofhome.com/recipes/sweet-potato-pie/.

ODD LAWS

In 2015, "Blackbeard's Law" was passed by the North Carolina legislature regarding photographs, videos, or other filmed materials capturing images of a shipwreck being surveyed by the state. Under the law, images of any such vessel, including its contents and historic artifacts, "in the custody of any agency of North Carolina government or its subdivisions" are deemed to be public record. It evolved from a copyright infringement suit by a videographer who documented exploration of the wreck of the *Queen Anne's Revenge*, flagship of the pirate Blackbeard who died in 1718. In 2020, the case made it all the way to the U.S. Supreme Court, which ruled in North Carolina's favor. It would seem that four centuries after his death, Blackbeard sails on.

It is not uncommon in many states for horse theft to be unlawful. The North Carolina legislature carried it a step further to include man's best friend. Along with horses or mules, anyone taking a dog without the owner's permission, even "with the intent to use such property for a special or temporary purpose," will be in violation of state law. For many Tar Heels, this means no borrowing someone else's dog to go hunting.

It is also unlawful to usurp someone else's kitchen grease. Under a 2013 North Carolina statute, it is unlawful to carry off waste kitchen grease that bears a notice on its container stating that unauthorized removal is prohibited without written consent of the owner. It is also unlawful to be so peeved at the inability to carry it off that the thwarted perpetrator decides to contaminate or damage the grease and/or its container. There are a number of grease-related subsections, specifying various penalties. Research reveals that the U.S. Department of Agriculture considers "yellow grease" to be a valuable commodity worth 30–40 cents a pound. Restaurants and authorized grease collectors went to state legislators about the problem of theft, with the result that today, for North Carolinians, "grease is the word."

UNUSUAL DESTINATIONS

At the **Museum of the Bizarre** in Wilmington, North Carolina, the unassuming building offers up a menu of the macabre. Oddities include a crystal skull and letters from serial killers, but the items belonging to celebrities tend to take center stage. Legendary magician Harry Houdini's Ouija board is joined by a lock of hair from superstar Founding Father Alexander Hamilton. There are also objects that will not be found in history books, such as an alleged footprint from Bigfoot, the hand of a chupacabra, the horn of a unicorn, and what is said to be the remains of a mermaid. The Museum of the Bizarre helpfully advises potential visitors that convenient parking is available adjacent to the building, possibly to reassure guests who may feel the need to run screaming from the premises.

It is difficult to imagine anyone who would run screaming from **Mount Airy, North Carolina**, unless it was fear of rejoining the "real world." As the hometown of the beloved actor Andy Griffith, Mount Airy has recreated itself to portray the fictional town of Mayberry, the setting for television's long-running comedy *The*

Andy Griffith Show, which can usually be found in reruns on any given day. Some people presume that Mount Airy was the inspiration for Mayberry, as they are happily transported to a simpler time and place, small-town-America style. Downtown Mount Airy is home to such landmarks as Floyd's Barbershop and the Mayberry Courthouse, with tours available in vintage police cars such as those on the TV show. A stop at the Mayberry Soda Fountain helps guests slow down into the comfort zone of an earlier age, even if it was fictitious.

People who read often do not take time to consider what makes reading possible at its most basic level: the alphabet. At the **Museum of the Alphabet** in Waxhaw, North Carolina, the chronological history of mainstream written language also pays attention to smaller, less-known minority languages. Those include the dialect of the Gullah communities of the southeastern coastal region of the United States as well as the Cherokee Syllabary developed by the Native American leader Sequoyah. The museum's homage to language takes visitors on a journey from the ancient Rosetta Stone to seeing their name in Klingon from the *Star Trek* universe.

Honorable mention goes to the **Stanley Rehder Carnivorous Plant Garden** in Wilmington. It is dedicated to flesh-eating plants such as the Venus flytrap. This spot in North Carolina provides one of the few places in the world where the microclimate permits year-round outdoor growth of such plants. As noted on travel sites, a helpful hint for visitors is to remember *not* to wear open-toed shoes.

DISTINCTIVE NORTH CAROLINA WORDS AND SAYINGS

Blue: In North Carolina, this is a trick question. Is it the light blue of the University of North Carolina or the dark blue of its rival, Duke University? The response can distinguish friend from foe.

Cheerwine: A cherry-flavored soft drink made in North Carolina for more than a century. It contains no alcohol, but claims the hearts of Tar Heels.

Field party: Usually in the autumn when nights are crisp, this festive gathering takes place around a bonfire on someone's farmland and often includes a lot of barbecue and Cheerwine.

OBX: The Outer Banks, which are the 200-mile string of barrier islands off the North Carolina coast that are known for their prime beachfront property.

Tobacco Road: Referring to the region's history as a major tobacco producer, it's a nickname for U.S. Highway 15-501, separating college rivals Duke, North Carolina State, University of North Carolina, and Wake Forest by just a few miles.

Further Reading

Fortson, Ben. *A Nutshell History of North Carolina*. Charleston, SC: History Press, 2016.

Tise, Larry, and Jeffrey J. Crow (editors). *New Voyages to Carolina: Reinterpreting North Carolina History*. Chapel Hill: University of North Carolina Press, 2017.

Wilson, Patty A. *Haunted North Carolina: Ghosts and Strange Phenomena of the Tar Heel State*. Mechanicsburg, PA: Stackpole Books, 2009.

North Dakota

FACT BOX

Nicknames: Peace Garden State, Flickertail State, Roughrider State
Statehood Granted: 1889
Capital: Bismarck
Population: 762,000
State Motto: "Liberty and Union, Now and Forever, One and Inseparable"
What Natives Call Themselves: North Dakotans

STATE HISTORY

For thousands of years, North Dakota was home to Native Americans before the coming of Europeans. When white explorers arrived, they encountered tribes of people such as the Crow, Lakota, and Mandan.

The first white man who was documented as reaching today's North Dakota was a French Canadian trader named Pierre Gaultier, Sieur de La Vérendrye, who led an expedition that arrived in 1738. As with many of the French-speaking explorers, he was primarily interested in fur trading with the Native Americans.

Some of the Native tribes the French encountered lived in permanent villages near the Missouri River and its tributaries. Others were migratory, following the great herds of bison on the Dakota plains.

Decades after the arrival of the French traders, events half a world away from today's North Dakota altered its destiny. In 1803, Napoleon Bonaparte, emperor of France, wanted money to fight a war. He lost interest in owning a great swath of land west of the Mississippi River in faraway North America. Napoleon offered what is known today as the Louisiana Purchase to the fledgling United States for $15 million. Covering more than 800,000 square miles, the deal came to about three cents an acre and doubled the size of the United States.

Today's North Dakota was included in the Louisiana Purchase, along with all or some current American states such as Arkansas, Colorado, Iowa, Kansas, Louisiana, Minnesota, Missouri, Montana, Nebraska, New Mexico, Oklahoma, South Dakota, Texas, and Wyoming.

U.S. president Thomas Jefferson was curious about what America had just bought, so he sent an expedition under William Clark and Meriwether Lewis to check it out and see if they could reach the Pacific. Their "Corps of Discovery," otherwise known as the Lewis and Clark Expedition, lasted from 1803 to 1806.

During their cross-country trek, the Lewis and Clark Expedition spent more than 200 days in North Dakota, passing more time there than any other place on their journey. It was in North Dakota that their Native American guide Sacajawea was returned to her home.

Through most of the 1800s, the region that became known as the Dakota Territory was very thinly settled by white people. However, that changed with the coming of the railroad in the late 1800s. Promoting heavily to Easterners and Europeans, land in the Dakotas was presented as being ideal for agriculture. Insofar as the quality of the land, that was true. However, the weather in North Dakota, abutting the Canadian border, often tends to be an issue where farming is concerned.

Although she had just given birth, Sacagawea traveled with the Lewis and Clark Expedition thousands of miles as a guide and interpreter. On the return trip through North Dakota, she was eventually returned to her home. (Joe Sohm/Dreamstime.com)

Temperatures in North Dakota have been said to range from 120° to 60° below zero, therefore hardly ideal for agriculture much of the year. However, the people who settled there did their best to make a success of it, which remains a continuing tradition. Even today, almost 90 percent of North Dakota land is utilized by farms and ranches.

In March 1861, on the eve of the Civil War, the U.S. Congress formally established the Territory of Dakota. Its name was taken from the Dakota branch of the Sioux tribe, the people who were living in the region at the time. Along with today's North Dakota and South Dakota, the original Dakota Territory included much of present-day Montana and Wyoming.

In late 1889, the territory was reorganized and then split into North Dakota and South Dakota. On November 2, 1889, both Dakotas attained statehood.

From the time North Dakota became a state, it attracted a large number of immigrants, especially Germans and Scandinavians, which eventually led some

Blind Justice

President Benjamin Harrison (1833–1901) was a lawyer and a politician as well as the grandson of former president William Henry Harrison and the great-grandson of Benjamin Harrison V, a signer of America's Declaration of Independence. Therefore, Benjamin Harrison was no stranger to diplomacy. In 1889, when it came time to sign the documents conferring statehood on North Dakota and South Dakota, he knew it could result in hard feelings if one of the would-be states felt slighted by being second in line—which might translate into a loss of votes. Harrison had both statehood proclamations hidden by sheets of paper that covered all but the signature line. He then shuffled the documents before signing, which he did without knowing which was first. It was a solid political move, since the actual order in which he signed was never recorded. However, since that time, the alphabet has taken over where politicians feared to tread. With the letter *N* coming before *S* alphabetically, North Dakota is usually listed as the 39th state with South Dakota following as number 40.

jokesters to refer to the state as "Norse Dakota." Some raised cattle, although most became wheat farmers. Both endeavors were suited to the new state, since they both require a lot of land, something North Dakota could certainly boast.

Large numbers of settlers were needed to populate all those wide open spaces, leading to an accolade of which North Dakota could be proud. In an era when most American females had few rights, generally being forbidden to own property, women were among the first farmers in North Dakota. Thousands of single women held homestead claims in North Dakota, owning their own farms. Just like male farmers, the women handled horses, operated machinery, tended farm animals, and worked in the fields.

The Homestead Act of 1852 offered 160 acres of free land to a person who improved the site by building a house, cultivating the land, and living there for five years. The tradition of North Dakota women owning their own farms has remained through the 21st century. The Agricultural Census, which is performed by the U.S. Department of Agriculture every five years, indicates that several thousand women continue to operate their own farms in today's North Dakota.

Female farmers have no doubt contributed to a few of North Dakota's superlatives. For example, what was named the "World's Largest Hamburger" was consumed at Rutland, North Dakota, in 1982. It tilted the scales at over 3,500 pounds and fed more than 8,000 burger-lovers.

What any good hamburger needs, even the most supersized variety, is an order of fries. A record was set at Grand Forks, North Dakota, in 2015 with an event that earned the title of "World's Largest French Fry Feed" when more than 5,000 pounds of the succulent spuds were served.

Not to forget those who prefer sweets to meat and potatoes, in 2008, Fargo, North Dakota, grilled up almost 35,000 pancakes at the "World's Largest Pancake Feed."

Along with its massive meals, North Dakota has traditionally been known as a friendly place inhabited by nice people. Occasionally, however, that friendliness has been stretched to the limit by an unlikely source: the rivalry—for the most part, a friendly rivalry—with its neighbor South Dakota.

Periodically, that rivalry has seemed headed for an unsavory turn of events. Over the years, various proposals have reached the North Dakota Legislative Assembly to drop the word "North" from the state's name, leaving it simply as "Dakota," thus making South Dakota the "other" one. The proposals have always failed, but in any case, to some North Dakotans, their home state is the center of the universe anyway.

URBAN LEGENDS

A number of states boast their own Loch Ness Monster–type aquatic creature, but North Dakota's spooky swimmer may be among the most colorful. **Miniwashitu** is sometimes also known as the Missouri River Monster. According to the legend, it travels upstream in the springtime, breaking the winter buildup of ice as it goes. Reports have described it as a large creature that is covered in red bison-like hair, has a single eye that is topped by a horn, and has a long, jagged spine sticking out of its back. Not only is that description the stuff of nightmares, it is also said that anyone who looks directly at the creature will go insane and soon die. That prediction is based on anecdotal evidence that involved only one man who was indeed said to go mad and then expire. However, most North Dakotans prefer not to test the theory.

Riverside Cemetery in Fargo has built a reputation for being one of the most haunted spots in North Dakota. According to the legend, audio recordings made from atop a particular mausoleum seem to capture the sounds of knocking from inside. Another version maintains that the knocking sounds seem to come from near the doors of the mausoleum. An addendum to the legend is that visitors have also reported hearing voices coming from gravestones in the cemetery as well as a feeling of being watched when nobody else was nearby—in any case, nobody they could see.

Any place hosting what is called the **Stairway to Hell** is probably not to be trifled with. Founded in 1900 and almost completely abandoned in the 1970s, the town of Tagus, North Dakota, is said to have been home to a church that became a hot spot for Satan worshippers. Although the house of worship is in ruins today, said to have been torched by vandals, the urban legend maintains that a stairway to hell is ensconced under the foundation of the church. The legend goes further to claim that by standing in a certain spot, there are audible sounds of the screams of souls who have been condemned to the underworld. Adding to the story, there have been some reports of blood-red hellhounds appearing from out of nowhere, gravestones that glow, and even a demon train roaring down railroad tracks that run through the neglected, forsaken little ghost town. A tiny handful of tenacious residents still remain amid the sagging, once-lovely structures, including a farmhouse with an elegant turret. They have reported that the town is sometimes used as a party place for local teens, including one incident that attracted 300 partyers to what was called a Halloween trashing session. For sad little Tagus, that may be the unkindest curse of all.

ICONIC NORTH DAKOTA FOOD

Krumkake is a cone-shaped, waffle-type cookie made with ingredients including butter, cream, eggs, flour, and sugar. The best way to make them is by using a krumkake iron (similar to a small waffle iron). Krumkake can be enhanced with whipped cream, berries, or other fillings as well as being enjoyed without any filling at all. True to its origins among descendants of Norwegian immigrants in North Dakota, these sweet treats are often made at Christmastime.

Krumkake (Yields enough for 1 platter)
3 eggs
¾ cup granulated sugar
1 tsp ground cardamom
1 tsp vanilla extract
½ cup (1 stick) unsalted butter, melted
1 cup plus 2 Tbsp all-purpose flour, sifted
¼ cup heavy cream
½ tsp almond extract or cinnamon added to batter for flavor if so desired
Powdered sugar as needed

1. In large mixing bowl, beat the eggs with electric mixer on medium speed until thick, about 2–3 minutes.
2. Lower mixer speed, gradually adding sugar by ¼ cup portions at a time.
3. Add a third of the flour, and mix on low speed, until combined, then add half of the melted butter and repeat, ending with the flour.
4. Mix in cardamom and vanilla until combined, then let batter rest while krumkake iron heats.
5. When iron is hot, control thickness of batter by adding some heavy cream if needed.
6. Place 1 tsp of batter in center of krumkake iron. When edges are slightly browned, remove with spatula or knife, then quickly fold over a spoon handle to create the cone shape.
7. Cool finished krumkakes on a baking sheet, then fill, if so desired, dusting with powdered sugar just before serving.

Source: Adapted from https://commongroundnd.com/recipes/sarahs-norwegian-krumkake/.

ODD LAWS

North Dakota apparently takes certain vegetable products seriously. Under state legislative statutes, no aliens need apply to the North Dakota Dry Pea and Lentil Council. The focus of the group, as may be inferred by its name, is to promote commodities such as lentils and chickpeas, also known as garbanzos. All members of the organization, which was created in 1997, must be U.S. citizens. The organization goes further by dividing the state into five "dry pea and lentil districts," having a participating producer elected from each district. Even with North Dakota's close proximity to Canada, foreign lentil barons from the Great White North are prohibited.

North Dakota is known as a pleasant state full of charitable people. One of the allowable ways to raise money for good causes in North Dakota is by sponsoring poker games. However, the state's attorney general has seen it fitting to set some limits, even among the most well meaning. Charitable groups are indeed permitted to hold poker games to raise money, but they cannot go overboard. Licensed charitable organizations can only conduct such poker games on two occasions per year. Monthly tournaments are out of the question, no matter how much the group puts the "fun" in "fundraising." The charitable games must be held at an authorized site of the licensed organization, and the organization may supply the dealer. The attorney general goes further in corralling any high-roller tendencies among the players, even if it is for charity, stating that the maximum single bet is one dollar. In addition, there cannot be more than three raises, of a maximum of one dollar each, by all the players in each round. The statute specifies stud poker, but it is doubtful that the sky's the limit on Texas Hold 'Em.

UNUSUAL DESTINATIONS

The crowd-pleasing **Enchanted Highway Sculptures** of Regent, North Dakota, are not only award-winning works of art, but they also come with what Hollywood might see as a great backstory. In 1989, a former school principal saw his tiny farming town in Western North Dakota dwindling away, fearing it would become abandoned altogether. As in the many "Eureka!" moments that are central to popular films, a thought crossed his mind: "If you build it, they will come." He did, and people indeed showed up, along with the folks from the *Guinness Book of World Records*. With no experience as either an artist or a welder, he began fabricating giant metal figures that earned the title of the "World's Largest Scrap Metal Sculpture" by the authorities at Guinness. Gargantuan metal grasshoppers, geese, deer, and pheasants dot the landscape along the highway, serving as a magnet for photo-snapping tourists who might also indulge in a shopping spree at the nearby gift shop.

It's officially called the Stanley R. Mickelsen Safeguard Missile Complex, but most people refer to it simply as **Nekoma**, named for the nearby town. If that name is reminiscent of an exotic spot half a world away, the giant pyramid soaring above the flat, isolated North Dakota landscape seems to reinforce the notion.

Only when passersby learn the full story does the site become even more bizarre than the tale of any ancient Egyptian pharaoh. Built during the Cold War era of the 1960s, the pyramid rested atop a huge radar system surrounded by underground surface-to-air nuclear missile silos to fend off Soviet attacks. After millions of tax dollars were poured into its construction, the massive military facility closed after only three days of operation. It was named for Mickelsen, who joined the army in 1917, an age when wars were fought with bayonets, not ballistic missiles. Concerns about its expense and effectiveness rendered it obsolete almost immediately. Tourists are not allowed to enter the grounds, much less to explore the pyramid. However, those wishing to visit their old tax dollars can snap photos from outside the gate.

Simply put, **Tommy the Turtle** at Bottineau, North Dakota, is considered the world's tallest turtle riding the world's largest snowmobile. Higher than a three-story building, the towering Tommy was constructed of fiberglass in 1978. Like pandas and koalas, Tommy the Turtle is strangely lovable, especially among children who are allowed to join him aboard his vehicle. It is not known where the idea came from, since turtles are not generally seen riding snowmobiles, but somehow the concept works, turning tremendous Tommy into a terrific photo opportunity.

Honorable mention goes to the **KVLY-TV Mast** at Blanchard, North Dakota. Topping out at 2,063 feet, it is known as the tallest structure in the Western Hemisphere. By way of comparison, New York's Empire State Building is 1,454 tall to its very tip. Rising above the North Dakota plains in 1963, KVLY's broadcast tower was the first man-made structure to exceed a height of 2,000 feet. Even today, it's worth a look—as long as the viewer looks up . . . way up.

DISTINCTIVE NORTH DAKOTA WORDS AND SAYINGS

Bis-Man and **Wahp-Breck:** Cities that straddle rivers but are otherwise close together, such as Bismarck and Mandan ("Bis-Man") or Wahpeton and Breckenridge ("Wahp-Breck").

Flickertail: A squirrel or prairie dog, which some parts of North Dakota have in abundance. Not only is the expression descriptive of the way the animals rapidly move their hindquarters, but it has also become a state nickname.

Salad: Not a type of fresh, leafy, vegetable-based dish that contains greens, unless it is Lime Jell-O. North Dakotans prefer their salad ingredients to be canned fruit, gelatin, mayonnaise, and a hearty dollop of whipped topping.

Sundogs: In a place where temperatures drop as low as they do in North Dakota, these are not man's best friend. "Sundogs" mean the day is going to be especially cold, since they occur when air is frigid enough to form ice crystals that diffuse sunlight into a halo effect.

Further Reading

Aasen, Larry. *North Dakota*. Chicago, IL: Arcadia Publishing, 2000.

Lindgren, H. Elaine. *Land in Her Own Name: Women as Homesteaders in North Dakota*. Norman: University of Oklahoma Press, 1996.

Orser, Lori L. *Spooky Creepy North Dakota*. Atglen, PA: Schiffer, 2010.

Risjord, Norman. *Dakota: The Story of the Northern Plains*. Lincoln: University of Nebraska Press, 2013.

Ohio

> **FACT BOX**
>
> **Nickname:** The Buckeye State
> **Statehood Granted:** 1803*
> **Capital:** Columbus
> **Population:** 12,000,000
> **State Motto:** "With God, All Things Are Possible"
> **What Natives Call Themselves:** Ohioans or Buckeyes

STATE HISTORY

The asterisk (*) regarding the year when Ohio became a state highlights a little-known episode in its history. It is one that should appeal to trivia buffs facing a question about the date of Ohio's statehood.

The year that most sources use is 1803, when its boundaries were approved as the 17th state during the term of President Thomas Jefferson. Apart from the thirteen original colonies, that placed Ohio after only Vermont, Kentucky, and Tennessee in order of statehood during the early days of the nation.

However, the fledging U.S. Congress did not actually complete all the steps to grant statehood—it had *not* approved Ohio's constitution. The problem was discovered in 1953 by a group of Ohio teachers on the eve of the state's 150th birthday celebration. After a quick piece of legislation was passed, President Dwight Eisenhower backdated the document and signed Ohio's retroactive admittance to the Union in 1953.

Eons before that, statehood was not an issue for the Indigenous people who lived in today's Ohio. Archaeological evidence indicates that there were ancient Clovis and Folsom people in the Ohio Valley at least 13,000 years ago.

When French explorers arrived in today's Ohio, they encountered Native American tribes such as the Algonquin and Iroquois. Following explorer René-Robert Cavelier, Sieur de La Salle claiming the land for France in 1669, Frenchmen established trading posts in the region in order to transact the fur business.

The territory took its name from the Ohio River, originating from the Native word *ohi-yo*, meaning "great river."

After France was defeated in the French and Indian War (1754–1763), today's Ohio was ceded to Great Britain. With the thirteen British colonies planted on the

Atlantic coast, present-day Ohio was considered to be the wild frontier as part of the then remote Northwest Territory.

Britain lost the land in 1783 to the new United States of America after the War of Independence. An application for the Ohio Territory's statehood was submitted in 1803, which most people assumed was granted, at least until the gaffe was discovered in 1953.

Slavery had been banned in the Ohio Territory by the Northwest Ordinance of 1787. Therefore, Ohio entered the Union as a free state.

In 1833, Oberlin College was founded in the town of Oberlin, Ohio, having the distinction of being the first college in the United States to admit women as well as people of color.

Industry in Ohio grew during the 1800s, with the state having a strong transportation system via water and the growing railway. Both would be needed to move troops and supplies during the Civil War (1861–1865). Ohio manufactured many of the products needed for the North to fight the war. The state also provided the precious commodity of human lives. The number of Ohio soldiers proved to be larger per capita than any other state in the Union. Ultimately, Ohio suffered the loss of almost 35,000 men who died in the war.

After that conflict, Ohio continued to grow industrially, making use of international shipping on the Great Lakes, with raw materials coming in and finished products going out. In the late nineteenth and early twentieth centuries, Ohio attracted large numbers of European immigrants and African Americans seeking work in its factories.

Ohio is unique for its pennant-shaped "Ohio Burgee," seen here. It is the only non-rectangular state flag in the nation. (Diana Opryshko/Dreamstime.com)

> ### Hang On, Dorothy
>
> The official anthem of the Buckeye State is "Beautiful Ohio" from 1919. However, Ohio has a particular distinction in also having an official rock song. In 1985, the Ohio General Assembly issued a resolution complete with such formal verbiage as, "WHEREAS, the members of the 116th General Assembly of Ohio wish to recognize the rock song 'Hang On Sloopy' as the official rock song of the great State of Ohio." The resolution cites a rock group called The McCoys from Dayton, Ohio, whose recording of 'Hang On Sloopy' was a hit record in 1965. The legislation takes an interesting turn with, "WHEREAS, if fans of jazz, country-and-western, classical, Hawaiian and polka music think those styles also should be recognized by the state, then by golly, they can push their own resolution just like we're doing." The song's title was said to be inspired by a singer named Dorothy Sloop (1913–1998) of Steubenville, Ohio, who sometimes used the stage name Sloopy but did not receive any official mention by the legislature.

For almost a century after statehood, Ohio did not have its own official flag. In 1902, the state legislature approved the triangular, pennant-shaped "Ohio Burgee," the only nonrectangular state flag in the nation.

In 1953, the Ohio General Assembly pursued another important matter, approving the buckeye as the official state tree. It is America's only state honoring the buckeye tree and became a source of the nickname for Ohioans: "Buckeyes."

For many people, Ohio is the center of the universe due to several distinctions. In 1920, the first professional football league was formed in Canton, Ohio, as the American Professional Football Association. Later evolving into the National Football League (NFL), Ohio has been home to such NFL teams as the Cincinnati Bengals and the Cleveland Browns. In 1963, the Pro Football Hall of Fame opened in Canton.

Meanwhile, Cleveland disk jockey Alan Freed was the first to coin the phrase "rock and roll." Beginning in 1951, Freed promoted that emerging style of music on his radio show and organized what was called the first major rock concert, the Moondog Coronation Ball, held in Cleveland in 1952. With a nod to those historical firsts, Cleveland was chosen as the site of the Rock and Roll Hall of Fame, which opened in 1995.

Ohio regularly vies with Virginia as the state that has been home to the greatest number of American presidents. Depending on interpretation, Ohio can claim William Henry Harrison (America's 9th president; born in Virginia but moved to Ohio), Ulysses Grant (18th), Rutherford B. Hayes (19th), James A. Garfield (20th), Benjamin Harrison (23rd), William McKinley (25th), William Howard Taft (27th), and Warren Harding (29th).

Ohio may also lead the nation in memorials to lesser-known chief executives, including James A. Garfield's tomb, the Warren Harding presidential home and tomb, the William Henry Harrison monument, and the William McKinley presidential library and museum. It is also home to what is called the "Rutherford B. Hayes Birthplace Gas Station."

Of the eight U.S. presidents claimed by Ohio, only Grant served two full terms. Four (Garfield, Harding, McKinley, and W. Harrison) died in office, with Garfield and McKinley the victims of assassination.

URBAN LEGENDS

The **Cincinnati Music Hall**, home of the Cincinnati Symphony Orchestra, is said to also be the home of a ghostly legend that has given it a reputation as one of the state's most haunted places. According to the tale, the Music Hall, completed in 1878, was built over a massive burial ground for victims of an 1832 cholera epidemic as well as being the final resting place for the city's indigent poor. Over the years, rumors spread about the site being haunted by the ghosts of the unhappy souls who had been interred there. The urban legend grew after early excavations for the Music Hall revealed about a hundred skeletons, followed by an expansion of the building that uncovered 65 graves. In 1988, more than 200 pounds of human bones were found encased in concrete. According to the legend, there are reports of loud rapping noises at the Music Hall as well as the sound of unseen footsteps when no one else is around. Believers in the legend are of the opinion that this must be the manifestation of souls that did not rest in peace, or at the very least, music lovers from the Great Beyond.

The town of Loveland is sometimes called the "Sweetheart of Ohio," boasting the historic Loveland Castle as well as scenic nature paths. However, amid its charm, the area around the Little Miami River near Loveland is said to be the domain of the **Loveland Lizard Man**. Also called the Loveland Frogman, alleged sightings that date back to 1955 have been reported, including several in 1972 that were given additional credence since they came from police officers. The reports described a humanoid/reptilian creature that stood about four feet tall after rising from a crouching position to walk upright. Some experts claim that the reports were exaggerated and that the creature was a large iguana without a tail. However, the legend continues unabated with periodic sightings reported. The main question in the minds of true believers is whether the creature is a lizard that looks like a man or a man who looks like a lizard.

Near the modern-day town of Doylestown lies Ohio's version of the Headless Horseman. In an area that was a thriving coal mining village in the late 1800s, **Rogues Hollow** (spelled without an apostrophe) became notorious for criminals who holed up there, conducting illicit activities from that base of operations. With its eerie abandoned mines adding to the mystique, tales began to emerge of ghost sightings, shaking ground at the cemetery, and a headless horseman making his rounds. Some of the apparitions and strange sounds from below ground are said to be the spirits of dead miners who were killed on the job, still slashing away at veins of coal that are long played out. Some spoilsports claim that the tales were circulated by the outlaws themselves to keep outsiders away from their lair, but those who believe the urban legend attest to restless spirits stalking the hollow by dead of night.

ICONIC OHIO FOOD

Native Americans in what became today's Ohio are said to have named the tree species *Aesculus glabra* as the buckeye tree due to its oval, two-toned nuts that looked like the eye of a male deer, commonly known as a buck. The most iconic food in the Buckeye State is **Ohio Buckeye Candy**, colored and shaped to look like the nut of the aforementioned tree. Whether they do or not, it is difficult to argue with anything that is made from peanut butter and powdered sugar dipped in fudgy chocolate.

> **Ohio Buckeye Candy** (Yields 5–6 dozen depending on how big they are rolled)
> 1 stick butter, softened
> 18 oz jar creamy peanut butter
> 2 tsp vanilla
> 1 lb confectioners' sugar
> 2 lb candy chocolate, milk, and/or dark chocolate to taste
> 1 box toothpicks
> Waxed paper
> Disposable plastic gloves

1. After creaming together the butter, peanut butter, and vanilla, add sugar 1–2 cups at a time until desired texture is reached, generally somewhat crumbly but also sticking together.
2. Roll into balls about 1 inch in size, and place on cookie sheet that has been covered with waxed paper.
3. When all have been rolled into balls, insert a toothpick about halfway down in each before placing them in freezer for about 10 minutes to chill.
4. While they are chilling, melt the candy chocolate.
5. Remove chilled balls from freezer and quickly dip them into the melted chocolate about two-thirds of the way down, leaving light spot on top so they resemble buckeyes.
6. Set the dipped buckeyes on another piece of waxed paper to dry.
7. To avoid leaving fingerprints on the chocolate, use plastic gloves when removing the toothpicks and setting the buckeye candy on a plate.

Source: Adapted from https://www.justapinch.com/recipes/dessert/cookies/famous-ohio-buckeyes.html.

ODD LAWS

Like many states, Ohio is cited on innumerable websites for allegedly having silly laws. Some are completely fabricated and then copied repeatedly all over the internet. Others have a tenuous relationship with reality. Many sites claim that the state of Ohio has a law that bans dueling. That ancient attempt at settling a perceived insult is not specifically stated. However, under Ohio Revised Codes, it is unlawful to discharge a firearm on a lawn, park, playground, orchard, or "any other ground abutting a school, church, inhabited dwelling, the property of another, or property of a charitable institution." Therefore, if aggrieved parties choose one of those places to settle their differences with pistols, it would indeed be unlawful in Ohio.

The town of Bay Village is said to have an ordinance making it illegal to walk a cow down a thoroughfare called Lake Road. Again, that is stretching the truth a bit. Under a municipal ordinance, the town prohibits walking, jogging, or running along Lake Road as well as nine other streets in the city limits. Therefore, walking a cow is no more unlawful than walking solo. In the interest of full disclosure, according to the town historical society, there was a cattle-related law on the books many years ago because early farmers impeded traffic when herding their cows down Lake Road. Today, farm animals of any kind are prohibited in Bay Village, making the cow question "moo-t."

Canton, Ohio, has a problem with high grass, citing it as an offense that could land a property owner in jail. Further, the resident cannot attempt to keep the "grass police" away by installing an electrified fence or topping a fence with barbed wire, both of which are banned under the city code. Angry homeowners with unruly lawns who try to calm their nerves by practicing their golf swing at a local park are in violation of the law because the municipal code prohibits golf practice shots in city parks. In fact, those wishing to play games of any kind in a Canton park will need prior permission from the city parks superintendent.

Finally, Ohio is cited on numerous websites for banning the popular book, *Catch 22*, the story of a World War II soldier who is frustrated by the world around him. Indeed, the book was briefly banned in 1972 by one Ohio school library, not the entire state, on the grounds of offensive language. By 1976, the book was back on the shelves for readers who related to being frustrated by the world around them.

UNUSUAL DESTINATIONS

The proud history of the **Bun Museum** in Toledo began in 1972 when actor Jamie Farr of the television show *M*A*S*H* stopped by and autographed a hot dog bun at Tony Packo's restaurant. Both Farr himself and Max Klinger (the TV character he played) called Toledo home and claimed to be fans of the real-life café. From that simple beginning, over 3,000 more autographed buns were added to the collection and encased in plastic. They include U.S. presidents, actors, astronauts, comedians, musicians—a veritable celebrity Who's Who from Tony Bennett to Frank Zappa, as well as former British prime minister Margaret Thatcher.

Speaking of Britain, the inspiration for **Cornhenge** at Dublin, Ohio, seems to have crossed the Atlantic from its prehistoric stone counterpart in England. Completed in 1994 and officially called *Field of Corn (with Osage Orange Trees)*, the massive corn-themed sculpture was commissioned by the Dublin Arts Council. It consists of more than 100 concrete ears of white corn, each standing about six feet tall. Every 1,500-pound ear of corn is angled to look different to observers. The sculpture garden sits appropriately in a space that was a former corn field. Locals have taken it to heart to such a degree that weddings are often held there, "corny" or not.

The subject matter of some unusual destinations can be taken quite literally from their names. One is the **Pencil Sharpener Museum** in Logan, Ohio. The collection was amassed by a local resident. After his passing, the installation was taken over by the Hocking Hills Regional Welcome Center. Totaling almost 3,500 pencil sharpeners, there are no duplicates among the assortment, which is said to be the largest collection of pencil sharpeners in America. The handheld sharpeners range from utilitarian to character-themed such as a Barbie doll. They are displayed under a sign proclaiming "Keep Sharp . . . Be Sharp . . . Act Sharp . . . Look Sharp . . . Stay Sharp"—which seems to say it all.

Another collection that is named for exactly what it is can be found at the **Things Swallowed Exhibit** in the Allen County Museum in Lima, Ohio. They are more than 100 items that were swallowed—and removed—by two local doctors in general practice who retrieved the objects from inside their patients. Among the finds are buttons, dentures, various pins including a diaper pin, and a rather lengthy piece of rubber hose, all having been swallowed by people. Incidentally, the Allen County Museum claims to be the only county museum in Ohio accredited by the American Association of Museums.

Honorable mention goes to the **Grave of Dr. Fredric J. Baur** (1918–2008) at Arlington Memorial Gardens near Cincinnati. Baur's name may not be widely known, but his invention is beloved by snack food aficionados around the world. He designed the cylindrical container for the popular Pringles potato crisps. Baur was apparently so proud of his packaging innovation that he asked for his cremated remains to be buried in a Pringles can. His family honored the request.

DISTINCTIVE OHIO WORDS AND SAYINGS

"O-H": In a Buckeye State version of the game Marco Polo, saying the first two letters requires a spirited response of "I-O!"

Jake: Not a person, but a reference to the Cleveland baseball stadium called Jacobs Field but renamed Progressive Field in 2008. Some fans still cling to its former incarnation, as in, "We saw a game at the Jake."

Shoe, the: Another sports-related moniker, this time in Columbus, the home of Ohio State University. Its nickname reflects the facility's shape that is similar to a horseshoe.

Three Cs: The Ohio cities of Cincinnati, Cleveland, and Columbus, which are placed alphabetically here but usually ranked according to wherever the speaker resides.

Further Reading

Cartaino, Carol. *It Happened in Ohio: Stories of Events and People that Shaped Buckeye State History*. 2nd edition. Guilford, CT: Globe Pequot, 2019.

Cayton, Andrew. *Ohio: The History of a People*. Columbus: Ohio State University Press, 2002.

Kern, Kevin, and Gregory S. Wilson. *Ohio: A History of the Buckeye State*. Malden, MA: Wiley-Blackwell, 2014.

Oklahoma

FACT BOX
Nickname: The Sooner State
Statehood Granted: 1907
Capital: Oklahoma City
Population: 4,000,000
State Motto: *Labor omnia vincit* (Latin: "Work Conquers All Things")
What Natives Call Themselves: Oklahomans

STATE HISTORY

Many archaeologists believe that Indigenous people were present in today's Oklahoma as far back as the last Ice Age. Centuries later, people of the Caddoan Mississippian culture built mound complexes beginning around the year 850, such as those currently known as Spiro Mounds in Eastern Oklahoma. Apache people moved in between approximately 1300 and 1500, just before Europeans made contact. The Spanish conquistador Francisco de Coronado passed through today's Oklahoma in 1541 but apparently found nothing he wished to claim for Spain.

French explorers had no such hesitation, claiming the vast region of America's midsection for France in 1699. There was some land swapping back and forth between France and Spain until 1803, when French territory west of the Mississippi River was sold to the United States in the Louisiana Purchase.

With all that real estate changing hands, there was no noticeable thought given to the people who already lived in Oklahoma, including Choctaw, Comanche, Kiowa, Osage, and Quapaw tribes. The name "Oklahoma" is generally said to be derived from the Choctaw words *okla* and *humma*, meaning "red people."

After the Louisiana Purchase, the land currently known as Oklahoma was part of the Arkansas Territory from 1819 to 1828. Plans were made in Washington, DC, to forcibly move other Native Americans to the current state of Oklahoma by designating it as "Indian Territory." Under the Indian Removal Act of 1830, tens of thousands of Native people from the Southeastern United States were driven from their homes by the U.S. Army and expelled to Oklahoma where other tribes were already living. This forced removal to a barren land in the West became known as the "Trail of Tears," a harsh journey on which many Native Americans died.

During the Civil War (1861–1865), several major Native tribes sided with the Confederacy. Today's Oklahoma was the scene of a number of battles between the U.S. Army and Confederate forces, including the Battle of Cabin Creek, the Battle of Honey Springs, and the Battle of Middle Boggy Depot.

In the 20 years after the war, there was a lot of traffic through Oklahoma's Indian Territory by Texas cattle ranchers driving their herds to railheads in Kansas. Major trails such as the Chisholm, Great Western, and Santa Fe all crossed today's Oklahoma. White settlers began building trading posts and homes along the way, which was illegal under Indian Territory restrictions.

In 1927, an Oklahoma businessman campaigned for a new highway, Route 66. Ironically, Route 66 would soon be the permanent way out of the state for thousands of desperate Oklahomans in the Dust Bowl of the 1930s. (Maxim Grebeshkov/Dreamstime.com)

That growing white presence prompted the U.S. Congress to pass the Dawes Act in 1887, decreasing the amount of land that had been promised to Native Americans. Two years later, the stage was set for the Oklahoma Land Rush. When whites were permitted to homestead parts of Indian Territory on a first-come basis, about 50,000 people started gathering. The official starting time, noon on April 22, 1889, was to be designated by a starting gun. However, some would-be landowners unlawfully staked their claims in Oklahoma sooner than permitted. Termed "sooners," this led to the state's official nickname.

In 1907, Oklahoma became the 46th state to join the Union. At that time, the Oklahoma Territory was one of America's major oil producers.

Oklahoma businessman Cyrus Avery began a campaign in 1927 to create a new U.S. highway, to be called Route 66, using a stretch of road from Amarillo, Texas, to his hometown of Tulsa, Oklahoma. In an ironic development, this formed the original portion of Route 66, which in a few short years, would become the major pathway out of Oklahoma for the "Okies," Depression-era farmers whose land was decimated by the Dust Bowl of the 1930s.

Oklahoma bounced back, providing America with an impressive number of "firsts," some more beloved than others. For example, Oklahoma was the first state to utilize the parking meter, which was installed at Oklahoma City in 1935.

Arguably less reviled, today's shopping cart was invented in Oklahoma City. In 1937, a grocery store owner hoped to provide customers with a convenient way to

> **Motto or Not**
>
> According to official sources, Oklahoma's state motto is *Labor omnia vincit*, Latin for "Work conquers all things." The Oklahoma Historical Society states that the phrase was "referred to as a motto in the 1893 statute describing the Grand Seal of the Territory of Oklahoma." Further quoting the Historical Society, "The Oklahoma Constitution also includes the phrase in the description of the state seal but does not officially define it as a motto." A constituent group did some research and found no official vote regarding *Labor omnia vincit*. In 2012, a bill was introduced at the statehouse as follows: "Be it resolved by the House of Representatives of the 2nd session of the 53rd Oklahoma Legislature, the Senate concurring therein: That the official motto of the State of Oklahoma is hereby declared to be: '*Oklahoma—In God We Trust!*'" For most Americans, the phrase sounds vaguely familiar. However, even with the exclamation point for emphasis, official sources still cite *Labor omnia vincit*.

carry their groceries, enabling them to buy more items on a single visit. Remarkably, the shopping cart was not an immediate success. Male and female models were hired to push the new invention around the store before the carts gained popularity.

According to meteorologists, Oklahoma is regularly home to the greatest number of tornadoes per square mile in the United States. Therefore, it is fitting that America's first official tornado warning system began in Oklahoma on March 25, 1948. The warning was developed by two meteorologists based at Tinker Air Force Base in Oklahoma City. At first they were criticized for the potential to incite a panic. Later that same day, a supercell tornado indeed touched down, causing millions of dollars in damage but with no reported injuries. Coincidentally, the site of the March 25 tornado was Tinker Air Force Base.

URBAN LEGENDS

Oklahoma has its own Bigfoot legend, traced back to 1970 when some high schoolers from the town of Talihina were cruising a local back road one foggy night. Although the image of Oklahoma is a flat, treeless plain, there are thick forests in the southeastern part of the state. When one of the boys wandered away from the group toward a densely wooded area, he claimed to encounter what was later called the **Green Hill Monster**. The boy described seeing a huge, horrible creature covered in long, thick matted hair and standing taller than a human. Speeding with his friends to the local sheriff, a report was made. However, the subsequent investigation revealed only a large number of dead animals where the boy claimed to have spotted the monster. Nonetheless, locals were discouraged from visiting the area after dark since the creature was never caught, although there were periodic reports of sightings. The Green Hill Monster has attained an enviable degree of present-day celebrity through the annual Honobia Bigfoot Festival and Conference that is held at Beavers Bend State Park. Along with appearances by Bigfoot researchers and writers, part of the yearly event includes awarding scholarships to deserving students who might be said to go to college with a little help from Bigfoot.

At **Magnetic Hill** on the rural Pioneer Road in the town of Springer, it is said that a mysterious force will pull cars up the hill after being parked in neutral at the bottom. The story goes that the force field is from the ghosts of those who were killed in automobile crashes at the site, pulling the cars of the still-living away from the place where the dead met their doom. Others say it is a strange otherworldly magnetism that is strong enough to crash an airplane. Some spoilsports claim it is the result of an optical illusion, but believers continue to believe.

Shaman's Portal, a site popularly known as "Oklahoma's Bermuda Triangle," is located at Beaver Dunes Park in Beaver Sands. The urban legend maintains that numerous people have allegedly vanished there, never to be seen again. According to the story, it's an unidentified flying object (UFO) crash site known for strange occurrences that are said to go back to the days of the region's Spanish explorers. Reportedly, Native Americans tried to warn Coronado of its danger, but he refused to listen. According to what is said to have been written in Coronado's journal, three of his men mysteriously disappeared into flashes of green light. Purveyors of the legend maintain that the occurrences are clear evidence of the paranormal, with the unfortunate humans being sucked into an alternate dimension. Others claim that those who disappeared were victims of UFO abductions or at the very least, the supernatural residue of previous visits to Oklahoma by extraterrestrials.

ICONIC OKLAHOMA FOOD

In 1988, the Oklahoma legislature approved the "Official State Meal." While many states have an official food, or at least an iconic one, Oklahoma is unique in sanctioning a full meal. And quite a meal it is. In alphabetical order, it consists of barbecued pork; black-eyed peas; chicken fried steak; corn; corn bread; fried okra; grits; sausage served with a side of biscuits and gravy; and squash, strawberries, and pecan pie for dessert. It is said that depending on portion sizes, the meal probably contains about 2,700 calories, exceeding the recommended daily intake for the average person as well as surpassing guidelines for fat and sodium. The recipe below provides instructions for one element: **Chicken Fried Steak**, which, to the surprise of some non-Oklahomans, does not contain any chicken.

Chicken Fried Steak (Serves 4)
4 round steaks, cut thin
2 cups flour
2 tsp Kosher salt
1½ tsp garlic powder

½ tsp cayenne
2 eggs, beaten
½ cup milk
Cooking oil or fat for frying

Gravy:
3 Tbsp pan drippings
3 Tbsp flour
¼ cup whipping cream
1¾ cups milk
Salt
Black pepper

1. Using a meat mallet or rolling pin, pound the steaks about ¼ inch thick, then sprinkle each with dash of salt and pepper.
2. Using two wide, shallow dishes, whisk together eggs and milk in one and flour, salt, cayenne, and garlic powder in the other before soaking steaks repeatedly in both mixtures, then set all aside.
3. After heating about ¼ inch of oil to 350°F, lay each individual steak in the oil and spoon some hot oil on the top of the steak.
4. Fry about two minutes, until edges of the steak turn golden brown, then turn the steak over in the pan, frying for two minutes more.
5. Remove each from the pan, placing it on a wire rack in warm oven (about 200°). Repeat with remaining steaks.
6. For gravy, lower heat to medium, and remove most of the oil from the frying pan except about 3 Tbsp of oil. Whisk in 3 Tbsp flour, and let the mixture cook while stirring constantly for about 4–5 minutes, until it becomes the color of light chocolate.
7. When mixture is smooth, stir in milk and cream, whisking constantly and adding milk for desired consistency. Season with salt and pepper to taste before pouring over the steaks.

Source: Adapted from https://www.insp.com/blog/state-plate-recipe-oklahomas-chicken-fried-steak/.

ODD LAWS

Under current Oklahoma law, a person who is guilty of bad language, or what is termed in the statute to be "profane swearing," is in violation of the law. The fine is one dollar for each offense. It is not known who might be called upon to report the infractions as well as who substantiates them. Nor is it specified how the code is to be enforced, or what nonprofane swearing might be. In addition, it is unclear whether the law is also applicable to movies and television shows where profane swearing is simply business as usual.

Oklahoma not only prohibits bad language but also bans language that is loud. Potential malefactors should not even think about mouthing off in church. State law forbids willfully disturbing or interrupting any gathering where people meet for religious worship. The statute specifies what is considered to be criminal, including indulging in "profane discourse," making unnecessary noise, or committing what the statute terms rude or indecent acts either at the place of worship itself or in close enough proximity to disturb the solemnity of the worshipful group. Under the same section of the statute, it is forbidden to exhibit any shows or plays without a license by the proper authority within a mile of a place of worship. Racing animals or gaming of any kind are also banned within a mile's distance, along with obstructing traffic that would impede worshippers trying to get to their meeting.

In Bartlesville, the city's municipal code prohibits "objectionable environmental influences." Companies in its industrial district cannot emit heat, odors, noise, or smoke, which many citizens find to be reasonable restrictions to maintain the quality of life in their community. However, the statute also prohibits "vibrations," without specifying whether good vibes are included in the list of no-no's.

UNUSUAL DESTINATIONS

With more of a particular stringed musical instrument on display to the public than at any other collection, the **American Banjo Museum** in Oklahoma City is said to be the only museum in the world that celebrates this cheery sound. Not only does the museum exhibit individual instruments, it tells the history of today's banjo, having been invented centuries ago in Africa using such materials as gourds and animal skins. It was re-created in America by enslaved people beginning in the 1600s, going on to become a vital part of American culture. The museum displays several hundred banjos, from simple ones made by hand to what are called concert banjos. There is also sheet music and assorted memorabilia on exhibit. However, for many visitors, the high point of the tour is being given an opportunity by museum staff to attempt plucking on a real banjo themselves.

Proud boosters at locations around the world often consider themselves to be the center of the universe. However, Tulsa claims an anomaly that it calls the *real-* **Center of the Universe** where visitors can experience its strange properties for free. It's a small concrete circle within a larger circle of bricks that may not be long on fanfare but is definitely big on being a mysterious phenomenon. If a person stands in the middle of the small circle and makes a noise, the sound reverberates back many times louder than the original, with an effect similar to an amped-up echo chamber. Some say the strange acoustic anomaly is caused not by intergalactic energy but by sound reflecting off a nearby circular planter. However, experts have studied the cause of the odd acoustical vortex, apparently reaching no clear consensus. Some believers claim they can drop a pin in the center of the circle, and instead of hearing a tiny, tiny sound, the result is more like a loud gong. Conversely, making a loud sound in the center cannot be heard from those who are nearby but standing outside the circle.

For those who simply cannot get enough of political ads, the **Julian P. Kanter Political Commercial Archive** at Norman, Oklahoma, is the largest collection of political advertisements in the world. With about 80,000 recordings of political ads captured on film, video, and audio formats as well as the internet, it presents a fascinating timeline of American democracy in action, running from 1936 to the present day. Campaign ads, debates, and speeches are all here, running the gamut among congressional, gubernatorial, senatorial, and presidential races. According to the archive, there are still about 1,000 ads and 40 unopened boxes yet to be cataloged if any enthusiasts of all things political are interested in being elected for the task.

The **Toy and Action Figure Museum** in the apostrophe-free Pauls Valley, Oklahoma, claims to be the world's only museum devoted solely to action figures. It is probably an apocryphal story, but it's said that if a girl plays with a humanlike plastic figurine, it is called a doll while if a boy does so, it's an action figure. In any case, Oklahoma's Toy and Action Figure Museum includes more than 13,000 distinct action figures, ranging from those of the 1950s to the present. Many have not been removed from their original packaging, which is the gold standard in the toy world. The museum's central diorama displays what is basically an action figure universe of characters ranging from Spider-Man to representations like the set of Peewee's Playhouse. Although all action figures are created equal, some are more equal than others as seen in a separate display room that features nothing but Batman-related exhibits. The museum houses exhibits showing the creation of action figures, from the original idea to the manufacturing process. An annual Hall of Fame induction immortalizes worthy nominees. After being inspired by the vast array of items on display, visitors can enhance their personal collections by making a purchase at the museum's gift shop which—not surprisingly—is stocked with action figures.

DISTINCTIVE OKLAHOMA WORDS AND SAYINGS

Fraidy hole: An underground shelter offering protection from a tornado. Anyone living through one of those terrifying storms may have the right to be a bit of a fraidy cat.

OKC and **T-Town:** The state's major metropolises, Oklahoma City and Tulsa, respectively.

Twister: Not the party game, but a vicious tornado whipping across the plains. Incidentally, most Oklahomans know the difference between a tornado watch and tornado warning.

Honorable mention: True Oklahomans are able to correctly pronounce the names of towns such as **Eufaula, Tahlequah, Oologah, Okemah, Okmulgee, Nuyaka, Pawhuska,** and **Weleetka**, all of which are said to be derived from Native American terms. However, no definitive explanation is given for the town of **IXL**, located in Okfuskee County.

Further Reading

Baird, W. David, and Danney Goble. *Oklahoma: A History*. Norman: University of Oklahoma Press, 2011.

Bouziden, Deborah. *Oklahoma Off the Beaten Path: A Guide to Unique Places*. Lanham, MD: Rowman & Littlefield, 2015.

Goins, Charles Robert, and Danney Goble. *Historical Atlas of Oklahoma*. 4th edition. Norman: University of Oklahoma Press, 2012.

Oregon

FACT BOX

Nickname: The Beaver State
Statehood Granted: 1859
Capital: Salem
Population: 4,200,000
State Motto: *Alis volat propriis* (Latin: "She Flies with Her Own Wings")
What Natives Call Themselves: Oregonians

STATE HISTORY

Native American people such as the Chinook, Klamath, Nez Percé, and Shasta tribes made their home over the centuries in today's Oregon. However, compared to some, they were relative newcomers.

Preserved in an Oregon cave near Fort Rock, 70 pairs of sandals were discovered in 1938. What made the cache of footwear unique is that the sandals were dated at more than 10,000 years old, winning the title of being the oldest-known shoes in the world. In addition, experts state that no other site can boast the large quantity found there, ranging from child-size to those that had been worn by adults.

In the 1500s, European explorers and traders were in evidence along Oregon's Pacific coastline. By 1565, Spain was dispatching ships across the ocean from the Philippines, with the vessels probably being swept along by currents that carried them to the northern Pacific. In 1592, the Oregon coast first appeared on a Spanish map.

By the early 1700s, Spanish ships were regularly arriving on America's west coast. Some, like the 1707 wreck of the *San Francisco Xavier*, encountered fierce storms, coming aground on the shoreline of today's Oregon.

Mapping expeditions by French and Spanish explorers during the 1700s made Americans on the East Coast aware of the land in the northwest. When the Lewis and Clark Expedition established a presence in today's Oregon during 1805 and 1806, it caught the attention of the American government seeking to contain the British who were just across the Canadian border.

With the establishment of the Oregon Trail from Missouri to Oregon in the 1840s, settlers headed toward the region, drawn by the fur and lumber trade. In 1848, the Oregon Territory was formally recognized.

Cascadia the Beautiful

In a sentiment that goes back several centuries, periodically there are calls to establish a new country called Cascadia in the Pacific Northwest. The proposed nation would include all of Oregon along with parts of Idaho, Northern California, Washington, and British Columbia. Some claim the Cascadia movement is merely a regional identity, while others aim for full-fledged secession from the United States. Supporters cite an 1813 letter from Thomas Jefferson describing the settlement of Oregon as "the germ of a great, free, and independent empire on that side of our continent." Often included on lists of aspiring new nations around the world, Cascadia is perhaps the only one with a flag popularly called "Doug" in honor of the Douglas fir tree that forms its centerpiece. In further separatist feeling, some Southern Oregonians have been urging secession from the rest of Oregon since 1941 when they renamed the area "the State of Jefferson," complete with its own flag. However, their flag was not called "Jeff."

The rise of the nation's railroads in the 1800s connected Oregon to the rest of the country. Settlers continued to arrive during the 19th century, leading to Oregon's entry into the Union as the 33rd state in 1859.

Since that time, Oregon has generally prospered. Along with Alaska, Delaware, Montana, and New Hampshire, it is one of only five states with no sales tax.

A proposed new country called Cascadia in the Pacific Northwest would include Oregon. Cascadia's flag is popularly called "Doug" in honor of the Douglas fir tree at its center. (Gladder/Dreamstime.com)

Oregon's Mount Hood is often said to be one of the most-climbed mountains in the world, following only Japan's Mount Fuji. The state also has hidden depths, with Crater Lake being the deepest lake in the United States and one of the top 10 deepest in the world. It descends to around 2,000 feet, or deep enough to submerge a 200-story skyscraper.

One of the more curious oddities about Oregon is that no one is entirely sure how it got its name. Some claim the word is adapted from the Spanish *orejon*, colloquially meaning "big ears," while others call it an adaptation of the Spanish region of Aragon, where many early explorers allegedly came from. Some favor the French word *ouregan*, or hurricane, a nod to the region's fierce storms. There are a few supporters of the theory that the name stems from the Spanish origins of the word "oregano," a plant that grows in the region, which would no doubt delight the state's pizza lovers.

The earliest documented use of the actual word "Oregon" was on a 1765 petition to the English king seeking money for an expedition. The rest is history.

URBAN LEGENDS

Built in 1889, the **Geiser Grand Hotel** in Baker City is apparently the lodging of choice for some supernatural guests who never checked out. With its stained glass ceiling and Victorian-era chandeliers, the apparitions may enjoy a nostalgic sense of living in the past. According to the urban legend, the star of the paranormal parade is the Lady in Blue. There have been reports of her sashaying up and down the main staircase dressed in an ornate gown that appears to date from the late 1800s. When she reaches the bottom of the staircase, she allegedly vanishes into a wall. Sometimes called "Granny Annabelle," she is said to be the apparition of one of the hotel's early owners. Modern-day guests in Room 302, Annabelle's personal suite, report having their travel items moved and sometimes mischievously being awakened in the middle of the night by Granny's wanderings around the room. Other Geiser ghosts allegedly include a cowboy and a saloon singer. The hotel offers ghost tours at Halloween to help sort them all out.

The **Lafayette Curse** legend maintains that in the late 1800s, a woman named Anna Marple was accused of being an accomplice in a brutal murder at the small Oregon town of Lafayette. The charges against her were dropped due to lack of evidence, although in the process, she gained the reputation of being a witch. Her son was hanged for the murder although he proclaimed his innocence. Anna's alleged witchcraft could not save him from a torturous death during which he strangled for 18 long minutes when the rope failed to snap his neck. The accusations of witchcraft finally caught up with Anna, who was hanged for her alleged witchery. Before she died, she laid a curse on the town, shouting that it would burn and never thrive. Her ghost was then said to haunt the town cemetery. From there, she may have kept a gleeful eye on major fires in Lafayette that occurred during 1895, 1897, 1898, 1904, 1914, 1928, and 1946. Perhaps Anna finally decided to let bygones be bygones. Or possibly the cease-fire came because by 1946, the town of Lafayette was not built primarily of wood.

One of Oregon's most pervasive urban legends is called the **McMinnville UFO Sighting** that was said to have taken place in 1950. Allegedly, two photographs of a suspected flying saucer were taken on a farm near the town of McMinnville, subsequently being printed in major national publications. Some say the photos show evidence of the spacecraft being suspended by a string, ergo a hoax. However, others claim that the man and wife who reported the sighting were honest farm people who never sought to profit from the observation, maintaining until the end of their lives that the sighting and the photos were real. The story lives on through McMinnville's annual UFO Festival, which is the largest such gathering in the Pacific Northwest, and second only to Roswell, New Mexico, as the largest in the nation—high praise indeed.

One urban legend that has even true believers in the offbeat scratching their heads is **Polybius**. The story goes that it was a black-box arcade game that could be found in Portland suburbs around 1981. It was said to be so intensely addictive that it hypnotized its players, rendering them oblivious to strange happenings such as suddenly disappearing, only to find themselves miles from home in places such as the Tillamook State Forest or underground in Portland's infamous Shanghai Tunnels. Amnesia, hallucinations, insomnia, and nightmares were allegedly side-effects of the game. Polybius was said to be part of a mind-control experiment by the CIA. Some players were allegedly abducted by mysterious men in black. The urban legend emerged around the year 2000, by which time no actual Polybius game consoles could be found. According to some versions of the tale, those same mysterious men in black were responsible for its disappearance. Incidentally, a real-life ancient Greek historian named Polybius lived around 200 BC, and is known for espousing objective scientific methods in analyzing alleged facts. There is no surviving historical record concerning his stance on urban legends.

ICONIC OREGON FOOD

The marionberry has been described by Oregonians as sweet, tart, and delicious. They may be a bit biased because the marionberry was developed in Oregon, which remains one of the only producers of the fruit, said to be a cross between a blackberry, loganberry, and raspberry. Named for Oregon's Marion County, marionberries were brought to market in 1956. In 2009, a proposal to make the marionberry the official state berry was brought forward in the Oregon legislature. Although it was supported by all of the state legislators, the resolution was opposed by producers of other berries. To avoid a food fight, the resolution was tabled. However, there are few objections when **Marionberry Pie** appears on Oregon's dinner tables.

> **Oregon Marionberry Pie** (Serves 8)
> Prepared 9-inch piecrust, top and bottom
> 1 cup plus 1 tsp sugar, divided
> 2 Tbsp plus 2 tsp quick-cooking tapioca
> 1 Tbsp lemon juice

    4 cups fresh marionberries
    1 package (8 oz) cream cheese, softened
    ½ cup confectioners' sugar
    ½ tsp almond extract
    ½ tsp vanilla extract
    1 Tbsp heavy whipping cream

1. In a large bowl, mix one cup sugar with tapioca and lemon juice. Add berries; toss to coat. Let stand 15 minutes while oven preheats to 425°F.
2. In a small bowl, beat cream cheese, confectioners' sugar, and the extracts; spread over bottom of prepared crust, and top with berry mixture.
3. Cut top crust into ½-inch wide strips, and arrange them over filling in a lattice pattern.
4. Brush lattice strips with cream, then sprinkle with remaining sugar. Trim and seal strips at edge of bottom crust, fluting the edges.
5. Bake 15 minutes at 425° before reducing oven temperature to 350° and baking 50–60 minutes longer, until crust is golden brown and filling is bubbly. Cover edges with foil during last 15 minutes of baking to prevent over-browning. Cool on a wire rack before serving.

Source: Adapted from https://www.tasteofhome.com/recipes/oregon-s-best-marionberry-pie/.

ODD LAWS

Occasionally, there is material on the internet that may not be entirely true. A number of sites dedicated to "Stupid Laws" around the country include the entry that it is against the law in Oregon to fish using canned corn. There is generally no further information to indicate whether the unlawfulness includes both cooked and uncooked corn, creamed or otherwise. Actually, according to the state's Department of Fish and Wildlife, there is a kernel of truth in it. Corn is a popular bait to use when fishing for kokanee, a form of sockeye salmon, and using it as bait is permissible under current regulations. However, it's against the law set down by Fish and Wildlife to "chum" by dumping entire cans of corn into the water to attract masses of the corn-loving fish to the spot. There are also Oregon fishing holes specifically designated only to be used for fly-fishing or by using lures only, in which case, the use of corn or any other vegetable is prohibited.

    In the city of Portland, individuals who prefer motorized recreation over fishing are cautioned to be aware that the beloved decades-old American tradition of "cruising" is prohibited in some parts of the city between 9:00 p.m. and 5:00 a.m. Anyone spotted driving slowly more than twice in an area designated by signs declaring it a "traffic congestion thoroughfare" is in violation of the law. Those who object to the ordinance point to the popularity of such movies as *American Graffiti*, a virtual love letter to the fine art of cruising town in cars. Opposition forces counter with the fact that the film in question was set in California, a place that many Oregonians consider to be a different planet.

If would-be cruisers try getting their kicks on Portland streets in a slightly modified fashion, they will be disappointed as well. It is a violation of the city code to be towed behind a car on skateboards, roller skates, or other similar devices on wheels. Sleds are also off-limits. On certain city streets, even using human power is unlawful if skating, or presumably sledding, is performed on sidewalks.

Finally, Portlanders seeking a quiet spot to sit and ponder the regulations on recreational transportation also need to be careful where they take a seat. The scenic bridges that cross the Willamette River in Portland may look inviting, but under city code, people are prohibited from sitting on, standing upon, or leaning over a Willamette River bridge railing. Exceptions are helpfully available for those engaged in bridge maintenance work or otherwise authorized by what Portland considers to be an appropriate government agency.

UNUSUAL DESTINATIONS

Anyone who has ever yearned for the feeling of stepping onto another planet—one that is not very welcoming—can find a reasonable facsimile at Oregon's **Alvord Desert** near New Princeton. Experts state that many thousands of years ago, it was a lake measuring 200 feet deep. Through the centuries, the natural minerals in the lake water descended to the bottom. Receiving little rainfall each year, today the lake water has evaporated, leaving the Alvord Desert to resemble a desolate moonscape. The salty materials that were on the lake bottom solidified to form what is today the desert's surface. In addition, without an abundance of development in the area, the Alvord Desert enjoys very little light pollution. Stargazers report that at certain times of the year, the Milky Way presents a brilliant celestial panorama, reinforcing the feeling that the viewer is on a distant planet visited only by the starship *Enterprise*.

A very unimpressive name disguises an awesome natural wonder. The mile-wide **Hole in the Ground** at Lake County, Oregon, is a massive—there is no other word for it—hole. Among experts, there is a difference of opinion as to whether it was formed by an ancient meteor strike or by a prehistoric volcano blast from up to 100,000 years ago. It is theorized that if it was indeed a volcano, the violent eruption left a rim reaching about 100–200 feet above ground level along with a crater about 500 feet deep. Water is said to have reacted explosively with volcanic magma, leaving only a giant pit. The landscape is so desolate that NASA determined the crater to be similar to that of the moon. During the 1960s, the space agency sent astronauts to Oregon's Hole in the Ground to test equipment and spacesuits as well as to learn about geology. According to local historians, astronauts placed a piece of lava rock from the Hole in the Ground on the surface of the moon as a memento of their otherworldly training in Oregon.

Everything's coming up roses at the **International Rose Test Garden** in Portland. When the 10,000 individual plants are in bloom, their glorious scent welcomes visitors to what some feel is a bit of heaven on earth. The garden was created in 1915 in order to save varieties of roses that were being decimated in Europe during World War I in order to cultivate them for the future before the plants disappeared in the carnage. Today, the International Rose Test Garden is home to about 650 species, with new varieties of roses regularly being tested. There is no fungicide spraying, and the roses receive only basic maintenance. Apparently the plants are happy that way. Through the years, a virtual kaleidoscope of rose culture has blossomed at the garden, providing a unique treat for the senses. It's a place where even the most hardened cynic might be tempted to see the world through rose-colored glasses.

At the **Neskowin Ghost Forest** in Neskowin, Oregon, the scenery is so bleak that it is virtually the opposite of the Rose Garden's opulent beauty. About a hundred stunted remnants of an ancient forest rise eerily from under the sand and seawater of the Tillamook Coast. For thousands of years, they were 200-foot-tall Sitka spruce trees but eventually became submerged under the sand, devolving into a local legend about a phantom forest that dominated the area millennia earlier. Powerful storms in the late 1990s scoured the region, eroding the sand along the coastline to reveal the eerie ghost forest that had been buried there. Experts theorize that the 2,000-year-old trees were victims of a powerful earthquake in 1700 that caused the land to sink. Thick mud resulted from seawater pouring in, but served a valuable purpose by preserving what was left of the trees. Today, visitors can spot the petrified giants, perhaps lingering to ponder the vicissitudes of time and tide.

DISTINCTIVE OREGON WORDS AND SAYINGS

Cheese: In Oregon there is only one: Tillamook.

Drysider: Native of the less-rainy region of Eastern Oregon.

Elephant Ears: Known in other states as doughboys, fried bread, or fry dough, this is what Oregonians call the county fair staple.

Hood: Neither a gangster nor a head covering, it's the standard Oregon reference to Mount Hood, the state's tallest peak, as in "Yesterday we skied the Hood."

Honorable mention: **Californians**, known elsewhere as residents of the Golden State, but in Oregon, the feeling is best expressed on a popular bumper sticker: *"Californians—Welcome to Oregon. Now go home."*

Further Reading

Cox, Thomas R. *The Other Oregon: People, Environment, and History East of the Cascades.* Corvallis: Oregon State University Press, 2019.

Crutchfield, James A. *It Happened In Oregon: Stories of Events and People That Shaped Beaver State History.* 3rd edition. Lanham, MD: Globe Pequot, 2018.

Robbins, William G. *Oregon: This Storied Land.* 2nd edition. Seattle: University of Washington Press, 2020.

Pennsylvania

FACT BOX

Nickname: Keystone State
Statehood Granted: 1787
Capital: Harrisburg
Population: 13,000,000
State Motto: "Virtue, Liberty and Independence"
What Natives Call Themselves: Pennsylvanians

STATE HISTORY

Pennsylvania, along with Kentucky, Massachusetts, and Virginia, officially terms itself a commonwealth, rather than a state. According to *Merriam-Webster*, there is really no difference apart from the name alone. It is said that the term "commonwealth" was specified in some state constitutions just after the American Revolution because it had a democratic sound.

In any case, either as a commonwealth or a state, Pennsylvania is rich in American history. Because both the Declaration of Independence and the U.S. Constitution were created in Philadelphia, some consider the Keystone State to be the nation's birthplace.

However, its history goes back far earlier. For more than 10,000 years, Native American people lived there. When Europeans arrived in the 1600s, people such as the Shawnee, Susquehannock, and Lenni Lenape, also known as the Delaware, called it home.

In the 1630s, there was some incursion into Pennsylvania by Dutch colonists and those from the New Sweden colony on the East Coast. However, further colonization from those countries diminished after 1681, when England's King Charles II issued a land grant to the family of William Penn as compensation for a debt.

The king named the large region "Pennsylvania," or "Penn's Forest." William Penn, a Quaker, offered the vision of a society in Pennsylvania that promoted freedom of religion. Another aspect of Penn's governance was to deal fairly with the Native Americans, advocating their equal rights. After signing and adhering to a treaty, Pennsylvania's colonists and Natives generally enjoyed a peaceful coexistence.

Philadelphia enjoyed early, enduring success. In 1682, soon after the Pennsylvania colony's founding, the village of Philadelphia was established by William Penn, no doubt attracted by its prime location on the Delaware and Schuylkill rivers. Since Pennsylvania was the only one of the thirteen original colonies that did not border the Atlantic Ocean, water access was critical for its growth and prosperity.

In 1723, the 17-year-old Benjamin Franklin arrived in Philadelphia from Massachusetts. Over the years, this newcomer from Boston became closely identified with Pennsylvania.

As a burgeoning center of commerce, culture, education, and religious tolerance, along with its central location, Pennsylvania became an important hub for the thirteen original colonies. Convening in Philadelphia, the Continental Congress produced the Declaration of Independence in 1776.

In 1780, Pennsylvania passed the Gradual Abolition Act, aimed at emancipating enslaved people. It was the first abolitionist law to be passed in what became the United States.

The U.S. Constitution was created in Philadelphia in 1787, the year when Pennsylvania was granted statehood. Philadelphia served as the capital of the young nation in its early years, with presidents George Washington and John Adams residing there from 1790 to 1800, before the creation of Washington, DC.

Pennsylvania can boast a number of "firsts" in the nation's history, especially in finance. Due to a shortage of gold and silver, the Pennsylvania colony issued its own paper money beginning in 1764, a bold move that kept the colony solvent.

In 1790, the country's first stock exchange was created in Philadelphia, helping to support America's prosperity and westward expansion by raising funds for the development of coal mines and railroads. Then, in 1792, the U.S. Congress approved the creation of the nation's first mint in Philadelphia, becoming the first federal building to be constructed under the Constitution.

With all that financial expertise, Pennsylvania continued to prosper in the 1800s. The state's rich deposits of coal became a major part of its economy as well as fueling America, both literally and figuratively.

But even those successes were dwarfed in 1859. That year, near the Pennsylvania town of Titusville, the first commercially drilled oil well was a success, spurring the initial major oil boom in the United States.

Apart from commercial success, Pennsylvania was also home to the first hospital in the country (1751), the nation's first school of medicine (1765), and America's first school of pharmacy (1821). Not surprisingly, considering its oil boom, the oldest gas station in the United States opened in 1909 at Altoona, Pennsylvania, and, much like the Keystone State itself, has been in continuous operation ever since.

URBAN LEGENDS

Blue Mist Road in Pittsburgh is more formally named Irwin Road and is sometimes spelled as Blue Myst Road, possibly because it looks more intriguing. After

> ### Stephen King, Call Your Agent
>
> Tidying up before the annual Memorial Day celebration in 1962, volunteer firefighters in Centralia, Pennsylvania, lit a controlled burn at the local garbage dump as they had done in the past. This time, however, the fire ignited an underground seam of coal. It could not be extinguished and is still blazing today. The subterranean inferno is not expected to burn itself out for another 250 years. With smoke and toxic gas spewing from openings in the ground, the residents of Centralia had to be evacuated, leaving a ghost town. Even the groundwater is heated to boiling, so there is no vegetation. Only the town's cemeteries show any sign that there had been human habitation. Centralia could easily be a nightmare from horror writer Stephen King. In fact, his novel *Black House* includes a completely unrelated imaginary town named Centralia, fictionally located in Wisconsin. Some say Mr. King might look into the actual Centralia, with fire still burning under the eerily abandoned real-life Pennsylvania town like a hellish manifestation.

sundown, an eerie dense blue haze is said to descend on the roadway, shrouding it in an atmosphere that is fit only for ghouls. It is said that one evening, a man who lived on that street returned home from work and proceeded to slaughter his wife and children. Adding insult to injury, he hid their bodies in a septic tank. Their aggrieved spirits are said to roam the accursed roadway. In addition, near the street is an old stone foundation that is said to have been the residence of a witch who guarded her property with a legion of goblins that continue to chase intruders even after she is long gone. A kinder, gentler legend is that in an adjacent cemetery, the headstones of two dead lovers are said to lean and touch each other during a full moon.

The **Bus to Nowhere** sounds like it could be a good country song title, but actually it is an urban legend in Philadelphia that probably does not involve the city's public transportation system. It is said that when people have hit rock bottom, overwhelmed by despair for whatever reason—failed romance, loss of life savings, personal tragedy, extreme hopelessness—a mythical bus will appear. After boarding, the distraught passengers sit quietly, lost in their own misery while the bus travels aimlessly through the night. Any passengers who rally a bit from the heartbreak can pull the cord and get off, having no memory of their phantom transport. It is said that some ride for years, while others never leave.

When a roadway is so spooky that Hollywood director M. Night Shyamalan films a horror movie such as 2004's *The Village* in a nearby field, it gives the place a certain panache. Such is the case of **Devil's Road** in Chadds Ford Township. One version of the tale is that a wealthy clan resorted to incest in order to keep their fortune within the family. Deformed offspring were allegedly hidden in the nearby

"Cult House." It is said that nearby trees bend away from the place, as if trying to escape the full brunt of its horror.

Among many, the **House on Ridge Avenue** in Pittsburgh earned the reputation of being America's most haunted house. Also known as the Congelier House, it was allegedly the site of a forbidden affair gone horribly wrong. It is said that the lady of the house discovered her husband having a liaison with the family's maid. In a fit of jealous rage, the woman murdered both her husband and the maid. Perhaps out of remorse or possibly because good help is hard to find, a few days later, the murderess was discovered sitting in her rocking chair cradling the decapitated head of the former maid. In later years, after the house was sold to a reclusive doctor, a cache of women's severed heads was found in the basement. In its final incarnation, the structure became a boarding house for immigrant workers. It is said that they moved in but never moved out—not alive, anyway. Those who look for the house today are told by purveyors of the tale that it mysteriously exploded, possibly from the built-up effects of all that evil inside.

ICONIC PENNSYLVANIA FOOD

Many people swear by their own special comfort food, but the one that seems to have the greatest loyalty in the Keystone State is the **Philly Cheesesteak**. Said to have been born in South Philadelphia around 1930, there has been plenty of time for aficionados to form strong opinions. One dispute centers on making the choice among American cheese, provolone, or Cheez Whiz, but never all three. Some purists claim that the original Philly Cheesesteak did not even have any cheese, although the matter is hotly debated. In another major category, the question in Philly-speak is "wit or wit-out," an inquiry regarding onions. This recipe includes onions, although the individual chef is welcome to omit them if so desired.

> **Philly Cheesesteak** (Yields 4 sandwiches)
> 2 beef rib-eye steaks or top round
> 1 Tbsp vegetable oil
> Salt and pepper to taste
> 4 hoagie or Italian rolls
> 1 medium yellow onion, thinly sliced
> Choice of American cheese, provolone, or Cheez Whiz (choose only one)

1. Slice steak as thin as possible and season with salt and pepper (partially freeze to slice it even thinner if so desired).
2. Heat oil in a large skillet over medium heat and add sliced onion. Sauté about 5–7 minutes until soft.
3. Remove cooked onion and set aside, then add sliced steak to same pan.
4. Sear 1–2 minutes, then flip and sear the other side, chopping the steak with a spatula as it cooks.
5. Add cooked onions and reduce heat to low.

6. Top the chopped steak with choice of one: four slices of American, four slices provolone, or ½ cup Cheese Whiz.
7. Let cheese melt, transfer to rolls, and serve immediately.

Source: Adapted from https://thestayathomechef.com/philly-cheesesteak/.

ODD LAWS

A certain statute by the Pennsylvania Fish and Boat Commission is sometimes interpreted on the internet as making it illegal for people to catch fish by using body parts other than the human mouth. The actual regulation concerns body parts of the *fish*, specifically that it is unlawful to fish by what is known as foul hooking, snag fishing, or snatch fishing, by using a "device in, to, with, or around any part of the body of the fish." It is also illegal to try catching fish by utilizing dynamite, in which case, there might not be many usable body parts of the fish left. On the plus side, the Commission designates two "Fish for Free Days" each year when no fishing license is required. At that time, all other fishing regulations, including those involving dynamite, still apply.

It strikes some people as strange that in Pennsylvania, all liquor stores must be run by the state itself. A few exceptions exist, such as allowing up to two cases of beer to be purchased at beer distributors and/or wine in cases, which is permissible when bought from distributors of that beverage. The state's legal statutes inform interested parties that it is the Pennsylvania State Police's Bureau of Liquor Control Enforcement, and not the Pennsylvania Liquor Control Board, that enforces Pennsylvania's liquor laws. In any case, state-owned establishments selling alcoholic beverages earn hundreds of millions of dollars each year that end up in Pennsylvania's treasury, which may be an intoxicating benefit for the state's taxpayers.

Some people find it odd, if not silly, that Pennsylvania's traffic laws include provisions for what the driver of an automobile should do when encountering a horse-drawn buggy on the same road. However, with more than 80,000 Amish people whose primary means of transportation is via horse and buggy, the law makes perfect sense. Basically, it comes down to using caution, courtesy, and not frightening the horses.

UNUSUAL DESTINATIONS

The **American Treasure Tour** in Oaks, Pennsylvania, could best be described as a "collection of collections." With more than 100,000 square feet of floor space in a former tire factory, the museum seems like an immaculately kept supersized self-storage unit for a secret private collector who doesn't mind people checking out the stuff. With all that square footage, a tram is available to transport guests past a myriad of circus posters and other kitschy ceiling and wall hangings. Tens of thousands of items are divided into groupings including Christmas villages, circus memorabilia, clown statues, grandfather clocks, movie posters, nutcracker figurines, player pianos, porcelain dolls, stained glass windows, untold numbers of stuffed animals, vintage automobiles, and what appears to be a 25-foot-tall open-toed high-heel shoe. What strikes most visitors is how lovingly restored and preserved the items are, with an almost Smithsonian-type level of care for what the collector apparently felt were significant cultural artifacts.

At **Gobbler's Knob** near Punxsutawney, Pennsylvania, the greatest show on earth measures about 22 inches long and weighs around 20 pounds. By far, the town's most famous resident and tourist attraction is a nocturnal rodent named Punxsutawney Phil. His annual appearance in front of the nation's news media takes place on February 2, better known as Groundhog's Day, when the animal is expected to predict the weather. However, for the other 364 days a year, Punxsutawney remains a destination for those seeking offbeat attractions centering on a small mammal. At Phil's Burrow, Punxsutawney Phil lives with his wife Phyllis in what is said to be a climate-controlled environment that allows visitors to observe them through outside viewing windows. The town's Groundhog Club is full of Punxsutawney Phil memorabilia galore. In addition, the warm-weather Groundhog Festival takes place annually around July 4. There are Phantastic Phil statues arrayed around town all year, in case anyone happens to forget Punxsutawney's major claim to fame.

Like Punxsutawney, another small Pennsylvania town has one specific thing going for it, but it's one that is out of this world. It is a subject of debate whether the town of **Mars**, Pennsylvania, is named for the Red Planet, but there's no question about its relationship to the Fourth Rock from the Sun. The town's official stationery has flying saucers and little green aliens on it. Businesses sport names like Mars Agway, Mars Gourmet, Mars Hardware, and Mars National Bank. Residents cheer for sports teams from the Mars School District, home of the Planets. Strange alien figures peek from windows around town, which perhaps makes it a welcoming destination for fellow extraterrestrial travelers. The town has been the site of crop circles and reports of unidentified flying object (UFO) sightings. One supposedly tangible piece of evidence is a gray flying saucer that appeared one day on the town square and has apparently made a permanent landing. It's a popular spot for photo opportunities by tourists and is beloved by locals who aim to prove there really is life on—or in—Mars.

Philadelphia is home to a unique tradition that traces its roots back to Europe's Middle Ages. The city's **Mummers Museum** pays tribute to all things Mummer related. Held each year on New Year's Day, the Philadelphia Mummers Parade holds the title of the longest-running folk parade in the nation, an event that some say is even stranger than Mardi Gras. Tens of thousands of otherwise sedate Philadelphians strut down Broad Street in colorful, extravagant, and often bizarre costumes, many of which are displayed in the Mummers Museum. Some claim the name "Mummers" evolves from the practice by medieval European peasants of going from door to door silently begging for food and drink, ergo "keeping mum." There is nothing silent about the elaborate Mummers Parade, with its memorabilia housed in Philadelphia at what is said to be the only Mummer museum in the world.

Philadelphia, Pennsylvania, is home to the unique tradition of "Mummers." With colorful, extravagant, and often bizarre costumes, each year on New Year's Day, the Mummers Parade is said by some to be stranger than Mardi Gras. (Seashell317/Dreamstime.com)

Mechanical icons including C-3PO, Gort, WALL-E, and even the real-life Roomba automated vacuum cleaner hold places of honor next to Andy, called a "RoboThespian," who greets visitors at **RoboWorld** in Pittsburgh. Associated with the Robot Hall of Fame, the institution honors significant automatons whose technical innovation and/or cultural impact seem to have pointed the way to a technologically heavy future. As the first point of contact, the aforementioned Andy introduces visitors to such concepts as robotic sensing and thinking. Wandering among the robots on display, human visitors can interact with automatons that demonstrate speech and visual recognition, present a pleasant personality that can mimic friendly human behavior, and reveal the ability to conduct a conversation. As Gort, the celebrity robot from the movie *The Day the Earth Stood Still* might say, "Klaatu Barada Nicto."

DISTINCTIVE PENNSYLVANIA WORDS AND SAYINGS

Dutch: Not people from the Netherlands, but the Pennsylvania descendants of early German settlers once called "Deustch" and now Americanized.

   Gum bands: Known elsewhere as rubber bands, they are not for chewing.

   Heinz: Along with being a major Pennsylvania food manufacturer, it is also Heinz Field where the NFL's Pittsburgh Steelers play, as in "We have 50-yard-line tickets at Heinz this weekend."

Sheetz: This Western Pennsylvania convenience store is beloved by locals. It constitutes half of a rivalry, with its opposition being . . .

. . . **Wawa:** An Eastern Pennsylvania convenience store whose name is said to be derived from Native American dialect. Along with Sheetz, it is the other half of the geographical convenience store rivalry as to which is better.

Further Reading

Dekok, David. *Fire Underground: The Ongoing Tragedy of the Centralia Mine Fire.* Guilford, CT: Globe Pequot, 2010.

Klein, Philip, and Ari Hoogenboom. *A History of Pennsylvania.* University Park, PA: Penn State University Press, 1998.

Miller, Randall M., and William Pencak (editors). *Pennsylvania: A History of the Commonwealth.* University Park, PA: Penn State University Press, 2002.

Rhode Island

> **FACT BOX**
>
> **Nickname:** The Ocean State
> **Statehood Granted:** 1790
> **Capital:** Providence
> **Population:** 1,060,000
> **State Motto:** "Hope"
> **What Natives Call Themselves:** Rhode Islanders

STATE HISTORY

Rhode Island is known as the smallest state in the Union. It is also known for not actually being an island, a fact that often causes confusion among schoolchildren in geography class.

There are several theories as to how the name evolved. One is that in 1524, Giovanni da Verrazano was the first European to sail off the coast of today's Rhode Island. In his logs, he compared nearby Block Island with the Mediterranean island of Rhodes. The name was somehow also applied to the mainland.

Another account is that explorer Adriaen Block from the Netherlands sailed into the region of today's Rhode Island in 1614. He described the color of the land as reddish, or "rodlich" in 17th-century Dutch. It is said that autumn foliage may have explained the land's overall red appearance. However, it does not explain why the word "island" was appended since he had no problem recognizing Block Island, naming it for himself.

Today's Rhode Island was inhabited by Indigenous people for thousands of years. By the time the area was colonized by Europeans, the major groups were the Narragansetts, Pequots, and Wampanoags.

The Pequots attempted to defy the European settlers but were driven almost to extinction by the colonists. The less warlike Narragansett and Wampanoag people became the predominant tribes in Rhode Island, but the colonists began to prohibit them from cutting down trees or hunting deer, which the Indigenous people needed to survive. The resulting tensions led to the outbreak of King Philip's War in 1675 in which thousands of Native people were killed or sold into slavery.

290 STATE ODDITIES

In the Massachusetts Bay Colony, settlers such as Roger Williams began to disagree with the Puritans' religious views there. After being banished from Massachusetts, in 1636, Williams and his followers settled in what became today's Providence, Rhode Island.

The Rhode Island colony became known for its religious freedom. All were welcome, including fellow dissenters like Anne Hutchinson.

As more Europeans arrived, several colonial settlements in Rhode Island merged. In 1663, a charter from England's King Charles II gave the future state its name, "Rhode Island and Providence Plantations."

Rhode Island became a haven of free thought. Founded in 1764, today's elite Brown University in Providence was the first colonial college to accept students of different religious beliefs.

The colony also nurtured free political thought, including the idea of breaking with England. In 1772, a year before the Boston Tea Party, residents of Providence set fire to a British ship for enforcing trade regulations that angered the colonists.

Anne Hutchinson, depicted here, was welcomed to Rhode Island with its religious freedom. She questioned the Puritans' religious views in the Massachusetts Bay Colony, including the role of women, and had been banished from Massachusetts. (Library of Congress)

On May 4, 1776, a full two months before the creation of the Declaration of Independence, Rhode Island was the first of the thirteen colonies to officially deny allegiance to Great Britain. The first African American regiment to fight against the British in the American Revolution distinguished themselves during the Battle of Rhode Island in 1778.

Ironically, after America defeated the British, the last of the thirteen colonies to ratify the U.S. Constitution was Rhode Island. Although most other states approved the document in 1787, Rhode Island did not do so until 1790. However, it is said that Rhode Island's independent spirit was the reason for the delay, waiting for assurances that a Bill of Rights would be included.

Each July 4 since 1785, the town of Bristol, Rhode Island, has held the country's oldest Independence Day celebrations. In a further display of patriotism,

> **What's in a Name?**
>
> In the year 2020, the name of Rhode Island was changed to . . . *Rhode Island*. Ever since 1790, following the American Revolution, it had officially been the "State of Rhode Island and Providence Plantations." In those days, the name was derived from the merger of four colonial settlements: Newport, Providence, Portsmouth, and Warwick. "Rhode Island and Providence Plantations" was the state's official name for 230 years, where it could be found on governmental correspondence, formal citations, orders from the governor's office, official websites, and even the pay stubs of state employees. In 2020, an amendment to drop "Providence Plantations" was approved by voters 53 to 47 percent. Possibly, some of the voters against the name change included those who would have to redo all the stationery and websites. On the other hand, some believe that most state employees would be happy with whatever name is on their paycheck.

during the Civil War, Rhode Island was the first state to send troops to fight for the Union.

Boasting the nickname "the Ocean State" for its lengthy shoreline, Rhode Island has traditionally attracted pleasure boats to towns like Newport. During the late 1800s, it also attracted money. Gilded Age millionaires built elaborate "summer cottages" by the shore, with most of the enormous mansions springing up among their ultrarich friends in Newport.

Rhode Island has the dubious distinction of being home to America's first traffic law. Enacted in 1678, authorities banned horses from galloping on the streets of Newport. The state took it a step further in 1904 when the first jail sentence was ordered for speeding in an automobile, also with Newport leading the way.

URBAN LEGENDS

The **Athenaeum** in Providence is a library that is also an alleged hangout for the supernatural manifestations of such heavyweights in the world of gothic literature as H. P. Lovecraft and Edgar Allan Poe. Spending time at the Athenaeum to court a local woman after the death of his wife in 1847, Poe suffered a broken engagement to would-be wife #2 due to his heavy drinking. Less than a year later, in 1849, Poe died under mysterious circumstances. His ex-fiancée is said to have summoned Poe's spirit to the Athenaeum, where his ghostly presence has been reported in the library on a fairly regular basis. According to one popular legend, a disheveled man was found sleeping on the Athenaeum steps, and when asked to move, he allegedly shouted, "The Conqueror Worm!" before vanishing into thin air. The worm in question was the title of one of Poe's poems about death and dying. The Athenaeum is also said to be the haunting ground of horror writer H. P. Lovecraft, a Providence native who credited Poe for being his inspiration.

The **Biltmore Hotel** in Providence was later renamed as the Graduate Providence after its renovation. However, apparently whatever its name, the historic building is often listed among the most haunted hotels in America. There are enough stories of ghostly encounters, vanishing people, murder, and mayhem to rank it among the top Rhode Island urban legends. First opened in 1922, it is said to have been financed by a man who was rumored to be a Satanist. During the Prohibition era of the 1930s, the hotel allegedly housed a speakeasy in the basement, the site of mob activity as well as festive parties, with phantom laughter reportedly still echoing from its walls.

Many Rhode Islanders claim that their home state's very own horrifying creature **Fingernail Freddie** was the inspiration for the Freddy Krueger character of horror movie fame. The urban legend of the murderous man in need of a manicure has been a staple for those sitting around Rhode Island campfires over the generations. The tale evolves from an alleged incident in the 1800s when mischievous boys set fire to a house in the woods near Cumberland, killing the family inside and scorching the face of the father before he managed to escape. Horribly disfigured and consumed with vengeance, the man is said to have survived in the deep woods as a recluse. He returned to town only to kill the boys who were responsible, which some said he did by growing and sharpening his fingernails to act as murder weapons. Thought by some to have inspired the *Nightmare on Elm Street* movies, Freddy is said to haunt a local cemetery and to guard the burned-out remains of his former home, killing anyone who dares to approach.

The legend of the **Perron Home** in Harrisville is associated with not one but two popular Hollywood movies, *The Amityville Horror* in 1979 and 2013's *The Conjuring*. The Perron family moved into the two-story home not knowing that its history was rather dicey. Soon, they began experiencing strange happenings, such as household items going missing after just being used and fresh piles of dirt appearing on a freshly cleaned floor. Before long, all the family members claimed to have seen spirits. When the mother of the Perron household decided to look into the home's past, she found that each family who lived there across the generations had a history of tragedy, including children being mysteriously drowned, tenants committing suicide by hanging themselves in the attic, rape, murder, and even several occupants who froze to death. The Perron family brought in the investigators who had looked into the hauntings at the Amityville Horror house. The psychic sleuths claimed the Perron family's problems were caused by the evil spirit of a 19th-century woman accused without substantiation of being a witch. The life of that wronged woman was ended when she was hanged from a tree outside the house. Eventually, the Perrons were able to move, after which reports of supernatural spirits in the house quieted down, but it is said they did not disappear completely.

ICONIC RHODE ISLAND FOOD

The humble clam may be small, but it is big in New England and is *huge* in Rhode Island, especially the variety of clams called quahogs (pronounced "KO-hogs").

This rounded clam lends itself to what is considered the signature Rhode Island dish: **Stuffies**. Rhode Island Stuffies can be found throughout the state, from fancy restaurants to street vendors. Just as with the Thanksgiving turkey, the bread-based stuffing can be made from scratch using the cook's favorite recipe, or it can be created using a prepared mix, as seen in the recipe below:

> **Rhode Island Stuffies** (Yields 15–20 individual Stuffies)
> 1 package prepared stuffing mix
> ½ lb chopped quahogs, reserving shells
> 1 pint clam juice
> 2 cups chopped celery
> 1 cup chopped onions
> ½ lb butter
> Salt, pepper, and garlic to taste
> Add-ins before cooking as preferred, such as bacon, Romano cheese, and/or chourico (Portuguese sausage), plus lemon and/or Tabasco sauce when serving
>
> 1. Preheat oven to 350°F.
> 2. Prepare stuffing mix according to directions.
> 3. Sauté celery and onions in butter until soft.
> 4. Combine cooked stuffing, chopped quahogs, and clam juice in a mixing bowl, adding salt, pepper, and garlic to taste.
> 5. Add the sautéed celery and onions, mixing well.
> 6. After the mixture cools, stuff into quahog shells.
> 7. Bake in oven for 30 minutes.
> 8. If desired, serve with lemon and Tabasco sauce on the side.

Source: Adapted from http://www.quahog.org/factsfolklore/index.php?id=181.

ODD LAWS

Some people hesitate to miss a meeting since there is a chance they will be appointed to a committee or leadership position in their absence. That would seem to be the case according to an 1896 Rhode Island law that was updated in 2012. It states that anyone who is appointed to the position of town sergeant and refuses to serve will be penalized by a fine of seven dollars. As a centuries-old holdover from England, the town sergeant serves for seven years as a law enforcement officer for small towns, including those in today's Rhode Island. Back in 1896, the seven dollars fine amounted to more than $200 in today's money, a significant amount. However, there is no explanation as to why the fine was not increased from seven dollars when the statute was updated in 2012. The infraction of this law also begs the question of who enforces the penalty, which would normally be the town sergeant, if the accused person—that same individual—refuses to serve.

A person who refuses to serve as their municipality's town sergeant might be subject to criticism, even harsh words that could be considered slander. Under Rhode Island law, in cases of libel or slander, if the defamed person files a legal action, the slanderer can be found innocent if the nasty words can be proven to be the truth. However, the Rhode Island law goes further than most state laws regarding libel or slander. In Rhode Island, even if the defendant can prove the statements were the truth, it is not a sufficient defense if the words had a malicious intent. Some people might argue that all slander is malicious, especially if it is directed at them, but that is a question for legal experts.

Slander can sometimes lead to physical acts of violence beyond the spoken word. However, if it leads to a duel, the situation can get dicey. Rhode Island law states that anyone who voluntarily engages in a duel with any dangerous weapon "to the hazard of life" can face a $1,000 fine or prison term. This is a law that was enacted in the early days of Rhode Island's history; it is not only still on the books, but it is also enforced well into the 21st century. That is because this law not only bans the principals from dueling but also prohibits anyone who encourages the fight, such as a recent case in which a parent encouraged their offspring to fight another child. Health-care providers may wish to note that standing by as a "surgeon" is also subject to this law.

UNUSUAL DESTINATIONS

The **Big Blue Bug**, which can be found facing Interstate 95 in Providence, often manifests itself not only as an unusual destination for visitors but also as an important part of local directions, as in "Take the next exit after the Big Blue Bug." This landmark has become a cultural icon not just of the city but also a badge of honor for the state. At almost 60 feet in length, the bright blue replica of an eastern subterranean termite is about as long as the height of a six-story building. Officially named "Nibbles Woodaway," the Big Blue Bug was originally constructed in 1980 to promote a local pest control company but has figuratively taken on a life of its own. Locals often bring out-of-town guests to see the city's giant mascot, especially when the Big Blue Bug is dressed for holidays such as Christmas when he appears with reindeer antlers. No one really likes to bring up the point that Nibbles represents a company dedicated to killing his kin; they just prefer to enjoy his unusual charm.

When it comes to things that are unusual, the **Musée Patamécanique** in Bristol takes it to a whole new level. This private institution is by appointment only for selected individuals and is considered to be something apart from the traditional museum trip. Fans claim it is definitely worth trying to experience the full effect. Founded in 2006, the first point of contact for prospective visitors is the website (museepata.org) since the actual location of this cabinet of curiosities is kept secret, just that it is somewhere in Bristol's historical district. The tours, which begin at sunset, comprise both indoor and outdoor venues. They are prearranged for a specific place and time, which always changes. A guide appears, providing wireless headphones and a map for the visitors before departing, leaving them to listen to the tour, which will lead them to the secret indoor location. Aficionados prefer not to disclose too much about the exhibits, but the word is that they include everything from animatronic singing chipmunks to what is said to be a machine for capturing the dreams of bumblebees.

Bees that happen to expire may find a home at the **Edna Lawrence Nature Lab**, often called "a library of dead things." It is located at the renowned Rhode Island School of Design (RISD) in Providence. The facility was created by artist Edna Lawrence in 1937, a RISD faculty member who wanted to familiarize students with the beauty of nature's forms, colors, and textures. In addition to dried plant specimens from around the world, there are animals represented from axolotl to zebra, as well as lions and tigers and bears. The Nature Lab is said to be a remarkably unique merger of art, science, and nature. Even the building where it is housed, constructed in 1885, is unique, attracting artists and historians to marvel at its hand-carved features, remnants of craftsmanship's bygone age.

Honorable mention goes to a destination that is also a reminder of a bygone age, namely the 1960s when the hugely popular gothic television series *Dark Shadows* thrilled millions of viewers with its array of ghosts, monsters, witches' curses, and vampire heartthrobs. Newport's spooky-looking **Seaview Terrace**, also known as the Carey Mansion, was the exterior stand-in for the *Dark Shadows* manor house where the ghouls were in residence. Built in 1925, Seaview Terrace was the last of Newport's great "summer cottages" to be constructed. Today the mansion is strictly private and not open for tours, but remains a destination to be observed from the roadway by dedicated fans for whom a foggy night makes the experience even better.

DISTINCTIVE RHODE ISLAND WORDS AND SAYINGS

Awful Awful: Known statewide, these silky, thick milkshakes are sold by the Newport Creamery, where the name is said to stand for "Awful Big, Awful Good."

Cabinet: Instead of being a piece of furniture, in Rhode Island this is what's known elsewhere as a basic milkshake—but *not* an Awful Awful (see Awful Awful).

Coffee milk: This is Rhode Island's official state drink and is composed of milk flavored with coffee syrup; it's said that doubters will understand the appeal after trying one.

Downcity: The downtown area of the city of Providence.

Rotary: Not the civic club, but a circular traffic intersection known elsewhere as a roundabout.

Further Reading

Davis, Deborah. *Gilded: How Newport Became America's Richest Resort*. Hoboken, NJ: Wiley, 2011.

Laxton, Glenn. *Hidden History of Rhode Island: Not-to-Be-Forgotten Tales of the Ocean State*. Charleston, SC: History Press, 2009.

McLoughlin, William. *Rhode Island: A History*. New York: W. W. Norton, 1986.

South Carolina

FACT BOX
Nickname: The Palmetto State
Statehood Granted: 1788
Capital: Columbia
Population: 5,200,000
State Motto: *Dum spiro spero* (Latin: "While I Breathe, I Hope")
What Natives Call Themselves: South Carolinians

STATE HISTORY

Many schoolchildren are familiar with South Carolina due to its repute as the first state to secede from the Union, which it did in late 1860, several months prior to the official onset of the Civil War (1861–1865).

However, that was relatively late in the game for the future state. There is evidence that people were living in today's South Carolina as far back as 40,000 years ago. When Europeans began arriving in the 16th century, the predominant Native American tribes in the region included the Catawba and Cherokee.

In 1526, the Spaniard Lucas Ayllón arrived, landing near today's Georgetown, South Carolina. By founding the San Miguel de Guadalupe colony that year, Spain is often regarded as the first European nation to establish a foothold in North America. However, the San Miguel colony was abandoned the following year due to an uprising of the Native Americans who were already there and the African slaves whom the Spaniards had brought with them. Those enslaved people are often regarded as the first African slaves transported to today's United States.

Upon the abandonment of San Miguel de Guadalupe in 1527, St. Augustine, Florida, founded by Spain in 1565, is usually credited with being the first permanent European settlement in the continental United States. Thereafter, Spain's interests lay to the south, creating an opportunity for England to colonize today's South Carolina.

Like its neighbor to the north, South Carolina was originally part of the English Province of Carolina, which was created in 1629. It was named for England's King Charles I ("Carolus" being Latin for "Charles"). The town of Charleston, South

Carolina, founded in 1670, honored King Charles II. In 1712, the huge province was officially divided into North and South Carolina.

Among the swaying Palmetto trees, from which the state takes its nickname, English settlers built rice plantations near the seacoast in what is called South Carolina's Low Country.

For free labor in the rice fields, African people from areas such as Angola were enslaved. It is said that those people had more of a resistance to mosquitoes and the malaria the insects carried than the white slave-owners, who were often absentee landlords.

Because of this, a unique community evolved, one that remains culturally distinctive to the present day. Called "Gullah" (reportedly from the word "Angola"), these were the enslaved African people and their descendants living in South Carolina's Low Country and Sea Islands. They were able to preserve more of their African language and heritage than any other African American group in the United States, such as those on cotton plantations elsewhere in the South. Today, South Carolina's Gullah people maintain their own unique culture of arts, crafts, foods, folkways, music, and storytelling that reflect strong African influences.

Although there were also relatively poor farmers, especially those of the inland region, South Carolina became one of the richest of the thirteen colonies. During the American Revolution, it was one of the top three regions where fighting took place, following only New York and New Jersey as battle zones.

When the war was won by the American side, in 1788, South Carolina joined the Union as its eighth state.

Between 1800 and 1860, South Carolina's prosperity increased significantly. One of its major assets and one of the first waterborne trade routes to be established in America was the Santee Canal, opening in 1800 to connect the seaside Charleston with the inland state capital, Columbia.

After it seceded from the Union in 1860, many historians

In 1827, legendary master of the macabre Edgar Allan Poe enlisted in the Army after becoming destitute. Stationed near Charleston, Poe evoked his time in South Carolina through such works as his story "The Gold Bug." (Courtesy of the Library of Congress.)

> ## Rich Man, Poe Man
>
> In 1827, when his first book of poems did not sell, legendary master of the macabre Edgar Allan Poe was virtually destitute. Under an assumed name, "Edgar A. Perry," the 18-year-old Poe enlisted in the army. Stationed at Fort Moultrie on Sullivan's Island, near Charleston, South Carolina, Poe worked as a clerk. This was likely due to the fact that unlike many enlisted men at the time, he could read and write. Some of his later works evoke the South Carolina influence, including his story "The Gold Bug." Today, Poe's time in South Carolina is commemorated on Sullivan's Island at places like Poe's Tavern, even though he only stayed at Fort Moultrie for about a year. The writer then briefly attended West Point, where he was soon court-martialed and expelled. Therefore, Poe's further military career might be summed up in one word: "Nevermore."

cite South Carolina as the place where the Civil War began. The location was Fort Sumter in the harbor at Charleston. It was shelled by Confederate forces on April 12–13, 1861, when federal troops who were stationed there refused to leave.

In 1865, Union general William Tecumseh Sherman followed his "March to the Sea" in Georgia by moving into South Carolina with a brutal wave of destruction. Like Atlanta during the march through Georgia, South Carolina's capital of Columbia was also burned. Some historians claim that the campaign in South Carolina led to the surrender of the Confederacy, marking the end of the war.

South Carolina's postwar fortunes were much like those of the rest of the former Confederacy, rising and falling with the tides of time. Eventually, the state's economy shifted from agriculture to other industries. Tourism became a major profit center, especially along South Carolina's beaches and barrier islands such as Hilton Head. Part of the attraction for tourists is the wealth of history that can be found all across South Carolina, including a significant number of "firsts" that are claimed by the Palmetto State.

South Carolina claims to have had the first library in America when one was established in 1700 in what was then called Charles Towne. Soon after, the city's name began to generally be written as Charlestown, later Charleston. Whatever name it was under, the first documented opera performance in today's United States was also in Charleston. Called *Flora*, it was performed in the town's courtroom in 1735.

Fans of Charleston's St. Cecilia Society claim that the group established America's first real symphony orchestra in 1766. Once again in the wealthy city of Charleston, an institution often regarded as America's first museum, the Charleston Museum, was founded by the Charleston Library Society in 1773 and has been in continuous operation ever since.

With its origins also in 1773, South Carolina's Silver Bluff Baptist Church was established, going on to become one of the oldest African American Christian congregations in the United States.

It is a point of pride in the Palmetto State that it produces more peaches than neighboring Georgia. South Carolinians are also proud to say that in 1743, a shipment of 432 golf balls and 96 clubs were sent from Scotland to Charleston, the city that claims to be the site of the first game of golf played in today's United States.

URBAN LEGENDS

According to a Gullah legend, **Boo Hag** is a creature of the night that creeps around in order to steal the life force from humans. While vampires are famed for drinking blood, Boo Hag obtains energy from sucking human breath. In addition, while the traditional vampire aims for the neck, Boo Hag rides the chest of sleeping victims, inhaling energy that way. The victim is said to awaken in the morning feeling tired and listless. Moreover, Boo Hag is said to have no skin, being blood red in color. With such an appearance being rather conspicuous, Boo Hag will therefore also try to steal human skin. It is said that waking up during the breath-sucking process will result in the aforementioned skin removal. The good news is that placing a broom next to one's bed can keep Boo Hag away during the night, since the creature will become preoccupied by counting the straws in the broom for hours, missing the window of opportunity from dusk to dawn.

The **Ghost Treasure of Folly Island** is said to be guarded by a dead pirate who, despite being deceased, watches over it to keep treasure seekers away from the loot. This legend goes back to the Civil War era when a young soldier was told by a Folly Island resident that several treasure chests were buried nearby, allegedly full of gold, silver, and jewels stolen by pirates. Furthermore, locals had heard that when the pirates finished digging a hole in which to bury the treasure chests, their leader plunged a knife into one of the men. Throwing the dead body on top of the treasure, the now deceased crewman was ordered to keep watch over it. After hearing the tale and discounting the curse, that night the soldier began digging in the spot where the treasure was reported to be buried. Suddenly, a storm whipped up thunder and lightning. During one of the brightest bolts of lighting, the ghostly figure of a pirate was illuminated, scaring the treasure seeker away from the spot where the loot allegedly remains to this day.

South Carolina's **Lizard Man** is said to be covered not only with green reptilian-like scales on its hands, face, and feet but he also sports dark matted hair on the rest of its body. Described as being red-eyed, muscular, and about seven feet tall, the Lizard Man is said to have only three fingers on each hand and three toes on each foot. However, the lack of digits does not reduce his power, which is said to be so strong that he can rip a car to smithereens, leaving his distinctive three-clawed scratches as a calling card. It also does not impede his ability to travel around the Palmetto State, reportedly being spotted in various South Carolina locations, shredding defenseless autos and scaring their drivers.

ICONIC SOUTH CAROLINA FOOD

It is important to know that **Frogmore Stew** contains no frogs. It is also not a traditional type of stew that is eaten with a spoon. Eating Frogmore Stew is meant to be a "hands on" culinary experience. Sometimes called Low Country Boil, it is a delectable combination of shrimp, sausage, red potatoes, and ears of corn. Frogmore Stew is said to be named for a tiny South Carolina community called Frogmore, which in turn was christened by an early settler in honor of his ancestral home in England. Some say the original dish was created by local shrimpers who added easily available food items. Individual cooks may improvise by adding their own choice of ingredients, such as fresh crab, to this basic recipe:

> **Frogmore Stew** (Yields 8 servings)
> 1½ gallons water
> Juice of 1 lemon
> Salt to taste
> 3 Tbsp Old Bay seasoning
> 2 dozen small red potatoes
> 2 lb sausage such as andouille or kielbasa, cut into ½-inch slices
> 10–12 ears of shucked corn on the cob, broken into 3-inch sections
> 4 lb uncooked jumbo shrimp, in shell

1. Boil the water, lemon, salt, and Old Bay seasoning, uncovered, in a very large stock pot over medium-high heat.
2. Add red potatoes, and continue boiling for 20 minutes, until potatoes remain firm but can be easily pierced with a knife.
3. Add sausage, and lower heat, gently boiling about five minutes.
4. Add corn, and continue boiling an additional five minutes.
5. Add shrimp, and boil an additional 3–5 minutes, making sure not to overcook the shrimp.
6. Remove from heat, drain immediately, and serve with lots of napkins or paper towels along with side items such as melted butter for the corn, cocktail sauce for the shrimp, and sour cream or ketchup for the potatoes.

Source: Adapted from https://whatscookingamerica.net/Soup/frogmorestew.htm.

ODD LAWS

South Carolina law forbids a male over age 16 from promising marriage to an unmarried woman, romancing her, and then not following through with the nuptials—but only as long as she is not "lewd and unchaste." The offender can be fined and/or sent to jail. Incidentally, the law also includes the statement that the man cannot be convicted due to the uncorroborated testimony of the woman. In other words, there has to be a witness to the proposal or some public demonstration of his dubious intent, possibly a billboard.

In a further attempt to protect the females of the Palmetto State, it is punishable by fine and/or jail time to send anonymous obscene messages to women. The South Carolina statute does not specify whether the law applies equally to the gender of whoever sends it. However, it does contain language stating that it is unlawful to communicate an immoral message in writing or by other means "except by telephone," leaving law-abiding citizens to wonder if obscene phone calls are OK.

In order to help curb such impulses, under a South Carolina statute, the state's public schools must observe Frances Willard Day on the fourth Friday of October each year. In the language of the law, schools must present a program so that children are taught "the evils of intemperance." For those who are curious, Frances Willard was president of the Woman's Christian Temperance Union from 1879 to 1898. She hailed from Rochester, New York, and it is unclear if she ever set foot in South Carolina. Still, in the Palmetto State, her influence lingers on, at least on the fourth Friday in October.

UNUSUAL DESTINATIONS

Some of America's great museums have begun with a bequest from a benefactor, such as the Smithsonian. Others began with a dream. In the case of the **Button Museum** in Bishopville, South Carolina, it all started with the lack of a dream. A Bishopville resident suffered from insomnia, the inability to fall asleep. He decided to find something to do as a substitute for simply lying awake through the night. For lack of anything else that was handy, he began attaching random buttons on one of his suits. Each night, the time passed quickly, and before he knew it, the garment was adorned with thousands of colorful buttons. From there, he progressed to shoes, followed by his collection of guitars, and then basically attached buttons to anything he could lay his hands on. Before long, television fame ensued for the self-proclaimed "Button King." His button-emblazoned collection was stored in a nearby hangar building and opened to the public, where the items currently on display for visitors include cars, a button-covered hearse (accessorized by button-covered caskets), and a button-festooned outhouse.

At the **Kazoo Museum** in Beaufort, it should not come as a surprise that the musical instrument being honored is the often underappreciated kazoo. By creating a buzzing sound when the player hums into it, the kazoo provides a festive, almost childlike quality to tunes being played on it. But its history is far from being simply child's play. Having been used for ceremonial purposes in Africa, a simpler form of the instrument was refashioned by enslaved people in America. The museum houses about 200 kazoos and kazoo-related items, including some that are century-old antiques and even some that are electric-powered. According to the museum, the kazoo is one of the few musical instruments to be homegrown in America. After taking a guided tour, which can take up to an hour, most visitors come away with a lot more respect for the lowly kazoo.

When it comes to respect, unidentified flying objects (UFOs) are often shown very little by skeptics. Still, at the **UFO Welcome Center** in the town of Bowman, that is no reason not to display some South Carolina hospitality. If visiting aliens need a place to crash—metaphorically speaking—this unique facility offers them a spot to freshen up, grab a quick shower, use the restroom (however those alien needs are met), and even watch a little television as they kick back after their long trip. Tourists from around the country or around the galaxy just need to look for a sign proclaiming "UFO Welcome Center" spray-painted on a fence in Bowman. After paying the owner an admission fee (in American dollars, not Martian moolah), they can all enjoy being welcomed, Planet Earth style.

If aliens from outer space ever do visit South Carolina, they may enjoy planning their trip so they arrive in the month of April. That is when the town of Saint George holds its annual **World Grits Festival**. For three gritty days, visitors can get up close and personal with the coarsely ground grain dish that is made from boiled cornmeal. There are the kinds of events that can be found at innumerable local festivals across the country, such as arts and crafts, beauty queens, dancing, music, a parade, and lots of food. But the World Grits Festival comes with its own unique spin: the Rolling in the Grits contest. The object of the competition is to trap as many grits on your clothing as possible by rolling in them for 10 seconds. A kiddie pool is filled with moistened grits. Then, contenders are weighed before and after they take the plunge, with the prize awarded to the most grit-filled contestant.

DISTINCTIVE SOUTH CAROLINA WORDS AND SAYINGS

Cackalacky: According to the state's Department of Tourism, this is an affectionate nickname for South Carolina, especially when goofy things happen there.

Carolina: South Carolinians call North Carolina by its full name, or simply "North." Displaying state pride, this is the preferred name for what some in the Palmetto State often consider the "real" Carolina.

Chuck: Hip version of referring to the city of Charleston. As opposed to . . .

. . .**Chunk**: To throw an object.

Sandlapper: Resident of the South Carolina lowlands.

South, the: Terminology that is specific to the Palmetto State, limiting Dixie to South Carolina, North Carolina, and occasionally Georgia. Nearby Florida does not make the cut.

Further Reading

Bass, Jack, and W. Scott Poole. *The Palmetto State: The Making of South Carolina*. Columbia: University of South Carolina Press, 2009.

Brown, Alan. *Haunted South Carolina: Ghosts and Strange Phenomena of the Palmetto State*. Mechanicsburg, PA: Stackpole Books, 2010.

Carmichael, Sherman. *Forgotten Tales of South Carolina*. Charleston, SC: History Press, 2011.

South Dakota

FACT BOX

Nickname: The Mount Rushmore State
Statehood Granted: 1889
Capital: Pierre
Population: 885,000
State Motto: "Under God the People Rule"
What Natives Call Themselves: South Dakotans

STATE HISTORY

Today's South Dakota encompasses rugged expanses such as the Badlands, which earned the foreboding name due to the rocky terrain, lack of water, and extreme temperatures that can be found there. Even before white men arrived, the Lakota people dubbed this region *mako sica*, or "bad lands."

Millions of years before that, however, the South Dakota Badlands appeared a bit more inviting to fabled creatures such as the dinosaurs, saber-toothed tigers, mammoths, and Tyrannosaurus rex that roamed there.

In relatively more recent times, today's South Dakota was populated by Native people for thousands of years, including tribes with the mellifluous-sounding names of Dakota, Lakota, and Nakota. After European and American settlers arrived in the 1700s and 1800s, the region was later named for the Dakota, a word said to mean "friend."

In 1743, French explorers Francois and Louis-Joseph de La Vérendrye were the first Europeans to arrive in today's South Dakota after traversing the territory's northern region. South Dakota was claimed by France as part of "La Louisiane," named for the French king Louis XIV. La Louisiane also encompassed all or some of other present-day states such as Arkansas, Colorado, Iowa, Kansas, Louisiana, Minnesota, Missouri, Montana, Nebraska, New Mexico, North Dakota, Oklahoma, Texas, and Wyoming.

Most of the Frenchmen arriving in South Dakota in the late 1700s were fur traders, carrying on commerce with the Natives and setting down few roots. In 1801, an outpost that was meant to be permanent, Fort aux Cedres, was constructed near

Mastodons, Mammoths, and More—Oh My!

South Dakota is a phenomenally rich source of ancient fossils, which are widespread throughout the state. Why South Dakota? Because far from looking the way it does today, the current state of South Dakota was submerged for eons during the Paleozoic era by a shallow sea. Its lush shoreline became a haven that attracted guests such as mammoths, mastodons, saber-toothed tigers, and the horned dinosaur called Triceratops. The latter earned the title of South Dakota's state fossil, a distinction millions of years in the making. The Mammoth Site at Hot Springs, South Dakota, contains the largest collection of woolly mammoth bones ever discovered. Even more unique, the bones have not been moved from their primeval resting place. South Dakota's Mammoth Site is the continent's only late Ice Age dig and the only one in the world that has been left exactly as it was found. This allows visitors to see the bones that were left after the massive creatures checked into this prehistoric Club Med but never checked out.

South Dakota is rich in ancient fossils. It was submerged for eons by a shallow sea that attracted prehistoric creatures. The Mammoth Site at Hot Springs, South Dakota, contains the largest collection of bones from woolly mammoths (illustrated here) ever discovered. (Fredweiss/Dreamstime.com)

the location of current-day Pierre, South Dakota. However, the fort was destroyed by fire in 1810.

The destruction of that French outpost ultimately became a moot point. La Louisiane became a pawn of international affairs in 1803 when France's emperor Napoleon Bonaparte wanted money to fight a war in Europe. He therefore offered the land that France claimed west of the Mississippi River to the young nation of the United States. The price for more than 800,000 square miles was $15 million, or about three cents an acre. What came to be called the Louisiana Purchase doubled the size of the United States.

The Lewis and Clark Expedition of 1803–1806 explored the newly purchased land. They passed through South Dakota in 1804 and again on the return trip in 1806. They documented some of the wildlife common to present-day South Dakota that astonished them, such as thousands of bison covering the plains.

It took the Lewis and Clark party five weeks to catch their first live coyote. Later, the tenacity of that species was honored by being named South Dakota's state animal.

Lewis and Clark were also intrigued by small creatures that burrowed in the ground to form a "village," naming them "petite chiens" ("little dogs") or today's prairie dog. Today, South Dakota is home to a prairie dog colony measuring 100 by 250 miles, containing an estimated 400 million prairie dogs.

Continuous American settlement of the region began in 1817. One of the outposts, Fort Pierre, later became part of today's metropolitan district of Pierre, South Dakota, the state's capital. Taking the name from the Dakota branch of the Sioux tribe, the U.S. Congress formally established the Territory of Dakota in 1861.

The rise of the railroads in the late 1800s brought settlers into the Dakota Territory. When gold was discovered in the Black Hills in 1874, prospectors unlawfully poured onto Indian land. Moreover, the discovery was said to be placer gold found in shallow deposits, relatively easy to find without the need for expensive equipment. Untold numbers of prospectors swarmed over land that was sacred to Native Americans.

During this Black Hills gold rush, a settlement called Deadwood sprang up illegally on Lakota Sioux land. Named for the dead trees surrounding it, in the boomtown atmosphere between 1876 and 1879, Deadwood boasted a population that soared to about 5,000. In its heyday, the town attracted such Old West icons as Wyatt Earp, Calamity Jane, and Wild Bill Hickok.

The emerging print technology of the late 1800s in America saw an explosion in the kind of books known as "pulp fiction." The town of Deadwood, South Dakota, attained national fame through the fictional exploits of a character named "Deadwood Dick" in a series of stories published between 1877 and 1897.

However, when the easy-to-find placer gold started to run out in the late 1800s, prospectors and the transient residents of towns such as Deadwood departed for points unknown. More recent citizens of Deadwood took a look at what was left of their town and turned it into a National Historic Landmark, complete with frontier architecture from the late 1800s. Deadwood, South Dakota, arguably gained an even higher pinnacle of fame in popular culture through the gritty cable television series *Deadwood*. Today, the town is a major tourist attraction.

In 1889, North and South Dakota attained statehood. To avoid contention, then president Benjamin Harrison signed the official documents after covering everything but the line where he would sign. Therefore, North and South Dakota joined the Union simultaneously on November 2, 1889, without anyone knowing which came first. Based on alphabetical order, North Dakota is usually listed first, with South Dakota as the 40th state.

With the Dakota name said to mean "friend" in Native American dialect, that designation took on a certain irony in 1890 when the Wounded Knee Massacre took place at South Dakota's Pine Ridge Indian Reservation. With the death of several hundred Native Americans, it is said to be the final clash between the U.S. Army and the Indigenous people of the Plains.

As reflected in the state's nickname, South Dakota can claim Mount Rushmore, one of the most iconic features of the American West. Carved into the mountainside between 1927 and 1941, it features the faces of four American presidents: Thomas Jefferson, Abraham Lincoln, Theodore Roosevelt, and George Washington. A nearby work in progress is the privately funded Crazy Horse Memorial honoring the Oglala Lakota warrior, Crazy Horse. Plans depict him on horseback pointing to his tribal land, set to become the world's largest sculpture when completed.

Although some people claim that Kansas is the center of the United States, the South Dakota town of Belle Fourche is known as America's actual geographic center when including the states of Alaska and Hawaii. Designated as such by the National Geodetic Survey, a metal pole marks the spot in a field near Belle Fourche. Many South Dakotans would go further, feeling their state is actually the center of the entire universe.

URBAN LEGENDS

According to the legend, the **Bigfoot of Sica Hollow** is native to a spot that literally has evil in its name. The word *sica* (pronounced "SHE-cha") is said to mean something bad or evil in Dakota Sioux dialect. Located near Sisseton, South Dakota, the tales center around the pure malevolence of Sica Hollow, a place where few want to venture. One exception is an alleged Bigfoot-type creature that is said to be responsible for a rash of disappearances in the area. In addition, some visitors claim to have heard disembodied Native American chants and war cries. Sica Hollow is said to be so cursed that the water in the boggy creek runs red, leading some to believe they were seeing the blood of ancient warriors. Rotting tree stumps are said to have a greenish glow, presumably due to supernatural forces. Observers also claim that the stumps look even eerier in the misty miasma that appears periodically in Sica Hollow. However, spoilsport scientists have attributed the phenomena to iron deposits that tint the water red, to phosphorous making the stumps look green, and to swamp gas giving the place its otherworldly fog. Science or not, true believers continue to believe, so the urban legend lives on.

Gitchie Manitou, in the southeastern corner of South Dakota near Sioux Falls, is an area that spreads into nearby Iowa, along with sharing its urban legend. Many believe it is haunted by the spirits of four South Dakota teens who were murdered there while camping in 1973. On top of that, it is noted for the ancient burial mounds of Native Americans, who called the place Gichi-Manidoo, for "great spirit," "great mystery," or "great force of nature," all of which are encompassed in the urban legend that casts a pall over the place.

It is often said that good things come in small packages. According to the legend of the **Little Devils**, bad things can also come the same way. Located near Vermillion, South Dakota, the Spirit Mounds site was held in trepidation by Native Americans for hundreds of years. According to the legend, anyone attempting to climb the Spirit Mounds will be attacked with razor-sharp arrows that are shot by "little devils" about 18 inches tall with fierce humanoid features. It is said that in the mid-1700s, Native American warriors tried to destroy the malevolent little creatures but ended up massacred themselves. When the Lewis and Clark Expedition arrived at today's Southeastern South Dakota in 1804, Native Americans warned them against ascending the Spirit Mounds because of the diminutive devils. There is no documentation that anyone in the Lewis and Clark party was waylaid by the mini-monsters, although they did record that there was a nice view from atop the hill. Still, the tale of the lethal archery-wielding little fiends lives on.

UNUSUAL SOUTH DAKOTA FOOD

When a dish is named the state's "Official Nosh," attention must be paid. In 2018, **South Dakota Chislic** (pronounced "CHIZ-lick") was indeed designated the notable nosh, and it has been said that no single dish is more strongly associated with South Dakota than Chislic. Outsiders from beyond the state sometimes confuse it with shish kebab, but as is often the case, the difference is in the details. Shunning vegetables, Chislic consists of half-inch cubes of meat such as beef, mutton, or venison that are deep-fried and served either on skewers or arrayed on toothpicks in a dish. The town of Meridian Corner, South Dakota, holds an annual Chislic Festival where guests might dine on cuisine similar to this recipe:

> **South Dakota Chislic** (Serves 6)
> 2 lb cubed beef, mutton, or venison
> 1 Tbsp garlic salt
> Oil for frying
>
> 1. Cut meat into half-inch cubes before dusting with garlic salt.
> 2. In a deep fryer or heavy pot, add enough oil to submerge the meat cubes and heat the oil to 350°F.
> 3. Pat the meat dry with paper towels, setting some towels aside for the finished Chislic to drain.
> 4. Carefully drop about ½ pound of the meat cubes at a time into the fryer, letting it roil in the hot oil for about two minutes.
> 5. Remove fried meat cubes to paper towels, adding more meat until all are cooked and drained.
> 6. Serve with condiments as desired, such as blue cheese dip or hot sauce.

Source: Adapted from https://honest-food.net/south-dakota-chislic-recipe/.

ODD LAWS

Under South Dakota law, it is illegal to use a spotlight while hunting between sunset and sunrise. In the words of the statute, hunters cannot shine a motor vehicle headlight or other artificial light onto a highway or into any field, pasture, woodland, forest, or prairie, which sounds fairly comprehensive. However, there are a few exceptions to the rule. For example, the nocturnal hunter can turn on a spotlight if they are hunting raccoons and claim they need the light to keep track of their dog. Furthermore, a flashlight can be employed if "the person is on foot, to take raccoons after the raccoons have been treed by dogs." If South Dakota seems to have a grudge against raccoons, law enforcement officers fare better, being exempted from this statute in the performance of their duties.

Under South Dakota law, liquor stores cannot sell a "confection or candy" containing more than 0.5 percent alcohol by weight. Furthermore, the law states that if said candy contains more than one-half of 1 percent alcohol by weight, the confection or candy is "deemed adulterated for the purposes of this title." The law has had the unintended consequence of alerting some demographic groups that such sweet treats, adulterated or otherwise, even exist.

In Huron, South Dakota, it is against the law to create static. Some pranksters are appalled that this ordinance would prohibit the kind of hair-raising fun and sudden shocks that are usually created by rubbing their feet along a carpet and then accosting an unsuspecting victim with the ensuing zap of static electricity. However, purveyors of practical jokes can rest easy knowing they are probably safe from prosecution. The actual ordinance makes it unlawful to create static with a "machine or device" that would interfere with radio or television broadcasts. The ordinance only makes it illegal to create such static interference between the hours of 7:00 a.m. and 11:00 p.m., apparently on the belief that there's not much worth watching or listening to at any other time.

UNUSUAL DESTINATIONS

At the **Ardmore** ghost town, the only things that remain are abandoned businesses, vehicles, and homes. Founded in 1889, Ardmore is called a modern-day photographer's dream because it looks frozen in time. Its 19th-century founders saw nothing but prosperity ahead, since the town was designated as a stopping point for the railroad. However, Mother Nature put a damper on things. The local creek, which was intended to supply water for both the town and the trains, turned out to be too acidic for human consumption. Trains would therefore have to haul water and leave it for the residents. Drought then left the farming town high and dry, forcing residents to move elsewhere. All that remains today amid the melancholy reminders of broken dreams are decaying structures such as downtown buildings with large signs proclaiming "Saloon," but without any thirsty patrons banging through the creaking doors.

Topping the scales at six tons, the **Giant Prairie Dog** at the Badlands Ranch Store in Cactus Flat, South Dakota, lives up to its name. Said to be the largest in the world, this husky-looking concrete critter has stood in its 12-foot-tall majesty since 1959. Today, it continues to serve as a kind of modern-day Colossus of Rhodes towering over the nearby colony of real-life prairie dogs, none of whom are said to exceed normal, diminutive prairie dog size. For visitors who stop by, the store has feed available (called "prairie dog chow") for the live prairie dogs, which appear quite healthy, no doubt due to the tourist-provided buffet.

As a reminder of what are said to have been at least 1,000 nuclear missile launch sites dotting the Plains, the **Minuteman Missile Visitor Center** at Philip, South Dakota, illustrates the cold facts of the Cold War. Artifacts and displays concerning the Minuteman Intercontinental Ballistic Missile System are available for viewing. One of the most-photographed items is a sign resembling that of a nationally known pizza delivery firm, complete with a logo featuring colorful dominoes along with a graphic of a Minuteman Missile. The inscription reads: "Worldwide delivery in 30 minutes or less . . . or your next one is free."

Hopefully a bit less daunting to younger visitors is what is known as the **World's Largest Pheasant** in the town of Huron, South Dakota. The fiberglass and steel bird weighs in at 22 tons, standing almost three stories tall and 40 feet wide. Like the Giant Prairie Dog previously mentioned, the plus-size pheasant was also created in 1959. It was intended to affirm Huron's status as a premier pheasant hunting location. According to the Huron visitor's bureau, photo opportunities are encouraged, especially just before the annual pheasant season opener when local residents release a live bird in hopes of ensuring a good hunt.

DISTINCTIVE SOUTH DAKOTA WORDS AND SAYINGS

"**Banana Belt**": Sheltered somewhat by the Black Hills, this refers to the Rapid City area where residents can bask in balmy 2° temperatures when it's 10° below zero in the rest of the state.

Eastside vs. Westside: Not a rivalry in New York City but in South Dakota where the Missouri River essentially divides the state between the more-populated side that lies east of the river and the rugged west side.

Peer: It's the way South Dakotans pronounce the name of their capital city, Pierre. Although it was named for French fur trader Pierre Chouteau, those who suggest that it should be pronounced "Pea-AIR," as in France, are presumed to be outsiders.

Taverns: In South Dakota, these are not necessarily places to consume distilled beverages, but rather the name of a sandwich that other states call a Sloppy Joe.

Further Reading

Hoover, Herbert T., and Edward P. Hogan. *A New South Dakota History*. Sioux Falls, SD: Center for Western Studies, 2009.

Shadley, Mark, and Josh Wennes. *Haunted Deadwood: A True Wild West Ghost Town*. Charleston, SC: History Press, 2012.

Tennant, Brad. *On This Day in South Dakota History*. Charleston, SC: History Press, 2017.

Tennessee

FACT BOX

Nickname: The Volunteer State
Statehood Granted: 1796
Capital: Nashville
Population: 7,000,000
State Motto: "Agriculture and Commerce"
What Natives Call Themselves: Tennesseans or Volunteers

STATE HISTORY

Some people question Tennessee's choice of the state motto, "Agriculture and Commerce." Their reasoning is that the mountains near Knoxville in East Tennessee produced bluegrass; Nashville in the state's midsection is the ancestral home of the Grand Ole Opry, and Memphis in the west gave us both the "Father of the Blues" W. C. Handy *and* Elvis Presley, the King of Rock and Roll. Therefore, many people think "Music" should be added somewhere in the state motto.

In any case, a popular maxim is that the Mississippi River delta begins in Memphis, specifically in the lobby of the city's Peabody Hotel. Long before that lobby existed, complete with the daily walk of its famed ducks, today's Tennessee was home to prehistoric people who lived there about 12,000 years ago, around the end of the last Ice Age. Before that, many historians believe Tennessee reverberated not with the sounds of country music or the blues, but with the massive hooves of mastodons.

The first recorded visit to Tennessee by Europeans was led by Spanish explorer Hernando de Soto in 1540. Juan Pardo, another Spaniard, arrived in 1567. He recorded the name of a local Indian village as "Tanasqui," from which the state's current name is said to have evolved.

The Spaniards did not stay. After England established the thirteen original colonies on North America's east coast through the 1600s and 1700s, some early settlers from places like the Carolinas pushed westward into today's Tennessee. Fort Loudoun, one of the earliest British fortifications on what was then the frontier, was established just west of the Great Smoky Mountains in 1756.

When Europeans came to today's Tennessee, the Indigenous people who lived there included the Cherokee, Chickasaw, Choctaw, and Shawnee. As more white settlers arrived, the Native people were pushed out.

> **The Sound of Music**
>
> It comes as no surprise that Tennessee should take pride in its rich songwriting tradition, from Memphis blues to the country sounds of Nashville to the folk tradition in the mountains of East Tennessee. In 2003, a resolution in the state's General Assembly designated songwriting as an official state art form. Perhaps to assuage all the different artists within the musical world, Tennessee currently has a whole handful of official state songs: "My Homeland, Tennessee" (designated as the official state song by the General Assembly in 1925), "When It's Iris Time in Tennessee" (designated in 1935), "My Tennessee" (1955), "Tennessee Waltz" (1965), "Rocky Top" (1982), "Tennessee" (1992), "The Pride of Tennessee" (1996), "Smoky Mountain Rain" (2010), and "Tennessee" (2011). In addition, a rap number titled "A Tennessee Bicentennial Rap: 1796–1996" was designated the state's official bicentennial rap song in 1996. The General Assembly also considered a resolution to designate "So I'll Just Shine in Tennessee" as a state song in 2010, but took no action, perhaps feeling that having 10 official state songs was sufficient.

A year after the American Revolution (1775–1783) in which the colonists emerged victorious, the spirit of independence inspired the people of Eastern Tennessee to try forming the State of Franklin in 1784. This proposed new state would have been the first to join the Union after the thirteen original colonies. The Franklinites formed their own government, but it was never recognized as a separate state by federal officials and was dissolved in 1789. Ironically, John Sevier, the governor of Franklin, went on to become the first governor of Tennessee.

In 1796, Tennessee was admitted to the Union as the 16th state. It became known as the Volunteer State during the War of 1812 after sending about 1,500 volunteers to help defeat the British.

As Southern states seceded from the Union, Tennessee was the last to join the Confederacy, which it did by referendum in June 1861. Its people were divided between the Northern and Southern causes, and when the Civil War ended in 1865, Tennessee was the first state to rejoin the Union.

As its official nickname attests, in the late 1800s and early 1900s, Tennessee sought to balance its economy between agriculture and commerce. However, like the rest of the South, it remained in poverty, especially during the Great Depression of the 1930s. This began to change in 1933 when President Franklin Roosevelt's New Deal created the Tennessee Valley Authority (TVA) to provide electricity, flood control, and jobs to aid Tennessee's economy, encouraging new industries to locate in the state.

Partially due to access to electricity from the TVA as a public utility, during World War II, Tennessee was home to a secret city that did not officially exist. Hidden deep in the Tennessee hills, a new town called Oak Ridge was unknown to the rest of the world. Tens of thousands of average Americans from across the country kept the secret of what they were doing: creating fuel for the atomic bomb.

The Grand Ole Opry in Nashville is home to the longest-running live radio broadcast in the world. A very small sample of legendary Opry talent includes Brad Paisley, Dolly Parton, Minnie Pearl, and Charley Pride. (Arne Beruldsen/Dreamstime.com)

Music has been a constant in Tennessee. Since the origination of Nashville's Grand Ole Opry in 1925, it has been home to the longest-running live radio broadcast in the world.

Some Tennessee cities have notable sobriquets. Memphis became known as the Cotton Capital of the World, Columbia as the Mule Capital of the World, and Lebanon as the Appalachian Square Dance Capital of the World.

Possibly more significantly, Knoxville became known as the "First Dumpster City" in 1937. This came after the Dempster Brothers patented the dumpster in 1935, a move that caught on their hometown of Knoxville and was implemented there before becoming a catchall for the world.

URBAN LEGENDS

No look at Tennessee's urban legends would be complete without including the **Bell Witch**. It is said that the witch was the evil spirit of a woman who was a neighbor of the John Bell family near the town of Adams, Tennessee. From 1817 to

1821, her poltergeist allegedly tormented the Bell clan, eventually killing John Bell outright with a vial of poison. The reputation of the Bell Witch was so daunting that even the otherwise fearless president Andrew Jackson claimed to be spooked. Today, it is said that the spirit of the Bell Witch haunts a cave next to the former John Bell farm. Ghost hunters are often disappointed to be unable to investigate the cave, which is on private property. However, they can seek out the Bell Witch through a string of Hollywood movies including *The Bell Witch Haunting* (2004), *An American Haunting* (2005), *Bell Witch: The Movie* (2007), *The Bell Witch Legend* (2008), and a 2013 remake also called *The Bell Witch Haunting*. Many people feel that the most famous film version of the Bell Witch was the original, a surprise hit movie in 1999 called *The Blair Witch Project*, said to be a fictionalized "docudrama" inspired by Tennessee's Bell Witch. Incidentally, the total cost of the latter film was around $750,000, going on to earn about $250 million worldwide. If it was indeed inspired by the Bell Witch, there is no documentation as to whether her evil spirit sought a piece of the profits through an equally scary lawyer.

Some of the Civil War's bloodiest battles took place in Tennessee. One of them was Chickamauga in 1863, where about 35,000 men were killed. In the aftermath, the severed head of one of the young soldiers was found amid the carnage. Today, well over a century later, it is said that his spirit continues to haunt the battlefield, possibly in search of the rest of his body. Anyone walking the battlefield at night will allegedly be followed by **"Old Green Eyes,"** a pair of glowing eyeballs named for the mangled man whose spirit cannot seem to leave the place where he so horribly met his death.

In the small town of White Bluff, near Nashville, the **White Bluff Screamer** stands tall in local lore. While most residents have heard the story, some old-timers claim to have actually seen the massive beast. According to the tale, a backwoods couple had a child who was horribly disfigured. They kept the unfortunate offspring hidden in a basement space beneath their cabin. Being so far back in the woods, the couple did not have to worry about nosy visitors hearing screams coming from under the cabin. What they *did* have to worry about was what would happen when the child grew up. It allegedly escaped its basement prison, killed the parents, and fled into the woods. This is the malevolent creature that is said to kill pets and livestock, shrieking with a bloodcurdling scream on chilly evenings as it performs its evil deeds. Whether or not locals claim to believe the tale, many tend to keep pets indoors at night and make sure the deadbolts on their doors are securely locked.

ICONIC TENNESSEE FOOD

In the Volunteer State, "Hot Chicken" does not refer to poultry that is served warm. **Tennessee Hot Chicken** is said to have originated in Nashville before its fame spread statewide. The dish is adaptable to any cut of chicken, including relatively less expensive chicken thighs. It also lends itself to adding more cayenne pepper to make it even zestier for those who just can't get enough heat. In Tennessee, it is said that a Hot Chicken dinner is not complete without a few pickles plus some white bread on the side.

Tennessee Hot Chicken (Yields 8 servings)
4–5 boneless, skinless chicken breasts
2 cups flour, divided
2 tsp salt
1 tsp black pepper
1 Tbsp blackened seasoning
1 cup buttermilk or whole milk
2 eggs
2 tsp hot sauce
8–10 cups peanut oil

Hot Sauce Coating
1 cup peanut oil
1 Tbsp cayenne pepper
2 Tbsp brown sugar
1 tsp chili powder
1 tsp each garlic powder and paprika

1. After rinsing and patting chicken dry, set it aside while making the coating in three wide, shallow bowls.
2. In first bowl, mix one cup flour with salt and pepper.
3. In second bowl, whisk eggs, buttermilk, and hot sauce together.
4. In third bowl, whisk the other cup of flour with blackened seasoning.
5. Place one piece of chicken into first bowl of flour, salt, and black pepper, shaking off excess.
6. Then dip chicken piece into buttermilk mixture in second bowl before dredging it in final bowl with flour and blackened seasoning.
7. Place prepared chicken on baking sheet, then continue with the rest of the chicken pieces.
8. Using a heavy-bottomed pot or large cast iron skillet, heat about 3–4 inches of oil over medium-high heat until it reaches 325°F.
9. Turning occasionally, fry 2–3 pieces of chicken at a time, about 15–18 minutes, until they are crisp and golden brown, about 165° on a meat thermometer. Transfer cooked chicken to wire rack set inside a baking sheet.
10. Whisk cayenne, brown sugar, chili powder, garlic powder, and paprika together in a medium bowl, then carefully add a cup of the frying oil before brushing fried chicken with the spicy oil.
11. Serve chicken immediately, preferably on white bread with pickle slices.

Source: Adapted from https://www.thecountrycook.net/nashville-hot-chicken/.

ODD LAWS

Tennessee residents who disagree with what is called the Tennessee Login Law point out that one of its drawbacks is that while visiting a friend or family member, it is illegal to log into their streaming account such as Netflix in order to watch movies. The statute renders it unlawful to share login information such as passwords for movie or music sites. As with many laws, the legislation began with the best intentions. It was added in 2011 to update the state's old cable TV theft laws, being aimed at hackers and thieves who sell passwords. However, the law's sponsors acknowledged that it could be interpreted to be used against private citizens hungry for some entertainment on a friend's or relative's subscription account. Some have asked cynically whether authorities might have other crimes to contend with, other than the sharing of Netflix passwords among friends. While that is arguably a relevant point, those willing to risk it may wish to note that they could face up to a year in jail and a fine of $2,500.

The Tennessee Constitution makes it clear that like Netflix passwords, some things may not be meant to be shared. It states that the doors of the legislature, both the House and Senate as well as committees, must be kept open "unless when the business shall be such as ought to be kept secret." Supporters of open government claim that the law could be employed in many cases to justify closed-door meetings to keep them private, away from the eyes and ears of the citizens, i.e., the ones being governed.

Another constitutional caveat in Tennessee might also lend itself to a wide interpretation. It states that voters must not receive any gifts or rewards in exchange for their votes, including "meat, drink, money or otherwise." A gift of money, also called bribery, is completely understandable to most people. However, the bone of contention to those who are aware of this law is the part that specifies meat and drink. Like those in other states, many Tennessee politicians would be severely hampered in their quest for election without the lure of free hot dog dinners, barbecues, and other time-honored edible-based events to connect with voters.

UNUSUAL DESTINATIONS

Anyone who has watched television programs such as *Heavy Rescue* knows that vehicle recovery of any kind, especially mammoth tractor-trailer trucks on frozen freeways, is no piece of cake. It's a dangerous occupation, whether in the isolated wilderness, a 50-car highway pileup, or even having to tow the car of an angry auto owner from city streets. The **International Towing and Recovery Museum** in Chattanooga shines a light on this underappreciated aspect of the car culture, also honoring those who died while trying to clear roads and save lives. Trivia buffs may wish to note that according to the museum, the first tow truck was invented in Chattanooga in 1916. Therefore, it is fitting that this museum opened in the city where it all began. Artifacts and memorabilia are displayed along with antique salvage trucks and cranes. However, for many, the most moving exhibit is the statue of a driver and child being rescued from a car that is sinking under water, with only its taillight showing. Surrounding it are the names of those who died trying to save the lives of strangers as part of their average workday.

A historic site with its information hub spelled "Visitor Centre" leads guests to suspect either poor spelling or a nod to British usage. In the case of the **Rugby Colony** in Rugby, Tennessee, it is the latter. Rugby Colony was the site of a utopian dream of a better life for its British inhabitants who began arriving in 1880. As the Industrial Age transformed the lives of average people, British author Thomas Hughes, who wrote the classic novel *Tom Brown's Schooldays*, founded the Rugby Colony. The goal was for it to be a thriving agricultural community based on the cooperation of its residents. He envisioned a cultured lifestyle that was not controlled by the strict British class system. By 1884, the colony was flourishing, boasting almost 70 Victorian-style buildings and more than 300 inhabitants. However, by 1900, after bouts of disease, financial problems, fires, and the kind of extreme weather that hampers agriculture, most residents left. A few did remain, and their legacy is this Victorian village frozen in time.

The Great Smoky Mountain National Park near Elkmont, Tennessee, outside Gatlinburg, is enchanting any time of year, but for a truly unusual encounter with Mother Nature, visitors may wish to plan a trip around the first of June. At that time, what is called the **Synchronous Fireflies of the Smoky Mountains** put on quite a show. Starting nightly around 10:00 p.m., the lightning bugs bring on their illuminated display with more precision than an Olympic synchronized swim team. After six seconds of total darkness, thousands of fireflies light up six rapid times in a three-second period before going dark again for six more seconds, all perfectly in sync. Only about a dozen firefly species around the world can synchronize their flashes. Scientists call the phenomenon by the fireflies to be "coupled oscillation," but it is the town of Elkmont that has it down to a science. During late May or early June, trolleys run from the visitor center to the park. There is a lottery for space, with an average of more than 20,000 people clamoring each year to see the fireflies' dazzling show.

For fans of the hit play and movie *Inherit the Wind*, honorable mention goes to the **Rhea County Courthouse** in Dayton, Tennessee. It was the site of the famed Scopes "Monkey" Trial in 1925 when renowned legal advocates William Jennings Bryan and Clarence Darrow debated whether to teach evolution in schools. Today, figures of both men are displayed on the courthouse lawn. Inside the courthouse is an exhibit about the case along with the actual courtroom on the second floor that is open to the public, arranged much like it was in 1925.

DISTINCTIVE TENNESSEE WORDS AND SAYINGS

Goo Goo: Not the musings of a baby, but a reference to the Tennessee-bred candy called the Goo Goo Cluster that is more than a century old.

NashVegas: An expression used by some Nashville visitors, but frowned upon by locals.

Play pretties: Children's toys.

"Rocky Top": Not just the gravelly high point on a mountain, but a song that many consider the ultimate Tennessee anthem.

Vols: Short for "volunteers" (as in the Volunteer State), this beloved abbreviation is used for University of Tennessee athletics programs.

Further Reading

Bergeron, Paul H. *Tennesseans and Their History*. Knoxville: University of Tennessee Press, 2007.

Brown, Alan. *Haunted Tennessee: Ghosts and Strange Phenomena of the Volunteer State*. Mechanicsburg, PA: Stackpole Books, 2009.

Jones, James B. *History in Tennessee: Lost Episodes from the Volunteer State's Past*. Charleston, SC: America through Time, 2018.

Texas

> **FACT BOX**
> **Nickname:** The Lone Star State
> **Statehood Granted:** 1845
> **Capital:** Austin
> **Population:** 29,000,000
> **State Motto:** "Friendship"
> **What Natives Call Themselves:** Texans

STATE HISTORY

Because of its complex history and storied mythology, it is often difficult to describe Texas in brief. Some sources begin with its size: not just "big" but "BIG." To put it in Lone Star State vernacular, it is "Texas sized."

Until Alaska was granted statehood in 1959, Texas could boast that it was nation's largest state. Since that time, the terminology has been adjusted to Texas being the largest in the *contiguous* United States.

Regardless of size, Texas proudly claims the nickname, "the Lone Star State," based on its former status as an independent country, having its own single-star flag.

The first inhabitants of Texas were Indigenous people including the Apache, Caddo, and Comanche tribes. From the Caddo word for "friend" (*táysha*), the name "Texas" is said to have evolved. After Spanish-speaking people arrived, the Native word *táysha* was adapted into "Tejas," (pronounced TAY-hoss), later becoming "Texas."

Spanish explorer Alonso Álvarez de Pineda is credited by most historians as the first European to arrive in today's Texas, which he did in 1520. He claimed the land for Spain, although it was of no particular interest to that country for well over a century.

In the late 1600s, squabbles and perceived threats among European countries led to a renewed interest in Texas by Spain. In 1685, the Frenchman René-Robert Cavelier, Sieur de La Salle, established a colony for France near Matagorda Bay, between today's Galveston and Corpus Christi. By doing so, France was seen to be creating a wedge that could divide territory from Spain's eastern and western holdings in North America.

That drew Spain's attention. A permanent settlement of Spaniards was authorized near the San Antonio River in 1718. The term "Six Flags Over Texas" started to become a literal description rather than an amusement park. Half a dozen countries claimed all or part of today's Texas. In chronological order, they were Spain (beginning in 1520 and then intermittently until 1821), France (1685–1690), Mexico (1821–1836), and the Republic of Texas (1836–1845). In 1845, Texas became the 28th state of the Union, but it seceded in 1861 to join the Confederacy. After the Civil War ended in 1865, Texas rejoined the Union in 1870.

In a state that large, there were few lawmen to keep the peace. The Texas Rangers, officially created in 1835, had statewide authority, becoming known as a daunting law enforcement team.

Even with the Rangers having statewide jurisdiction, Texas became known as a place in which to disappear. Those who wished to escape their past, including debtors and outlaws, as well as those simply looking for better lives, found Texas to be a good place to start over. The phrase "Gone to Texas" (or simply "GTT") was known around the country, often being found scrawled on abandoned homesteads.

By the mid-1830s, settlers in Texas began chafing for independence from Mexico. In 1836, a battle in San Antonio took place between the "Texian" rebels and the Mexican Army. The settlers, defending their stronghold at a mission called the Alamo, were overwhelmed by the Mexican forces. But their deaths gave rise to an

In 1836, a battle took place at a mission called the Alamo. Seeking independence, the "Texians" were overwhelmed by Mexican forces. Their deaths inspired a renewed spirit of rebellion in Texas with the expression, "Remember the Alamo!" (Bonnie Avonrude/Dreamstime.com)

> ### Marfa's Vineyard?
>
> On the barren desert plains of Southwest Texas, in an expanse that most sources call "desolate," lies the tiny town of Marfa, Texas, with a population of about 1,800 people. For many years, it was famous for the mysterious Marfa Lights, glowing orbs that appear to float through the desert skies. Lying roughly on the same longitude as Roswell, New Mexico, the Marfa Lights have never been explained to everyone's satisfaction and may simply be unidentified flying objects (UFOs) that flew a bit too far past Roswell. Marfa's other claim to fame is that it was the place where the classic movie *Giant* was filmed in 1956. Yet, today Marfa attracts celebrities other than movie stars as well as people from around the globe attracted to its thriving avant-garde artist colony. For some, isolated little Marfa seems to be the end of the world. To others, it's as vibrant a center of arts and culture as Martha's Vineyard in Massachusetts. Like art itself, Marfa's appeal is in the eye of the beholder.

expression that led to a renewed spirit of rebellion in Texas, one that would ring through the years: "Remember the Alamo!"

After winning independence and statehood, Texas relied on agriculture and cattle until 1901 when an oil field at Spindletop, near Beaumont, catapulted Texas into an era of almost unimaginable wealth.

In 1962, Texas heralded another new era, the Space Age, when America's Manned Spacecraft Center was established in Houston.

Still, much of Texas lore centers on its size, which is larger than any European country. A person in El Paso, Texas, is closer to Los Angeles, California, than the eastern border of Texas. Along with sheer acreage, the state's economy is also "Texas sized." According to the World Bank, the Texas economy is in world's top 10, higher than Australia, Sweden, or Switzerland.

However, there is also room for smallness in Texas, especially the whimsical kind. In an isolated stretch of desert near Marfa, Texas, lies the world's smallest Prada store, which is never open. Installed in 2005, it is meant to be a work of art, but is stocked with items from the luxury brand and is eye-catching amid the desolation, to say the least.

URBAN LEGENDS

The **Bragg Road Ghost Light** is sometimes called by other names, including the Ghost Road of Saratoga and the Saratoga Light. These mysterious lights in the town of Saratoga, Texas, are said to randomly appear and disappear at night over Bragg Road, a rural dirt road. Some skeptics dismiss them as swamp gas or headlights that are somehow being reflected, while true believers say those theories don't hold up. As in some similar types of occurrences around the nation, the urban legend is that the origin of the lights can be attributed to the ghost of a railroad worker as he walks around the spot along the tracks where he was decapitated in a train accident. The lights are said to emanate from the lantern he carries as he tries to find his lost head, even though the tracks are long gone.

The **Lake Worth Monster** also has an alias: Goatman. The creature has been described as being part goat and part human, having scales on its body and sporting long claws instead of fingers. Alleged sightings date back to 1969, with one report holding the creature responsible for throwing an automobile tire at a group of people. Others claimed that the creature leaped from a tree, landing on a man's car. Another witness reported the beast as being covered with white fur, helpfully providing a photo, but later ascribed it to being a prank. In any case, the Lake Worth Monster has a convenient home right in the neighborhood. It is said to live at the nearby Fort Worth Nature Center, where an annual event called the Lake Worth Monster Bash celebrates its most famous resident.

The **White Lady of Rio Frio** is said to appear as an eerie wisp of fog near the Frio River in the unincorporated community of Rio Frio, west of San Antonio. The tale goes back to the early 1900s when a beautiful young woman is said to have become the object of desire by her sister's husband. Spurning his advances, she declared her love for another young man. The obsessed brother-in-law lured her outside one night while she was wearing a white nightgown. He allegedly killed her instantly by shooting her through the heart. Today, her gentle spirit is said to roam the canyon where she lived her short life. There are stories that the ghostly woman in white looks after young children by protecting them from danger, perhaps in deference to the children of her own that she might have had if her life had not been cruelly taken from her.

Honorable mention among urban legends in the Lone Star State goes to its very own "Texas-sized" **Bigfoot**. Sightings of the huge, hairy, apelike monster have been reported all over the state, especially heavily forested regions such as the Big Thicket and the Piney Woods. That locale is perfectly understandable for a creature who prefers to live concealed among the trees. However, the wide open spaces of West Texas have also had their share of alleged sightings, including reports of the creature's footprints being photographed near Lubbock in Yellow House Canyon. The Lubbock-area Bigfoot has been dubbed the "Canyon Thang," utilizing Texas pronunciation. To help monitor Bigfoot sightings in the Lone Star State, the online Texas Bigfoot Research Center and an annual Texas Bigfoot Conference were established to help keep track of the state's Texas-sized monster.

ICONIC TEXAS FOOD

Although chili was named the Official State Dish of Texas in 1977 and while many people think of barbecue as quintessentially Texan, those two items are intensely personal. They can cause heated controversies over such issues as beans versus no beans in chili or how Texas is worlds apart from Kansas City and the Carolinas in the barbecue arena. Another iconic Texas dish that reflects the flavor of the Lone

Star State without as much of a food fight is **Smoked Brisket**. This is the procedure, which takes a while but is worth it:

Texas Style Smoked Brisket (Yields 24 servings)
1 untrimmed ("packer cut") beef brisket about 12–14 pounds
¼ cup ground black pepper
¼ cup kosher salt

1. Combine salt and pepper.
2. Trim the brisket's fat to ¼–½ inch thick, then rub the salt and pepper mixture all over the meat before letting it sit at room temperature for an hour.
3. Raise smoker temperature to 225–250°F. Fill a disposable aluminum pan with water, setting it on the smoker to create humidity. Keep water pan full during the smoking process.
4. Place brisket on the smoker, fat side up, and close the lid. With lid closed, smoke the brisket at least three hours, checking it every 30 minutes to make sure the dark color is developing, and spritzing brisket surface with water in a spray bottle if it starts looking dry.
5. After around 5–6 hours, when the brisket has a dark color and reaches internal temperature of 165–170°, wrap brisket in aluminum foil before placing it back on the smoker.
6. Continue to cook for several more hours until internal temperature reads 200–210°.
7. Remove wrapped brisket from smoker, and let it rest 1–2 hours until the internal temperature drops to 140–145°F, then slice against the grain and serve.

Source: Adapted from https://houseofnasheats.com/texas-smoked-brisket/.

ODD LAWS

Bigfoot is one of the most popular urban legends in Texas, with the state having sightings reported in numerous places as well as being the home of the Texas Bigfoot Research Center and the annual Texas Bigfoot Conference. Therefore, it would seem plausible that Bigfoot holds an elite status in the Lone Star State. However, according to the Texas Parks and Wildlife Department, the state agency that regulates hunting, it is legal to capture, hunt, and/or kill Bigfoot since the creature is not a protected species under state law. The law also does not provide a Bigfoot bag limit or possession limit. As a nonprotected, nongame animal that is not classified as an endangered species (although some would argue this point), there is no limit on Bigfoot. However, a valid Texas hunting license is required.

State residents in a budget crunch should consider other means of boosting their finances apart from selling their body parts. Under the Texas Penal Code, it is unlawful for Texans to sell human organs such as eyes, heart, kidneys, liver, lungs, or skin. Conviction can result in jail time up to a year and/or a fine up to

$4,000. The same law also pertains to anyone found guilty of purchasing body parts. On the plus side, when running short of cash, it is perfectly legal in Texas to sell human blood and hair, preferably one's own.

If someone is found guilty of selling their body parts and wishes to consult an attorney, a section of the Texas Penal Code titled "Barratry and Solicitation of Professional Employment" regulates how it can and cannot be done. Under its provisions, lawyers (along with chiropractors, physicians, surgeons, and licensed private investigators) cannot solicit employment for themselves or others. The law covers drumming up business either in person or by telephone. For laymen, "barratry" is a legal term that describes an attorney instigating a dispute or encouraging someone to file a frivolous lawsuit in order to profit from the resultant legal fees.

Some mention must be given to a Texas-Law-That-Never-Was. According to the Texas Legislative Reference Library, a proposed statute was introduced into the statehouse in 1973 but not passed. It would have required criminals to give their intended victim a 24-hour notice describing what crime the perpetrator would be committing against the targeted prey. To make what sounds like a surefire crime prevention measure easy for criminals to uphold, the notice to victims could have been given either verbally or in writing. Yet, despite that convenience, the proposal still did not become law.

UNUSUAL DESTINATIONS

Out on the plains of West Texas, Amarillo is the hot spot for those who find half-buried Cadillacs to be cool. Constructed in 1974, **Cadillac Ranch** is what has been called a "public art installation and sculpture." It comprises 10 Cadillac automobiles, nose down and tailfins up. The theme of the artwork is said to be a monument to the Golden Age of American cars, back when the automotive world was ruled by Chrysler, Ford, and General Motors, with the latter being the manufacturer of Cadillac luxury cars. Later, what the Caddies apparently needed to accompany them was a counterpoint: half-buried combine harvesters. Many farmers consider the combine (pronounced "COM-byne") to be the Cadillac of farm equipment, and at **Combine City**, also in Amarillo, this "homage" to Cadillac Ranch is reflected. More than a dozen of the retired hardworking giants are buried with their noses down and blades up, in a kind of salute to America's heavy-metal agricultural technology.

To some, the **Salt Palace** in Grand Saline, Texas, is a bit of a misnomer on both counts. The "palace" is a small, unassuming one-story building, and the tiny town of Grand Saline itself is hardly grand, being home to only around 3,000 residents. However, both pay tribute to a major industry: salt. Founded in 1845, the town of Grand Saline was built atop a huge natural salt deposit, thousands of feet deep, that is predicted to last 20,000 years. The current Salt Palace museum, constructed in 1993 after a few earlier incarnations, is built entirely of rock salt. Inside, artifacts, memorabilia, and photographs illustrate the kind of salt mining that a major corporation still operates below Grand Saline. There are no tours available of the working mine itself, but there is a film at the Salt Palace to show how it's done. To many guests, a high point of their visit is being photographed licking the walls.

Few people seem interested in licking the items on display at the **Toilet Seat Art Museum**. Created by retired master plumber Barney Smith, at last count there were more than 1,500 toilet seats, each uniquely painted or otherwise adorned with such items as assorted trinkets, belt buckles, coaxial cable, coins, flags, license plates from all 50 states and the U.S. Virgin Islands, shells, even shredded money. The collection, over 50 years in the making, started with a few toilet seats that were being discarded by a plumbing supply store. Smith noticed them while picking up parts for his plumbing business. He painted them, and flushed with success, created hundreds more, allowing the public to view them for free although none of the toilet seat art is for sale. The facility started out in Smith's hometown of San Antonio, but after this death in 2018 at age 98, the collection currently sits on display at The Colony, Texas, a suburb of Dallas. A good time to visit might be November 19, the official United Nations international observance to inspire progress in global sanitation, a salute called World Toilet Day.

Honorable Mention: This being Texas, there are countless "World's Largest" attractions in the Lone Star State boasting statues that visitors find to be perfect for "Texas sized" photo opportunities. These include the **World's Largest Blue Crab** (Rockport Beach), **World's Largest Cowboy Boots** (San Antonio), **World's Largest Killer Bee** (Hidalgo), and **World's Largest Spur** (Lampasas). At the **World's Largest Squirrel** (Cedar Creek), the massive rodent clutches a pecan bigger than a human head, although it does not measure up to Seguin, which, having a 10-foot nut, calls itself the home of the **World's Largest Pecan**.

DISTINCTIVE TEXAS WORDS AND SAYINGS

All hat and no cattle: Big talk, but nothing to back it up.

Do wut? Asking the speaker to repeat something. "Do wut now?" is appropriate for those who prefer to make the request in a lengthier format.

Hi-dee! Texas pronunciation of "Howdy," the standard greeting of the Lone Star State; said to be derived from the more formal "How do you do?"

Pert near: Pretty close. Basically, not perfect but close enough to be workable. It is similar to "Fair-ta-middlin," the response to an inquiry about one's health.

Proud of: Not exactly demonstrating pride, but rather an overpriced item that the seller seems to feel is worth a lot of money.

Sorry: Not always an apology, but can be a description of someone out of favor, as in "my sorry lowlife ex-boyfriend."

Further Reading

Brown, Alan. *Haunted Texas: Ghosts and Strange Phenomena of the Lone Star State*. Mechanicsburg, PA: Stackpole Books, 2008.

Fehrenbach, T. R. *Lone Star: A History of Texas and the Texans*. Boston, MA: Da Capo Press, 2000.

Harrigan, Stephen. *Big Wonderful Thing: A History of Texas*. Austin: University of Texas Press, 2019.

Utah

FACT BOX

Nickname: The Beehive State
Statehood Granted: 1896
Capital: Salt Lake City
Population: 32,000,000
State Motto: "Industry"
What Natives Call Themselves: Utahns

STATE HISTORY

For thousands of years, Indigenous people called Puebloans, also known today as the Anasazi, made their home amid the awe-inspiring landscape of the current state of Utah. They excavated homes in caves before disappearing from the region between the years 1200 and 1400.

Eventually, people including the Navajo, Shoshone, and Ute appeared. They were the inhabitants of today's Utah when Spanish explorers began entering the region. Some historians believe that Francisco Vázquez de Coronado, on his continuing quest for the rumored cities of gold, may have crossed into Utah in 1540. Finding none, he moved on.

Things were relatively quiet in Utah for the next two centuries. For the most part, the Native people coexisted and traded peacefully with each other.

In 1776, while revolutionary events were occurring thousands of miles away on the East Coast, Spain still held the Southwest. That year, a group of Spaniards passed through Utah from Santa Fe in hopes of finding an easy overland route to the Pacific, but like Coronado, they kept moving.

Fur trappers and traders were present in some parts of Utah by the early 1800s, with some establishing trading posts primarily near the Great Salt Lake. By that time, the name "Utah" was widely being used. It is said to have been derived from the Ute tribe who lived there, with their name basically meaning "people of the mountains."

Throughout the 1800s, white settlers were making their way westward. In 1846, the doomed Donner Party passed through the Salt Lake Valley, but kept moving, ultimately sealing their tragic fate.

Another group arrived in 1847, remaining in Utah and making a permanent impact on its history. Brigham Young led a group from the Church of Jesus Christ of Latter-day Saints (LDS), sometimes called Mormons, into the Salt Lake Valley.

The plan was to move beyond the borders of the United States, where they had experienced persecution and violence. At the time of their arrival, Utah was in Mexican Territory. It was isolated enough that LDS members felt they could safely practice their religion. Arriving in the Salt Lake Valley, church leader Brigham Young is reported to have stated that it was the "right place."

Salt Lake City was founded in 1847. Along with establishing schools and houses of worship, the new arrivals began building homes, carving out farms, and creating irrigation systems that they needed to survive. More than 70,000 pioneering Mormons settled in Utah over the next few decades, establishing such towns as Ogden and Provo.

Their legacy is a state in which about two-thirds of the population reportedly belongs to the same religion, the Church of Jesus Christ of Latter-day Saints, with its headquarters in Salt Lake City. This makes Utah the only American state that has an overwhelming majority of people who belong to a single religious denomination.

The early Mormon settlers struggled to survive amid Utah's harsh elements. Originally, they called their new homeland "Deseret." Some people think the name is adapted from the word "desert," since much of Utah is covered with arid land. However, the word "deseret" was said to have been found in the Book of Mormon religious text. The term has been described as an ancient word for "honeybee," the hardworking little creature that symbolizes industriousness and productivity.

After the arrival of the Mormons, for the most part, Utah was basically ignored by Mexico. However, things changed after the Mexican War ended in 1848. With a victory by the United States, much of Mexico's land in the Southwest was claimed by the American government as part of "Manifest Destiny," or expansion from the Atlantic to Pacific coasts.

People all across the nation became familiar with the name of the Utah Territory through two historic events in the 1860s. In 1861, Salt Lake City, the territorial capital, became the final link for the first transcontinental telegraph. Brigham Young and Abraham Lincoln were among the first to send messages via telegram.

In addition, the first transcontinental railroad was completed in 1869. The famed "Golden Spike" was driven at Promontory Summit in the Utah Territory, near the Great Salt Lake. It was symbolic of the final piece of construction on the track, initiating the great era of America's coast-to-coast rail system. It dramatically accelerated the settlement of the American West and enhanced the nation's growing prosperity by moving people, finished goods, and raw materials across the country's enormous distances.

Around this time, other parts of the Southwest that had formerly been held by Mexico, such as California, were applying for statehood. The original leaders of today's Utah had envisioned a state of Deseret, which would have been a large landmass encompassing almost all of Utah and Nevada along with portions of Arizona,

California, Colorado, Idaho, New Mexico, Oregon, and Wyoming. By the time the Utah Territory was created by Congress in 1850, the proposed Deseret region had been considerably whittled down. When Utah became the 45th state 1896, it took on the familiar boundaries of today's Beehive State. That particular nickname was chosen not because of a large number of bees in the state but because like the word "deseret," it was said to reflect hard work and industriousness.

In the early 1900s, people became curious about Utah, especially its natural wonders. Many were able to visit via rail or automobile and were amazed by its otherworldly looking national parks such as Natural Bridges and Zion, which were first set aside in 1908. Those were followed by national parks including Rainbow Bridge (1910), Dinosaur (1915), Bryce Canyon (1928), Arches (1929), Cedar Breaks (1933), and Capitol Reef (1937).

In the early part of the 20th century, Utah also became a prime location for the flourishing art of motion pictures. People around the world who could not visit the state in person became familiar with its scenic wonders.

URBAN LEGENDS

Ironically, the site of one of Utah's most pervasive urban legends is not in Utah at all. The **Disneyland Hearse** is an antique funeral carriage drawn by ghostly looking horses that is found at the entrance to the popular Haunted Mansion at

Millions of people have seen Utah even if they have never been there. Monument Valley set the scene for innumerable Western movies as well as *Jurassic World* and TV's *Doctor Who*. (iStockPhoto .com)

> **Monumental Achievement**
>
> Most Americans have seen Utah even if they have never been there. During the Great Depression of the 1930s, the struggling owners of a Utah trading post heard that movie director John Ford was looking for a place to shoot a Western. With their last few dollars, they drove to Hollywood, camping outside Ford's office. When they were finally able to show Ford pictures of the land around their trading post, the filmmaker knew he had found the perfect location. The place was called Monument Valley, and since then, Hollywood has been a regular visitor. Along with Ford's *Stagecoach* (1939), movies filmed there include *My Darling Clementine* (1946), *She Wore a Yellow Ribbon* (1949), *The Searchers* (1956), *How the West Was Won* (1962), *Easy Rider* (1968), *2001: A Space Odyssey* (1968), *National Lampoon's Vacation* (1983), *Forrest Gump* (1994), and *Jurassic World: Fallen Kingdom* (2018). Television's sci-fi hero *Doctor Who* also made a stop there, which was the first time the show was shot at a location in America.

California's Disneyland. The Utah urban legend is that it was used to transport the body of Brigham Young to his burial. However, according to officials at the Church History Museum of the Church of Jesus Christ of Latter-day Saints in Salt Lake City, documentation indicates otherwise. The dead body of Brigham Young was moved to his final resting place by being carried on a platform by men of the church, a directive that was among the instructions in Young's will. Furthermore, experts on antique vehicles have stated that Disneyland's hearse was manufactured in the 1890s, while Brigham Young died in 1877. But, as with many urban legends, facts rarely intrude on a good story.

Many people believe in the **Escalante Petrified Forest Curse**, especially if they feel that they have personally suffered its consequences. According to what is said to be an ancient hex, anyone removing pieces of petrified wood from the park as a souvenir will suffer grievous misfortune. It is not hard to see why absconding with a bit of the long-dead wood might be tempting. On the scenic trails that wind through the forest, there are pieces of petrified wood that are dated at millions of years old. Across the eons, minerals such as copper, iron, and manganese have tinted the petrified wood in deep, rich colors. Even the tree rings on some trees, marking their almost unimaginable age, can be clearly seen. Many of them lie exactly where they fell eons before humans walked the Earth. However, although it is tempting, it is also illegal to take anything, including bits of petrified wood, from the state park. According to the legend, park officials receive up to a dozen letters each year returning the purloined pieces. The letters describe stories of accidents, fires, illnesses, unemployment, and other misfortunes attesting, at least in the minds of the culprits, to the power of the curse—and asking that it be lifted after seeing the error of their ways.

The **Uintah Basin** is said to be a hot spot for extraterrestrial activity, with thousands of unidentified flying object (UFO) sightings being reported over more than 50 years. Believers are adamant that while none of the alleged sightings have actually been proven, the sheer number of reports must indicate the presence of UFOs, or at least some sort of supernatural activity. There was an especially high volume of sightings in the late 1960s that led some scientists to investigate. After studying various correlations, they came to a conclusion, publishing their findings in scientific journals. However, the scientists in question were not from NASA. Instead, they were entomologists—researchers who study insects. They determined that there was a direct connection between the UFO sightings of the 1960s and massive swarms of *spruce budworms*. The unusually large infestation of budworms during that time period appeared illuminated by electrically charged fields stimulated by thunderheads. Being nocturnal beings, the flight patterns of the bugs apparently put on quite a show for earthlings convinced they were being invaded by UFOs from outer space. Since spruce budworms are capable of devouring vast swaths of plant life in their paths, they may actually have been more of a threat than little green men.

ICONIC UTAH FOOD

Despite its name, the dish called **Utah Funeral Potatoes** can also be cheery on festive occasions. Its name evolved from commonly being served at after-funeral gatherings in the culture of the Church of Jesus Christ of Latter-day Saints. Today, it is said that there will be at least one pan of funeral potatoes at just about any potluck or other feast in Utah. Its countless variations depend on the individual cook, but the recipe below provides the basics. Some cooks start from scratch by using fresh potatoes, but others prefer the texture of frozen hash browns as seen here:

Utah Funeral Potatoes (Yields 8 servings)
1 stick butter, divided
½ cup diced onion
1 package (32 oz) frozen shredded hash browns, thawed
2 cups shredded sharp cheddar cheese
1 can (10½ oz) cream of chicken, celery, or mushroom soup
2 cups sour cream
½ tsp salt
¼ tsp black pepper
1 cup coarsely crushed butter-flavored crackers or corn flakes

1. Preheat oven to 375°F while coating a 9 by 13 inch baking dish with cooking spray.
2. In a small skillet, over medium heat, melt half the stick of butter. Add onion and sauté 4–5 minutes, or until soft.
3. In a large bowl, combine hash browns, cheese, soup, sour cream, salt, pepper, and onion; mix well before spooning into prepared baking dish.

4. In a small microwaveable bowl, melt remaining butter in microwave; stir in corn flakes or cracker crumbs, then sprinkle mixture over potatoes.
5. Cover baking dish with foil and bake 35 minutes, then remove foil and bake 10–15 minutes more until golden brown and heated through.

Source: Adapted from https://www.mrfood.com/Potatoes-Rice/Utahs-Best-Funeral-Potatoes.

ODD LAWS

It is understandable that Utah lawmakers would want to keep the state's sidewalks safe for pedestrians. A driver is prohibited from impeding or obstructing the ordinary use of the sidewalk by parking there. However, Utah law goes a step further to keep pedestrians on sidewalks safe from impediments. Not only is it unlawful to drive a car or truck onto a sidewalk, but animals also have to keep their distance. It is not known how big or how vicious the animal would have to be to place the owner on the wrong side of the law. On the plus side, animals can use the sidewalk when crossing to or from abutting property, which might be helpful for individuals taking their pet rhino for a walk.

Utah residents who avoid sidewalks but do not necessarily drive a car also have to follow certain rules. Those riding a bicycle must keep at least one hand on the handlebars at all times. The law becomes even more specific for bike riders carrying things, in which case, under the law, they may not carry any article, bundle, or package that prevents the use of both hands in the operation of the bicycle. This law would no doubt also apply to individuals planning to audition as a stunt rider for the circus.

While the "bike and bundle" statute might appear to some as a small thing, other Utah laws involved much bigger, dramatic situations—catastrophic, in fact. Just so its residents and visitors are aware, under Utah law, no one is allowed to cause widespread injury or damage by using a weapon of mass destruction. Infractions include causing an avalanche, the collapse of a building, explosion, fire, or flood. To stay within the law and avoid court appearances in Utah, visitors would be well advised to keep their weapons of mass destruction at home since violation of this law is a first-degree felony.

UNUSUAL DESTINATIONS

Back in the Pleistocene Age, about a million years ago, a huge body of water in today's Utah covered thousands of square miles, about the size of Lake Michigan. However, as the region's geology and climate changed, all that water evaporated, leaving 30,000 square miles of thick sediment that eventually became the **Bonneville Salt Flats**, near Wendover, Utah. Its blinding white appearance and disorienting flatness have made it the location for movies such as *Independence Day* and *Pirates of the Caribbean: At World's End*. Most of the time, visitors find that it can indeed seem like the world's end, as silent and desolate as a far-flung planet. However, several times a year, reality comes roaring in—literally. Automotive racers and spectators from around the globe come to experience an adrenaline rush on the hard-packed natural speedway. At that time, the decibel level far exceeds anything heard in the Pleistocene Age, including the now-extinct mammals whose fossils have been found there.

Speaking of other planets, the NASA-funded **Mars Desert Research Station (MDRS)** makes the most of Utah's eerie similarity to our neighboring planet, Mars. Project specialists might arrive in the nearby town of Hanksville, Utah, about seven miles away, but after settling in at MDRS, they may feel they are about 220 million miles from Earth, not on the red sands of Utah, but on the Red Planet. New technologies are tested with an eye toward a mission to Mars and possibly even eventual colonization. At any given time, about a half dozen crew members live in a habitat building, but must suit up in space gear any time they go outside. The MDRS facility also includes an engineering pod, greenhouse, solar observatory, and science building. Members of the public can sometimes spot one of the Mars simulations from a distance, but no tours are permitted, as the crews must also learn how to function in isolation. This Utah site would seem to be the place to do just that.

There are usually few good things to be said about a drought. However, at Utah's Great Salt Lake, near the town of Corinne, there is an art installation that only appears when the lake level is down. The **Spiral Jetty** is a 1,500-foot-long earthwork sculpture that was built by Robert Smithson in 1970. At the time, the lake level was down. But when the drought ended and the water rose, the artwork was submerged, impossible to see. Since that time, it only reemerges during severe droughts. At one point, it went unseen for more than 30 years. Only when the water drops, can it be enjoyed by the public. The Spiral Jetty was originally constructed of black basalt, but during its decades under water, it became encrusted with white salt and seems to have a pink-tinted color in the water surrounding it. Before his death just three years after completing the Spiral Jetty, the artist expressed an admiration for the power of Nature to change things. Many of his admirers feel he would be happy with his artwork's ever-changing look as well as its disappearing act.

DISTINCTIVE UTAH WORDS AND SAYINGS

Holy war: Athletic events between Utah's Brigham Young University and the University of Utah, with many LDS church members avidly supporting and playing for both teams.

Lagoon: Not a peaceful body of water, but Utah's most iconic amusement park.

Sluffing: Skipping school.

Slots: In Utah, these are hardly gaming machines. In the Beehive State, canyons are called "slots."

Sundance: Not a ritual by Indigenous people, but the annual independent film festival in Park City, Utah, which some people feel is the center of the universe, at least for 10 days each January.

Further Reading

Alexander, Thomas. *Utah, the Right Place*. Layton, UT: Gibbs Smith, 2003.
Stone, Eileen Hallet. *Hidden History of Utah*. Charleston, SC: History Press, 2013.
Wharton, Gayen, and Tom Wharton. *It Happened in Utah: Stories of Events and People That Shaped Beehive State History*. 3rd edition. Guilford, CT: Globe Pequot, 2018.

Vermont

FACT BOX

Nickname: The Green Mountain State
Statehood Granted: 1791
Capital: Montpelier
Population: 630,000
State Motto: "Freedom and Unity"
What Natives Call Themselves: Vermonters

STATE HISTORY

Vermonters have traditionally been known for their independent spirit. Indeed, the state was its own independent republic before joining the Union. Some people believe that part of the average Vermonter's personality is formed by the state's geography. The rocky Green Mountains run down the middle of the state from north to south, like a granite spine.

Vermont's geography also imparted a French Canadian influence from its northern border as well as characteristics derived from the British colonies to the south. A progressive spirit arose in Vermont, being an early advocate for the abolition of slavery, promoter of women's right to vote, and supporter of public education.

Perhaps that spirit also held elements of sweetness, as Vermont has traditionally been the top producer of maple syrup in the United States. Early settlers are said to have learned about the sweet treat from Native American people such as the Mohawk tribe who lived in much of the territory of today's Vermont.

Several origin stories exist to illustrate how lowly tree sap turned into something celestial. One version is that after a Native American man threw his tomahawk at a maple tree, sap ran out. His wife then boiled a piece of venison in the gooey liquid, discovering a new taste sensation. In another account, it is said that a group of Native Americans discovered tasty sap running from a broken maple branch, with no tomahawks involved.

By the 1500s, the first Europeans were arriving. In 1535, France's Jacques Cartier is thought to have made an initial foray into Vermont. He was followed by fellow Frenchman Samuel de Champlain who claimed Vermont as part of New

STATE ODDITIES

Vermont is known as America's top producer of maple syrup, with the popular maple leaf image being seen across the state. The production of maple syrup is one of Vermont's largest industries. (Janice Higgins/Dreamstime.com)

France in 1609. A French military unit built Fort Sainte Anne in 1666 to establish their authority.

Settlers from Massachusetts began moving into the area in 1724, creating the first permanent presence of English colonists in Vermont. During the cold northern winters, many farmers wished to supplement their income when nothing would grow. Enjoying relatively peaceful relations with the Native Americans, they began to learn about the aforementioned sap from maple trees, discovering that it was less expensive as a sweetener than molasses or sugar. It sweetened not only their foodstuffs but also their fortunes when they marketed it for sale. Collecting maple syrup went on to become one of Vermont's largest industries, along with mining and manufacturing.

But that was far in the future. For colonists in Vermont during the 1700s, they first had to cope with shifting allegiances.

In 1763, France was defeated in the French and Indian War. As a result, today's Vermont was part of the territory that was ceded to Great Britain by France. However, part of the future state would forever be French by virtue of its name. In the French language, "vert" is the color green and "mont" means "mountain," giving rise to "Vermont."

In 1770, Vermonter Ethan Allen recruited some friends and family members to form a militia. Calling themselves the Green Mountain Boys, their early goal was to protect local settlers. With the coming of the American Revolution in 1775, the Green Mountain Boys became known for their wartime exploits, such as helping to capture the British installation at Fort Ticonderoga in New York, a significant victory for the patriots.

Vermont's participation in the Revolutionary War was as an independent region called the Vermont Republic, which had been established in 1777. As a sovereign nation, the Vermont Republic abolished slavery, being the first of the future United States to do so. The independent republic of Vermont also issued its own monetary system and operated a self-sufficient postal service.

After the American Revolution ended in 1783, the Vermont Republic remained independent. In 1788, it adopted "Freedom and Unity" as its official motto, a phrase that remained after Vermont eventually joined the Union as the 14th state in 1791.

> ### Status Quo
>
> In 2015, an official Latin motto for Vermont was enacted by the legislature following the suggestion of a high school student who loved the classics. With Vermont being the 14th state to join the Union, the student came up with the Latin phrase *Stella Quarta Decima Fulgeat*, or "May the Fourteenth Star Shine Bright." However, as seen on the state seal, "Freedom and Unity" remains Vermont's official motto. The Latin phrase is considered a secondary Vermont symbol, joining the state bird, state flower, and state tree. Even so, the move to adopt a Latin phrase, even a secondary one, elicited some heated responses from citizens who thought "Latin" referred to Latino immigrants. It is not known if the protesters knew about other classical Latin phrases in America, including the nation's motto, "E Pluribus Unum," meaning "From Many, One," which is on the Great Seal of the United States as well as on its currency.

Vermont was the first American state that was not one of the thirteen original colonies. It has the distinction of joining only three other states that had formerly been sovereign republics: California, Hawaii, and Texas.

Vermont sent men to fight for the Union in the Civil War (1861–1865) and was the site of an unusual event during that conflict. In 1864, a small group of Confederates entered Vermont from Canada. During a raid on the town of St. Albans, Vermont, the rebels robbed a bank and tried to burn the town before escaping back into Canada. The fire did not ignite, and the money was later returned to St. Albans.

Trivia buffs may wish to note that Vermont is the only New England state without direct access to the Atlantic Ocean. However, being awash in all that maple syrup, Vermonters do not seem to mind.

URBAN LEGENDS

The **Frozen People** tale is said to have been recounted in a diary from the 1800s, although it is not known if the actual diary or the story it told have ever been authenticated. According to the legend, a poor Vermont family living in the isolated hills could not manage to feed all the members of the family during the harsh winter months when nothing would grow. After the first hard freeze of the season, their solution to the economic crunch was to drug the family's old people into unconsciousness. The comatose geriatrics were taken outside into the glacial cold, where they became quick-frozen. They were then thoughtfully placed in boxes packed with straw to avoid being a wintertime feast for predators. Regular snowfall kept the boxes cold (and hidden from prying eyes of neighbors) until the spring thaw. The stiff, cold bodies were then removed from their boxes and slowly revived, awakening by a roaring fire and given a nice hearty bowl of hot soup. The formerly frozen people remembered nothing and simply felt marvelously rested, as one might after a four-month nap. They then went about their lives in glowing good health with no ill effects. Usually the storyteller claims to have heard it from a friend whose uncle, an old-timer, allegedly witnessed the whole thing, thus presumably giving it credibility.

The **Hayden House Curse** recounts the ultimate mother-in-law story. Built in 1854, the Hayden House in Albany, Vermont, was home to the family of William Hayden. His mother-in-law, Mercie Dale, lent Hayden large sums of money, presumably to help his business and provide for her daughter. However, Hayden squandered the money away in very unbusinesslike ways, then refused to repay the loan. Their familial relations further soured when Mercie suspected Hayden of trying to poison her. On her deathbed, Mercie cursed the Hayden family name, dooming the Hayden line by proclaiming that it would soon die out. Over the course of a few years, the entire William Hayden family line did indeed expire due to what were said to be unexplained illnesses. Ironically, the deceased Hayden clan, along with Mercie Dale, lies buried in the family cemetery where it is uncertain whether they are resting in peace. Some feel that the moral of the story is "Never a borrower nor a lender be," particularly when it involves one's mother-in-law.

During the late 1800s, the town of **West Castleton** on Vermont's Lake Bomoseen was a thriving community of laborers, many of whom were employed at the town's slate quarries. However, the town began to dwindle in the 1930s and was eventually abandoned completely. Today, West Castleton is known as a ghost town, for more reasons than one. It seems that back when the town was booming, local workers enjoyed visiting a popular tavern on the other side of the lake. The quickest way to get there was by rowboat. One evening after work, three friends got in a boat as usual and began rowing toward the other side of the lake. They never got there. The only thing that remained by light of day was their empty rowboat floating on the calm waters of the lake with no signs of struggle or distress. After a lengthy search, neither their remains nor any clues as to their fate were found. Today, the waters of Lake Bomoseen on the West Castleton shoreline remain tranquil, but at the full moon, a ghostly rowboat that is completely empty of human life can be seen drifting across the lake in eerie silence, without its oars even making a ripple in the water.

ICONIC VERMONT FOOD

Even the name **Sugar on Snow** is evocative of Vermont. If there are two things Vermont has in large quantities, it is (a) snow and (b) sugary maple syrup. With the correct ingredients on hand, preparing this quintessential Vermont treat is relatively simple. Those ingredients are basically Vermont maple syrup and a supply of clean, fresh snow. Some people enjoy variations, such as rolling the drizzled ribbons of maple syrup onto a Popsicle stick or making it into a taffy-like candy. Others just enjoy eating it with a spoon in its purest state. There are usually plenty of variations to be found at the annual Vermont Maple Weekend, including the preferred accompaniments: dill pickles (for an acidic counterpoint) and plain donuts (for their buttery texture) to balance all that mouthwatering sweetness.

> **Sugar on Snow** (Serves 6)
> 1 cup dark robust Vermont maple syrup
> Fresh snow packed in a baking pan or large bowl
> ½ tsp butter
>
> 1. Place snow in freezer until needed.
> 2. Heat syrup and butter in saucepan to a low boil, about 10–15 minutes, turning the heat down if it threatens to boil over.
> 3. Test with candy thermometer until mixture reaches 235°F.
> 4. Remove from heat, and allow to cool slightly.
> 5. Take snow from freezer, and pack in smaller bowls, pouring syrup over the snow.
> 6. Eat immediately, served with pickles and plain donuts if desired.

Source: Adapted from https://www.food.com/recipe/sugar-on-snow-227739.

ODD LAWS

The year 1968 was a turbulent one. Perhaps lost in the maelstrom of world events was a law that was passed in the state of Vermont. It was the first in the continental United States to officially ban billboards. Recognizing that travelers sometimes want to know where nearby restaurants and lodgings are located, Vermont utilizes relatively small travel information signs. These signs are usually clustered together to minimize their visual effect and maximize the chance to enjoy an unobstructed view of the state's natural beauty. A small caveat is that businesses located along state roads can erect signage letting people know where they are, but only as long as the business conforms to local sign regulations.

Not only does Vermont have a ban on billboards, but it also has a ban on bans—in this case, any ban against clotheslines. It is illegal for groups such as neighborhood organizations or property owners associations to ban clotheslines, since a clothesline is officially considered by the state of Vermont to be an energy-efficient means of drying laundry. In fact, it's so official that the energy efficiency stipulation is cited by legislative statute. By law, clotheslines are defined as energy devices utilizing renewable solar power, and therefore, any governing body is forbidden from passing other laws prohibiting them. On the other hand, Vermonters do not appreciate the sight of people's wet clothes becoming an eyesore on wash day. The statute does not permit hanging laundry on balconies, terraces, or patio railings, which is considered to be unsightly in a state valued for its scenery.

Margarine is also addressed under Vermont law. It's perfectly legal for restaurants in the state to serve margarine, but it must be noted prominently on the menu that it is doing so. In 1871, a U.S. patent was issued for a product called "oleomargarine," which combined vegetable oils with animal fats. It was proposed as a butter substitute, with margarine being marketed as less expensive than butter, as well as lasting longer on grocery store shelves and in restaurant coolers. In its original state, margarine is white in color, which many people found unappealing. Therefore, some margarine manufacturers colored it yellow to look like butter. Butter-makers fought back in the subsequent "Margarine Wars," resulting in Vermont's ruling that nondairy butter substitutes had to be dyed pink to differentiate them from pure dairy butter. The pink color mandate traveled all the way to the U.S. Supreme Court where it was struck down as "forced adulteration." But Vermonters are still proud of their dairy products, leading to the current margarine-related prerequisite.

UNUSUAL DESTINATIONS

With Vermont's first permanent European settlement being founded in 1724, there are a lot of historic old cemeteries scattered around the state. However, one of Vermont's best known, attracting an unusual share of attention, was created several centuries later. **Ben & Jerry's Flavor Graveyard** in Waterbury, Vermont, has been called the sweetest cemetery in the state, if not the world. It's an offshoot of Ben & Jerry's Ice Cream, which was established in 1978. The company regularly introduces new flavors, decommissions others, and sometimes decides that a proposed new taste sensation just doesn't make the cut. The array of headstones in this tasteful graveyard allows visitors to pay their respects to the dearly de-pinted. As opposed to most cemeteries, this one allows flavor fans the opportunity to suggest resurrecting a loved one after seeing monuments to past glories such as Aloha Macadamia, Cool Britannia, Economic Crunch, Ethan Almond, This Is Nuts, and Vermonty Python.

At the Evergreen Cemetery in New Haven, Vermont, visitors do not encounter the flavor of the month but instead come across what can only be called a tomb with a view. The **Grave of Timothy Clark Smith** is the presumed final resting place of a 19th-century doctor who was not necessarily afraid of death but was terrified of being buried alive. Designing his own eternal accommodations, Smith's final instructions included being buried with a bell in his hand, a breathing tube, and a set of stairs enabling him to get back to the surface "just in case." Most memorable to visitors today is a thick square-glass window positioned on the tomb to look down on his face so loved ones could check on his status below ground. He died at age 72 in 1893 and presumably stayed put. However, it's hard to tell. Due to the age of the glass, discoloration, and moisture that has collected on it from inside, visitors cannot see very far into the crypt or actually come face to face with the current embodiment of Dr. Smith.

One more Vermont cemetery is worthy of mention as a unique destination for the living. The granite funerary monument sculptures at **Hope Cemetery** in Barre, Vermont, a town that calls itself the Granite Capital of the World, pay tribute not only to the deceased but also to their passions in life. Among thousands of monuments are statues attesting to their individuality by representing things that meant something to them in life. They include a baseball player, biplane, family portrait, motorcycle, race car, soccer ball, soldier smoking a cigarette, and perhaps most touching, a pajama-clad elderly couple sitting up in bed while holding hands. Stretched out in front of the stone is their grave.

Lest anyone think that the only unusual destinations in Vermont are cemeteries, what is billed as the **World's Tallest Ladderback Chair** in Bennington comes with its own resurrection story. At almost the height of a two-story building, the chair's first incarnation dates back to the 1940s when it was built to stand in front of a furniture store. By the year 2000, Vermont winters had taken their toll. After a brand-new replacement weighing more than a ton was erected, it stood proudly for *20 days* before collapsing in a windstorm. A new one was built and was found to be sturdier—but then the furniture store burned down. Fortunately, the resurrected chair was able to be moved to the store's current location. Today, curious onlookers make a point of checking on this beloved landmark, if only to see what will happen next.

DISTINCTIVE VERMONT WORDS AND SAYINGS

802: This number that is seen on bumper stickers, T-shirts, and sometimes even tattoos is Vermont's telephone area code—the only one in the state—and Vermonters are proud of it.

Creemee: What is known elsewhere as soft-serve ice cream.

Flatlander: Someone who is not from Vermont.

Mud season: A veritable fifth season that falls between winter and spring.

Vermonter: Someone born in Vermont, preferably the product of several generations of Vermonters.

Woodchuck: A backwoodsy Vermonter, with an example being the characters "Larry, Darryl, and Darryl" on the classic television series *Newhart*. For TV trivia buffs, the show's exterior shots were Vermont's Waybury Inn.

Further Reading

Bushnell, Mark. *Hidden History of Vermont*. Charleston, SC: History Press, 2017.

Klyza, Christopher, and Stephen Trombulak. *The Story of Vermont: A Natural and Cultural History*. 2nd edition. Lebanon, NH: University Press of New England, 2015.

Sherman, Michael, Gene Sessions, and Jeffrey Potash. *Freedom and Unity: A History of Vermont*. Barre: Vermont Historical Society, 2004.

Virginia

FACT BOX

Nickname: Old Dominion
Statehood Granted: 1788
Capital: Richmond
Population: 8,500,000
State Motto: *Sic semper tyrannis* (Latin: "Thus Always to Tyrants")
What Natives Call Themselves: Virginians

STATE HISTORY

For thousands of years before Europeans arrived, today's Virginia was home to Indigenous people. In 1570, about 30 Native American tribes merged under Chief Powhatan. The merger was intended to provide a stronger base for trade, but ironically, that same year, new arrivals on their shores began making trade secondary to survival.

Records show that it was in 1570 when Spanish Jesuits founded Ajacán Mission on the Virginia Peninsula. Their group was killed by hostile Native Americans, sparking retaliation by Spaniards who sailed up from their Florida territory for vengeance.

England's Queen Elizabeth I granted Walter Raleigh a charter to form a colony north of Florida. In 1584, Raleigh's expedition explored the region he named Virginia, which is generally said to refer to Elizabeth's sobriquet as the "Virgin Queen."

In 1607, America's first permanent English settlement was established at a site in Virginia called Jamestown, in honor of King James I. About half of the early settlers died during what was called the Starving Time in 1609.

However, those who survived were highly motivated to build the colony and make their fortunes. They discovered that they could profit from growing and selling tobacco to European markets. In 1619, the first enslaved Africans were brought to Jamestown to work the fields. By 1661, Virginia was passing statutes that officially condoned slavery, making it a hereditary condition for the descendants of enslaved people.

As one of the most prominent of the original thirteen colonies, Virginia prospered over the course of the next century. It established its own governing body,

Talking Turkey

Schoolchildren generally believe that America's first Thanksgiving was held in 1620 when the Pilgrims at Plymouth Rock in Massachusetts initiated a national day of family, food, and football. However, as acknowledged by two U.S. presidents (of both political parties), the first Thanksgiving was actually held by 38 English colonists at Berkeley Plantation, Virginia, before the Pilgrims even left port. Each November, the Virginia Thanksgiving Festival attempts to set the record straight, citing speeches by Presidents John F. Kennedy and George W. Bush that the first recorded Thanksgiving in the New World took place in 1619, more than a year before the Pilgrims carved their turkey. Virginia's Thanksgiving menu included ham and oysters, which are considered delicacies today, but scholars note that they were only consumed out of necessity since the alternative meal was moldy ship's rations. Virginia's Thanksgiving was also about prayer, not partying. Along with what some historians call better publicity, it's why many believe that the Pilgrims' food fest story is the version that prevailed.

called the House of Burgesses and eventually became a major hub of the movement advocating America's break from England.

Along with the other colonies, Virginia declared independence from Great Britain in 1776. The names of notable Virginians went down in history for their significant roles in the Revolutionary period, including Patrick Henry, Thomas Jefferson, James Madison, and George Washington.

In 1788, Virginia officially became the 10th state in the Union. At the time, today's Kentucky was part of Virginia, but split off in 1792 to become its own state.

In 1861, a little more than 70 years after Virginia joined the Union, the state seceded to become part of the Confederate States of America. Richmond, Virginia, was chosen as the

Walter Raleigh, seen here, was granted a charter by England's Queen Elizabeth I to form a North American colony. He explored the region he named Virginia, leading to America's first permanent English settlement at Jamestown, Virginia, in 1607. (Georgios Kollidas/Dreamstime.com)

capital of the Confederacy. It was Virginian Robert E. Lee who took command of Confederate forces, and over the course of the Civil War, more battles were fought in Virginia than in any other place.

Just as Kentucky had once been a part of Virginia, West Virginia split from Virginia during the Civil War since its people did not wish to be part of the Confederacy. West Virginia became its own state, joining the Union in 1863.

Virginia was the site of two events that many historians consider to be virtually the first and last of the Civil War: the First Battle of Bull Run near Manassas, Virginia, in 1861, and Lee's surrender at Appomattox, Virginia, in 1865.

Today, the state is officially called the Commonwealth of Virginia, a status it shares with Kentucky, Massachusetts, and Pennsylvania. However, according to *Merriam-Webster*, the distinction is in name alone.

Virginia's nickname of "Old Dominion" refers to its status as the first permanent English settlement in mainland North America. Its legislature is the nation's oldest continuous lawmaking body.

Today, Virginia is one of the dozen wealthiest states in the nation. Although its tobacco production has steadily been dropping, Virginia is still one of America's top three tobacco-producing states.

Ironically, the Virginia colony was originally planned to produce silk, as seen in a 1650 how-to guide titled *Virginia's Discovery of Silke-Wormes, with Their Benefit and the Implanting of Mulberry Trees*. After a fungus wiped out the trees on which the silkworms fed, Virginians switched their fate and fortunes to tobacco.

URBAN LEGENDS

The **Beale Treasure** continues to be a legend that inspires modern-day believers to grab their shovels along with cryptographic ciphers and head for the hills. As the story goes, in the early 1800s, a Virginia man named Thomas Jefferson Beale buried a treasure, estimated to be worth millions of dollars today, somewhere in Bedford County. Some say he then left town to try finding more loot out west. Beale allegedly left three coded messages as to the treasure's whereabouts in a locked box, which he gave to a friend along with the promise that he'd send the key to the cipher code at a later date. Neither Beale nor the cipher key was ever heard from again. However, in 1885, the three coded messages appeared in a pamphlet for sale to the public at a cost of about $14 in today's money. Since then, treasure hunters have tried their luck at finding Beale's buried treasure, ranging from attempts to conclusively break the code describing its location to simply digging in what they consider to be likely spots. Some sources euphemistically describe the Beale papers as being of "unproven veracity"; others simply call the whole thing a hoax. On the other hand, it has inspired a lot of people to enjoy the Virginia countryside while they dig it up.

Even stately Virginia has its own Bigfoot urban legend, this one called the **Beast of Gum Hill**. The big fellow has generally been reported in the mountainous area of Saltville, Virginia, a municipality with a town motto of "Preserving History for

Over 30,000 Years." The town is named for the nearby salt marshes that are said to have attracted wildlife for centuries, back when the region was populated by Native Americans who hunted there. If those Indigenous people ever spotted Sasquatch alongside their potential dinner, the reports were not documented. In more recent years, a tall hairy creature has allegedly been sighted running around the woods, including by one family group who reported that they saw the beast while they were camping in 1989. A pair of red eyes was spotted peering at them from the bushes. In 2014, a full 25 years later, a man from that very same group claims to have seen a Bigfoot-type creature when he was fishing. He claims that 25 years earlier, he had taken a shot at it, causing the creature to dash off through the woods, leaving it to cross paths with the same gunslinger another day.

Yorktown is famed as the place where the defeat of the British is said to have essentially ended the Revolutionary War. For some, an even more compelling reason to recognize Yorktown is due to the multiple urban legends of **Crawford Road**. The first concerns a brokenhearted bride-to-be who allegedly hanged herself from the road's overpass on her wedding day. Since that time, observers have reported seeing the spectral apparition of a woman in white swaying slowly below the bridge, as if swinging from a noose. Drivers who think they will be safe on Crawford Road if they just lock their doors may be in for a surprise. Some have claimed to feel the sensation of hands on their back or feeling their feet being stepped on. Others report that their car windows inexplicably fogged up, revealing unexplained handprints on the outside. Car batteries have been said to die under the Crawford Road Bridge. Apparitions have also been seen standing in the middle of the road. If drivers turn on soothing music or attempt to drive away demons with head-banging heavy metal, there have been reports that radios and CD players suddenly produce the sound of loud screams or a high-pitched screeching noise as they pass under the bridge, which continues after they drive past. It is said that local police patrol Crawford Road regularly—but they may not be the only ones.

ICONIC VIRGINIA FOOD

With a nod to famed Virginia ham, many sources consider the most iconic dish from the Old Dominion state to be **Virginia Peanut Soup**. Peanuts were grown extensively in the region for centuries. This soup was adapted by enslaved African people during Virginia's early days after being a staple of cuisine in such countries as Gambia and Senegal. Along with being creamy and smooth, this soup is extremely rich, so a small portion goes a long way. For that reason, it is often served in small cups as an appetizer as seen in this recipe:

> **Virginia Peanut Soup** (Yields 12 appetizer servings)
> ¼ cup butter
> 1 medium onion, chopped
> 2 celery stalks (without leaves), chopped
> ¼ cup all-purpose flour

8 cups chicken broth
2 cups smooth peanut butter
1¾ cups light cream
Dash of lemon juice or hot sauce for zestier flavor, if desired
Garnishes such as chopped peanuts, parsley, or sliced green onion, if desired

1. After melting butter in a large pot over medium-high heat, add onion and celery to sauté for 5–7 minutes until soft, but not brown.
2. Stir in flour until well blended, about a minute.
3. Add chicken broth, and bring to a boil, stirring constantly, then lower heat and simmer about 10 minutes until broth thickens slightly.
4. Remove from heat, and then puree.
5. Stir in peanut butter and cream to combine.
6. Simmer over low heat until peanut butter is melted and soup is hot, but not boiling.
7. Stir in lemon juice or hot sauce to taste if desired.
8. Spoon into small individual cups, adding garnish if desired.

Source: Adapted from https://www.theseasonedmom.com/virginia-peanut-soup/#recipe.

ODD LAWS

Virginians who wish to get a little exercise by strolling in the evening may wish to check both the legal statutes and the time of day. Under Virginia law, it is illegal to wander around a cemetery at night. No matter if it's a public or private graveyard, it is unlawful to enter a cemetery at night without specific permission from the proprietor or caretaker as well as the stroller being there for any purpose other than to visit the burial plot of a family member. As the 17th-century poet Andrew Marvell noted, *"The grave's a fine and private place / But none, I think, do there embrace."* In Virginia, Marvell might have included "wandering" as well.

It would be doubly serious if the would-be nocturnal cemetery stroller had to cross a highway to get to the graveyard, choosing to do so in a golf cart. Crossing a highway in a golf cart is unlawful in Virginia, and possibly not survivable if it is one of the busy, high-speed multilane freeways on the outskirts of the Washington, DC, metroplex. There are some exceptions, such as a highway where the speed limit is under 25 mph, although the Capital Beltway speed limit is considerably higher. In other cases, the highway's speed limit could be a maximum of 35 mph, but it is only permissible when the golf cart driver crosses at a traffic light. If population signs are posted, the driver of the golf cart could go joyriding if it is a town with fewer than 2,000 people and if there is a clearly marked golf cart crossing. Should golf cart drivers meet all those criteria, they must also have a valid driver's license, display a sign that says "Slow Moving Vehicle," and make sure they can get across during daylight hours.

Some laws appear odd to modern observers, but have a basis in historical fact that could, in certain instances, be tragic. A case in point is the Virginia statute making it illegal to use x-ray machines for fitting shoes. In the early years of the 20th century, people were excited about new technologies such as x-rays, with some seeing ways to make money. Shoe sellers spread the word that women would be bad mothers if their children's shoes did not fit properly, causing irreparable damage to young feet. Thus, they needed to take the child's measurements by using the store's x-ray machine, a wooden box with an opening for the foot. Often, the mother would use it first to show the child it was perfectly safe. It wasn't. Unbeknown to them, the ensuing x-rays could form a connection between radiation and cancer. Virginia did not pass this law until the 1950s, but it is still on the books in case history repeats itself.

UNUSUAL DESTINATIONS

For those who are not planning to go to England or even take a lengthy American road trip, they can combine three landmarks in one sojourn to Virginia. The first, **Foamhenge**, in Centreville, Virginia, eliminates a trek across the ocean to see Britain's Stonehenge. As may be surmised by its name, the real Stonehenge was constructed from massive columns of stone, each weighing tons. At Foamhenge, an artist built an exact replica of the ancient English monument, although the Virginia version is much lighter since it was created entirely from giant blocks of Styrofoam. Foamhenge is expertly painted to look like actual stone, even seen from a short distance. Some visitors in a position to compare the two landmarks claim that Virginia's Foamhenge is even more photogenic than England's Stonehenge. The good news is that the creators of Stonehenge probably don't mind the snub, being dead for about 5,000 years.

If a pilgrimage to Memphis, Tennessee, is not in the plans, the second destination, **Mini-Graceland** in Roanoke, Virginia, might suffice. Elvis fans should be forewarned that, as the name indicates, Virginia's version of Graceland is a miniaturized facsimile. For example, Virginia's replica of the Graceland pool is around the size of a hospital bedpan, while an average cat strolling by is about as tall as the second story of the mini-mansion. It should go without saying that the Memphis version is significantly larger, being life-size, as befitting the King of Rock and Roll. Mini-Graceland, sometimes known as Elvis City, was created in the 1980s by a family who loved the King, remaining loyal even after Presley passed away in 1977. Constructing it in their yard, they welcomed visitors. In subsequent years, the site passed through various caretakers, such as a local garden club and other family members. Thanks to their care, Elvis fans can't help falling in love with the diminutive, yet heartfelt tribute.

Finally, the only thing **Mount Trashmore** in Virginia Beach has in common with South Dakota's Mount Rushmore is basically a similar-sounding name. But Mount Trashmore has one advantage going for it: some people call it the greatest park ever made of trash, which is high praise indeed. In addition, as opposed to the stony presidential faces on the Mount Rushmore National Monument, which always seem to stay the same, the 165-acre Mount Trashmore Park reinvents itself periodically. Sometimes it's a child-friendly playground; or at other times, it's been a fishing hole; or at still others, it's a skate park. But it's always basically a garbage dump. Mount Trashmore was created by compacting layers of garbage, mixing it with clean soil, and covering it with a thick layer of rubber. Three flagpoles in the park are not only festive and patriotic, but they also act as vents for methane gas that is released by the rotting trash beneath the park's surface. Lightning once struck one of the flagpoles with the result that the gas being vented out of the pole caught fire, which visitors found quite eye-catching.

Honorable mention goes to a farm near Williamsburg, where the **Heads of Former U.S. Presidents**, from George Washington to George W. Bush, look thoughtfully into the distance. These remarkably accurate sculptures are all about the height of a two-story building, and each weighs around 20,000 pounds. They had been the centerpiece of a public park, but when the land was bought, the presidents had to be moved so as not to be destroyed. Although they are now on private property, occasional tours are available. A short documentary, *All the Presidents' Heads*, can be seen at https://www.youtube.com/watch?v=dxX5YYTSBaI for those unable to visit.

DISTINCTIVE VIRGINIA WORDS AND SAYINGS

DMV: Not the folks at the Department of Motor Vehicles, but the District of Columbia, Maryland, and Virginia tristate region.

Kings Dominion: Despite the unusual punctuation, it is not the realm of royalty but what is said to be Virginia's best-loved amusement park.

Metro: Not a reference to an urban area, but the rail transit system for Northern Virginia and Washington, DC, that is never to be called the "subway."

NOVA: Another geographic amalgamation, this one indicating Northern Virginia, home to about half the state's population.

VB: Virginia Beach, boasting 35 miles of coastline, the longest stretch of pleasure beach in the world according to the Guinness World Records.

Further Reading

Colbert, Judy. *Virginia Off the Beaten Path*. 12th edition. Guilford, CT: Globe Pequot, 2019.

Horn, James. *1619: Jamestown and the Forging of American Democracy*. New York: Basic Books, 2018.

Taylor, L. B. *Haunted Virginia: Ghosts and Strange Phenomena of the Old Dominion*. Mechanicsburg, PA: Stackpole Books, 2009.

Wallenstein, Peter. *Cradle of America: A History of Virginia*. Lawrence: University Press of Kansas, 2014.

Washington

FACT BOX

Nickname: The Evergreen State
Statehood Granted: 1889
Capital: Olympia
Population: 7,600,000
State Motto: *Al-ki* (Chinook: translated roughly as "By and By" or "Hope for the Future")
What Natives Call Themselves: Washingtonians

STATE HISTORY

Today's state of Washington is considered by many to be an extremely attractive place to live. Apparently, that was also the feeling in the distant past. In Kennewick, Washington, the remains of a prehistoric resident dubbed Kennewick Man were discovered in 1996. Scientists claim that his skeleton, dating to about 10,000 years ago, is one of the oldest and most complete ever found.

When people of European ancestry began arriving in today's Washington during the late 1700s, the Indigenous tribes they encountered included the Spokane, Suquamish, and Yakama. Although the Native people themselves often did not survive the influx of whites due to disease and/or dislocation, a large number of place-names in Washington reflect the presence of its Native American past.

In 1775, the first documented European to land on the Washington coast was Don Bruno de Heceta, an explorer from Spain. He declared that the Pacific Ocean was a "Spanish lake," and therefore, everything it touched belonged to Spain—at least according to Don Bruno.

Other European countries saw things differently. An English fur trader named Charles William Barkley arrived in 1787, leading to disputes over the territory between Britain and Spain. By the early 1800s, Spain was backing away from its claims of exclusivity to the region.

Traders and settlers came from Europe and Russia, as well as the United States, which won its independence from England in 1783 after the American Revolution.

The American government dispatched a group of explorers called the Corps of Discovery, but more popularly known as the Lewis and Clark Expedition. They entered today's state of Washington in 1805. Paddling canoes down the Columbia

River, it was the final leg of their cross-country journey, which would eventually lead to their arrival on the coast of the Pacific Ocean.

As the 1800s progressed, there were ongoing territorial disputes in the Pacific Northwest between Britain and the United States. However, by the mid-1800s, the United States felt secure enough in its ownership to start naming various locales in the region.

In 1853, there was a proposal for the Northwestern territory to be named "Columbia" in honor of the Columbia River, which was vital to the region. However, a U.S. congressman objected, finding that name to be too similar to the District of Columbia, the nation's governmental zone on the East Coast.

The name that was adopted instead was "Washington." It is not known if the same U.S. congressman who objected to "Columbia" protested again, on the grounds that the proposal of "Washington" also duplicated the name of the nation's capital of Washington, DC.

The naming issue came up again in 1889 when the territory was in the process of seeking statehood. Some people proposed the state name to be "Tacoma" to avoid confusion with the nation's capital. However, things were ultimately just left as they were.

Many residents of the state in the Pacific Northwest consider their home turf to be *the* Washington, while they refer to the nation's capital by its full designation of "Washington, DC," or, simply, "DC." Elsewhere, the state of Washington is sometimes referred to as "Washington State" to make sure everyone understands which is which.

Today's Washington remains the only U.S. state named after a president: in this case, George Washington, the nation's first.

In 1889, Washington became the 42nd state to join the Union. It continued to prosper through the lumber industry until the early decades of the 20th century brought a new economic engine to the state: power itself. To produce electricity, hydroelectric dams were constructed as part of President Franklin Roosevelt's New Deal public works program during the Great Depression. They included Washington's massive Grand Coulee Dam on the Columbia River, built in 1933.

The small town of Tenino, Washington, attained national fame during the Great Depression of the 1930s and continues to be of interest for its unique approach to economic hard times. Like many around the United States, Tenino's local bank closed in the Depression. The town may not have had a lot of cash on hand, but it did have plenty of wood. Utilizing its abundant supply of lumber, the town's government began issuing a temporary form of money called "scrip" that was made from thin slices of wood. The idea was for people to use it to keep the livelihoods of local residents afloat. Ironically, most of the wooden money was never redeemed, becoming a latter-day collector's item.

Fortunately, with Microsoft headquarters and other high-tech industries located in the state, such economic hard times may not be a threat in Washington's immediate future.

Look to the Skies!

Proving the phrase "Timing is everything," several unfortunate coincidences occurred in Washington one night in 1938. Hydroelectric power meant that residents in remote areas of the state had radios, bringing programs to them from around the country. On October 30, 1938, there was a radio broadcast of *The War of the Worlds* by Orson Welles and his Mercury Theatre. The fictional account of a Martian invasion sent many Americans into a panic. In Concrete, Washington, a poorly timed thunderstorm and transformer explosion at the local power plant during the broadcast plunged the town into darkness. Despite the heavy downpour, some of the 1,000 residents of Concrete ran through the streets in terror, while others fled into the mountains to hide. By morning, news media and public officials managed to get the word out that the invasion was fictitious, leaving a wake of anger and embarrassment among townspeople. But at least, they were safe from Martians . . . for the time being.

URBAN LEGENDS

At the popular Pike Place Market in Seattle, people's attention is sometimes diverted from the famed flying fish in time to see the **Indian Princess of Pike Place**. The legend is that the ghost of Princess Kikisoblu, renamed Angeline in English, appears at the market. She was said to have been born near today's Seattle in the early 1800s as the daughter of Chief Seattle of the Suquamish people. As she grew, her angelic beauty and regal bearing inspired her to become known as Angeline. In the 1850s, the U.S. government forced her people onto a reservation far from their home. However, she was granted permission to stay in Seattle and was allowed to live in a cabin near today's Pike Street. The story is that nowadays, people at Pike Place Market occasionally see an old Native American woman sitting on a blanket with woven baskets for sale. When would-be shoppers approach her, they find that the lady has completely vanished.

An allegedly bottomless pit called **Mel's Hole** is said to exist near Ellensburg, Washington. According to the story, a man named Mel Waters called in to a radio show claiming that there was a bizarre sinkhole on his property that had strange powers, including the ability to being the dead back to life—at least deceased canines. The man said he had thrown his dead dog into the hole only to see the same dog come sauntering by soon afterward, very much alive and looking unperturbed at having been tossed into the abyss. The reanimated hound did not reveal how he made it out of the deep pit, so Mel began an investigation. Tying fishing line together, he said he let it go down at least 15 miles before touching bottom (or running out of fishing line, depending on the story). Mel is said to have been a frequent caller on the radio show, gaining a following until a local newspaper reported that there was no evidence of anyone named Mel Waters living in the area. Apparently miffed at having his identity questioned, Mel stopped his call-ins, never revealing to listeners the exact location of the pit. However, it is said that since its existence was not entirely disproven, people still visit what they believe is the approximate site to try finding this life-saving sinkhole.

A number of other states boast legends of a Bigfoot-type creature on their turf. However, when it comes to large hairy monsters, the **Sasquatch** of Washington may be the superstar of this genre. It is said that there have been more reported sightings of the creature in Washington than anywhere else. Some tally the total number of observations to more than 500. The reports go back to the days when Indigenous people lived in the Pacific Northwest. In fact, the Sasquatch name is said to have been derived from the word "Sasquits" in the language of the Salish people. After white settlers arrived, they heard the stories. Reports claimed that seven-foot-tall humanoids were seen stalking the woods and mountains. The hairy creatures frightened campers, hikers, and even manly lumberjacks, who sometimes became quite hairy themselves. At least two municipalities in Washington, Skamania County and Whatcom County, have passed ordinances declaring themselves to be a Sasquatch protection and refuge area. In addition, the Western Air Defense Sector, Washington Air National Guard, adopted Bigfoot as its mascot. This military unit claims that it monitors the skies of almost three-quarters of the United States and Canada, adding that much like the Bigfoot of legend, they are rarely seen or heard, but with their motto of "BELIEVE in Preparedness," they quietly observe.

ICONIC WASHINGTON FOOD

Despite New York's claim to being called the "Big Apple," Washington is the nation's top apple producer. In addition, with Washington's official fruit being the apple, many people feel it best represents the Evergreen State. By the early 1800s, settlers discovered that Washington's apple crop was being well nourished by the fertile soil that was rich in lava ash. With cool mountain water, plus an arid climate that led to fewer disease and insect problems, Washington became known for ideal apple growing conditions and bountiful orchards. Today, the state provides the nation with such varieties as Fuji, Gala, Granny Smith, Honeycrisp, Pink Lady, and Delicious, the latter in both red and golden varieties. This recipe for **Washington Apple Pie** from the Washington Apple Commission (motto: "No Other Apple Comes Close") shows off the state fruit to its best advantage:

> **Washington Apple Pie** (Serves 8)
> 2 prepared crusts for 9-inch pie
> 6 golden delicious apples, peeled, cored, and sliced thin
> ¼ cup sugar
> 2 Tbsp flour
> 1 tsp vanilla extract
> ½ tsp cinnamon

¼ tsp ground ginger
⅛ tsp ground mace
2 Tbsp butter
Small saucer of cream or whole milk

1. While heating oven to 425°F, line a 9-inch pie pan with half the crust pastry.
2. In a large bowl, combine apples, cinnamon, flour, ginger, mace, sugar, and vanilla; toss well until blended.
3. Transfer apple mixture to pastry-lined pie pan, and dot with butter.
4. Cover apple filling with remaining pastry; pinch together edges of bottom and top crust to seal.
5. Brush top crust with cream or milk, then cut several slits to vent steam.
6. Bake 20 minutes at 425° before lowering heat to 375° and baking 30–35 minutes more or until apples are tender.

Source: Adapted from https://bestapples.com/recipes/classic-apple-pie-2/.

ODD LAWS

There is a Washington law on the books that would-be grunge rockers in the adolescent age range may wish to know. It concerns traveling in the family car with parental figures. Along with toddlers, the law states that young people under four feet nine inches tall and younger than age 13 must be secured in a booster seat. When transporting a surly preteen who is under 13 years old, the driver must make sure the young person is in the back seat "where it is practical to do so." An exception can be made if the vehicle only has lap belts, such as those found in older cars that were made prior to 2007, as opposed to the more recent diagonal shoulder harness. Large preteens taller than four feet nine inches can evade the mandate, while many others may presumably want their parents drop them off well away from their junior high as they climb out of their booster seat.

Fans of the movie *Ferris Bueller's Day Off* as well as many adult members of the workforce are familiar with the tactic of "calling in sick" from school or work. If they actually are exhibiting symptoms of a condition such as the common cold, Washingtonians experiencing a guilty conscience about doing so should be relieved to know that they are simply doing their civic duty by staying home. Washington law states that people with an infectious disease (such as what is called the common cold) must avoid contact with others, even on the street, and must not expose anyone to the symptoms without their knowledge. The statute declares the crime to be a misdemeanor, but does not elaborate on the penalty, possibly not wishing to add to the misery of a cold sufferer.

Last, but certainly not least, according to the law in Washington's Skamania County, a particular life-form called Bigfoot or Sasquatch is considered to be an endangered species. Therefore, it is against the law for individuals in that county who come across the creature to kill it. There is a $1,000 fine as well as possible jail time for up to a year. When the law was enacted in 1969, the fine could be up to $10,000 plus up to five years in jail, so the fervor for Bigfoot-related criminalization may have ebbed in the last half century. Fortunately for some people, provisions of the law also protect innocent large, hairy humans who may be mistaken for Sasquatch.

UNUSUAL DESTINATIONS

At Goldendale, Washington, there sits a French chateau, an odd museum, and a replica of England's Stonehenge. They were part of a proposed utopian community that failed to attract utopians. The **Maryhill Museum of Art and Stonehenge** was built by a gentleman named Sam Hill, who some credit with being the basis for the expression "What the Sam Hill?" (i.e., "What on earth is going on here?"). Mr. Hill was a Quaker who dreamed of establishing a peace-loving Quaker community in Washington during the early 1900s. He provided the funding, but few other Quakers were as interested as he was. Nevertheless, he proceeded with the construction of a mansion overlooking the Columbia River in a rough approximation of a French Chateau. Today, that mansion houses the Maryhill Museum of Art, which is a bit more eclectic than most. There is artwork from the Belle Époque (French for "beautiful age") of the late 1800s, including original sketches, statues, and plasters by Auguste Rodin, famous for his sculpture *The Thinker*. Visitors will also come upon unusual chess sets, unique furniture, and Native American baskets. Hill was friends with the exiled Queen Marie of Romania, who donated her crown jewels, Orthodox icon collection, royal artifacts, throne, and wedding dress. Outside, it is the full-scale replica of England's Stonehenge that attracts much attention. Built in 1918 to honor those who died in the carnage of the First World War, it is said to be the earliest World War I memorial in North America.

Seattle's distinctive landmark, the 600-foot tall Space Needle, was opened in 1962. Amid the nation's "Space Race," the iconic observation tower was created as part of that city's 1962 World's Fair. (Photoquest/Dreamstime.com)

Death of a different kind inspired the **Nutty Narrows Bridge** in Longview. Called the

World's Narrowest Bridge, it is only wide enough for squirrels to cross in order to avoid the automobile traffic below. Local citizens noticed that the animals had to run across a busy street to find food, with many perishing in the attempt. After obtaining approval from the city council, compassionate people pooled their resources to build the bridge in 1963. It is said that adult squirrels have been observed instructing their young on the art of using the overpass instead of trying to cross the traffic-filled street in a display of youthful bravado that could be their last.

It takes a certain amount of bravado to open an establishment such as the **Rubber Chicken Museum** in Seattle, but it has become almost as much of a crowd-pleaser as seeing someone assaulted with a fake fowl in the name of comedy. Among the plastic poultry is said to be the world's largest rubber chicken as well as the world's smallest. According to the museum's website, the institution is intended to be more than just a chuckle-fest by including what is said to be a scholarly essay by a renowned rubber chicken expert that puts the artifact in its proper historical context. Brave souls are encouraged to inquire about the owner's locked "Room 6" collection in which some sort of secret treasures are kept.

In South Bend, Washington, which calls itself "the Oyster Capital of the World," the **World's Largest Oyster** can be found. This concrete sculpture of a halved oyster shell is said to be a must-see for a photo opportunity when passing through South Bend. Being free, it's a pearl of a deal.

DISTINCTIVE WASHINGTON WORDS AND SAYINGS

Cascade Concrete: Hard, icy snow found in the Cascade Mountains, where it melts during the day and refreezes at night.

Needle: Nothing to do with a vaccination, but rather the iconic 600-foot-tall Space Needle that has been a Seattle landmark since it opened in 1962.

STP: The annual 200-mile Seattle-to-Portland bike ride that attracts thousands of riders.

"The Mountain is out": A day in rainy Washington when it is clear enough to see Mount Rainier.

Vancouver: Not the Canadian city but the one in Washington that was founded in 1825, predating Canada's version by more than 60 years.

Volcano, the: Mount St. Helens, Washington's active volcano that erupted in 1980 and has been the site of volcanic activity ever since, although it remains popular with fearless hikers.

Further Reading

Hardina, Nicole. *Little Washington: A Nostalgic Look at the Evergreen State's Smallest Towns.* Cambridge, MN: Adventure Publications, 2020.

Kirk, Ruth, and Carmela Alexander. *Washington's Past: A Road Guide to History*. Seattle: University of Washington Press, 1995.

Ritter, Harry. *Washington's History, Revised Edition: The People, Land, and Events of the Far Northwest*. Portland, OR: WestWinds Press, 2003.

West Virginia

> **FACT BOX**
> **Nickname:** The Mountain State
> **Statehood Granted:** 1863
> **Capital:** Charleston
> **Population:** 1,800,000
> **State Motto:** *Montani semper liberi* (Latin: "Mountaineers Are Always Free")
> **What Natives Call Themselves:** West Virginians or Mountaineers

STATE HISTORY

In the Mountain State's distant past, today's West Virginia was a favored hunting ground for a number of Indigenous tribes. Archaeological research has pointed to evidence of human habitation in West Virginia dating back more than 12,000 years.

Thousands of archaeological sites, such as ceremonial mounds built by ancient mound builders, have been unearthed in West Virginia.

In subsequent centuries, Native American cultures evolved from nomadic tribes to those that established communities near rivers and streams. Eventually, the powerful Iroquois tribe arose, claiming regions in today's West Virginia as their hunting ground. Other tribes, such as the Cherokee and Shawnee also claimed those lands, with the Iroquois driving many others out of the region by the mid-1600s.

However, there were developments on the East Coast that were going on at the same time, making strife between warring Native American tribes an exercise in futility.

After Jamestown, Virginia, was founded by England in 1607, today's West Virginia was considered part of the Virginia Colony. By the early 1700s, it was not only English settlers who arrived in the colony's western mountains but also Germans, who founded a settlement called New Mecklenburg, or today's Shepherdstown, West Virginia. There was a steady flow of white settlers, both from Europe and from other nearby colonies such as Pennsylvania.

In the latter 1700s, survey teams from Eastern Virginia traveled the western mountainous region. There, they encountered neither a plantation economy nor the kind of relatively sophisticated society that could be found in the east.

Inhabitants in the western part of the colony led a hardscrabble existence in small isolated communities scattered in the mountains.

Based on the surveyors' findings that the mountainous west was a completely different entity from the tidewater east, there were proposals to create a fourteenth American colony in the current West Virginia. The name put forward at that time was "Vandalia." It was a nod to the wife of England's King George III, Queen Charlotte, who claimed descent from the Vandals of Europe through her German ancestry.

The Vandalia plan was put forward in 1774, just when revolutionary fervor was heating up, making King George and his family unpopular in America. Vandalia did not come to be.

In the watershed year of 1776, another proposal was put forward to create a new state in the mountains of Western Virginia. Although its proponents came up with another name, "Westsylvania," it also did not come to pass. From the time of the American Revolution to the Civil War, today's West Virginia remained part of the state of Virginia.

After the Civil War began in 1861, Virginia seceded from the Union. However, the residents of Western Virginia felt that the state's government was controlled by wealthy tidewater plantation owners from the east. Most inhabitants of the western part of the state were small farmers who carved out their existence in the hills, thinking of themselves not as elite planters but as simple "mountaineers."

Therefore, at the Wheeling Conventions of 1861, counties in today's West Virginia voted to become an independent entity, breaking away from the Confederate state of Virginia. This time it worked—they succeeded in seceding from secession.

With combat already taking place in the Civil War, the U.S. government saw the benefit of adding a new state to the Union. This time around, there were a number of proposed names from which to choose. These included Allegheny, Augusta, Columbia, New Virginia, Western Virginia, and West Virginia. Vandalia was proposed again, and Kanawha had a lot of support, but ultimately West Virginia was chosen.

West Virginia was admitted to the Union in 1863 as the 35th state, an occasion that represented a number of unique elements. West Virginia was the only state east of the Mississippi to be admitted to the Union during the Civil War. It was admitted under a directive from President Abraham Lincoln, the only state to be admitted to the Union under a presidential proclamation. It was the only one to be formed by seceding from a Confederate state and was the first to be created by separating from an existing state since Maine had split from Massachusetts in 1820.

West Virginia was hit particularly hard by the Civil War, with the state sending about an equal number of soldiers both to the Union and to the Confederate armies. West Virginians were therefore often fighting each other, personifying the tragedy of "brother against brother."

After the war, West Virginia developed an economy based in large part on its natural resources such as coal mining, an industry that continues to this day.

> ### Heavenly
>
> In 2014, West Virginia named "Take Me Home, Country Roads" as its official state anthem. The move proved so popular that in 2018, the state's tourism campaign centered around the song with its iconic verse "Almost Heaven, West Virginia." In 2021, the state's new vacation guide was a special edition celebrating the 50th anniversary of the song's release. The tune is one of the most beloved from singer John Denver, who recorded it in 1971. Along with "Rocky Mountain High" in Colorado, it is the second official state song credited to Denver, who died in 1997. "Take Me Home, Country Roads" has been called a perfect love letter to the state, with the line "Almost Heaven, West Virginia" being known to millions worldwide who can sing along from memory. Today, the song is played at athletic events and other functions in West Virginia, even some funerals. At football games, fans are encouraged to sing the song along with the team. Perhaps if the late John Denver has made it past "almost" Heaven to the real thing, he must be proud.

In perhaps the ultimate bad neighbor situation, after the Civil War, the state of Virginia, from which West Virginia had separated, bore a grudge. It claimed that West Virginia owed a large debt from before the war. When West Virginia declined to pay, it became a heated issue between the two states. The squabble escalated all the way to the U.S. Supreme Court in 1915. The court ruled that West Virginia owed $12 million, plus interest. The then-astronomical sum is the equivalent of about $312 million in 2020. It took West Virginia until 1939 to pay it off.

URBAN LEGENDS

According to the legend of the **Dingess Tunnel**, the mile-long underpass is inhabited by the souls of those who perished there. It was built in 1892 for the railroad, which at the time was the only way to connect the remote mountain community of Dingess with the rest of the world. It was a world to which some local inhabitants did not wish to be connected. Legend has it that the locals shot anyone who looked different from them, especially African American and Chinese laborers tasked with hacking the tunnel out of the unforgiving rock. Townsfolk also killed about 20 lawmen who were charged with keeping the peace. Many workers died during the tunnel's construction, and at least two trains collided inside the narrow shaft. Today, it is an automobile tunnel in which drivers report hearing the sounds of wailing and seeing ghosts within its dark, narrow rock walls.

A dark night in 1952 proved to be a memorable one in the small community of Flatwoods, West Virginia, giving birth to the legend of the **Flatwoods Monster**.

The story goes that some local boys saw a bright light in the sky and headed in the general direction to investigate. Near the spot where they assumed it had landed, they saw pulsating red lights. Amid the glow, they then reported seeing a monster with a black humanoid body that was at least 7–10 feet tall. It too seemed to glow and was reported as floating above the ground. The monster then allegedly let out a shriek and flew toward them, causing the boys to scatter. Later investigations reported that the bright light was most likely the same meteor that was also seen in other states that night. Their findings suggested that the red lights came from an aircraft or a hazard beacon, as well as the speculation that the creature was a barn owl perched on a tree limb. Nonetheless, the town embraced the legend, erecting several "monster chairs" as a photo opportunity for tourists.

The superstar of West Virginia monster lore is the Mothman. The huge winged creature crossed with a humanoid was first reported in 1966. In recognition, West Virginia hosts an annual Mothman Festival. (Seenunseen/Dreamstime.com)

The Flatwoods Monster Museum and annual "Flatwoods Days" festival also pay homage to this legend, which maintains its hold on the town.

As intriguing as other West Virginia urban legends may be, the superstar in the Mountain State's monster lore is no doubt the **Mothman**. Hailing from Point Pleasant, this hybrid of a huge winged creature crossed with a humanoid was first sighted in 1966 by several men who were said to be digging a grave at a cemetery. They reported that a winged creature flew out from the nearby trees, soaring over their heads. A few days later, two couples reported seeing a winged monster with glowing red eyes. After the word got out, more sightings were reported, eventually totaling about a hundred through 1967. Due to its insect-type wing configuration, the creature was dubbed the Mothman. Even after the 1960s passed into history, the Mothman lived on as an urban legend. His reputation was no doubt enhanced by a 1975 book called *The Mothman Prophecies* and a 2002 horror film of the same name. Both combine the Mothman legend with theories about unidentified flying objects (UFOs) and supernatural phenomena, making it even more memorable.

ICONIC WEST VIRGINIA FOOD

When it comes to the state food of West Virginia, some people might picture biscuits and gravy, buckwheat pancakes, skillet corn bread, or other down-home country dishes. In fact, the actual winner is the **West Virginia Pepperoni Roll**, in which the down-home country in question is Italy. It is said to have been created by a baker in Fairmont, West Virginia, in 1927. He was an Italian immigrant whose previous job was mining. There, he had seen other miners needing a simple but tasty lunch they could carry in their pockets and eat with one hand if need be. His creation, the Pepperoni Roll, became so iconic of West Virginia that it is commemorated in the town of Fairmont by a historical marker from no less than the West Virginia Humanities Council and has inspired not one but two annual festivals.

> **West Virginia Pepperoni Rolls** (Yields 12)
> 1 package frozen "thaw, rise, and bake" yeast dinner rolls
> 6 oz pepperoni, sliced
> 16 oz shredded mozzarella cheese
> Small bowl of butter, melted

1. After spraying baking sheet with nonstick cooking spray, place 12 frozen dough balls on the baking sheet.
2. Cover dough balls with plastic wrap that has also been sprayed with nonstick spray before letting dough thaw completely, approximately two hours.
3. After dough has thawed, press each ball into a flat disc, and spread four pepperoni slices in the center of the dough.
4. Top pepperoni slices with about a tablespoon of mozzarella.
5. Roll the dough into a cigar shape, folding ends inward.
6. Spray a 9 by 13 baking dish with nonstick spray, and place each pepperoni roll on it, seam side down.
7. Allow the dough to rise until it doubles in size, about an hour.
8. Place into a 350°F oven for 25–30 minutes.
9. Immediately brush each pepperoni roll with melted butter when they have finished baking, then let cool in the pan before serving.

Source: Adapted from https://www.thekitchenwife.net/2018/06/simple-west-virginia-pepperoni-rolls.html.

ODD LAWS

The abundant natural beauty of West Virginia can sometimes leave a person feeling breathless as well as having worked up quite a thirst. People who are in the mood to buy a refreshing soft drink should know that under the law, their purchase will help increase the state's coffers by about a penny. As part of West Virginia code, soft drinks are subject to an excise tax not only on bottled nonalcoholic beverages, carbonated or not, but also on syrups and dry mixes to make them. The statute is quite specific, naming names: the brands Coca-Cola, Dr. Pepper, and Pepsi Cola are called out, along with carbonated water, fruit juice, ginger ale, lemonade, lemon/lime sodas, orangeade, root beer, and soda water.

If people in West Virginia happen to get into a debate regarding the fairness of taxing their soft drink, they may wish to settle their differences verbally if they plan to run for public office in the Mountain State. A legislative statute in West Virginia makes it clear that a person who has ever participated in a duel may not hold public office. Would-be public servants are prohibited from doing so whether the altercation with deadly weapons takes place either in-state or elsewhere. Neither shall they act as a second, nor they knowingly assist in such a duel. In West Virginia, the penalty is being barred from holding any office "of honor, trust or profit in this state."

Some lists of alleged "silly laws" often list one in West Virginia that may seem unusual on the surface but has a darker backstory. It can be found under a 2005 West Virginia statute titled, "Display of Red or Black Flag Unlawful." The lawmakers did not necessarily have anything against those color schemes. The statute prohibits the display of any "flag, emblem, device or sign" that indicates support for hostility against the state of West Virginia or the Constitution of the United States, which those flags are said to do.

UNUSUAL DESTINATIONS

Average Americans enduring a nuclear attack in the Cold War era as they huddled underground in cramped fallout shelters may have been surprised to learn that the U.S. Congress continued legislating in the lap of luxury. Accommodations in the huge subterranean **Congressional Fallout Shelter** at the Greenbrier Resort in White Sulphur Springs, West Virginia, even contained underground chambers for the House and Senate to meet. During the nuclear scare of the 1950s, members of Congress secretly arranged for a spacious taxpayer-funded shelter to protect themselves beneath the luxurious Greenbrier. Their spouses and children were not invited. It was a state secret until 1992 and today is a tourist attraction that is often called the "Graceland of Atomic Tourism." Amid the amenities of the shelter, there was a special room to calm members of Congress who needed to be soothed. There are those who say it's lonely at the top, or in these underground accommodations, the bottom.

Guests of the Greenbrier with its mineral baths have traditionally called their stay "taking the waters." A spa experience of a different kind is found at **George Washington's Bathtub** in Berkeley Springs, West Virginia, called "the only outdoor monument to presidential bathing." When the future first president was a young surveyor, he is said to have enjoyed relaxing in the local warm spring baths that were carved out of stone. Apparently, he liked it so much that he bought property there and returned periodically for a good soak, although it is not known if those dips included his wife Martha. Sticklers for historical accuracy may wish to note that the current version of Washington's Bathtub is a modern replica since his actual stone soaking spot has been lost over time. The waters, however, are a reasonable facsimile of the ones that have poured out for eons. In the month of March, an annual event is held at Berkeley Springs to mark Washington's first dip back in 1748.

There are those who might say that West Virginia's most famous urban legend deserves a venerable institution in his honor, and the **Mothman Museum** in Point Pleasant fits the bill. This museum is said to be the only public collection devoted solely to the mysterious monster that was reported in West Virginia in the 1960s, giving Bigfoot some serious competition in the weird creature niche. At the museum, the mystery of the Mothman is documented through newspaper clippings from the time of the alleged sightings as well as other memorabilia. Perhaps coincidentally, the museum gift shop includes a book about the Mothman written by the museum's owner. A military discount is offered at the facility, which is the focal point of the annual Mothman Festival each September. A 12-foot-tall metallic statue of the Mothman creature is nearby for those who wish total immersion in the cryptid-related experience.

A hushed honorable mention goes to the town of **Green Bank,** West Virginia, which is billed as a place for "Wi-Fi Refugees." Due to a nearby astronomical facility, no electronics are allowed in Green Bank. That prohibition includes what is called cellular radiation from devices such as laptops and smart phones. Green Bank, populated by fewer than 200 people, is located in the National Radio Quiet Zone, with transmissions being restricted by law. That law is enforced by "radio police" who use specialized equipment to detect outlawed electronics.

DISTINCTIVE WEST VIRGINIA WORDS AND SAYINGS

Eers! Visitors to West Virginia University athletic events wonder why fans shout the name of auditory organs. They don't—it's "Eers," short for the school's nickname, "Mountain*eers*."

Holler: Nothing to do with yelling, these are the remote valleys, or "hollows" of mountains where many small West Virginia communities were built.

Poke: If a West Virginian wants one, it means a bag to put something in, not sticking that person with a finger.

Ramp hunting: Forget the parking garage, this is a springtime search for ramps, the wild onions for which West Virginia is famous.

Sauce'n'slaw: Pronounced as a one-word request, it's the preferred topping on a true West Virginia hot dog, indicating chili and coleslaw.

Further Reading

Snell, Mark. *West Virginia and the Civil War: Mountaineers Are Always Free.* Charleston, SC: History Press, 2011.
Steelhammer, Rick. *West Virginia Curiosities: Quirky Characters, Roadside Oddities and Other Offbeat Stuff.* Guilford, CT: Globe Pequot, 2010.
Swick, Gerald. *West Virginia Histories: Unique People, Unusual Events, and the Occasional Ghost.* Nashville, TN: Grave Distractions Publications, 2017.

Wisconsin

FACT BOX

Nickname: The Badger State, also known as America's Dairyland
Statehood Granted: 1848
Capital: Madison
Population: 5,900,000
State Motto: "Forward"
What Natives Call Themselves: Wisconsinites

STATE HISTORY

Wisconsin earned its name from the Native American dialect. With the Kickapoo, Ojibwa, Pottawatomie, and Winnebago living there for generations, the term was first applied to the Wisconsin River. However, before the word "Wisconsin" reached its present spelling, it went through a multilingual transformation.

Today's Wisconsin attracted its first inhabitants dating back to the end of the Ice Age, about 12,000 years ago. The retreat of the glaciers left Wisconsin with an appealing landscape of forests and waterways, attracting large prehistoric creatures such as mammoths and mastodons. Eventually, they were followed by nomadic human hunters, visualizing dinner.

Even after the large prehistoric mammals died out, later Indigenous people in today's Wisconsin thrived on fishing as well as hunting smaller animals like deer and bison. They were also able to grow crops such as beans, corn, and squash. Communities emerged along Wisconsin's waterways.

After thousands of years, life in today's Wisconsin would eventually change. In 1634, the first-known European in the region was the Frenchman Jean Nicolet. His mission was to establish a fur trading network with the Native people and, incidentally, to find a water route to Asia.

Traveling via canoe, Nicolet indeed found huge bodies of water, but they were the Great Lakes, not the Pacific Ocean.

French explorer Jacques Marquette became the first European documented to have reached the Wisconsin River, which he did in 1673. His journal recorded the word "Ouisconsin," Marquette's interpretation of the Native pronunciation of the waterway.

The French established a network of fur trading posts throughout the region, but following France's defeat in the French and Indian War in 1763, Britain won control. The French "Ouisconsin" was anglicized by the British into "Wisconsin."

Like the French, the British at that time were more interested in the fur trade than permanent colonial settlements. After Britain lost the territory to the United States in the War of 1812, America's presence was established in today's Wisconsin.

Early pioneers were enticed by Wisconsin's rich deposits of lead. Mining replaced fur trading, with wheat farming also helping to sustain new groups of permanent settlers.

The Wisconsin Territory was formally created in 1836, when the completion of the Erie Canal helped bring more settlers westward into the region. The territorial legislature made the current spelling of Wisconsin official in 1845, and in 1848, Wisconsin entered the Union as its 30th state.

During the antebellum era, Wisconsin was a center of abolitionist sentiment. Following an 1854 incident in which Wisconsinites helped a runaway slave escape to Canada, the Wisconsin Supreme Court declared the nation's Fugitive Slave Law unconstitutional.

After the Civil War, Wisconsin farmers moved from wheat to dairy production, which was more profitable. Since that time, cows and their by-products have been a cornerstone of the state, popularly known as "America's Dairyland."

Today, Wisconsin has more dairy cattle per square mile than anywhere in the United States. About 90 percent of the milk is used to make cheese, producing more cheese than any other state. The town of Monroe, Wisconsin, claims to be the only place in America that produces the strong-smelling cheese known as Limburger.

Wisconsin residents can eat their cheese and wear it too. Big yellow "cheesehead" hats are often worn to support the state's Green Bay Packers football team. (Hannah Babiak/Dreamstime.com)

Wisconsinites can eat their cheese and wear it too, in the form of big yellow "cheesehead" hats in support of the state's Green Bay Packers football team.

During the 20th century, Wisconsin's natural beauty spurred the growth of tourism. This was especially the case in the early 1900s when Wisconsin's breezy lakes and rivers attracted urbanites from nearby cities such as Chicago, Detroit, and Milwaukee escaping the summer heat.

In 1962, one Wisconsin town attracted something else, when a 20-pound piece of the Russian satellite Sputnik IV crash-landed in Manitowoc. Determining it was not

> ### A "Capital" Investment
>
> Wisconsin has its share of towns that are self-proclaimed "Capitals of the World," such as Bloomer (Jump Rope Capital of the World), Mercer (Loon Capital), Mount Horeb (Troll Capital), Norwalk (Black Squirrel Capital), and Park Falls (Ruffed Grouse Capital). Possibly because a piece of *Sputnik* chose to land in Wisconsin, the state boasts *three* towns that call themselves the UFO Capital. Belleville, Dundee, and Elmwood, Wisconsin, each point to alien encounters that boost their claim. Belleville cites reports of mysterious lights in the sky in 1987 that were allegedly backed up by local police. Dundee boasts the additional element of a crop circle and what is said to be an alien in a jar, which was ostensibly found in a cave near the legendary UFO hotspot of Roswell, New Mexico. Elmwood asserts that a local police officer got up close and personal with what was said to be a flying saucer, not once, but twice, with a few Elmwood residents reporting that their television sets went out for 10 minutes around that same time. Incidentally, all three towns have annual UFO events to underscore their "Capital" status, at least with tourists.

a hostile attack, the town currently celebrates its moment in the Space Race with an annual Sputnikfest.

The Badger State also holds a cherished place in American culture with the make-believe town of Willows, Wisconsin, being the fictional hometown of the Barbie doll.

URBAN LEGENDS

Few states do *not* claim to have their own homegrown Bigfoot-type creature, and Wisconsin is no different—except that it has an **Abominable Snowman**. In 1998, some teenage boys were said to be walking in the woods when they heard a horrific shriek. The boys saw a shaggy white creature running toward them in pursuit. They sprinted away, evading capture. It was later said that around the same time, the mother of one of the boys claimed she also heard a weird sound. She described it as being similar to a train going by, although there was no known rail traffic in the area at that time. The story gained a greater following on the internet when an alleged announcement from the Wisconsin Department of Natural Resources made the rounds. The official-looking bulletin declared that there were recent Sasquatch sightings around the Kettle Moraine State Forest, so campers should be on the alert. It suggested that vacationers making contact with the abominable beast should not try to run but instead should stay calm. It also encouraged them to take a photograph if possible, noting the time and area of the sighting. No time-stamped photos were turned in by unruffled campers, and the post turned out to be false.

According to legend, the **Hodag** is a frightening creature with dinosaur-like spines down its back and large horns on its head. Featured prominently in Paul Bunyan stories, the Hodag is said to have been born from the ashes of oxen that had been cremated. According to an 1893 newspaper article in the town of Rhinelander where it was said to have been discovered, the Hodag had sharp claws on thick, short legs; a horned frog's head; and the face of a grinning elephant. Adding greater credibility, a group of locals posed for a photo standing around what looked like the charred remains of something undetermined. Their leader, a local surveyor, said they had required dynamite to kill the monster. A few years later, the same man claimed he used chloroform to subdue another Hodag, which he then captured alive. After the story was repeated nationally, scientists from the Smithsonian are said to have announced they would go to Wisconsin to inspect the discovery. Before they arrived, the surveyor admitted his Hodag story was a hoax.

Several Wisconsin towns have legends of highway hauntings. The **Phantom Hitchhiker** on the highway around Baraboo has been reported as thumbing a ride. After driving past the hitchhiker in his tattered green jacket, drivers who decline to pick him up look back in their rearview mirror and are astonished to find him gone. But the Phantom Man in the green jacket keeps being reported on the roadside, waiting for a ride that never stops. Wedding nights can prove fatal, as drivers on the **Stevens Point Bloody Bride Bridge** may attest. According to legend, a newlywed couple drove over the bridge on a rainy night just after their wedding but had a terrible auto wreck in which the new bride was killed. Soon after, there were reports of the deceased bride in her bloody wedding dress wandering forlornly across the bridge at night, noting that she could be seen most often in rearview mirrors on rainy nights. A further would-be corroboration of the tale involves an alleged police officer who thought he ran over a woman and went back to help her. Running to the point of impact, he claimed that surprisingly, no one was there.

ICONIC WISCONSIN FOOD

Visitors to Wisconsin hearing the word "Booyah!" accompanied by a fist pump can be sure is it something good. **Booyah** is both a celebratory expression and a thick soup or stew to keep Wisconsinites warm in winter. Cooks in the Badger State maintain that there is no wrong way to make it, as it can contain any combination of beef, chicken, pork, and vegetables. The recipe below is a standard example. The name is said to be the result of a misspelling after a local reporter asked a cook who had prepared the dish for a potluck dinner how to spell "bouillon," one of the ingredients. The response was "b-o-o-y-a-h," which is how it was printed in the newspaper. The name stuck.

Wisconsin Booyah (Yields about 8 qt)
3 Tbsp olive oil
1 lb boneless, skinless chicken thighs
1 lb beef stew meat

1 lb pork loin meat
1½ cups chopped onion
1 Tbsp coarse salt
½ tsp pepper
1 beef bouillon cube
4 cups water
1½ cups sliced celery
1½ cups chopped carrots
1½ cups shredded cabbage
2½ lb chopped potatoes
2 (14.5 oz) cans diced tomatoes
1 cup frozen green beans
1 cup frozen corn
1 cup frozen peas
4 cups water, divided
2 bay leaves
1 Tbsp Worcestershire sauce
½ Tbsp soy sauce
Oyster crackers as topping

1. In a large pot, heat olive oil to medium-high, then add meat and onions, allowing to simmer about five minutes.
2. Combine with salt, pepper, bouillon cube, and half the water, bringing it to a boil.
3. Cover pot, reduce heat, and simmer for two hours, breaking up meat as needed.
4. Add vegetables, bay leaves, remaining water, and Worcestershire and soy sauces, simmering for two more hours.
5. After removing the bay leaves, serve hot with oyster crackers on top.

ODD LAWS

Wisconsin famously calls itself America's Dairyland, so it should come as no surprise to learn that its lawmakers take matters concerning dairy products rather seriously. The Badger State also has a certain attitude toward nondairy items. It's against state law to substitute margarine, a non-dairy-based substance, for butter in a restaurant unless the customer specifically requests it. Also under state law, it is prohibited to provide margarine to schoolchildren or to prisoners, as well as to hospital patients unless a doctor has ordered it. Those committing a first offense risk being fined between $100 and $500 and/or being jailed for up to three months. Repeat offenders could face a fine of $500–$1,000 and up to a year in prison, where, under the law, they will *not* be served margarine.

As noted previously, Wisconsin's lawmakers make it their business to protect the Badger State's dairy industry since it is such a vital part of the state's economy.

According to the Wisconsin Department of Agriculture, Trade and Consumer Protection, there are strict guidelines in place to maintain the integrity and reputation of Wisconsin cheese. Under the rules, cheese is presented in distinct legal terms. For example, the formal definition of "cheese" is that it is a dairy product prepared from the pressed curd of milk. There is a section of the law governing specific requirements for the taste of different cheeses. Wisconsin's Grade AA cheddar must be "highly pleasing," while Grade B cheddar need only be "fairly pleasing." However, there are no definitions provided for those terms, so "highly pleasing" and "fairly pleasing" might be in the eye (or taste buds) of the beholder. This could prove daunting for individuals who never met a cheese they didn't like.

Moving away from the green pastures of dairy cows, there are also laws in Wisconsin that apply to the green lawns of homeowners. The municipal code in Sheboygan states that it is unlawful for the city's residents to "sprinkle their property in any manner to the distress or annoyance of others." It should be noted that there is no restriction on watering one's lawn, but doing so cannot annoy the fellow Sheboyganite next door. The statute does not spell out exactly what would constitute such aggravation, but presumes that Sheboyganites would know it when they see it.

UNUSUAL DESTINATIONS

At the **Bobblehead Hall of Fame and Museum** in Milwaukee, thousands of bobblehead figures nod and wobble their way into the hearts of visitors. It claims to be the world's only repository entirely dedicated to bobbleheads, providing a helpful historical perspective to the evolution of this popular head-nodding doll. Among the diminutive bobbling depictions of celebrities, politicians, sports figures, and cartoon characters, there is also a six-foot-tall bobblehead. However, for many visitors, the chance to design a custom-made plastic bobbler in their own likeness proves to be a heady experience. The museum claims to house the world's largest collection of bobbleheads from all genres and periods, with exhibits illustrating how bobbleheads are made. As part of the museum's mission, the National Bobblehead Hall of Fame invites nominations for an annual slate of the "best of the best." Many bobbleheads nod, but few are chosen to join this plastic pantheon. The museum shop conveniently offers merchandise for sale, not surprisingly including a wobbling rainbow of bobbleheads.

One of the most touching sights in the Badger State is **Fred Smith's Wisconsin Concrete Park** in the town of Phillips. Untrained in art, Fred Smith worked most of his life as a lumberjack, but had to retire for health reasons. At age 62, he began creating sculptures out of concrete, placing them in his field. For decoration, he used shards of broken beer bottles, of which Wisconsin is said to have quite a few. His body of work eventually grew to more than 200 concrete sculptures, with subjects encompassing figures from folklore, history, and nature along with animals, lumberjacks, miners, soldiers, and sweethearts. Smith's artwork can best be described as primitive, in the sense that the high-priced paintings of Grandma

Moses were considered primitives. Even though the figures that Smith made are boxy-looking and extremely unrealistic, most visitors feel it only adds to their charm.

Anyone hoping to spice up their trip to Wisconsin should squeeze in a visit to the **National Mustard Museum** in Middleton. The collection includes displays of more than 6,000 varieties of mustard from all around the world. The exhibits are categorized as both contemporary and historical, so there are lots of items for visitors to relish. Touches of whimsy are pure gold, such as a movie screening area called "MustardPiece Theatre" where guests can get a taste of the film *Mustard: The Spice of Nations*. Also on display are hundreds of items including antique mustard pots, memorabilia, mustard tins, and a tasteful array of vintage mustard ads. Mustard aficionados find a honey of an experience at the museum's Tasting Bar where the museum's Confidential Condiment Counselors will curate personalized palate-pleasers. Mustard fans may wish to schedule their trip to the museum on the first Saturday in August, which is National Mustard Day. At this annual jamboree, museum staffers spread themselves thin by painting the town yellow for the event, which can be both spicy and sweet.

It should be noted that the Mustard Museum was originally located in the town of Mount Horeb, Wisconsin, until it moved to nearby Middleton. However, Mount Horeb can still bask in the golden glow of fame, billing itself as the **Troll Capital of the World**. Described by many as "weirdly wonderful," the community is decorated with dozens of painted wooden trolls. These goblin-type figures originating in Scandinavian folklore can be seen scattered throughout town. Many inhabit Mount Horeb's Main Street, which has been dubbed the Trollway. That is only fitting, since it was the coming of a four-lane bypass that threatened the town's economy by leaving Mount Horeb in the dust. When some local shop owners placed several eye-catching trolls outside their store, they attracted both customers and visitors. An idea was born, with Mount Horeb developing into a troll-based tourist destination. It is only fair to warn easily spooked visitors that not all the little hobgoblins are made of wood—some seem to have magically come to life in the person of a costumed mascot who trolls the streets during local events such as the town's annual Troll Fest.

DISTINCTIVE WISCONSIN WORDS AND SAYINGS

Dells: Neither a popular line of computers nor places where "The Farmer" of nursery rhyme fame hangs out, but Wisconsin's "Waterpark Capital of the World" that is said to attract about 4 million visitors each year.

"Start with me last": Someone in a group of Wisconsinites who cannot seem to decide what to order in a restaurant.

Stop 'n' go lights: What people in places outside the Badger State refer to as traffic lights.

TYME machine: Not a portal to another era, but the former name for ATMs in Wisconsin that stands for "Take Your Money Everywhere." Even after the provider changed to another interbank network with a different name, TYME stood still in Wisconsin.

Further Reading

Godfrey, Linda S. *Haunted Wisconsin: Ghosts and Strange Phenomena of the Badger State.* Mechanicsburg, PA: Stackpole Books, 2010.

Janik, Erika. *A Short History of Wisconsin.* Madison: Wisconsin Historical Society Press, 2010.

McCann, Dennis. *The Wisconsin Story: 150 People, Places, and Turning Points That Shaped the Badger State*. 2nd edition. Madison: Wisconsin Historical Society Press, 2019.

Wyoming

FACT BOX

Nickname: Equality State
Statehood Granted: 1890
Capital: Cheyenne
Population: 580,000
State Motto: "Equal Rights"
What Natives Call Themselves: Wyomingites

STATE HISTORY

Trivia buffs may wish to note that Wyoming is the least densely populated state in the contiguous United States. Also, it is one of only two—the other being Colorado—whose geographical shape is a neat rectangle.

Wyoming retains much of the flavor of the Old West. It is not difficult to imagine the isolation that early settlers felt, even amid the scenic splendor of the state's rugged mountains and vast prairies.

For centuries, today's Wyoming provided wide open spaces for Native American tribes such as the Arapaho, Crow, Lakota, and Shoshone. They depended on migratory animals such as bison for their food, clothing, shelter, and tools. By following the great herds of bison, also known erroneously today as buffalo, the Indigenous people generally lived a nomadic life, residing in tepees that could easily be moved from place to place.

They did not know that events taking place thousands of miles away would eventually decimate them. Through the 1700s and early 1800s, the land was claimed by European countries including Spain, France, and Great Britain, soon to be followed by Mexico and the United States.

However, Wyoming generally remained sparsely settled through the late 1700s, serving as the domain of roaming French Canadian trappers who traversed the region. Their presence can be seen today at places in Wyoming named from the French language such as the Belle Fourche River, Grande Téton Mountains, and Gros Ventre River. Even the fabled Old West town of Laramie was named for Jacques La Ramée, a French Canadian trapper.

That would all begin to change in the early 1800s. As part of the Louisiana Purchase in 1803, the United States bought the Louisiana Territory from France, a huge piece of real estate that included a large part of Wyoming.

Historians note that explorer John Colter, a member of the Lewis and Clark Expedition, entered Wyoming in 1807. Colter, known as the first documented "mountain man," veered off from the others on the famed expedition to explore on his own. He discovered today's Yellowstone with its remarkable geysers, although at first it was thought that his reports of such astonishing natural wonders were merely tall tales. He was vindicated 65 years later when Yellowstone was designated as the nation's first national park in 1872. In fact, it was the first national park in the world and can boast more geysers than any other geyser field around the globe.

The first permanent settlement in Wyoming was Fort Laramie, which was established in 1834. At the end of the Mexican War in 1848, portions of the territory were ceded by Mexico to the United States. It is said that more than a hundred thousand people traveled through Wyoming between 1840 and 1870 on their way west. Many stayed.

The Wyoming Territory got its name from a U.S. congressman from Ohio named James M. Ashley who proposed "Wyoming" in 1865. He had been born in Pennsylvania where he became familiar with the state's Wyoming Valley, the subject of a popular 1809 poem titled "Gertrude of Wyoming." After actually visiting today's state of Wyoming, the lawmaker discovered it was nothing like Pennsylvania. He was dismayed by Wyoming's towering mountains and other non-Pennsylvania-like features. Nevertheless, the name stuck.

Following the end of the Civil War, the growth of the transcontinental railroad brought more people to the Wyoming Territory. Some remained in permanent settlements, while others tried their hand at mining the region's rich natural resources. However, mining was often a boom-and-bust endeavor. Once-vibrant mining communities turned into ghost towns, with Wyoming's population remaining sparse and often "wide open" for outlaws who could hole up in its remote canyons.

Women were seen as essential for permanent settlement, which was required for eventual statehood. To attract more females as well as to foster the growth of families, the Wyoming Territory was the first in the nation to extend voting rights for women, which it did in 1869.

Wyoming was admitted into the Union as the 44th state in 1890. Its women had been voting for more than half a century before 1920, when American women nationwide earned the right to vote.

In 1925, Wyoming carried it a step further when Nellie Tayloe Ross became the first female governor in the United States.

No look at Wyoming can omit Devil's Tower. Many people around the world became familiar with this extraordinary mountain formation due to the hit film, *Close Encounters of the Third Kind*, with a focal point of the plot being this legendary Wyoming landmark.

When Harry Met Leroy

The hit movie *Butch Cassidy and the Sundance Kid* launched a young actor named Robert Redford into megastardom. Redford's movie role as the Sundance Kid led to his founding such cultural institutions as the Sundance Institute for Film Studies as well as the annual ultra-trendy Sundance Film Festival. Wyoming played a role in it all. After stealing a horse in 1887, a young small-time criminal named Harry Alonzo Longabaugh served 18 months in a Wyoming jail, his first and only prison time. After his release, the 20-year-old was a full-fledged outlaw. Calling himself the Sundance Kid, Longabaugh went on to make an important connection when he met Robert Leroy Parker, a fellow criminal. Parker became better known as Butch Cassidy, with Longabaugh gaining fame as a sharpshooter under the name of the small town where he had been in jail: Sundance, Wyoming.

Wyoming is home to the famous rock formation called Devil's Tower. In the classic film, *Close Encounters of the Third Kind*, this legendary Wyoming landmark was a focal point of the plot. (Corel)

URBAN LEGENDS

With all its mountains and deep woods, it is not surprising for Wyoming to claim a **Bigfoot**-type creature prowling its vast expanses. It is said that Bigfoot has been spotted at several places in Wyoming, including Snow King Mountain, Teton Forest, Wind River Mountains, and even the venerable Yellowstone. At the latter location, there is a grainy photo online of four bears allegedly being stalked by Bigfoot, although the Sasquatch in the shot could also be a shadow. There have been unverified reports of a large hairy creature commandeering campsites, but no reliable photo has captured his image. It is said that the most common misidentifications have come from seeing large bears, of which Wyoming has plenty.

According to a Wyoming legend that began in the early 1800s, the **Death Ship of the Platte River** appears in a miasma of thick, white mist, with a ghostly crew aboard that is covered in frost. From those tell-tale signs, it should be obvious this is no pleasure cruise. Encountering the ship is said to foreshadow death on the same day. An additional detail is that observers on the riverbank can see their own corpse on the deck of the ship. A variation is that the person will not necessarily see their own corpse, but one belonging to a loved one who will soon die. One story cites a trapper who sighted the ship and spied the body of his fiancée lying on the deck. Believing her to be safe and well at home, he discounted the omen until later that day when his unfortunate ladylove inexplicably passed away.

It is said of the **Lady in Green** that during frontier days, when Fort Laramie served as a trading post, the commander brought his daughter with him to take up residence. Because of the area's unsettled conditions, he would not allow her to ride her horse away from the post. One day when he was away, she disobeyed him. Wearing a long green riding habit, she took her black stallion outside the post for a ride. When the father returned, to his horror he learned that both horse and rider had vanished. The legend grew that her ghost appears every seven years, riding the trail near Fort Laramie. Mounted atop her phantom black stallion, she can be seen wearing the same green riding attire as the day she disappeared. It is not known why she apparently chose this particular "seven year itch" as her time frame to reappear.

With its charming name, the **Sweetwater County Library** in Green River would seem to be an unlikely candidate for dark doings. But that is exactly the case. It opened its doors in 1980, having been built on top of a former graveyard. Since that time, the library is said to have experienced such unusual activity as books inexplicably flying off the shelves, computers turning on and off by themselves, objects being moved, light switches being turned on without any human touch, and strange noises where "Silence" should be the rule. None of this is standard library procedure. There are reports by staffers and patrons who say they heard their name being whispered. The site on which the library was built was Green River's city cemetery. The cemetery was moved to a different location and its occupants thought to have been removed for burial elsewhere, but more remains were unearthed on the property during construction. The library sponsors Ghost Walk tours in October, just in time for Halloween. Although the alleged spirits of the former occupants under the building are honored in that way, it is not known if they are offered library privileges.

ICONIC WYOMING FOOD

Many Wyomingites think of one of their favorite comfort foods, **White Chicken Chili**, as a kinder, gentler version of Texas chili. The Wyoming variety calls for relatively mild chile peppers, especially Hatch chiles, which some cooks feel offer an ideal balance of sweetness and spice. For heat-seekers, extra chile peppers can be added. The dish can also be made with chopped pork instead of chicken if so desired. This recipe calls for a slow cooker, although a large stock pot simmering on low could be also used. Topping the dish with Monterey Jack cheese makes it ideal on a cold Wyoming night.

> **White Chicken Chili** (Yields 4–6 servings)
> 2 cups chopped boneless, skinless chicken
> 1 Tbsp extra-virgin olive oil
> 1 medium onion, chopped (about 1½ cups)
> Dash salt and freshly ground pepper to taste
> 2 cloves garlic, minced
> 2 Tbsp chile powder
> ¼ tsp cayenne pepper
> 1½ tsp ground cumin
> 3 cups chicken stock, leftover or canned
> 8 oz Hatch chiles, fresh, freeze-dried, or canned
> 2 (15-oz) cans white beans, drained
> 1 bay leaf
> 1½ cups grated Monterey Jack cheese
> ⅓ cup fresh cilantro, coarsely chopped
>
> 1. In a large, heavy frying pan, heat chicken in oil over medium heat, slightly browning the meat.
> 2. Add onion, salt, and pepper, sautéing until onion is soft.
> 3. Add garlic, chile powder, cayenne, and cumin, stirring together for 2–3 minutes.
> 2. Transfer contents to slow cooker or stock pot, adding chicken stock, chiles, beans, and bay leaf. Allow to cook for 6–8 hours.
> 3. Remove bay leaf before serving the chili in bowls, with Monterey Jack topping and cilantro garnish.

Source: Adapted from https://farmflavor.com/recipes/white-bean-chicken-chili/.

ODD LAWS

Those who misquote a certain Wyoming law allege that all new buildings must allocate 1 percent of their cost to artwork. That interpretation only has a tenuous relation to the actual law, which was passed in 2013. The law pertains to state-funded government buildings, and only those that cost over $100,000. It also states that while the public art displays should cost an amount equal to 1 percent of the building's total construction costs, the artwork itself cannot tip the financial scales at more than $100,000.

Some spurious websites devoted to "silly laws" claim that Wyoming makes it unlawful to wear a hat that blocks people's view in places of entertainment. Either it was a statute that was on the books in the past when all men and women wore hats outside the home, some of which were on the large side, or Wyomingites are courteous and would remove a gigantic hat anyway, making such a law unnecessary. However, a current Wyoming law does deal with obstructing someone's sight lines, just not while watching a movie. It is unlawful for passengers to ride in a vehicle in such a manner that they interfere with the driver's ability to see in front or on the sides. The statute also specifies that having more than three people in the front seat is unlawful, if not uncomfortable. The law neglects to address visibility behind the vehicle, possibly in the mindset of many race car drivers, that what's behind you is not important. Of course, that does not pertain to vehicles with a siren and blue lights.

It is not known that there was a widespread practice that made such a statute necessary, but under a 2013 Wyoming law, a junk dealer may not do business with a person who appears to be intoxicated. The law applies the prohibition to anyone buying or selling junk metals, rubber, rags, or paper. The ruling also applies if a junk dealer is caught doing business with an individual who is a known thief or has been convicted of larceny. Even if the junk dealer claims ignorance of the seller's rap sheet, the stolen property must be returned at no charge to its rightful owner.

UNUSUAL DESTINATIONS

A mysterious circle of stones called the **Bighorn Medicine Wheel** at Lovell, Wyoming, is said to have been built by Native Americans centuries ago to predict astronomical events. Sitting at an altitude of more than 10,000 feet, it is covered by heavy snow most of the year. Only in the summer months does the rock pattern reveal itself. Measuring 80 feet across, the stones are arranged in the shape of a wheel with 28 spokes emanating from the ring-shaped pile of rocks at its center. While most sources believe the wheel's purpose was astronomical, it is said that it was also used in ceremonial rituals. Experts studying the formation state that the Bighorn Medicine Wheel is an accurate predictor of the summer solstice. The site is a registered National Historic Landmark and is monitored by an archaeologist through the summer. Visitors are not discouraged from coming to see it, although they are asked to respect the site and not disturb it.

At the **Parting of the Waters** in Moran, Wyoming, an average-looking creek is actually the source of a remarkable phenomenon. Water that flows in the creek here has a 50/50 chance of ending up either in the Atlantic Ocean to the east or the Pacific Ocean to the west. In other words, a well-informed trout could choose between its desired destination by heading for either the Atlantic or the Pacific when the stream splits in two. Two small tributaries grow ever larger, flowing into rivers that are progressively bigger the farther they run. Heading west, the 1,353-mile trip would take the aforementioned trout to the Pacific via the Snake and

Columbia Rivers. The other route is considerably longer, almost 3,500 miles that would take the fearless fish to the Yellowstone, Missouri, and Mississippi Rivers and finally the Gulf of Mexico to the Atlantic.

Near Cheyenne, Wyoming, sits the only accessible Peacekeeper Missile Alert Facility left in the nation. The **Quebec 01 Missile Alert Facility** was operated as a nuclear launch site by the U.S. Air Force from the Cold War era of 1964 to its waning days in 2005. Being repurposed, it opened to the public in 2019 as a museum to educate people about the Cold War and the military strategy of nuclear deterrence. Visitors can get a taste of what it was like to work 50 feet underground on a day-to-day basis while maintaining readiness to launch nuclear warheads, which Air Force personnel had to anticipate at any given moment. Knowledgeable staffers conduct tours of the facility, which the Wyoming State Parks department says was "hidden in plain sight."

As seen through the statuary around Douglas, Wyoming, the history of the jackalope is a tangled one. That backstory is even more significant since the creature is completely mythical, but that does not stop the citizens of Douglas from venerating it. Calling itself the "**Jackalope Capital of the World**," the town is the unofficial birthplace of the make-believe creature. Jackalopes were "born" in the 1930s when local taxidermists attached antelope horns to the stuffed dead bodies of jackrabbits. They created a niche market by selling them as Western décor to area hotels, no doubt dazzling impressionable tourists from the East. This decorating trend caught on. Jackalopes, some with deer antlers if the supply of antelopes ran low, flourished as wall mountings throughout Wyoming. As the epicenter of this ornamental boom, Douglas is home to several monuments in its honor. The town's original "World's Largest Jackalope" statue was eventually mangled by a car. A taller, sturdier concrete statue was erected in the town's Jackalope Square, where it remained as the largest until a version that was five feet taller appeared on a hill overlooking Douglas. Townspeople discovered that the hilltop's taller figure was only a black silhouette, clamoring for something more substantial. A larger one today proudly looks over the town, which offers jackalope hunting licenses, although the hunting season is only on June 31 (a month with 30 days). Incidentally, a jackalope logo was adopted by the Wyoming Lottery for its lottery tickets, with the tagline, "Just Maybe."

DISTINCTIVE WYOMING WORDS AND SAYINGS

Bison: What the rest of the country calls a buffalo. Wyomingites know better.

Cold and Wind: The two seasons that are said to be found in Wyoming.

Devil's Tower: Nothing evil about what is arguably the most recognizable rock formation in America.

Dout: What Wyomingites do to put out their campfire, similar to the word "douse," and having nothing to do with dubiousness.

Greenies: Visitors to Wyoming from Colorado, with its distinctive green license plates. Not usually a positive reference.

Snowsuit: Warm apparel that in other states might be worn by children, but which Wyomingites of all ages keep in their vehicle all year, "just in case."

Further Reading

Holscher, Patrick T. *On This Day in Wyoming History*. Charleston, SC: History Press, 2014.
Larson, T. A. *History of Wyoming*. 2nd edition. Lincoln: University of Nebraska Press, 1990.
Rainey, Alli. *Wyoming*. Woodstock, VT: Countryman Press, 2012.

Appendix A: Timeline of the Thirteen Original English Colonies

1. Massachusetts

In 1606, King James I of England grants a charter to establish two colonies on the East Coast of North America: Jamestown to the south and Popham in the north.

Popham Colony is established in 1607 at present-day Phippsburg, Maine, but due to cold weather, poor relations with the Natives, and lack of food, it is abandoned in 1608.

Plymouth Colony in Massachusetts is established in 1620.

Massachusetts Bay Colony is established at Salem in 1630.

Province of Maine is established in 1622 by the Council for New England; patent is reissued by England's King Charles I in 1639.

Province of Maine is absorbed by Massachusetts Bay Colony in 1658.

Plymouth Colony and Massachusetts Bay Colony merge in 1691.

2. Virginia

Chartered in 1606 by the London Company, becomes first permanent English colony in the New World after the founding of Jamestown, Virginia, in 1607.

3. New Hampshire

Province of New Hampshire is established in 1629, merges with Massachusetts Bay Colony in 1641 and rechartered as royal colony in 1679.

4. Maryland

Established in 1632 with charter granted to Lord Baltimore to provide religious toleration for England's Roman Catholics.

5. Connecticut

Saybrook Colony is established in 1635.

Connecticut Colony is formed at Hartford in 1636.

New Haven Colony is founded in 1638.

Saybrook Colony merges with Connecticut Colony in 1644.

New Haven Colony merges with Connecticut Colony in 1664.

6. Rhode Island

Providence Plantations is established by Roger Williams in 1636.

Portsmouth settlement is founded in 1638.

Newport settlement is created in 1639 after split with Portsmouth.

Warwick settlement is founded in 1642.

Providence, Portsmouth, Newport, and Warwick settlements merge to form the Colony of Rhode Island in 1663.

7. Delaware

Established as an English colony in 1664 after British seize New Netherland from the Dutch.

8. New York

Established as an English colony in 1664 after British seize New Netherland from the Dutch.

9. New Jersey

Established as English colony in 1664 after British seize New Netherland from the Dutch.

10. North Carolina

Province of Carolina is established in 1663, splits into North Carolina and South Carolina in 1712, with North Carolina rechartered as royal colony in 1729.

11. South Carolina

Province of Carolina is established in 1663, splits into North Carolina and South Carolina in 1712, with South Carolina rechartered as royal colony in 1729.

12. Pennsylvania

Established in 1681 by royal land grant to William Penn, a Quaker, who seeks religious freedom for Quakers.

13. Georgia

Carved out of South Carolina by King George II in 1732 with charter granted to James Oglethorpe who envisions a colony for "the worthy poor" and prisoners jailed for debt.

Appendix B: Quick Reference Guide to Statehood Dates and State Capitals

State	Statehood Granted	Capital
Alabama	1819	Montgomery
Alaska	1959	Juneau
Arizona	1912	Phoenix
Arkansas	1836	Little Rock
California	1850	Sacramento
Colorado	1876	Denver
Connecticut	1788	Hartford
Delaware	1787	Dover
Florida	1845	Tallahassee
Georgia	1788	Atlanta
Hawaii	1959	Honolulu
Idaho	1890	Boise
Illinois	1818	Springfield
Indiana	1816	Indianapolis
Iowa	1846	Des Moines
Kansas	1861	Topeka
Kentucky	1792	Frankfort
Louisiana	1812	Baton Rouge
Maine	1820	Augusta
Maryland	1788	Annapolis
Massachusetts	1788	Boston
Michigan	1837	Lansing

APPENDIX B

State	Statehood Granted	Capital
Minnesota	1858	Saint Paul
Mississippi	1817	Jackson
Missouri	1820	Jefferson City
Montana	1889	Helena
Nebraska	1867	Lincoln
Nevada	1864	Carson City
New Hampshire	1788	Concord
New Jersey	1787	Trenton
New Mexico	1912	Santa Fe
New York	1788	Albany
North Carolina	1789	Raleigh
North Dakota	1889	Bismarck
Ohio	1803	Columbus
Oklahoma	1907	Oklahoma City
Oregon	1859	Salem
Pennsylvania	1787	Harrisburg
Rhode Island	1790	Providence
South Carolina	1788	Columbia
South Dakota	1889	Pierre
Tennessee	1796	Nashville
Texas	1845	Austin
Utah	1896	Salt Lake City
Vermont	1791	Montpelier
Virginia	1788	Richmond
Washington	1889	Olympia
West Virginia	1863	Charleston
Wisconsin	1848	Madison
Wyoming	1890	Cheyenne

Selected Bibliography

INTRODUCTION

Englebert, Robert, and Guillaume Teasdale (editors). *French and Indians in the Heart of North America, 1630–1815*. East Lansing: Michigan State University Press, 2013.

Hakim, Joy. *A History of US: The First Americans: Prehistory–1600* (Book One). New York: Oxford University Press, 2007.

Hakim, Joy. *A History of US: Making Thirteen Colonies: 1600–1740* (Book Two). New York: Oxford University Press, 2007.

Hakim, Joy. *A History of US: From Colonies to Country: 1735–1791* (Book Three). New York: Oxford University Press, 2007.

Remini, Robert. *A Short History of the United States: From the Arrival of Native American Tribes to the Obama Presidency*. New York: Harper Perennial, 2009.

Sapp, Rick. *Native Americans State by State*. New York: Chartwell Books, 2018.

Thomas, Hugh. *The Golden Empire: Spain, Charles V, and the Creation of America*. New York: Random House, 2011.

ALABAMA

Bridges, Edwin C. *Alabama: The Making of an American State*. Tuscaloosa: University of Alabama Press, 2016.

Encyclopedia of Alabama. Accessed November 7, 2021. http://www.encyclopediaofalabama.org/.

Lacey, T. Jensen. *Amazing Alabama: Amazing Stories, Historical Oddities and Fascinating Tidbits from the Yellowhammer State*. Fairhope, AL: Moon Howler Publishing, 2019.

Wilson, Mary Johns. *100 Things to Do in Alabama before You Die*. St. Louis, MO: Reedy Press, 2019.

ALASKA

Borneman, Walter. *Alaska: Saga of a Bold Land—From Russian Fur Traders to the Gold Rush, Extraordinary Railroads, World War II, the Oil Boom, and the Fight over ANWR*. New York: HarperCollins, 2003.

Rennicke, Jeff. *National Geographic Treasures of Alaska: The Last Great American Wilderness*. Washington, DC: National Geographic, 2010.

Ritter, Harry. *Alaska's History: The People, Land, and Events of the North Country*. Portland, OR: Alaska Northwest Books, 1993.

State of Alaska. Accessed November 7, 2021. https://alaska.gov/.

ARIZONA

Guinn, Jeff. *The Last Gunfight: The Real Story of the Shootout at the O.K. Corral and How It Changed the American West*. New York: Simon & Schuster, 2011.

Heller, Chris. "Whatever Happened to the Wild Camels of the American West?" *Smithsonian*, August 6, 2015. https://www.smithsonianmag.com/history/whatever-happened-wild-camels-american-west-180956176/.

Sheridan, Thomas E. *Arizona: A History*. Revised edition. Tucson: University of Arizona Press, 2012.

State of Arizona. Accessed November 7, 2021. https://az.gov/.

Trimble, Marshall. *Arizona Oddities: Land of Anomalies and Tamales*. Charleston, SC: History Press, 2018.

ARKANSAS

Anderson, Layne. *Haunted Legends of Arkansas: Thirteen Historic Sites in the (Super) Natural State*. Little Rock, AR: Plum Street Publishers, 2016.

Encyclopedia of Arkansas. Accessed November 7, 2021. https://encyclopediaofarkansas.net/.

Hendricks, Nancy. *Senator Hattie Caraway: An Arkansas Legacy*. Charleston, SC: History Press, 2013.

Jones, Janie, and Wyatt Jones. *Arkansas Curiosities: Quirky Characters, Roadside Oddities and Other Offbeat Stuff*. Guilford, CT: Morris Book Publishing, 2010.

CALIFORNIA

Bishop, Greg, Joe Oesterle, and Mike Marinacci. *Weird California: Your Travel Guide to California's Local Legends and Best Kept Secrets* (Volume 7). New York: Sterling, 2009.

California State Guide. Accessed November 11, 2021. https://www.ca.gov/.

Hoover, Mildred, and Hero Rensch. *Historic Spots in California*. 4th edition. Palo Alto, CA: Stanford University Press, 1990.

Starr, Kevin. *California: A History*. New York: Modern Library, 2007.

COLORADO

Colorado Encyclopedia. Accessed November 11, 2021. https://coloradoencyclopedia.org/.

Dallas, Sandra, and Kendal Atchison. *Colorado Ghost Towns and Mining Camps*. Norman: University of Oklahoma Press, 1988.

Ferguson, William M. *The Anasazi of Mesa Verde and the Four Corners*. Boulder: University Press of Colorado, 1996.

Wyckoff, William. *Creating Colorado: The Making of a Western American Landscape, 1860–1940*. New Haven, CT: Yale University Press, 1999.

CONNECTICUT

Boynton, Cynthia Wolfe. *Connecticut Witch Trials: The First Panic in the New World*. Charleston, SC: History Press, 2014.

Connecticut. Accessed November 11, 2021. https://www.ctvisit.com/.

D'Agostino, Thomas, and Arlene Nicholson. *Connecticut Ghost Stories and Legends*. Charleston, SC: History Press, 2011.
Schechter, Stephen (editor). *Roots of the Republic: American Founding Documents Interpreted*. Lanham, MD: Rowman & Littlefield, 1991.

DELAWARE

Colbert, Judy. *Maryland and Delaware Off the Beaten Path: A Guide to Unique Places*. 9th edition. Guilford, CT: Globe Pequot, 2010.
Munroe, John A. *History of Delaware*. Newark: University of Delaware Press, 1993.
Official Website of the First State. Accessed November 11, 2021. https://delaware.gov/.
Wiener, Roberta, and James R. Arnold. *Delaware: The History of Delaware Colony, 1638–1776*. Chicago, IL: Raintree, 2005.

FLORIDA

Clark, James C. *Hidden History of Florida*. Charleston, SC: History Press, 2015.
Knowlton, Christopher. *Bubble in the Sun: The Florida Boom of the 1920s and How It Brought on the Great Depression*. New York: Simon & Schuster, 2020.
Lower, Catherine, and Cynthia Thuma. *Haunted Florida: Ghosts and Strange Phenomena of the Sunshine State*. Mechanicsburg, PA: Stackpole Books, 2008.
Visit Florida. Accessed November 12, 2021. https://www.visitflorida.com/en-us/visitor-services.html.

GEORGIA

McDonald, Jonah. *Secret Atlanta: A Guide to the Weird, Wonderful, and Obscure*. St. Louis, MO: Reedy Press, 2020.
Michaels, Brenna, and T. C. Michaels. *Hidden History of Savannah*. Charleston, SC: History Press, 2019.
Miles, Jim. *Weird Georgia: Close Encounters, Strange Creatures, and Unexplained Phenomena*. Nashville, TN: Cumberland House, 2000.
New Georgia Encyclopedia. Accessed November 12, 2021. https://www.georgiaencyclopedia.org/.

HAWAII

Allen, Helena G. *The Betrayal of Liliuokalani: Last Queen of Hawaii 1838–1917*. Honolulu, HI: Mutual Publishing, 1991.
Kapanui, Lopaka. *Haunted Hawaiian Nights*. Honolulu, HI: Mutual Publishing, 2005.
Loomis, Jim. *Fascinating Facts about Hawaii*. Honolulu, HI: Watermark Publishing, 2019.
Official Website of the Aloha State. Accessed November 12, 2021. https://portal.ehawaii.gov/index.html.
Queen Liliuokalani. *Hawaii's Story by Hawaii's Queen*. Honolulu, HI: Hui Hanai, 2013.

IDAHO

Visit Idaho. Accessed November 12, 2021. https://visitidaho.org/.
Weeks, Andy. *Forgotten Tales of Idaho.* Charleston, SC: Arcadia Publishing, 2015.
Weeks, Andy. *Haunted Idaho: Ghosts and Strange Phenomena of the Gem State.* Mechanicsburg, PA: Stackpole Books, 2013.
Young, Virgil. *The Story of Idaho: Millennial Edition.* Caldwell, ID: Caxton Press, 1990.

ILLINOIS

Encyclopedia of Chicago. Accessed November 12, 2021. http://www.encyclopedia.chicagohistory.org/pages/467.html.
Enjoy Illinois. Accessed November 12, 2021. https://www.enjoyillinois.com/.
Johnson, Raymond. *Chicago History: The Stranger Side.* Atglen, PA: Schiffer Publishing, 2014.
Kleen, Michael. *Haunting Illinois: A Tourist's Guide to the Weird and Wild Places of the Prairie State.* Holt, MI: Thunder Bay Press, 2014.

INDIANA

Indiana. Accessed November 12, 2021. https://www.visitindiana.com/.
Nunemaker, Jessica. *Little Indiana: Small Town Destinations.* Bloomington, IN: Quarry Books, 2016.
Wicentowski, Danny. "The Final Flight of Martin McNally." *Riverfront Times*, January 11, 2017. https://www.riverfronttimes.com/stlouis/the-final-flight-of-martin-mcnally/Content?oid=3137418.
Willis, Wanda Lou. *Haunted Hoosier Trails: A Guide to Indiana's Famous Folklore and Spooky Sites.* Covington, KY: Clerisy Press, 2004.

IOWA

Bergman, Marvin (editor). *Iowa History Reader.* Iowa City: University of Iowa Press, 2008.
Maulsby, Darcy Dougherty. *A Culinary History of Iowa: Sweet Corn, Pork Tenderloins, Maid-Rites and More.* Charleston, SC: History Press, 2016.
Pohlen, Jerome. *Oddball Iowa: A Guide to Some Really Strange Places.* Chicago: Chicago Review Press, 2005.
Travel Iowa. Accessed December 10, 2021. https://www.traveliowa.com/.

KANSAS

Coopers, Beth. *Ghosts of Kansas.* Atglen, PA: Schiffer Publishing, 2010.
Kansapedia. Accessed November 12, 2021. https://www.kshs.org/kansapedia/kansapedia/19539.
Zink, Adrian. *Hidden History of Kansas.* Charleston SC: History Press, 2017.

KENTUCKY

Hogeland, William. *The Whiskey Rebellion: George Washington, Alexander Hamilton, and the Frontier Rebels Who Challenged America's Newfound Sovereignty.* New York: Simon & Schuster, 2010.

SELECTED BIBLIOGRAPHY

Klotter, James, and Craig Thompson Friend. *A New History of Kentucky*. Lexington: University Press of Kentucky, 2018.
Ludwick, Cameron, and Blair Thomas. *My Old Kentucky Road Trip: Historic Destinations and Natural Wonders*. Charleston, SC: Arcadia Publishing, 2015.
Welcome to Kentucky. Accessed November 12, 2021. https://www.kentuckytourism.com/.

LOUISIANA

Bernard, Shane K. *The Cajuns: Americanization of a People*. Oxford: University Press of Mississippi, 2003.
64 Parishes Encyclopedia. Accessed November 12, 2021. https://64parishes.org/encyclopedia.
Stuart, Bonnye. *More than Petticoats: Remarkable Louisiana Women*. Guilford, CT: Globe Pequot, 2009.
Taylor, Troy. *Haunted New Orleans: History and Hauntings of the Crescent City*. Charleston, SC: History Press, 2010.

MAINE

Judd, Richard, Edwin Churchill, and Joel W. Eastman. *Maine: The Pine Tree State from Prehistory to the Present*. Orono: University of Maine Press, 1995.
Maine: An Encyclopedia. Accessed November 12, 2021. https://maineanencyclopedia.com/.
Stansfield, Charles. *Haunted Maine: Ghosts and Strange Phenomena of the Pine Tree State*. Mechanicsburg, PA: Stackpole Books, 2007.

MARYLAND

Cottom, Ric. *Your Maryland: Little-Known Histories from the Shores of the Chesapeake to the Foothills of the Allegheny Mountains*. Baltimore, MD: Johns Hopkins University Press, 2017.
"Maryland at a Glance." *Maryland Manual On-Line*. Accessed November 12, 2021. https://msa.maryland.gov/msa/mdmanual/01glance/html/mdglance.html.
Maryland Office of Tourism. Accessed November 12, 2021. https://www.visitmaryland.org/.
Okonowicz, Edward. *Haunted Maryland: Ghosts and Strange Phenomena of the Old Line State*. Mechanicsburg, PA: Stackpole Books, 2007.

MASSACHUSETTS

D'Agostino, Thomas. *Haunted Massachusetts*. Atglen, PA: Schiffer Publishing, 2007.
Massachusetts. Accessed November 12, 2021. https://www.massvacation.com/.
Official Website of the Commonwealth of Massachusetts. Accessed November 12, 2021. https://www.mass.gov/.
Roach, Marilynne. *The Salem Witch Trials: A Day-by-Day Chronicle of a Community under Siege*. Lanham, MD: Taylor Trade Publishing, 2004.

MICHIGAN

North, Tom. *Mackinac Island*. Charleston, SC: Arcadia Publishing, 2011.
Pattskyn, Helen. *Ghosthunting Michigan*. Covington, KY: Clerisy Press, 2012.

Pure Michigan. Accessed November 12, 2021. https://www.michigan.org/.
Sonnenberg, Mike. *Lost in Michigan: History and Travel Stories from an Endless Road Trip*. Saginaw, MI: Etaoin Publishing, 2017.

MINNESOTA

Atkins, Annette. *Creating Minnesota: A History from the Inside Out*. St. Paul, MN: Minnesota Historical Society Press, 2008.
MNopedia. Accessed November 12, 2021. https://www.mnopedia.org/.
Mohr, Howard. *How to Talk Minnesotan: Revised for the 21st Century*. New York: Penguin Books, 2013.

MISSISSIPPI

Busbee, Westley, Jr. *Mississippi: A History*. Malden, MA: Wiley-Blackwell, 2015.
McDowell, Gary, and Ruth A. McDowell. *Mississippi Secrets: Facts, Legends, and Folklore*. Lincoln, NE: iUniverse, 2007.
Mississippi Encyclopedia. Accessed November 12, 2021. https://mississippiencyclopedia.org/.
Wilkerson, Isabel. *The Warmth of Other Suns: The Epic Story of America's Great Migration*. New York: Vintage, 2011.

MISSOURI

Missouri Encyclopedia. Accessed November 12, 2021. https://missouriencyclopedia.org/.
Offutt, Jason. *Haunted Missouri: A Ghostly Guide to the Show-Me-State's Most Spirited Spots*. Kirksville, MO: Truman State University Press, 2007.
Spencer, Thomas (editor). *The Other Missouri History: Populists, Prostitutes, and Regular Folk*. Columbia: University of Missouri, 2005.

MONTANA

Donovan, James. *A Terrible Glory: Custer and the Little Bighorn—The Last Great Battle of the American West*. New York: Back Bay Books, 2008.
Montana. Accessed November 12, 2021. https://www.visitmt.com/.
Spritzer, Don. *Roadside History of Montana*. Missoula, MT: Mountain Press, 1999.
Stevens, Karen. *More Haunted Montana: Haunted Places You Can Visit—If You Dare!* Helena, MT: Riverbend Publishing, 2010.

NEBRASKA

Garrison, Gretchen M. *Detour Nebraska: Historic Destinations and Natural Wonders*. Charleston, SC: History Press, 2017.
History Nebraska. Accessed November 12, 2021. https://history.nebraska.gov.
Partsch, Tammy. *It Happened in Nebraska: Stories of Events and People That Shaped the Cornhusker State*. 2nd edition. Lanham, MD: Globe Pequot, 2019.

NEVADA

Bowers, Michael W. *The Sagebrush State: Nevada's History, Government, and Politics*. Reno: University of Nevada Press, 2015.

Schumacher, Geoff. *Sun, Sin and Suburbia: The History of Modern Las Vegas*. Reno: University of Nevada Press, 2015.

Travel Nevada. Accessed November 12, 2021. https://travelnevada.com.

NEW HAMPSHIRE

D'Agostino, Thomas. *Haunted New Hampshire*. Atglen, PA: Schiffer Publishing, 2007.

Discover New Hampshire. Accessed November 12, 2021. https://www.visitnh.gov/.

Rogers, Barbara, and Stillman Rogers. *New Hampshire Off the Beaten Path*. 9th edition. Guilford, CT: Globe Pequot, 2019.

Tree, Christina, and Christine Hamm. *New Hampshire: An Explorer's Guide*. 7th edition. Woodstock, VT: Countryman Press, 2010.

NEW JERSEY

Genovese, Peter. *New Jersey Curiosities: Quirky Characters, Roadside Oddities and Other Offbeat Stuff*. 3rd edition. Guilford, CT: Globe Pequot, 2011.

Lurie, Maxine, and Richard Veit. *Envisioning New Jersey: An Illustrated History of the Garden State*. New Brunswick, NJ: Rutgers University Press, 2016.

New Jersey. Accessed November 12, 2021. https://www.visitnj.org/.

Zwillenberg, Elias. *New Jersey Haunts*. Atglen, PA: Schiffer Publishing, 2010.

NEW MEXICO

Hillerman, Tony. *The Spell of New Mexico*. Reprint edition. Albuquerque: University of New Mexico Press, 1984.

Kessell, John L. *Pueblos, Spaniards, and the Kingdom of New Mexico*. Norman: University of Oklahoma Press, 2010.

New Mexico True. Accessed November 12, 2021. https://www.newmexico.org/.

Roberts, Calvin, and Susan A. Roberts. *A History of New Mexico*. 4th edition. Albuquerque: University of New Mexico Press, 2011.

NEW YORK

Burns, Ric, James Sanders, and Lisa Ades. *New York: An Illustrated History*. New York: Knopf, 2021.

New York Visitors Network. Accessed November 12, 2021. https://www.visitnewyorkstate.net/.

NYC: The Official Guide. Accessed November 12, 2021. https://www.nycgo.com/.

Reitano, Joanne. *New York State: Peoples, Places, and Priorities: A Concise History with Sources*. New York: Routledge, 2015.

NORTH CAROLINA

NCpedia. Accessed November 12, 2021. https://www.ncpedia.org/.
Pitzer, Sara. *North Carolina Myths and Legends: The True Stories behind History's Mysteries.* Guilford, CT: Globe Pequot, 2015.
Powell, William S. *North Carolina: A History.* Chapel Hill: University of North Carolina Press, 1988.
Ready, Milton. *The Tar Heel State: A History of North Carolina.* Columbia: University of South Carolina Press, 2005.

NORTH DAKOTA

Hargrove, Zachary. *Abandoned North Dakota: Weathered by Time.* Charleston, SC: America through Time, 2019.
North Dakota. Accessed November 12, 2021. https://www.nd.gov/.
Piepkorn, John. *Abandoned North Dakota: Glimpses of the Past.* Charleston, SC: America through Time, 2020.

OHIO

Gurvis, Sandra. *Ohio Curiosities: Quirky Characters, Roadside Oddities and Other Offbeat Stuff.* 2nd edition. Guilford, CT: Globe Pequot, 2011.
Ohio History Central. Accessed November 12, 2021. https://ohiohistorycentral.org/w/Welcome_To_Ohio_History_Central.
Stansfield, Charles, Jr. *Haunted Ohio: Ghosts and Strange Phenomena of the Buckeye State.* Mechanicsburg, PA: Stackpole Books, 2008.

OKLAHOMA

Dorman, Robert L. *It Happened in Oklahoma: Stories of Events and People That Shaped Sooner State History.* 3rd edition. Lanham, MD: Globe Pequot, 2019.
Encyclopedia of Oklahoma History and Culture. Accessed November 12, 2021. https://www.okhistory.org/publications/encyclopediaonline.
Ricksecker, Mike. *Ghosts and Legends of Oklahoma.* Atglen, PA: Schiffer Publishing, 2011.
Smith, Robert Barr, and Laurence J. Yadon. *Oklahoma Scoundrels: History's Most Notorious Outlaws, Bandits and Gangsters.* Charleston, SC: History Press, 2016.

OREGON

Hayes, Derek. *Historical Atlas of Washington and Oregon.* Oakland: University of California Press, 2011.
Oregon Encyclopedia. Accessed November 12, 2021. https://oregonencyclopedia.org/.
Schlosser, S. E. *Spooky Oregon: Tales of Hauntings, Strange Happenings, and Other Local Lore.* Lanham, MD: Globe Pequot, 2009.

PENNSYLVANIA

Bressi, Marlin. *Pennsylvania Oddities.* Mechanicsburg, PA: Sunbury Press, 2018.

DeLeon, Clark. *Pennsylvania Curiosities, Quirky Characters, Roadside Oddities and Other Offbeat Stuff.* 3rd edition. Guilford, CT: Globe Pequot, 2008.
Myers, Kathy. *Historic Tales of the Pennsylvania Wilds.* Charleston, SC: History Press, 2021.
Pennsylvania. Accessed November 12, 2021. https://www.visitpa.com/.

RHODE ISLAND
Conley, Patrick T. *Rhode Island Founders: From Settlement to Statehood.* Charleston, SC: History Press, 2010.
D'Agostino, Thomas. *Haunted Rhode Island.* Atglen, PA: Schiffer Publishing, 2005.
Rhode Island. Accessed November 12, 2021. https://www.visitrhodeisland.com/.
Warren, James. *God, War, and Providence: The Epic Struggle of Roger Williams and the Narragansett Indians against the Puritans of New England.* New York: Scribner, 2018.

SOUTH CAROLINA
Edgar, Walter B. *South Carolina: A History.* Columbia: University of South Carolina Press, 1999.
Schlosser, S. E., and Paul Hoffman. *Spooky South Carolina: Tales of Hauntings, Strange Happenings, and Other Local Lore.* Guilford, CT: Globe Pequot, 2011.
South Carolina Encyclopedia. Accessed December 10, 2021. https://www.scencyclopedia.org/sce/.

SOUTH DAKOTA
Ames, John E. *The Real Deadwood: True Life Histories of Wild Bill Hickok, Calamity Jane, Outlaw Towns, and Other Characters of the Lawless West.* New York: Chamberlain Brothers Publishing, 2004.
Encyclopedia of the Great Plains/South Dakota. Accessed November 12, 2021. http://plainshumanities.unl.edu/encyclopedia/doc/egp.pg.077.
Hunhoff, Bernie. *South Dakota Curiosities: Quirky Characters, Roadside Oddities and Other Offbeat Stuff.* Guilford, CT: Globe Pequot Press, 2010.

TENNESSEE
Finch, Jackie Sheckler. *Tennessee Off the Beaten Path: A Guide to Unique Places.* Guilford, CT: Globe Pequot Press, 2013.
Guy, Joe. *The Hidden History of East Tennessee.* Charleston, SC: History Press, 2008.
Tennessee Encyclopedia. Accessed November 12, 2021. https://tennesseeencyclopedia.net/.
Tennessee Encyclopedia of History and Culture. Accessed November 12, 2021. https://tennesseehistory.org/publications/the-tennessee-encyclopedia-of-history-and-culture/.

TEXAS
Calvert, Robert, Arnoldo De Leon, and Gregg Cantrell. *The History of Texas.* 5th edition. Malden, MA: Wiley-Blackwell, 2014.
Handbook of Texas Online. Accessed November 12, 2021. https://tshaonline.org/handbook.

Pohlen, Jerome. *Oddball Texas: A Guide to Some Really Strange Places*. Chicago, IL: Chicago Review Press, 2006.

Williams, Scott, and Donna Ingham. *Texas: Famous Phantoms, Sinister Sites, and Lingering Legends*. Guilford, CT: Lone Star Books Imprint of Globe Pequot, 2017.

UTAH

Cogley, Christopher, and Rich Briggs. *Utah's Greatest Wonders: A Photographic Journey of the Five National Parks*. Springville, UT: Plain Sight Publishing, 2017.

Utah History Encyclopedia. Accessed November 12, 2021. https://www.uen.org/utah_history_encyclopedia/.

Weeks, Andy. *Haunted Utah: Ghosts and Strange Phenomena of the Beehive State*. Mechanicsburg, PA: Stackpole Books, 2012.

VERMONT

Morrissey, Charles T. *Vermont: A History*. New York: Norton, 1984.

Vermont. Accessed November 12, 2021. https://www.vermontvacation.com/.

Wilson, Robert F. *Vermont . . . Who Knew?: Quirky Characters, Unsung Heroes, Wholesome, Offbeat Stuff*. Saxtons River, VT: Wilson McLeran Publishing, 2018.

VIRGINIA

Encyclopedia Virginia. Accessed November 12, 2021. https://www.encyclopediavirginia.org/.

Heinemann, Ronald, John Kolp, Anthony Parent Jr., and William G. Shade. *Old Dominion, New Commonwealth: A History of Virginia, 1607–2007*. Charlottesville: University of Virginia Press, 2007.

Taylor, L. B. *Ghosts of Virginia's Tidewater*. Charleston, SC: History Press, 2011.

Woolley, Benjamin. *Savage Kingdom: The True Story of Jamestown, 1607, and the Settlement of America*. New York: Harper, 2007.

WASHINGTON

LeWarne, Charles Pierce. *Washington State*. 3rd edition. Seattle: University of Washington Press, 2003.

Stansfield, Charles, and Alan Wycheck. *Haunted Washington: Ghosts and Strange Phenomena of the Evergreen State*. Mechanicsburg, PA: Stackpole Books, 2011.

Washington: The State. Accessed November 11, 2021. http://www.experiencewa.com/.

WEST VIRGINIA

West Virginia. Accessed November 11, 2021. https://wvtourism.com/.

Williams, John Alexander. *West Virginia: A History*. Morgantown, WV: West Virginia University Press, 2003.

Wittenberg, Eric, Penny Barrick, and Edmund Sargus Jr. *Seceding from Secession: The Civil War, Politics, and the Creation of West Virginia*. El Dorado Hills, CA: Savas Beatie, 2020.

WISCONSIN
Huhti, Thomas. *Wisconsin*. 7th edition. Berkeley, CA: Moon, 2017.
Revolinski, Kevin. *Backroads and Byways of Wisconsin*. 2nd edition. New York: Countryman Press, 2020.
Travel Wisconsin. Accessed November 11, 2021. https://www.travelwisconsin.com/.

WYOMING
Federal Writers' Project with James R. Dow, Susan D. Dow, and Roger L. Welsch (editors). *Wyoming Folklore: Reminiscences, Folktales, Beliefs, Customs, and Folk Speech*. Lincoln: University of Nebraska Press, 2010.
Lightner, Sam, Jr. *Wyoming: A History of the American West*. Lander, WY: Summits and Crux, 2020.
WyoHistoryOrg. Accessed November 11, 2021. https://www.wyohistory.org/.

Index

Page numbers in **bold** indicate location of main entries.

Acadians. *See* Cajuns
Adams, John, xxiv, 157, 282
Adams, John Quincy, xxiv, 25, 64
Ajacán Mission, 340
Alabama, **1–8**
   distinctive words and
      sayings, 8
   iconic food, 5–6
   odd laws, 6–7
   state history, 1–4
   unusual destinations, 7–8
   urban legends, 4–5
Alamo, xv, xxv, 319–320
Alamogordo, New Mexico. *See* Manhattan
   Project
Alaska, **9–15**
   distinctive words and sayings, 15
   iconic food, 12–13
   odd laws, 13–14
   state history, 9–11
   unusual destinations, 14–15
   urban legends, 11–12
Albany, New York, xv, xxi, 235, 237, 380
Albuquerque, New Mexico, 229, 232, 233
Aleutian Islands, 9, 11, 12, 13
Aleuts (Native American people), 9
Algonquin (Native American people), 258
Allen, Ethan, 334
American Revolution, xviii, xxiii, 3, 48, 56, 57, 104, 142, 149, 154, 157, 163, 198, 213, 215, 221, 236, 238, 244, 245, 281, 290, 291, 297, 311, 334, 347, 355
Anasazi (Native American people), 39, 40, 325
Androscoggin (Native American people), 214
Andy Griffith Show, The (television program), 248, 249
Annapolis, Maryland, 148, 149, 154, 379

Apache (Native American people), 18, 229, 266, 318
Apalachee (Native American people), 63, 71
Arapaho (Native American people), 117
"Area 51" (region in Nevada), 89, 208
Arizona, **16–22**
   distinctive words and sayings, 22
   iconic food, 19–20
   odd laws, 20–21
   state history, 16–18
   unusual destinations, 21–22
   urban legends, 18–19
Arkansas, **23–30**
   distinctive words and sayings, 30
   iconic food, 28–29
   odd laws, 29
   state history, 23–27
   unusual destinations, 29–30
   urban legends, 27–28
Arkansas Possum Pie, x, 28
Arkansas Post, 23
"Arkansas Traveler" (song and painting), 24–25
Aroostook County, Maine, 141, 147
Atlanta, Georgia, 71, 72, 73, 75, 77, 193, 298, 379
Atomic bomb, 96, 228, 229, 311
Attucks, Crispus, xxiii, 157
Augusta, Georgia, 74
Augusta, Maine, 141, 142, 379
Austin, Minnesota, 172, 175, 176
Austin, Texas, 318, 380
Ayllón, Lucas, 296

Bagels, 238–239
Baltimore, Lord, 16, 148, 149, 377
Baltimore, Maryland, 149, 150, 151, 154, 155, 246
Banneker, Benjamin, 151

Barrow, Clyde, 111, 138
Basketball, 158
Baton Rouge, Louisiana, xvii, 133, 379
"Beast of Boggy Creek." *See* Fouke Monster
Bell Witch, 312–313
Bering, Vitus, 9, 32
Bering Land Bridge, 9
Bierock, 120–121, 205
Big August Quarterly, 57
Bigfoot, x, 11, 27, 51, 57, 76, 128, 146, 154, 159, 165, 187, 216, 223, 230, 248, 268, 269, 306, 321, 322, 342, 343, 350, 351, 352, 360, 363, 371
Bismarck, North Dakota, 250, 256, 380
Bison, xii, 192, 193, 198, 250, 253, 305, 361, 369, 375
Blackbeard (a/k/a Edward Teach), 74, 244, 248
"Bleeding Kansas," 118
Block, Adriaen, 289
Bluegrass, 125, 126, 132
Bodega Bay, California, xvii, xxiv, 33
Boise, Idaho, xvii, 86, 87, 92, 379
Bonaparte, Joseph, 222
Bonaparte, Napoleon, 110, 134, 250, 354
Booth, John Wilkes, 150, 153, 154
Booyah, 364
Boston, Massachusetts, xxiii, 156, 157, 158, 160, 161, 162, 215, 222, 282, 290, 379
Boston Baked Beans, 160
Bourbon, 5, 126, 127, 132
Brown, Margaret "Molly," 41
Brown v. Board of Education, xxviii, 111, 119
Buckeyes (candy), 262
Buffalo Soldiers, 119
Buffett, Warren, 199–200
Burgoo, 127

Cabot, John, 55
Caddo (Native American people), 133, 266, 318
Cahokia (Native American complex), 94, 184
Cajuns, 133, 134, 135, 139, 140
California, **31–38**
   distinctive words and sayings, 37
   iconic food, 35
   odd laws, 35–36
   state history, 31–34
   unusual destinations, 36–37
   urban legends, 34–35
Camels (in American Southwest), 18
Canada, xii, 17, 86, 134, 141, 142, 191, 217, 255, 335, 350, 353, 362

Cape Canaveral, Florida, 65–66
Capone, Al, 66, 96, 97, 201
Caraway, Hattie, xxvii, 25
Carson City, Nevada, 206
Cartier, Jacques, 333
Cascadia (proposed state), 275
Cassidy, Butch. *See* Sundance Kid
Catawba (Native American people), 296
Centralia, Pennsylvania, 283
Champlain, Samuel, 333
Charles I, King of England, 148, 244, 296, 377
Charles II, King of England, 1, 48, 220, 244, 290, 297
Charleston, South Carolina, xxvi, 296, 297, 298, 299, 302
Charleston, West Virginia, 354, 380
Charlotte, Queen of England, 355
Cheese Frenchees, 202
"Cheesehead" hats, 362
Cheney Clow's Rebellion, 56
Cherokee (Native American people), xii, 71, 73, 243, 249, 296, 310, 354
Cheyenne (Native American people), 117
Cheyenne, Wyoming, 360, 375, 380
Chicago, Illinois, xvii, 22, 95, 96, 97, 109, 111, 240, 362
Chicago-Style Hot Dog, 97–98, 99, 100
Chickasaw (Native American people), 1, 23, 310
Chicken Fried Steak, 269
Chile Pepper Institute (New Mexico), 232–233
Choctaw (Native American people), 266
Chumash (Native American people), 33
Chupacabra, 230, 246, 248
Church of Jesus Christ of Latter-day Saints, 206, 326
Cibola. *See* Seven Cities of Cibola
Cioppino, 35
Civil War, xxvi, 3, 10, 18, 24, 41, 56, 58, 111, 118, 126, 127, 142, 149, 153, 158, 161, 178, 182, 185, 206, 228, 240, 244, 245, 246, 251, 259, 267, 291, 296, 298, 299, 311, 313, 319, 335, 342, 355, 356, 362, 370
Clark, George Rogers, 95
Clemens, Samuel Langhorne. *See* Twain, Mark
Clovis culture, 227
Clow, Cheney. *See* Cheney Clow's Rebellion
Coca-Cola, 72, 73, 359
Coeur d'Alene (Native American people), 86
Coeur d'Alene, Idaho (city), 87, 91

Colorado, **39–46**
   distinctive words and sayings, 45
   iconic food, 43–44
   odd laws, 44
   state history, 39–42
   unusual destinations, 44–45
   urban legends, 42–43
Colter, John, 370
Columbia (proposed state), 348
Columbia, South Carolina, 296, 297, 298, 380
Columbia River, 348, 352, 372
Columbus, Christopher, xi, xii, xiii, xiv, xxi, 39
Columbus, Ohio, 258, 264, 380
Comanche (Native American people), 117, 266, 318
Commonwealth (designation), 126, 158, 160, 161, 281, 342
Concord, Massachusetts, 157, 215, 245
Concord, New Hampshire, 213, 380
Confederate States of America, xxvi, 3, 24, 126, 127, 178, 228, 267, 298, 311, 319, 342
Congressional Fallout Shelter, 359
Connecticut, **47–54**
   distinctive words and sayings, 53
   iconic food, 51–52
   odd laws, 52
   state history, 47–50
   unusual destinations, 53
   urban legends, 50–51
Connecticut Western Reserve, 48
Constitution of the United States, xviii, xxiii, xxiv, 48, 57, 72, 179, 185, 215, 221, 237, 244, 281, 282, 290, 359
Cook, James, 79–80
Coronado, Francisco, xiv, xv, xxi, 16, 117–118, 227, 266, 269, 325
Corvette (automobile), 127
Crab Cakes, 152
Creek (Native American people), 1, 71
Crow (Native American people), 250, 369
Custer, George Armstrong, 192, 194
"Custer's Last Stand." *See* Little Bighorn, Battle of

Dakota (Native American people), 171, 303
Dare, Virginia, 244
Davis, Jefferson, 18, 127
De La Warr, Baron, 56
De León, Ponce, xiv, xxi, 1, 63–64
De Niza, Marcos, 16, 17
De Soto, Hernando, 1, 133, 178, 310

De Tonti, Henri, 23
Declaration of Independence, xxiii, 237, 244, 252, 281, 282, 290
Delaware, **55–62**
   distinctive words and sayings, 61
   iconic food, 58–59
   odd laws, 59–60
   state history, 55–58
   unusual destinations, 60–61
   urban legends, 58
Denver, Colorado, 39, 42, 45, 379
Denver, John, 42, 356
Des Moines, Iowa, xvii, 110, 116, 379
Deseret (Utah), 206, 326, 327
Detroit, Michigan, xvii, 164, 165, 167, 168, 235, 362
Devil's Tower, 370, 371, 375
D'Iberville, Pierre, 178
Dinosaurs, 40, 131, 168, 303
Disney, Walt, 187
Douglass, Frederick, xxv, xxvi, 150–151, 158
Dover, Delaware, 55, 56, 379
Dred Scott Decision, 185
Du Pont family, 57
Dubuque, Iowa, 110
Dutch East India Company, 55

Earp, Wyatt, 17, 118, 305
Edison, Thomas, 66, 223
Einstein, Albert, 223
Elias, Eulalia, 17
Elizabeth I, Queen of England, 56, 243, 340, 341
Elizabeth II, Queen of England, 125
Ellis Island, 237
Erie Canal, 96, 362
Eskimos (Native American people), 9, 15
"Esteban," 17

54th Massachusetts Infantry, 158
Fitzgerald, F. Scott, 150, 171
Florida, **63–70**
   distinctive words and sayings, 69
   iconic food, 67–68
   odd laws, 68
   state history, 63–66
   unusual destinations, 68–69
   urban legends, 66–67
Florida Land Boom, 65
"Florida Man," 66
Fort Christina, Delaware, 55

Fort Loudoun, Tennessee, 310
Fort Louis de la Mobile, 2
Fort Sumter, South Carolina, xxvi, 298
Fouke Monster ("Beast of Boggy Creek"), 27
Fountain of Youth, xiv, 64
Frankfort, Kentucky, 125
Franklin (proposed state), 311
Franklin, Benjamin, 149, 282
Freed, Alan, 260
French and Indian War, xvi, xxiii, 3, 95, 104, 110, 134, 163, 178, 258, 334, 362
French Canadians, xviii, 86, 103, 104, 136, 184, 250, 333, 369
Frogmore Stew, 300
Futuro House, 60, 61

Garcés, Francisco, 206
George III, King of England, 355
Georgia, **71–78**
    distinctive words and sayings, 77
    iconic food, 75
    odd laws, 76
    state history, 71–73
    unusual destinations, 76–77
    urban legends, 74–75
"Georgia on My Mind" (song), 74
Gone with the Wind (book and movie), 72
Grand Canyon, xiv, 16, 17
Grand Ole Opry, 179, 310, 312
Great Chicago Fire, 95
Great Depression, xxvii, 65, 106, 115, 311, 348
Great Lakes, xxiii, 104, 163, 165, 259, 361
Great Salt Lake, 325, 326, 331
Greenbrier Resort. *See* Congressional Fallout Shelter
Guinness World Records, 7, 45, 104, 192, 255, 346
Gumbo, 133, 136, 209

Hamilton, Alexander, 222, 248
"Hang On, Sloopy" (song), 260
Harrisburg, Pennsylvania, 281, 380
Harrison, Benjamin, xxvi, 252, 260, 305
Harrison, William Henry, xxv, 104, 252, 260, 261
Hart, Richard, 201
Hartford, Connecticut, 47, 49, 377, 379
Hatfields vs. McCoys (feud), 126
Hawaii, **79–85**
    distinctive words and sayings, 85
    iconic food, 83
    odd laws, 83–84
    state history, 79–81
    unusual destinations, 84–85
    urban legends, 81–83
Heceta, Don Bruno, 347
Helena, Montana, 191, 196, 380
Henrietta Maria, Queen of England, 148
Henson, Jim, 182, 183
Hollywood, California, 31, 32, 33, 34, 53, 91, 108, 200, 222, 231, 235, 255, 283, 292, 313, 328
Homestead Act of 1862, 199
Honolulu, Hawaii, 79, 80, 379
Hoosier Pie, 106
Hoosiers (Indiana nickname), 102, 106, 108
Hopi (Native American people), 16, 18, 227
Hot Brown (sandwich), 129
Hot Springs, Arkansas, 25, 27
Hutchinson, Anne, 290

Idaho, **86–93**
    distinctive words and sayings, 92–93
    iconic food, 89–90
    odd laws, 90–91
    state history, 86–88
    unusual destinations, 91–92
    urban legends, 88–89
Illini (Native American people), 94, 97, 103
Illinois, **94–101**
    distinctive words and sayings, 100–101
    iconic food, 97–99
    odd laws, 99
    state history, 94–96
    unusual destinations, 99–100
    urban legends, 96–97
Indian Removal Act of 1830, 72, 73, 266
Indiana, **102–109**
    distinctive words and sayings, 108–109
    iconic food, 106
    odd laws, 107
    state history, 102–104
    unusual destinations, 107–108
    urban legends, 104–106
"Indiana Jones" (fictional character), 105
Indianapolis, Indiana, 102, 103, 107, 108, 379
Industrial Revolution, 3, 41, 142, 158, 245
Inuits (Native American people), 9
Iolani Palace, 80, 81
Iowa, **110–116**
    distinctive words and sayings, 116
    iconic food, 113–114

odd laws, 114–115
state history, 110–112
unusual destinations, 115–116
urban legends, 112–113
Ioway (Native American people), 110
Iroquois (Native American people), xii, 235, 258, 354
Iroquois Confederacy, 235

"Jackalope," 375
Jackson, Mississippi, 177, 380
Jacksonville, Florida, 4
James I, King of England, 340, 377
James II, King of England, 236
Jamestown, Virginia, xxi, xxii, 142, 156, 340, 341, 354, 377
Jefferson, Thomas, xxiv, 250, 275
Jefferson City, Missouri, 184, 380
Joliet, Illinois, 99
Jolliet, Louis, 110
Juneau, Alaska, 9, 379

Kahanamoku, Duke, 80
Kamehameha I, King of Hawaii, 79, 80
Kansas, **117–124**
  distinctive words and sayings, 123
  iconic food, 120–121
  odd laws, 121–122
  state history, 117–119
  unusual destinations, 122–123
  urban legends, 119–120
Kansas-Nebraska Act, 118
Kaskaskia, Illinois, 95
Kennebec (Native American people), 141
Kennewick Man, 347
Kentucky, **125–132**
  distinctive words and sayings, 131–132
  iconic food, 129–130
  odd laws, 130
  state history, 125–128
  unusual destinations, 131
  urban legends, 128–129
Kentucky Derby, 125
Key, Francis Scott, 149
Key Lime Pie, 67–68
Key West, Florida, 79, 100
Kickapoo (Native American people), 361
King, Martin Luther, Jr., xxvii, 73
King, Stephen, 41, 144, 283
King Crab, 12–13
King Philip's War, xxii, 157, 289

Klondike Gold Rush, 9
Krumkake, 254

"La Louisiane." *See* Louisiana Territory
La Ramée, Jacques, 369
La Salle, René-Robert Cavelier, xvi, xxii, 23, 95, 103, 125, 134, 171, 258, 318
Lake Itasca, Minnesota, 171
Lake Pend Oreille, Idaho, 69
Lake Wobegon, Minnesota (fictional town). *See Prairie Home Companion, A*
Lakota (Native American people), 250, 303, 305, 306, 369
"Land of 10,000 Lakes" (Minnesota slogan), 170, 171
Lansing, Michigan, 163, 167, 379
Laramie, Wyoming, 369, 370, 372
Las Vegas, Nevada, 22, 84, 206, 207, 208, 209, 210, 211, 212
Lenape [Lenni] (Native American people), 55, 56, 148, 220, 235, 281
Lewis and Clark Expedition, 86, 192, 251, 305, 307, 347, 370
Liliuokalani, Queen of Hawaii, 80, 81
Lincoln, Abraham, xxvi, 10, 16, 24, 94, 95, 96, 126, 127, 150, 153, 306, 326, 355
Lincoln, Mary, 126
Lincoln, Nebraska, 198, 199, 204, 380
Little Bighorn, Battle of, 192, 194
Little Rock, Arkansas, x, 23, 25, 27, 29, 379
"Live Free or Die" (New Hampshire state motto), 213, 214, 215
Lobster Rolls, 144–145, 209
Long, Huey, 135
Longabaugh, Harry Alonzo. *See* Sundance Kid
Los Alamos, New Mexico, 96, 228
Los Angeles, California, xv, 32, 33, 34, 37, 49, 53, 79, 320
Lost Colony (Roanoke, North Carolina), xxi, 243–244
Louis XIV, King of France, xvi, 23, 134, 303
Louisiana, **133–140**
  distinctive words and sayings, 140
  iconic food, 136–137
  odd laws, 137–138
  state history, 133–135
  unusual destinations, 138–139
  urban, 135–136
Louisiana Purchase, xvi, 24, 40, 110, 118, 134, 185, 192, 250, 266, 305
Louisiana Territory, xxiv, 110, 118, 134, 370

Lovecraft, H. P., 291
Low Country Boil. *See* Frogmore Stew
Ludington, Sybil, 48
Lynyrd Skynyrd. *See* "Sweet Home Alabama"

Mackinac Island, Michigan, 165, 169
Madison, Wisconsin, 361, 380
Maidrite (sandwich), 113–114
Maine, **141–147**
   distinctive words and sayings, 147
   iconic food, 144–145
   odd laws, 145–146
   state history, 141–143
   unusual destinations, 146–147
   urban legends, 143–144
Mall of America, 172
Mammoths (prehistoric animals), 37, 211, 303, 304, 361
Mandan (Native American people), 250
Manhattan Island, xvi, xxii, 37, 235, 236, 237, 238, 240, 241
Manhattan Project, 228
Manifest Destiny, xxv, 228, 326
Maple syrup, 333, 334, 336, 337
Mardi Gras, 2, 3, 6, 7, 135, 286, 287
Margarine, 337–338, 365
Marionberry Pie, 277–278
Marquette, Jacques, 94, 97, 110, 361
Mars Hill Church, 111, 112
Marshall, Thurgood, 151
Maryland, **148–155**
   distinctive words and sayings, 154–155
   iconic food, 152
   odd laws, 152–153
   state history, 148–151
   unusual destinations, 153–154
   urban legends, 151–152
Maryland heraldic banner, 148, 149
Mason-Dixon Line, 56, 64, 149
Massachusett (Native American people), 156
Massachusetts, **156–162**
   distinctive words and sayings, 162
   iconic food, 160
   odd laws, 160–161
   state history, 156–158
   unusual destinations, 161–162
   urban legends, 158–160
Massachusetts Bay Colony, xxii, 157, 160, 290, 377
Massasoit, 156, 157
Mastodons, 168, 304, 310, 361
Mayaimi (Native American people), 63

Mayflower (ship), xvii, 63, 156
Mayflower Compact, 47–48
Mayo Clinic, 171
Mesa Verde, Colorado, 39–40
Mexican War, 33, 206, 228, 326, 370
Miami, Florida, 63, 66
Michigan, **163–169**
   distinctive words and sayings, 169
   iconic food, 166–167
   odd laws, 167–168
   state history, 163–165
   unusual destinations, 168–169
   urban legends, 165–166
Michigan-Style Pasties, 166–167
Microsoft Corporation, 229, 348
Minneapolis, Minnesota, 171, 172, 176
Minnesota, **170–176**
   distinctive words and sayings, 176
   iconic food, 173–174
   odd laws, 174–175
   state history, 170–173
   unusual destinations, 175–176
   urban legends, 172–173
Minnesota Hot Dish, 173–174
Minuit, Peter, xvi, xxii
Mission Trail (California), xv, 33
Mississippi, **177–183**
   distinctive words and sayings, 183
   iconic food, 180–181
   odd laws, 181
   state history, 177–179
   unusual destinations, 182–183
   urban legends, 179–180
Mississippi Delta, 177, 178, 183, 310
"Mississippi in Africa" (colony), 178
Mississippi Mud Pie, 180–181
Mississippi River, xvi, xxii, xxiii, 7, 23, 24, 64, 71, 97, 116, 119, 125, 133, 134, 135, 147, 171, 177, 178, 180, 183, 184, 185, 187, 194, 250, 266, 304, 310, 375
Missouri, **184–190**
   distinctive words and sayings, 190
   iconic food, 187–188
   odd laws, 188–189
   state history, 184–186
   unusual destinations, 189–190
   urban legends, 186–187
Missouri Compromise, 142, 185, 198
Missouri River, 116, 184, 191, 198, 201, 250, 253, 309
Mobile, Alabama, 2, 3, 4, 6

Mohegans (Native American people), 47
Montana, **191–197**
   distinctive words and sayings, 197
   iconic food, 195
   odd laws, 195–196
   state history, 181–194
   unusual destinations, 196–197
   urban legends, 194–195
Montana Wild Huckleberry Pie, 195
Montgomery, Alabama, 1, 3, 379
Montpelier, Vermont, 333, 380
Monument Valley, 16, 327, 328
Moores Creek Bridge, Battle of, 245
Mormons. *See* Church of Jesus Christ of Latter-day Saints
Mothman, 146, 357, 360
Motown, 164
Mount Washington, New Hampshire, 215
Mummers, 286, 287

Naismith, James. *See* Basketball
Narragansetts (Native American people), 289
Nashville, Tennessee, 178, 310, 311, 312, 313, 316, 380
Natchez (Native American people), 133, 177
Natchez, Mississippi, 178, 179
Natchez Trace, 178
National Aeronautics and Space Administration (NASA), 65, 279, 329, 331
Navajo (Native American people), 16, 17, 18, 19, 227, 230, 325
Navajo Fry Bread, 19–20
Nebraska, **198–205**
   distinctive words and sayings, 204–205
   iconic food, 202–203
   odd laws, 203–204
   state history, 198–200
   unusual destinations, 204
   urban legends, 201–202
Nevada, **206–212**
   distinctive words and sayings, 212
   iconic food, 209–210
   odd laws, 210–211
   state history, 206–208
   unusual destinations, 211
   urban legends, 208–209
New Deal. *See* Roosevelt, Franklin
New England, xxii, 141, 156, 292, 335, 377
New France, 2, 6
New Hampshire, **213–219**
   distinctive words and sayings, 219
   iconic food, 217
   odd laws, 217–218
   state history, 213–216
   unusual destinations, 218–219
   urban legends, 216–217
New Haven-Style Clam Pie, 51–52
New Jersey, **220–226**
   distinctive words and sayings, 226
   iconic food, 223–224
   odd laws, 224–225
   state history, 220–222
   unusual destinations, 225–226
   urban legends, 222–223
New Madrid Earthquake, 24
New Mexico, **227–234**
   distinctive words and sayings, 233–234
   iconic food, 230–231
   odd laws, 231–232
   state history, 227–229
   unusual destinations, 232–233
   urban legends, 229–230
New Netherland, xv, xvi, xxi, xxii, 47, 220, 235, 236, 378
New Spain, xiv, xv, 17
New Sweden, xvi, xxii, 281
New York, **235–242**
   distinctive words and sayings, 241
   iconic food, 238–239
   odd laws, 239–240
   state history, 235–237
   unusual destinations, 240–241
   urban legends, 237–238
Nez Percé (Native American people), 86, 87, 192, 274
Nickajack (proposed state), 3
Nicolet, Jean, 361
North Carolina, **243–249**
   distinctive words and sayings, 249
   iconic food, 247
   odd laws, 248
   state history, 243–246
   unusual destinations, 248–249
   urban legends, 246–247
North Dakota, **250–257**
   distinctive words and sayings, 256
   iconic food, 254
   odd laws, 255
   state history, 250–253
   unusual destinations, 255–256
   urban legends, 253–254
Northwest Territory, 104, 259

Nuclear testing, 208

Oak Ridge, Tennessee, 311
Oberlin College, Ohio, 259
Oglethorpe, James, 72, 378
Ohio, **258–265**
    distinctive words and sayings, 264
    iconic food, 262
    odd laws, 262–263
    state history, 258–261
    unusual destinations, 263–264
    urban legends, 261
Ohio "Burgee" flag, 259, 260
Ojibwe (Native American people), 171
O.K. Corral, 17, 18
Oklahoma, **266–273**
    distinctive words and sayings, 272
    iconic food, 269–270
    odd laws, 270–271
    state history, 266–268
    unusual destinations, 271–272
    urban legends, 268–269
Oklahoma City, Oklahoma, 266, 267, 268, 271, 272, 380
Olympia, Washington, 347, 380
Oregon, **274–280**
    distinctive words and sayings, 280
    iconic food, 277–278
    odd laws, 278–279
    state history, 274–276
    unusual destinations, 279–280
    urban legends, 276–277
Orlando, Florida, 66
Osage (Native American people), 23, 266

Paiute (Native American people), 86, 206
Pamlico (Native American people), 243
Pardo, Juan, 243, 310
Parker, Bonnie, 111, 138
Parker, Robert Leroy. *See* Sundance Kid
Peach Cobbler, 75
Peanut Soup, 343–344
Penn, William, xvi, xxii, 281, 282, 378
Pennacook (Native American people), 214
Pennsylvania, **281–288**
    distinctive words and sayings, 287–288
    iconic food, 284–285
    odd laws, 285
    state history, 281–282
    unusual destinations, 285–287
    urban legends, 282–284

Penobscot (Native American people), 141
Peoria, Illinois, 95, 96
Pequots (Native American people), 47, 289
Philadelphia, Pennsylvania, 281, 282, 283, 284, 286, 287
Philly Cheesesteak, 284–285
Phoenix, Arizona, 16, 191, 379
Pikes Peak, 40
Pineda, Alonso Álvarez, 318
Piscataway (Native American people), 148
Plaquemine culture (Native American people), 177
Plymouth, Massachusetts, xvii, xxii, 156, 377
Plymouth Rock, 63, 227, 341
Poe, Edgar Allan, 150, 291, 297, 298
Poe, Virginia, 150
Poi, 83
Popham Colony, 142, 377
Posole, 230–231
Pottawatomie (Native American people), 361
Poutine, 217
Powhatan, Native America chief, 340
Prairie Home Companion, A (radio program), 170
Presley, Elvis, x, 29, 82, 179, 208, 212, 310, 345
Pro Football Hall of Fame, 260
Providence, Rhode Island, 289, 290, 291, 292, 294, 295, 378, 380
Pueblo (Native American people), xii, 40, 227, 325
"Punxsutawney Phil" (groundhog), 286

Quahogs (seafood), 292–293
Quapaw (Native American people), 23, 266

Radisson, Pierre-Esprit, 170
Raleigh, North Carolina, 243, 245
Raleigh, Walter, 340, 341, 380
Rankin, Jeannette, xxvii, 194
Reconstruction, xxviii, 72, 126, 178
Reno, Nevada, 206, 208, 209
Research Triangle, North Carolina, 245
Revere, Paul, 48, 215
Revolutionary War. *See* American Revolution
Rhode Island, **289–295**
    distinctive words and sayings, 295
    iconic food, 292–293
    odd laws, 293–294
    state history, 289–292
    unusual destinations, 294–295
    urban legends, 291–292

"Rhode Island and Providence Plantations," 290, 291
Rhode Island Stuffies, 293
Rhyolite, Nevada, 211, 212
Richmond, Virginia, 3, 340, 341, 380
Rock and Roll Hall of Fame, 260
Rockefeller, Winthrop, 25
Roosevelt, Franklin, xxvii, 311, 348
Ross, Nellie Tayloe, 370
Roswell, New Mexico, 228, 231, 233, 277, 320, 363
Route 66 (highway), 190, 240–241, 267
Ruth, George Herman "Babe," 246

Sacajawea, 251
Sacramento, California, 31, 379
Saguaro (cactus), 20, 21, 22
Saint Louis Cemetery No. 1 (New Orleans), 138, 139
Saint Paul, Minnesota, 380
Salem, Massachusetts, 48, 151, 157, 160, 377
Salem, Oregon, 274, 380
Salt Lake City, Utah, 325, 326, 380
San Francisco, California, xv, xvii, xxi, xxiv, 32, 33, 34, 35, 36, 37, 77, 241
San Miguel de Guadalupe, South Carolina, 296
Sandwich, Earl of, 79–80
Santa Fe, New Mexico, xxi, xxii, 64, 227, 228, 229, 325, 380
Santa Fe Trail, 118, 185
Sasquatch, 76, 128, 146, 216, 343, 350, 351–352, 363, 372
Seaview Terrace, 295
Seven Cities of Cibola, 17, 227
Seven Years' War. *See* French and Indian War
Seward, William, xvii, 9, 10
Shakespeare, William, 214
Shasta (Native American people), 33, 274
Shawnee (Native American people), xxiv, 103, 104, 125, 148, 281, 310, 354
Sherman, William Tecumseh, 72, 298
Shoshone (Native American people), 86, 88, 206, 325, 369
"Show Me State" (Missouri nickname), 184, 186, 188
Shrimp Cocktail, 209–210
Siegel, Benjamin, 207
Skinwalkers, 19, 230
Sleepy Hollow, legend of, 238
Slippery Dumplings, 58–59
Sloop, Dorothy. *See* "Hang On, Sloopy"

Smith, John, xxi, 56
Smithsonian Institution, 25, 286, 301, 364
"Sooners" (Oklahoma nickname), 266, 267
South Carolina, **296–302**
  distinctive words and sayings, 302
  iconic food, 300
  odd laws, 300–301
  state history, 296–299
  unusual destinations, 301–302
  urban legends, 299
South Dakota, **303–309**
  distinctive words and sayings, 309
  iconic food, 307
  odd laws, 308
  state history, 303–306
  unusual destinations, 308–309
  urban legends, 306–307
Southdale (mall), 172
Space Needle, 352, 353
Spam (meat product), 172, 175–176
Spokane (Native American people), 347
Springfield, Illinois, 94, 95, 379
St. Albans, Vermont, 335
St. Augustine, Florida, xv, xxi, 64, 67, 296
St. Croix Island, Maine, 141–142
St. Louis, Missouri, 184, 185, 186, 187, 190
St. Michaels, Maryland, 150
Stark, John, 213
Sugar on Snow (Vermont dish), 336–337
Sundance Kid, 371
Sunken Land (region in Arkansas), 24
Supreme Court of the United States, xxv, xxvii, xxviii, 111, 118, 151, 185, 237, 248, 338, 356
Suquamish (Native American people), 347, 349
Susquehanna (Native American people), 55
Susquehannock (Native American people), 281
"Sweet Home Alabama" (song), 4
Sweet Potato Pie, 237

Tallahassee, Florida, 63, 379
Teach, Edward. *See* Blackbeard
Tecumseh (Shawnee chief), xxiv, 104
Tenino, Washington, 348
Tennessee, **310–317**
  distinctive words and sayings, 316–317
  iconic food, 313–314
  odd laws, 315
  state history, 310–312
  unusual destinations, 315–316
  urban legends, 312–313

Tennessee Hot Chicken, 313–314
Tennessee Valley Authority (TVA), 311
Texas, **318–324**
    distinctive words and sayings, 324
    iconic food, 321–322
    odd laws, 322–323
    state history, 318–320
    unusual destinations, 323–324
    urban legends, 320–321
Texas Rangers, 319
Texas Style Smoked Brisket, 322
Thanksgiving (holiday), 156, 157, 293, 341
Toasted Ravioli, 187–188
Tobacco, xviii, 107, 148, 204, 249, 340, 342
Toledo War, 163
Tombstone, Arizona, 16, 17, 18, 19
Topeka, Kansas, 117, 119, 121–122, 379
Trail of Tears, xxv, 72, 267
Transcontinental railroad, xxvi, 18, 41, 326, 370
Triple Divide (Montana), 191
Tubman, Harriet, xxv, 150, 151
Turner, Ted, 72, 193
Tuscarora (Native American people), 243
Twain, Mark, 184, 185
Twice Baked Potatoes, 89–90

Underground Railroad, xxv, 111, 112, 151
Unicameral (Nebraska legislature), 200
Unidentified Flying Objects (UFOs), 45, 159, 208, 228, 230, 301–302, 320
Union Church of Africans, 57
U.S. Air Force, 21, 208, 216, 228, 268, 375
Utah, **325–332**
    distinctive words and sayings, 331
    iconic food, 329–330
    odd laws, 330
    state history, 325–327
    unusual destinations, 330–331
    urban legends, 327–329
Utah Funeral Potatoes, 329–330
Ute (Native American people), 325

"Vandalia" (proposed state name), 355
Vérendrye, Pierre Gaultier, 250, 303
Vermont, **333–339**
    distinctive words and sayings, 339
    iconic food, 336–337
    odd laws, 337–338
    state history, 333–335
    unusual destinations, 338–339
    urban legends, 335–336
Vermont Republic, 334
Verrazano, Giovanni, 215, 289
Vicksburg, Mississippi, 177, 179
Virginia, **340–346**
    distinctive words and sayings, 346
    iconic food, 343–344
    odd laws, 344–345
    state history, 340–342
    unusual destinations, 345–346
    urban legends, 342–343

Walmart, 26, 30
Wampanoags (Native American people), 289
War of 1812, xxiv, 24, 142, 150, 198, 311, 362
War of the Worlds. *See* Welles, Orson
Washington, **347–353**
    distinctive words and sayings, 353
    iconic food, 350–351
    odd laws, 351–352
    state history, 347–348
    unusual destinations, 352–353
    urban legends, 349–350
Washington, DC, 149, 151, 186, 282, 344, 346, 348
Washington, George, xxiii, 57, 149, 222, 237, 246, 282, 306, 341, 346, 348
Washington Apple Pie, 350–351
Washington Crossing the Delaware (painting), 56, 221
Welles, Orson, 226, 349
West Virginia, **354–360**
    distinctive words and sayings, 360
    iconic food, 358
    odd laws, 358–359
    state history, 354–356
    unusual destinations, 359–360
    urban legends, 356–357
West Virginia Pepperoni Rolls, 358
"What Did Della Wear?" (song), 57
White Chicken Chili, 373
Williams, Roger, 290, 378
Wilson, August, 171
Wisconsin, **361–368**
    distinctive words and sayings, 367–368
    iconic food, 364–365
    odd laws, 365–366
    state history, 361–363
    unusual destinations, 366–367
    urban legends, 363–364
Witch hunts, 48

Wordsworth, William, 214
World War I, xxvii, 49, 56, 194, 204, 280, 352
World War II, xxvii, xxviii, 9, 25, 65, 82, 91, 119, 154, 194, 207, 228, 240, 263, 311
Wright, Orville and Wilbur, 104, 245
Wyoming, **369–376**
   distinctive words and sayings, 375–376
   iconic food, 372–373
   odd laws, 373–374
   state history, 369–370
   unusual destinations, 374–375
   urban legends, 371–372
Wyoming Valley, Pennsylvania, 370

Yakama (Native American people), 347
Yellowstone (national park), 92, 370, 371
Young, Brigham, 326, 328

Zwaanendael, 55, 56, 61

About the Author

Nancy Hendricks, PhD, is an award-winning author whose book *Senator Hattie Caraway: An Arkansas Legacy* was named by *Cosmopolitan* as one of the "Twenty Political Books Every Woman Should Read."

Hendricks is the author of several books for ABC-CLIO, including *America's First Ladies: A Historical Encyclopedia and Primary Document Collection of the Remarkable Women of the White House*; *Daily Life in 1950s America*; *Haunted Histories in America: True Stories behind the Nation's Most Feared Places*; *Ruth Bader Ginsburg: A Life in American History*; *Daily Life of Women in Postwar America*; and the two-volume *Popular Fads and Crazes through American History*. She is also author of the Civil War novel *Terrible Swift Sword: Long Road to the Sultana*.

Her writing can be seen on Smithsonian.com. Among other honors, Hendricks earned the National Society Daughters of the American Revolution "Women in American History" Award and the White House Millennium Award.

www.ingramcontent.com/pod-product-compliance
Lightning Source LLC
Chambersburg PA
CBHW082020300426
44117CB00015B/2291